A Comparative History
of
World Philosophy

A Comparative History

of

World Philosophy

From the Upanishads to Kant

✳

Ben-Ami Scharfstein

STATE UNIVERSITY OF NEW YORK PRESS

Published by
State University of New York Press, Albany

Printed in the United States of America

For information, address State University of New York Press,
State University Plaza, Albany, N.Y., 12246

Production by Marilyn P. Semerad
Marketing by Dana E. Yanulavich

Library of Congress Cataloging-in-Publication Data

Scharfstein, Ben-Ami, 1919–
    A comparative history of world philosophy : from the Upanishads to
Kant / Ben-Ami Scharfstein.
        p.   cm.
    Includes bibliographical references and index.
    ISBN 0-7914-3683-7 (alk. paper). — ISBN 0-7914-3684-5 (pbk. :
alk. paper)
    1. Philosophy, Comparative.   I. Title.
B799.S37   1998
109—dc21   97-19489
                                                                CIP

10   9   8   7   6   5   4

To my teachers and students

He who asks questions cannot avoid the answers.

—Cameroonian proverb

Contents

�

Preface

❈

Because I hope that newcomers to the history of philosophy will be
among the readers of this book, I have taken care to explain whatever
I think they need to know. The book begins with the reasons for studying
philosophy comparatively and with the difficulties raised by such study,
and it ends with a view of philosophy that is personal but that rests on
all of the preceding discussion. The philosophers dealt with represent
certain attitudes, schools, and traditions, but they are remembered most
interestingly and accurately as individuals. So even though I have had to
omit a great deal and make schematic summaries, I have in each instance
tried to suggest the philosopher's style, density, and order of thought. In
its later chapters the book tends to grow more difficult and elaborate, like
the philosophies it deals with; but the early chapters prepare for the later
ones, and, whatever the difficulty, I have always written as simply and
clearly as I can.

To avoid making a long book forbiddingly longer, I have limited not
only the number of philosophers dealt with but also the range of thought
by which each of them is represented. Plato, for example, is limited to his
theory of Ideas and Kant (except in the later discussion) to his *Critique of
Pure Reason*. In keeping with the needs of a particular comparison, I have
sometimes drawn a broad sketch and sometimes entered into details. When
it has seemed natural, I have shared my own views with the reader—there
is no good reason to pretend that I am a neutral, disembodied voice. But
however I judge each philosopher's thought, I have committed myself to
expound it with a minimum of bias.

My interpretations of individual philosophers are not meant to be
new in any basic sense, and they are bound, as I have implied, by the old
ideal of accuracy. Disproportions in the number of pages allotted to different

philosophers are not a measure of the importance I ascribe to them but of the varying need for clarification. If the quality of my accounts is uneven, this is at least to some extent a reflection of the unevenness of the literature on which I have depended. But though I have depended so much on others, for my part and, I hope, the reader's, what lies ahead is a genuine quest.

Acknowledgments

I am deeply grateful to all the friends and friendly acquaintances who checked parts of my manuscript and saved me from more than a few mistakes and misapprehensions. They range from doctoral candidates to seasoned philosophers and scholars. In alphabetical order, without indication of their academic titles, they are: Yoav Ariel, who has spent much of his life in company with Confucius, Mencius, Chuang Tzu, and their contemporaries, and who made a meticulously close examination of everything I wrote on Chinese philosophy (except on Chu Hsi); Shlomo Biderman, who reviewed all I wrote on Indian philosophy with a literary and philosophical sense for what matters most; Eli Franco, who reviewed almost everything on Indian philosophy and read and reread the text on Dignaga and Dharmakirti, in the light of his intimate acquaintance with both Bahmanical and Buddhist texts—a rare double accomplishment; Lenn Goodman, who read the account of Alfarabi, Avicenna, and Maimonides with a scholar's exactness and a philosopher's acuity; Irene Iber, expert in the development of Chinese culture, who read an early version of a number of chapters and proposed amendments, most of which I accepted; the late Yehuda Landa, who seemed to know Plato and Aristotle by heart, and who went over everything on Greek philosophy; Muhsin Mahdi, the editor of a number of Alfarabi's works, who was kind enough to check the account of Alfarabi and Avicenna; Galia Patt-Shamir, who preserved a Confucian courtesy in her comments on my account of Chu Hsi; Karin Preisendanz, who read the whole of the first chapter and the account of Upanishadic thinkers in the second, all with illuminating care, and who was my exceptionally painstaking savior in all that relates to Nyaya-Vaisheshika thought; Hilary Putnam, who, with Ruth Anna Putnam, helped me decide on the plan for the book, and who made helpful comments on the book's Afterword; Ornan Rotem, who made scholarly and philosophical comments on everything related to Buddhist thought, his specialty, as well as useful comments on the book's first chapter and the Afterword, and who, for good measure, helped with matters of style; and Zvi Tauber, who, thanks to his scholarly knowledge of European philosophy, saved me from errors and was ready to play the role of the Western philosopher open enough to take non-Western philosophy seriously. Finally, I thank my daughter, Doreet, for designing the cover of this book.

Chapter 1

The Three Philosophical Traditions

What, in This History, Is Considered to Be Philosophical?

There are three great philosophical traditions, the Indian, the Chinese, and the European. Before I describe them, I want to ask and answer, very briefly, what a philosophical tradition is, why I say that there are only three such traditions, and why it is best to study them together, as they are studied here, rather than separately or successively.

What is a philosophical tradition? A chain of persons who relate their thought to that of their predecessors and in this way form a continuous transmission from one generation to the next, from teacher to disciple to disciple's disciple. Or rather, because a whole tradition is made up of many subtraditions, it is one and the same tradition because all of its subtraditions share common sources and modes of thought and develop by reaction to one another. A tradition is by nature cumulative and it progresses in the sense that it defines itself with increasing detail and density. I define the tradition as philosophical to the extent that its members articulate it in the form of principles—if only principles of interpretation—and of conclusions reasonably drawn from them; and I define it as philosophical to the extent that its adherents defend and attack by means of reasonable arguments—even those that deny reason—and understand and explain how they try to be reasonable. As history demonstrates again and again, no philosophy is purely rational, pure rationality being an unreasonable, impossible ideal. Matters of religion, communal loyalty, reverence for teachers, and cultural habits, not to mention individual psychology, have always limited rationality, so that philosophical subtraditions or schools are rational by tendency rather than in any absolute way.[1]

I go on to my second question: Why say that there are only three great philosophical traditions? To claim this, one must put aside the correct but, for our purpose, insufficient definitions of philosophy as wisdom or as the group of principles, either stated or implied, by which any person or community views life. In keeping with the original meaning of the term *philosophy, love of wisdom*, philosophers, one supposes, have wanted to be wise, yet experience has taught that there is no good reason to think that they are necessarily so except, circularly, by their own definitions, and no good reason to think that nonphilosophers cannot be equally wise, that is, perceptive, farsighted, and sagacious, in the ways that their particular lives have taught them. Nor is there any good reason to suppose that traditions that are not philosophical by the definition I have adopted have not had their own depth of sophistication and practical intelligence (which is implicitly also theoretical).

Let me pause briefly to give a few examples of what I mean by this last statement. The definition of philosophy that is adopted here implies that ancient Mesopotamia and Egypt had no philosophical tradition. This implication holds true even though the Mesopotamians' religious texts show that they were trying to grasp universal and permanent principles that lie below the surface of things. On the basis of these principles they erected often fantastic hypotheses from which they could extrapolate what could or should happen. A different, more modest kind of understanding can be extrapolated from the Mesopotamian epic of Gilgamesh. Like Greek drama, the epic warns against the attempt to overcome the nature of things. In the end, the hero gets, though maybe refuses, the advice (accepted by Voltaire's Candide) to relax his heroics, accept the unheroic pleasures of life, and submit to the fate of all humans. The quite dissimilar *Dialogue of Pessimism* is a debate of a man with himself in which he makes contrary judgments on how he should act. It ends, it seems, with a skeptical, gloomy, yet humorous acceptance of all the contradictory positions— what is good is bad and what is useful is harmful. As in *Ecclesiastes*, the reason appears to be that a human being understands too little to know what it is best to do. Like the wisdom literature of the Egyptians and Hebrews, that of the Mesopotamians teaches the lesson of a temperate acceptance of life and life's duties.[2]

All this suggests the intellectual accomplishment of the Mesopotamians, which is matched by that of the other great, equally ancient civilization, the Egyptian. To give one of many examples, the Egyptians explain the world with the help of the cosmic goddess Maat, who unites in her person the values of order, equilibrium, truth, and wisdom, and so keeps the world tolerable to the human beings who tenant it. Yet god as conceived by the Egyptians remains ambiguous in number: except for the twenty years during which the pharaoh Akhenaten tried to force monotheism on the Egyptians, god for them remained both one and many, always being discovered in new manifestations. By their refusal to regard monotheism and polytheism as exclusive of one another, the Egyptians expressed their tacit conviction that nature has a certain unity but cannot be summed up in a fixed number of gods or forces.[3]

All this, I repeat, is not philosophy as I mean it here. If we accept a more general definition and think of philosophy as wisdom in the face of the difficulties of life, we discover that "primitives," as we have miscalled them, can be our equals. Let me justify this judgment with the example of the answer given by an Eskimo shaman to the explorer Knud Rasmussen when Rasmussen pressed him to justify his religion. Taking Rasmussen outside, the Eskimo first asked him why the blizzard was so cruel and then showed him a sick woman and asked why the innocent must suffer. When Rasmussen hesitated, the Eskimo said:

> You see, you are equally unable to give any reason why we ask why life is as it is. All our customs come from life and turn towards life; we explain nothing, we believe in nothing, but in what I have shown you lies our answer to all you ask.[4]

This answer shows that a cold climate and apparently simple life can produce wisdom; but so can a hot climate, as is proved by African proverbial thought, at times as pointed as anything in La Rochefoucauld or Nietzsche. "Those who are absent are always wrong," says an African proverb; and "Wisdom is like mushrooms that come after you have finished eating (too late!)"; and "A healthy ear can stand hearing sick words."[5]

Such proverbs are akin to African dilemma tales, which put arguable, humorous problems to a group of listeners. Take the example of the Nigerian tale in which a blind man accompanied by his blind wife, blind mother, and blind mother-in-law, finds seven eyes. Two he gives to his wife, two he takes for himself, one he gives to his mother, and one to his mother-in-law. He is left with a single eye in his hand. If he gives the remaining eye to his own mother, his wife—who is there looking at him—will make him feel ashamed, but if he gives it to his wife's mother, he will be afraid, because one's mother is not to be trifled with. The teller of the tale challenges the audience to make and justify the choice, which is not unlike the choices we try to work out in philosophical ethics or, more practically, in the medical dilemmas now discussed by philosophers and hospital committees.[6]

Why are such profound myths, clever proverbs, and dilemma tales not philosophy in the sense intended here? The myths are not because, relying on traditional narratives and on imagination, they do not usually make their meaning explicit and never justify it by careful reasoning—the meaning remains basically implicit. The *Dialogue of Pessimism* is not philosophy as meant here because the speaker does no more than state the opposing views between which he is caught, the Eskimo's insight is not because it is not developed, and the African proverbs and dilemma tales are not, for the same reason, and also because they are not related with enough care to explicit principles—at least to principles by which situations may be analyzed.*

Yet mythology, debate against oneself, existential emotion, proverbial sharpness, and exercise in hard choices all join philosophy in the sense used here when, in keeping with the definition that has been adopted, they are argued out reasonably; or when the principles on which they rest are distinguished from the conclusions built on them—or it is reasonably argued that there are no such principles; or when the methods of argument are themselves justified; or when the story, emotion, cleverness, or confrontation with oneself or others is put in a relatively unbroken sequence of reasonings. This spelling out of reasons is not necessarily to the good, or all to the good: The tendency of reason to devalue what it has not succeeded in making verbally explicit and logically consistent makes it apt to miss a great deal to which imagination has given the form of mythology, religion, and art. Where abstraction displays clearly defined but skeletally bare principles—one logical lever openly moving another—imagination, as tradition develops it, displays complex images and ambiguous relations that are less easy to analyze or enchain deductively but are far more suggestive.

---

*In a book that influenced many African intellectuals, the Belgian missionary Placide Tempels argued that the thought of the Bantus (of central and southern Africa) is a consistent, rational, and therefore "philosophical" vitalism based on the principle that all being is hierarchically organized force. Another influential figure, the Rwandan priest Alexis Kagame, argued that the Rwandaise language shows an implicit, particularly dynamic notion of structure. Further, the French anthropologist Marcel Griaule attributed to the Dogon, of central Mali, a rich cosmology and a "metaphysics" expressed in rites and actions (*Conversations with Ogotemmeli,* p. 3).

In essential agreement with the restrictive definition of philosophy I have given here, Kwasi Wiredu, an Oxford-educated philosopher from Ghana, considers traditional African thought, however humanistic, to be only a "folk philosophy." An African philosophy distinct from traditional world-views is still to be created, he says (*Philosophy and an African Culture,* pp. 6–8, 33–36). And the French-educated philosopher Paulin Hountondji denounces "ethnophilosophies" as European constructs unknown to the Africans to which they have been attributed and insists that the theoretical creativity of the African peoples, arrested by colonialism, is yet to be liberated (*African Philosophy,* pp. 45, 54, 67, 101, 164).

Why Are There Only Three Philosophical Traditions?

I have still not explained why I have said that there are only three philosophical traditions, the Indian, the Chinese, and the European. What about such others as the Jewish, Muslim, Japanese, and Tibetan? Well, yes and no, as philosophers say, these are and are not separate traditions. The matter is more complicated than it seems at first. To begin with, it is possible to argue that even the Indians, Chinese, and Europeans never arrived at points of view unified enough to justify classifying them as distinct traditions. In all three, there are obvious and unobvious points of cleavage. To mention only the most obvious, in India, the Indians who regarded themselves as orthodox tried to delegitimize, that is, read out of their tradition, the philosophies they classified as unorthodox; in China, the Taoists mocked the tradition that Confucians revered, and during China's later history, orthodox Confucians saw Buddhism as deeply foreign to Chinese tradition; and in Europe, it is not hard to distinguish the different national traditions—philosophy that is in a French, English, German, Italian, or other tradition.

To justify classifying each of the three great traditions as distinct, one therefore has to show that it has a unity that prevails over all the internal differences it exhibits. Or if the attempt to show that unity prevails seems tenuous or subjective, one has to show that each of the three has pervasive habits of thought and a history of self-reference—of person to person, of intellectual group to group, of intellectual group to authoritative person, tradition, or text, and so on. This would demonstrate unity in two separable senses, that of continuity and that of self-reference. Continuity is the relationship that makes everything subsequent in the tradition lead back to the same beginnings in time, place, or attitude—the Vedas, say, in India,

---

In contrast especially to Hountondji, Kwame Gyekye, of the University of Ghana, argues that there are cultural ideas common to the African peoples, so that it is justifiable to speak of African philosophy. African philosophers should therefore "turn their gaze on the *intellectual foundations of African culture and experience.* . . ." (*An Essay on African Thought*, pp. 189–90, 212 [quoted]).

It has also been argued that the distinction between folk philosophy and formal philosophy rests on a parochial idea that "captures only the contemporary analytic tradition" (P. Ikunobe, "The Parochial Universalist Conception of 'Philosophy' and 'African Philosophy,' " pp. 194–95, 207).

H. Odera Oruka, whose philosophical training is American, has conducted research in Kenya on what he calls "sage philosophy," which he regards as a logical, critical, didactic form of wisdom distinct from that taught by folk-sages, who are uncritical. He protests that it is only prejudice that grants a Greek sage such as Heraclitus the name *philosopher* but denies it to a contemporary African sage such as Mbuya Akoko (*Sage Philosophy*, p. xxv). Okura's book contains brief life histories of seven Kenyan sages and interviews designed to exhibit the critical quality of their reasoning.

Bibliographical data for this footnote are given in note 6, above.

the godlike culture heroes in China, and the Greek philosophers in Europe. Self-reference, in contrast, is the quality that makes any isolated statement or philosophy difficult to understand without setting it in the contextual web that determines what is internal to the tradition and what is external to it, belongs to another world of thought and, no doubt, action.

What obscures and what strengthens the unity of each of the three traditions? Even China, which alone of the three traditions has had a single government for much of its history, has undergone dramatic changes of dynasty and probably of the character we identify as Chinese; and, like India and Europe, it has always contained a great variety of territories, people, languages, and cultural traditions. All the same, most Chinese thinkers have shared the same classical language, same historical reference points, and (in imperial China) same education, which was essential to their prestige and to their usual competition for government office.

The unity of India and Europe has been more tenuous. However, the great old classics of the one were Sanskrit and of the other were Greek and Latin, and just as classical Chinese was the learned language of educated Chinese, Sanskrit remained that of learned Indians and Latin of learned Europeans, so that, in each tradition, reference to the past would normally be to the same classical literature. As for Japanese thought, philosophically it depends mainly on the Chinese, as the Tibetan depends mainly on the Indian, that is, Buddhist, while Jewish and Muslim thought, though each has its own history and dogmas, draw their philosophy proper from the same Greek and Roman sources and, in this limited but real sense, are part of the European tradition.*

Philosophy, it turns out, had just three territorial origins, three beginning languages, three historical pasts, and three webs of self-reference. That there have been just three major philosophical traditions is, therefore, a fact, a brute fact, I would say. Whoever is so minded can emphasize the breaks in each and the vagueness at times of the borders between them,

---

*No doubt, pride in one's Jewish or Muslim heritage may prompt one to minimize this dependence on European, that is, Greek and Roman thought. The dependence is explained in chapter 9, which discusses, among other philosophers, Al-Farabi, Ibn Sina (Avicenna) and Maimonides. Each of the three has his own, sometimes considerable degree of philosophical independence, but the thought of no one of them can be conceived without the Aristotelian and Neoplatonic principles that underlie it. As will be explained, the Muslims themselves reserve the term *philosophy* for thought based on these Aristotelian-Neoplatonic principles. The often philosophical theology that departs from the principles is called *kalam,* which may be translated *dialectical theology.* For its logic, *kalam* depends on Hellenistic, especially Stoic logic, and for its practices of debate and its dissociative kind of atomism—which denies natural causality— perhaps on Indian philosophy.

borders like those of diffuse clouds; but the notions themselves of breaks and borders imply something that is single enough to be broken and separate enough to have borders of some kind.[7]

Why Is It Best to Study the Three Traditions Together Rather than Separately or Successively?

As the interrelationship between human beings everywhere grows stronger and more visible, it grows more obvious that a point of view that takes account of no more than a single culture is to that extent provincial. This provincialism has been shared by persons of otherwise great intellectual distinction, too proud, I suppose, to realize how narrow-minded they were, or still are. I do not hesitate to say that anyone who believes that philosophy (in the relatively technical sense adopted here) has been confined to Europe is demonstrating either ignorance or prejudice. So far as I know, this belief is never held by those who have studied Indian or Chinese thought with care.

Granted that there are three philosophical traditions and that interest in them all is justified, why claim, as I do, that is it best to begin by studying them together or—to diminish the claim—to begin by comparing characteristic examples of all three in revealing detail? One reason is that each of the traditions is so great in extent and depth that if any one of them really seizes your interest, you sink into it and the chances of studying another tradition seriously are greatly diminished; and if you do take up another, it is likely to be as a subject of only minor interest. That is, by concentrating exclusively on any one tradition, you in practice tend to prejudge its importance and reduce the likelihood that you will be able to understand it in just relationship to the others.

A second reason for learning the three together is that you then become aware of a much greater variety of positions. The result is that every philosophy is seen in the light of more contrasts, and more contrasts yield a greater variety of interpretations and, it is reasonable to hope, a greater ability to modulate any point of view. And if the three are learned together, it is easier to explore the possibility that there are philosophical positions and arguments that are truly universal or that, taken together, make up a kind of periodic table of the elements of philosophy. This possibility is one in favor of which, on pragmatic, psychological, and personal grounds, I myself incline. But the opposite, I should say, more romantic inclination, makes things even more interesting: By changing your eyes, you see things—meanings, relationships, and values—to which you have so far been blind. A perceptive traveler in philosophy learns to grasp what has been invisible because it is too familiar or, on the contrary, too distant, and is led to take greater care in discriminating exact meanings.

Let me give an example: The Chinese philosopher Hsün-tzu, of the third century B.C.E., says, "The nature of man is evil; his goodness is the result of his activity," and the German philosopher Kant, of the eighteenth century, says, "The question here is: whether man is *good* by nature, or *evil* by nature, or whether he is by nature equally receptive to good and evil, according as one or another hand happens to mould him." Anyone curious enough to explore the likeness between both statements must first learn their contexts. To begin with, one must ask what both mean by *good*, *evil*, and *nature*? And then one must ask how much of the similarity is the result of translation from, respectively, Chinese and German, into the same standard English? The questions are not trivial nor the answers simple.[8]

Yet even if what I have been contending is true, there remains a practical objection, which is that no one knows enough to teach the three traditions together except very superficially. In answer, I admit that no person can know all three in great depth—I certainly do not pretend to. Yet those who make this objection ought to think further and take into account that much the same argument applies to the history of even a single tradition. It is easy to make an arithmetical estimate to show that no person, however industrious, has nearly enough time to make a more than superficial study of the works of all the philosophers and schools considered important in either the Indian, the Chinese, or the European tradition. Our human limitations are such that it is an accomplishment to learn even a single philosopher really well. How difficult it is to bend one's understanding to fit that of someone else, especially someone different in culture and experience, someone who may have written thousands of pages and made acknowledged and unacknowledged shifts of position and have shown all the coherence and incoherence of which a thinker is capable! If a fully adequate knowledge of the sources was required, it would be extremely unlikely that anyone could write a history of modern European philosophy or, for that matter, write any history of any kind of any extended period or large area. I have heard a specialist in Hellenistic philosophy say that it is now impossible for anyone to know even Greek philosophy—scholarship has grown too detailed. But since we have and need general histories, it stands to reason that they can be written only because their authors are ready to contend with their relative ignorance. Unless they were willing to do so, in history, as in other fields of learning, we would be left with the work of specialists too narrow to see anything whole and would be unable to see any subject in a wide yet relatively informed perspective. To study or write the history of philosophy of *any* tradition or period, one must be ready to omit very much, to take more than a little on the authority of others, and to try to make clear to oneself what is of great and what of less importance.

The total number of philosophical works that can possibly be studied by a historian who deals with all three traditions is no greater than the number that can possibly be studied by a historian of any one of them, so that the selectivity of the comparative historian must be greater, as must surely be the dependence on other scholars—the mere linguistic competence demanded grows almost beyond human possibilities. I am confident, however, that once the philosophical classics of each of the three traditions are more widely known, their strangeness in the other two traditions will wear off and the easier texts will be as accessible in translation as the easier native ones. The denser or more technical texts, whether native or foreign, will always need elaborate commentaries.[9]

A Distant, Preliminary View of the Three Traditions

This first view of the three traditions begins with a chronological chart of the philosophers to be discussed here.* In choosing just these philosophers, I may have been influenced by their suitability for comparison. But this influence, conscious or not, can only have been marginal because most of those listed are indispensable to the traditions to which they belong and which they largely define; and though I hope not to forget the philosophers' individuality, it is the part their ideas play in creating their respective traditions that I intend to emphasize. That is, I have ordinarily adopted what I take to be each tradition's retrospective view of its own development and of the contribution that each of its philosophers made to it. I must concede that a few of the persons who appear in the chart— Confucius is the most conspicuous example—are not philosophers by the definition I have adopted, but they belong here because they are the fathers of their respective philosophical traditions. I must also concede

---

*A good many of the dates I give are doubtful, and some, especially of the Indian philosophers, are known only vaguely—all that is really known of the dates of Uddalaka and Yajnavalkya is that they precede the Buddha. As for the Buddha, there are scholars who go beyond minor adjustments of his dates and situate him a full hundred years later. In this chart, which aims at maximal simplicity, I have not allowed myself more than two question marks nor used the abbreviation *c.* or *ca.* to indicate approximation. Vasubandhu may represent two philosophers rather than one, but this is not the place to discuss dividing him. While a number of undoubtedly great philosophers do not appear in this chronology, some of the philosophers I do write about are absent here because I could not stretch the notion of a great philosopher enough to include them. As explained in the text, Alfarabi, Avicenna, and Mainmonides are considered to belong to the European tradition. For the sake of a perhaps quixotic and merely relative neutrality—the birth of Christ is still the chronology's starting point—I use the abbreviations B.C.E. and C.E.

that, to write a coherent history of a practical size, I feel compelled to leave out more than a few philosophers that I take to be great. Besides, the philosophers that do appear are not invariably great, and a number of them, chosen to represent certain points of view, might have been exchanged for others.

The italicized names on the chart are those of philosophers I should have taken up if I had wanted to make this history more nearly complete and, especially, if I had continued it up to our own times. In spite of their relatively early date, I do not deal with the Buddhists Hui-neng, Fa-tsang, and Dogen. This is because Hui-neng and Dogen, who are, respectively, Chinese and Japanese Ch'an (Zen) thinkers, are best compared with Europeans such as Kierkegaard and Nietzsche, these four comprising a group, as I see it, of postmetaphysical irrationalists. And Fa-tsang, with his philosophy of all-in-all, would make a particularly interesting pair with Hegel.

Now, to begin with, look not at the names of the particular philosophers but at the way in which the names cluster at some points and are absent at others (see Figure 1.1).

The names we see clustered at the top of the three columns express the fact that all three traditions went through an early period in which there was enough conflict and enough freedom to encourage the simultaneous appearance of many quite different points of view. Competition between these points of view stimulated the intellectual self-assertion that constitutes philosophy. In all three traditions, this was a time of the breaking and building of social structures that encouraged adventurous intellectuals to think aloud, to play, pray, and dream in the mode of reasoning. In response to their own ambition or the urging of their disciples or rulers, they dueled with neighbors of like philosophical or other ambitions, neighbors who varied, according to distinctions then already drawn, from hidebound conservatives to wild radicals and damnable sophists.

It is not chance that in the geographical areas of each of the three traditions there were then many small states rubbing shoulders in amity or enmity. In some of these states—in Europe, Athens is the best example—the habit of freedom was strong enough for it to be possible to argue almost anything—though in Athens, Anaxagoras, Socrates, and maybe others paid for the freedom they exercised. The upshot was that in all three traditions there were sages or intellectuals, typically with entourages of followers, to argue for or against the already existing tradition of a golden age, for or against this-worldliness, and for or against altruism or egoism. However religious or traditional India and China may appear to later eyes, everything sacred and everything profane could then be mocked by those of a turn for mockery, or debated by those of a mind to debate. These wars waged with reasons led to the development of thought about

Chronology of Great Philosophers

INDIA	CHINA, JAPAN	EUROPE
B.C.E.		
Uddalaka (?8th cent.)		
Yajnavalkya (?8th cent.)		
Mahavira (599–527)		Heraclitus (fl. 500)
Buddha (563–483)	Confucius (551–479)	Parmenides (b. 515)
	Mo-tzu (480–390)	Socrates (470–399)
		Democritus (460–370)
	Chuang-tzu (4th cent.)	Plato (428–348)
	Mencius (371–298)	Aristotle (384–322)
		Pyrrho (365–270)
		Epicurus (341–270)
	Hsün-tzu (298–238)	Arcesilaus (315–241)
	Han Fei-tzu (280–233)	
		Carneades (214–129)
		Lucretius (99–55)
C.E.		
Nagarjuna (fl.200)		Plotinus (205–270)
		Sextus Empiricus
Asanga (fl. 350)		(3rd cent.)
Vasubandu (fl. 350)		
		Proclus (410–485)
Bhartirhari (450–510)		
Dignaga (480–540)		
	Hui-neng (638–713)/	
Dharmakirti (600–660)	Shen-hui (670–762)	
Shankara (700–750)	Fa-tsang (643–712)	
Jayarashi (fl. 800)		Al-Farabi (870–950)
Udayana (fl. 1050)		Avicenna (980–1037)
Shriharsha (fl. 1150)	Chu Hsi (1138–1200)	Maimonides
		(1135–1204)
	Dogen (1200–1253)	Aquinas (1225–1274)
		Duns Scotus (1266–1308)
Gangesha (fl. 1320)		William of Ockham
		(1285–1347)
Raghunatha (fl. 1500)	WangYang-ming	
	(1472–1529)	
		Descartes (1596–1650)
Gadadhara (fl. 1650)		Spinoza (1632–1677)
		Locke (1632–1704)
		Leibniz (1646–1716)
		Berkeley (1685–1753)
		Hume (1711–1776)
		Kant (1724–1804)
		Hegel (1770–1831)
		Kierkegaard (1813–1855)
		Nietzsche (1844–1900)
		Peirce (1839–1914)
		James (1842–1910)
		Dewey (1859–1952)
		Husserl (1859–1938)
	Nishida (1878–1945)	Russell (1872–1970)
		Wittgenstein (1889–1951)
		Heidegger (1889–1976)

thought, by which I mean about the hows and whys of reasons and reasoning. Not only do we find the beginnings of an almost formal logic but, along with it, a conscious playing about with paradoxes, the players happy as children with glittering new intellectual toys, and a readiness to demonstrate virtuosity as such in the logic or rhetoric of debate.

The philosopher Karl Jaspers calls this period the axial age because so much on which human thought turns was originated in its course—ours, he says, is another such age, the first in which history ceases to be a collection of local histories and becomes world history.[10] Jaspers takes as his starting point the eighth century B.C.E.; but if we restrict ourselves to the sixth and fifth centuries alone, we find not only the sages and philosophers listed in our chart, but writers, artists, and scientists who were equal creators of the three traditions, and, beyond these three, creators of other traditions, such as the prophets Ezekiel and Second Isaiah, who also helped to extend human thought—philosophy taken in its broader, more simply human sense.[11]

I go on to the relative emptiness of the chart for Europe during the period beginning with the first century C.E. and ending (Muslims and Jews apart) in the thirteenth. It should not be supposed that there are no names to fill the gap, which reflects the judgment that these are not the names of the great creators of the philosophical traditions (for Europe, I have probably been unjust in omitting the leading Stoics and Augustine). As the chart implies, there was a great change in Chinese philosophy that took place when Buddhism became acclimatized to its Chinese home and when Confucianism had to reconstruct itself in competition with Buddhism. But this intermediate period—intermediate from our position in time—is just that of the flourishing of Buddhist philosophy in India, as well as of its philosophical opponents, all of them sharpening one another's philosophical wits by means of their rivalry. It was through the now sophisticated Buddhist philosophy that India made the thought of China, Japan, and Tibet far more varied and subtle than before. For India, however, the chart becomes empty from about the twelfth century.

As compared with the crowded column of European philosophers, the near emptiness of the Indian and Sino-Japanese columns from the seventeenth century and on has an involved explanation, not all of which I am sure. At least some of it is likely to be the result of Western ignorance in general and my own ignorance in particular. I mean that the Indian and Chinese thinkers of this time have been studied in the West far less than their predecessors. To the best of my knowledge—I've confessed my ignorance—the only classical Indian school that continued to be visibly creative, as opposed to just increasingly intricate, was the logic-emphasizing school, in this period called, with reason, the "New Logic" (Navya-Nyaya).

The school of Vedanta may, more hesitantly, be added. But other classical schools also remained alive, and the verdict that their later work was uncreative may be the result of our inattentiveness to distinctions that they perceived and that we, too, may sometime come to perceive to be of genuine interest. Or perhaps we already perceive them so but are unaware that others have preceded us in recognizing their interest.

An example of possibly unjust omission is that of the Chinese "searchers for evidence." They were the members of a seventeenth- and eighteenth-century group of reform-minded thinkers. Using philology as their instrument, they hoped to recover ancient truths, purify them of later metaphysical dross, and, with these truths, go about reforming society. The "searchers for evidence" (k'ao-cheng) advocated the use of empirical criteria such as stone and bronze inscriptions, genealogies, and chronologically precise biographies; and they discussed Chinese astronomy and mathematics in relation to the European. Some of them (such as Tai Chen [1724–1777]) tried to legitimize this European science by assigning it a Chinese origin. By and large, the skeptical and empirical tendencies of these thinkers served the purpose of reconstructing the antiquity they revered. Their closest European analogues were the Renaissance scholars whose passion was to recover and relive Greco-Roman antiquity. But for all his courage and importance, Tai Chen seems to me not to show an intellectual intensity great enough to be classed as a great philosopher. However, my verdict may be the result of insufficient knowledge.

This whole late period, during which European philosophy flourished and non-European philosophy appears, rightly or wrongly, to have lessened its creative intensity is also the period that experienced foreign rule. Such rule may well have sapped the life of the Indian and then the Chinese philosophical tradition by weakening their social power and by impelling them in the direction of an at first necessarily crude encounter with Western thought. In India, Muslim raiders and conquerors exercised an increasing influence from the early eleventh century. Some Muslim rulers were simply intolerant, while others were tolerant either out of conviction or for merely pragmatic reasons—the extraordinarily tolerant emperor Akbar created a monotheism based on Hinduism and Christianity as much as on his native Muslim religion. In wartime, Muslim rulers often demonstrated their piety by desecrating or destroying Hindu temples, which in the villages were centers of social life and of potential resistance. In retaliation, a Hindu rebellion was likely to result in the same treatment of mosques. The clash was not between peoples who felt themselves to be equals because, to the intolerant on either side, the other was composed of the uncivilized or dangerous, of infidels, as the Muslims saw the Hindus, or of barbarians, as the Hindus saw the Muslims. The fact that the center of the school of New Logic was in Northeast India, which had remained untroubled by the earlier, more fanatical Muslims, may help explain the school's continued creativity.

It is not a priori unlikely, as modern Indian Muslims have claimed, that the Hindus who willingly converted to Islam were those who felt themselves most victimized by the caste system; and the mystical sects of Islam might pull at already mystically inclined Hindus. But for Hindus generally, the contact with the Muslims was external because the Muslim religion was imageless, ruled by dogma, and relatively egalitarian, while they, the Hindus, worshiped images and belonged to hereditary groupings, *jatis*, into which they were born and in which they lived, worshiped, worked, and died. To leave or be expelled from such a group was to become culturally naked and humanly isolated.

I have been speaking of the Hindus in relation to the Muslims, but when the British became dominant, as happened in the later eighteenth century, the results were just as complicated and hard to summarize as those of Muslim dominance. I allow myself to avoid any detail here and to say only that, in the long run, European thought proved to be a dangerous, sometimes demoralizing rival to the traditional thought of India.[12]

In China, the first great outside influence, which came from India in the form of Buddhism, was quite peaceful. By about the fourth century C.E., Buddhism had been transformed from a foreign into a native, Chinese religion. However, in the eyes of orthodox Confucians it was offensive and even dangerous because, they argued, a Buddhist was encouraged as such to transfer allegiance from the family and from the Confucian hierarchy of teachers and officials to the Buddhist monastery, and was encouraged, at least in principle, to renounce marriage and even the most usual and innocent animal pleasures—all the goals that most ordinary humans pursue without question. As it was actually lived, Buddhism proved far more pliant than such orthodox complainants could admit, and many individuals were Confucian and Buddhist (or Taoist) at once, with a feeling, attested to by poets and artists, of inward wealth rather than inward contradiction.

As a result of the different form of life it encouraged, of the shift in allegiance it demanded of those deeply faithful to it, and of its heavy involvement in court politics, Buddhism aroused strenuous opposition and was subjected to persecution, though not of the most drastic kinds practiced in Europe. The monasteries' wealth was confiscated and their monks were dispersed, causing the decline of all but two sects, Ch'an (Zen) and Pure Land.[13]

The Europeans who first influenced the Chinese were the missionaries. Their influence was mostly on the scholars or court officials who were intrigued by their foreign learning or by the clocks and other devices they brought with them. However, the missionaries were eventually expelled and their converts subjected to persecution. It was not until the middle of the nineteenth century that a serious contest began between the Chinese who favored tradition and those who wanted to introduce Western learning or practices. This contest, like the contests elsewhere between traditionalists and Westernized reformers, was fierce and bred great fears and hopes.

We have to leave such political contests and go back to philosophy proper and to the causes for its real or apparent loss of creativity in India and China. In both traditions, threats from the outside have led to repeated retreats inward. The kind of retreat I mean is to an orthodoxy that demonstrates its faithfulness to tradition by insisting on remaining fixed, that is, by ignoring or pretending to ignore the worth of everything that is foreign to it. Such a retreat was possible because the Indian and Chinese traditionalists were unable to conceive that there could be languages equal in refinement and exactness to Sanskrit—taken to be utterly sacred and beautiful—or, in the case of China, to classical Chinese—taken to be incomparably superior in every way—and unable to conceive that there could be other philosophical cultures that might at all approach the richness and rightness of their own. As the Indians and Chinese understood it, their thought had undergone a process that began in inspired wisdom and continued by way of the differentiation, refinement, and expansion that made each culture inexpressibly right and deep, so that those who had formed themselves by its means could retire into its depths without feeling any sense of narrowness, that is, of provinciality or loss of universal truth. Both the Chinese and Indian traditions of philosophy have functioned as "a sophisticated theoretical structure of self-universalization and self-isolation."[14] The European tradition, too, has usually exhibited this narcissistic attention to itself. But this should not lead us to forget the obvious, that a community preserves itself by excluding from power any foreigners and foreignness that endanger its unity, such as it may be.

History shows that the Buddhists were able to look outward more than the Hindus but unable to survive in India itself. Deeply Hindu or deeply Confucian philosophers felt alienated from Buddhism. It was rare for them to acknowledge any need to consider a foreign tradition as if it could teach them anything of intellectual or spiritual value. By the twentieth century, of course, such a view had become implausible to an increasing and finally dominant number of intellectuals.

Despite what I have said, it should not be assumed that the Hindus isolated themselves completely from Muslim thought; but the mutual influences of various kinds were never of great importance to classical philosophy. Finally, however, whether earlier or later, Western thought, along with Western commerce and Western arms, became a subversive influence everywhere. The effect of the West became so dominant that a Hindu or Chinese was (and is) likely to accept Western values while insisting that his native tradition developed their equivalents earlier, or at least by itself: Everything Western worth anything was already there in the Upanishads or *The Book of Changes*. To give a more subtle though more doubtful example, researchers into the intellectual life of seventeenth-century China point out, as I have implied, that it resembles European thought in being oriented (ironic word here) toward the critical, empirical, and even material. It is true that the Chinese have always had an interest in history, philology, and archeology, all of them needed to subject documents and ideas to a critical analysis. But perhaps the researchers were tempted by the desire to show how far the Chinese tradition could go toward an educated empiricism by means of its own resources alone.* The play of pride and shame in one's tradition never disappears. And of course, both Indian and Chinese nationalists have responded to humiliation by outsiders by stressing the essential superiority of their native thought.[15]

Is the Conception of Philosophy the Same in the Three Traditions?

We are still not clear of initial problems. This is because in speaking of philosophy I have been making the perhaps mistaken assumption that such an enterprise or profession in fact exists in India and China. One interesting though much too simple way of testing the assumption is to ask whether terms for *philosophy* exist in Sanskrit and Chinese, and if they appear to exist, whether their meanings are close enough to the

---

*Modern Western philosophy is said to have first entered Chinese intellectual life in the form of an article on Francis Bacon, written by Wang Tao (1822–1897), who collaborated with the missionary James Legge on a pioneering translation of the Chinese classics. Wang Tao's article on Bacon was published in 1873, and a translation of Bacon's *Novum Organum*, in 1877. In 1889, an essay competition in a Shanghai college ("supervised" by Wang Tao) was based on the unusual question, in what does the Chinese way of "investigation things and extending knowledge" differ from and resemble that initiated in the West by "the Englishman Bacon," whose ideas "affected the writings of two other [English] intellectuals, Darwin and Spencer. Since their works have proven to be so beneficial, can you provide a detailed account of the sources of these influences?" The four answers that have been preserved show a basic understanding of Bacon, and two of them, a basic understanding of Darwin as well. After the abolition, in 1905, of the imperial examination system, Bacon's ideas were widely accepted among intellectuals (Yuan Weishi, "A Few Problems. . . . ," pp. 164–66, 174–75).

European meanings to justify their use as equivalents. Although I am committed to saying yes, this answer is not self-evident. The moment of word investigation that follows gives a useful reminder of the kind of difficulties that comparative philosophy faces.

It soon becomes evident that the Sanskrit or Chinese terms that Westerners have perhaps thoughtlessly used to translate *philosophy* and *school of philosophy* have meanings that are unique to their own languages.[16] This mismatching has sometimes been a source of both pride and shame, and it has made it easy to declare that not only the terms but also the subject matter and the institutions of the European tradition, such as its schools of philosophy, are unique to Europe. But while it is true that, by a philologist's standards, the terms themselves for *philosophy* are different in meaning, observation of their use shows that this difference is not in itself crucial. It might have been crucial if each tradition had permanently fixed the technical meanings of its philosophical terms. Sometimes equivalents were stabilized by the need for exactness in translation. In China— notably in the seventh century under the direction of Hsüan-tsang—Sanskrit originals were translated by large groups of specialists. In Tibet, the meanings of Sanskrit terms came to be fixed either by usage or official decree: according to the late eighth-century *Word Combination*, misleading translations were revised and terms whose meaning "had to be fixed in accord with an interpretation" were given official equivalents.[17] All the same, the meanings of general philosophical terms have varied a good deal in all three traditions, so even though the terms' webs of relationship vary, there is a good deal of overlapping. As long as the likelihood of similarity-in-difference is understood and it is taken for granted that philosophically important terms are clarified when studied in context, no great misunderstanding need arise from the equation of a term like *philosophy* with the terms it translates. It can be just as misleading to be overexact, by insisting on distinctions finer than the context makes necessary, as to be careless; and the level of abstraction—of distance of terms from their local associations—should be appropriate to the translator's particular aim.

Let me spell out what I have just said in enough detail to make the point convincing. I begin with Greece, where the term was invented.[18] There, in Greece, the word *wisdom* (*sophia*) could be used, as it was by Plato, to distinguish between true wisdom and the false wisdom taught, he complained, by the sophists. Aristotle used the word to name the highest intellectual virtue, which he contrasted with practical wisdom. As for *philosophia, the love of wisdom*, Socrates explains in the *Apology* that what he does is to persuade young and old to care less for body or money than for excellence of soul. Later, in the *Phaedo*, when he speaks of his impending execution by the Athenians, he explains that God has laid on him the duty of living a life of philosophy and examining both himself and others, and that because he believes that he has spent his life in this way, he is confident that he will be greatly blessed after death. For this reason, he goes on, all those rightly engaged in philosophy are training themselves for dying—philosophy is the proper training for death! But *philosophia* is also used in the Platonic dialogues to name the search for true knowledge in the sense of the discovery of the unchanging principles of knowledge. Afterward, the Greek concept of philosophy becomes whatever the history of Western philosophy had made it become—there are very many variations.

Perhaps to our astonishment, we find no term in traditional India for *philosopher* as distinguished from *sage*, *saint*, or the like (for *logician* there is the rough equivalent *tarkika*). But there are two old terms, *anvikshiki* and *darshana*, that can be equated with *philosophy*.[19] The first of these, still sometimes translated by *philosophy*, appears to have meant a method of reasoning or science of investigation. Considered to be "a source of light for all sciences, an instrument for all activities, a foundation for all religious and social duties," it was appropriated by the Logic School (Nyaya) as a self-description; but it continued to be used in the neutral sense of *logical reasoning*.[20] Since it was associated with logic, the term could also be associated with sophistry and with secular, antitraditional points of view, and its nuances were sometimes unfavorable. The more orthodox or believing philosophers kept such analytic reasoning in its place by insisting that it could always be corrected or refuted and therefore could not reach the absolute truth, which only the authority of scripture or intuition could establish.

It appears to me that, except for the Logic School, orthodox Indian philosophers were more likely to use logic in order to bare contradictions in their opponents' views than to establish their own positive doctrines. In the usual ways of metaphysicians, these doctrines were simply proclaimed at the start or were accepted as the revealed truth, the *Veda* intuited by the sages who founded their respective schools. The doctrines were then defended by logical counterattacks on those who had attacked them logically. To interject my own opinion, I think that it was sensible of these philosophers to use logic to attack and refute rather than to prove, because logic finds flaws in reasoning but cannot build philosophies by its own power alone.

Darshana, the other Sanskrit term equated with *philosophy*, is taken etymologically to mean *(the act of) seeing*. When extended to mean *realization*, the term has been used to strengthen the presumption of Indians that their tradition is superior to the analytic, wholly theoretical interests they (mistakenly) attribute to Western philosophy in general.[21] However, some

Westerners have claimed that the difference between the Indian and Western terms shows that the Indian tradition has lacked the very concept of philosophy as the West has understood it.

In time, especially for the purpose of classifying their philosophies, most Indians came to prefer the term *darshana* to designate an Indian *view, doctrine,* or *system.* In the nineteenth century, when the Indians began to study European philosophy, they used *darshana* to translate *philosophy.* But not all of them have been happy with the translation. Sometimes they have complained that it helps to deprive Indian thought of its native difference from Western ways of thought. Sometimes, too, they have proclaimed that all philosophy should be understood in the light of the spiritual doctrine of India, which defines philosophy more profoundly than philosophy itself is able to—the true (more than) philosopher is the seer.

What of China?[22] It turns out that China, too, lacked an exact equivalent to *philosophy.* The invention of a new term for it, by a Japanese, makes another illuminating footnote to comparative philosophy. The story of the term begins in 1862, when a young Japanese named Nishi Amane was sent to study in Leiden, from where he brought books by Comte, Mill, Montesquieu, Hegel, and other philosophers, along with the ambition to reform Japanese thought in their light. Back in Japan, he joined a group of "Illuminists" dedicated to encouraging Western liberalism in Japan. One of the group said sarcastically that all that Japan had to be proud of was its scenery. Another member of the group favored Western science on the grounds that it was not Western but universal, and said, in addition, that only Western-style, constitutional government conformed with human nature. As always, such sentiments provoked a conservative reaction.

Nishi himself, who favored and translated Mill's *Utilitarianism,* created (or transcribed phonetically into Japanese) much of the philosophical terminology the Japanese were to use. Long before, when preparing to lecture on Greek and European philosophy at the Center for the Investigation of Barbarian Books, he had tried to approximate the Greek meaning of *philosophy* by abbreviating the Japanese words *science of questing wisdom* into the term *kitetsugaku.* But then he had applied the word to philosophy in the Western sense alone. Now he decided to coin a more general word. To this end, he analyzed the Western concept of *philosophy* and found a possible Chinese analogue, an old word composed of a character of two hands and an axe (meaning, perhaps, *to break open,* as with an axe) and another character, for mouth (meaning *by using thought or speech*). As a whole, the word means, roughly, *to speak with deliberation* or *to conceive.* Having discovered the concept of philosophy, as he thought, in classical Chinese, Nishi felt justified in abbreviating his earlier term to *tetsugaku,* to be applied to philosophical thought universally, Sino-Japanese (Confucian,

Taoist, Buddhist, etc.) and Western alike. Invented in 1874, the term proved very successful and was widely adopted in East Asia, including China, though only, of course, in its ideographic, pictorial form, the Chinese sound of which is transliterated *che-hsüeh* (in pinyin *zhe-xe*.)[23]

Not only *philosophy* but also *school* (of philosophy) creates a problem. In Chinese, the nearest old term is *chia*, literally *family*, used in the sense of *scholarly lineage*, which implies that the task of those it designates, like that assumed by an Indian school, is to keep an intellectual and spiritual heritage. The Indian schools kept their heritage by a method that made their philosophies grow, like trees, in concentric rings of argument and counterargument. That is, although they supposed that their respective positions expressed a truth that was timeless, they kept investigating it in increasing detail, mostly, it seems, to defend their versions of the truth against the always renewed objections of their rivals. Indian philosophers were likely to conceal their originality, much as did medieval Jewish, Muslim, and Christian philosophers, who had committed themselves to preserve rather than renew the truth—Maimonides and Aquinas and their followers are good examples.

The view that one should concentrate on preserving an already revealed truth must often have lowered interest in the philosophical changes brought about by individuals. To the extent that it did so, the present history's concentration on individual philosophers reflects a distinctly Western rather than Indian point of view. But this statement, too, has to be qualified because the story of Indian (including Buddhist and Jain) philosophy, as the Indians themselves tell it, is filled with incredibly able heroes. Characteristically, the Chinese accounts are historicized, although they too begin with mythically improved or invented ancestors.

Such comments on Indian, European medieval, and Chinese philosophers are not meant to imply that the present account succeeds in neutralizing the biasses of the modern West. If—as I am not sure—the desire to understand those different from oneself and the desire to go beyond stereotypes are predominantly Western, then I do not really want to escape completely. In any case, whatever our ideal, we cannot wholly avoid remaining the persons we early grew up to be.[24]

What I have told of the relation between the Indian, Chinese, and European terms for *philosophy* and *school of philosophy* implies that an exact correspondence of such concepts is impossible but that a working correspondence is not hard to reach. This is because, as I have noted, the old terms were subjected to such a variety of interpretations that if one wants to be as exact as possible, the meaning of every use, Indian, Chinese, and European, has to be worked out in detail. Such understanding profits by conscious analysis, but the more usual and subtle learning is by way of the tacit understanding that comes with the actual study of particular texts.*

Telltale Sign of Philosophy: Logic

Well-articulated reasoning, I have said, is the test of philosophy. The clearest overt sign of such reasoning is the adoption of logical rules, that is, rules by which to ensure the strictness of the reasoning. The ability to use an explicitly logical method can therefore be used as a criterion, though not the only one, by which to judge whether or not a tradition is truly philosophical in the sense adopted here.[25] Now if the basis of explicitly logical thinking is the law of contradiction (of a pair of contradictory statements, one is true and the other false) then all three traditions are philosophical because they all not only recognize the law implicitly but use it at times in different conscious variants.** In ancient India an at least semitechnical use of the term *mutual prohibition* or *contradiction (viprati-shedha)* begins some time between the fifth and third centuries B.C.E.[26] The philosophers of the Logic School (Nyaya) assume the law of contradiction in their discussions and give it practical expression in their arguments. Indian philosophers who qualify the law of contradiction for their own doctrinal reasons argue that there is a kind of negation that, not being exclusive, does not give rise to self-contradiction.[27] Occasionally the law of

---

*"The correct method . . . is not one of seeking a more or less literal translation for a word, but rather to find those *homeomorphic equivalents* which describe the possible correlative activity or activities in other cultures. . . . Each real word in any language opens up a whole field of meanings, with diverse connotations and denotations, which is practically impossible to cover with another single word of another linguistic universe (Pannikar, "Śapathaprajna," p. 21 [see note 19 above]).

**The just preceding note (note 25) recalls a number of recent essays on the different philosophical conceptions of rationality. It seems to me that they all acknowledge that to be rational or (if a distinction is made) to be reasonable, one must think intelligibly. Intelligible thought implies consistency in the use of ideas, and consistency requires the use, implicit or explicit, of the law of contradiction. Philosophers like the Neoplatonists, Spinoza, and Hegel, who believe that the world is or has a logical structure, may take the law of contradiction, along with all formal logic, to be subordinate to the inexpressible source of logic, or enveloped within a metaphysically higher kind of logic (for Hegel, see the compact account in M. Inwood, *A Hegel Dictionary*, Oxford: Blackwell, 1992, pp. 268–71). But these philosophers do their best to reason consistently. Of course, there are those who prefer to deny that logic has access to any reality. But to fit the category of philosopher, a skeptic or irrationalist such as Chuang-tzu, Nagarjuna, Kierkegaard, or Nietzsche has to make an intelligible defense of the contention that reason, including the law of contradiction, is empty or misleading. The problem that arises, of the skeptic's overt self-contradiction, is dealt with here in chapter 8, on developed skepticism.

contradiction or the companion law of excluded middle are stated explicitly. Both occur together in the following eleventh-century text:

> There is no other sort, when there is mutual opposition. The opposed cannot be [in] one and the same, since the very utterance would be contradictory. A kind other than the positive and the negative is not possible, for they are of the nature of mutual affirmation and negation. By merely denying the positive, the negative is affirmed.[28]

The ancient Chinese have a different cast of mind.[29] Because their language is not inflected (its characters do not change their forms), they at first conceived of their sentences as only a succession of "names," as they called words. The earliest explicit recognition of the importance of word order in sentences or, rather, strings of words, occurs in a text of the third century B.C.E. When referring to the logical relation between a pair of words, the ancient Chinese of a logical cast of mind may say that the words follow from one another or "dismiss" (are inconsistent with) one another, or that if one is inadmissible, so is the other. In one text, the law of excluded middle takes the form of the statement that when two men contradict each another in a disputation and one opinion is right ("fits the fact"), the other is necessarily wrong (does not "fit the fact"). Use is made of the term *pei* to state that something is inconsistent, illogical, or self-falsifying. A good example is that of an ancient, logically inclined Chinese who, unhappy with Chuang Tzu's statement that to accept a proposition from one point of view is to reject it from another, retorts, "To deem all saying self-falsifying is self-falsifying"—a retort that Chuang Tzu, always logically brazen, shows he understands.[30]

Unlike either the Europeans or the Indians, the Chinese have no explicit, developed, formal logic; and they neither theorize about the truth as such nor are tempted to hypostatize it. It is said, quite rightly, that ancient, classical Chinese philosophy "does not generate any theory of something resembling the Euclidean process," and therefore has no basis for the use of a concept "strongly similar to the core concept of reason." Taken together, the words *no basis*, *strongly similar*, and *core* make these words both hard to refute and probably misleading.* Whatever the exact

*The cited view is that of Chad Hansen. He concludes that Chinese thinking is "non-contrastively rational," by which he means that "no classical Chinese theorist is either a rationalist or an anti-rationalist." This seems to me closer to the elusive truth; only the unyielding *no* is not quite plausible. If Hansen would modify the sentence and say that no classical Chinese philosopher "is either a *complete* rationalist or a *complete* anti-rationalist"—a verdict that, on close analysis, fits all Indian and all European philosophers—he would be right. If he modified the sentence and said "is *ever* a rationalist or an anti-rationalist," he would be wrong. Chinese philosophers do have description of their logic, the ancient Chinese of course have the verbal means to agree with what we speak of as a true statement and disagree with a false one. The Chuang Tzu book complains that "the disputers of this world all say: 'The finest substance has no form. The greatest thing cannot be encompassed.'" The answer is the rhetorical question, Is that the reliably real state of affairs?[31] Naturally, the ancient Chinese use a variety of terms to express their sense of what is true, right, or real. Tones omitted, the terms include *shih*, meaning *be this, be it, be right*, which pairs with its opposite, *fei*, meaning *not be this, not be it, be wrong*; *shih*, meaning *be solid, be real*, the opposite of which is *hsü*, meaning *be empty, be tenuous, be unreal*; *jan*, meaning *be so, be the case*, the opposite of which is *fou*, meaning *be not so, not be the case*; and so on.[32]

Though the Chinese had no developed formal logic, interpreted understandingly, their arguments seem as logically consistent as ours do; and it is not difficult to recast the more explicitly logical (Later Mohist) writing in European logical forms and—risking cultural distance—to recast them in syllogisms.[33] Some of the Chinese were logically playful or logically serious enough to act the sophist and defend paradoxes. The following two paradoxes are reminiscent of Zeno: "No matter how swift the barbed arrow, there are times when it is neither moving nor at rest"; and "Take a pole one foot long, cut away half of it every day, and at the end of ten thousand generations there will still be some left."[34] The most famous of the Chinese sophists, Kung-sun Lung, was "a man of Chao who enjoyed hair-splitting and paradoxical talk." He wrote essays on themes such as "a white horse is not a horse," "ice is not cold," and "coals are not hot."[35] His notorious exclusion of a white horse from among horses inspired an anecdote about an would-be tax evader: A man argued with a customs inspector that he did not have to pay the tax on horses because the horse he was riding was not a horse but a white horse. Kung-sun Lung is right only if one supposes that *white horse* is conceptually so different from *horse*, so much a creature of another kind, that the term *white horse*

---

rationalistic impulses at times. See Hansen's "Should the Ancient Masters Value Reason," in Rosemont, ed., *Chinese Texts and Philosophical Contexts*, p. 192. In answering Hansen (in the same book, pp. 291–97), Angus Graham finds more analytic sharpness in Chinese philosophy than Hansen is able to—where Hansen softens contrasts, Graham hardens them. In *A Daoist Theory of Chinese Thought*, Hansen applies his view to the whole of ancient Chinese philosophy. The controversy surrounding Hansen's views is taken up in the essays in Lenk and Paul, eds., *Epistemological Issues in Classical Chinese Philosophy*, and also in Peerenboom, *Law and Morality in Ancient China*, pp. 57–61. Peerenboom (p. 60) is sure that the author of the *Huan-Lao Boshu* (Silk Manuscripts of Huang-Lao), written in the fourth or third century B.C.E., "is adamant that language corresponds to reality" and "is concerned . . . with the *truth* of the matter in the old fashioned sense of 'fitting the facts.'"

cannot ever be subsumed under the term *horse*. Perhaps the sophist's trick was no more than to shift when under attack from the ordinary, paradoxical meaning of "a white horse is not a (kind of) horse" to "(the meaning of) *a white horse* is not (the meaning of) *a horse*." But, even if right, this solution is too easy to satisfy for long and Kung-sun Lung's paradox, as developed in his simply worded but enigmatic essay, has proved an irresistible challenge to exegetes.[36]

It is true that the early exploration of logical problems and paradoxes soon dies out, to be revived, in a different spirit, when Buddhism takes root. From the start, however, Chinese thought shares the logic implicit in the structure of the Chinese language. The extreme brevity and extreme ambiguity of the classical language are countered by context, to be sure, but also by fixed rules for word order and by a pervasive parallelism, supplemented by antithesis, of words, phrases, longer passages, and topics.[37] The lack of interest of later Chinese philosophers in logic as such is compensated for by their concentration on the lessons that history teaches for social and political thought—in China, even the Buddhists were relatively uninterested in logic and, unlike the Tibetans, had few translations of logical works.[38] This concentration, natural to persons who are themselves most probably in government service, is used to exercise persuasion on others like themselves and, not infrequently, high officials or rulers, likely to be attuned to case histories and other historical evidence. In Europe too, historical evidence, which is not demanded for epistemology or metaphysics, finds its natural place in social and political theory and is drawn on, in the form of precedent, for legal purposes.

It is typical of Greek and most later European philosophers to make a sharp distinction between inductive reasoning—the accumulation of particulars in order to arrive at a necessarily uncertain generalization—and deductive reasoning—at its most effective, the derivation of true particular conclusions from a true generalization or a universal. In contrast, Indian philosophers never make this sharp distinction. Deduction is to them incidental to the process of accurate induction. The explicit distinctions the Indians make are between reasons that are contradictory, or inconclusive, or certain, certainty being established by the absence of counterexamples that would prove the induction to be doubtful. To formalize the process of induction, the Indians use their traditional reasoning procedure, usually, though misleadingly, considered to be a syllogism. It is natural enough to use the name *syllogism* because the Indian form has an appearance like that of a European syllogism. Furthermore, although in its complete guise, including a nonsyllogistic example, it has five rather than three members, it is easy—too easy—to translate the Indian form into a European syllogism with the usual two propositions followed by a conclusion.* Certainly, the name *syllogism* is applicable if we adopt Aristotle's very wide definition of a syllogism as "a discourse in which, certain things being stated, something other than what is stated follows of necessity from their being so."[39] However, the Greek problem is not the Indian one. The problem of the Greek syllogism is whether two propositions imply a third, which is the conclusion deduced from them (as from "all men are mortal" and "Socrates is a man" it is deduced that "Socrates is mortal"). In other words, the problem is whether the "middle term" (the humanity common to all men and to the man Socrates) makes it logically necessary to ascribe the property in question (mortality) to the subject in question (Socrates). In contrast, the problem of the Indian form is whether or not one property (such as "possessing fire"), occurrences of which have been reliably observed, pervades or encompasses another property (of "possessing smoke"), instances of which have also been observed. How, in our cognitive acts, do we infer this? the Indian asks. When we look at smoke, is our awareness of the cognitive structure, the "universal," of smokiness pervaded or encompassed by awareness of the cognitive structure of fieriness? Or: If we see smoke on a mountain and know from other evidence—like the positive evidence of a kitchen stove and the negative evidence of a lake—that wherever and only wherever there is fire there is also smoke, then we know that the instance of smoke we see is accompanied, like smoke in general, by fire. The "proving property" of smokiness ensures that the

---

*In its complete form, used for debating mostly epistemological issues, the Indian "syllogism" has the following five members:

    (1) Hypothesis: The mountain possesses fire.

    (2) Reason: Because it possesses smoke.

    (3) Example: Where there is smoke there is fire, as in a kitchen.

    (4) Application: This mountain is similar (possesses smoke).

    (5) Conclusion: Therefore the mountain is similar (possesses fire).

In practice, in "inferring for oneself," the Indian "syllogism" is usually abbreviated to: "This mountain possesses fire, because of smoke." Stated in a three-member form like that of the European syllogism, this Indian "syllogism" becomes:

    (1) This mountain is a locus of smoke.

    (2) Every locus of smoke (instance of smoke-possession) is a locus of fire.

    (3) Therefore this mountain is a locus of fire.

Whatever pervades—fills, encompasses—something else occurs in all or more than all the loci of that something else that it pervades.

Nyaya philosophers are preoccupied with the attempt to give pervasion (*vyapti*) a detailed, fully satisfactory definition. Because the Indian form expresses the pervasion of one property by another, there is no need for the middle term of the Aristotelian syllogism. (Ingalls, *Materials for the Study of Navya-Nyāya Logic,* pp. 32–33; Goekoop, *Logic of Invariable Comcomitance,* pp. 11–12; Potter, ed., *The Tradition of Nyāya–Vaiśeṣika up to Gaṅgeśa,* pp. 180–206; and Wada, *Basic Concepts in Navya-Nyāya,* pp. 32–36.)

property of fieriness, which overlaps and contains the property of smokiness, is really possessed by the subject, the mountain that is the "property possessor." Note how in the Indian example there is a coincidence of the two senses of smoke and fire, the extensional sense, referring to the class of sites or objects (the places where there is fire or smoke) and the intensional sense, referring to attributes (of fire or smoke). The extensional sense, that of the inclusion of one meaning-location in another meaning-location, is apparent in such a sentence as "Whatever is a locus of smoke is also a locus of fire." This can be translated into the statement that any instance of the class of smoke loci is included among the instances of the class of fire loci. But the Indian regards the locus as smoke possessing or fire possessing, that is, as having a certain quality or property. He refers to cognitions and uses the language not of class and class membership but of occurrence and possession.[40] I have spoken of awareness as pervaded or encompassed. To pervade, which is literally to pass through, means, to penetrate or permeate. It conveys the sense that the terms—the smoke and fire—are related to each other by their meanings. To encompass, to include by surrounding, conveys the terms' extensional relationship.

To the Indian thinker, the main, inductive function of logic is to ascertain with formal care if a certain property really belongs to a certain subject or if the connection is only accidental, imaginary, or illusory. His most difficult question is whether or not we can discover the conditions of pervasion for making an inference free of error. The insistence on an example agreed to by all, rules out of discussion premises that are not accepted by all as true. This is reminiscent of Kant's insistence that a geometrical proof must involve the actual construction of a geometrical figure.[41]

The Indian process of "reasoning for others" obviously merges logic as pure, formal reasoning with a theory of perception or cognition, the theory being clear enough to be represented as an abstract rule.* This makes the rules of logic into rules of perception as well.[42] Likewise, the Indian insistence on an acceptable example fits the style of Indian debating and introduces into logic what in the West is separated as what we now call epistemology. Given the factors that the Indians consider relevant to logic, it is not surprising that the Indian form is structurally so different from the European that it can reasonably be denied the name of *syllogism;*

---

*Put as such a rule, the elementary Indian logic of induction is this: "For any knower S, if S has a perceptual cognition, Fx, and then remembers the rule 'Wherever there is F, there is G' as instantiated in the uncontroversial case O, and then perceives in x the same F as before but this time as figuring in the remembered rule 'Wherever there is F, there is G,' then S will experience an inferential cognition of the form Gx, provided that there is no relevant hindrance" (Mohanty, *Reason and Tradition in Indian Thought,* p. 111).

but the convenience of the name has so far prevailed over the demand for terminological strictness.[43]

There is some justification for considering the induction-oriented logic of the Indian philosophers to be a kind of deduction—in a not very helpful way, Aristotle himself claims that induction is based on deduction.[44] One of the usual forms of Indian logic (tarka), regarded as an aid to inductive generalization, is rigorous formal implication that begins from an if-then premise. But Indian inductive logic also becomes rigorous. This happens in the philosophy of the Buddhist philosopher Dignaga, of the fifth or sixth century C.E., who recognizes that the validity of reasoning as such depends—as Aristotle recognizes it to depend—on the rightness of its form, not the truth or falsity of its premises. As in Aristotle's logic, formal reasoning is taken by Dignaga to compel assent only when carried out in an ideal way. His logic tests whether or not the chosen property of one class of individuals is incompatible with (disjoined from), is in part compatible with (is "erratic" with respect to, only overlaps), or is fully compatible with (completely fills or pervades) the property being considered of another class of individuals.[45] Dignaga's logic is an attempt, conveniently represented by Venn diagrams, to match classes by their intensions. It confirms the absence of error in the inference by which the "arguable property" is shown to pervade the class of individuals with which the inference is concerned.*

It must in candor be added that Dignaga's logic, though an impressive achievement, is not very satisfactory and that the tests he sets for induction are so difficult that they have aroused the suspicion that they are designed to show that no actual human procedure could meet them with complete success, that is, make an unquestionable induction. The suspicion makes it possible to guess that Dignaga's logic is akin to a Buddhist's intellectual variety of meditation, that it is, in other words, an exercise meant not for empirical assurance but for a stringent, dispassionate insight into the illusoriness of human judgment.[46]

My description of Dignaga's logic is too quick and vague to do more than indicate that it has a formal structure. In any case, by the time the

---

*In India, unlike Europe, "linguistics developed early and logic late. The earliest logical investigations in India pre-date the classical Nyaya and are due to grammarians such as Patanjali." Frits Staal, who points this out, suspects that there was no one comparable to Frege, Tarski, or Gödel among Indian logicians because these logicians never developed an artificial language. However, says Staal, the grammarian Panini (fl. c. 400 B.C.E.) did so, though in a different way. "Panini is still regarded as the greatest linguist of all times. There simply is no other candidate. No one else has constructed an almost complete grammar of a natural language using linguistic principles in a principled manner" (Staal, "The Sanskrit of Science," Journal of Indian Philosophy 23.1 [March 1995], p. 88).

New Logic School (Navya-Nyaya) flourished, in the fourteenth century, Indian logic was already abstract enough to be translatable into contemporary symbolic logic. But once it undergoes the translation, it loses interesting subtleties.[47] To the Nyaya philosophers, unlike (probably) the Buddhist, Dignaga, the point of complicating and formalizing the logic of induction is to show that freedom from error, or to put it as they do, the determination of *invariable concomitance*, is an achievable ideal for practical life. The Nyaya philosopher believes he can create a logical freedom-from-error formula, one that tells how to forestall the danger of a deviation (the logical contradictory of a pervasion) and so to make counterexamples—even future counterexamples—extremely improbable, even impossible (the philosopher may hope). But a theoretical formula can be difficult to apply, and if one wants to apply it perfectly, too difficult. As the Indian philosopher is well aware, a deviation from an inductive conclusion is not self-contradictory and so always remains logically possible. Necessity is therefore weaker than as usually conceptualized in the West.[48]*

As long as we see that Indian logic is meant to define the logical conditions for eliminating inductive errors, it seems unimportant if we classify it as inductive or deductive, or, for that matter, extensional or intensional. This issue of classification should not obscure the fact that the logic is an explicitly formal one (though, to draw a fine distinction, its formality is meant to convince rather than to reach a logically incontrovertible conclusion).

One logical characteristic does stand out as unique to European philosophy. It is the parallel between philosophical reasoning and Euclidean geometry, by which I mean the adoption of the idea that to prove something one must begin with definitions and axioms and continue, in

---

*Correspondingly, the intensive study of the logic of induction is earlier than in Europe. The first European philosopher, it is said, to recognize induction as an independent problem and discuss it elaborately was Hume. Despite Whewell, Herschel, and Mill, "it was left to Pierce in the late nineteenth century to bring out the value of hypothesis (calling it abduction and distinguishing it from deduction and induction)." Some traces of the link between causation and counterfactual conditionals are found in Hume, but "no detailed and systematic study of them is found in any Western writing before this century. The same, further, applies to the principle of economy . . . Similarly, a systematic study of inference to the best explanation is emerging only in some very recent publications" (Chakrabarti, *Definition and Induction,* p. 209 [see just preceding note 48]).

The ancient Indian logician's view has been put so: The "concept of an acceptable (set of) beliefs or theorems was relative in the sense that its intention lies in telling us which beliefs or theorems should be regarded as acceptable *given* a certain (default)-theory. But it was not meant to let us know whether a proposition should be accepted or not absolutely, without qualifications . . . Indian theories of inference and proof were always closely linked up with epistemological issues" (Oetke, "Ancient Indian Logic . . . ," p. 484).

principle without error, by way of a chain of demonstrated proofs to a conclusion that cannot logically be denied. This method, historically most familiar in Spinoza's philosophy, goes back, of course, to the Greeks, especially Aristotle, and came into some vogue during the sixteenth and seventeenth centuries.[49] But although European philosophers have often accepted the method as an ideal, it has been more effective in stimulating the metaphysical imagination—witness Spinoza again—than in attaining its goal. Judged by its aim to attain certainty, it has always failed. The truth, I believe, is that philosophers, although often very careful in their reasoning, do most of it by the same informal and fallible methods as laymen. Even if a philosopher agrees to accept the verdicts of logic, arguments can be restated in arguably defensible forms. Despite the deductive ideal they have often held, European philosophers, including Aristotle himself, have rarely tried and have nowhere ever succeeded in composing genuinely deductive philosophies; even in science, Newton's *Optics* is quite exceptional.[50] The philosophers' difference from laymen lies less in the formal consistency of their reasoning than in their dependence on philosophical tradition with its legacy of analyses and technical terms, which can give philosophies such a formidable appearance to outsiders. Seen from the inside, the philosophies are always vulnerable.

Telltale Sign of Philosophy: Disputation

The subject of logic, which so often distinguishes philosophy in its professional aspect, is related to a social form that has often sustained philosophy as a profession. I am referring to philosophical debates conducted in accord with a set of rules. The object of such rules has been to ensure the contestants an equal opportunity, to define what kinds of reasoning are acceptable or unacceptable, and to provide a method for deciding the winner. Such formal debates were held in all three traditions.

I begin with philosophical debating in China.[51] We know that in the late fourth century B.C.E., philosophical disputes (*pien*) emphasizing logic and paradox were held, at least sometimes for no more serious reason than sport. As mentioned earlier, the interest in logic as such died out. In a later age, in the third century C.E., a more literary kind of discussion or debate came into vogue. The obvious reason was the politics of the time. Intellectuals had been taught by their tradition that they were responsible for the morality of the government, but conditions were then so difficult for them that many became disillusioned with politics. Making what might be an anguished choice, not a few of them rejected traditional morality in favor of one or another kind of mysticism. One of these intellectuals writes in a poem that, having left riches and honor behind, his heart is ashes in a withered, immaterial, mystic house. Now, at last, he is able to forget his troubles; but can he be sure, he asks, that he can leave his social self and humanity behind and live in the mystic void alone.[52]

Such intellectuals practiced what the Chinese called "pure talk." The phrase refers to the conversations in which the disillusioned intellectuals met to think and banter "purely," free of the yoke of now corrupted social obligations. They took pleasure in the cleverness and irreverence of their banter, and they drank, took drugs (to prolong their lives), speculated on transcending moral doctrines by means of spontaneity, practiced un-confucian naturalness by going nude, mocked the heroes of Confucianism, and talked anarchistically and Taoistically against despotism. What matters here is that some of their talk was in the form of debates, with a formal thesis, refutation, and rebuttal, and some was concerned with abstract subjects such as speculative cosmology, Taoistic or Buddhistic "nothing-ness," the existence of immortals, the identity and equality of all beings, and the like. The echoes of such talk and debates helped make the third century a memorable one in Chinese intellectual history.

What of Greek and later European debates?[53] In Greece, debates were essential to the political life of the democratic city-states, as we know best in the case of the Athenian assembly (*ecclesia*) and people's court (*dikasteron*). By the classical age, disputation had its teachers and hand-books. Thucydides' *History of the Peloponnesian War* contains political debates conducted, like those of the sophists, in pairs of contradictory speeches. Such debates are central to Aristophanes' *Clouds*, the farcical yet bitter attack on sophistical argument and its supposed teacher, Socrates.* Plato's dialogues are, of course, largely composed of debates. He calls one type of debate *eristic*, by which he means argument for the sake not of truth but victory, and the corresponding art of winning arguments by means of fallacy, ambiguity, and other verbal fighting skills. Plato uses the term *antilogy* (*anti-logia*) for the technique of contradiction by which one forces an opponent from a statement (*logos*) to its contrary or contradic-tory, a practice, he says, that amuses young men who enjoy tearing with words all those who approach them. Of the various forms of argument, Plato prefers *dialectic*, which aims at the truth beyond the senses.[54] Aristotle, who elaborates on both the proper and the deceptive strategies of debate, makes it clear that in his own school there are debates conducted by rule,

---

*In Athens, the "city of words," persuasive speech "had become a desideratum of a uniquely intense and peculiarly Athenian kind, entailing nothing less than 'change in attitude towards the use of words in this period' and a privileging in the lawcourt of 'artificial proofs' . . . that is rhetorical supporting arguments over 'inartificial' ones such as exculpatory oaths and evidence given under torture" ("Fowl Play: A Curious Lawsuit in Classical Athens . . . ," P. Cartledge, in Cartledge, Millett, and Todd, eds., *Nomos*, pp. 49–50).

the defender of a thesis being attacked by a questioner, who tries to push the defender to make a statement that is on its face untrue or absurd.[55] Aristotle assumes that philosophers have to learn argument by practicing it—he says that if we have nobody else to argue with, we ought to argue with ourselves; and he gives the advice not to argue with casual persons, because this will lead to a debased, merely contentious kind of discussion.[56]

Despite the importance of debate to the ancient Greeks, its use in philosophy does not seem to have become as elaborately institutionalized as in medieval Europe. There, in university disputations held on subjects set in advance, a student would answer a question that the presiding master had put, and would then answer objections to the answer he had given. The "free questions" kind of disputation, which had no subject announced in advance, was open to everyone, and gave the opportunity to show off one's logical dexterity or play out one's personal rivalries. All disputations were supposed to be based, as Aristotle had recommended, on commonly agreed presuppositions and—as the medievals agreed—on authoritative quotations, the arguments being developed by means of syllogistic or like reasoning. But formal disputation lost its vitality in the later fourteenth century, and it had no consistent parallel in the rough-and-tumble of European philosophy after the Middle Ages.

For debate, India was the most developed of the traditions.[57] The rules were more elaborately worked out than elsewhere, and the practice of debating had a deep, culturally pervasive influence. To give some sense of the types and rules of debate, I follow the Logic School, which is nothing if not systematic. It divides debates into three basic types, those of *discussion, disputation,* and *wrangling.* In the first of these, discussion, the persons engaged are set on attaining the truth rather than on winning. To attain the truth, thesis is set against thesis, proof is based, point by point, on a combination of evidence and argument, and no argument known to be untrue is used—what kind is true and what untrue is clearly specified. In contrast to Western philosophy, though not Western law, the rules of evidence include a careful assessment of the verbal testimony relied on. The defeated side is said to harbor no anger.

Indian "disputation" is different in that it consciously aims at victory. For this reason, even though it holds to the same standards of reasoning as "discussion," it allows the use of "quibbles"—ways of assigning argument-destroying meanings to the opponent's words—as well as other tricks meant to demolish the opponent's case (tricks of the kind Aristotle deals with in his *Sophistical Refutations*). Finally, in "wrangling," a debater does nothing to establish his own position but only criticizes and condemns his opponent's arguments. Because no thesis need be defended, this is the form of debate a thorough skeptic would have to choose—examples will be given in the chapter on developed skepticism.

Held in a monastery or a royal court, a debate between eminent philosophers was a great public entertainment. There are many well-known stories according to which the losers of a debate and his disciples became followers of the winner. It seems that a victory could determine the allegiance of a king—he no doubt had political motives of which the stories tell us nothing—and the dominance of the winning side throughout his realm. As an example we can take the story, a typical glorification legend, that tells of the debating skills of the seventh-century Buddhist philosopher Dharmakirti. The story shows that a philosopher was expected to prove his greatness by overcoming and converting opponents.

To develop his skill against Hindus, the story says, Dharmakirti concealed his identity and studied with Hindu teachers. The most eminent of these was the great Mimamsa master, Kumarila. From him, Dharmakirti learned the art of refutation so well that in a three-month series of debates he, one by one, defeated and converted to Buddhism the five hundred experts in the six Hindu systems of philosophy. Furious, Kumarila insisted that Dharmakirti debate him and demanded that, if Dharmakirti lost, he should be killed. But Dharmakirti refuted each of Kumarila's five hundred theses with a hundred arguments and converted Kumarila.

After further victories over other eminent philosophers, Dharmakirti went to Dravali, a center of Hindu learning, where he rang a bell and publicly challenged anyone there to debate him. Most of the local Hindu philosophers ran away, while others kept silent out of fear of defeat. Then the great Vedanta philosopher Shankara sent a message announcing that he wanted to debate Dharmakirti. In the presence of the king, Shankara said to the assembled people that if he, Shankara, won, they would decide if Dharmakirti should be drowned or converted to Vedanta. But Shankara was repeatedly defeated and in the end had nothing more to say. He urged his disciple, Bhatta, an expert in logic, to go on arguing and defeat the shaven-headed Buddhist. Even if Bhatta lost, he said, he would be reborn as his son and go on fighting Dharmakirti. Then he jumped into the Ganges and died. Dharmakirti converted many of Shankara's followers, while others ran away.

As Shankara wished, his death did not end the debate. For three years, Bhatta propitiated his god, for three years more he studied the Buddhist arguments and how to refute them, but he too was completely defeated and jumped into the Ganges and died. A thousand Hindus were then converted and others, including Shankara, reborn as Bhatta's younger son, fled to the east. What happened afterwards to this reborn Shankara is not described, but Shankara was reborn still again, this time with a still sharper intellect and still greater debating skill, and aided this time by the full vision of his god. At the age of fifteen or sixteen, in the presence of the king and an audience of five thousand, he debated Dharmakirti a second time, with the same result and the same suicide by drowning.

All the same, the debate was renewed. Toward the end of Dharmakirti's life, Shankara was born once again, now as the son of Bhatta's elder son, his intellect even stronger than before. On this occasion, his god gave him personal lessons and sometimes even merged with him and taught him still unknown arguments. A young prodigy of twelve, he refused to wait for more experience before debating Dharmakirti because, he said, "Without defeating him there can be no real fame in debate." This time both the debaters agreed that the one defeated would adopt the other's religion. Neither Shankara's successive lives, nor his augmented intellect, nor the lessons he got from his god were enough. Dharmakirti won and converted him to Buddhism.[58] Of course, what actually happened in India was that Buddhism, not Hinduism, was defeated.

Not everyone approved of public debates. The Buddha himself, whose manner was that of calm, authoritative reason, had stressed how cruel it was to attack opponents in debate and how useless it was to debate metaphysical questions. Metaphysical debate was useless to him because, on one interpretation, it dealt with insoluble problems, and on another, perhaps better one, because it prevented people from accepting the solution to existential pain that he was teaching. And besides, why debate the questions with non-Buddhist philosophers, who had never learned the Buddhist truth? Such is the moral of the famous Buddhist parable of the blind men and the elephant, which tells of the king who assembled all the men blind from birth and let them feel an elephant. The blind men who had felt the elephant's head said he was like a water pot, those who had felt his ears said he was like a winnowing basket, those who had felt his tusks said he was like a plowshare, those who had felt his trunk said he was like a plow pole, and so on. The blind men fell to arguing and fighting with their fists, a sight that delighted the king. The moral of the parable is: "The heretics who do not know good from evil or right from wrong, brawl, wrangle, and strike one another with the daggers of their tongues."[59]*

---

*Philosophical debate is still an integral part of the education of a Tibetan aspiring to the degree of "spiritual guide" (geshe). "The primary method of examination is oral debate, in which a monk must be able quickly to size up a wide range of philosophical positions, defend any of them against any other, and trimph (or at least hold his own) in a no-holds-barred intellectual contest. The debates are generally very lively, with monks enthusiastically jumping, pivoting, shouting, and sometimes even pushing their opponent. Some debaters will use techniques designed to undermine the assurance of their opponents, such as raising eyebrows in mock surprise, intending to cause opponents to question the wisdom of their positions. The stated purpose of the exercise is to develop the intellects of the monks, and it is felt that direct dialectical confrontation accomplishes this goal by training monks to defend philosophical positions, to think on their feet, and to critically examine their doctrines and positions" (J. Powers, An Introduction to Tibetan Buddhism, Ithaca: Snow Lion Publications, 1995, p. 413).

The Three Traditions in Themselves:
Unique, Alike, and Neither

Having adopted a moderately stringent definition of philosophy, we have seen that philosophy did in fact exist in all three traditions and that, in all three, philosophers were consciously aware of logic and engaged in formal disputations. We have also seen that Chinese logic, though it developed for a brief period, remained mostly implicit and that Indian logic was never detached from epistemology. As for disputations, in China, it seems, they were relatively infrequent and of indecisive importance; in Greece they were frequent, but their importance for philosophy is hard to estimate; in medieval Europe they were both frequent and important; and in ancient and later India they were frequent and sometimes of great social and perhaps even political importance.

On the surface, then, we find both general similarities and particular differences among the traditions. The natural question that follows is how deep the similarities and differences may go. In answering, it is possible to stress either similarities or differences, or try to strike a balance between the two. My own answer is that both the similarities and the differences run very deep and are of extraordinary interest, and that, to confound the simplifiers, there is no similarity not tinged with difference nor difference not tinged with similarity.

To begin with differences, it is possible to take an extreme position and claim that each of the traditions is incommensurable with the others, that is, that no tradition can be grasped at all by means of the categories and habits of thought of the others. This extreme is empirically implausible and the attempt to argue in its favor entails its own denial: Whoever goes beyond the mere assertion and undertakes to explain how and why traditional Indians, Chinese, and Europeans were—and, to later interpreters, remain—impenetrable worlds apart, is most probably assuming the ability to enter into each of the worlds far enough to show that they are closed to one another. The explanation explains what, it is claimed, is impossible to explain.

Therefore the belief in total incommensurability, if anyone really holds it, seems to me implausible and I will not deal with it any further here.[60] Besides, the relations between the traditions have not justified it. Yet there are claims that the differences are so pervasive that every crosscultural comparison of philosophies is necessarily a reductive one. One of the direct implications of such a claim is that each of the philosophic terms involved in a comparison has a meaning or group of meanings that a substitute in another philosophic language necessarily distorts; and it is implied that the successive distortions end in a basic misunderstanding of the philosophy as a whole. Possible examples of distortion are easy to point out. We have already mentioned the misrepresentation of the Indian "syllogism" by the Greek syllogism, the losses that occur in the translation of later Indian logic into symbolic logic, and the misleading attribution to the ancient Chinese of an understanding of propositions in the sense given them by Western logic.

The danger of misunderstanding can be illustrated with the help of some current interpretations of Chinese philosophy. Earlier, I suggested a comparison between the statements of Hsün-tzu and Kant that human beings are by nature evil. But Hsün-tzu's mode of argument, with its stress on ethical precedent and the exact application of terms, is not at all Kantian. Nor is Hsün-tzu at all Kantian when he recommends a way out of pressing ethical situations for which there are no accepted rules of conduct. In such situations, he advises, one should guide oneself by the indirect means the Chinese term for which, *t'ui-lei*, has been translated *analogical projection*. To make such a projection, one must pay careful attention both to the issues involved and to the terms with which to characterize them, and then, having found the most appropriate traditional analogy, one must apply it to the situation in question. By projecting the analogy with such care, the situation is put into the measured, rational context that tradition has created. "Each analogical projection is basically an attempt to specify the concrete significance of *tao*, and it thus represents a temporal mediation between the ideal of *tao* and the actual world."[61]

In keeping with such an analysis, it is stressed that in the Chinese tradition problems are solved not by abstract reasoning but by the considered extension of old, historically fixed norms. Since everyone who denies the norms is taken to be unreasonable, rationality is measured by obedience to the norms.[62] It is therefore the goal of all the most ancient Chinese philosophers to teach how language should be used to guide action effectively. They therefore see their task as the identification of a constant *tao*, that is, a kind of discourse that guides behavior quite reliably.[63] Western philosophy, it is argued, bases itself on the ideal of a Euclidean kind of proof, and on the ideal of the individual whose self-rule requires free rational choices, not tradition. In contrast, Chinese philosophy is based on the belief that language, which is created by convention, must be used to reinforce the social good. When thinkers such as the Taoists diverge from this model, they move not toward the "argumentative theater" of other philosophers but toward poetry and painting.[64]

Suppose that for the moment we assume that there are great intellectual gaps between the philosophical traditions, gaps expressed by differences of the kind that I have just stated. If so, we can assume not only particular differences between Indian, Chinese, and Western logic, but also general differences between India, where interest has been focused on strategies of living and redemption, China, where interest has been focused on concrete ethical problems, and Europe, where interest has been focused on abstract proofs, theories, and entities. Do such not unfair assumptions separate the three traditions so widely that any direct comparison, guided, to begin with, by surface likenesses, must prove illusory?

I think not. My counterassumption is that there is a level at which the differences between traditions grow less isolating and comparisons grow genuinely illuminating. I say this for the simplest of reasons: the biological likeness between human beings, the similarity of their social needs, and their similar ways of fulfilling themselves, intellectually and otherwise. Philosophies everywhere have been the more stringently logical counterparts of the social opposition between compliance and revolt—often simultaneously of both. In this not at all trivial sense, philosophies are alike, and therefore their comparison, if not simplistic, can be rewarding. It is still a great challenge to demonstrate which logical forms are universal, or to show the similarity of the basic mechanisms of philosophical argument—which seem to me quite few—or of the basic elements of political thought or esthetic response. But whatever the challenge, the crudeness of the initial comparisons is the inevitable condition for learning how to refine them. The moral is only that the beginnings of understanding should not be mistaken for its final conclusions.

While the initial similarities between traditions may have a misleading simplicity, so may the initial contrasts. The (non-Buddhist) Indian philosophers are true to the Vedic tradition, one repeats; but they invariably interpret the tradition in favor of their school, their point of view, so that their faithfulness to tradition is not much more than the faith that tradition must verify what their group has made of it. Of all the Indian schools, only the *Mimamsa*, meaning (School of) *Investigation* (to interpret the ritual intention of sacred texts) is seriously and literally faithful to the Veda's ritual injunctions. One may repeat that the Chinese philosophers, as well, are faithful to tradition. Yet in the relatively brief period, from the sixth to the third centuries B.C.E., when indigenous Chinese philosophy is at its most creative, only the Confucians, in no way then dominant, are seriously faithful to tradition. All the schools appeal or at least refer to history, but invariably interpret it to support the particular positions they have arrived at. And European philosophers, who are said to be individualists, have often regarded themselves as faithful to a tradition. There were organized groups of philosophers faithful to Plato, or to Aristotle, or to Epicurus. Medieval philosophers were, of course, faithful to their respective traditions of Judaism, Christianity, and Islam. Later, there were considerable if relatively short-lived subtraditions of Cartesians, Kantians, and

Hegelians. All told, if there is a great divide between East and West, it is not faithfulness to tradition as opposed to unqualified individualism.

Nor is the great divide the use on the Chinese side of analogy, projected or not. Analogy has been essential to the thought of everyone everywhere. The analogical projection of traditional moral judgments is the instrument by which tradition has developed as such, as witness, among others, the Talmudists and the thinkers of medieval Europe and Islam; and it has at all times been essential to ethics, political theory, and the practice of law.[65]

Nor is the European faithfulness to abstract entities and deductive ideals as great a divide as it may seem in a stereotypical polarization. Aristotle himself, the inventor of formal logic and a rationalistic proof of God's existence, does not fit the stereotype. Instead, he emphasizes that the "philosophy of human nature," by which he means the ruling art of politics (including ethics) is no exact, demonstrable science. This philosophy, he says, depends on practical wisdom and on the early inculcation of good habits—"The end aimed at is not knowledge but action."[66] Furthermore, as I have pointed out, very few of the European philosophers who adopted the ideal of consistent deduction tried seriously to achieve it in their own philosophies. To be sure, syllogistic reasoning was very influential during the Middle Ages, but it disciplined the form of philosophy more often than it determined its substance. And so, for all the differences between the three traditions, it is difficult to distinguish between them in terms of sweeping global abstractions such as traditionalism, or individualism, or dependence on analogy, or, in practice, on deduction.

I supplement this protest against excessively polarized differences with a few examples of interesting similarities: The ladderlike structure of nature that Aristotle describes is unmistakably like that of Hsün-tzu. Both the Greek and Indian atomists defend their belief that matter cannot be infinitely divided by arguing that unless matter is composed of atoms in some sense finite in size, the infinitely continued division of matter would end in the total disappearance of matter. Greek and Indian skeptics often hit on the same intellectual mechanisms for refuting certainty of any kind. Sophists and materialists appear in all three traditions.[67] The standard Buddhist arguments against substance and, especially, a metaphysical self are essentially the same as those of Hume. A Buddhist philosopher and Kant both argue for a critical philosophy (in the Kantian sense) with essentially the same attack on the ability of consciousness to give an objective representation of what is taken to be the external reality.

But even if such examples are granted, they are fragments isolated from unique traditions. Does the uniqueness of each tradition not determine the uniqueness of everything that belongs to it? My answer is this:

The practitioners of any one philosophical tradition are attuned to its subtleties and dismayed by a comparatist's possibly careless "It's all the same!" The philosophers' disputes—with themselves and their opponents—are in and through the tradition or subtradition that has come to constitute their intellectual substance. Because of its emotive, intellectual, and perhaps social effect, the difference over which a philosopher disputes with a near philosophical neighbor is likely to be of great immediate importance to both; but for an outsider it is likely to be no more than an intellectually negligible quibble. As the person within a certain tradition sees it, to try to compare its philosophy with that of another tradition is like trying to play two discordant games at the same time. However, the comparatist is not the practitioner of any one philosophy but a theme-and-variation philosopher, whose interest is in the varieties of philosophies. Among other questions, such a philosopher asks: What is the activity (or what are the activities) of which these philosophies are the varieties? The natural answer is: A common name implies some congruity. But in what, and how much, and why? And if philosophies and games prove to be incongruous with others of their respective designated kinds, why has language accorded them a misleading verbal congruity? Depending on how it is practiced, the comparatist's pursuit may or may not be predominantly philosophical. The history of philosophy and the sociology of knowledge may be seductive, and neither is in itself philosophy. If the pursuit is philosophical, it is so in a special way. My conclusion is that the philosophical traditions are either unique or alike depending on one's position in relation to them—inside or outside—and the standard of judgment one adopts, that is, the kind and degree of abstraction one allows oneself in order to deny or justify comparison. Both sides are quite right, if one wishes, or neither, if one insists.*

If we turn from these issues to the usual ones of metaphysics, we find certain striking differences between traditions. One of these concerns the belief in God. The later European philosophical tradition generally assumes an all-powerful creator-God, the Indian tradition often opposes it, and the Chinese tradition puts natural forces and Heaven in God's place.

---

*Although mathematics is comprised of a group of sciences of extreme abstraction, it has its own problems of loss of uniqueness as its level of abstraction rises. When two mathematical theories that have seemed merely analogous prove to be aspects of the same, more general theory, says the mathematician André Weil, "the separate identities are lost and with them the strange and wonderful sense of similarity and difference which attracts and perplexes the investigator." Weil, who regrets the passing of analogy, with its illusiveness and mystery, into clear knowledge, has been influenced by Indian poetry and philosophy and connects his regret with the philosophy of the *Bhagavad Gita* (D. Reed, *Figures of Thought: Mathematics and Mathematical Texts,* Routledge: London, 1995, pp. 152, 180 [note 8]).

To begin with Europe, from the Middle Ages on, most European philosophers have depended for their moral and metaphysical arguments on the belief in God, the creator and ruler of the universe. In the popular religion of India and China, reward and punishment by gods is usual, but in both traditions taken philosophically, there is an often impersonal attitude according to which reward and punishment are akin to what Europeans take to be natural law. More exactly, in some Indian philosophical systems the powers and person of God are like those usual in Europe. In other Indian systems, God creates in that he rearranges matter, but matter exists as absolutely as he does; and in still other systems, the world-creator, the personal God who is the object of human devotion, is an emanation of (and identical with) the unqualified, featureless, unknowable reality that is God in the final sense. Though unknowable, he is of a nature much discussed by European philosophers and theologians. So classical Indian and Chinese philosophy can be atheistic in the sense that they leave human fate mainly to impersonal forces that are intrinsic to the universe, that is, to matter, karma, *tao*, Heaven, or the Supreme Ultimate, and to the understanding, intuition, yogic exercises, or meditations supposed to affect, detach, abolish, surpass, or attain them.

From a Western standpoint, what is most strange about the Indian conception of God or gods is that some of the most devout groups have been totally atheistic—the gods they acknowledge are part of nature and subject to its laws. Much of Buddhism has been of this sort, though not consistently, and so has Jainism, and so has the orthodox, ritualistic school of Mimamsa.

To experience the energy a Mimamsa philosopher might put into the refutation of the belief in a creator-God, consider the following summary of arguments against such a God: In order to create the world, God would have to have the desire to create it; to have any desire at all, including the desire to create, he would need a body; if he had a body, the body would have to have been created by a preceding creator; if his body was eternal, the matter of which it was made would have to be as eternal as he was; if it was possible for him to have no body, it would be impossible for him to influence matter, that is, the atoms of the world. Furthermore, if he had no body, he could not know anything, because to know something, just like to desire something, one needs sense organs, but sense organs, knowledge, and desire are all material; and so on. And if God created the world out of compassion, there was no one to be compassionate to before living persons were created; and if he created them out of compassion, then why did he not create only happy beings? If he could not create only happy beings, he is not all-powerful. And if it is argued that we know he created the world because he said that he did, he may have said this only to emphasize how powerful he is; and so on. As for the holy words of the Vedas, the truth of which is self-evident and uncontradicted by experience, they need no author or guarantor other than themselves. Besides, no witness was present to see God create them; and so on. While later adherents of Mimamsa thought of God as the supervisor of the law of karma, that is, of rewards and punishments, it is clear that, to the Mimamsa philosopher whose views I have repeated, belief in a creator-God could only weaken and denature religion.[68]

India and all Buddhist countries are also distinguished from Europe by their belief in the law of karma, according to which every act committed with either a good or evil purpose is rewarded or punished, by the very nature of the universe, in either the present life or a future one, so that each person's fate is the accumulated result of previous acts going back indefinitely far. It is widely believed that a god or a Buddha of mercy may intervene to change one's fate, and believed that under certain circumstances karma can be transferred, like money, from one person to another. But in principle, karma is understood as Europeans understand natural law. Philosophers worked out its theory in some detail.[69]

Yet despite the endless life and the possibility of accumulating the rewards granted by virtue of good karma, the ideal of the Indian philosophical systems—materialism and related skepticism excepted—is to break out of the cycle of birth and death. The Indians seem to fear not only the endlessly returning pains but also the exhausting pointlessness of cosmic circulation. The way out, as the orthodox systems and Buddhism and Jainism agree, is to end the cycle by getting rid of the ideas, emotions, and desires— the worldly elements—that perpetuate it, and then to remain in a transcendent state of rapture, if that is the right word, or, as others believe, of total neutrality or higher indifference. The analogous ideas of Western religious philosophy are not developed with the same persistent attention to detail.

China differs both in its religion and its metaphysics (or protoscience). Its lasting native theories do not postulate God but only natural forces and the equilibria between the forces, which, if disturbed, have to be restored; otherwise, humans suffer disaster. The extreme Chinese reverence for ancestors is cultic, although in Western eyes such reverence is only weakly religious. This reverence is supported, especially among the Confucians, by an impersonal, politicized cosmology. For the Confucians grow to be deeply concerned with the fate of the prevailing dynasty. This is because, they believe, its rise and fall are critical to the fate of all the Chinese; and because its rise and fall are determined by Heaven, which works according to infallible rules of justice. Sooner or later, the Chinese know, the dynasty will grow unrighteous, its vitality will be sapped, and Heaven will decree that it be replaced.[70]

This whole Chinese mode of thought, from which an omnipotent creator and lawgiver is excluded, construes nature, including humankind, as a web of forces in the changing rhythms of which everything moves and flourishes or decays. In addition, the parallel between microcosm and macrocosm is widely accepted. Chinese thought can therefore be classified as a species or group of species of organicism. The result is that, unlike Westerners and many Indians, the ancient Chinese do not believe they are directed by a transcendent God who gives them orders from above. Instead, they see themselves as natural organisms pervaded by the nature that comprises them. One consequence of this attitude is that they have little if any of the idea of natural laws, in the sense of definite rules that God imposes on nature as he does on human beings. There is no full Chinese equivalent to "And God said, 'Let there be lights in the firmament of the heavens to separate the day from the night; and let them be for signs and for seasons and for days and nights, and let them be lights in the firmament of the heavens to give light upon the earth.' "[71]

Once again, one should avoid exaggerated polarization. "Heaven," which is the Chinese equivalent of *providence* and the *supreme principle of nature*, is like the West's God in that it issues decrees, those, already mentioned, that determine the fate of dynasties. Though never regarded as a creator, Heaven was worshiped by the Chinese emperors and often somewhat personalized, like the earlier Shang Ti, the God on High—this is the term for *God* in Protestant translations of the Bible. Surprisingly, the philosopher Mo-tzu, of the late fourth or early third century B.C.E., expresses himself like a European philosopher who is justifying God's ways. Mo-tzu writes:

> Moreover there is a basis for my knowing how generously Heaven loves the people. It is the fact that it [Heaven] has orbited the sun, moon and stars in order to illumine and lead [the people]. It has instituted the four seasons of spring, autumn, winter and summer in order to guide and untangle them. It sends down snow, frost, rain and dew to grow the five grains, hemp and [mulberry leaves] for silk, thereby enabling the people to gain and be benefited by them . . . It has created kings, dukes, marquises and earls, causing them to reward the worthy and punish the violent.[72]

Not only does early Chinese philosophy contain occasional passages implying that there is an organizer or ruler of the universe, but there are two known occurrences of the phrase *laws of Heaven* (*t'ien fa*), which in the one instance, relating to human affairs, can be translated *natural law*, while in the other, relating to the human body, the state, and the physical universe, can be translated *laws of nature*.[73] The general conclusion is that the absence in China of the idea of a lawgiving God and of laws of nature is not absolute and not reason enough for an unyielding contrast between the thought of China and Europe. Furthermore, it is clearly not true that organicism is Chinese rather than European. To sharpen the contrast is to forget that organicism of a kind is not unknown to Plato, that Aristotle is strongly influenced by (non-reductive) biology, that the Stoics' universe is a form of organicism, that Leibniz believes profoundly in it, and that Kant makes philosophical use of it. It is Kant who states that "pure speculative reason has a structure wherein everything is an organ, the whole being for the sake of every part, and every part for the sake of all the others."[74] There is no reason to go on to Schiller, Goethe, Schelling, Hegel, and a host of estheticians and biologists in order to show that organicism, although always rivaled by analytic or reductive philosophies, has had a great influence on the history of European thought.[75]

The Three Traditions in Themselves:
Spiritual Transcendence against Positivistic Curiosity?

The distinctions I have just made between the three traditions are of great importance to both religion and philosophy. I feel it necessary to supplement them with a warning, a warning against the most common distinction made between India or China, on the one hand, and Europe, on the other, or, more comprehensively, between East and West. As mentioned in relation to India, the distinction is as follows: Eastern philosophy is spiritual and integral with life, while Western philosophy is abstract, materialistic or positivistic, and split off from life. In one exposition of this view, it is said that Greek philosophy studies society and man, which are the outer reality of human life, while Indian philosophy denies outer things in favor of an undeniable, ultimate, inner reality. Modern Western philosophy, it is said, represents the triumph of the objective or outward attitude, which, however helpful morally and politically, must be balanced by truly religious consciousness, which is the deeper, inward, Indian one.[76]

Such a view is seriously misleading. To see this, recall that in all three traditions, especially in the Indian and European, philosophy in the more technical sense came to be the province of specialists whose doctrines were usually unintelligible or pointless to most people, just as they are today. In each of the traditions, the tie between philosophy and religion remained strong—although even in the medieval universities of Europe there was a clear distinction, often accompanied by a struggle for influence, between the faculties of theology and philosophy. Typically, philosophers in all three traditions have claimed that their doctrines give those who study them a better understanding of what is true and worthwhile and how this desired goal can be attained. This holds true even of the positivists or materialists, well-known exponents of which are found in each of the traditions, and even of the philosophical skeptics in each of them, though not necessarily of the combative or playful reasoners we name sophists.

If we think of the Western philosophers listed in the preceding chronology, the opinion that they are concerned mostly with outward matters, meaning material, social, and political ones, can be plausibly held of only a few of the thirty-four, most unambiguously of two Greeks, Democritus and Epicurus, one Roman, Lucretius, and one Englishman, Hume, to whom Russell may possibly be added; and it can be made of the various kinds of positivism that were widely though far from exclusively accepted by Western intellectuals from about the time of the French Revolution. But it cannot ever be made of Western philosophy as a whole. This is the fact.

The fact is also that, East and West, most philosophy has been concerned with salvation, whether this-worldly or other-worldly. However, the interest of Hindu and Buddhist philosophers in salvation is different because it is so often tied up with the belief that to live is basically to suffer. This attitude is not characteristic of Indian philosophy at the start but begins at about the time of the origin of Buddhism—did conditions then make it especially easy to draw attention to suffering?—and remains prominent in most of the classical philosophies of India, to which reason appears valuable mostly because it helps humans to escape suffering. Take, for example, the basic text of the classical school of *Samkhya* (*samkhya* means, roughly, *enumeration* of the categories of existence and—extended to refer to a school— *the school that analyzes by means of enumeration* of these categories). The text begins by stating that because human beings are tormented by the three kinds of suffering, they want to know how to get rid of it, something that can be permanently accomplished not by material or by revealed, Scriptural means, but only by a discriminating understanding.

Each Indian school having adopted different means for such a purpose, Indian philosophy can be understood, almost as a whole, as a kind of transcendent utilitarianism, one that does not exhibit curiosity for its own sake and seeks transcendent experience. Yet transcendent experience and intellectual conviction are not really separated by the Indians but (very often) supposed to support one another and, finally, to be in effect the same—Spinoza uses a different machinery of thought, but is he so different in this particular conviction? European philosophy does not ordinarily lay so great an emphasis on suffering—the Stoics, the Neoplatonists, and thinkers like Pascal and Schopenhauer are among the not infrequent exceptions—but European philosophical thought, like the Indian, has usually expressed the hope for transcendence. And in thinking of the emphasis of Indian philosophy on suffering, we should remember that the suffering or, better, the negative quality it attributes to life, is not suffering in its merely ordinary sense but in that meant by Spinoza, having to do with the objective nature of the universe and the philosopher's ability to distinguish between the transient, on the one hand, and the eternal on the other.

This need to be objective and renounce the suffering that results from the painful impermanence of everything worldly is the moral of the Buddhist parable about Kisa Gotami. When her young son died, she took his body on her hip and went from door to door asking for medicine to cure him but was met only with derision. When she asked the Buddha for the medicine, he in compassion told her to make a round of the whole city and bring him mustard seeds from any house in which no one had ever died. When she failed to find even one such house, she understood that her boy was not the only person who had been overtaken by death, but that all things are impermanent and that death is a law common to all mankind. Seeing this, she became reconciled to death and cast her boy into the burning-ground.[77]

It is doubly deceiving to make the distinction between philosophy as pure inquiry for the Europeans and as the science of liberation for the Indians or, for the Chinese, of morally differentiated action, moral merger with humanity, or intuitive unity with nature. Consider again the view that Chinese philosophy is interested in "erecting, initiating, motivating, and insinuating actions and action-oriented attitudes, not in describing a transcendent world independent of actions and consciousness."[78] Even if we take this description to be accurate, it remains true that the Chinese philosopher is at times motivated by curiosity and always by the desire to express himself and to create a body of interesting thought. It also remains true, I am sure, that the philosophers of India and Europe use their descriptions of transcendent worlds, and so forth, to insinuate actions and action-oriented attitudes. No philosophy is without its social dimension and effect.

I say this not because I suppose that Indian or Chinese thinkers agree with the Europeans who agree with Aristotle that the contemplation of the truth, the theoretical life, is the best of all lives. But Indian philosophy exhibits structures and refinements that, inspired or not by the need for liberation or defense against rival schools, lead to an analytical sharpness the exercise of which is its own reward; and the public victories it may bring have an additional, this-worldly sweetness. Sharp and detailed as contemporary philosophers may be, it does not take much reading in the sources to learn that many of their Indian (and medieval European) predecessors were their matches.

This equality cannot be tested by resurrecting medieval Europeans, but it is still possible to question traditional Indian philosophers. Accordingly, not long ago, an experimental five-day dialogue was held, in Sanskrit and English, between a group of Indian pandits of the Navya-Nyaya school and a group of contemporary, Western-oriented Indian philosophers. The participants were at first disconcerted to discover that "there were so to speak, no philosophically uncommitted or neutral words in Sanskrit which could serve as even rough equivalents of what was sought to be conveyed through the English terms."[79] For the subject of the dialogue, the experimenters chose Russell's doctrine of propositions as expounded in the *Principles of Mathematics* (in a technical sense, propositions are ignored in Indian philosophy). Russell's main points were summarized, a Sanskrit translation was made for the pandits who knew no English, and translators into and from Sanskrit were provided. Challenged to depart from the mere defense and exegesis of their traditional positions, some of the pandits suggested how Nyaya might be developed in new directions. Some of the pandits were later introduced to modern Western logic and some of the Western-oriented philosophers studied Navya-Nyaya logic. Each side is said to have developed a profound respect for the other and to have discovered philosophically exhilarating differences.* The moral drawn is that a contrasting analysis that leads in a different direction and that over millennia gradually builds an imposing philosophical structure is something whose possibility one cannot even conceive if one is confined to a single philosophical tradition. One inevitably treats the only known tradition as the only possible one and hence as universally paradigmatic in character.[80]

I am convinced that the analytical sharpness and constructive complexities of Indian philosophy show the operation of curiosity working for its own, nondoctrinal, nonsalvational reasons, trying to build reality as it

---

*But given the pandits' habitual defense of their philosophy, it is not surprising that (with the exception I note below) there was no obvious change in their position—changes in the positions of the modern philosophers are not recorded. But each side in the dialogue appears to have arrived at an at least fairly clear understanding of the other, and the discussion is detailed, analytical, and pertinent. The pandit who at the end summarizes the Nyaya response holds that "the postulation of a separate kind of entity called 'proposition' is groundless" and adds that, if he understands Russell correctly, "such a theory does not deserve to go unattacked." Russell's temperament was such that, had he been available, he would not have foregone an answer, supplemented, no doubt, with a cutting witticism. (The quotations are from Krishna et al., eds., *Samvada* [see note 79, this chapter], pp. 212–13.)

can and solving the intellectual difficulties it has revealed in the process. The need for salvation stimulates philosophical thought but is also the opportunity and excuse for immersing oneself in the pleasure of exercising one's mind: When intense, philosophy is a habit of thought, a calling, and a passion, the stubborn search for either a detailed rational objectivity or a philosophical escape from it.

Not surprisingly, therefore, a sharp distinction between Indian salvational and Western nonsalvational philosophy is deceptive. Even recent European philosophy, whether of the Existentialist or Wittgensteinian kind, has searched for escape from unnecessary pain (for Wittgenstein himself, the pain that results from philosophical bewitchment by words). Or it has searched for salvation of a sort by means of the acceptance of one's own finiteness and death, or by means of the renewed illumination of Being in a world darkened by objectivity, utility, and science (the first aim is that of the early Heidegger, the second, of the late one).

How the Constraints of Orthodoxy
Can Intensify Philosophical Reasoning

These last words are a reminder that both Wittgenstein and Heidegger come close to repudiating the whole of philosophy. But as was said in the beginning, their repudiation is considered philosophical when philosophy is defined to include reasonable arguments that deny reason, whether in general or in its philosophical guise. Wittgenstein remains a philosopher even when he tries to dissolve away the content of philosophy and leave only a critical method of examining what is said, especially by philosophers, and Heidegger remains a philosopher even when he turns to poetry to reveal Being or, for the sake of that revelation, turns back to pre-Platonic thought. Chuang Tzu, Ch'an (Zen) monks, and Kierkegaard find their truths not by means of philosophical solutions but philosophically intractable paradoxes, although the reasoning more often implied than stated in Ch'an Buddhism is that articulated in earlier, more explicit Buddhist philosophy. All these revelers in paradox draw their sustenance from the philosophy they repudiate. What, in its absence, would they have to say?

I have been making essentially the same defense for studying the orthodox philosophical theologies of Hinduism, late Buddhism, Judaism, Islam, and Christianity as forms of philosophy. However, there is not only their religious orientation to consider, but their orthodoxy as such. By definition, religious orthodoxy and, for that matter, any orthodoxy, is opposed to the free use of reason and in this sense inhibits the pursuit of philosophy. A skeptic, disbeliever, or believer in reason alone is therefore apt to claim that religious orthodoxy is the antithesis of any philosophy worthy of the name. But as I have said in different ways, the ideal of reason alone has never been fulfilled. The problems with which philosophers have dealt have always been so far beyond a provable solution (as their critics have shown) that *any* stand a philosopher takes must incorporate assumptions, explicit or implicit, that are neither proved nor, it has so far appeared, provable. Therefore whatever stand one takes (including the one now being taken) is incompletely reasonable or, to someone unsympathetic to it, arbitrary or foolish. Except for the rules or technical arguments whose power to convince is independent of any system—the law of contradiction is the simplest example—a philosophy must reflect not reason as such but reason in accord with one's social heritage and individual experience. From this standpoint, a philosophy is the intellectually formulated projection of a tradition or personality, or, to be more exact, of both at once.

Given the power to do so, orthodoxy suppresses any reasoning that conflicts with its dogmatically held tenets. But the human intellect is never wholly servile for long. The person who is orthodox and, at the same time, philosophical is like a musician or painter who creates within the confines of an accepted style. Particular dogmas and methods of thought being inescapable, the person's self-expression is limited to variations on the accepted position. Since nothing else is allowed, the creative impulse is confined to the exploration of this position in increasing detail or intensity, by which I mean an intensively, even microscopically directed attention. The individual thinker then uses the permitted style of thought in order to express the most intensive variations allowed, often different enough in their variety or intensity to be fiercely resisted by unintensive or differently intensive thinkers. The restriction itself can act as a powerful stimulus. In the long run, therefore, even the most restricted style allows original thought to live and, not infrequently, to flourish.

Of course, orthodoxy is not confined to religion. If we think of philosophical orthodoxy as, minimally, the commitment to remain faithful to a particular standpoint, then there have been many truly or ostensibly orthodox exponents of many great philosophers, the list of which ends for the while with Heidegger and Wittgenstein. What is lost by orthodoxy is compensated for, more or less, by what is gained. Considering the history of thought in the light of human limitations, philosophers impoverish themselves excessively if they insist that philosophy should exclude thought that is dominated by traditional religion or by orthodoxy of any particular kind. One ought not to forget that philosophical attacks on orthodoxy are deeply indebted to it—as I will repeat, the more truly independent the line of thought, the more likely it is to be primitive. In all three traditions, the attacks owe their structure and technical resources to the dogmatically developed thought that they intend to undermine. In the heat of battle against an orthodoxy, the intellectual debt owed it by its opponents is not easy for them to acknowledge. Of course, an orthodoxy increases its ability to survive by making use of the resources its unorthodox opponents put at its disposal.

The Three Traditions in Themselves: Their Uniqueness of Style

Is it possible to grasp the differences between the three philosophical traditions in a summary way? I'm not sure that anyone in the position to accept the challenge ever resists it, but it's a mistake to put much trust in a formula designed to sum up any one of the three. To venture such a formula is to undertake an exercise in the disclosure of a nonexistent essence, to confuse the intricate variations within variations of intellectual history with the formulaic brevity possible to mathematics or the magical compactness ascribed to mantras. How could an aphoristic sentence or two capture any tradition that has grown over thousands of years and has engaged persons of so many degrees of philosophical creativity and so many types—wise, sharp, scholarly, bibliomaniacal, confrontational, conciliatory, narcissistic, rebellious, compulsive, and just plain weird? True, many of these philosophers were in the service of teachers the contradiction of whom was a sin against reverence and loyalty. But the human lust to think as an individual is not easily denied, and so what one could not say against tradition or in one's own name was attributed to an old sage or put down as a mere elucidation of the accepted text, until subterranean change after change made the tradition something it had never been before.

Yet in spite of the failure of the formulas, whose inescapable shallowness I have stressed, only a coward of a comparatist would evade the attempt to characterize the different traditions, to see them summarily, if only as a beginning on which to elaborate. After all, each of the three has its individuality, which can be recognized though not put into quite satisfactory words. One recognizes a fragment of Indian, Chinese, or European philosophy as one recognizes a voice in a babble of voices or a face in a crowd, without any hesitation. The identifying characteristic may be the particular abstract message, but I think it is less usually the abstraction in itself, which is likely to have counterparts in the other traditions, as its style, which is in part comprised of its manner of approach to the subject, of the rhythm, emphasis, and style of compression or expansion in which it progresses from idea to idea to conclusion (how does one give a description of a voice or a face good enough for it to be recognized?). Yet for the same reason that mathematicians recognize one another's styles in mathematics, there must also be something in the nature—the principles and the organization—of the logic per se by which to identify the philosophical tradition, perhaps the subtradition, and even the individual philosopher.

All that is quite vague. Can I describe, briefly and simply, some of the individual characteristics of the Indian, Chinese, and European styles of philosophizing? To make an answer more nearly possible, I confine myself to the standard or classical doctrines. Well, then, very inadequately, an Indian philosophical system is likely to depend on a source (which opens and closes with an invocation to the patron sage or god) that is so abbreviated that, taken by itself, it is near impenetrable. It is so brief probably because it is meant for memorizing in a predominantly oral culture and certainly because it is meant for elucidation by a teacher and a commentary.

In a typical Indian discussion of a philosophical problem there is a systematic, if only formal fairness in that the text repeats and responds to the views of all the rival schools. The frequent compression of the text is likely to face the interpreter with the problem of deciding whether a statement represents the opinion of the writer or of the view the writer means to refute—a mistake in identification is as serious as confusing *yes* with *no*. The to and fro of argument is signaled by an armature of phrases such as:

> But what is the proof?; but in this case; well, then (how would you respond) if (we say)?; if it were so, exactly this should also be the case; this is not right, because; but would this not be similar?; no (this is not so) because; others, however, say; this is also incorrect; well, then (how do you respond) if?; but how can there be?; this is not so; well then, let us admit that; that (dilemma); and it is not so; but then, if; and one should not say; if one assumes that; well, then (let us say that); with this (argumentation); well, then (let us say that); that may be enough.[81]

It is Indian style, as well, for the philosopher to put arguments in verse, accompanied by a commentary written either by himself, a follower, or, sometimes, a member of a rival school. The commentaries and subcommentaries are technical and often ambiguous because they are meant for teachers and students who are used to the issues and the style in which they have traditionally been put. Like the Indian philosophical treatises, they are, at their best, dry, direct, sharply reasoned, pious, and acidulous—a laborious pleasure to those who have acquired the Indian taste. In accord with the Indian taste, philosophical texts are given an imaginative punctuation by means of stock analogies such as the rope mistaken for a snake, the shell mistaken for silver, the mirage of water, the hare's (nonexistent) horns, and the (impossible) son of the barren woman.

Because I cannot do so briefly enough, I refrain from reviewing the characteristic assumptions and modes of analysis of Indian philosophers, who, not unlike the Chinese, love to work with numbered categories.[82] But they have shown an ability far beyond any of the Chinese (except, maybe, the Buddhists) or Europeans to go explicitly inward and distinguish, often with perceptive care, between the objects, conditions, and functions of perception and conception. The kinds of perception between which they distinguish include those that are preverbal, postverbal, normal, abnormal, illusory, supernormal, and divine, and of each separate sense and all the senses together; and include self-perceptions and perceptions of space, time, and universals. The kinds of cognition between which they distinguish include those of dreams, memories, recollections, recognitions, imaginations, reveries, and trances. They also distinguish between different desires, aversions, and emotions—emotions of attachment, clinging, yearning, lust, detachment, love, joy, anger, resentment, dejection, fear, greed, longing, conceit, hatred, forbearance, contentment, equanimity, tranquillity, endurance, wonder, and *rasa*. And among kinds of consciousness, they distinguish between the subliminal, the supraliminal, the supernormal, and the transcendental.[83]

There is much that is artificial in this inward analysis, yet, all told, it shows how intensely the Indians are able to concentrate on these very elusive processes. It is not surprising that the Indians' fascination with inward life is related to their interest in transcendence and the yogic methods for arriving at it. Their earliest philosophy already shows an intense appreciation of the ability to dream whole rich worlds, a sign to them that the ego can, by itself, both create and identify itself with everything it experiences, which is to say, with all perceptible reality, which is (often) to say, with a cosmic ego in nature identical with the personal one. When a person is asleep, Indians explain, he is like a king, who moves everywhere as he likes—the dreamer is everything that his self invents. This view of the power of the dreaming self makes it natural for the mystical Indians to believe that deep, dreamless sleep, which they take to be the highest level, is a way of attaining certainty and peace by going beyond the lower, dreaming consciousness—which still differentiates things—and by leaving the individual unlimited by anything or anyone else, his borders having vanished in the undifferentiated common reality.

What of the style of classical Chinese thought? It is equally if not more compressed than the Indian, besides which it lacks many of the grammatical indications that are considered essential for clarity in Sanskrit or in Greek, Latin, and other European languages. Let me give as an example a short passage in which Hsün-tzu, in the course of his attack on the view that human beings are by nature good, defines what is meant by good and evil:

> All men in the world, past and present, agree in defining goodness as that which is upright, reasonable, and orderly, and evil as that which is prejudiced, irresponsible, and chaotic.

This passage is, on its face, fully intelligible; but try to understand the following approximately literal substitution of English words for Chinese characters. Needless to say, the Chinese is more compact and, in the original, unedited text lacks punctuation.

> Everybody past-present Heaven-below's
> that-which called good-ones:
> alignment pattern equableness good-order are;
> that-which called evil-ones:
> One-sidedness irregularity turbulence disorder are.[84]

Such clarity as is inherent in the Chinese language comes largely, as I have said, from the way the characters are organized. The characters march across the page in their fixed and parallel order and unchanging (uninflected) shape, like so many logical/esthetic symbols—each symbol's meaning to be chosen from among a variety of possibilities in accord with the immediate context, the general context of which is the whole of classical Chinese literature. The reader sees the phrases echo and enchain one another into rhythms and meanings such as these taken from Lao-tzu:

> The whole world recognizes the beautiful
> as the beautiful, yet this is only the ugly;
> the whole world recognizes the good as
> the good, yet this is only the bad.
>> Thus Something and Nothing
>> produce each other;
>> The difficult and the easy complement each other;
>> The long and the short off-set each other;
>> The high and the low incline towards each other;
>> Before and after follow each other.
> Therefore the sage keeps to the deed
> that consists in taking no action and practices
> the teaching that uses no words.[85]

To those who have not learned a classical text in the classical way, the text contains a set of riddles to be solved by finding the most probable combination of meanings and intended associations. The process is not unlike solving subtle crossword puzzles, because the texts, compiled by thinkers each of whose memories retained a great part of the classical literature, are quite certain to quote, paraphrase, or hint at other, unnamed texts the reader is assumed to know; if the assumption proves false, the thinker—the thinker's text—abandons the reader as unworthy of any subtle understanding.[86]

But there are also comparisons, stories, conversations, and historical instances to lighten the way.

As shown by the passage from Lao-tzu, the correlative style of Chinese writing and thought, with one thing or idea set alongside or against another, creates a rhythm like that of the changing correspondences by which, the Chinese believe, the universe functions. Subtlety rules even their frequent stereotypes. Take as an example the Confucian notion that human nature is good but requires considerable education, and that a familylike harmony, achieved by unequal but faithful reciprocity, is the social and universal ideal. But the Chinese are very sensitive to the nuances of these deceptively modifiable stereotypes. The obtuse will miss the subtlety concealed within the platitude that allows it to enter another's mind without jarring it. As classical Chinese philosophers say, the correct application of language is the key to ethical behavior, because the mind— the heart—acts according to the distinctions of the words it uses. Is this a hypersimple or hypersubtle view? Something of both, maybe. Taken as a whole and at its best, the Chinese view expresses an ideal of actively personal and impersonal harmonizing like that achieved by the calligrapher who infuses the poem he writes, sometimes on the painting he himself has made, with the forces whose entangled contrariety catches and inspires an intensive quality of life.

I've forgotten Chinese queerness, crudeness, heartbreak, hatred, and other traits, which come to expression in philosophy as in other media; but I cannot say it all. Nor can I show in adequate detail that most of the indigenous Chinese philosophy was written not in a special philosophical language, but in the usual literary style, as essays, letters, conversations, and expansions of a master's words. I mention this, as I earlier mentioned the Indian style of commentaries and of treatises intended for technical precision, because European philosophy seems to me to have been extraordinarily varied—often, like the Chinese, merging indistinguishably with literature in general, but often written, like the Indian, in learned styles impenetrable to laymen.

Given the brevity I must observe, I can only hint at the great variety of European styles. The main point I want to make is that, the Middle Ages excepted, the philosopher's pride is more in his individual position than in his school, if he is at all willing to recognize himself as belonging to one. There is such a great variety of styles of philosophizing that it is much harder than for India or China to point out what is common to them. To say this in the form of a brief reminder: At the very beginning there is the style of epic poetry chosen by Parmenides and, later and differently, by Lucretius. Also at the beginning, there is the contrary, aphoristic style, of Heraclitus, and, later, are the aphoristic styles of Francis Bacon—an aphorism, he said, is a seed of thought—and of Pascal, Nietzsche, and Wittgenstein. Toward the beginning, there are the drama style of Plato and the contrary style of (the surviving) Aristotle, who is always analyzing and always discovering systematic connections but always correcting himself, so that he never gets to a finished system. There are the dialogue-treatises of Cicero, the discourses of Epictetus, and the meditations of Marcus Aurelius; and the style of free, imaginative, often eloquent composition of Plotinus and the copious commentary style of Proclus, carried over into the commentary style of the Middle Ages. But Proclus also has a Euclidean style, which Descartes uses for a sketch and Spinoza elaborates in his *Ethics*. This Euclidean style is paralleled in later philosophers who, like Wolff, Hegel and, in one book, Wittgenstein, stress formal structure. Then there is the style of the free essay, which we find in Plutarch, in the quotation-patchwork intimacy of Montaigne, and in many others. The detailed treatise cannot, of course, be forgotten. In Kant and those who follow him, it is often made up of convoluted sentences, furnished with special technical terms, that go from one deep difficulty to another. And now, to make the barest mention of the present, many write and think like the academic professionals they are, whether in the style of Wittgenstein, Heidegger, or some other philosophical mentor; but they nearly all aspire to the clear victory by argument that none of them ever wins.

Everything I have said up until now is by way of introduction, by way, that is, of reflection on the kind of work to be done, but it is not the work itself. If, as a result of the work, we will come to see that the philosophy of the other traditions shares a good deal with ours, this will teach us something we surely ought to know. But the discovery of what has been common to philosophically thinking humans is unlikely to invigorate philosophy as such. This is because the contemporary philosopher is far less interested in recovering variations of old thoughts than in thinking ahead, as far and as exactly as possible, into unknown territory.

What can push thought ahead in comparative philosophy is not the similarity one finds or misses but the strain one undergoes in the finding or missing, and, when a similarity is found, the strain in showing it for what it is and marking out its limits. It is possible for us to think ahead in the forms that we have inherited and, no less, in those that others have inherited, with our kinds of insight and theirs, so that the friction between them makes them sharper, more subtle instruments of understanding than philosophers have had before. Will this possibility ever really tempt many of them?

Chapter 2

✳

The Beginnings of Metaphysical Philosophy
Uddalaka, Yajnavalkya, Heraclitus, Parmenides

From now on, this book will practice a moderate philosophical austerity. I mean that, with justifiable exceptions, each chapter will focus
more on ideas than on personalities, circumstances, or social surroundings. This is for two reasons. The first is concern with the philosophers'
influence on their respective traditions. It is natural for a tradition to
ignore philosophical views that turn out to be inconvenient, and to turn
the philosopher into a character given the same name as the original but
recreated, as in a play, to fill the role the tradition requires. I hope to
protect the individual against this eviction from his thought, but I am also
committed to explain what tradition made of it.

The second reason for focusing mainly on ideas is to allow us to
begin at a level of abstraction high enough to allow the ideas to be compared at all. This freeing of the ideas for comparison—equivalent to the
clearing away of "noise" that makes the exact sciences possible—requires
us to disregard as temporarily irrelevant the ideas' simply local or individual characteristics. Otherwise everything to be compared has a raggedly
individual shape that makes clear analysis problematic or, strictly speaking, impossible. A truly full analysis would be an endless recital of inex-
haustibly many details and inexhaustible nuances of quality.[1] But once we
have compared the abstracted ideas, we can qualify them in order to make
them as individual or local as we prefer. To consider the ideas inherently
beyond comparison is to negate their intended nature as abstractions. But

when they are scrutinized in close detail, they become more individual and begin to reveal the extent to which they share in the uniqueness of those who held them.

The Theme: The Search for What Is Primary, Basic, or Real

Now that these preliminary remarks have been made, I can state the theme of the present chapter. The theme, which neither philosophy nor religion has ever abandoned, is the relation between the unity of the world and its variety, and between its permanence and the changes it undergoes. These four traits can be paired in another way to express the theme as the relation between unity and permanence and between variety and change. Together, the four concepts—unity, variety, permanence, change—are involved in any attempt to understand how and why the world is or appears to be as we experience or appear to experience it. To think about the four concepts is to be attracted, almost by instinct, to the further distinction between what is primary, basic, or real, and what is secondary, dependent, or unreal.

Considering that human beings, even highly philosophical ones, are practical as well as theorizing creatures, the attempt to understand is also an attempt to gain a practical goal, which is power in some sense, whether over nature, over others, or over oneself. These goals, the search for which is guided by curiosity and example and driven by desire, are, of course, evident in the four philosophers we are about to discuss. They do not distinguish or distinguish very little between the theoretical and the practical, or, in the Indian instances, between the theoretical, practical, and ritual. Yet in each of these individuals we catch sight of the philosophical impulse as it first becomes visible to us in the history of civilization. Whatever traditional ideas these individuals may have inherited, there is the (maybe misleading) feeling of the creation of something philosophical from nothing philosophical; and however naive or arbitrary the expression of this impulse may seem to us now, it shows the thrusting boldness of the human intellect as it begins to awaken to its power to create and destroy by means of purely abstract thought.

Uddalaka (8th [?] Century B.C.E.):
Everything Is the Subtle Essence, the Existent

This first encounter with Indian philosophers has five protagonists: Uddalaka Aruni (son of Aruna), his son Shvetaketu, his student Yajnavalkya, Maitreyi —the more philosophical of Yajnavalkya's two wives—

and king Janaka of Videha, the Bihar of today, who was Uddalaka's disciple and Yajanavalkya's patron.[2] Their discussions dealt with here, discussions of unknown and unknowable authenticity, are from two ancient Upanishads, the *Brihad-Aranyaka Upanishad* (Great Secret Teaching of the Forest) and the *Chandogya Upanishad* (Secret Teaching of the Chandogyas).[3]*

I have chosen to represent Uddalaka's and Yajnavalkya's ideas by means of some justly famous passages. The relative clarity of my accounts of these passages and the sharpness of contrasts I derive from them seem to me to be possibly misleading. If one wants to understand such old, sacred texts, one ought to be wary of later interpretations, usually meant to support one or another traditional position. Even if one has the philological ability to interpret the texts on their own, in the light of only earlier or presumably contemporary texts, there is much that must remain inexact, if not mysterious—every clarification or expansion risks too violent reduction of mythical or quasi-mythical conceptions to merely logical form.

Regardless of the moderate philosophical austerity adopted here, it would be cruel to resist an anecdote that fixes a philosopher in one's memory. I therefore take the liberty of repeating a traditional story of how Uddalaka got his name: After his teacher sent him to repair a breach in a dike, he failed to return. His teacher then went to the site of the dike and called out. He heard him and got up out of the breach, in which he had been lying—he had been able to stop it only with his own body, he explained. Because he opened the breach again by getting up, the teacher gave him the name Uddalaka, Puller of the Stop, and said: "Since you obeyed my word, you shall obtain the highest good. All the Vedas will be manifest to you and all the books of the Law."[4] Of Uddalaka's son Shvetaketu, his partner in the memorable series of dialogues to be discussed, I repeat only that he is said to have broken the rule for orthodox students by insisting on eating honey.

Uddalaka is the person I would like to dramatize as the first philosopher. He may have lived earlier or later than the date I assign him, the eighth century B.C.E., but it is safe to assume that he preceded the earliest Greek philosophers. Much of his philosophical thought comes to expression in the

---

*The term *Upanishad*, used as the name of a kind of text, has most often been taken by scholars to mean *confidential instruction*, *secret teaching*, or *secret text*. Other meanings are *secret word* and *secret significance*. The word is made up of *upa* (near), *ni* (down), and *sad*, an etymology that indicates that the original meaning was probably *a sitting near* (a teacher, for instruction). However, the philosopher Shankara, who is discussed in a later chapter, derives the meaning of *upanishad* from *destroy* (because it destroys inborn ignorance) or from *conduct* (toward Brahman). There seems to have been no ancient canon of Upanishads, but collections of them were in time formed, first one of 34, then another of 52, and, much later, one of 108. For further information on the term and on its sources, see note 3, just preceding.

conversations between him and his son Shvetaketu. Because his ideas make a more natural impression in the context of these dialogues, my paraphrase echoes something of their form.

The dialogues form a series of lessons in which Uddalaka teaches Shvetaketu what he failed to learn during the twelve years of study from which he has just returned, now twenty-four years old and full of conceit.[5] Has he learned what is of true importance? To test him, Uddalaka asks him if he has learned the rule by which the yet unheard could be heard, the yet unthought could be thought, and the yet not understood could be understood. To Shvetaketu's question what the rule is, the father answers that it is the one by which a person can know everything made of a certain substance by knowing only a small portion of it, for instance, everything made of earth by knowing a single one of its clods.[6]

Uddalaka goes on to teach an early Indian theory of the origin of the different substances and of the universe they make up. According to his theory, there are three basic elements, each of which is a power or, as he also calls it, a divinity. The elements are heat (which is also light), water, and food (food meaning plants). This choice of elements shows that Uddalaka is thinking primarily of the cosmic elements that become the elements that make up living things, that is, the living things' heat and the water and food they need for their existence.

Uddalaka is following precedent when he begins his account of the origin of things with the primal Existent (sat) or the primal Being, which is what exists solely and completely by virtue of its own power of existence. He contends that the Existent cannot come, as some think, from the Non-Existent, from Nothing (asat), the unordered chaos that others assume preceded the cosmos, which is by nature ordered.[7] As the sequel shows, he believes that the Existent or the Being is alive, that is, has the conscious desire to be many—"to propagate" powers, or, to use a more cautious term, to emanate powers from itself. The Existent, Uddalaka believes, is these powers' own power of existence. Following a traditional theme, Uddalaka is in effect arguing that there must be some fundamental something by virtue of which anything can at all exist. In accord with this tradition, he believes that the process of creation is catalyzed by the conscious and at least vaguely personal desire to create. The ruling analogy, I suppose, is that of a father longing for children. This longing aside, much the same problem concerning primary and secondary existence arises in European philosophy, very explicitly in the odd-sounding question—a tribute to the stubbornness of curiosity—Why is there anything at all?

To return to the scene of primal creation, because the Existent had the desire to become many, it emanated heat/light from itself. Then heat/light, having the same desire, emanated water from itself—which explains why a person sweats when hot. Having the same desire, water emanated food from itself, which explains why there is plenty of food when it rains. Then the Existent or the Being had the desire to make individual things. In Indian thought, as it happens, an individual person or thing is made up of an inward nature or "name" (naman) and an outward appearance or "form" (rupa), that is, a visible (colored) shape. Thinking in terms of such an analysis into name and form (nama-rupa), Uddalaka explains that the Existent entered into heat, water, and food (that is, plants), as their life, with this essential living part of itself, its own living self. In entering, it caused each of these elements to contain something of the other two, so that what we actually see is not wholly composed of any one element but of the triad of elements in different proportions. Fire, for example, contains not only heat but the other elements as well. But we know Fire basically when we know its indwelling nature of fire, which is visible in the redness of its red form. Therefore, Uddalaka concludes, whoever knows the three elements knows the truth of everything visible, which is made of them alone.[8] His idea that to understand anything one must understand the elements that make it up continues to be an elementary, irreplaceable tactic of thought.

In accord with his doctrine of elements, Uddalaka tells his son that human beings, too, are composed of heat, water, and food, each of which has three different degrees of fineness. The highest human functions are composed of the finest degrees of the elements: the organ of thought is composed of the finest degree of food, the life-breath of the finest degree of water, and speech of the finest degree of heat—the doctrine is, at least in part, a vitalistic materialism. To demonstrate the truth of this theory, Uddalaka makes an experiment by asking Shvetaketu to stop eating for fifteen days. At the end of the fifteen days, Shvetaketu finds himself unable to recite the hymns, sacrificial formulas, and chants that he knows by heart. His father explains that it is as if a great fire in Shvetaketu has burned out and left only a firefly-sized ember. When Shvetaketu eats again, as his father orders, his organ of thought is renewed by the food that makes it up, and he remembers everything he is asked.[9]

In the context of the Indian speculation of his time, this three-element doctrine of Uddalaka is a highly original invention. Because the text of Uddalaka's instruction was well known and because its teaching resembles later Indian doctrines, it is reasonable to assume that it influenced them. But Uddalaka is most vividly remembered by tradition for his doctrine that the essential component of everything that lives is one and the same invisible Self or Atman (in deference to the translation I am using, I capitalize atman only here). As he teaches the doctrine to his son, Shvetaketu, each time he finishes a demonstration that everything is without exception constituted by this reality, he drives the point home by repeating, "That is you!" *"tat tvam asi,"* words that were to become a cardinal formula of a number of Indian schools.*

Uddalaka explains himself: When a human being sleeps, he enters into his own, that is, he is united with the Existent. A bird tied by a string flies in one direction after another but finds no resting place until it alights just where it is tied, in the same way as the human being's thought-organ (*manas*) flies in one direction after another but finds no resting place until it alights on the life-breath, just where it is tied.[10]

Shvetaketu says, "Tell me more," and Uddalaka answers with the analogy of the rivers flowing from ocean into ocean, in each ocean becoming indistinguishable. Uddalaka then gives the analogy of honey. The bees make honey, he says, out of the juices of various trees but reduce this juice to a unity, and no one of the juices can distinguish itself as that of a particular tree. Just so, when any creature—tiger, lion, wolf, boar, worm, moth, gnat, or mosquito—merges with the Existent, it no longer knows that it is a particular individual but feels merged with the Existent.[11]

Shvetaketu again says, "Tell me more," a phrase he repeats before each new lesson his father gives him. Pointing to a great tree, Uddalaka says that because it is through and through pervaded with living Self, wherever it is hacked, in its middle, which is alive, or at its top, which is alive, its sap will flow out of it. If life leaves one of its branches, that branch withers, and if life leaves the whole tree, the whole tree withers. "What loses life dies, but life itself does not die."[12]

From all the examples he has given, Uddalaka draws the same conclusion: "That which is that subtle essence is nothing other than this universe. That is the real, that is the self (*atman*), that is you, Shvetaketu!"[13]

The lesson is extended with the help of a fruit from a banyan tree. Following Uddalaka's directions, Shvetaketu extracts fine seeds from the tree's fruit and splits one of them. When Shvetaketu finds nothing that explains anything inside the seed, Uddalaka says, "Because of that subtle essence that you do not perceive this great banyan tree continues in existence," and he ends again with the formula, "That is you, Shvetaketu!"

---

*This traditional translation is now disputed, and "That's how you are" is suggested in its place. The argument for the change is that, by the rules of Vedic grammar, "the neuter pronoun *tat* ('that') cannot stand in apposition to a masculine noun or pronoun (here *tvam*, 'you'), even when the antecedent of 'that' may be a neuter word. Thus, if the author had wanted to assert the identity between 'that' and 'you,' he would have used the masculine of 'that'; the phrase would then have read *sa tvam asi* . . . The phrase, therefore, does not establish the identity between the individual and the ultimate being (*sat*), but rather shows that Shvetaketu lives in the same manner as all other creatures, that is, by means of an invisible and subtle essence." However, "it may also . . . to some degree, indicate the cause of his existence," as it does in the analogy, given just below, of the subtle essence of the seed of the banyan tree (Olivelle, *Upaniṣads*, p. 349, drawing on the grammatical analysis of J. Brereton). The ambiguity allowed seems plausible and the "to some extent" allows a less dramatic persistence of the hallowed old meaning.

Then, following his father's directions, Shvetaketu puts salt into water and waits a day. Told to bring the salt to his father, he tries to touch it in order to take it out but fails because the salt has all dissolved. Following his father's directions, Shvetaketu verifies this by tasting it from one side and another—the water is salty everywhere. The lesson is that although the Existent is not perceived, it is everywhere. It is the subtle essence that is this universe, the truth, the self, and Shvetaketu as well.[14]

Uddalaka strengthens his lesson by describing the process of dying: A dying man is able to know his relatives as long as his speech does not retreat into his organ of thought, his organ of thought into his life-breath, his life-breath into his heat/light and his heat/light, into the highest power, the divinity. After this succession of retreats has taken place, the dying person no longer knows his relatives because his life has retreated into the subtle essence that is the Existent and has vanished from his body. Uddalaka repeats the refrain, "That is you, Shvetaketu!" and repeats it again at the end of the final lesson, which is an analogy of a different kind: Unlike a lying criminal who undergoes the ordeal of grasping a heated axe, a person who is not guilty and covers himself with the truth, the real, does not perish but is released by his accusers.[15] This seems to mean that in covering himself with truth, the innocent man is delivered from danger by his coincidence with the Existent.

To summarize the series of lessons: By using analogies and empirical observations, Uddalaka has shown that this whole varied world arises and continues to exist, like a banyan tree, from the invisible essence that he calls the Existent or the Being; has shown that the Existent, like salt dissolved in water, is present everywhere even though it is imperceptible; has shown that the disappearance of consciousness in death is a step-by-step return to the imperceptible Existent; and has shown that the truth, the real, can protect a person who is undergoing a judicial ordeal. Although later ascribed a much broader significance, this last lesson seems meant only to give an explanation of why judicial ordeals are able to distinguish between the guilty and the innocent.*

---

*The traditional controversy concerning Uddalaka's phrase "That is you!" can be put simply enough, though it will become clearer when the relevant philosophy, that of Shankara, is discussed. Shankara gives the phrase a far-reaching interpretation: The self, the *atman*, is completely indistinguishable from Brahman, so that to think of them as in any way different is to be under the spell of illusion. Other schools dispute this interpretation. For example, that of Ramanuja (c.e. 1055–1137) claims that for the self to be a particular form of Brahman or to be essentially dependent on Brahman is not the same as to be absolutely identical with it. The phrase *that is you* is therefore taken to mean that although God dwells within the human soul, there is a real difference between him and human beings. Otherwise their individual identity would be annihilated, which is absurd. (See J. B. Carman, *The Theology of Rāmānuja*, New Haven: Yale University Press, 1974, pp. 124–25; and E. Lott, *Vedantic Approaches to God*, London: Macmillan, 1980, pp. 28–37.)

Yajnavalkya (8th [?] Century B.C.E.): Reality Is Experienced in Deep Dreaming But Can Be Described Only by Negation

Yajnavalkya is represented as the great expert in ritual procedures and secrets, a man who strikes fear into those who dispute such matters with him.[16] He follows Uddalaka here because of the sources that describe him as Uddalaka's student. Endowed with a poetically philosophical cast of mind, he at times makes the impression of blatant pride. Once, when asked by King Janaka, the patron of philosopher-ritualists, if he has come to the debate for the sake of the cattle put up as the prize or for the sake of questions with subtle solutions, he answers frankly, "Both, O great king."

Like Uddalaka, Yajnavalkya insists that all existing things comprise an invisible unity, one that words, he is sure, are too limiting to express. Together with King Janaka, he explores the nature of reality. As a favor to the king, he allows him the privilege of asking any question he wants. Aiming at a truly revealing answer, the king begins by asking, with apparent innocence, what it is that serves as light to men here in this world. He is first given a series of obvious answers: the sun; and when the sun sets, the moon; and when the moon sets, fire. Then, when the king asks what serves as a light when the sun sets, the moon sets, and the fire is out, he gets the less obvious answer, speech—because, even in the darkness, a person moves in the direction of a voice. Then the king asks a deep question: What serves man as a light when the sun and moon have set, the fire is out, and speech has ended? Yajnavalkya answers, the Self. This is because, Yajnavalkya says, "It is by the light of the self that man sits, walks, works, and returns home." The king asks what the Self is and gets the answer: The Self is the light that is the inner person (purusha) lodged within the heart. He consists of intelligence, which is the inner light within the vital breaths. This inner person has two states, one in this world, and one in the other. When he is born and attains a body, he is joined with evils; when he dies, he abandons evils. But there is a third state, that of dreams. In this state, this person sees both the evils of this world and the joys of the other.[17]

Yajnavalkya goes on: When the inner person, the Self, falls asleep, he takes material from the waking world, cuts it down and builds it up, and so is able to dream by his own radiance and light. In sleep, the inner person proves that he is able to create everything for itself: wagons, teams of horses, roads; joys, delights, happinesses; pools, rivers, lakes. He creates this all for himself, "For he is the Creator." He takes many forms, has his pleasure with women, laughs, and, it seems to him, sees terrifying sights.[18]

Like a great fish that swims from the closer to the farther banks of a river, the inner person, the Self, alternates between the dream state and the waking state. The highest dream state is that of desireless, dreamless sleep, in which the inner person can be entirely at peace, as unconscious of anything inner or outer as a man embraced by a beloved woman. Unaffected by good and evil, nothing exists for him any longer, no father, mother, worlds, gods, Vedas, sacrifices, nor anyone who is by nature blameworthy or praiseworthy. This is because there is no longer any difference between the person who senses and knows and that which is sensed and known. When sensing and knowing, this person does not really sense or know: there is no longer anything separate for him to sense or know.[19]

This description by Yajnavalkya of the passage from the state of wakefulness to that of conscious dreaming and then to an unconscious, unitary state was to be incorporated into the Indian theory of the four states of the self, which are: waking; shallow, dream-filled sleep; deep, dreamless sleep; and union with the ultimate (Brahman) that underlies everything.[20] To make a comparison with a Greek view of dreaming, in Homer's epics, dreaming is represented as passive and the dreamers are visited, they believe, by dream figures that exist independently of themselves—"the Greeks never spoke of *having* a dream, but always of *seeing* a dream."[21]* In the Indian tradition, too, dreams may be seen, but Yajnavalkya believes that dreams are active projections of the self. To him, this is evidence that dreaming shares the creative nature of reality in itself.

The subject of sleep and dreams having been ended, Yajnavalkya explains the nature of death to the king. He does this rather fearfully, because the king has been extracting too many of his secrets from him. Death is preceded by coma. The sensory powers, which are the different life-breaths, are received by the soul-person that (according to an old belief) lodges in the eye, and they descend together into the heart. The heart's tip lights up, and by its light the Self leaves the body along with

---

*One should always beware, I suppose, of making such contrasts too categorical. "In Homer we find only a very special kind of dream. The dreams in Homer are 'literary dreams' used to further the story and, as such, cannot be taken as informing about the whole real dream-experience of the early Greeks . . . Homer only reports those dreams with a message," of a kind related to the Gods and purported divine messages . . . "Although we do not find in Homer the activities of a dream soul, its absence does not necessarily presuppose its nonexistence"(Bremmer, *The Early Greek Concept of the Soul*, pp. 18–20).

As might be expected, Indian philosophers have many different theories of dreaming. Some believe that dreams are created independently of the external sense organs and some that they are memories of waking experience. Different physiological causes are recognized and external stimuli are often taken into account—a sleeping man may dream that a light brought near his eye is a bonfire. (See Sinha, *Indian Psychology*, vol. 1, chap. 5; the example is from p. 320.)

the central life-breath and the sensory powers—the other life-breaths—
which together comprise consciousness. The Self, which has got rid of this
body and cast off ignorance, weaves a new form for itself, whether of god,
man, or another creature—the Self is really Brahman and therefore consists of everything that exists. In its succeeding life, the Self becomes
something that accords with its particular actions and its conduct in general, whether good or evil. But the life-breaths of someone who is without
desire, who desires only the Self, collect within him. Being Brahman himself, he attains Brahman while still in this world and becomes immortal.[22]

Describing the Self by a series of negations, Yajnavalkya says it is
not, not (neti, neti)—not graspable, not destructible, not attached, not
disturbed by anything good or evil done by himself, not tormented by
what he has not done. Whoever knows this truth remains "controlled, at
peace, patient, full of faith." When he knows the truth, "everyone comes
to be his Self" and "he becomes the Self of everyone." Subduing all evil,
he is free of evil, free of age, free of hunger, and free of thirst.[23]

In the end, Yajnavalkya decides to become a wandering ascetic.
Maitreyi, his wife with an interest in philosophical discussion, asks him a
last question: If all the wealth of the world was mine, would that make me
immortal? After he answers "no," she asks what she should do with that
which does not make her immortal. He answers that she is dear to him
and so she should weigh his words with care. He says: A husband is not
dear for himself, nor is a wife dear for herself, nor are sons, possessions,
the brahman caste, the warrior caste, the world, the gods, the Vedas, the
sacrifices, the creatures, dear for themselves—nothing such is dear for
itself. Everything that is loved is loved for love of the Self, the atman.
Everything that is seen, heard, thought, and meditated on is the atman.

Yajnavalkya begins to explain by giving a list made up mostly of
human activities and what includes them: the sea is the sole location of all
water; the different kinds of sensation are located, respectively and solely, in
the skin, the nostrils, the tongue, the eye, and the ear; all resolves are located
in the thought organ, all sciences in the heart, all deeds in the hands, all
journeys in the feet, all delights in the genital organ, all evacuations in the
anus, and all speech—speech as holy—in the Vedas. By his own line of
reasoning, Yajnavalkya should have ended this list with the ultimately inclusive place, the Self, which is the sole location of all things. For the great
element, the Self, he says immediately afterward, is nothing but a mass of
intelligence with no boundaries, in the same way as a lump of salt is nothing
but a mass of flavor with no inside or outside. Arising out of the elements,
the Self perishes into them—meaning, it seems, that like salt dissolved in
water, it enters into them and cannot be separated out again. "After death
there is no consciousness"—consciousness does not separate out again.[24]

Maitreyi does not understand this last sentence, so Yajnavalkya goes on explaining: The Self is certainly not destroyed. If there was somebody other than the Self, one could see, smell, taste, talk to, hear, think of, touch, or know something else. But when in death all of someone has become just the Self, what means are there by which the Self could see, smell, taste, talk to, hear, think of, touch, or know; and what or who would be there to be seen, smelled, tasted, talked to, heard, thought of, touched, or known? By what means could one know the Knower, apart from whom there is nothing and nobody?

Having explained the subject of immortality, Yajnavalkya leaves.[25]

Heraclitus (fl. 500 B.C.E.): Nothing Is Still

Heraclitus is immodestly critical of men both great and small.[26] To him, learning is not enough for understanding, nor is poetic imagination enough—Homer, he says, should be expelled from the poets' competition and be beaten with a rod. It is reported that when the people of his city, Ephesus, asked him to make laws, he refused on the grounds that the city was too much in the grip of a bad constitution. Whether true or maliciously invented, the end assigned him by tradition sounds as if it was repayment for his pride and his disparagement of others: Having become a misanthrope, he wanders about on the mountains, where he lives on grass and herbs, but this makes him sick and, when his disagreeable attempt to cure himself fails, he dies.[27]

What is left of Heraclitus is a set of striking, often barely comprehensible aphorisms. These may have been no better connected or more intelligible in antiquity, when he was called "the dark "and "the riddler." To show of what fragments I have pieced together my account of him, I follow each of them by its standard number.[28] As I have intimated, Heraclitus makes frequent, usually lapidary complaints. He states, complainingly, that people hear like the deaf and are absent while present (1). Even after they hear the true account, the *logos* of how all things come to pass, they fail to comprehend (2). But he, Heraclitus, went in search of himself (28); and he has come to know that nature loves to hide (10). One truth he discovers is that all things are one (36). For the universe always was, is, and will be an ever-living fire that is kindled in measures and in measures goes out (38). The world arises from this fire, the sea first and the earth from the sea (39). All things are in repayment for fire and fire for all things, in the same way as goods are in repayment for gold and gold for goods (40). The cosmic exchanges are kept within their proper limits by the Furies, who are the ministers of Justice (44). This justice of limits is needed because things always change in the way other and still other waters flow on those who step into the same rivers (50).

With respect to politics and ethics, Heraclitus says that people must fight for the law no less than for the walls of their city (65). Of life in general he says that it is best that human beings should not get all they want because health is made sweet by disease, satiety by hunger, and rest by weariness (67). The world is such that war is the father and king of all, making some slaves, others free—everything occurs and is judged by conflict (83).

Of souls, says Heraclitus, the dry one is a gleam of light and wisest and best (109). What awaits men at death, they cannot imagine (84), the living and the dead, the waking and the sleeping, and the old and the young being transposed into one another (93). Whole and not whole, convergent and divergent, consonant and dissonant, from all things one and from one thing all (124). They all are ruled by the divine, this "wise one" who knows the plan by which it steers all things through all things (54). This divine is alone, willing and unwilling to be spoken of as Zeus (118).

All of Heraclitus' views invite explanation, but here I need go into only those that concern the *logos*, god and the cosmic fire, and change.

Logos is a common Greek word for *speech*, *account*, and *reason*. In one especially ambiguous aphorism (31), Heraclitus says that thinking is shared by all, and in another (35) that the vital principle or soul, the *psyche*, has no limits. Maybe he means that, like fire, the soul is universal because it reaches everywhere or that because all things are alive, they are within the soul's reach. To *logos* as a cosmic principle Heraclitus assigns the function of creating order in the warring tensions of the world.

From *logos* we go on to the divine and to the cosmic fire. The divine, which Heraclitus personalizes as "the wise one," possesses the plan by which all things are steered. The wise one is alone in the sense of being unique or supreme and, as such, fits and does not fit the traditional conception of Zeus and might be called, just as appropriately, by other names. His thunderbolt is his fire that orders and guides by means of the oppositions, the polar strife, of all: fire will discern and catch up with all things as they move from diversity to full unity and back again (119–22).[29]

Finally there is the doctrine of the universality of change, which gives Heraclitus his fame in the history of philosophy. His metaphor of the river whose waters are always changing has already been cited. His best known version of the metaphor is that one cannot step twice into the same river (51). Cratylus, whose Heracliteanism is said to have reduced him to silence—because, maybe, words imply permanence—had words enough to criticize Heraclitus and say that it is impossible to step into the river even once—presumably because the river changes too fast at every point to ever be the same river.[30] It is reasonable to interpret Heraclitus' metaphor to mean, as Plato and Aristotle agree, that while a river continues to have the same form, its contents are always changing—changing in a way, Aristotle adds, that escapes perception. Plato expresses this Heraclitean idea when he says that a man is called the same from childhood to old age even though everything of him has changed, his hair, flesh and bones and blood, and all his body.[31] A like idea of the preservation of identity in change is implied when Heraclitus speaks of the continuity between the sleeping and the waking and the living and the dead. It is in this vein that Plato declares that opposites come to be from opposites, as when souls are born from the dead.[32] As best we can now make out, in holding that all things change, Heraclitus means that because even static-seeming things eventually change, they too are subject to the laws of tension, opposition, and process.

Parmenides (b. c.515 B.C.E.): What Is, Cannot Not Be

Parmenides was a native of Elea, a city-state in southwest Italy.[33] He is said to have been the first to declare that the earth is spherical and situated in the center of space, the earth having no reason to move in one direction rather than another. He is also said to have made laws for his city that were so good that every year the citizens insisted that the magistrates they elected should swear to abide by his laws. In Plato's dialogue given Parmenides' name, we are told that Parmenides, then a distinguished looking man of about sixty-five, visited Athens together with his disciple Zeno, who was nearly forty. An independent source speaks of Zeno's presence in Athens, and, whether or not Parmenides accompanied him, the date Plato assumes for the dialogue must be about 450 B.C.E. Plato tells us that Socrates, then very young, heard Parmenides develop some magnificent arguments and impressed Socrates as having an altogether noble sort of depth.[34]

The fragments of Parmenides that remain are some hundred and fifty lines from a long poem, one that draws on the *Iliad* and the *Odyssey* for the form of its verse, its vocabulary, and its images. The fragments come from four successive parts of the poem. In the prologue, the poet, drawn by "sagacious" mares and escorted by the daughters of the sun is brought into the presence of an unnamed welcoming goddess. She says to him that he must be informed both of persuasive reality and of the mistaken beliefs of mortals.[35] Is Parmenides using the goddess merely as a literary device or does he mean to say that his words are inspired? I find it hard to decide.

The diction in which the goddess lays down her proofs is obscure, so the poem faces the reader with one puzzling statement after another; but the general tenor of the argument is almost clear, and later philosophers have made a great deal of it. The goddess contrasts the path that leads to the truth with the usual, false path taken by mortals, whose bewilderment makes them deaf and blind. The goddess tells Parmenides to gaze steadily and not cut off *being* from *being*, not to be misled by "an unseeing eye and a noisy ear and tongue."[36] Ordinary mortals follow both paths, but the choice between them is stark and exclusive. It is the choice between what is and "cannot not be" (between "what is" and what "is not for not being") and what is not and cannot possibly be (what "is not" and "must needs not be")[37]* The goddess clearly implies and almost enunciates the law of contradiction—a proposition cannot be *both* true and false—and the law of excluded middle—a proposition can be *only* true or false. She argues that whatever there is for speaking and thinking about either exists or does not; but if the speech or thought are to make sense, their object can be only what exists. The nonexistent can neither be thought nor spoken of intelligibly.[38] In other words, it is self-contradictory to assert that what does not exist—which is nothing at all— can really be the object of intelligible thinking. One *cannot* really refer to— direct one's attention at—what does not exist: to say that something, some thing, is nothing, no thing, is self-contradictory. Therefore (just as in Euclidean geometry) the impossibility of choosing one of two possible alternatives makes the choice of the other alternative logically necessary:

---

*Parmenides' is (*esti*) is very difficult to translate because it has no subject—he does not say what, if anything, is. Does *is* here mean *that which is*, or *there is something that is* (*real* or *true*), or *there is existence—existence exists*? It is almost amusing to see how much trouble so few simple Greek words—*esti* and *einai*—give the translators of Parmenides' fragment 2. Take, for example, the following four contemporary translations: "What is there to be said and thought must needs be; for it is there for being, but nothing is not" (Kirk, Raven, and Schofield, p. 247). "The one—that [it] is, and that [it] cannot not be . . . The other—that [it] is not and that [it] needs not be" (Gallop, p. 55). "The one, that a thing is, and that it is not for being . . . the other, that a thing is not, and that it must needs not be" (Coxon, p. 52). "How it is and how it is not possible that it should not be so" and "how it is not and how it is right that it should not be so" (Mourelatos, p. 71).

Mourelatos, who explains the problems involved in detail (chap. 2 and appendix 2), regards Parmenides' *esti* as an example of "speculative predication," predication that more or less combines the *is* of identity (which simplifies by eliminating distinctions) with the adjectival *is* (*is really*) of discovery and with *is* as the copula of classification. Speculative predication answers the question, What is it? by giving an answer that is meant to be a final explanation. (See *The Route of Parmenides*, pp. 56–61.)

What is not nothing must be something, that is, it must exist, and is there to be spoken of and thought of.

I have put the contrast between the Way of Truth and the Way of Seeming, as the two paths are usually called, more clearly than Parmenides' syntax allows because here, as elsewhere, his struggle to put new abstract ideas into metrical form results in extreme syntactic obscurity. But one point can be immediately and certainly clarified. When the goddess refers to what is not, she is not thinking of dreamed objects or imagined objects such as mermaids but is implying something far more extreme, that the objects we sense and speak of cannot, in truth, be spoken of or thought, because they cannot exist at all—logic shows their existence to be impossible. Their existence is impossible because of their plurality and change. To take a Greek example of alternative possibilities, this is because to speak of hot and cold requires us to say that when it is hot now, it is not cold. As has been established by the goddess, the reference to what is not is a nonsensical one. All such pairs of alternatives are therefore impossible. In truth, all mortal talk of the sensible world is meaningless because it implies a self-contradiction, or is no more than a dim, hardly comprehensible echo of true, comprehensible talk.

Having said this—if the suggested interpretation is right—the goddess proceeds to prove that *being* is ungenerated and imperishable, entire, unique, unmoved, and perfect.[39] Her argument is as follows: Whatever is, is now all at once and one and indivisible. To drive this home, the goddess asks, What origin can there be to look for, how and from what might whatever exists have grown, and what necessity could have urged whatever exists to begin and spring up from nothing? *Being*, she reminds us, can never not have been, either in whole or part. If it once existed only in part, that of it that did not exist would have been nothing; and if it came into existence altogether, it would have come into existence from nothing. The truth is that what exists now cannot have not existed in the past. For similar reasons, it cannot possibly not exist in the future. What is cannot arise from what is not, because what is not cannot be at all. There is, therefore, no genesis.[40] And if, all the same, something did arise out of nothing, no reason could be given for its arising at one particular time rather than another because no reason at all for arising is involved. So whatever is must exist now, all at once and continuously, and in the past and future as well.

Not only does what is exist as a continuous indivisible whole, but it must be all equally existent or, literally, "full of what is."[41] In other words, it can have no qualitative or quantitative gaps but must be the same throughout all of its being. That is, it cannot have any degrees, cannot exist any more at one point than another. From this the conclusion is drawn that it cannot change in any quality because a change of white to black, for instance, like any other change, would require white to perish and black to come into existence. So what exists must also remain firmly where and what it is; and it cannot change in the sense of moving, either.[42] The goddess also insists that what exists must not lack anything. It is not lawful, she says, that *being* should be incomplete, that is, defective.[43] Since *not-being* lacks everything, she probably means that to be incomplete in any way is to be nonexistent in that way, which is impossible for *being*, which has been "bound fast by fate to be entire and changeless."[44]

Having proved that what exists cannot go in or out of existence, change in any way, move at all, or be incomplete, the goddess reaches the rather mysterious conclusion that *being* is "in a state of perfection like the volume of a spherical ball," which is in every direction equally related to its center. If the goddess means to say that *being* is a real, space-occupying sphere with a limit in space, she may have difficulty answering the question, What lies beyond the boundary of the sphere? It makes more sense to suppose that in referring to a sphere she means only that whatever exists must be perfectly symmetrical in every way: *being* is qualitatively like a sphere in being equal with itself from every view and in every respect: it is a self-determined perfection.[45]

Having finished teaching the truth of the unchanging fullness of *being*, her "reliable discourse," the goddess says to the poet that she will also order her words deceptively and teach him about what mortals have taken to exist.[46] Does she mean to create a theory of pervasive illusory phenomena or secondary reality, of the kind so usual in Indian thought?[47] Maybe she wants no more than to equip the poet with the most persuasive cosmology that mortals can create so that he should be better prepared to show its inadequacy.

I am afraid that, given the evidence at our disposal, we cannot explain why Parmenides (or his goddess) makes the—to him (or her)—self-contradictory cosmology of nothing, which follows in the poem. Like the other ancient Greek cosmologies, that of Parmenides is of interest to the historian of thought, but I will not go into it at all because it is only Parmenides' doctrine of what *is* that has given him his great influence. Despite the difficulties in interpreting him, it is clear that he gives the first example of the use of consecutive formal logic designed to reach a metaphysical conclusion. His conclusion is metaphysical in a double sense, because it assigns to logic the power to contradict the most evident testimony of the senses.

I will not go into the plausibility of Parmenides' argument, though I take it to be specious. Together with his fragmentary thoughts, the historically, grammatically, and philosophically complicated verb *to be* became central to European philosophy. Nothing more need be said of his view because so much of the subsequent history of philosophy is a commentary on it.

Discussion

There are two obvious ways in which to compare Uddalaka and Yajnavalkya with Heraclitus and Parmenides. The first is by means of the societies in which they lived.[48] The second is by their conviction that all things are one.

What was alike in the respective societies of these Indians and Greeks? The two Greeks, at least, were city dwellers; but both the Indian and Greek philosophers lived among a population consisting mostly of farmers and herders. In India, the old organization by tribes (tribal organization in Greece, too, was old and influential) was giving way to small kingdoms. Indians and Greeks alike were organized in clearly if not very rigidly hierarchical class structures. The hierarchy of the Greeks was headed by aristocrats and by the generally wider, usually hereditary, class of citizens, who were of various degrees. The hierarchy of the Indians was headed by warriors, among them the king, and by priests—that is, brahmans. At the times in question, both Indian and Greek life was caught up in a process of social and economic transformation. The process inspired controversy and a questioning, sometimes radically innovative attitude, evidence for which is given by the four philosophers. Considered as individuals, all four are proud, intellectually competitive, and oracular. Perhaps, too, there is something analogous in their thought, for instance, the tendency to see abstractions as metaphysical realities, because Sanskrit and Greek are analogous languages.

The most general difference between the two pairs of philosophers is also a function of their social surroundings. It rests on the sharp difference between the Indian monarchy, with its ruling king and priests, their power symbolically rooted in religious ritual, and the independent Greek city-state, with its ruling aristocrats and citizens, their power rooted in a civic constitution. Not surprisingly, therefore, the source of the earliest Indian philosophical tradition lies largely in religious ritual, while that of the Greek is related to civic life. The reasons why the Greek city-states developed in such various, often consciously invented or reinvented ways, and why they became relatively free religiously are too complex to repeat here. But their growing—though still relative—freedom from religion can be exemplified by the fact that, about 600 B.C.E., a Cretan city-state could justify its constitutional decisions by saying that they were "pleasing to the city," and that, at about the same time, Solon felt no need to attribute his code to the gods.[49]

When I say that the source of Indian philosophy is mainly ritual, I mean, to begin with, that men such as Uddalaka and Yajnavalkya are brahmans (the word is accented on the first syllable), members of the social order that masters the sacred doctrine of Brahman (accent on the last syllable). Not all persons of this period who engage in philosophical dialogues or disputations are brahmans—on one memorable occasion, King Janaka demonstrates that he is superior in understanding, first to Shvetaketu and then his father, Uddalaka. It seems reasonable to assume that members of the ruling order with a particular interest in religious matters were likely to believe that, important as these matters might be to them intellectually, they were all-important to their rule and to the prosperity of their land. But the texts give no evidence that King Janaka's quest for knowledge was meant for political or social advantage.

The overriding concern of the brahmans with ritual thought explains much of the manner in which they philosophize. The ideas of Uddalaka and Yajnavalkya that have been singled out are not in themselves ritualistic; but even when the two go beyond ritual problems, they organize their thought on analogical patterns of an Indian ritual type. This is because ritual to the brahmans is a set of techniques by which they imitate or, rather, perform cosmic processes in order to impel them to work to human advantage, so the brahmans are always trying to connect ritual acts and formulas more effectively with the unseen sources of reality. For this purpose, they undertake complicated speculations and turn up esoteric correspondences of very many kinds.* As they see it, the universe is a profound riddle compounded of lesser riddles the solutions to which are the powerful analogies they intuit or learn from others.

The medium of early Indian philosophy is therefore very often the correspondence or analogy. It is this, Uddalaka says, that proves the omnipresence of the subtle essence, the Self, that constitutes everything

---

* Such identifications, deductions, and correspondences are really "equations in terms of a more or less consistent classificatory system. They are the key-stone of the brahmanic science . . . When 'the man who knows' understands one of the entities which are declared identical he knows, and wields power over, the other or the others . . . The priest who kindles the sacred fires is the spring, and that is why there are forest-fires in spring" (Gonda, *Vedic Literature*, p. 372).

In all the ritual equations, the connecting concept is Brahman. Derived from the root *brh*, meaning *to be firm, to be strong*, and the like, Brahman is that by which everything is supported and by and in which everything is metaphysically identical. Brahman can therefore be seen as a connective power that is condensed into the enigmas the brahmans try to solve. These enigmas are "the equation between human behavior and natural phenomena, the connection between rite and cosmos"(Smith, *Reflections on Resemblance, Ritual, and Religion*, pp. 71–72, depending on L. Renou, "Sur la notion de *brahman*").

alive. The Self is revealed by the uniformity of honey, by the life that pervades the banyan tree, by the salt invisibly present all over the water—everywhere one finds resemblances that lead beyond themselves to the Self. As Yajnavalkya puts it, everything on every scale but the last, incommensurable one is found to be metaphysically encompassed within something identical with it but superior to it (like fractals, each of which breeds an endless sequence of identical forms on different scales and makes extraordinary patterns on patterns).

Traditional religion and ritual are clearly less important for the Greek thought that concerns us. That is, in Heraclitus and Parmenides, as in the other of the earliest Greek philosophers, there are evident echoes of Greek religion, but these are never as close as are the Indian exercises in ritual piety or magic to the thought of Uddalaka and Yajnavalkya. In the Greek city-state there are no dominant priests to make their preoccupations central to life at all times. Those responsible for religious practice are probably citizens like the others, members of an intellectual elite all familiar with one another and apt to influence one another. We do not know what intellectual company Heraclitus had in Ephesus—assuming that he wanted human company at all—or Parmenides had in Elea, so, to avoid anachronism, we had best forget that the poets, playwrights, historians, mathematicians, doctors, orators, and philosophers lived in one another's company in later Athens. In India, professional knowledge, the grammar, medicine, law, and other specialties of India in Upanishadic time, all serve or coalesce with religion—such is the impression conveyed by the sources, which are themselves religious.[50] Unlike the Indians, Heraclitus, Parmenides, and the other Greek philosophers of the time make much use of models taken from the work of craftsmen, doctors, and mathematicians. It appears significant that the Greek term for *knowledge* is *episteme*, meaning (true, scientific) *knowledge*, *theoretical knowledge*, and, as well, *manual skill*, so that *knowing* has the sense of *skillful doing*.[51] Skillful doing in morality, like that in artisanry, is constructive and therefore good; and the skillful deed is based on the plan in the craftsman's mind, as Socrates was to emphasize, or in the understanding of the moral person.

When I say that the philosophy of the early Greeks is heavily influenced by their interest in civic politics, I mean that there are many reasons for them to engage in political thought. One reason is the need to devote effort to decide in advance just how the colonies they establish should be organized. A second reason is the contact between city-states with different forms of government—constitutional monarchy, oligarchy, and democracy—and the frequency of constitutional upheavals. A third reason, perhaps the most fundamental, is the nature of the more democratic city–states, in which citizens share the tasks of government and themselves make the important political decisions, which they, of course, debate among them-selves. Greek citizens—a minority of the population, one should remem-ber—develop the feeling that they rule themselves and have to invent their own institutions and regulations as they themselves think best.

Although Heraclitus and Parmenides are not, as we know them, primarily political, they have an interest in the laws of their states. Heraclitus scorns most men, says that "one man is ten thousand if he is the best," and contends that the Ephesians deserve to be hanged because they drove out their best man; and he also believes, as I have said, that "the people must fight for the law as for their city wall." And Parmenides is regarded by his fellow citizens as a legislator whose laws cannot be bettered.[52] In the light of the political color of Greek thought, it is instructive to compare Heraclitus' ever-living Fire and his triad of *logos*, *justice (dike)*, and *god (Zeus)* with Uddalaka's primal Existent and the triad of heat, water, and food the Existent propagates, and, as well, with the invisible essence that is the life and inseparable unity of everything. The contrast is almost that between the universe conceived in relation to fundamental civic law and conceived in relation to fundamental human biology. Yajnavalkya's dyad of Self and Brahman are really a marvellous monad conceived mainly in relation to the psychobiology of living things and the mystery of their death. Parmenides' Being stands apart in that it is wholly static in itself and cannot possibly have any effect. It is the substance of the cosmos con-ceived in terms of the sharp oppositions of nascent Greek logic.

Heraclitus' Fire, Uddalaka's Existent, and Yajnavalkya's Self are still ar-chaic, and they share degrees of either desire or consciousness. Logos and Justice are, however, close to impersonal. *Logos* is the more or less mathemati-cal rule of proportion by which change functions. And Justice—guaranteed by Zeus—also means *compensation* and *legal proceedings*, and is by nature related to the legal codes of the city-states, which are defined in writing. The Indian concepts imply a world order but are not immediately related to ethics (except as ritual acts), certainly not to the behavior of free individuals, the idea of which seems foreign to the ancient Indians. The relation of the Greek concepts to the civic life of the city-states becomes open and at times domi-nant in philosophy, but only in a later age, that of Socrates.

It is notable that the Indian pair of concepts reflect subjective expe-rience far more than do the Greek. Yajnavalkya's idea of the Self is satu-rated with a richness of experience extrapolated from every conceivable human pleasure and ability to perceive, conceive, remember, and dream (though not from evil, lack, or pain, which are found along with pleasures only in the inferior stages of experience, those of waking and dreaming). As Yajnavalkya conceives it, the Self embraces the imagined maximum of human inwardness. Its inwardness is imagined so complete that its object is identical with its subject: words are unnecessary, inexpressive, and, to be paradoxically exact, are impossible; for the Self's "experience" is inexpressibly free of the subject-object relationship. In compensation, if that is the right word, for the lack of such an intense inwardness, Heraclitus has a sense of the enormous complexity of the world, that is, of its tensional "warfare," and a belief that Zeus's thoughts are inexpressibly beyond what is possible to human beings.

Not surprisingly, then, it is characteristic of Greek (and later European) philosophers to devote far more detailed thought than most Indian philosophers to ethical and political problems. However, relatively unintrospective as it is, Greek thought is more distant than Indian thought from the intimate interior of human experience. This generalization needs to be qualified, but it holds broadly true.[53]

Now for the Indian and Greek identity of things: Thinkers such as Uddalaka and Yajnavalkya reach the conclusion that the differentiation of things is inexplicably but necessarily overborne by their identity. Uddalaka's Existent remains "identical" with its unceasing emanations. Yajnavalkya stresses that everything alive—isn't everything in some sense alive to him?—is intelligence, which is consciousness, which is the Self, which is Brahman, and therefore is consciousness, which contains everything as the sea contains all the waters that emerge from it and reenter it. This old Indian theme of cosmic unity requires Uddalaka and Yajnavalkya to try to demonstrate that the universe is one despite its many forces, functions, objects, and persons that it contains or appears to contain. For Uddalaka, the Existent is not the essence of things simply, but is heat/light, which is water, which is food (plants), and is the names–and–forms that constitute all individual things. To the imagination, this unity in the Existent may be not unlike the view of modern physics that, in the final analysis, matter and energy are the same and comprise everything of every kind that exists.

Yajnavalkya's scheme has been described in his account of dying. His privileging of consciousness apparently rests on the Indian perception, not at all foreign to Europe, that to try to think consciousness away is much the same as to try to think oneself away and, in doing so, to make the world vanish along with it and cancel out the very thinker who is thinking of himself thinking himself away. This has the psychological quality of an impossible suicide, equivalent to the most extreme violation of the law of contradictions. Fully realized consciousness is already conceived as—paradoxically—enclosed all within itself, with no separate object to be conscious of. Though superlatively conscious, it is not conscious *of* anything. Is it, then, superlatively "unconscious" consciousness?

I conclude this chapter by returning to its theme, the attempt to understand the relation between the unity and the variety of the world, between its permanence and change and, equivalently, between what is basic or real and what is not. Heraclitus and Parmenides give answers that are, with respect to the absoluteness of the world's unity, very similar to the Indians', and are in other respects very different. It is interesting though not relevant to early Indian thought that Heraclitus' Fire, like the fire of later Indian doctrine, is the power in whose flames the world repeatedly appears and vanishes. There is even a striking image in Heraclitus of the self as an inner light that matches an equally striking one in which Yajnavalkya responds to King Janaka. Heraclitus says, "A man strikes a light for himself in the night, when his sight is quenched. Living, he touches the dead in his sleep; waking, he touches the sleeper." Equivalently, when the king asks Yajnavalkya what serves man here as a light when the sun has set, the moon has set, the fire is extinguished, and speech has ended, Yajnavalkya answers: "The Self, O king . . . For it is by the light of the Self that he sits down, walks about, does his work, and returns home."[54] But these passages reflect less of similarity of doctrine, I feel, than of poetic apprehension.*

As for Parmenides, the polarity he conceives is that between truth and *being*, on the one hand, and falsehood and variety, on the other. His *being*, like that of the Indians, necessarily exists, its necessity established by the law of contradiction. For the first time in philosophy, existence is proved by sheer logic. In this sense, logic is the universal principle of both truth and existence.

Uddalaka proves the true, undeniable existence of the Existent in these words:

---

*The importance in Indian thought of fire, the god Agni, makes suggestive comparisons possible. Heraclitus' cycle of fire everlasting that is kindled and goes out (fragment 37 in Kahn) is like the Indian cycle of worlds that begin and end in fire. There is even a fragment (43A) that attributes to Heraclitus belief in a cycle, like those of later India, of great cosmic years each a flood for winter and a world conflagration for summer; but such a fragment can be suspected of being Stoic rather than Heraclitean. At any rate, there is some likeness between Uddalaka's cosmic process in which the heat—its form the red of fire—becomes water, which becomes food (in India associated with earth), and Heraclitus' cosmic process (as I take it to be) in which fire becomes sea and sea becomes earth (fragments 38–39 in Kahn). There is a report that Heraclitus said that as fire thickens it turns moist and condenses into water, which thickens and condenses into earth (Diogenes Laertius, *Lives* 9.9). The Upanishadic conception almost always has a ritualistic analogy or purpose that distinguishes it from the Presocratic. In India, what fire does is assimilated to the ritual of sacrifice. Shvetaketu is taught that "this world . . . is a sacrificial fire; the earth is its fuel, the fire is its smoke . . . In this fire, the gods make an offering of the rain. Out of this sacrificial offering arises food" (*Bṛhādaraṇyaka Upaniṣad* 6.2.11, in Deussen, *Sixty Upanishads . . .* , vol. 1, p. 527).

Now some say: The non-existent only was this universe in the beginning, one alone, without a second; from that non-existent the existent was born . . . How could the existent be born from the non-existent, as they say? On the contrary, the existent only . . . was this universe in the beginning, one alone, without a second.[55]

In the same vein, Parmenides' goddess says that she will not allow him to say or think that "anything is not; and then what necessity in fact could have urged it to begin and spring up later or before from Nothing? Thus it must either be entirely or not be at all."[56]

The logical point of Uddalaka's and Parmenides' texts is abstractly the same. But while Uddalaka must assume, along with Yajnavalkya, that the Existent or Being cannot be added to or subtracted from or begin or end, his Existent has desires, and emanates the population of the world as if it was bearing children. Parmenides, however, takes the crucial logical point to prove that change of any kind is impossible—a notion so obscure that I assume we do not really understand his point—and likens this unchanging truth or reality to the complete symmetry of a sphere. The resemblance in philosophies is unmistakable, the difference profound. Heraclitus' cosmic fire is alive; but his *logos*, like Parmenides' *one*, has a nature that resembles that of the concepts of mathematics or physics, not of human desire or consciousness.

Yet there is a philosophically fateful similarity to add. Parmenides already thinks of ordinary experience as wholly illusory. Uddalaka and Yajnavalkya say nothing of this kind that is so radically explicit. Uddalaka's one and only Existent is the origin, life, and support of the protean, multifarious world; and Yajnavalkya's Brahman, though it can retreat from multifariousness into superlative unity, is that for the sake of which everything else is loved. But Uddalaka's thought and, more so, Yajnavalkya's lead easily to a philosophy for which the sensed, variable world is an illusion, and so the two will be taken by later Indian philosophers to be prototypical monistic mystics.

Chapter 3

The Beginnings of Moral Philosophy

Confucius/Mencius, the Buddha, Socrates

Theme: Confucianism, Buddhism, and Socratism Bear the Imprint of Their Inventors' Characters

The desire to concentrate on ideas more than on persons or circumstances should be relaxed for Confucius, the Buddha, and Socrates, whose enormous influence has stemmed at least as much from their characters as from their ideas. Confucius was not a philosopher but a sage—a title he denied he deserved—and a humane and forceful teacher. His acutely sensitive concern for decent, stable human relations made a profound impression on his direct students and, in time—fostered by rulers who found in him an often excessively moral ally—on the Chinese tradition as a whole. Like Confucius, the Buddha cannot be recovered in historical detail, but no one can read the early Buddhist dialogues without feeling his profound sympathy with human suffering in every sense and his stubborn desire, that of someone who was by nature an analytical and yet empathic physician, to help humans to cure themselves by neutralizing their desires. And Socrates (for whose view I suggest the equivalent name of *Socratism*) exerted his still active influence on the European tradition less by his abstract ideas, which were few and not very developed, than by the resoluteness with which he forced people to take moral stock of their actions, by the calm courage with which he faced the charges against him, and by the eminence of his philosophical disciples, especially Plato, in whose dialogues he continues to live as our close intellectual neighbor rather than a merely literary creation.

Confucius (551–479 B.C.E.) and Mencius (371–289 B.C.E.): Backward-Looking Hierarchical Humanitarianism

According to the traditional biography written by Ssu-ma Ch'ien, Confucius—Kung Fu-tzu (Master Kung) in Chinese—was born in a poor family of noble descent.[1] His father died soon after his birth. The love for ceremony that saturates his thought began early; even as a child he performed play sacrifices and ceremonies. As a young man, he studied the traditional history and literature, with the evident purpose of becoming a government official. However, his career was cut short by his scruples. Having been advanced in the country of his birth, Lu, from post to post, he was made Grand Secretary of Justice. In this office, he had a corrupt minister executed, with the result that Lu became peaceful and safe. But his success made Ch'i, a neighboring state, afraid that Lu might grow too strong. Ch'i therefore sent Lu's ruler the gift of pretty dancers and fine horses. The gift so distracted the ruler from his duties that Confucius was prompted to resign. A more prosaic reason for the resignation is given by Mencius, who reports that Confucius was not given his share of the sacrificial meat of a ritual.

Together with a few disciples, Confucius then wandered from one court to another, often answering rulers' questions on good government but never given an actual post. After some thirteen years of wandering during which rulers ignored or repulsed him or criticized his views, he lost his desire for office. His time was spent in studying the old form of worship and social intercourse, which he felt had degenerated, and tracing the history of the early dynasties. At the age of sixty-eight, realizing that he would never get the chance to put his political ideals into practice but unwilling to die without accomplishing something creditable in the eyes of posterity, he used existing historical accounts and state archives to write the annals called *Spring and Autumn*. In these annals, he chose his words so as to imply approval or criticism of the acts he described, because his hope was that unrestrained rulers would learn shame and self-restraint from it, and that a great king might some day appear, read the book, and adopt the principles it implied. Hoping to reform society by means of the ways of the ancient kings, "he set forth his writings so as to constitute the institutions, usages, and laws for the whole world" and "handed down to posterity the comprehensive record of the Six Classics."[2]

To his three thousand students, seventy-two of them considered advanced, Confucius taught the old poetry (interpreted as moral lessons), and the old historical documents, rites, and ceremonies (including the related ceremonial music). He proposed to teach his students the knowledge, attitudes, and skills needed to make them administrators good in every sense. Character, he taught his students, was of extreme importance; and he exhorted them to avoid merely facile solutions, not based on an understanding of the ordinary people whose welfare was at stake. Irrespective of their origin, his students were required to learn to become persons who were morally and politically exemplary. Their training included the specialized arts—ritual, music, archery, charioteering, calligraphy, and mathematics—but only as these served the virtues of an "exemplary person."

It is said that Confucius taught about four things: literature, human conduct, being one's true self, and honesty in social relationships. As such teaching required, he also denounced or avoided arbitrariness of opinion, dogmatism, narrowmindedness, and egotism. His teaching was not much occupied with the subject of the will of Heaven or of the profit to be gained by the conduct he recommended; and he would try to stimulate a person's thought only if he believed that the person really wanted to find out the truth. In private life, he was gentle and refined, we are told; in places of public worship and at courts he was eloquent and yet careful in his words; and everywhere his conduct was careful and considerate. As a teacher, he took full advantage of the individuality of his students.* His biographer comments that, unlike those who, famous during their lives, came to nothing after their deaths,

> Confucius, who was but a common scholar clad in a plain gown, became the acknowledged Master of scholars for over ten generations. All people in China who discuss the six arts, from the emperors, kings, and princes down, regard the Master as the final authority. He may be called the Supreme Sage.[3]

It is generally agreed that Confucius' voice is most clearly heard in his *Lun Yü* or *Selected Sayings*, the book that has come to be known in the

---

*Not everyone appreciated Confucius' ability to adapt his advice to different persons and conditions. Writing about 80 C.E., the literal-minded, often rationalistic Wang Ch'ung complained of Confucius' inconsistency in thought and action. According to the (unreliable) text of the *Analects,* he said, Confucius gave incomplete, inexactly phrased, or contradictory answers to his disciples, and so there are matters on which "later generations have been left in doubt." Furthermore, complained Wang, unlike a sage, Confucius was unable to accept Heaven's fate with equanimity, and he let his sympathy for others interfere with the consistency of the rules he himself set (M. Nyland, "Han Classicists Writing in Dialogue about Their Own Tradition," *Philosophy East and West* 47.2 [April 1997], pp. 142–43).

West as the *Analects* (the numbers in the following account refer to it by book, "chapter"—sometimes only a single sentence—and, when necessary, by sentence within the chapter). An often disorderly collection of twenty "books" of different dates put together by his students or students' students, the *Analects* has a generally authentic ring. This is because the conversations in it are so nearly ordinary, so obviously meant for particular interlocutors asking particular questions, and so unsystematic that it is hard to believe that they were remembered as anything but the talk of the unforgettable teacher. In the *Analects*, Confucius is still an ordinary, unpretentious human being and not the all-knowing sage into which he was later transformed. The only praise he allows himself is that he loves the learning he wants to transmit, that he always tries to go on observing and learning in order to improve himself, and that he insists on the traditional morality. But for all his love for tradition, he prefers, he says, to reject moral preconceptions and remain undogmatic and flexible (18.8, 9.4). An advocate of simplicity, he finds joy, he says, in eating coarse rice, drinking water, and pillowing himself on his elbow (7.16).

For Confucius, the only sure reward the good man may realistically hope for is his own self-respect (2.4)—trying to identify which K'ung was being talked about, a gatekeeper once asks if he was the one who kept working away at something hopeless (14.38). The gatekeeper's question is apposite because to Confucius, taught by his frustrations, worldly success is uncertain, as is, apparently, survival after death. A disciple says that the heavy burden put on the good man ends only with his death (8.7), while Confucius himself says that the good man's benevolence may require him to accept death (15.9). Those whose strength is inadequate fall out along the way (6.12). To a disciple who asks about serving the gods and the spirits of the dead, Confucius answers that he, the disciple, cannot even serve man, so how can he serve the spirits? When the disciple persists and asks about death, Confucius answers that the disciple does not understand even life, so how can he understand death (11.12). But Confucius shares the old belief in the "decree of Heaven" in the sense of an impersonal cosmic justice that establishes the destiny of every individual and dynasty. This justice may be quite mysterious and can only be accepted (12.5, 11.7).

The matter of self-respect is of quite extraordinary importance to Confucius and, thereafter, to all Confucians. I would like to exemplify this by way of a somewhat conjectural interpretation of the first sentence of the *Analects*, which reads:

> The Master said, "Is it not a pleasure, having learned something, to try it out at due intervals? Is it not a joy to have

friends come from afar? Is it not gentlemanly not to take offense when others fail to appreciate your abilities?" (1.1)

These English words do not translate the peremptoriness of the
Chinese question-form—*pu I . . . hu?*—which does not allow a negative
response. The sentence therefore shows some internal tension. Why did
whoever compiled the *Analects* choose it to open the book? To answer, one
should recall that among Confucius' students there were those who had
abandoned their lives as merchants, family members, military men, and
court officials. But although they dedicated themselves to study, as Confucius
prescribed, judged externally, they failed to get the social and political
status that was their aim. It is therefore natural for them to ask what point
there is in being a member of the Confucian community. Confucius reas-
sures them by saying in effect: we have both the pleasure and the psychological defense of progress in study, joy in friendship, and moral ability not
to take offense when unappreciated.

What is most important, Confucius is implicitly saying, is the relation of a person with himself, his ability to receive a friend from whom
he has been parted for a long time and take joy, not alone in his friendship
but in his transformation for the better. What proves to be essential in this
self-recognition is the steadfast goodness *(jen)* for which Confucius uses
the image of the mountain—for knowledge he uses the image of water.
The happiness he finds in the presence of others is the negation of Taoism
(taken up in the next chapter) with its preference for the asocial solitude
of "nothingness." Confucius and Confucianism begin in social relations
and enter into politics naturally and by conviction. All this—learning,
humanity, society, and politics—are, in theory, divorced from the expectation for any reward but an internal one. In taking such a position, Confucius
is the first thinker we know of in Chinese history to divorce philosophizing from particular situations. Consequently, his *Analects* is the first Chinese book we know in which the tie to the particular situation is to a
great extent broken and timeless moral and humanistic generalizations are
made.[4]

The particular subjects that Confucius stresses may be summarized
under the following headings: goodness; superlative character; superior
character; filiality; respectful keeping of the rites; truthfulness; the
rectification of names; and rightness. I take these up briefly one by one.

Goodness, benevolence, humanity: One of the terms that Confucius
uses often is *jen* (pronounced *ren*; a different Chinese character from the
similarly transliterated word for *man*). This has the broad sense of *good* or
(ideally) *human*, having the virtue of *humanity* (but not, in the *Analects*,
kind or *tender-hearted*). As Confucius means it, the term includes a great

many good qualities. It applies to someone who is unselfish, courteous, diligent, unworried, observant of ritual, able to overcome his own egotism, brave, and loyal, and also wise, wise meaning sure about the difference between right and wrong and a good judge of character. It is possible for a person to be born with all these qualities, but such superlative humanity is most likely to be the result of study. Unlike his disciples, Confucius does not find any recent paragons of such goodness, which he ascribes in full only to the ancient, godlike sages such as the Emperor Yao, whose contagious influence alone was enough to make others moral (8.19). He himself does not presume to be a sage, he says (27.34). However, when some high official remarks that Confucius is surely a sage because otherwise he would not have so many skills, Confucius does not protest and says that the official understands him well; but he takes care to deny that his many skills are the mark of the sage and explains that, unlike an exemplary person, a *chün-tzu*, he is skilled in many menial things because, when young, his circumstances were humble (9.6).

Superlative character: To Confucius, the sage's level of humanity, *sheng jen*, characterizes only the traditional ancient creators of civilization.[5] But though he refuses to rank himself with them, to his disciples he is surely the sage because he is the living repository of the ancient virtues he teaches. As has been implied, the sage is not an easily described ideal but, rather, one of a group of human paradigms. Perhaps the term itself can teach us something of what it means to be a sage. The term—the Chinese character—contains the radical meaning *ear*, which creates an association with hearing, with someone whose ear is attuned or in accord, as Confucius says of himself (4.2). In the *Analects*, to hear (*wen*) is used very often—far more often than *to see*—to mean *to learn*.[6]* Perhaps, then, a sage is implicitly someone who hears with particular sensitivity, who hears the nuances of his message and of the responses to it, and—from their words and manner of expression—hears what other people are and communicates to them what they should be. As Confucius says, whoever does not understand words, does not understand people (20.3). The words of the sages

---

*A word of caution: It is all too easy to mistake a term's etymology for its meaning in use. Furthermore, in Chinese, a semantic and a merely phonetic element of a word—a character—may be difficult to distinguish. However, in the present instance it is helpful to know that the oldest Chinese etymological dictionary, *Explanations of Simple and Compound Characters* (*Shuo-wen chieh-tzu*), compiled about A.D. 100, defines *sheng* as "to communicate with, to be conversant with, to penetrate, to connect," and adds, "It derives semantically from *erh* . . . 'ear.'" Etymology apart, the character *sheng* has often been understood in terms of a differently written but homophonic word meaning *to sound*, or *sound*, or *voice*. "Hearing the sound," an ancient source says, the sage "knows a thing's nature and conditions" (Hall and Ames, *Thinking Through Confucius*, p. 258).

are to be held in awe, he says, because, like the decree of Heaven, they transform the world (16.8).

Exemplary character: The word for this quality is *chün-tzu*, which is derived from *ruler, chün*. Meaning, at first, the descendant of a ruling house, *chün-tzu* comes to apply to any member of the upper classes. Then the term is extended to anyone whose superiority is not only of birth but also of character and, finally, superiority of character alone. Someone is therefore a *chün-tzu* (often translated *gentleman*, but who now knows what that is?) if he behaves with decency, openness, and care. Yet the connection with ruling is retained because such cultivation of character is undertaken in order to help pursue an official career, though never, to Confucius, at the expense of principles. Service in government, for the welfare of the common people, is the exemplary man's duty (13.19–20). To the question how to govern well, Confucius answers that what is needed is enough food, enough weapons, and the trust of the common people. To the further question, which of the three is most important, he answers, the weapons should be given up first, and then, if necessary, the food—death has always been with us—but not the trust, because without trust, the common people have nothing to stand on (12.7).

The *chün-tzu* is serious, flexible, helpful, respectful, and always on the side of the moral and the good in others; and he is never arrogant or extreme in word or act (1.8, 12.16, 4.18). A true *chün-tzu* is free of violence—as his composed face shows—is trustworthy—as his honest face shows—and, in word and tone, avoids coarseness and unreasonableness (8.4). Such good character is a matter of holding the delicate balance between too much and too little of the good qualities. This balance is created by the love of learning that teaches one to consider things carefully, that is, in the light of precedent, good sense, and the understanding of human nature (17.8). When Confucius says, "There is one single thread binding my way together," the disciple who understands him explains that the Master's way is to use oneself as a gauge, that is, to assume that one's own reaction is a gauge for that of everyone else (4.15). Three times in the *Analects* Confucius says (or is said to have said), without elaborating, that one should love one's fellow men (1.5., 17.3 or 4, 12.22). It is possible that the words *fellow men* apply primarily to exemplary, cultivated humans, but the object is always to rule by understanding, by example, and by inspiring trust. The ruler corrects his subjects, but to do so effectively, he must himself act correctly (13.6). If he does, the people, guided by virtue and the rites, will have a sense of shame and reform themselves (2.3).

Filiality: Confucius' term, *hsiao*, refers to piety toward both one's dead ancestors and one's living parents. Such piety contrasts with the recommendation of the philosopher Mo Tzu (468–376 B.C.E.) that one should love and care for everyone equally. To the Confucians, love for the members of one's family comes first, because, the Confucians are sure, love decreases with familial, social, and geographical distance. The most essential family relations, as Confucius believes, are those between a father and his son and between an older and younger brother. The very root of a man's character, he holds, is to be a good son and an obedient young man (1.2).

Ceremony and music: In Confucius' eyes, the "rites" are rules that reflect the moral insight of the past and that ought to govern life in every respect. Rites understood in this broad sense include not only ritual matters such as sacrifices and seasonal observances, but also rules of correct behavior. Rites are close in Confucius' view to literature, the poetry of the *Odes*, for example, which are sung and which, he thinks, are to be interpreted as moral lessons. Rites are also close to music, for the most part as it performed for court ceremonial and sacrifices. At its best, music is a performance whose perfect beauty is the perfect medium for its perfect goodness. Correspondingly, wanton music, like subversive talk, is morally dangerous (3.25, 15.11, 17.10–11). Beautiful music is moral, that is, has a moral effect, because it is a harmonious, harmonizing medium (3.23, 25). According to a famous passage of the *Analects*, Confucius once heard such good, beautiful music that for three months he was unaware of the taste of the meat he ate and said that he had never dreamed that music could reach such heights (7.14).

Truthfulness, faithfulness, reliability (hsin): This virtue requires the keeping of promises and faithfulness to one's own words and resolutions. Therefore the *chün-tzu* is ashamed if, by boasting, he allows his words to outstrip his deeds (14.27–28). Men in antiquity were wary of speaking (4.22). The *chün-tzu* puts his words into action before he speaks them out (2.13).

The rectification or ordering of names: This phrase, which occurs in the *Analects* has been suspected of reflecting the concerns of a later time, but the *Analects* often refers to the issue itself, which is close to that of faithfulness and is heavily emphasized in the Confucian tradition. Because Confucius is faithful to the old royal house and its morality, he is very antagonistic to the encroachments of the feudal nobles on the king's authority, which, by Confucius' time, is no more than nominal. To preserve the old order and morality, Confucius insists that all definitions of functions and prerogatives be carefully preserved, so that when he is asked by a feudal ruler about government, he answers that the key is for the prince to be a prince, the minister a minister, the father a father, and the son a son. A ruler who does not follow the proper Way of a ruler does not merit the name, and a minister who neglects the responsibilities of his office empties the concept of the office of its content (12.11). When names are not used correctly, what is said sounds unreasonable—does not fit the situation—acts are not carried out as they should be, propriety and music fail, punishments do not accomplish what they are intended for, and the people have no idea how to act (13.3, 5). To Confucius, the ordering of names is a performance whose correctness—conformity with the traditional but sensitively adapted standard—is the condition for maintaining an effective and truly human society.[7]

Rightness, rectitude: This general virtue, *yi*, applies to the moral rightness of an act under particular circumstances, not to the frame of mind or character of the person who carries out the act. An absolute standard, it is the objective counterpart of true goodness or humanity.

Next to Confucius himself, Mencius—Meng-tzu in Chinese—has been the most revered of Confucian teachers.[8] As happened with Confucius, his father died when he was young. Among the anecdotes about Mencius and his mother, there is a famous one that tells how she impressed her son by cutting the web she was weaving in order to demonstrate that to be indifferent to one's studies is to cut the web of learning, a lesson which, being Mencius, he took deeply to heart.[9]

A great deal of Mencius' life was spent as an adviser in different courts of a still much divided, increasingly war-ridden China. Intent, like Confucius, on extolling the Sage Emperors, he could not get along with the rulers of his own times and he retired to Confucian studies and the company of his disciples. His position as the model Confucian, officially recognized only in the eleventh century, must rest largely on his deep compassion for the common man and his bitterness against those who care more for war and politics than for the people who suffer because of them. Extraordinarily radical for a Chinese in showing such compassion and bitterness, he goes so far as to say that bad rulers ought to be deposed (*Mencius*, 5.B.9, 7.A.31). He also hopes that if the natural virtues are cultivated well enough, the Mandate of Heaven may change for the better and a cycle of good order will replace the bad.[10] A good king, he says, is overdue, but Heaven has not yet so decided, and he is alone in his times to work for the coming of a cycle of peace and order (7.B.38.1–4; 2.B.13.4–5).

Although Mencius depends on Confucius, he is far more the philosopher. His conversations, compiled by his students, are more developed and his reasoning appears conscious of the dialectic already deployed by other Chinese philosophers. Much of his most famous doctrine, an extension of the concept of true goodness (humanity), is that humankind is good by nature and that its goodness ought to be reflected in the humanity of the government. It is of extreme importance to him that this truth should be realized so that the moral capacity of everyone is developed. The *chün-tzu*, he says, retains his original, true heart, the purpose of learning being to repossess it (6.A.10, 6.A.11); but everyone shares in an innate, disinterested compassion, which Mencius puts in the hypothetical example, famous in China, of a man who suddenly sees a young child about to fall into a well: "He would certainly be moved to compassion, not because he wanted to get into the good graces of the parents, nor because he wanted to win the praise of his fellow villagers or friends, nor yet because he disliked the cry of the child (2.A.6)."[11]

This innateness of morality is the subject of an extended debate between Mencius and one Kao-tzu, who holds that righteousness (*yi*) is not innate, but "external," by which he means that it is learned. According to Kao-tzu, the appetite for food and sex is natural, and so, too, is affection for a brother; but human nature itself prefers neither good nor bad any more than water by nature flows east or west. So when he sees an old man, whose age is unrelated or external to his own life, he treats him with the deference due him because he has been taught to do so, not for any other reason. The man's oldness is as external to him as his perception that the man is white.

Mencius answers Kao-tzu image by image and point by point. Water, he says, shows no preference for east or west but by nature flows down in the same way as a man by nature does good—although, just as water can be splashed up or forced to stay uphill, a man, in contradiction to his nature, can be made bad. White is the same white whether it is the white of feathers, snow, or jade. But when the word *nature* (*hsing*) is used to apply to different living things, the sense of the word is affected by the kind of living thing of which it is the nature, whether a dog, an ox, or a man. In such cases, the identity of the generic term does not imply identity in fact: animal nature is not the same as human nature.[12] Mencius is evidently arguing on the basis of the doctrine expressed by logicians of his time who insist on exactness in distinguishing between analogies of different kinds: "A small square is analogous to a large square; a small horse is analogous to a large horse; but inferior intelligence is not analogous to superior intelligence."[13]

Mencius does not suppose that the innateness of moral feeling is enough by itself to make human beings moral. What he believes is that the energy (*ch'i*) of growth in general is also the energy of moral growth; but while moral energy develops independently of a person's will, it flourishes or decays as the person's acts are in or out of moral accord with it. The result is that any human being will be moral if guided to think and act along moral lines; but even though spontaneous acts of kindness are natural, education and effort are necessary to develop the human virtues fully.

Mencius' view that human beings are innately good came to dominate Confucianism, even though the great Confucian philosopher Hsün-tzu (298–230 B.C.E.), whose opinion I have cited along with Kant's in the first chapter, argues, in agreement with Kao-tzu, that Mencius does not understand the difference between human nature and what humans can acquire only by means of conscious effort.[14]

The Buddha (563–483 B.C.E.): Waking Up to No Self

He has a host of names, of which the familiar *the Buddha* will be used here.[16] However, even early Buddhists believe that he was preceded by other Buddhas, meaning Enlightened Ones—the root *budh* means *to wake, to perceive, to understand.* Before the Buddha leaves home, his personal name (in tradition) is Siddhartha. When he is an ascetic, his fellow ascetics call him Gautama, meaning, it seems, *of the Gautama clan,* a name also used by brahmans in referring to him; and he is often referred to as Gautama Buddha to distinguish him from earlier presumed Buddhas. Another name current in the Buddha's time is Shakyamuni, Sage of the Shakya tribe. When he preaches after his enlightenment, he refers to himself as the Tathagata—perhaps then a name for spiritually accomplished persons—meaning *(the one) thus gone.** His disciples may call him by such names as Lord, Great Sage, Victor, or, more impressively, Perfectly Enlightened One, or, most impressively of all, Unsurpassed and Perfectly Enlightened One. That is not all, but I think he has been named more than enough for the still human if superlative person he was presumed to be in his own lifetime.[16]

The story of the Buddha's life is told and retold in lovingly fabulous variations.[17] The beginning goes back far before his conception, though I begin only there. The start of his conception is his entry into the womb of his mother in the form—as she dreams but as also happens in fact—of a white elephant with a silvery lotus in its trunk. To understand the

---

* *Thus gone* is the literal meaning, to which *thus come* was assimilated. Perhaps the term originally applied to a person who would no longer be reborn, as in the question, Does a Tathagata exist after death? Used by the Buddha to refer to himself, it was soon confined by Buddhists to him, and then later applied to Buddhas generally. Etymology and conjecture apart, in early Buddhism, the term has meanings like *perfected one,* i.e., someone who has attained wisdom or "suchness" and can lead others to it. In Mahayana Buddhism, *tathagata* is given metaphysical and cosmic senses that are inappropriate to the present context. (See Vetter, *The Ideas and Meditative Practices of Early Buddhism,* p. 8, note 2; and Horner, trans., *The Middle Length Sayings,* vol. 1, pp. xvii–xviii.)

dream, the king summons sixty-four eminent brahmans, who explain that it means that a son will be born who will become either a universal king or a Buddha. At the moment of conception, all the ten thousand worlds shake, everyone, however maimed, becomes whole, everyone speaks mildly, and all flowers bloom. After ten months, the Buddha emerges, spotless and pure, walking out of his upright mother as if coming down a stair.

During the Buddha's childhood, he goes into a spontaneous meditative trance while he is watching his father and others engaged in ceremonial plowing. His father, disturbed by the prophecy that the child may become a holy man, tries to keep him preoccupied with pleasure and gives him a palace for each of the three seasons, forty thousand dancing girls, self-sounding musical instruments, and a beautiful wife, who bears him a son. But the king's attempt fails as a result of the four outings in which, on successive occasions, the prince sees an old man, a sick man, and a dead man, learns that he, too, will grow old, sick, and die, and then meets a monk who praises renunciation. At home in the palace, he wakes to see his beautiful singers asleep and repulsively grinding their teeth and muttering or showing their loathsome nakedness; the magnificent apartment seems to him like a cemetery. On his great shining white horse, to whose tail his faithful charioteer clings, he flees the palace. He is nineteen years old at the time, or, by a variant tradition, twenty-nine.

The next dramatic set of episodes concerns the Buddha's life as a seeker after truth. Two meditative trances do not lead to enlightenment. Attended by a group of five wandering ascetics, he then undertakes austerities for six relentless years.[18] Trying to dominate his mind, he clenches his teeth and presses his tongue against his palate with such force that sweat pours from his armpits. He breathes through his nose and ears till his head aches fiercely. He holds his breath till he feels as if a butcher was cutting through his stomach and he burns as if he was set over a fire. He eats so little that his ribs stick out like the crooked rafters of an old shed and when he touches the skin of his belly he takes hold of his spine. But he still is not enlightened.

Then the Buddha—not yet the Buddha—remembers the rapturous meditation of his childhood. He asks himself, *Could this be, perhaps, the way to enlightenment?* and thinks, *Why should I be afraid of this happiness that has nothing to do with objects which awaken desire and nothing to do with harmful qualities?*[19] So the Buddha chooses the way of meditation again. Too weak to meditate, to the disgust of the five ascetics he takes some rice and milk and grows strong enough to meditate (in the same way as Yajnavalka was able to remember after he broke his fast). Quieting his mind, he rises from meditative stage to stage until he gets rid of joy and anguish and is calmly mindful and gains enlightenment. He is thirty or, by the variant tradition, thirty-five. He now sees himself in his former lives, now knows how beings arise and pass away, now knows about pain and how to destroy it, is now emancipated from sensual desire, the desire to exist, and ignorance. He has had no teacher but has enlightened himself. He is now the Buddha.

At first the Buddha is reluctant to teach others because he is sure they will not understand him—ignorant of the truth, they are too inflamed by the lusts of life. But having become all compassion and therefore able to venture outside of himself, he realizes that people are different from one another and that at least some of them can learn, and he gains confidence and decides to help others.[20] Seeing the five ascetics in the Deer Park, he tells them he is now a Tathagata and convinces them of this by means of the sermon, his first, that he preaches to them. The sermon is against the two extremes, of pleasure and of ascetic pain. He states the four noble truths: the first, that all life is painful (or, by an alternate translation, is suffering); the second, that the cause of pain is the multiple craving that leads to rebirth, life, and death; the third, how pain is ended and craving renounced; and the fourth, how to get to the end of pain by the joint means of right views, right intention, right speech, right action, right livelihood, right effort, right mindfulness, and right concentration.*

I will no more than mention the Buddha's subsequent preaching throughout central India, the growth of his community of monks, or the plots against him by his evil disciple Devadatta, the first schismatic. But the events that precede his death and his death itself are cardinal to understanding who and what he is.[21]

His favorite disciple, Ananda, becomes afraid that the Buddha will die without teaching all he knows, but the Buddha tells him that he is now eighty, that his body is as rickety as an old cart, and that he has always

---

*I have used the word *pain* more often than its alternative, *suffering*, because it seems to me to have a wider scope, that is, to reach the level of suffering only when it is acute. If one distinguishes pain from suffering in terms of modern neuropsychiatry, then *suffering* is the more appropriate word, because some persons can undergo considerable pain in a physiological or psychiatric sense without responding to it by suffering in the emotional sense. For example: Someone who has undergone a brain operation to relieve physical pain or who has suffered damage to the prefrontal brain may undergo physiological pain—feel in pain—but not suffer from it, that is, remain cheerful because unconcerned with the pain. In the state of what is called "la belle indiffrence," persons in an extremely inconvenient or difficult situation (such as hysterical blindness or a wholly incapacitating paraplegia) may remain quite unconcerned with it. And the rare person born with no ability to experience physical pain may remain unperturbed even when cut, burned, or otherwise injured. (See A. R. Damasio, *Descartes' Error*, New York: Putnam's Sons, 1994, pp. 262–67; R. Melzak and P. Wall, *The Challenge of Pain*, rev. ed., Harmondsworth: Penguin, 1982, pp. 294–98A. M. Nicholi, Jr., ed. *The New Harvard Guide to Psychiatry*, Cambridge: Harvard University Press, 1988, p. 252.)

taught all he has to teach, so his disciples now have to take refuge in themselves and in the truth. His life, he knows, is drawing to its close, but he goes on traveling and teaching. A grateful listener invites him to a meal the Buddha knows is tainted but he eats it to honor the man's hospitality and becomes deathly ill. Calmly, he predicts the time and place of his death and asks that his body be ceremoniously burned, like that of a dead king. Then he addresses his assembled disciples asking that word should be spread of his impending death so that anyone who wants to visit him for the last time will be able to. Then, just before his death, he stands before his assembled disciples and he says once, twice, and three times that if any one of them has any doubt or misgiving as to him, the Buddha, the doctrine, the path, or the method, he should ask, without excessive reverence for the teacher, because this is the last chance to question him. They remain silent. His last words are that all composite things pass away and that they, the monks, should continue striving vigilantly. Entering into a meditative trance, he rises up, then down, and again up the ladder of trances and dies in the last, nirvanic stage. There is a terrifying earthquake, the heavens thunder, and Brahma, the highest of the gods, breaks into praise of the Buddha and his teaching.

I have now told as much of Buddha's traditional story as space allows. As scholars have proved by attempting the impossible, there is no way to get behind the legend to the historical person, at least to more than the barest outline of his life. We cannot avoid remaining doubtful of the storyteller's protected prince and the formulaic series of adventures by which he is set on his religious quest. Furthermore, there is no way of knowing which of the words attributed to him are really his, because everything he is said to have said is only what his disciples claimed to remember. And the Buddha can hardly have spoken in the enormously repetitive style of many of his dialogues. All the same, the early Buddhist literature portrays a Buddha-person with sympathetic traits. One is his love of truth and dislike of coercion.

It is easy to believe that the historic Buddha, like the mythical one, had this respect for the truth. His modestly human truthfulness is expressed in a tale in which the Buddha-to-be is one of three brothers who try to get the keeper of a lake, who, unfortunately, no longer has a nose, to give them some of the lotuses that grow in the lake he guards. Two of the brothers try to put him into a giving mood by telling him that his nose will grow back if he is generous. He gives them nothing. The future Buddha disagrees with his brothers and says that only fools say that noses grow back, because a nose once lost is lost forever. His truthfulness gains him the lotuses.[22]

Of the many doctrines of early Buddhism, I will take up the four that appear to me of the greatest philosophical interest: the Buddha's "rationalism" in relation to the limits he sets on metaphysical discussion; his doctrine of selflessness, that is, of no soul; his conception of a human being as an interrelated series of psychophysical processes; and his ideal of nirvana.*

The Buddha's rationalism as related to the limits he sets on metaphysical discussion:[23] Some of the Buddha's opponents believe in the authority of their scriptures and traditions, some in critically reasoned metaphysics, and some, like himself, in the intuitive grasp of the truth. There are early Buddhist texts that deny that anyone, even the god Brahma, is omniscient.[24] There are other, probably later, texts in which the Buddha is taken to be omniscient—to know everything in past, present, and future—and others in which he limits his extraordinary knowledge to his past births, clairvoyance, and the way to nirvana. In still other texts he speaks modestly and says that there are some questions the right and wrong of which one cannot settle without making qualifications. When he is asked how, in view of the contradictions between different authoritative persons, truth can be distinguished from falsehood, he answers that one should not be guided by hearsay, common opinion, tradition, the authority of scripture, speculation, attractive theories, or the impression made by the personal merits or authority of a master. The only guide should be one's own ability

---

*All of the evidence I draw on here for the Buddha's doctrines comes from the canon of the Theravada ("Teaching of the Elders"), which has remained widespread in Southeast Asia. Confinement to this evidence is natural because, of all the schools of Hinayana ("Small Vehicle"), only Theravada has survived—the name Hinayana was invented by Mahayana ("Great Vehicle") to express contempt for what it took to be an inferior doctrine, but it has proved too convenient to fall into disuse. The only other Hinayana school of whose canon much survives (survives in Sanskrit, Tibetan, and mostly in Chinese) is that of the Sarvastivada ("The Teaching that All Exists"). Luckily, in what concerns us in the present chapter, the doctrines of Theravada and Sarvastivada appear to be fairly similar.

The literary character and relatively simple doctrine of the Hinayana *sutras* (discourses attributed to the Buddha), which are consistent with what we know to have begun as a purely oral teaching, have led most scholars—in agreement with the Theravadins—to regard Hinayana as the original form of Buddhism, out of which the more literary and complex Mahayana *sutras* developed. But if we take into account that both the Hinayana and Mahayana texts were first put into writing about the time of Christ, it remains possible, as some scholars maintain, that Mahayana, having continued the tradition of the Mahasangikas (the "Majority Group" that split away early from the other schools), may be no more distant than Hinayana from the historical Buddha's doctrine. Mahayana accepts that the Theravada *sutras*, written in Pali, were in fact taught by the Buddha, but it takes them to express a doctrine meant only for those unable to understand the fuller, more accurate Mahayana truth. (See N. R. Peat, "The Historical Buddha and His Teachings," in *Abhidharma Buddhism to 150 A.D.*, ed. K. Potter, Delhi: Banarsidass, 1996, pp. 23–26.)

to recognize what should be rejected, rejected because it leads to misfortune and suffering.[25] If this passage is consistent with others in which faith in the Buddha is praised, it is because the Buddha insists that, regardless of scripture or teacher, a person should come to recognize what is better and worse and not rely on uncomprehending faith. Faith comes by way of the words the Buddha speaks; the truth is something that is heard from him, who is saturated with it.[26] There is no sign that the Buddha thinks that he himself is ever wrong.

The Buddha often rejects philosophical debate that deals with problems that appear to him not only, perhaps, insoluble but also distracting from the great, soluble one of pain. Systematized neatly, these problems appear in the Buddha's discourses as four sets of contradictory theses: the world is eternal, is not eternal; the world is finite, is not finite; the self or soul is identical with the body, is not identical with the body; and the Tathagata exists after death, does not exist after death, and neither exists nor does not exist after death. These theses reflect the views of various teachers or schools of the Buddha's time.[27]

On one memorable occasion, when a disciple complains to the Buddha that he is dissatisfied because these questions have been ignored, the Buddha answers with a simile: It is as if a man was shot by a heavily poisoned arrow but refused to allow the doctor to draw out the arrow until he knew the name, clan, color, and village or town of the man who shot him, and until he knew with what kind of bow, bowstring, and arrow—of what the arrow was made, what feathers it was shafted with, and so on. The chances are, says the Buddha, that the man would die before he got the information. Whatever the answer to the metaphysical questions, the fact is that there are birth, aging, dying, grief, suffering, and despair. He has not explained the metaphysical problems, he says, because they do nothing to calm, give the necessary insight, or lead to nirvana.[28]

On the surface, the metaphysical questions the Buddha refuses to consider resemble Kant's antinomies (which will come up later). It has been assumed that, like Kant, the Buddha considers them beyond the limits of human intelligence. But it is nowhere stated in the Buddhist dialogues that these questions do not, in fact, have categorical answers—except insofar as there are no merely verbal solutions. For example, the alternative logical possibilities relating to the existence after death of the Tathagata miss the elusive, no doubt ineffable truth because what pertains to nirvana is beyond the ability of our concepts to grasp.

The Buddha's doctrine of selflessness or no soul (anatman):[29] The Buddha denies that human beings have permanent selves or souls. This denial is in direct contradiction to the view of Uddalaka, Yajnavalkya, and most non-Buddhist Indian philosophers. As against the others, the Buddhists contend that everything, composite or not, is impermanent. To make this contention plausible, they analyze the individual human being—body and mind together—into components or functions of five kinds, five groups or aggregates (*skandha* in Sanskrit, *khanda* in the Pali of the texts under discussion).* The groups or aggregates are the following: the physical body (as furnished with sense organs); sensation (classified as pleasant, painful, and neutral); perception/conception (the creation of mental images and ideas); volition (the forming of impulses, predispositions, attitudes); and consciousness (the power to recognize and judge). As usually translated, the list is: form (*rupa, body as visible*), sensation (*vedana*), perception (*samjna*, in Pali, *sanna*), mental formations (*samskara, sankhara*), consciousness (*vijnana, vinnana*). Because everything in all of these groups is in constant change, the Buddhists argue, the person, who is wholly composed of them, is necessarily in constant change.

This analysis is a decisive factor in the Buddha's argument against a permanent self. If the self, the *atman*, he says, was the all-powerful, indestructible existence that non-Buddhist philosophers take it to be, it would have to be identical with (or included in) one of the five groups that constitute the human being. If, for example, the self was the body, as a materialist would hold, the body would not be subject to sickness or any other imperfection. The Buddha repeats this argument for the other "groups," including, finally, the most likely candidate, consciousness. But consciousness, too, is subject to imperfection and impermanence and is unable either to be or avoid being however one pleases.[30]

A second argument against a soul/self begins in a discussion of trance, understood to be the temporary cessation of consciousness. How is this cessation to be explained? Some say it is without any cause or condition; some say that a person's self is consciousness, which comes and goes; and some say that powerful brahmans or gods draw consciousness in and out of a person. But the state of trance is best explained not as

---

* "The dialect of Middle Indo-Aryan which is found in the texts of the Theravadin Buddhists and usually called 'Pali' by European scholars is nowhere so called in the Theravadin canon." Apparently, "the name 'Pali' is based upon a misunderstanding of the compound *pali-bhasha* 'language of the canon' . . . The commentaries state that the language spoken by the Buddha, which is the language of the canon, is Magadhi. This is referred to as the *mula-bhasha*, the root language of all languages, and the language which a child would speak naturally if it heard no other language spoken . . . What we know of Magadhi as described . . . in later times . . . enables us to say that Pali is not Magadhi," though the Buddha is said to have preached in Magadha on occasion. At the councils held to recite the canon, its language must have been more or less normalized. "Since this normalized language was an 'ecclesiastical' one, recited by monks who spoke in a variety of languages or dialects, there is no necessity to assume that it coincided exactly with any one particular spoken language" (Norman, *Pali Literature*, pp. 1–4).

anything having to do with a consciousness-soul that comes and goes or that is inserted into or taken out of a person.* Trances, says the Buddha, are the end result of a natural process, as we see when we consider how training influences some ideas to arise and others to pass away. Training shows how, at each meditative step, consciousness of a particular kind arises while the preceding kind ends. When the meditator reaches the highest stage of consciousness, he may come to think that conscious thought of any kind is an inferior state and may stop thinking and imagining, and "so he touches cessation." This cessation of conscious ideas has been achieved gradually, step by step, by means of a causal process—a soul has nothing to do with it.[31]

A third kind of argument used by the Buddha is aimed against the idea that the self is material or, more seriously, that it is consciousness in the sense of consciousness identical with knowledge. This view is wrong, the Buddha argues, because experience shows that knowledge is conditioned: it must have a cause, that is, it must be learned. First consciousness arises and only then does knowledge arise. Therefore consciousness must be one thing and knowledge another.[32] Even if the self was regarded as a formless soul made of consciousness, consciousness would arise first and knowledge would arise out of it. A person always recognizes that knowledge has come to him as the result of one cause or another.

A fourth argument used by the Buddha against a fixed self of any kind, material or immaterial, is reminiscent of a famous section of St. Augustine's *Confessions*. Consider the temporal nature of the self as it is experienced: A person believes that he once existed in the past, exists in the present, and will exist in the future. Once, the past that is now unreal to him was real. But the once real past has become unreal and the once unreal future has become real in the form of the present; and there still

---

* *Consciousness* translates *sanna*, which can also be translated *perceptions* (as in Walshe, *Thus Have I Heard*), giving the passage a different resonance. Not only do the Pali terms not match English ones exactly, but until they are fixed by scholastics, they show a great deal of semantic overlap. It may be misleading to give a fixed interpretation of the still untechnical terms of earlier Buddhism. Early texts use two words, *sanna* and *vinnana*, for ordinary consciousness or perception. In later, scholastic doctrine, *sanna* is specialized to mean the nonmaterial process by which the sense organs "touch" their object, or to mean the effect that impact produces by the coming together of the object of sensation, the sense organ, and the sensation. *Vinnana* comes to be the dominant word for ordinary, discriminating consciousness. In Buddhist fashion, *vinnana* is said to depend completely on the conditions that cause it, and to disappear along with them; but it is also said to descend into the mother's womb and to transmigrate from individual to individual. Each sense organ is granted its own *vinnana*. In later, scholastic Buddhism, its main function is to gain a first, vague perception of matter. (See E. R. Sarathchandra, *Buddhist Psychology of Perception*, pp. 4–28; and Johansson, *The Dynamic Psychology of Early Buddhism*.)

is the future, at present unreal, time. Which time is fully real? The words we use for our selves at each temporal stage of our experience are mere names or conventional designations, good only for ordinary talk. There is no fixed self or substratum; there are only qualities that keep changing in their causal order as they influence one another.[33]

The no-self theory creates intellectual problems, the most immediate of which is the nature of whatever it is that is affected by karma and transmigrates. The answer is a theory of continuity—resembling that of Heraclitus or contemporary physics—exemplified by a stream of water or a flame, which change constantly and yet remain in form the same continuous stream or flame. The developed answers to the problem of continuity belong to a later period and will not be pursued here.

The Buddha's conception of the human being as an interrelated series of psychophysical processes:[34] The Buddhist holds that a human being is nothing other than a chain of interdependent processes. This chain of causation is called "dependent origination" or "dependent co-arising." It consists of twelve linked processes that form a spiral-like succession of existences. Each of the twelve processes of one segment of the spiral arises from the process that comes before it. What is of interest here is not the doctrine in its exact detail, which must appear to us somewhat arbitrary, but the psychophysical vision.

For the record, the following is the most usual form of the chain: Each process-stage or link is impermanent, without any self—the permanent reality that is assumed by philosophical opponents. A process comes into existence from the preceding process and goes out of existence just as its predecessor does. Ignorance, which starts the whole process, is the condition for mental formations, which are the condition for consciousness. In turn, consciousness is the condition for name–and–form (*nama-rupa*, body), name–and–form for the six senses, the six senses for sense contact, sense contact for feeling, feeling for craving, craving for grasping, grasping for becoming, becoming for birth, and birth for old age and death, distress, grief, suffering, sorrow, and unrest.[35]

To make this scheme easier to grasp, we might eliminate the details of its progression and put it quite generally: A person begins as a complex transmigrating consciousness that descends into the mother's womb and plants itself and grows there, watered by its cravings, in the field of its actions. Impelled by the force of its desiring, this consciousness–seed of the person collects images, sensations, and activities, and so prepares its own birth. After it is born, it continues to crave stimuli and gather karma and memories and prepare its next birth; or it can become more independent of stimuli, more understanding, purer, emptier, so that the life-creating force will be diminished and less likely to go on to a new rebirth.[36]

Such a conception is modern because everything in the person interacts with everything else, because knowing is joined with craving and both are joined with remembering, because conscious and unconscious processes run into and affect one another, and because the embryo craves and collects experiences no less than the child and the finally old man it becomes. In spirit, the whole is not unlike modern neuropsychology and developmental psychology.[37]*

The Buddhist ideal of nirvana:[38] The word *nirvana*, which is composed of *nih* (*out*) and *va* (*blow*), has the literal meaning of *blowing out*, and is used to signify transcendent calm not only by Buddhists but by Hindus and Jains as well. In Buddhist use, nirvana always signifies the ending of sorrow, suffering, or pain, as the word *duhkha* is variously translated. Often described with the help of words such as *without characteristics* and *deathless*, nirvana is taken to be the result of the successful effort to extinguish one's sense of self and escape from the suffering that is inherent in embodied existence. Early Buddhist literature makes it quite clear what nirvana is not. It is not death, which is only an incident in transmigration. Nor is it a condition possible to reach only at or after death—it can be attained, as the Buddha attained it, during one's lifetime as "nirvana with phenomenal existence." Nor is nirvana an Indian heaven, an impermanent abode that one enters and leaves. Nirvana is nowhere. The Buddha explains that if a fire would go out and someone would ask in what direction it went, east, west, north, or south, the answer would have to be that direction was not at all relevant. "Exactly in the same way . . . visible form, feeling, apperception, dispositions and perception, by which one could designate a Tathagata, are now given up and once and for all uprooted. 'Come into being' does not apply, 'not come into being,' does not apply, 'come into being as well as not come into being' does not apply, 'neither come into being nor not come into being' does not apply."[39]

All the same, the idea of nirvana is not, or not consistently, all negative. The idea of blowing out that the word embodies relates it to the

---

*Compare the Buddhist view with that of the neuropsychological researcher who writes: "The neural basis for the self, as I see it, resides with the continuous reactivation of at least two sets of representations. One set concerns representations of key events in an individual's autobiography, on the basis of which a notion of identity can be reconstructed repeatedly, by partial activation in topographically organized sensory maps . . . The second set of representations underlying the neural self consists of the primordial representations of the individual's body . . . At each moment the state of self is constructed, from the ground up. It is an evanescent reference state, so continuously and consistently *reconstructed* that the owner never knows that it is being *remade* unless something goes wrong with the remaking" (A. R. Damasio, *Descartes' Error*, New York: Grosset/Putnam, 1994, pp. 238–39).

blowing out of a fire. There is an ancient Indian idea according to which fire exists invisibly before it has been kindled and after it has been extinguished, changing only its form or modality. In one Upanishad, a comparison is drawn between Brahman and fire, whose material form is not perceived when the fire lies latent in its source, the firewood, but remains there in its invisible, subtle form until caught again by means of the firedrill.[40] It is therefore not surprising that in some Buddhist texts what *does not exist* is interpreted as *is not perceived* and nirvana is understood to be a pure, subtle, everlasting "island" or "realm." In fact, in early Buddhist literature, phrases used by the Brahmans to describe the joy of *atman* merged with Brahman are used by the Buddhists to describe nirvana or the joy of the meditator on its verge. Even in early, relatively unmetaphysical Buddhism there is some tendency to see nirvana as the perfect dimension of existence; and there is also, perhaps, the beginning of a view of nirvana as a something beyond space, time, and causality.

To reach nirvana is always to undergo a dramatic change arrived at by meditative concentration and intellectual insight. In nirvana, all needs and emotions—obsessive sensuality, incessant change, irrelevant speculation—are replaced by total calm, insight, and freedom. Consciousness is now undisturbed and the mind fluctuates only superficially, so that sensation no longer leads to emotions and desires, karma is no longer accumulated, and there is nothing to flow on into a new existence. These early, perhaps inconsistent views of nirvana become the province of debate and help divide Buddhism into rival schools of thought and practice—a complex matter that will not be discussed here.

This is the moment at which a too-brief word should be said about the Buddhist perception of life as suffering. This perception divides Buddhism from Confucianism and, in its uncompromising intensity, from most Western thought. The logic of Buddhism obviously depends upon its account of the painfulness—the painful results—even of pleasure, and on the universality of the law of karma, which itself depends upon belief in transmigration. But the Buddha does not expect of laymen what he expects of those who want to become, like himself, fully dispassionate and compassionate. To laymen he preaches that morality, in the usual sense, will gain them great wealth by careful attention to their affairs, a reputation for good conduct, self-assurance among people of every kind, a death without anxiety, and a place after death in a heavenly world.[41] To an ordinary laymen, the Buddhist master of dispassion and compassion is less a person one wants to emulate than a distant ideal, which may influence one's thought and conduct, but probably in a subtle rather than obvious way.

Socrates (470–399 B.C.E.):
Gadfly by Induction

Socrates' father was a sculptor and his mother a midwife—Socrates calls himself a midwife of the soul.[42] In his youth, he studied geometry and astronomy. He was notably brave, as was proved in three military campaigns; at Potidaea, it is said, he won the prize for bravery. His moral integrity was proved when, under the democratic regime, he refused to put the unprecedented proposal to condemn all the generals who had won a naval battle but failed to rescue two thousand men from their wrecked ships. A second proof of moral integrity was his refusal, under the new oligarchy of the Thirty, to call Leon of Salamis before them for execution without trial. He also showed a rather truculent modesty, and when the oracle of Delphi called him the wisest man in Greece, he said that the pronouncement was hard at first to understand. Aristophanes must have found the pronouncement unintelligible, for to him Socrates was the image of socially destructive, self-important absurdity.

Socrates' wife Xanthippe, famous in antiquity as a shrew, bore him the son Lamprocles.* Myrto (if it is true that he was ever married to her) perhaps gave him two other sons. He was or became poor. Xenophon reports that it was Socrates' regular habit to dance because he thought that such exercise kept the body in good condition, and that in his old age he learned to play the lyre. Although he had a Silenus face and an unbeautiful body, he was magnetically attractive. Plato called him the bravest, wisest, most upright man of his time, and Xenophon, the best and happiest of men.

The most notable event in Socrates' life was the trial for impiety that ended in his execution. About fifty years earlier, the philosopher Anaxagoras had been exiled from Athens, ostensibly for saying that the sun, regarded as a deity, was no more than a fiery stone; Protagoras is said to have been convicted of impiety and his books burned in the marketplace; Aristotle left Athens rather than face a trial on political grounds, it appears; and

---

*The relations between Xanthippe and Socrates gave birth to misogynous, often cautionary tales. When Abelard promised to marry Heloise, she tried to dissuade him from a step she thought would disgrace him, burden him, and prevent him from philosophizing. She exhorted him to "remember Socrates' marriage and the sordid episode whereby he did at least remove the slur it cast on philosophy by providing an example to be warning to his successors. This too was noted by Jerome, when he tells this tale of Socrates in the first book of his *Against Jovinian*: 'One day after he had withstood an endless stream of invective which Xanthippe poured out from a window above his head, he felt himself soaked with dirty water. All he did was to wipe his head and say: "I knew that thunderstorm would lead to rain" ' " (*Abelard & Heloise*, trans. B. Radice, London: Folio Society, 1977, pp. 29–30; the translation is also published by Penguin Books).

there are other, though doubtful stories about philosophers' trials. Yet speech was then relatively free in Athens—(Plato's) Socrates declares that there is more freedom to talk in Athens than anywhere else in Greece.[43]

Socrates seems to have been regarded by many Athenians as one of the intellectuals, often foreign, who were subverting democracy and respect for traditional values. The animus against Socrates had both political and religious grounds. Political suspicion was aroused by his association with Critias, the leader of the cruel oligarchic uprising, and with Alicibiades, who despised democracy. It was easy to assume that Socrates' teaching had been responsible for their conduct.* It has often been said that the amnesty for the oligarchs made it inexpedient to level any openly political accusation; but this is not certain.[44] In any case, the charge against Socrates was restricted to a religious one. The charge was that Socrates refused to recognize the gods recognized by the state and introduced other, new *daimona*—new *daimons*, that is, divinities or, perhaps, new "daimonic" practices. The actual wording of the indictment may be that preserved in the text of Diogenes Laertius:

> This indictment and affidavit is sworn by Meletus, the son of Meletus of Pitthos, against Socrates, the son of Sophroniscus of Alopece: Socrates is guilty of refusing to recognize the gods recognized by the state, and of introducing other new divinities. The penalty demanded is death.[45]

As far as we know, such a charge was the first of its kind ever made in Athens. It is unlikely that the religious accusation was aimed at any belief—Athenian beliefs were many, various, and unsystematized—but it may have been aimed at neglect of the public religious practices that honored the gods on whom Athens depended. What is most obviously pertinent, however, is the prohibition against the unsanctioned introduction of

---

*The decision to prosecute an old man for saying and doing what he had been saying and doing unmolested for so many years must have been a response to the wounds of recent history: a lost war, a lost empire, an oligarchic *coup*. The problem is to decide whether the Athenians' diagnosis was more specific—'Socrates taught subversives'—or more general—'Socrates embodies the moral malaise that has brought Athens low' " (Parker, *Athenian Religion*, pp. 201–202).

Xenophon reports that Socrates' accuser (perhaps the sophist Polycrates) held that Socrates encouraged his associates to despise the established constitution by saying that it was foolish to appoint public officials by lot rather than ability (see the *Protagoras* 319b), and that such arguments incited young men to despise the established political order. Xenophon says that the accuser also argued that Critias and Alcibiades, having become associates of Socrates, had done the city great evil (Xenophon, *Memorabilia*, 1.2.9, 12). But Polycrates' accusation against Socrates was published years after Socrates' trial and he is not mentioned as among those "who wrote the indictment" (Brickhouse and Smith, pp. 173–74; see also Parker, *Athenian Religion*, pp. 206–207).

new public cults, meaning, ordinarily, the worship of a god not yet officially recognized. Socrates' references to his inward sign or "divinity" may have been taken to imply worship of such a god. This "divinity" is Socrates' *daimonion*, as it is called in two Platonic passages, or, as called elsewhere by Plato, Socrates' divine sign or customary oracle, or, most simply, his inner voice. Later supposed to be a "genius" or spirit, the *daimonion* seems to be only an instinctive voice or sign that warns Socrates not to say or undertake something particular, often quite trivial. At least once, however, the sign has the more general effect of keeping Socrates away from politics. The *daimonion* has no dogma to teach and warns not of moral consequences but of misfortune.[46] But the jurors may have understood the *daimonion* to be a strange oracle that only Socrates, a lone individual, could consult. Such a privileged consultation might be doubly incriminating to those who suspected his political leanings and resented his sharply critical presence.[47] The conclusion of the trial and the imminence of death elicit from Socrates the view, so foreign to the Greeks of his time, that one "ought not return injustice for injustice or do ill to any man, no matter what one may suffer at their hands" (*Crito* 49d).[48]*

Socrates' most obvious traits as a philosopher are his manner of argument by persistent questions, his profession of ignorance, and the use of the questions and the profession to attempt to gain an exact understanding of virtue. In Aristotle's words:

> Socrates believed that knowledge of virtue was the final aim, and he inquired what justice is, and what courage and every other kind of virtue. This was reasonable in view of his conviction that all the virtues [kinds of excellence] were sciences, so that to know justice was at the same time to be just; for as

---

*"It was not the Athenian custom to disguise hatred, and neither party to a case hesitated to declare his adversary deserving of death . . . The attempt to retaliate upon an enemy being justified . . . successful retaliation was a joy, and failure a horror; a man might be respected for attempting revenge and denigrated for making no attempt." But "obstinate insistence on justice" was sometimes repudiated in favor of "kindly magnanimity" (*Gorgias*, fragment B6). Sometimes, a considered tolerance influenced political conduct. When democracy was restored in Athens in 403, it was decided that it was best "not to recall ills," meaning, not to bear grudges or retaliate. These words are later described (by the Athenian orator Aeschinas) as "the noblest words which civilization can utter." The Athenians' magnanimous decision gave them great satisfaction.

Protagoras, a relativist, insists on distinguishing between rational punishment, meant to deter, and "mindless vengeance" (Plato, *Protagoras* 342a–b). Yet Aristotle continues to believe that one should do good to friends and evil to enemies—to do good to enemies is as objectionable, he says, as to do evil to friends (*Topics* 113a2–9). Aristotle believes that it is just, and therefore noble, not to come to terms with one's enemies but to take revenge on them (*Rhetoric* 1367a19–20). (See Dover, *Popular Morality in the Time of Plato and Aristotle*, pp. 182 [quoted], 191 [quoted], 193); and Vlastos, *Socrates*, pp. 187–89.)

soon as we have learned geometry and architecture we are architects and geometricians. For this reason he inquired what virtue is, but not how or from what it is acquired. (*Eudemian Ethics* 1216b)[49]

To Socrates, virtue (*areté*) as a whole is made up, as he says, of manliness (courage), moderation, justice, piety, and wisdom.[50] To understand these is a matter of supreme importance because, despite his profession of ignorance, he is convinced that virtue (*areté*) is knowledge—to have courage, for example, is to know and, because one knows, to act on what really is and is not to be feared. To do wrong is to be ignorant, and to be ignorant is not to know how to live or be happy, while to be virtuous is to know how to live well, that is, to be happy, a self-justifying goal not at all the same as merely having pleasure.[51]

The Socrates we know best, the one who appears in Plato, cannot be cleanly separated from his creator. But the earlier, more Socratic dialogues tend to be shorter, more bantering, and more optimistic in spirit. And, name apart, the Socrates of the earlier dialogues is different from the Socrates of the later ones. To put the difference in negations, the earlier Socrates, the one I am considering to be Socrates, does not deal with other than moral issues, does not claim to know anything, reaches few and only very general conclusions, does not philosophize except by questioning and refuting others, does not believe in separately existing (Platonic) Ideas or Forms, is not, until after his trial, much concerned with life after death, and expresses religious belief only in the *daimonion*, in the oracle, in an undefined moral god, and, sometimes, in uncharacterized "gods."[52]

Socrates' philosophic traits run together in a way unprofitable to separate. When in the course of searching for the exact definition of a virtue, he questions someone, he will often ask which of the two of a pair of traits is better, for example, whether justice is better than injustice. He himself never or almost never says what any of the virtues are because, he claims, he does not know and hopes to learn by eliciting the truth from the person he is questioning. He bears down on those he questions, even rudely, always convicting them of giving examples rather than viable definitions and of reasoning circularly. Always, they break down under his questioning, sometimes because of the possibly dubious intellectual tactics he uses.

The nature of Socrates' intellectual tactics is a delicate matter, not only because of the honor in which we hold him but because, if he himself thought them questionable, he might regard them as in themselves an obstacle to the truth—can a sophistical distinction be used to harry someone into eliciting a possible truth from himself? The matter is particularly delicate because Socrates is an inveterate ironist and one is not always sure (I am not always sure) if he is not being so marginally ironical in relation to himself that he can say opposite things and, probably with qualifications, mean both.[53]

Consider, in this light, Socrates' repeated declaration that he knows nothing, that he has nothing to teach, that he does not engage in politics. This means, as he says, that he is not a craftsman, doctor, orator, or other specialist and therefore has no special knowledge to impart, and that his inquiries do not touch directly on political matters. But he does believe and argue that wisdom and virtue should be practiced. He says, forthrightly, "To do injustice and to disobey my superior, god or man, this I know to be evil and base" (Apology 29b).[54] And once, referring to his statement that men would rather do than suffer injustice, he even asks whether it has not been proved that what he said was true (Gorgias 479e). Carried beyond his usual profession of ignorance, he adds that "these things," his relevant conclusions, have been, to speak crudely, "clamped down and bound by arguments of iron and adamant." Then, qualifying, he goes on that, with respect to himself, his position is always the same: he does "not know how these things are," but he has never met anyone who has spoken otherwise of injustice without being ridiculous (Gorgias 508e–509a).[55]

Socrates' reference to arguments of iron seems no more than a brief moment of logically excessive enthusiasm. Still, if he knows that he knows nothing, why does he always seem so sure of himself? Maybe he professes ignorance because he refuses to use the word know to characterize his own beliefs, which are justified, he thinks, by their ability to withstand argument, but reserves the word for the self-evident, logically guaranteed certainty that Parmenides, for one, attributes to true philosophy. Or perhaps he thinks that to know is to have a godlike grasp of the whole of moral knowledge, with all its interrelated virtues.* Under pressure, when facing the jurors who will decide his fate, Socrates explains that, in a human sense, he does know something. The oracle named him the wisest—the most knowing—of men, he says, because he is better as he is—neither wise with the knowledge that the craftsmen have nor ignorant with their

---

*By one interpretation, Socrates thinks that what he knows is true in the sense that it has stood up to argument and is consistent with other plausible beliefs, but that this is not logically self-evident and not enough to prove his beliefs to be absolutely true (Vlastos, "Socrates' Disavowal of Knowledge," in Socratic Studies). By another interpretation, Socrates is conscious of how little he knows of the sum total of truths that is necessary for certainty to be reached (Penner, "Socrates and the Early Dialogues," pp. 143–44. See also Brickhouse and Smith, Plato's Socrates, pp. 30–38).

ignorance or the ignorance of others. He is better than all those who believe that they are wise about everything. Very likely, what God means by his oracle is that human nature is of little or no worth, so that anyone is wisest if, like this fellow, Socrates, he realizes that, in respect to wisdom, he is truly nothing (*Apology* 22d-23a).[56]*

Now consider the way in which Socrates questions his interlocutors. Not only is he persistent, but he rejects both hypothetical arguments and attempts to argue merely for the sake of victory. Say what you really believe, he says, do not agree with any view against your own opinion (*Crito* 49d) or adopt different arguments for different occasions (*Gorgias* 482a). Along with sincerity, he demands consistency—regardless of others, he refuses to be an out-of-tune lyre, discordant with himself (*Gorgias* 482b–c). As one distinguished Athenian general, Nicias, explains to another, Lysimachus:

> Whenever anyone comes face to face with Socrates and has a conversation with him, what invariably happens is that, although they may have started on a completely different subject at first, Socrates will keep heading him off as they're talking until he has him trapped into giving an account of his present life-style, and of the way he has spent his life in the past. And once he has him trapped, Socrates won't let him go before he was well and truly cross-examined him on every angle. (*Laches* 187e-188a)[57]

First, Socrates gets his partner in conversation to say what he thinks about some virtue; he presses him for more statements; he shows his further statements to be inadequate and to lead to contradictions or circularity. Almost always, he refutes, according to Plato with invariable success. Abstracted from its twists and turns, the process is roughly this: Socrates asks what some virtue is. His interlocutor answers with an ex-

---

*I use both *wisdom* and *knowledge* to translate *sophia*. In its early use, *sophia* most often means *skill*. For its later use, the most convenient translation is usually *wisdom*. But this translation can be misleading because the Socratic *sophia* does not mean *wisdom* in its most usual sense, that of the breadth of view or the equanimity or tolerance that reflect experience or prolonged reflection. Instead, it means the kind of competence the craftsman shows in the pursuit of his craft and Socrates seeks in a more general form by way of the understanding of the virtues. In his early, more Socratic writing, Plato is said not to distinguish in principle between *episteme* (knowledge as opposed to belief), *phronesis* (ethical wisdom or insight), *techne* (skill, craft), and *nous* (intelligence). The opposite of *sophia* is not so much foolishness as ignorance (*agnosia*) or, especially, conceited ignorance (*amathia*). What Socrates thinks that he, like other humans, lacks is God's (perfect) knowledge. To know oneself is therefore to know that one is only human. (See Strycker and Slings [who translate *sophia* with *cleverness* or *understanding*], *Plato's Apology of Socrates*, pp. 62–68, esp. note p. 61.)

ample. Asked for a standard by which to recognize the virtue, the interlocutor gives a definition. Socrates shows that the definition conflicts with
some idea on which both he and the interlocutor agree (the holy cannot
be simply what the gods love because the gods disagree). The interlocutor
changes his definition (the holy is what *all* the gods love). Socrates asks
a question that suggests the direction he thinks is right (is the holy loved
by the gods because it is holy or is it holy because they love it?). Socrates
wants to know, he says, what the nature and reality of the holy is. Eventually, after long leading questions, very brief answers, and more attempts
at definition, the interlocutor admits his ignorance. He does not know, he
agrees, because his initial definition has been shown to conflict with beliefs
that both he and Socrates accept without question. As long as these beliefs
are not shown to contradict others that he accepts—unless someone un-
binds and looses the relevant arguments—the beliefs are to be regarded as
true (*Gorgias* 509a). Speaking logically or empirically, they may not be true,
Socrates admits; but at this point he appears sure of himself. He continues
"examining," "investigating," "inquiring," "questioning," until what is, in effect,
his refutation—refutation by question and answer, the Socratic elenchus—
leads to a deduction from his interlocutor's belief that contradicts that belief:
his interlocutor is refuted out of his own mouth.[58]

Does Socrates' constant practice of refuting imply a general hostility to
others, or is it a recurring demonstration for himself of his superiority over
the people he questions? Speaking psychologically, I cannot answer. In the
Apology Socrates contends that it is the gods who have imposed on him the
duty to understand himself and others. Like a gadfly stinging a noble but
sluggish horse, he wants to shame the Athenians into realizing that the
virtue of the soul is more important than anything else. His death will not
release them from the duty of examining their lives. Other, younger, harsher
men will follow him and trouble them the more (*Apology* 23ab, 29de, 39c).

If Socrates confined himself to questioning others in order to demonstrate their unhealthy moral ignorance and if he thought of himself as
not knowing anything beyond doubt, the Socrates who appears in the
dialogue *Meno* is a new, more Platonic one. There is no evidence that the
mature Socrates was ever much interested in mathematics. In the *Meno*,
however, he shows that—helped by adversarial questions, by leading
questions, and by the crucial diagonal line he draws—the apparently ignorant slave boy he is questioning has an intuitive knowledge of geometry.
The problem in the demonstration is a decidedly technical one: What is
the side of a square with an area double that of a square with sides two
feet long? This problem, related to the Greek discovery of the incommensurability of the diagonal, is discussed with the help of specialized terms
taken from the then developing field of axiomatized geometry. What is

new is Socrates' elaborate use of geometry (of "the application of areas") to show how moral philosophizing should proceed, his willingness to borrow the method of hypothesis from the geometers, his emphasis on recollection of what the soul has always learned in its many previous lives, and his implication, so foreign to the Socrates described earlier, that reasoning can lead to mathematically infallible moral conclusions.[59]

Aristotle gives a plausible account of Socrates' philosophical accomplishment: By questions that help to overcome Heraclitus, Socrates leads to Plato's theory of Ideas and his, Aristotle's, theory of essences. As Aristotle explains, Heraclitus' doctrine that all sensible things are in a state of flux makes it impossible for knowledge to exist unless there are entities other than sensible ones (*Metaphysics* 1078b). Having said this, Aristotle summarizes the limited but pioneering contribution of Socrates. It is that Socrates was the first to try to find a general definition of the moral virtues, and because the starting point of all logical reasoning is the essence, Socrates inquired into the essence of things.

> There are two innovations which may fairly be ascribed to Socrates: inductive reasoning and general definition. Both of these are associated with the starting-point of scientific knowledge. But whereas Socrates regarded neither universals nor definitions as existing in separation, the Idealists gave them a separate existence, and to these universals and definitions of existing things they gave the name of Ideas. (*Metaphysics* 1078b 17–32)[60]

Naturally, this summing up of Socrates' innovations is colored by Aristotle's sense of the progress of philosophy. But the impression that Socrates made on people had little to do with Platonic Ideas or Aristotelian essences. It was not these that persuaded Antisthenes to walk to Athens every day to hear Socrates. He walked the five miles because Socrates was so impressively hardy, so much a wrestler, so (unlike Plato) without conceit, so sure that virtue was teachable, so remote from evil, so deserving to be loved.[61] The early Christians such as Justin Martyr thought that Socrates should be considered a Christian because, like them, he defied the state, exhorted people to become acquainted with the still unknown God, and suffered a martyrdom he could have escaped.[62]

Because Socrates was in everything an individualist, the individualists among philosophers, ancient and modern, have measured themselves against him, whether with praise or blame. Nietzsche shifts from unqualified admiration for Socrates' wisdom and courage to the rhetorically sharp question, why Socrates was a monomaniac with respect to morality. Severely but not unreasonably, he adds that all the Socratics, including Plato, are opposed because of the profound instinct that human beings cannot be made better by telling them that virtue is demonstrable and asking them for reasons.[63] Kierkegaard makes the point that Socrates is invulnerable to punishment by society (as Kierkegaard himself wants to be). The Athenian court, he says, failed to understand that it could not inflict punishment on Socrates, because Socrates, knowing nothing at all, did not know death to be harsh and painful.[64] Kierkegaard, who cultivates one kind of silence by means of anonymous publication and another by embracing paradox, particularly admires Socrates' silence, his refusal to give answers:

> For the observer, Socrates' life is like a magnificent pause in the course of history: we do not hear him at all; a profound stillness prevails—until it is broken up by the noisy attempts of the many and very different schools of followers to trace their origins in this hidden and cryptic source. With Socrates the stream of historical narrative, just like the river Guadalquivir, drops underground for some distance, only to rush out again with renewed power.[65]

Bertrand Russell, himself rebellious, atheistic, and scientistic, admires Socrates' courage but criticizes him for wanting to prove the universe agreeable to his own ethical standards. This desire, says Russell, is treachery to the truth, for which Socrates should be consigned to a long residence in a scientific purgatory.[66] Wittgenstein, who sees only pain and illness in the questions philosophers ask, finds Socrates beyond reparation. "Reading the Socratic dialogues," he says, "one has the feeling: what a frightful waste of time! What's the point of these arguments that prove nothing and clarify nothing?"[67] To end, as is only fair, with a more appreciative judgment, I cite Karl Popper, who favors pointed, unrelenting questions and responsible freedom:

> From Socrates' apology and from his death there sprang a new idea of a free man: the idea of a man whose spirit cannot be subdued; of a man who is free because he is self-sufficient; who is not in need of constraint because he is able to rule himself, and to accept freely the rule of law.[68]

Discussion

Confucius, Mencius, the Buddha, and Socrates talk about matters of concern to ordinary persons and adopt a way of argument, didactic or agonistic, that is natural to conversation.* They all often proceed by the simple iteration of examples. Of course, there are differences among the strategies and aims they pursue in conversation: Socrates invokes the arguments that demonstrate the essential identity of all instances of each of the different virtues; Confucius invokes the sages whose words and acts demonstrate the variation and socializing power of the different virtues in different situations; and the Buddha invokes the analyses that dissolve the illusion of fixed objects and selves and show how the different virtues can join one another in curing human suffering. But at its most philosophical, the conversation of all three is usually about something, some quality, principle, supposed reality, or method being searched for, defined or applied more exactly, or, in the Buddhist case, perhaps denied. Such conversation is mostly in the mode of argument from analogy that Aristotle calls *induction* and finds exemplified in Socrates.

Let me give examples taken from among those already cited, this time, for exactness' sake, word for word. The first is from the discussion between Kao-tzu and Mencius on whether or not the feeling of humanity is inborn. Mencius, it will be recalled, is making the point that the use of the same word, *nature*, should not be taken to imply identity in what it designates. Its sense changes when it is applied to human, moral issues. Similarly, the meaning of a morally used term such as *rightness* varies with the object to which it is applied, unlike a term such as *whiteness*, which is morally indifferent.

> "Treating as white" is the same whether one is treating a horse as old or white or a man as white. But I wonder if you would think that "treating as old" is the same whether one is treating a horse as old or a man as elder? Furthermore, is it the one

---

*"Just as Confucius keeps at a prudent distance from cosmological or religious speculations, so Socrates, in Cicero's formula, is the Greek who 'drew philosophy away from the hidden secret of nature' in order to apply it to the duties of ordinary life." Furthermore, both avow their ignorance, and neither presents himself as the possessor of a doctrine (see *Analects* 2.17; 9. 7). Neither makes speeches nor talks much, yet both train disciples zealously (*Analects* 7.18). "For, while recognizing that they are not the guardians of any wisdom, they draw from deep within themselves the consciousness of a vocation that surpasses them (that comes from 'Heaven,' from the 'demon') and gives them confidence to face the threats of their contemporaries . . . Finally, while showing the same respect for established religious practices, they both seem to aspire to a more internal religion, of which their own moral experience makes them aware (see *Analects* 7.34) . . . But one does not see Confucius pretending to adopt his adversary's position, as Socrates commonly does in order to push his interlocutor to develop it to its end and, by doing so, to make its incoherence or inanity suddenly appear (the situation of 'aporia')" (F. Jullien, *Le détour et l'accès: Stratégies du sens en Chine, en Grèce*, Paris: Grasset, 1995, pp. 253–54).

who is old that is dutiful, or is it the one who treats him as elder that is dutiful? (*Mencius* 6.A.3–4.)[69]

Compare this conversation with that between Socrates and Meno on what virtue may be—on the unity of the different instances of each virtue, Meno has just admitted that there are many kinds of virtue, and Socrates is making a point exactly the opposite of Mencius' because he wants to discover the common nature of the virtues, not the difference possibly concealed by their common name:

> Do you think it is only true of virtue that it is one thing for a woman, another for a man, and so on? Or is this also true of health and size and strength? Do you think health is one thing for a man, and another for a woman? Or is health, if it is to be health, the same character everywhere, whether in man or anything else? (*Meno* 72d–e)[70]

In the following example, the Buddha uses the technique of examining instances to see if *atman* can be discovered by means of its inherent impregnability and omnipotence. He believes he is conducting a decisive, that is, complete induction because, as he and his interlocutors are agreed, he is basing his reasoning on an exhaustive enumeration of the components that make up a human being, so he repeats the same argument with respect to body, sensation, perception/cognition, volition, and consciousness. Since the argument is everywhere identical, I give it for consciousness only, with the omission of the self-evident answers given by the listening monks:

> If consciousness were the soul, this consciousness would not be subject to sickness, and it would be possible in the case of consciousness to say, "let my consciousness be thus, let my consciousness be thus." Now because consciousness is soulless . . . it is not possible in the case of consciousness to say, "Let my consciousness be thus, let my consciousness be thus" . . . Is it fitting to consider what is impermanent, painful, and subject to change as, "this is mine, this am I, this is my soul?"[71]

In each of the three examples I have cited, there is a search to find, verify, or falsify a real definition or true concept. All the examples are relevant to what the Confucians, beginning with Confucius himself, see as the "rectification of names." If one reads these examples in their context, one sees that it is the Buddhist who makes the largest assumption—that the enumeration of what constitutes a person is accurate and exhaustive.

In the examples given here, Mencius and Socrates are on about the same level of sophistication (the geometrical examples of the *Meno* go much further, of course). The equivocal nature of concepts may be clearer to Mencius, but Socrates pursues his argument at greater length and with more energy. Seen now, all the arguments are primitive. I mean not that they are mistaken—they can be remade on a higher level of sophistication—but that they are very incomplete.

We have seen that the knowledge that is sought is not the same. The Buddha searches for the knowledge that overcomes pain, and Socrates, for the knowledge of the essences of the virtues, which he believes will necessarily transform those who know them. But Confucius searches not for knowledge in any abstract sense, but for historical paradigms of goodness, whose moral stature he wants to analyze in order to be able to assimilate and teach it. So Socrates searches for fixed, still undiscovered definitions, to clarify morality that is still only instinctive and therefore inconsistent; the Buddha teaches the fixed laws he has discovered for escaping pain, including the law that nothing in ordinary life but the law itself is fixed; and Confucius teaches traditionally fixed but neglected truths, which he presses home in tautological-seeming maxims: the ruler must be a ruler, the subject a subject, the father a father, the son a son (*Analects* 12.11).[72]

The human attractiveness of the four protagonists of this chapter rests, I think, on their combination of moral with intellectual responsiveness, on their fatherly, teacherly, tenderly objective concern. Measured though he is, Confucius requires his fellow men to love one another, and he says forthrightly, "Do not impose on others what you yourself do not desire" (*Analects* 15.24).[73] Mencius insists that "whoever is devoid of the heart of compassion is not human" (*Mencius* 1A.6).[74] The Buddha exhorts monks not to kill any living thing, to lay aside the cudgel and sword, and to live in compassion and kindness to all living things.[75]

Confucius' remarks are directed toward the educated, who are at least potential officials. As usual, Socrates lends his words intimations of justice: he says that doing ill to anyone is always wrong in order to explain his refusal to flee the city that has unjustly sentenced him to death. And as usual, the Buddha means to help his monks on the road to enlightenment. Confucius, with a vivid sense of near failure, looks for his reward in his own approval of his actions and the approval of still unwritten history; the Buddha, theoretically above reward and punishment, gets his satisfaction from the help he give others and his certainty of nirvana; and Socrates, who hopes to be rewarded by God, also says that he is answering to his own conscience. Despite their differences, each of these fathers of philosophy is willing to give up everything, including life—the Buddha, this particular life—for the sake of his sense of the humane and the just.

Of the four, only the Buddha leaves testimony of a severe struggle with his own desires and doubts, but he, too, arrives at certainty and, like the others—even the Socrates who knows nothing for sure—teaches in the mode of certainty. Each of the teachers lends his disciples the assurance that disciples need and the certainty that virtue, being identical with knowledge, can be learned from them and give at least inward peace and security.

Chapter 4

❋

Early Logical Relativism, Skepticism, and Absolutism

Mahavira, Chuang-tzu, Protagoras, Gorgias, Plato

Theme: Can Being, Negation, and Becoming All Be Reconciled?

The Existent of Uddalaka is superlatively creative life, the Self of Yajnavalkya is superlatively internalized experience, and the *being* of Parmenides is logical, superlatively fixed existence. All three philosophers create an antithesis between what unchangeably *is* or remains unchangeably *what* it is—even as the universal creative force—and between what becomes or changes or (in Parmenides' case) appears to become or change. As against these three believers in *being*—vitalistic, selflike, or logical— there is Heraclitus. Heraclitus, it is true, says that all things are one, but in the sense that the cosmos is a living fire that is lit and goes out by some law of proportions that determines how fire and all things "requite" one another. To Heraclitus, the world is a perpetually dynamic process: what seems to remain the same is really in incessant change—only the law that governs change remains the same. When Heraclitean doctrine takes a radical turn in Cratylus (fifth–fourth century B.C.E.), the contrast between being and becoming reaches an extreme the starkness of which invigorates the philosopher in Plato. But *being* of the philosophers contrasts too flagrantly with ordinary experience to attract any but a special kind of thinker. Change and uncertainty are everywhere too obvious. Furthermore, the clashes between different points of view remain too obviously unresolved for any doctrine, whether of static being or of change, to remain unchallenged. The result is that ordinary doubts develop into relativism and skepticism, whose partisans speak in this chapter along with their special enemy, Plato.

A word on the two terms I have just used: The relativist, who claims that nothing can be understood except in relation to its context, is not the same as the skeptic, who says that nothing can be known without serious doubt. The one says: Each moral position can be philosophically justified in terms of the person or group that holds it. The other says: no moral position at all can be persuasively justified in any simply rational way. But relativism has most often abetted skepticism by showing that commonly held opinions are doubtful because they are merely relative—if there is no justification that is good everywhere, there is no justification that is good in general, so that anyone who is aware of this can suppose that skepticism has won its case. Historically, therefore, extreme relativism and extreme skepticism join, and they are opposed by their enemies as if they were a single evil meant to subvert tradition, decency, common sense, and philosophical understanding—a formidable sum of fears!

Here, in the present chapter, Mahavira and other early Jains teach a relativism of viewpoints and a synthesis of being and becoming, along with belief in the adequacy of the way in which they do so and belief in the truth, of course, of their religion. Protagoras represents relativism along with belief in progress and in the teachability of virtue. Gorgias represents the (verbally) immoderate skeptic or the revealer of the paradoxical potential of strictly philosophical language. Chuang-tzu, just as clever, is extremely relativistic and makes a sharp opposite to Plato, who is usually extremely opposed to relativism and skepticism. However, both philosophers, having learned to be discriminating about negation, make an extraordinary attempt to reconcile all the extremes.[1]

Mahavira (599–527 B.C.E.): Viewpoints, Maybes, Qualifications

Jainism is named after the twenty-four "conquerors" or *jinas* in whom tradition sees the origin of this religion.[2] The last of the *jinas*, the surely historical personage and founder or, perhaps, reviver of Jainism, is Mahavira, a title meaning Great Hero. Mahavira's life overlaps that of the Buddha, and much in their careers and religion is parallel. As in the story of the

Buddha, it is foretold that Mahavira will be either a universal monarch or an all-knowing saint. Like the Buddha, Mahavira finds his way essentially alone. His parents having died, at the age of thirty he gives away all he owns and becomes an ascetic. During his twelve years as a naked wanderer, the privations he inflicts on himself are sharpened by those inflicted by other human beings and by nature. He never loses patience or gives in to hatred but, like a hero in battle, withstands everything. He meets and for six years is friendly with the ascetic Gosala, founder of the Ajivikas, an ascetic and deterministic sect; but the friendship turns to hatred. One summer night on the banks of the river Rujipalika, after twelve years, six months, and fifteen days of his ascetic search, when he is forty-two years old, Mahavira meditates and reaches a state of complete enlightenment. He is now omniscient, a *jina*, with perfect knowledge of what he has known imperfectly before. For the next thirty years he preaches his doctrine. He meets the same kings as the Buddha, but never the Buddha himself, and the Buddha, we know, condemns his teachings.[3]

Like the Buddha, Mahavira puts great emphasis on suffering. Suffering, he says, is the result of the bondage caused by ignorance, and ignorance is the desire that attaches humans to sensuous things. Human beings, so he preaches, should learn to be free from emotion and desire and should practice noninjury. In injuring others, he teaches, one injures oneself: "You yourself are the (being) which you intend to kill; you yourself are the (being) which you intend to ill-use; you yourself are the (being) which you intend to insult."[4]

Mahavira does not take the Buddhist way of meditation on the absence of self but of harsh penance—which, he believes, annihilates karma—and of self-restraint, equanimity, noninjury, and nonattachment. All these, he insists, break the tie between one's infinitely conscious "life" and the matter that obscures its knowledge and bliss and keeps it in bondage.[5]

For our present purpose, Jain philosophy is particularly interesting because of its advocacy of the doctrine of interrelatedness or *non-onesidedness* (*anekanta-vada*), which is largely made up of the doctrine of *viewpoints* (*nyaya-vada*) and the doctrine of *maybe* (*syad-vada*). These articulate the position that everything has innumerable aspects. Reality cannot be fully described from any one viewpoint, so that many views, each with its necessary qualification, are true at the same time.

Were these doctrines formulated by Mahavira himself? As in the case of the Buddha, it is not possible to distinguish between his own and his early followers' views. It is possible, however, to distinguish earlier from later sources and set aside any that were obviously elaborated much later.[6] Of Mahavira himself, we can be sure that, out of concern not to cause suffering, he refuses to force a truth on anyone because even this act results in suffering. A Jain monk is therefore forbidden to be careless and categorically assert or negate statements, and a wise man is enjoined to explain with the help of conditional expressions. Jainism is unusual in assuming that if someone thinks in a different way, there *must* be a plausible reason for the difference.

It follows that for Mahavira there are plausible reasons for opposite philosophical views. When asked by a disciple if the world is eternal, Mahavira answers yes, it is eternal—it has never ceased to exist, exists now, and will always exist—but it is also noneternal—it regresses, progresses, and regresses again in temporal cycles.[7] To the question whether the world is finite or infinite, Mahavira answers from four points of view. From the point of view of substance, he says, the world is one and, in this numerical sense, finite. From the standpoint of area, it is finite because, in keeping with the Jain cosmology, its length and breadth are known and its area can be calculated. From the standpoint of time, however, it is infinite because it has never ceased and will never cease to exist. And from the standpoint of modification, the world is infinite, that is, beyond numerical calculation, because it has countless modifications of color, smell, taste, touch, figure, heaviness, lightness, and other, formless modifications. Likewise the soul is both finite and infinite. It is finite because, being one, it is countable, and also because, by Jain belief, it has parts and a knowable size. But the soul is infinite because, by Jain belief, it is eternal and so has "infinite modifications of knowledge, infinite modifications of direct insight, infinite modifications of character, infinite modifications of formless quality. It has no end at all."[8]

It is evident that Mahavira practices what Buddha sometimes recommends: he separates an unanswerable because ambiguous question into several straightforward, answerable ones. In the examples above, it is clear that Mahavira is pointing out that to answer a question, one must know in what respect its terms are being used. To give another example from Mahavira's conversation, when asked if the soul is identical with the body, he answers: It is identical in that it suffers from injuries to the body, but it is different in that it outlives the body. Changeable in one sense, it is static in another.[9] Once this is understood, it is possible to answer contentious philosophical questions both *yes* and *no*, with the provision that each answer is from a certain viewpoint. One viewpoint can be positive, another negative, and a third, both positive and negative.

According to the doctrine of *viewpoints* or *standpoints* (*nyaya-vada*), clearly formulated by about the second century A.D., there are five philosophical standpoints, which are: "the common person's view, generic view, practical view, linear view and literal view."[10]* The common person's view is inexact because, taking things from a remote conceptual distance, a person may see in a forest only wood—trees only as material for building or for fuel—or, looking from very close by, the person may see the forest in terms of the hole stumbled into, the forest becoming for the while a place in which one stumbles. Or, to give another, simpler interpretation, the common person's view is any statement that, in a rough and ready sense, can be understood but is vague. Or, the common person's view is inexact because it does not distinguish between the generic and the particular—when you see a bamboo or say *bamboo* you are probably not thinking of what exactly distinguishes bamboos (technically a variety of grass) from various kinds of trees or other tall plants.

The generic view collects various instances under a general heading. To give directions, it may be enough to say, "Turn when you get to the tree," without specifying which particular tree or kind of tree. By this view a particular city is considered only a collection of many buildings. Or, in an absolutist philosophy, the result may be the statement that "everything is only *being*."

The practical view concentrates on function and (says the old commentary) explains by the use of metaphors: these trees are a treasure (when cut and sold). The practical view was later understood as the practical complement of the general view, that is, as a particularizing standpoint: "I don't want a fruit. I want a mango."

The linear ("straight thread") view takes as real only what exists here and now, what a thing is at the moment. A thing's past and future modes are not considered real. While the old commentary does not say so, this would be the view ascribed to the usual Buddhist analysis.

The fifth, verbal or literal view, takes words at their face value and assumes that their particular meaning signifies what is real:

> Even changing the gender, number, word-ending or tense of a word is thought to change its meaning and, therefore, to change the object to which it refers. So it is not appropriate to use words in different genders, number etc., to refer to the same object or event.[11]

---

*These are the words of the Jain thinker Umasvati, probably of the second century A.D. He is held in reverence by both of the two Jain sects, the Shvetambara and the Digambara, but their received texts of Umasvati are somewhat different. A variant of this sutra (set of aphorisms) adds two standpoints, the etymological view and the actuality view, making a total of seven, which is the number accepted by the developed Jain tradition. The five-view variant seems the more ancient. (See the translator's introduction to Umasvati, *Tattvārtha Sūtra*, p. xxiii, and his remark on p. 27.)

Likewise, two words with different etymological origins cannot mean exactly the same thing. Every word has only one meaning and every meaning only one word that fits it; there are no absolute synonyms.*

I am not sure that I have not intruded late or foreign meanings into my explanations, but the idea that we see and refer to things from different viewpoints is in itself quite clear. The doctrine of viewpoints is a complement to that of *maybe* or *in a sense (yes) (syad-vada)*.[12] Perhaps the first Jain to put the doctrine of *in a sense* in a developed philosophical way is Kundakunda (fourth century C.E.). He uses the doctrine to solve the problem of being or permanence as against becoming or change. This he does by means of a synthesis of the two: A substance is anything with qualities and modifications that originates, persists, and decays without changing its "own-nature," its nature as *sat, being* (the discussion of Aristotle will return to a similar notion of substance). Whatever originates, says the philosopher, must be destroyed, and vice versa; but both processes are impossible unless something underlying them continues to exist.[13] As a commentator of Kundakunda explains, to make a pot, one destroys a lump of clay, but both the destruction and the origin are a persistence of clay substance. If not for this persistence, which connects and makes possible destruction and origination, the changes—the destruction of the clay, the origination of the pot—could not occur because they either would have no cause or have an absurd, illusory, nonexistent cause.[14] Therefore, as the Jains say—considering the relation between origin, destruction, and persistence—from one viewpoint, a thing *is*; from a second viewpoint, a thing *is not*; and from a third viewpoint, a thing *both is and*—in turn—*is not*. A further, more entertaining possibility is that, in contradiction to logic, a thing *is and*—simultaneously—*is not*, making it *indescribable*.[15]

To sum up in the words of a sixth-century Jain logician:

All the standpoints are right in their own respective spheres—
but if they are taken to be refutations, each of the other, then

---

*Since nouns are inflected in Sanskrit, the *king* in the sentence "The king *(raja)* sees the boy" can be said to have a different meaning than in the sentence "The boy sees the king *(rajanam)*." Furthermore, the king as he *was* is now nonexistent and therefore quite different from the king as he is. Time can change meanings also in the sense that a cook is literally a cook only when cooking, not when sleeping. Finally, when we refer to the king as *rajan* we refer to him as one who has the royal insignia, but when we refer to him as *bhupa* we refer to him as one who protects the earth. (See Matilal, *The Central Philosophy of Jainism*, pp. 45–46.)

The doctrine that there are no absolute synonyms is also held by the Greek sophist Prodicus, who takes care to distinguish between such terms as *esteem* and *praise, will* and *desire, doing* and *making*, and *fearless* and *brave*. (See Plato, *Protagoras* 337a and 340a, *Charmides* 163b, and *Laches* 197b.)

they are wrong. But a man who knows the "non-one-sided" nature of reality never says that a particular view is absolutely wrong.[16]

Chuang-tzu (4th c. B.C.E.):
Saying Says Something but Not Something Fixed

Writing during the second century B.C.E., the historian Ssu-ma Ch'ien tells us that Chuang-tzu was a native of Meng, that his personal name was Chou, and that he was employed in Lacquer Garden (either a garden or the city given its name).[17] The historian tells us that King Wei of Ch'u, who reigned from 339 to 329 B.C.E., was so impressed by Chuang-tzu's reputation that he invited him to become prime minister, but Chuang-tzu refused because the position was dangerous and because he preferred to follow his own inclinations: "His chief doctrines were founded upon the sayings of Lao Tzu . . . His literary and dialectical skill was such that the best scholars of the age were unable to refute his destructive criticism of the Confucian and Mohist schools."[18]

The kind of impression Chuang-tzu made on one of his disciples (how remote we cannot tell) can be gathered from an anecdote about his lack of political ambition: Finding him wearing a coarse, patched gown and shoes tied up with string, the King of Wei remarks that Chuang-tzu has fallen into a miserable state. No, says Chuang-tzu, not into a miserable state but into poverty and unlucky times. Haven't you seen how a monkey swings and frolics in the cedars, catalpas, and camphor trees? he asks. But when it's among prickly bushes and trees, he goes on, it moves cautiously and keeps looking aside and quivering in fear. It's not that its sinews have gone stiff, but the situation doesn't allow the monkey to show how agile it is. If I'd lived under a degenerate ruler and unscrupulous minsters, how could I avoid falling into a miserable state? The proof is that Pi-kan had his heart cut out by the tyrant Chou.[19]

The book named *Chuang-tzu* seems to have been compiled during the second century B.C.E., but the text as we now have it goes back to about 300 C.E., by which time many of its words were already obsolete. Since it represents a number of distinctly different positions, contains anecdotes describing Chuang-tzu in the third person, and ends with a survey of philosophy in which he is spoken of in the third person, it is an obviously composite book. In spite of Ssu-ma Ch'ien, who thinks that Chuang-tzu is a disciple of Lao Tzu, the pairing of the two in the same, Taoist school was relatively late. This is clear from the "inner chapters," written by Chuang-tzu himself, in which Lao Tzu is a minor figure, mentioned only twice.[20]

The original distance between the nebulous figure or figures of Lao Tzu and the rather more definite one of Chuang-tzu is of importance for the interpretation of Chuang Tzu's thought. This is because Chuang-tzu is often understood to believe in Lao Tzu's kind of ineffable "constant" *tao* (way, path, nature). Chuang-tzu does often speak of *tao,* but as usual in ancient Chinese, the text has neither the definite article *the* nor any indication of singular or plural, so it is only by a translator's decision that *tao* can be transformed into *the (one) tao,* or, alternatively, into the plural, *taos.* Such a choice signals a decisive turn in interpretation. It appears to me that, as a whole, the text of the inner chapters is more naturally taken not as a denial of surface appearances in favor of a single mystic reality, but as a subtly individual, skeptical—but incompletely skeptical—kind of relativism, with the relativistic/mystical refusal to see the world either as many or as one because, as Chuang-tzu holds, it is misleading to describe it numerically.*

The exposition of Chuang-tzu that follows is based largely on the book's second chapter, its most remarkable combination of poetry and abstract argument. The subject of the chapter is the spontaneous reciprocity of things, the falsifying of this reciprocity by unnatural, divisive distinctions, and the way in which relativism can equalize the distinctions that humans have tried to impose on nature. Chuang-tzu's relativism is one that favors the unprejudiced acceptance of *all* natural possibilities. What

---

*Chad Hansen, who favors an interpretation of Chuang-tzu that is not mystical or monistic but wholly relativistic, writes: "Dao [tao] remains a general term in the Zhuangzi [Chuang-tzu], not a singular one. The Zhuangzi contains references to great dao, extreme dao, mysterious dao, the ancient king's dao, its, his, or their dao, emperor's dao, human dao, human dao, the dao of governing, moral dao, the dao of long life, the master's dao, the dao you cannot (or do not) dao, the gentleman's dao, this dao, authentic dao, artificial dao, my dao, ancient dao, the Yellow Emperor's and Yao and Shun's dao, Shendao's dao, Confucius' dao, and Mozi's [Mo-tzu's] dao. He speaks of learning, hearing, saying, forgetting, having, lacking, losing, gaining, naming and daoing dao" (Hansen, A Daoist Theory of Chinese Thought, p. 268).

Hansen's interpretation, which is both radical and consistent, does not seem to me to fit the text well enough, but his insistence that tao is not a singular but a general term is in most instances hard to refute. In any case, since the language does not require Chuang-tzu to go beyond a general tao, unqualified by the, a, or any number, there is usually no reason for him to concern himself with a problem that English forces on the translator.

Hansen takes pleasure in the theory that he is the Utah-born reincarnation of Chuang-tzu. But since Chuang-tzu does not believe in any authority, he would not approve of deferring even to himself as an authoritative interpreter of his own thought. (See Hansen, A Daoist Theory of Chinese Thought, pp. x–xi.)

he argues against is artificiality, which he takes to include anything fixed in language, logic, morality, or vision of the world.

The chapter begins with the musings of one Tzu-ch'i of Nan-kuo. He is leaning on his armrest and looking up at the sky. He sighs vacantly. He has lost his counterpart—his companions, his wife, himself, who can tell? Someone there asks him what this condition of Tzu-ch'i can be. Can the body be made to be like withered wood and the heart/mind like dead ashes? The man leaning on the armrest is not the same as the one who was leaning on it before. Tzu-ch'i answers, I have lost myself. He is hearing, he says, the winds, the shouting whistling, screeching, moaning noises of nature, the pipes of Heaven. These are the sounds of the myriads of things that, unlike the pipes blown on by men, are allowed to be themselves. Who can their blower be? What were they all born from? Are they separate from myself? It seems that they have a true master, but we have no clues to it. There is something there, but it is without any form.[21]

This summary misses the great poetic exuberance of the original but serves to introduce two subjects, that of spontaneous, indeterminate mutuality, and that of the real and yet indeterminate meaning of words. The musing questions go on: Let me consider if anything rules myself, the body I am. Of its hundred joints, nine openings, and six organs, which are your kin, which your servants? Or are you equally pleased with them all? If so, maybe there is no one among them that can rule, or maybe they take turns being rulers and servants. Or maybe there is a true ruler among them. To look for one and not be able to identify him neither adds to nor detracts from his genuineness.[22]

The words that have been used, with their ruler-servant distinction, have not clarified anything. Well, words are not just a blowing of breath. Whoever uses words, says something with them. But what he means by them is not yet determined. Do they, in fact, say anything? Or are they useless attempts? If we take them to be different from the twitterings of fledglings, is there or is there not a clear distinction? The Confucians and Mohists argue: How can *tao* be hidden—there *are* distinctions between genuine and false. How can words be hidden—there *are* distinctions between *yes*—*that's it*—and *no*. How can *tao* go on and not be present? How can words be there and not be acceptable? But *tao* is hidden by petty formulations, words, by the show of glory. And so there are the *yes-no* distinctions of the Confucians and Mohists, who each say *yes* to the other's *no* and *no* to the other's *yes*. If we do want to contradict, to say *yes* to someone's *no* and *no* to *yes*, clarity, illumination, is needed.[23]*

As the sophist would say, everything can be seen from contrary viewpoints. There is nothing that cannot be said to be *that*—to be other— and nothing that cannot be affirmed to be *this*. *That* or *this*, whichever way you see something provokes the contrary way of seeing it. And so the negation of otherness comes out of affirmation—*that* comes from *this*— while *this*, affirmation, comes out of *that*. The *that-this* relation is explained by the theory of simultaneous births, the theory that opposites arise simultaneously. Births are simultaneously deaths, and deaths are simultaneously births.** Likewise, what is allowable from one standpoint is, from another, simultaneous standpoint, not allowable, and vice versa. Anything from any standpoint can be affirmed or denied of anything from another standpoint. Circumstances that lead to *yes*, affirmation, *that's it*, also lead to the opposite, *no*, negation. The sage, however, does not accept the simultaneous splitting of acts and positions into *this* and *that*, but illuminates them all by the light of Heaven, says both yes and yes and no to everything. Then every *this*-affirmation is also a *that*, and vice versa— neither is split away from the other and neither is simply affirmed or denied. The ideal condition in which neither *this* nor *that* holds, where

---

*To fall into the spirit of these paraphrases, it may help to take account of three simple but critical words, *pien, shih,* and *fei.* The word *pien* means *to argue alternatives, to dispute.* A cognate word, transliterated in the same way, means *to distinguish* or *to discriminate* in the sense of discoursing in a discriminating, rational way. In rational discourse, one distinguishes the correct alternative, *shih (this, is this, this-yes, yes)* from *fei (is not, no).* Applied to the ethical problems, those which most concern Chinese thinkers, *shih* and *fei* mean morally *right* and *wrong,* or *fitting* and *unfitting.* Given a different, more logical nuance, *shih* and *fei* mean *true* and *false,* or, as verbs, *to affirm* and *to deny.* To get beyond mere opinion, one tries "to hit right and wrong adequately." (See Roetz, "Validity in Chou Thought," pp. 85–86; Graham, *Disputers of the Tao,* p. 36; Wu, *The Butterfly as Companion,* p. 159.)

Of course, Chuang-tzu is answered in scornful kind. For example, the Confucian Hsün-tzu (3rd century B.C.E.) repays Chuang-tzu with the words, "Chuangtze was prejudiced towards Nature, and did not know man" (*The Works of Hsüntze,* trans. H. H. Dubs, London: Probsthain, 1928, p. 264 [book 21]).

**The last chapter of *Chuang-tzu* lists the paradoxes of the sophist Hui Shih. One of them is the following: "Simultaneously with being at noon the sun declines, simultaneously with being alive a thing dies." These and other paradoxes appear to depend on Hui Shih's use of the idea of the dimensionless point. If something ends at the same point at which something else begins, the ending and beginning are simultaneous, so life is simultaneous with death. The births and deaths of the text above are metaphors for all beginnings and ends. If they are also meant for literal births and deaths, these may be considered simultaneous because, at every stage of life, something of life vanishes, and so—from one point of view—life consists of constant small dyings away that culminate in a great one, which is itself, at one point, simultaneous with life. But this explanation is little more than a guess. (See A. C. Graham, *Later Mohist Logic, Ethics and Science,* Hong Kong: The Chinese University of Hong Kong, and London: School of Oriental and African Studies, 1978, pp. 58, 341.)

both join and there is no opposition, is called the pivot of *tao* (*tao shu*). This pivot is set in the midpoint of its circle—is it the world's circle?—so that the direction of the motion around it, now *yes*, now *no*, leaves the pivot just as it is. At the pivot, we find the illimitable state of the interdependence and mutuality of judgments and things.[24]

The distinctions made by reason and morality all lead to paradoxes. Where to begin? Try to think of any beginning: There is what begins. So there is also what-has-yet-to-begin of what begins. And so there is also what-has-yet-to-begin of what-has-yet-to-begin of what begins. The admission that there is what there is, implies that there is also what is not (not yet)—*something* implies *nothing*, which is the state of the (some)thing's absence but is also the potentiality for a something. This implies that there is what-has-yet-to-begin of what is not (yet). This implies that there is what-has-yet-to-begin of what-has-yet-to-begin of what is not (yet). (We've fallen into two infinite regresses, each of which implies the other, the one regress beginning with an actual beginning—a something—and what preceded it, and what preceded what preceded it, and so on, and the other regress beginning with what did not begin—a nothing—and what of the same nothing-kind preceded it and preceded what preceded it, and so on.) To continue: Suddenly, because we have *something*, we have *nothing*. But I do not know which of the two, something and nothing, is or is not (does *nothing* or a [possibly pregnant] absence or potentiality exist, or exist on a par with *something*?). And I do not know if, in referring, I have really referred to something or to nothing.[25]*

Begin again. Try now to think of the unity of things. It has been said (by the sophist Hui Shih) that heaven and earth count as one unity. True, the myriads of things and I together make one. Now that I have called them one, have I not said something? But by calling them *one*, have I not added the word *one* to the total one of things? And the one and the one make two, and the two and the first one make three; and so on, beyond

---

*To Chuang-tzu, as to other early Taoists, *nothing* is what we can take to be a positive concept. I have been careful to use *something* and *nothing* here rather than *existence* and *nonexistence*. The Chinese words in question are *yu* and *wu*. *Yu* means *have, there is, something;* and *exists, existence*. *Wu*, the opposite of *yu*, means *not to have, there is not, nothing;* and *nonexistence*. The dominant sense is that of having or not having, so *something* and *nothing* are often convenient translations. Chuang-tzu's *nothing* is not nonexistence in the Western sense but is potentially something. *Yu* meaning *nothing* describes what is limited or imperfect; when *tao* is said to be nothing, it is the nothing that precedes the distinction between something and nothing. That is, the whole, out of which everything comes, is indeterminate and limitless, neither something nor nothing. When the void (nothing) is added to something, there still remains what-has-yet-to-begin-to-be. But serious metaphysical arguments over *yu* and *wu* are considerably later than the present text, the paradoxical force of which may depend on the plasticity of the terms *wu* and *yu*. (See Graham, *Chuang-tzu*, note pp. 52–53; and *Disputers of the Tao*, pp. 410–11. Wu, in *The Butterfly as Companion*, objects [note, p. 164] and uses *existence* and *nonexistence* freely.)

what a skilled calculator, let alone an ordinary person, is able to sum up.[26] Altogether, those who distinguish between alternatives leave out what is not included in either alternative. The sage embraces them all without discrimination; most people make the distinctions. And so I say that to make distinctions is to fail to see something.[27]

Who knows what's right? People who sleep in the damp get backaches and paralysis, but do eels? People up in trees tremble and draw back with fear, but do monkeys? People eat animals that feed on hay or grain, deer eat grass, centipedes relish snakes, and owls and crows crave mice. Baboons mate with gibbons, bucks go with does, eels roam with fish. Mao Ch'iang and Lady Li were admired by people as beauties, but fish that saw them plunged deep, birds that saw them flew high, and bucks and does that saw them leaped away. Which of all these knows what is the right place to live, the right food to eat, and the right kind of beauty? From my standpoint, the rules of benevolence and duty, the paths of approval and disapproval are tangled and confused. How can I understand the distinctions they make?[28]

Are we arguing? But arguments cannot really be settled. Suppose I argue with you and you win, are you really right and am I really wrong? And if I win, am I really right and you really wrong? Or is one of us right and one of us wrong? Or are both of us right or both of us wrong? And if I and you can't settle the argument between us, others will be equally in the dark. Who can tell us what is right? If the judge shares your opinion, how can he decide which opinion is right, and if he shares mine, how can he decide which is right? And if he shares both our opinions, how can he decide which is right? And if I, you, and another man can't arrive at a mutual understanding, can we find anyone else?[29]

Is anything really distinguishable from anything else? Can dreaming be distinguished from wakefulness? Once Chuang Chou—I myself— dreamed a butterfly. So flitting, flitting, he was a butterfly, visibly doing as it pleased, not aware of Chou. Suddenly, he awoke. Then he was utterly and completely Chou. But he does not know—did Chou dream the butterfly or the butterfly dream Chou. Chou and the butterfly—there must be a distinction. This is what is called the transformation of things.[30]

Chuang-tzu's dream story is less easy to interpret than it may seem at first.[31] It is possible to assume that the point of the story is that experience is so fluid, so easily transformative, that the attempt to make a strict division between butterfly and human and waking and dreaming only puts us into a dilemma—we cannot rationally decide exactly what we are or in which state. It is therefore wisest to escape the dilemma by enjoying the transformations without attempting to divide them from one another.

It is possible and, I think, preferable to go beyond this interpretation. The story concerns two very different creatures, a human and a butterfly, and two distinctly different states, of waking and of dreaming. The dreamer (in Chuang-tzu) thinks it/he is awake and does not reflect that it/he may be dreaming. Only the awakened human makes this reflection: To begin with, he is surely himself and awake, but then he reflects and becomes uncertain what he is and in what state. He cannot make the final separation, which is also perhaps one between the genuineness or solidity of waking experience and the illusiveness or nothingness of dreaming. The conclusion is not that the distinctions should be disregarded but that they should be accepted as inevitable, as part of the creative bounty of nature. The fact that only waking human beings are reflective does not tilt the balance in favor of being human and awake, because it is just this condition that raises the problem of identity and shows it to be insoluble. Chuang-tzu's solution is to accept everything without prejudice—varying identities, varying states, and reflective doubts—so that, in the end, he believes, there are only the many distinctions and spontaneous mutual transformations.

I am afraid that this interpretation, which fits the butterfly-dream well, does not fit a later passage, in which Chuang-tzu speaks of the great or ultimate awakening from the dream of life. He adds that Confucius (called, without respect, by his familiar name) is a dream and then tells his auditor, "I call you a 'dream'—I, too, am a dream."

Without himself undertaking to explain the mystery of dreams, Chuang-tzu says that once in a great while a sage appears who understands it.[32]

This passage, helpful to those who see Chuang-tzu as a full-fledged mystic, reflects his love—not unlike Plato's—for vividly metaphorical, mythlike stories. Chuang-tzu is not constructing a system and—again, not unlike Plato—may well have moved from one point of view to another without committing himself fully to any. However, all things considered, it appears most likely that Chuang-tzu does not (usually) object to distinctions as such. They cannot be avoided, and so, naturally, should not be avoided; they are the variety of life. But distinctions should never be allowed to rule and become exclusive.

Trying, always unsystematically, to express how we can think about things without lapsing into rigidity, Chuang-tzu uses such phrases as "lodging words" (yü yen), "weighty words" (chung yen), and "goblet words" (chih yen). To use "lodging words" is to "borrow a standpoint outside in order to sort a matter out," to "lodge" for a while at someone else's standpoint. When you adopt the other person's way of seeing things, he responds. In giving up your own position for the while, you put the responsibility for the standpoint on the other person. But lodging does not exclude weighting. One 'weights' what one says by giving it the weight of experience. The weightiest words are therefore those of a venerable teacher, though age alone is far from enough to grasp the root and branch of things. As for "goblet words," they are responses that remain spontaneous and adaptable. The name apparently comes from the kind of goblet that when too full tips over and then rights itself. To spill over in the sense of goblet words seems to be to speak in such natural words and with such spontaneous changes of meaning that no one is confused, because the meaning turns itself right side up as the words flow on naturally. It says most when it says least. Let the stream find its own channels.[33]

The last chapter of the *Chuang-tzu* book says that Chuang-tzu

> was not arrogant toward the myriad things. He did not make demands with a "That's it" and "That's not," and so he got along with conventional people . . . Above, he roamed with the maker of things; below, he made friends with those for whom life and death are externals and there is neither end nor beginning.[34]

Protagoras (485–410), Gorgias (483–376): Man Is the Measure of Everything, Words Capture Only Words

Plato, who emphasizes the negative connotations of the word *sophist*, sees them as mercenaries who sell their logical and rhetorical skills without caring for the truth.[35] According to Xenophon, Socrates called them prostitutes for selling their intellectual favors.[36] In Plato's *Sophist* there is a hunt for a definition of the sophist that makes him out to be the hired hunter of rich young men, the retail merchant of learning as soul nourishment, the athlete of specious debating, the (perhaps useful) purifier from conceits that block understanding, and the counterfeiter of philosophy. With all the elements of sophistry joined in comically miscellaneous definition, sophistry turns out to be

> the art of contradiction making, descended from an insincere kind of conceited mimicry, of the semblance-making breed, derived from image making, distinguished as a portion, not divine but human, of production, that presents a shadow play of words. (*Sophist*, 268c)[37]

The sophists are too free and freely contentious to accept Plato's fixed, eternal principles. Professional knowers and teachers, they come from all over Greece to Periclean Athens not to profit from philosophical truth but from rich clients and an active intellectual life. By Socrates' time, they are professional teachers who give a higher education to those who can afford to pay for it. This education furnishes information on many subjects, including the science of the times. It is particularly useful to those who are anxious to achieve success in the courtroom and in politics. Although, like Confucius and Mencius, the important Greek sophists have their retinues of students, they are less concerned, broadly speaking, to improve their character or increase their wisdom than to teach them the arts of persuasion. These arts include rhetoric and argument by antithesis, especially in what concerns politics and ethics. To this end, they teach how to analyze problems into their components, each of which can then be considered and dealt with separately, pro or con. Generalizations about the sophists are likely to be misleading because they are individuals, not to say, individualists, each with his own specialties. But their very presence serves to put old dogmas and ways of conduct in question.

Much the most famous sophist is Protagoras of the city of Abdera. He appears to be close to Pericles, who chooses him to write the code of laws for the Athenian colony of Thurii. In Plato's dialogue named after him, he is treated humorously but with respect, even affection. An arguer by profession, Protagoras claims the ability to make the weaker argument the stronger. According to Aristotle, Protagoras holds that contradictory statements about the same thing are true, and that it is possible either to assert or deny something of every subject (*Metaphysics* 1007b18). It is in keeping with this position that Protagoras' lost work *On the Gods* began, we are told, with words that led the Athenians to banish him and burn his books.* The possibly fateful words are: "Concerning the gods I cannot know either that they exist or that they do not exist, or what form they might have, for there is much to prevent one's knowing: the obscurity of the subject and the shortness of man's life."[38]

---

*Diogenes Laertius (9.52) reports that because of the introduction to Protagoras' book, saying that the existence of the gods was unknowable, the Athenians expelled him, had a herald collect all the copies of his works, and burned them in the marketplace. Philostratus also reports (*Lives of the Sophists* 1.10) that the Athenians banished Protagoras. But according to Sextus Empiricus (9.55–56), the Athenians voted the death penalty, after which Protagoras fled and then died at sea. Hard as it is to ignore these reports, it seems strange that Plato can know of such drastic punishments, openly debated and voted on, and yet have Socrates state in the *Meno* (91e–92a) that during Protagoras' forty years of practice as a sophist and up to the present—a dramatic date of about 402 B.C.E.—his reputation has been consistently high. This is not to deny that Aristophanes' *Clouds* and other evidence shows that conservatives felt menaced by the views of both philosophers and sophists, not a few of whom compounded their philosophically unsettling radicalism by their sinfully foreign birth. (See Burkert, "Athenian Cults and Festivals," pp. 246–48, and Ostwald, "Athens as a Cultural Centre," pp. 367–69.)

Protagoras' lasting impression on European philosophy comes from the statement, as reported by Plato, that "of all things man is the measure, of things that are that they are, and of things that are not that they are not." To give an example, the same wind seems cold to one person and not to the other. Because the degree of cold appears different to each person and because appearance and perception are the same, everything that appears to anyone is real in relation to him. In other words, reality is determined individually.[39]* Plato's Socrates asks: If this is so, by what evidence can he and his partner in discussion be sure they are awake rather than asleep and dreaming the conversation in which they are engaged?[40] If it is the individual's experience that determines reality, Socrates continues, why did Protagoras not say that the measure of all things is the pig or the baboon? Why did we stand in awe of him if, in fact, he was no more intelligent than other men or even a tadpole?

Speaking in Protagoras' name, Socrates answers: A wise man is one who can change someone to whom bad appears. The doctor cures the sick man to whom food is distasteful. In the same way, the sophist uses his discourse to change someone's state that is, for that person, depraved, unsound, or sickly to a sound, healthy state. The difference is not one between falsehood and truth but between worse and better.[41]

Gorgias, a native of Leontini in Sicily, travelled a great deal, but often stayed in Athens. He died at the notable age of at least one hundred and five (of the philosophers dealt with in this book, only Hsün Tzu comes near to competing with him in longevity). He was admired for his rhetorical and sophistical skills, which earned him high fees—under the influence of rhetoric, he claims, all are made slaves not by force but willingly.[42] With rhetorical emphasis, he praises the powers of speech and says:

> The effect of speech on the condition of the soul is comparable to the power of drugs over the nature of bodies. For just as different drugs dispel different secretions from the body, and

---

*Protagoras was later charged with contending, in effect, that the wind is both cold and warm, each person perceiving one of the two coexisting contradictory qualities. The charge rests on his saying "that the reasons [logoi] of all appearances are present in the matter, so that the matter is capable, as far as lies in its own power, of being everything that appears to everybody. For the man whose condition is natural grasps, out of what is contained in matter, what can appear to those in a natural condition, whereas the man whose condition is not natural grasps what can appear to those in his condition" (Sextus Empiricus, Outlines of Pyrrhonism 1.216; trans. Sprague, ed., The Older Sophists, p. 11). Both Democritus and Plato object to Protagoras' relativism on the ground that he is bound by his doctrine to admit that if every person's opinion is true for that person, then those who hold that Protagoras is wrong are right for themselves (Theaetetus 171a). (See Kerferd, The Sophistic Movement, pp. 107–109.)

some bring an end to disease and others to life, so also in the case of speeches, some distress, others delight, some cause fear, others make the hearers bold, and some drug and bewitch the soul with a kind of evil persuasion.[43]

Gorgias teaches the habit, Plato says, of answering any question in a fearless, confident style. "For he offers himself for questioning to any Greek who wishes, on any subject he pleases, and there is no one he does not answer."[44] Not all Athenians admired him. A line in Aristophanes—no lover of intellectuals—names Gorgias as one of the rascally race of sycophants who live by their tongues and who, when sacrificed anywhere in Attica, have their tongues cut out.[45]

In addition to various orations, some on political matters, Gorgias wrote a book called *On the Nonexistent or On Nature*. A surviving fragment of this book is the most sustained example we have of the technically exact reasoning of the sophists of the time. In this fragment Gorgias says that the truth concerning the real world cannot be transmitted by words (or thoughts, or reasonings, as *logoi* may be translated). This, he says, is because words can never *be* the reality they appear to capture about the world. The purpose of his argument is not self-evident.* It seems to me that it is intended to display the power of tricky logic to force assent to even absurd conclusions. I say this because it appears immediately self-refuting to argue in order to persuade others that arguments cannot be conveyed from one person to another—Gorgias says elsewhere that skill in *logoi* can be used in a good cause. But since Gorgias' reasoning is apparently meant to show that a Parmenidean kind of logic of *it is* and *it is not* is self-refuting, the idea that tricky logic can be led absurd conclusions is an example of the very point he is trying to make. In any case,

---

*One question is whether or not the argument takes the verb *to be* in a purely existential or in a predicative sense. Unfortunately for us, in Parmenides and even Gorgias it may retain something of both senses. A closely related question is whether the argument is about the reality represented by the verb or about the difficulties involved in the verb's use. If it is about the reality, the argument may be a reduction to absurdity of ontological pronouncements like those made by Parmenides. But if the argument is about predication, then Gorgias "is arguing that there is no way in which the verb 'to be' can be applied to a subject without contradictions arising and he is thinking primarily of statements about phenomena." On this interpretation of Parmenides' argument, the contradictions he and the other Eleatics identify in the use of negative statements are extended by Gorgias to positive statements as well. (See Kerferd, *The Sophistic Movement*, p. 96.)

Since I see no way by which to decide between the interpretations, I adopt what seems to me to be the simplest hypothesis: The argument is, at once, about the verb *to be* and the reality it represents. What it demonstrates is that, when used by a sophisticated enough sophist, logical, especially Eleatic language can be led to absurd conclusions.

his arguments, patterned on Parmenides-like antitheses, create a logical mechanism, often borrowed by subsequent skeptics, for putting causation into doubt.

According to Gorgias' argument, which will be quoted later, nothing really exists. Having demonstrated this radical thesis to his own satisfaction, or enough for the sophistical purpose of his argument, he goes on to reason that even if anything exists, it cannot be known by thought, and if it can be known by thought, what is known cannot be transmitted to anyone else. In complete contradiction to common sense, Gorgias argues so: It is our eyes that determine what is visible; we do not deny the existence of visible things because we do not hear them. By analogy, if thought, like vision and hearing, was its own criterion for existence, everything we think should be known to exist simply because it is thought. But this is absurd because we think of many impossible things. Therefore the testimony of thought cannot have the veridical force of that of the senses; and we must conclude that whatever, for the sake of argument, we assumed to exist cannot be grasped by thought.

Gorgias ends his argument by contending that even if anything exists and is grasped by thought, it cannot be communicated. The reason is that if we assume that there are externally existing objects of vision, hearing, and the senses in general, the visible things among them are apprehended by vision, not hearing, and the audible ones by hearing, not vision. How, then, can things seen or heard be revealed to another person? After all, the means by which we believe we reveal them is *logos*, which is speech or thought; but *logos* is not the same as the existing things it is supposed to reveal. Actually, therefore, we reveal to others not external existing things, but only *logos* (speech or thought), which is quite different from them; for just as visible things cannot become audible, so the assumed external things cannot become our *logos*; and because they are not *logos*, they cannot be revealed to another person.[46]

I cut Gorgias' argument short to summarize it: Each sense is the unique medium for what it alone can convey. In other words, each sense is unlike any other sense and is unable to convey what any other sense conveys. The medium of words, too, is unique and is different from that of any of the senses, which alone convey external reality—speech or thought cannot convey what the senses do. One kind of speech may be better than another, but speech is unable to convey external reality because it cannot *be* that reality. To convey external things, words or thoughts would have to correspond with them, or be the same as they are, or, briefly, to *be* them. But this is impossible, for words or thoughts are too different from things, so what *is* cannot be thought or expressed. Parmenides had identified being, thinking, and saying. Now Gorgias separates them by making them radically and paradoxically incompatible with one another.

Plato (428–348 B.C.E.): The Friend, the Critic, and the Reconciler of Ideas[47]

There is a group of old stories that assign Plato, like the Buddha, a miraculous birth. In Plato's case it is said to be by the agency of Apollo and, some versions say, by way of a dream (Christian authors claim that this story shows that there were instances of virgin birth in ancient Greece). As an omen of future eloquence, bees left honey on the infant Plato's lips.[48] A more credible story tells that young Plato first intended to write tragedies, but on his way to enter his tragedy in a competition, he heard Socrates and threw his play into the fire.[49] From that time on, the story says, Plato, then twenty years old, was Socrates' pupil. The story may remind us that, to Plato, writing is a problematic. Socrates wrote nothing, but Plato, who wrote a good deal, retains a suspicion of written words because, as Socrates says in a dialogue, these words talk as if they were intelligent, but if you ask books anything about what they have said, they just repeat themselves. Writing, which is indiscriminate and gets unfairly treated, needs a parent to come to its help; so writing is not really serious but a pastime good for memories in one's old age. Better to select a person of the right kind, says the Socrates who is Plato, and by dialectics sow words based on knowledge and able to defend themselves and lead on to blessedness. At best, writing is a way of reminding those who already know the truth that the only serious lessons on justice, honor, and goodness are those written in the soul of the listener.[50]

Such words may explain why Plato never writes any system but always varying dialogues in which—after the first, Socratically indecisive ones—a teacher and a disciple usually find their dialectical way toward a truth of the sort that may well vanish when written down. Speaking of himself in the third person, Plato is careful to mention that he was present at Socrates' trial and, again, that he was not present at Socrates' death— reporting on the event, Phaedo says that he thinks that Plato was ill at the time.[51] But Plato does not otherwise participate as a character in the dialogues he writes and we can be sure of little about his own preferences except that they change as the characters he invents or half-invents talk themselves into as close an imitation of true dialectical conversation as one can arrive at in written-down philosophy. Therefore we cannot summarize Plato's system of philosophy—no such system exists in the dialogues taken as a whole—but only note how his preoccupations change with each different cast of characters and how the writer Plato shifts from comedies of philosophical ignorance to dialectical dramas favoring the hypothesis of Ideas, immortal souls, virtue as harmony, and a universe ruled by justice. As Plato grows older, the problems and solutions he deals with grow more complex, the expositions grow more technical, and the favorite hypothesis, that of Ideas, is subjected to sharp criticism though never abandoned. Aristotle at one point speaks of the account Plato gives in his so-called unwritten teaching, and Aristotle is reported to have said that Plato lectured on the one Good.* There is no reason to doubt this report; but the unwritten teaching, whatever it was, cannot be reconstructed from anything so vague. Besides, there is no good reason to suppose that Plato considered his unwritten teaching more important than his dialogues, or that his unwritten views were more fixed than those that his dialogues teach.[52] He remains a creator who speaks through always different situations and voices.

If any conception can be singled out as Plato's almost constant philosophical preoccupation and heritage, it is that of the Idea or Form. In Greek, the terms *eidos* and *idea* mean *appearance, shape,* or *form,* and take on the additional meaning of *characteristic property* or *type*.[53] As I have said, Aristotle explains that Plato was attracted in his youth to the radically Heraclitean doctrine of Cratylus that everything sensible is always in flux and cannot really be known. Having accepted Socrates' belief in the universal—the general definition—in ethical matters, Plato applied the belief more widely. He claimed, says Aristotle, that because sensible things were always changing, general definitions can only be of something else, which he called Ideas. He said that sensible things are named and given their identities by means of their relation to the Ideas, a relation he called *participation*. Unlike Socrates, Plato and the Platonists give their universals or general definitions a separate existence.[54]

The separating off of certain general ideas into a realm of their own was not a new philosophical practice because the Pythagoreans had already separated off numbers from everything physical. That is, they had equated numbers with geometrical shapes and musical intervals and considered the numbers to be either actual (though nonphysical) constituents of nature or laws of relationship imported into nature. Put very freely in

---

*The report is by Aristoxenus, who says that Aristotle used it to show that a lecturer should, unlike Plato, preface his lecture so as make his audience receptive to what follows. "Themistius reports the anecdote to illustrate the point that the true philosopher does not seek public acclaim and that his discourse has the same force whether delivered to a crowd or in solitude . . . Simplicius also makes mention of the lecture on the Good and reports that Xenocrates, Speusippus, Aristotle, Heracleides, Hestaiaios, and others were present and wrote up the notes that they took during the lecture" (Reginos, *Platonica*, p. 125).

the latter sense, the Pythagoreans' basic notion is that there are numbers in themselves—say two, four, and six, or better, the abstract natures *twoness*, *fourness*, and *sixness*, and so on, of numbers in themselves. These abstract essences are, each one alone and in relation to the others, so perfectly exact and so completely unaffected by time and place—they neither age, break, nor vary from one locale to another—that they must be regarded as quite different from physical objects. Physical objects have numerical qualities, a definite number and numerically specifiable size, weight, and so on. But physical objects are also invariably subject to aging, breakage, and inexactness and have none of the purity of numbers in themselves. The physical objects' numerical qualities and relationships cannot come from the objects themselves but must depend on the qualities we know exactly in numbers in themselves, the nature of which is, so to speak, imported into or shared by material objects. Nature is discovered to obey, so to speak, the immaterial, absolute laws of mathematics. Therefore the Pythagoreans say, as Aristotle reports, "that things themselves are numbers," or, more conformably to the account I have been giving, that existing things owe their being to the imitation of numbers.[55]

In his dialogues, Plato compares or identifies an Idea (a Form) with a plan or model, or with a number or ideal geometrical shape. An Idea is like the plan by which, for instance, a house is made. More exactly, it is the eternal model (*paradeigma*) of which the physical object (the *aistheton*) is a kind of copy (*eikon*). In the *Timaeus*, Plato thinks of the world as the work of a god-craftsman who makes everything from Ideas, which he uses as plans for universal creation. Like mathematical objects such as numbers or ideal geometrical shapes, the Ideas are in no place and not subject to time, even though all physically existing things are copies of them and "participate" in them. Sensible objects are always changing, fluctuating, impermanent. Knowledge, on the contrary, has to be stable in order to be knowledge at all; if its very nature would change as a physical change was taking place, there would be no knowledge because there would be no stable person to know and nothing stable enough to be known: "If that which knows [the soul] and that which is known [the Idea, the Form] exist forever, and the beautiful and the good and every other thing also exist, then I do not think that they can resemble a process of flux (*Cratylus* 440b)."[56]

Of course, an Idea is not the same as that to which it lends itself. To give one kind of example (reminiscent of but contrary to Uddalaka's doctrine), heat and fire are not the same, nor are cold and snow, but fire can never as such admit cold nor snow heat, so that the name of the Idea is always attached as a distinguishing characteristic to whatever always has the Idea.

The Ideas are grasped by reason. Human beings come to know them by bringing dispersed particulars under a Form—for example, the many instances of love under the Form of Love—and, by means of this ability to collect like instances, they see what belongs together and learn to be clear and consistent in their thought. Because a comprehensive Idea contains others of narrower scope, the philosopher divides the comprehensive Idea according to its "natural joints" until a contained Idea has been divided off clearly (*Phaedrus* 265d–e). This method of collection and division, to which Plato gives the name *dialectic*, is the germ of the notion of scientific classification.

Plato needs and tries out hierarchical schemes of Ideas. In the *Republic*, the Good is the highest, in the *Symposium*, the Beautiful, and in the *Parmenides*, the One. In the *Sophist*, to which I will return, he takes up the problem of how the Ideas are related to one another. This problem may be dramatized as that of the celestial architect who has to decide which Ideas are needed to make a world, and once he has chosen them, how to combine or blend them, all without violating the laws of logic, which are those of possibility. Plato takes on quite a job and, being no demiurgos, is not up to it; but for a merely human being, his efforts are quite remarkable.

Actually, in creating and recreating his hypothesis of Ideas, Plato becomes quite aware of its difficulties. He exposes these in the *Parmenides*, in which a young, hesitant Socrates defends the hypothesis in a discussion with Zeno, Parmenides' disciple, and then, more searchingly, with Parmenides himself. In Plato's sense of the word, Parmenides' critique is a dialectical one, that is, it considers the Ideas from one viewpoint, another, and then another, testing each viewpoint for weaknesses and venturing cures until a tentative solution emerges. As logical laws are applied to test the hypothesis, Socrates falters. Sometimes Parmenides puts in a positive, helpful word, and in the end he lays the failure of the arguments in favor of Ideas to Socrates' youth—to defend Ideas, he says, one has to have both wide experience and natural ability. Parmenides even adds that if someone denies that there are Ideas of existing things—a character for each single thing—he is denying the necessary sense of a thing's sameness with itself and "will utterly destroy the power and significance of thought and discourse" (135c).[57] So while the hypothesis of Ideas has been shown to be subject to various dilemmas, it seems to be assumed that they can be overcome.

I abbreviate all this argument between Zeno, Parmenides, and Socrates but retain its very simple vocabulary and its characteristic transitions. To begin at the argument's beginning: Speaking for Parmenides, Zeno defends his teacher's belief in absolute unity by saying that things cannot be many because, if they were, they would be both like and unlike one another, and this is a logical absurdity. True to Parmenides' radical way of arguing, Zeno identifies the logical characteristics of likeness and unlikeness with the whole nature of objects that are alike (in being identical with themselves) and unlike (in being unlike other objects). Zeno points out that an object cannot suffer the coexistence in itself of sameness and difference.

Socrates answers by distinguishing sharply between the logical characteristics in themselves, that is, the Ideas, and the objects that share in them: Opposite Ideas—heat and cold, equality and inequality—cannot qualify one another, but they can simultaneously qualify sensible objects. In this vein, Socrates answers Zeno that the difficulty is solved if there are two separate and different Ideas, one of likeness and another of unlikeness, of which things get certain shares, so that some could be both like and unlike. The Ideas suffer no change—one and many are always what they are—but I, Socrates, am one and many, with a right side, a left side, a front, a back, and so on, so that I, who am one by being Socrates, am also many (127d–130a).[58]

Parmenides enters the discussion and says that Socrates separates characteristics, such as the Just, the Beautiful, and the Good, from the things that share them. What, he asks, about Man, or Fire, or Water (Uddalaka would accept these Ideas, though his *names* are not identical with Ideas).

Socrates says he is perplexed about these possible Ideas; and he gives the same answer to the following question if there are separate Ideas of ridiculous things such as hair, mud, and dirt (130a–131a).

Parmenides then asks if each thing that gets a share of an Idea gets a share of the whole Idea or gets only a part of it. How, he asks, can the same one thing—the Idea—be wholly present in many things and there-fore separate from itself? What can sharing be if the sharing is of a kind that does not diminish what is shared, as it would have to diminish it if what was shared was either the whole Idea or a part of it? If we share in the Idea at all, what is left of it for itself? If anything shares in a part, that part is unique to what shares it and is unlike other parts in other things that share the particular Idea. But if participation is neither in the whole Idea nor in part of it, in what sense can there be participation at all? If things did participate in the whole of an Idea, the Idea would be separated from itself.

Socrates answers: The Idea could be like one and the same day, which is in many different places at once and yet not separate from itself (131a–c). But, asks Parmenides, can such an Idea as largeness in itself be divided into parts that are larger and smaller? And what about something being given a small part of the equal? Will it be equal to anything by means of a share of equality that is less than equality itself? And if a small object gets a share of smallness, will the addition of the smallness make it smaller than it was? And what about the pluralizing of every Idea? asks Parmenides. For example: If largeness is large as are the large things that share in it, then the likeness between largeness in itself and something that is large is still another largeness, and so largenesses will multiply without end (131d–132b).

Socrates answers: But what if each of the Ideas is a thought that exists nowhere but in minds, so it can remain one and not be multiplied?

No, says Parmenides, the thought has to be *of* something known to exist, which is not merely a thought, and to be common to a number of things, and it is this common nature that is the Idea. Furthermore, if the Idea is a thought, because it is the same Idea all over, whatever is composed of thoughts must be purely thought, nothing else (132b–c).

Socrates answers: But still, Parmenides, the Ideas are paradigms fixed in the nature of things that things resemble.

But then, Parmenides answers Socrates, if the likeness that is in us is different from likeness in itself, there will be likenesses of likeness without end: there will be the Idea, Likeness; there will be the things that are like each other; and there will be the likeness in the things that are like each other. Parmenides adds: The greatest of the difficulties is this, that the relations between the Ideas are confined to one another and therefore are not the same as the relations among ourselves, including such relations as are supposed to be gained from sharing in the Ideas. A slave is the slave of his master, not of the Idea of Master, any more than the master is master of the Idea of Slave. So Ideas such as Beauty in itself and the Good in itself are unknowable for us. Persons are related to persons and objects, while Ideas are related to Ideas. So if Ideas are what we take them to be, they are unknowable to us because they pertain to the absolute truth, not to the truth as we know it in our world, which is relative only to the things that exist in our world. Only the god has exact enough knowledge to know the Ideas. But what the god knows is not the same as knowledge among us, so knowledge in the god's world and knowledge in our world are separate, strangely enough (132d–134d).

Parmenides' conclusion is that Socrates has a noble, even divine impulse toward argument but has undertaken to mark off Ideas too soon, before he has been properly trained (135d). Parmenides is begged by those present to play what he calls the "laborious game" of hypothesizing and show them what proper training is like. He proposes to begin with his own hypothesis about the one and what must follow if one is or one is not (136a–137b). Parmenides' training exercises—the source of wisdom to the Neoplatonists but a matter for endless, inconclusive debates among modern interpreters—do not concern us here.

In the *Sophist* and other late dialogues, Plato takes up the difficulties shown in the *Parmenides* and tries to fit Ideas to one another and to the world more plausibly. In the *Sophist*, he works out a scheme to show how Ideas can participate in and exclude one another, and how such relations and nonrelations between Ideas are reflected in the world of phenomena. According to Plato's scheme, a set of very general Ideas dominates the rest, and Ideas are made up of interwoven elements (remember Uddalaka's much simpler formulation).

Taking on the guise of an Eleatic Stranger, Plato says: Some of the Ideas (now called Kinds) combine with one another, and some do not combine; and some combine with a few others and some with many; and some pervade all. Movement and Rest, for example, are incompatible with one another—if combined, Movement would come to a standstill and Rest would be in movement (251c–252d). The Ideas combine or not just as the letters of the alphabet combine or not, the vowels being especially good for pervading the others. And just as the art of the musician is needed to understand which sounds can or cannot be blended, a science is needed—that of dialectic or philosophy—to distinguish the different Kinds (Ideas) from one another and discover how one Kind unites many others or runs through and divides a Kind into other Ideas. Reality and the Ideas that together make it up, have a structure that philosophy can make clear (252e–254b).

The Stranger then establishes that there are five very important Kinds: Being (or Existence), Rest and Motion, and Sameness and Difference. It is hard to tell if by Motion the Stranger means physical motion alone or also the self-motion of life elsewhere attributed only to souls. Whatever he exactly means by the term, he says that Rest and Motion can never blend with one another because if they did, Motion would be at rest and Rest in motion; but both Rest and Motion surely *are*, so it is clear that Being blends with both. But though each blends with Being and also with Sameness, Being and Sameness are distinct—because while Rest and Motion both *are*, both exist, they are not the same as one another but distinguished by Difference. And so on (254d–255d).

One point more, having to do with the tricky matter of *is* and *is not*: The Eleatic Stranger says that each Idea clearly *is*; but since, by the nature of Difference, it is neither Being itself nor any Idea it is different from, every Idea not only *is* but also *is not*. Actually, even Being is not, meaning, is not any other Idea. Parmenides is therefore wrong in saying that that which *is* cannot not *be*. Why? Because in establishing that even Being is not, all that we establish is that it is different from other Ideas. When we say that something is not tall we mean that it is shorter than or equal to something else. In the same way, what is not beautiful is contrasted not with what does not exist but with what we take to be beautiful. When we say that something is not, we mean not that it does not exist at all but that it is different from whatever we are going to mention. So Father Parmenides is refuted (and Father Mencius, with his stress on the equivocality of words, is vindicated) (255e–259b).

Plato's changing doctrines show the difficulties a philosopher runs into in analyzing and judging the world by means of logic that is assumed to be identical with reality as such. At this point I stop my discussion of Plato, without venturing a contemporary analysis of the strengths and weaknesses of his theory of Ideas or of the arguments repeated from the *Parmenides*, which often have the sound of sophistry-by-antithesis but which Plato later often retains or tries to remedy. My excuse for stopping at this point is only that this is not primarily a book of critical analysis, and I have to stick fairly close to my job and not dissipate it in something else.*

Discussion

I begin with a memorandum consisting of brief, sometimes abbreviated quotations:

> Mahavira: The world is, Jamali, eternal . . . The world is, Jamali, non-eternal.[59]

> Samntabhadra (600 C.E.): A thing *is* existent—from a certain point of view. It is *non*-existent—from another point of view. It is *both* existent and non-existent *in turn*—from a third point of view. It is *indescribable* (simultaneously existent and non-existent)—from a fourth point of view. It *is* existent and *indescribable*—from a fifth point of view. It is *non*-existent and *indescribable*—from a sixth point of view. It is *both* existent and *non*-existent and *indescribable*—from a seventh point of view.[60]

---

*In a discussion of various interpretations of the *Sophist*, a scholar adopts what he calls "the indeterminacy position" meaning that there is no demonstrably true interpretation of past philosophical texts but only a range of "more and more plausible interpretations." I do not know if this scholar wants to imply that, in contrast with past texts, those of living philosophers are not subject to such indeterminacy. Could a resurrected Plato give a true interpretation of his own philosophy? Who, as Chuang-tzu would ask, would be the right judge of the demonstration— Plato would be prejudiced in his own favor—and what judge would be the right one to judge the judge to be right? (See Pelletier, *Parmenides, Plato, and the Semantics of Not-Being*, chap. 1 [p. 6 quoted].)

Chuang-tzu (and Hui Tzu): No thing is not "other," no thing is not "it"...Hence it is said: "'Other' comes out from 'it,' 'it' likewise goes by 'other,'" the opinion that 'it' and 'other' are born simultaneously. However, "Simultaneously with being alive one dies," and simultaneously with dying one is alive, and simultaneously with being allowable something becomes unallowable and simultaneously with being unallowable it becomes allowable. (chap. 2)[61]*

Protagoras: He said that of all things the measure is the man, meaning simply that what appears to each person also *is* positively the case. But once this is taken to be so, the same thing turns out both to be and not to be, and to be bad as well as good, not to mention the other opposites. (Aristotle, *Metaphysics* 11.6)[62]

Gorgias: The nonexistent does not exist; for if the nonexistent exists, it will both exist and not exist at the same time. Moreover, the existent does not exist either. For if the existent exists, it is either eternal or generated. If the existent is eternal, it does not have any beginning, and not having a beginning, it is without limit, and if it is without limit, it is nowhere. Moreover, neither can the existent be generated, for if it has come into being, it has to come either from the existent or the nonexistent. But if it is existent, it has not come to be, but already exists. (*On the Nonexistent or on Nature*).[63]

Plato: We have not merely shown that the things that are not, are, but we have brought to light the real character of "not-being." We have shown that the nature of the Different has existence and is parcelled out over the whole field of existent things with reference to one another; and of every part of it that

---

*The ambiguous brevity of the above translation represents the very terse original relatively well. A more expanded, less ambiguous translation reads: "Everything is 'that' in relation to other things and 'this' in relation to itself. We may not be able to see things from the standpoint of 'that,' but we can understand them from the standpoint of 'this.' Therefore, it may be said that 'that' derives from 'this' and that 'this' is dependent upon 'that.' Such is the notion of the cogenesis of 'this' and 'that.' Nonetheless, from the moment of birth death begins simultaneously, and from the moment of death birth begins simultaneously. Every affirmation is a denial of something else, and every denial is an affirmation of something else' (Mair's translation, p. 15).

I do not understand the "nonetheless" of the next-to-last sentence of this translation.

is set in contrast to "that which is" we have dared to say that precisely that is *really* "that which is not." (*Sophist* 258d–e)[64]

These philosophers play with negation as if it was the key to every room, lighted and dark, full and empty, in the home of *being*. Aided by negation, they study how concepts are related to one another, are related to everyday reality, and are related to human judgment. Their study requires them to answer whether or not philosophical concepts contradict what most people take their experience to be. Hence the clash between, on the one side, an objectivizing philosophy, which accepts changeless truth as the unperceived but sole reality, and, on the other side, relativistic and skeptical philosophies, which refuse to go beyond the rival values, disorder, and doubt they see everywhere. What Mahavira, Chuang-tzu, and Plato all learn from the clash is to use the term *nonexistence* to mean *other than*. But Plato by no means forgets the sense in which the nonexistent is impossible; Mahavira (or the Jains) understand self-contradiction both in the sense of the illusory and the inexpressible; and Chuang-tzu, who rejects the logical sense, plays with the others.

Of the philosophers discussed here, Protagoras and Chuang-tzu appear concerned less with relativism in general than with ethical and other forms of evaluation. While it is not certain if Protagoras means relativism to apply only to individual humans or also to humans as compared with other species, Chuang-tzu applies it happily to both individuals and species, and, going further than Protagoras, is his own kind of anarchist. Both he and (probably) Protagoras say that it is possible to assert and deny something of every subject, that is, that contradictories can both be true, a view that the later Jains include in their doctrine of viewpoints.

Compared with both Protagoras and Chuang-tzu, Gorgias, taken literally, is a skeptic who doubts the most elementary abilities of sensation, perception, conception, and learning. Taken less literally, he is demonstrating the impotence of a philosophically common kind of language. Taken literally, his intellectual tactic resembles that of Parmenides (and, later, Descartes) in that he conceives of sensory perception and of thought (put into words) as closed realms unable to make contact with each other (though Descartes, of course, allows thought to take extended things as its objects). That is, empirical abilities such as sensory perception and verbal thought are conceived almost as if they were logical contradictories such as (for him) *existence* and *nonexistence*—an approach that Plato criticizes in Parmenides and himself tries to escape. Or perhaps Gorgias too is demonstrating the need to escape.

Mahavira, or rather the typical Jain philosopher, has much of the relativist in him but is, at bottom, a refined absolutist because he insists that his particular understanding of relativity is quite correct; yet he suggests more than he allows himself to believe. Like the older Plato, Kundakunda tries to create a synthesis of abstractions that fits the problem of *being* and *becoming*. The Jains are engaged, after their own fashion, in the same work as the participants in Plato's *Sophist*. Freeing themselves from the tyranny of the logical *yes* or *no*, they join with the aging Plato and the ageless Chuang-tzu in learning how these antithetical terms can be applied at once to the same thing—from a certain standpoint.

Chuang-tzu bears at least some comparison with Socrates. Both of them are familiar with the paradox-breeding logic of sophists and both take advantage of this knowledge to combat the sophists. Socrates uses ordinary craftsmen as his favorite examples of people who, when confined to their trade, know exactly what they are doing. Chuang-tzu makes a similar choice, of a butcher, whose intuitively easy but exact work he describes in knowing detail, down to the need of the less expert to replace the knife that gets chipped because they lack intuitive dexterity.[65] Socrates speaks of his warning *daimon* (which, according to Xenophon, does more than warn), while, according to one translation, Chuang-tzu speaks of the "utmost man" as "daemonic"—the Chinese word is *shen, spirit*; another translation speaks of "the ultimately arrived man" as "spirit-filled."[66] In both cases, Greek and Chinese, the source is supposed to be mysterious, more than human, and beyond the reach of reason. The last and deepest resemblance is the frequency in both Socrates and Chuang-tzu of the persistent but unanswered question and the readiness, even eagerness, to profess ignorance.[67] It is Chuang-tzu who asks, "How do I know that what I call knowing is not ignorance? How do I know that what I call ignorance is not knowing?" And again—but in a question about ineffable *tao*—"Is it by not knowing that you know? Is it that if you do know you are ignorant? Who knows the knowing which is ignorance?"[68]

Now there is no doubt that Chuang-tzu is, if not a mystic, closer to mysticism than Socrates, who has such strong aspirations for rational knowledge. But both Chuang-tzu and Socrates have an unflinching readiness to proclaim their ignorance as itself an important kind of knowledge. The unfrightened ignorance of both in the face of death also seems psychologically akin to me. In the *Apology*, Socrates wonders if to die is like a dreamless sleep, which seems good to him, or like a journey to the place of the great dead, with whom he will be able converse. Then, as we cannot forget, come the last, defiant words to the jurors, "Who of us goes to the better is unclear to all but God." Chuang-tzu's question is: "How do I know that loving life is not a delusion? . . . How do I know that the dead do not wonder why they ever longed for life?"[69]

It seems to me that in both Socrates and Chuang-tzu this fearlessness reflects not some fixed, saving truth, but the certainty of a person who has thought and felt things through to the end that is possible to him:

the fear is conquered, or at least lessened, by the fearlessness of the attempt to understand or (for Chuang-tzu) to coincide with, and, as a result,
to give in to—or take pleasure or confidence in—what cannot be
understood.

Still, it cannot be pretended that Chuang-tzu and Socrates are very
much alike in their basic philosophical views, because the one is a relativist in morality and the other takes morality to be objective. In relation
to Plato, I should like to begin by saying the obvious, that Chuang-tzu, the
nearly complete relativist, and Plato, very often, it appears, the complete
absolutist, are opposites. Although Plato remains interested in the relativist's
arguments, he even plays with something like the idea of the rectification
of names, in his case, the idea that each segment of reality has exactly one
matching *logos,* and that names or words in general have an inherent
rightness.[70] Chuang-tzu detests such ideas. Yet there is something alike in
the two, an impulse not to be so consistently onesided as to miss what is
(in Chuang-tzu's case) sometimes steady or (in Plato's case) often changing.
On the balance, therefore, Chuang-tzu—without, he would say, conscious
effort—and Plato—with acknowledged conscious effort—are doing the
trickiest, most difficult intellectual work of all the philosophers who share
this chapter. Seen in perspective, their work is to create a reasonable
synthesis of relativism and skepticism with what is, in Plato's case, metaphysically fixed or, in Chuang-tzu's case, just stable enough to explain why
people can communicate and, with luck, chance, purpose, or intuition,
understand one another. Chuang-tzu's interest in alternatives and refusal
to decide between them, which, at least superficially, resembles the Socrates
of Plato's early dialogues, offers a challenge truly like Plato's: What is the
position, if any, with which he identifies himself?

As between Chuang-tzu (in my description) and Plato, I would choose
the former for subtlety, by which I mean the ability to come closer to the
abstraction-resisting qualities of human perception, thought, and conduct,
and Plato for power, achieved in his case by testing, that is, by internally
debating, far-reaching abstractions both separately and in different combinations. Is it incidental that both he and Chuang-tzu are richly imaginative
and think of philosophizing as a kind of play, which, to be serious, needs
the freedom to explore without any self-imposed limit? On changing,
playful impulses, they vary the characters that appear and vanish, the
themes that are taken up and dropped, and the literary modalities they
use, from logic chopping to more human talk, to metaphors, and to tales.
These impulses force the reader on into small whirlpools of contrariety
and abstraction and on again into the current of imagined talk, some
small, some big. But Chuang-tzu, unlike Plato, never turns stern; his often
happy, even rhapsodic kind of relativism is unique. To make fittingly odd

comparisons: I find something of a parallel for Chuang-tzu's human grotesques in Rabelais or Dickens, and, for the relativizing breadth of his sympathies, in Montaigne, and, maybe, for his unrestricted and ecstatic acceptance of everything natural, Walt Whitman—each of these, of course, far more profuse than Chuang-tzu, the original and the derived together. For his readiness to move with the natural wind and his insistence that everything be allowed to be itself, uncaged in alien rules and systems, he breaks through whatever bars may confine Chinese thinkers to their own great but only Middle Kingdom.

One last comparison, this one in mystical quality, something I would like to distinguish from mysticism in any formal sense: Like Uddalaka, Yajnavalkya, and Parmenides, Plato often requires us to reverse the commonsense identification of reality with what the senses show us. The four philosophers I have just named, especially Parmenides and Plato, are men with both highly poetic and highly logical minds, capable of inventing a poetically logical or logically poetic way of grasping the world and of distinguishing between the more and less real in it. They end in something that is at least close to a logically defended mysticism. The same can be said of Chuang-tzu, although his particular poetically logical sense draws him not at all to abstract principles and little to a ruling unity but to an unburdened naturalness, a radical freeing of self that drives him, too, in the direction of mysticism, in his case toward empathy with the unseen forces of nature, which are no different from ourselves because they are our immediate natures as well.

Chapter 5

✳

Early Rational Synthesis

Hsün-tzu, Aristotle

Theme: The Conceptual Integration of Cosmos,
Society, and Individual

Most of the philosophers so far discussed unify the world by reducing its intricacies to a single, sweeping, easily wielded idea. This process of what may be called disintrication draws attention by its ruthlessness. The philosopher's imposed simplicity accentuates how much has been sacrificed and stimulates others to invent concepts flexible enough to allow intricacy to return, though hardly enough to fit the world whose measure they are meant to take. Uddalaka, Yajnavalkya, and Parmenides each knows a truth so great that it overwhelms other possible truths (Heraclitus, who also speaks in sweeping truths, remains too enigmatic for me to put him confidently in the same disintricating company). And Confucius, Mencius, Buddha, and Socrates each have a method for salvation that rests on very nearly a single theme—that of Confucius and Mencius on the formation of a superior, reverent character, that of the Buddha on the cure of all pain by means of a studied, full dispassion, and that of Socrates on the disclosure of the nature of the virtues. Mahavira, Chuang-tzu, Protagoras, and Gorgias attack such single-minded certainties, Mahavira by his viewpoints, Chuang-tzu by his relativizing, Protagoras by his individualizing, and Gorgias by his parodic attack, using the philosophers' own methods, on all philosophical certainties. Plato attempts to integrate the human being into the world, but he is often held captive by the prejudice that there are no concepts by means of which change can be known. Both Hsün-tzu and Aristotle represent a moment in the development of tradition in which philosophers are able to get over their intoxication with powerful principles and abstractions. Conscious of the philosophers who preceded them, they are able to reach a more cautious, plausible balance. For this they have to take account of the individual, of society, and of the world that encompasses them. The systems of Hsün-tzu and Aristotle are early not only in time but in their unfinished quality. They show a sense of the whole and have concepts to connect concepts and form hierarchical relationships, but, considered structurally, their systems are unfinished. They change from occasion to occasion and not infrequently at least seem to contradict themselves. These flaws in system show that the philosophers are engaged not only in exhibiting but also in exploring the truth. But for whatever reasons, including the editorial hand of their students, the systematic thought of both philosophers leaves their systems more nearly potential than actual.*

It seems to me no accident that the tentative syntheses of Hsün-tzu and Aristotle are predominantly secular. Each of them seems to be living in a rare kind of hiatus between forms of belief that in one serious way or another disavow rationality, and so—because they avoid religious dogma, mysticism, and magic—they deserve the epithet *rational*. It quickly becomes obvious that Hsün-tzu's rationality, like that of the other pre-Buddhist Chinese, lacks a detailed equivalent to Aristotle's logic and science. The interest in comparing the two philosophers therefore lies in some of their general attitudes, in their views of language, in their ethical thought, and in their ability to create broad syntheses, however incompletely systematic, at an early stage of their traditions' development.

---

*Speaking of Aristotle's concern for system, a scholar says: "First, he constantly employs a whole framework or network of concepts, in terms of which he formulates the problems of a given field . . . And second, in working in any one domain he seems to carry with him a web of specific theory developed in other domains so that the ramifications of one part of knowledge on other parts of knowledge are always near the surface" (Edel, *Aristotle and His Philosophy*, p. 30). Another scholar says: "I do not suppose that the whole Corpus expresses a unified philosophical system; and in particular I have argued that Aristotle changes his mind on some fundamental issues about the nature of his arguments. None the less, I eventually suggest that his later works develop views that are connected enough to count as systematic" (Irwin, *Aristotle's First Principles*, pp. 471, 480).

Hsün-tzu (c. 310–c. 210 B.C.E.):
Goodness Is the Result of Conscious Activity.

Hsün-tzu lived during the aptly named Warring States period.[1] Its lack of stability and its endless hostilities explain why he so detested corrupt rulers and emphasized the need for a society made stable by inbred, ritually supported Confucian principles. As a Confucian, he believed that a ruler took on a responsibility that should be carried out in the spirit of the traditional founders of civilization, the virtuous sage-kings. By his mid-thirties, Hsün-tzu's reputation had earned him the title of "most eminent elder scholar" in the state academy of Ch'i.[2] It was no doubt his reputation as a scholar of political conduct that led to his invitation to several courts, notably that of Ch'in, whose great potential he was able to recognize. But the king of Ch'in rejected his advice that, to succeed, a ruler should rely not on the force of arms but on rectitude, particularly his own, and should nurture filial piety and human welfare. Although the king praised Hsün-tzu's advice with a polite "well argued," he took the opposite, warlike course, for a time with disconcerting success. It is not surprising that Hsün-tzu, unlike most Confucian thinkers, undertook to study the principles of war.[3]

Taught by the victory of the three armies that had united and succeeded in defeating Ch'in, Hsün-tzu argued that their success depended on true, intelligent loyalty rather than blind adherence to instructions. Such loyalty was needed, he realized, because there were no sage kings in his time; to be effective, political advisers would now have to learn the art by which to counter the mediocrity of actual rulers.[4] His own political fortunes varied as he was appointed, dismissed, and reappointed as a magistrate—reappointed in spite of his sardonic protest that a king (poor king!) is in so difficult a position that he deserves the pity even of a leper. He hoped to counter the linguistic and therefore moral confusion caused by the sophists and reinstate the correct use of "names." After the treacherous assassination of the de facto ruler of Chu, the state in which Hsün-tzu served as magistrate, Hsün-tzu was abruptly dismissed. He now began to stress the need for stringent, objective "law" and exactly calculated punishments, and to advocate economy in government and the priority of fundamental occupations over those that he took to be merely parasitic.

By then in his middle seventies, Hsün-tzu retired to devote himself to teaching and preaching. This was the time when the state of Ch'in, under the extraordinarily bold leadership of its king and of Hsün-tzu's student, Li Ssu, made a rapid conquest of the whole of China and took dramatic steps to unify its culture. Offered a nominal position by Li Ssu, Hsün-tzu refused it with the prediction that his student "would fall into unfathomable disasters," as he did. When Hsün-tzu died, he was at least in his late nineties; he may have reached the age of one hundred.[5]

As a writer, Hsün-tzu is orderly, serious, and intense. Although the text of his works sometimes seems pieced together, there is little evidence in it of interpolation.[6] Two of his educational principles were to have great practical success. The one was that learning should be based on the recitation of the (not yet standardized) Confucian classics. The other was that learning should above all aim to produce Confucians of exemplary character. Hsün-tzu's explicit influence remained powerful only during the short-lived dynasty of Ch'in (221–206 B.C.E.) and its successor, the earlier Han dynasty. His dour view of human nature and the influence of his students on Ch'in, which became a byword for cruelty, must have helped lead to the later dominance of Mencius.[7] Yet whether or not one admires him or his principles, Hsün-tzu is the most wide-ranging, well-integrated, and rational—unsupersititious—of the early Confucians, in fact, of all early Chinese philosophers.

The Confucian ideal that Hsün-tzu nurtures has three human levels: that of the scholar, that of the superior person (the *chün-tzu*), and that of the sage, a rare and ancient human paragon. In Hsün-tzu's view, what a scholar studies and commits to memory is the epitome of human experience. It is the scholar's ability to assimilate this experience that allows him to become a true human being rather than an animal. Hsün-tzu insists that study should leave its mark on behavior. Anyone who fails to grasp that moral obligations are one with the principles of humanity has not mastered the learning he professes.[8]

To explain Hsün-tzu's thought, I take up six of its themes: (1) The nature of language and discussion; (2) rationalism; (3) the contention that man is evil; (4) the organization of society; (5) immoderation; and (6) self-cultivation.

1. *The nature of language and discussion:* As might be expected, Hsün-tzu emphasizes the need for the "rectification of names" or, in more normal English, the correct use of names, that is, words.[9] He recalls with what care for tradition the great kings fixed names for punishments, titles, and ceremonies and favored words that were already current. Having said this, Hsün-tzu gives examples of the definitions of words such as *(human) nature, emotions, awareness,* and *knowledge.*[10] To understand Hsün-tzu's concern for the uniformity of words, one must remember that the Chinese language was not yet standardized—the Ch'in empire, which enforced standardization, was just coming into existence. To tamper with language, Hsün-tzu says, by "hair-splitting wordings" and making up new ones on one's own authority is as socially damaging as forging credentials or tampering with weights and measures. Careless language confuses the grasp of the realities to which words refer, multiplies arguments, and blurs the distinction between right and wrong.[11]

To explain, Hsün-tzu goes back to the way in which names (*ming*), that is, words, are initially assigned their meanings. To name things, one uses the testimony of the senses and begins by classifying those "that belong to the same category of being or have the same essential characteristics," as the senses testify.[12] The eye distinguishes shapes, colors, and designs; the ear distinguishes pitch, timbre, modal keys, rhythm, and noises; the mouth distinguishes sweet and bitter, salty and bland, pungent and sour tastes; the nose distinguishes the various scents; and the body distinguishes pain and itching, cold and heat, smoothness and roughness, and lightness and heaviness. And the heart—the mind—distinguishes all the various emotions.[13]

Given this evidence, we name particular things. If a single name is not enough, we use a compound one, and we go on to more and more broad or general terms until, when we reach a term such as *things*, we can go no further. Sometimes this process is reversed and we go from the most general term to words like *bird* or *animal*, which distinguish broadly, and draw distinction within distinction until we stop because there are no further distinctions to be made. Because the names given have no intrinsic rightness for their purpose, they have to be agreed on; and if they grow customary, they are accepted as appropriate. In using the names, one must be careful to retain them when the same things appear in different places or when things undergo some transformation but remain essentially the same.[14]

Naming alone is often not enough. When a name alone is not enough to convey the defined meaning, the meaning is completed by explanation. When the explanation is not completely understood, dialectics comes into use, that is, alternatives are discussed or argued. Given the names, which define different realities, we link them by stringing them together into compositions. "When both the use and the links between names are grasped, we are said to know the name." When names are used correctly, as they have been defined, when propositions conform to explanations, when explanations conform to the mind, and when the mind conforms to the Way, the true qualities of things are clearly conveyed.[15]

> Divisions and differences should be made but not so as to introduce errors. Inferences should be made from the characteristics of the category of a thing, but not to the point of introducing fallacies. Then when we listen, it will conform to good form, and when we engage in dialectics, we will fully express all that inheres in things.[16]

Hsün-tzu is confident that the sophists' arguments can be countered by testing their statements in the light of the essential function of naming, of the testimony of the senses, and of dialectics, which is the logic of argument. To know the function of naming, he says, is to exclude a statement such as "to kill a robber is not to kill a man." To use the testimony of the senses is to exclude paradoxes such as "mountains and marshes are level." And to make proper use of names and of dialectics is to exclude paradoxes such as "the flying arrow does not pass the pillar" and "a white horse is not a horse."[17] It is of extreme imporance to resist the sophists' misuse of language, Hsün-tzu believes, because when they trade on the disparity between words and realities, they turn intellectual into moral confusion by depriving the mind of its ability to control desire—the mind is simply blinded. Clarity of thought is necessary for people to act as they believe is right; as a general rule, they all accept what they think is allowable and reject what they think is not allowable. There is no example of anyone who understood the Way and did not follow it.[18]

2. *Rationalism:* Philosophical Chinese of Hsün-tzu's time think of the cosmos as made of a number of great forces, each with its role in a harmony of reciprocating opposites.[19] The forces include Heaven—to Hsün-tzu, the dominant force—and Earth, which sustains what Heaven begets. The forces also include the antithetical pair, Yin and Yang, whose alternations and modulations cause change in everything. There is also the energy substance of the cosmos, *ch'i*. Finally, there is *li* (*pattern*), which is the principle of rational, that is, hierarchical order. Unlike those who think that *li* rules in the cosmos as a whole, Hsün-tzu confines it to human life. It is the *chün-tzu*, he believes, who supplies the (moral) pattern that Heaven and Earth themselves lack.[20] To Hsün-tzu, the Way or *Tao*—*Tao* in the singular—is not usually a natural force but the unvarying principle by which a human being weighs the alternatives of good and evil.

The cosmos made up of these forces or principles is considered by most Chinese of Hsün-tzu's time to be predictable by means of omens, manipulable by magic, and responsive to human behavior. Hsün-tzu rejects the magic, the omens, and the responsiveness. His rationalism may not be fully consistent: to him, *Heaven*, his synonym for *nature*, is still colored by the same sense of *ruler* that we find in our own phrases, "nature decrees" or "the laws of nature." But though not quite all of a piece, his rationalism or naturalism is very emphatic.*

Heaven is *t'ien*. Knoblock, whose translation I have used extensively, often prefers the translation *Nature*, so I have often followed him. Knoblock explains: "The word is a common term and is used in this book in several different senses; thus it is best translated by a different word for each separate meaning, even though the Chinese conceived all of them as 'one thing.' The abstract, objective *tian* [in Pinyin transliteration] is translated 'Nature'; when a moral, directive sense is implied, the word is translated 'Heaven'; and where celestial events are involved it is rendered 'heaven.' Further, in many contexts, particularly where man is contrasted with Nature, *tian* is short for *tiandi*, 'Heaven and Earth.' The idea of 'Nature' is the philosophical rationalization of the older, fundamental notion of a directing Heaven" (Knoblock, *Xünzi*, vol. 3, p. 3). Maybe it would be best to use *Heaven* everywhere, leaving the ambiguity unresolved except as (one thinks or sees) it is resolved by context. (On the varying, possibly contradictory senses of Heaven in Hsün-tzu, see Eno, *The Confucian Creation of Heaven*, pp. 154–65.)

The course of Nature, says Hsün-tzu, is constant. It is not affected by either good or bad emperors. If the response to its constancy is good government, there will be good fortune. Having adapted to its course, you will be well off, your nutrition will be complete, and you will not be troubled with disease; and you will be able to survive floods and droughts.[21] But Heaven itself does not respond to human beings. It does not suspend the winter because men dislike the cold. "You pray for rain and it rains. Why? For no particular reason, I say. It is just as though you had not prayed for rain and it rained anyway." Falling stars, creaking trees, and eclipses of the sun and moon are not evil portents but natural events, the results of the changes of Heaven and Earth and the mutations of Yin and Yang. What *are* to be feared are such human portents as bad plowing, poor weeding of fields, and the failure of crops that causes grain to be imported and sold at high prices and cause people to die by the roadside of starvation.[22]

But although Hsün-tzu, unlike Confucius and Mencius, regards Heaven as indifferent to human beings, he stresses that it has given them faculties they can use to their own, human advantage. When he says this, he sounds like an optimistic evolutionist or an exponent of the so-called *anthropic principle*, by which one draws attention to the special conditions for human development that Nature has provided.[23]

According to Hsün-tzu's vision of the world, the human emotions and faculties, each of which is different and necessary, are the work of Heaven. For this reason they are rightly called *Heavenly* (for *Heavenly* the reader may substitute *natural* [with a small *n*] and both gain and lose something). Likewise, the heart or mind, which lodges in the center and rules the faculties, is called *the lord provided by Nature*. The decrees of Nature or the Heavenly dictates establish that only whoever lives in accord with the nature of the human species will be fortunate.[24]

Knowing this, the sage, the perfect man—the counterpart of Chuang-tzu's sage—does not try to penetrate into the work of Nature. Instead of indulging in this competition with Heaven/Nature, he preserves the heavenly accomplishment by purifying his natural "lord," rectifying his natural faculties, completing his natural nourishment, and nourishing his natural emotions. In this way, he completes what Heaven has achieved. For "Heaven has its seasons; Earth its resources; and Man his government. This, of course, is why it is said that they 'can form a Triad.'" When a man tries to be something more or different from the human member of this triad, he suffers from delusion. Each of the myriad things grows by means of its harmonious relation with Nature. We see the result but not the invisible, formless process by which Nature achieves it. One needs to be a sage to act without trying to understand of Heaven what cannot be understood.[25]

More strongly, and, for emphasis, in rhymed verse, Hsün-tzu writes:

Instead of magnifying Heaven and contemplating it,
Why not domesticate and curb it?
Instead of being subservient to Heaven and singing its
    praises,
Why not curb its decree and put it to use?
Instead of looking out for the seasons and awaiting their
    bounty,
Why not respond to them and make them serve you? . . .
Instead of contemplating things in their independence,
Why not make them a pattern from which none escapes?[26]

This time there is no qualification, nothing one should refrain from understanding. If one can forget that the words are written in rhyming Chinese characters and in the context of a faithful Confucianism, one is reminded of Francis Bacon. Hsün-tzu, too, has a method, at least a rhetorical one, by which, he supposes, individuals can achieve empirical results, escape uncertainty, and fulfill their basic desire. To achieve all this, they must accept reasonable limits, avoid any obsessive interests, rely on the natural unity of the mind, and find the most effective ways of overcoming doubt. Hsün-tzu enumerates many causes of doubt: Darkness obscures vision, drunkenness disorders thought, a pressed eyeball gives double vision, and distance diminishes size. One learns not to use moving water, with its deceptive reflections, as a mirror, or to accept the testimony of a blind man that there are no stars—doubtful means cannot settle doubts.[27]

Everyone has a natural, inborn understanding, and it is part of the natural order of things that they can be known. But the search to understand the natural principles of order—of ethics or of science—will fail unless one takes care to limit the search. The reason is that, to be productive, thought must be well focused, undistracted, and not too emotionally forced. Therefore, when humans pursue their desires, they should deliberate carefully, distinguish the relevant from the irrelevant, always "considering the long view of things and thinking of the consequences."[28] An undisturbed pan of water reflects one's face clearly, but not when stirred by the wind. One must keep the rational principle clear and not allow things to tilt it and muddy the truth. For Hsün-tzu is sure that "if one guides the mind by li [in the sense of reason] and nourishes it with clarity and does not allow any extrinsic things to upset it, then the mind is quite capable of determining right and wrong and resolving doubts."[29]

3. Man is evil: Hsün-tzu says "Man's nature is evil; any good in humans is acquired by conscious activity."[30] It is this view for which Hsün-tzu is best known and most violently denigrated in the Chinese

philosophical tradition.* Just as nothing profoundly metaphysical is intended by Mencius' "human nature is good"—a statement that occurs, directly or indirectly only twice in his writings—nothing profoundly metaphysical is implied in Hsün-tzu's "man's nature is evil"—a statement he makes only, though repeatedly, in the chapter that bears this title. It seems as though Mencius' infrequent but rhetorically effective words on human goodness arouse Hsün-tzu to use rhetorically contradictory ones. Hsün-tzu is led to such rhetorical emphasis just because both he and Mencius think rather alike. Both hold that ordinary human beings need a thoroughgoing education. The difference is primarily that Mencius says this in a believing, optimistic temper, and Hsün-tzu, in a way that one can interpret as either realistic or misanthropic. Whatever the interpretation, to Hsün-tzu the difference is profound, and he is very blunt in his attack on Mencius:

> Mencius considered that "since man can learn, his nature is good." I say this is not so. It shows that Mencius did not reach any real understanding of what man's inborn nature is and that he did not investigate the division between those things that are inborn in man and those that are acquired. As a general rule, "inborn nature" embraces what is spontaneous from Nature, what cannot be learned, and what requires no application to master. Ritual principles and moral duties are creations of the sages. They are things that people must study to

---

*"Man's nature is evil" translates *hsing o p'ien*. Evil is *o* (fourth tone) in the Wade-Giles transliteration, used in this book, and *e* in Pinyin. The dictionary meanings of the character are *bad, evil, wicked, vice*. There is a related meaning—in effect, another word—*hate, hatred*; and there is a related group of words referring to ugly or deformed people. Out of curiosity, I have consulted ten ostensibly independent translations, dating from Legge's in 1861 to Hansen's in 1992 and Knoblock's in 1994. Of the ten translators, only two, Cua, in 1985, and Graham, in 1989, prefer *bad*. Graham translates, "Man's nature is bad, the good in him is artifice." I suppose the translation chosen depends on euphony and context—*bad* suggests the kind of language used of or by a child, while *evil* may suggest, as it should not, an Augustinian kind of original sin. Hsün-tzu's text goes on to say, in Graham's translation, "from birth he has jealousy and hatred in him" (Graham, *Disputers of the Tao*, pp. 245–46). Watson (p. 157) translates, "He is born with feelings of envy and hate." If this is what Hsün-tzu believes, the translation *bad* is too weak.

Hansen takes up the suggestion that the often repeated phrase or the chapter that contains it is interpolated. He believes that "it is a partisan interpretative gloss" and, whether it is so or not, its translation misleads modern readers by reminding them not of Confucian but Christian or Buddhist views. (See Hansen, *A Daoist Theory of Chinese Thought*, pp. 336–37, and p. 417, note 84; and Graham, "The Mencian Theory of Human Nature," pp. 57–59. On the condition of the text, Knoblock writes only, "The order of the text of this book [book 23] is seriously disturbed" [*Xunzi*, vol. 3, p. 280].)

be able to follow them and to which they must apply themselves before they can fulfill their precepts. What cannot be
gained by learning and cannot be mastered by application yet
is found in man is properly termed "inborn nature." What
must be learned before a man can do it and what he must
apply himself to before he can master it yet is found in man
is properly called "acquired nature." This is precisely the distinction between "inborn" and "acquired" natures.[31]

Hsün-tzu's explanation is that human beings are born acquisitive,
envious, and full of the desire to see and hear. If they are allowed to
indulge in these wants, they become aggressive and greedy, they violate
the natural order of class distinctions, and a cruel tyranny develops. Making
an analogy that became famous, Hsün-tzu writes:

A warped piece of wood must first await application of the
press-frame, steam to soften it, and force to bend its shape
before it can be made straight . . . Now, since human nature is
evil, it must await the instructions of a teacher and the model
before it can be put right, and it must obtain ritual principles
and a sense of moral right before it can become orderly.[32]

4. *The organization of society:* Human beings have no choice, says
Hsün-tzu, except to organize themselves into a society. If authority is
equally distributed, there is no unity, so if society is not divided on hierarchical principles, the result is quarreling, chaos, insecurity, and a weak,
fragmented state. Ritual principles are therefore necessary. These are, we
know, the filial relation between son and parents and brother and brother,
and the equivalent relations between social superiors and inferiors, that is,
between the ruler and his subjects. A true ruler is someone able to organize humans so that everything finds its proper place and is done at the
proper time, so that the common people are unified and worthy men offer
their services to the government. In everything, a sense of order and
humanity is necessary, as well as patience and common sense. More particularly, it is necessary to guard the natural environment, to censor writing and music with care, to administer adequate and just punishments, to
provide for moral education, and to attend to agriculture and commerce.
And finally, it is necessary that the king himself behave decently and
intelligently. Hsün-tzu suggests the assignment of clear responsibility to
each of the important officials, up to and including the king himself, who
is not the right person to be king, he says, if the world is not unified and
the feudal lords are rebellious.[33]

I have stated all these requirements of good government briefly, but because of current interest, I recall some details of the precautions Hsün-tzu recommends for the care of the natural environment. For example, he wants laws enforced for conserving the grasses and trees, fish and turtles, and other edibles of the mountain forests, lakes, and marshes. With respect to the marshes, he urges that nets and poisons be banned during the season when the turtles and fish are depositing their eggs, so that they remain abundant. And with respect to the mountain forests, he urges that they should not be cut when they are flowering or putting out new growth, so that the forests are not denuded and people have enough timber.[34]

5. *Immoderation:* Hsün-tzu makes a sustained attack on immoderation of all sorts. He begins by saying it is a common human flaw to be blinded by attention to some small point of the truth. Such blinding, he says, comes from many sources: desire or aversion, interest in the beginnings or ends of things, or in what is remote or near, or in breadth or shallowness, or in the past or present. Unlike the single-minded sages, feudal lords now follow different theories of government and philosophers teach a hundred different doctrines.[35]

Among the philosophers Hsün-tzu considers to have been blindly onesided, he recalls: Mo-tzu, who was blinded by his interest in utility from understanding ritual gradation and form; Shen Pu-hai, who was blinded by his concern with the technique of ruling from understanding the role of knowledge; Hui-tzu, who was blinded by his interest in propositions and his assessment of everything by logical argument from understanding realities; and Chuang-tzu, who was blinded by his reliance on Heaven (Nature), on things as they simply occur, from understanding human beings. But Confucius, humane and wise, was free of obsession. Therefore his study of the methods of producing order can be considered the equal of that of the great ancient kings. "Such are the blessings of not being obsessed."[36]

Self-cultivation: This ideal leads to Hsün-tzu's treatment of the theme, common in China, of cultivating oneself. He relates the theme to current attempts to prolong life and he recommends controlling the "vital breath" (*ch'i*) as a way of cultivating character and strengthening self. Possibly referring to breathing exercises, he says that if the vital breath is conserved by the reduction of one's desires and by proper foresight, it nurtures the mind. But if one lacks unity of purpose, the vital breath is dissipated in undisciplined action and vehement emotion, and one grows old prematurely. Therefore one should calm one's impulsiveness and unify excessively penetrating knowledge with the qualities of ease and sincerity.[37]

According to Hsün-tzu, apart from a good teacher and the reduction of one's desires, the most potent cure for what ails human beings is ritual (in the broad Confucian sense).[38] To preserve order and by order to preserve life and ability, one should choose a journey with an end, avoid sophistical debates, and find a worthy model for one's life. "When your emotions find peace in ritual and your knowledge is like that of your teacher, then you will become a sage."[39]

This ideal of a path of moderation, study, internalized decency, and studied decorum may not appear especially attractive now, in an age that does not value decorum highly. However, Hsün-tzu testifies that the ideal makes possible an intensely pleasurable peace of mind and a resoluteness that expresses inner power. When the *chün-tzu*

> has reached the limit of such perfection, he finds delight in it. His eye then finds greater enjoyment in the five colors, his ear in the five sounds, his mouth in the five tastes, and his mind benefits from possessing all that is in the world. Therefore, the exigencies of time and place and consideration of personal profit cannot influence him, cliques and coteries cannot sway him, and the whole world cannot deter him. He was born to follow it, and he will die following it.[40]

Aristotle (384–322 B.C.E.): The Primary Objects of Desire and Thought Are the Same.

Aristotle was the son of the physician of King Amyntas of Macedon, the grandfather of Alexander the Great.[41] At seventeen, he went to Athens to study in Plato's Academy. A stranger, without a citizen's rights, he sometimes found it difficult to remain there. It is reported that he left the Academy while Plato was still alive, but we know he felt close to him, as he shows when he says that he finds Ideas difficult to criticize because they were introduced by his friends.[42]

When King Philip of Macedon was looking for a tutor for his son Alexander, he turned to Aristotle. It is plausible to assume that, like the Confucians and Plato, Aristotle would be happy to advise a ruler or future ruler. The *Politics* has a passage that might have been directly addressed to Alexander. It says that the inhabitants of the cold areas of the world are spirited but unintelligent and unskilled, and although relatively free, they are politically unorganized and incapable of ruling over others; and the natives of Asia are intelligent and inventive but, lacking spirit, are always in a state of subjection. But the Hellenic race, which is intermediate, is both high spirited and intelligent. "Hence it continues free, and is the best governed of any nation, and if it could be formed into one state, would be able to rule the world."[43] Aristotle addressed a book to Alexander—

Cicero says he has it—and gave him the advice, which he did not follow, to "play the part of a leader to the Greeks and of a master to the barbarians, [to] care for the former as friends and kinsmen, and treat the latter as beasts or plants."[44]

After an absence from Athens of many years, Aristotle returned and for twelve years conducted mostly biological research, lectured, and collected a large library. His institution was at least as scientific as philosophical in our sense. It would be strange and unreasonable, Aristotle says, if we did not get great satisfaction from contemplating the works of nature when we are able to make out their causes—"in all natural things there is something to move wonder."[45] Very aware of the intricacy of the world, he assigned different assistants to different lines of research, including botany, medicine, the history of the exact sciences, and mathematics and astronomy (which went together).[46]

When Alexander died in 323 B.C.E. and the Athenians hoped to regain their independence, Aristotle's Macedonian connection was enough, it seems, for a charge of impiety to be leveled against him. Rather than undergo a trial, he left Athens for Chalcis, where he died after about a year, at the age of sixty-three. In his will, he leaves his daughter and son, Nichomachus, in the care of a guardian, asks that his freedwoman, who has shown him steady affection, be taken good care of and given a talent of silver and servants, and that his dead wife, Pythia, be buried, as she had instructed, together with him.[47]

Aristotle's popular works, only fragments of which remain, were written in a flowing, ornate style. As Cicero shows by his acknowledged imitations, at least some of Aristotle's popular works were dominated by the long monologues of the main character. Of Aristotle's work, about a third remains. The whole—comprising 445,270 lines—was catalogued and arranged into treatises, we are told, by Andronicus of Rhodes (first century B.C.E.).* Most of Aristotle's remaining work is written concisely and with

---

*For reasons obscure to us, Aristotle's major philosophical works had become hard to find. "Andronicus of Rhodes set out to remedy this situation by preparing a new, critical edition of these works," in part from "copies of Aristotelian manuscripts which had found their way into the library of a certain Apellicon and had been taken from Athens to Rome by Sulla after his sack of Athens in 86 B.C.E. . . .

"Andronicus presented Aristotle's philosophy as a system like those of the Stoics and Epicureans, which his adherents were expected to understand and propagate, with such additions as might be needed from time to time. It has been suggested [by Ingmar Düring and others] that this entailed a distortion of Aristotle's thought. But while it is true that many of Aristotle's books were not originally written for the context in which Andronicus placed them, and Andronicus ignored and probably had no way of knowing the dates at which particular books were composed, a systematic tendency was inherent in Aristotle's thought from the start" (H. B. Gottschalk, "The Earliest Aristotelian Commentators," in Sorabji, ed., Aristotle Transformed, pp. 54, 65).

many breaks, as if composed of notebook entries or rough drafts.* The sayings attributed to him sound disabused; but when he is asked what he has gained from philosophy, he gives an answer of a kind we might expect from a more prosaic twin of Hsün-tzu, "This, that I do without being ordered what some are constrained to do by the fear of the law."[48]

Aristotle's curiosity seems without limits. He takes up, always in an inquiring, constructive spirit, the subjects of logic, the nature and proper development of science in general, and physics, meteorology, psychology, embryology, botany, and perception and memory, and, as well, metaphysics, ethics, politics (especially constitutional theory), rhetoric, and poetics. He classifies and he collects—not only books, but also maps, models for use during lectures, and biological specimens. Temperamentally calmer, less aesthetic, and less visionary than Plato, he is more persistently analytical, and his hunger to understand is often much humbler and more empirical than Plato would find possible. In approaching a problem, he sets it out carefully, reviews others' opinions, and tries to hit on the questions that lead to a deep understanding. Usually his analysis is tentative and he is always ready to correct it; and, at the same time as he analyzes a subject, he reflects on the processes by which he analyzes it.** Since he has so many interests and is so rich in ideas and variations of ideas that have been explored in detail over many centuries, the exposition that follows—less selective than for many of the other philosophers—is more sketchy than usual in these pages.

To see Aristotle in the context of his tradition, we should remember that up to his time it had one great abstract problem and one great practical one. The great abstract problem is, of course, the relation between *being* and *becoming*; the practical problem is the organization of the city-state. Aristotle deals with both problems analytically. To that of *being* and *becoming* he responds with three pairs of related concepts, all at least hinted at by Plato: potentiality and actuality, matter and form, and substance and accident. As a framework for philosophy as a whole he also develops a theory of science.

---

*The roughness of style "is not unpleasing (and if you love Aristotle's thought, you will come to love his style), but it is undeniable: the syntax is spare, ornamentation is rare, transitions are abrupt, and connections opaque. . . . Reading Aristotle, as the poet Thomas Gray put it, is like eating dried hay." The ancient admirers of Aristotle's style probably had in mind his "exoteric," not his "esoteric" works (Barnes, "[Aristotle's] Life and Work," pp. 11–12).

**Aristotle's "actual practice suggests that he was less concerned with striving for univocity than with exploiting the stretch of the concept, with exploring the very different types of phenomena and processes he encompasses under the same polyvalent rubric." For Aristotle, "when it comes to a conflict between theory and practice, it is the practice that speaks the louder of the two" (Lloyd, *Aristotelian Explorations,* pp. 103, 222).

Potentiality and actuality: Not surprisingly, Aristotle observes that between being and not-being there is always the intermediate state of coming-to-be, *genesis*, so that between that which is and that which is not there is always the developing subject.[49] Aristotle uses the word *dynamis* to name whatever it is in the subject that directs its development. In ordinary Greek *dynamis* means *power* or *ability*, but he gives it the special sense of *potentiality*, that is, the innate principle in every natural object by which it becomes what its nature aims at. In relation to a living thing, potentiality is equivalent to its genetic constitution, which establishes its traits as the member of a species and its development in the course of its lifetime. Since, by Aristotelian standards, nature does nothing in vain, what the natural object becomes defines what it is. More explicitly, what the natural object becomes defines what the object is by nature suited to be and to do and, as well, what it will or should actually become, which is its *actualization* or *energeia*. So it is the nature of each natural object— an object with an internal source of change—to change toward the final state or goal that defines what it is. A boy is by nature a potential man and is fully actual only when he has become a man; an eye being formed is actual only when it fulfills its function of seeing. That *nature* exists is a self-evident fact of experience it would be absurd to try to prove.[50]

Matter and form: Aristotle's idea of potentiality needs the additional, though more or less synonymous, concept of matter. Like the Jains and like Plato in the *Parmenides*, Aristotle finds himself forced to assume that what undergoes change is a persistent substratum. For this substratum Aristotle uses the word *hyle*, translated *matter*. While it is observation that suggests the concept of matter, the matter we observe is always to some extent actual, in some way formed. The concept of matter is therefore theoretical and a twin to that of potentiality. Just as potentiality makes no sense in the absence of actuality, matter makes no sense in the absence of the correlative notion of form or *eidos*; as Plato says, it is the form of a thing that makes it intelligible. To Aristotle, a thing's form is, therefore, its intelligible essence, its nature as reason knows it, its actuality. Except at their theoretical extremes—pure matter or potentiality and pure form or actuality—matter and form are relative: the fibers of a plant have their own matter and form, but they are the matter of which the plant is made. A living creature is, in fact, a hierarchy of levels of increasingly compli-cated combinations of matter and form—in today's language, rising from subatomic particles to atoms to molecules to cells to organs, to the whole creature.[51]

Substance and accident: The concepts of matter and form—the two always or almost always coexisting with one another—require the further concept of substance, that which is made up of both matter and form. A substance is an individual something or other, with its characteristic attributes and its ability to undergo a succession of contrary changes. The term Aristotle uses for *substance* is *ousia*. To him, the primary sense of *substance* is that of something particular, but the term also has the usually secondary sense of *form* or *essence*. Like the grammatical subject in a sentence, *substance* is the independent element to which all the rest refers. A quality that belongs to a substance but is inessential to it is regarded as a mere accompaniment or *accident (to symbebekos)*. Aristotle gives as examples of accidents the finding of treasure when one digs a hole for a plant, the whiteness of a musical man, and going to Aegina because carried there by a storm. What plays no necessary role in the understanding of something can play no role in scientific understanding. It is an accident if a person is white or not—the color of a human being is no part of the definition of a human being—but a human being is necessarily a kind of animal.[52]

Theory of science: According to Aristotle, knowledge is either practical or theoretical. The object of science is theoretical knowledge, *episteme*. Theoretical knowledge is necessary and, as such, is eternal, unchanging, and capable of being taught and learned. Its instrument is logic, which deals with the formal correctness, that is, the consistency and truth of an argument. The word Aristotle uses for scientific demonstration or reasoning is *syllogismos*, meaning deductive reasoning, the drawing of conclusions from premises. It must have premises because all reasoning and teaching begin from something already known. Aristotle continues:

> By demonstration I mean a syllogism which produces scientific knowledge, in other words one which enables us to know by the mere fact that we grasp it . . . Demonstrative knowledge must proceed from premises which are true, primary, immediate, better known than, prior to, and causative of the conclusion. (*Posterior Analytics* 71b)[53]*

---

*Aristotle says (*Sophistical Refutations*, 183b) that, before him, nothing at all existed of a systematic account of correct inference. "As such, Aristotle was the founder of logic. This makes the extent of his logical theories all the more remarkable. His *Prior Analytics* contains the complete exposition of a theory of inference (usually called the 'syllogistic'), developed with a striking mathematical rigor. History's first logic has also been its most influential, with an unparalleled importance in post-Hellenistic philosophy, medieval Islamic philosophy, and especially mediaeval European thought: indeed, for many generations of philosophers, Aristotelian logic was identically logic. Not until the twentieth century was it finally supplanted as a result of the work of Frege and his successors . . . Recent studies have revealed a strong kinship in methods and interests between Aristotle and present-day logical theory, even if his actual results are wanting by modern standards" (R. Smith, "Logic," in Sorabji, ed., *The Cambridge Companion to Aristotle*, p. 27).

The most basic principles of knowledge, which cannot themselves be proved, are the laws of contradiction and excluded middle. Such principles are intuited by means of induction, which is the intellectual intuition by which one grasps the universals within the objects we sense:

> Demonstration is from universals, and induction is from particulars, and it is impossible to contemplate universals except through induction . . . and induction is impossible for one not having perception. For perception is of individuals. (*Posterior Analytics* 81a40–b7)[54]

Close to sense experience, induction is more convincing, clear, and easily learned than deduction, but deduction can be more effective in argument.[55]

Not everything of importance to us can be known scientifically, so we need practical as well as scientific knowledge. Like sensation, ethics and politics are concerned with particular facts, and it is clear that one learns to be ethical or to take part in politics mainly by practical experience, not abstract reasoning. In such fields, what one tries to achieve is practical wisdom (*phronesis*), which in ethics consists of the virtues that depend on the habit of choosing the mean between extremes or vices.[56]

The only remaining Aristotelian conception that needs to be brought up now is what Aristotle calls *first philosophy* and, rarely, *theology*. Its object is to grasp what *being* is in its full sense. The cosmos that Aristotle envisages in first philosophy is a successor to that described in Plato's *Timaeus*— both Plato's and Aristotle's worlds are unified systems all the motion of which is derived from a single eternal source.[57]

Aristotle's theology rests not only on his philosophical principles but also on his conception of the cosmos as a set of nested spheres each carrying a planet or, in the case of the outermost sphere, the fixed stars. Instead of trying to work through enough details to make this scheme appear plausible, I will state Aristotle's theology in the simplest, most dogmatic way. I allow myself to do this because Aristotle's reasoning on this matter is of little importance to the comparisons about to be made.

Without explanation, then: Everything in the physical world contains matter and is therefore also potential, meaning, not fully actualized. Aristotle—thinking deductively and hierarchically—reasons that change or motion in the world is caused by the great transparent concentric spheres that carry the planets with them. He reasons further that although the motion of these spheres is eternal, it can be caused only by something fully actual, and something fully actual, having no potentiality or matter, is itself unmoving, that is, unchanging. Aristotle identifies this being as God, the first, unmoved mover, whose activity, fully actual, can only be the activity of thinking. Since this thinking excludes potentiality—excludes anything outside itself toward which it develops—the object of this thinking can only be its own thought—it is thought thinking itself.*

Discussion

In most of what I have described of Aristotle's philosophy there is little that resembles Hsün-tzu's, who has no formal logic, no developed theory of science, and no detailed physics. However, as I have said, the rational syntheses of Hsün-tzu and Aristotle have comparable, sometimes rather similar basic characteristics—in ways that repay consideration, the Chinese philosopher and the Greek philosopher were surprisingly alike. As might be expected, Hsün-tzu is much more attentive to history than Aristotle, though often the examples he uses are predetermined by the moral interpretation he gives them. He is attentive to the natural world around him—his understanding of ecology is fairly detailed—but Aristotle is obviously much more the scientist, both theoretical and empirical. Aristotle is also the more individualistic, unchecked by reverence. In the passage in which he declares that friendship makes it hard for him to criticize Ideas, he goes on to say that, especially for philosophers, truth must be honored above friendship.[58] Hsün-tzu criticizes Mencius in such a spirit, but, unlike Aristotle in relation to Plato, he is all reverence toward Confucius. The most interesting difference between Hsün-tzu and Aristotle is that Aristotle prefers a meditative grasp of the truth over moral or political activity. He knows by definition that the philosopher will be a morally superior person, but he separates the activity of philosophizing from that of politics. In contrast, Hsün-tzu, like other Confucians, finds such a separation impossible, the whole point of study being to strengthen social harmony.

---

*Here it is enough to point out that the conception of God is extrapolated by Aristotle in order to complete his cosmos. As will be seen in later chapters, this conception of God became standard for a long time in Neoplatonic and medieval philosophy, whether Christian, Moslem, or Jewish. In the *Great Ethics*, the *Magna Moralia*, the authenticity of which is disputed, there is a passage (1213a) that dwells on the difficulty of believing in a god who thinks either of something other than himself or of himself. As to God's self-contemplation, says the text, "if a human being surveys himself, we censure him as stupid. It will be absurd, therefore, it is said, for god to contemplate himself." The difficulty is not addressed, the text adds, because it is not the subject under discussion. (See *The Complete Works of Aristotle*, ed. Barnes, vol. 2, p. 1920. On the interpretation of the Aristotelian passage discussed above see T. de Koninck, "Aristotle on God as Thought Thinking Itself," *Review of Metaphysics*, March 1994.)

I compare Hsün-tzu and Aristotle under the following heads:
(1) discourse and argument; (2) rationalism; (3) the ladder of being;
(4) the relation of ethics to politics; (5) the ideal of moderation; (6) the
human and philosophical ideal.

1. *Discourse and argument*: As we have seen, Hsün-tzu insists that
names, especially those by which we characterize human relationships and
functions, should be rid of ambiguity and used in accord with their exact
references as established by tradition, by common usage, by sensory evidence, and by moral effect. Having no intrinsic rightness of their own,
these words are based on pure convention. Applied in accord with the
testimony of the senses, they are arranged in either an ascending order of
increasing generality or a descending order of increasing particularity. The
correct words should be formed into combinations and understood in
accord with the true circumstances underlying their use. And the differences between the words should be carefully distinguished and analogies
or inferences drawn that are neither forced or false.[59]

Aristotle agrees that "a *name* is a spoken sound significant by
convention . . . none of whose parts is significant in separation . . . because
no name is a name naturally but only when it has become a symbol."[60]*
He, too, believes that the reference of words is based on the testimony of
the senses—"induction" (in his sense), which is for most people the easiest
and most convincing form of knowledge. And Aristotle, too, speaks of the
different levels of generality of terms and, like Hsün-tzu, insists that, to
avoid falling into fallacies, the exact sense of the terms used in argument
must be clear. Of course, Aristotle is quite different from Hsün-tzu in that
he favors formal deduction—in its place.[61]

Both philosophers make much of rhetorical considerations. Hsün-
tzu's advice is to

> introduce the topic with dignity and earnestness, dwell on it
> with modesty and sincerity, hold to it with firmness and
> strength, illustrate its meaning with parables and praiseworthy
> examples, elucidate its significance by making distinctions and
> drawing boundaries, and present it with exuberance and ar-
> dor. If you make of it something precious and rare, valuable
> and magical, your persuasion will always and invariably be

---

*"'Name' gives the original and central meaning of the Greek *onoma* . . . In some contexts it is
tempting to write 'word' or 'noun,' but only 'name' can do duty in all contexts. Moreover, the use
of 'name' in the translation will serve to remind the reader of the primitive nature of Aristotle's
view of meaning: 'Philo' and 'man' are names of different sorts of things but are both just
names"(*Aristotle's* Categories *and* De Interpretatione, trans. Ackrill, p. 115 [note to 16a19]).

well received, and even if you do not please them, none will fail to esteem you.[62]

Aristotle's equivalent advice is that one should concern oneself not alone with the argument as such but also with the impression made on the audience. This is because listeners are affected by the kind of person they take the speaker to be and the attitude they ascribe to him. Aristotle discusses how to arouse the audience's emotions and how to adapt oneself to the audience's character. He also takes up rhetorical devices, including examples and maxims. Aside from logical demonstration, he says, there are three things we trust, which make a speaker persuasive to us:

> These are practical wisdom and virtue and good will; for speakers make mistakes in what they say or advise through [failure to exhibit] either all or one of these; for either through lack of practical sense they do not form opinions rightly; or through forming opinions rightly they do not say what they think because of a bad character; or they are prudent and fair-minded but lack good will. (*On Rhetoric* 1378a)[63]

My only comment is that much of Aristotle's advice is the kind a sophist would give, while Hsün-tzu remains consistently on the moral level and, in giving advice, sounds more the practiced rhetorician than does Aristotle.

Rationalism: Both philosophers prefer to depend on empirical evidence and reason. Hsün-tzu, persuaded of the human and political damage caused by superstition, spends a good deal of effort in denouncing it. Aristotle does not, and it is therefore not surprising that among the writings traditionally (in this case wrongly) attributed to him there is a book, *Physiognomics*, that tells, among the rest, that the whole animal kingdom gives evidence that proves that "soft *hair* indicates cowardice, and coarse hair courage."[64] In sharp contrast, Hsün-tzu makes an eloquent attack on physiognomics, which, for the believing Chinese, gives insight not only into character but into the future as well. He depends on historical examples to show that physical appearance is no indication of character. One of his examples is the courage with which a revolt was put down by Prince Gao, the Duke of She, who "was so frail, small, short, and skinny that when he walked it looked as if he could not support even his clothes."[65]

The philosophers' attitude toward God or (for Hsün-tzu) Heaven is a measure of the different quality of their rationalism. Aristotle's God is a bold extrapolation based on a metaphysical principle. It represents an extreme idealization of the philosophers' activity of thinking for the pleasure of thinking alone—the philosopher is as much like God as is possible to him. Hsün-tzu, wary of extrapolating human characteristics, wants to confine thought about Heaven and Earth to what is recurrent or of pragmatic interest. Heaven and humankind fit together. Humankind has resulted, in an impersonal sense, from Heaven's activity, but humanity is unique in its ability to be moral. Hsün-tzu is apparently not fond of the cosmic speculations of the protoscientists, if that is the right name for them. As he says, "One needs to be a sage not to try to understand of Heaven what cannot be understood."[66]

3. *The ladder of being:* Hsün-tzu has a clear idea of a natural hierarchy of beings. Everything in the world, which "gets what is congenial to it, what nourishes its potentialities," is arranged so that water and fire have *ch'i* but no life, plants and trees have life but no knowledge, birds and beasts have knowledge but no sense of right and wrong (*yi*); humans have *ch'i*, life, knowledge, and a sense of right and wrong. Therefore they are the noblest of all that is in the world. They are weaker than the ox and slower than the horse, yet horse and ox are put to use by them. How so? Because humans are able to form societies and they are not . . . How are they able to form societies? By making hierarchical distinctions? How can such distinctions be put into effect? By the sense of right and wrong. If they use this sense to make hierarchical distinctions, there will be harmony; if there is harmony, there will be unity; if there is unity, there will be power; and if there is power, they can overcome all things.[67]

Compare this ladder with Aristotle's, who explains that there is a rising scale of souls—forms or actualities—of living things. On this scale, each higher step presupposes the lower ones, plants having only the power of nutrition, animals having sensation and desire as well. On the basis of these powers, successively higher powers are added, the last and most rare of which is the power of reason, which is confined to humans and possible superior beings. The power of reason to become what it is thinking of includes the ability to argue, to calculate, and to intuit truth.[68] Aristotle says that "nature proceeds little by little from things lifeless to animal life" and that "there is observed in plants a continuous scale of ascent toward the animal."[69] Elsewhere he says that plants exist for the sake of animals and goes on, "If nature makes nothing incomplete, and nothing in vain, the inference must be that she has made all animals for the sake of man."[70] To this he adds that man, the most political of animals, is the only one with the gift of speech, and

> the power of speech is intended to set forth the expedient and inexpedient, and therefore likewise the just and the unjust. And it is a characteristic of man that he alone has any sense of good and evil, of just and unjust, and the association of

living beings who have this sense makes a family and a state . . . In the first place there must be a union of those who cannot exist without each other; namely, of male and female, that the race may continue . . . and of natural ruler and subject, that both may be preserved. (*Politics* 1253a, 1252a)[71]

For all the differences in nuance, both philosophers have an analogous scale of nature leading, by way of human morality, to a naturally and justly hierarchical society.

4. *The relation of ethics to politics*: The connection is already clear in the passages above. Hsün-tzu's views on the connection have been explained, so I add those of Aristotle. He, too, believes that the good for the individual and for the state require a similar harmony and that the happiness of the individual is the same as that of the state. And he believes that because the individual is not self-sufficient, he is like a part in relation to the whole. This means that the state is a creation of nature and prior to the individual. Hence the connection with politics and laws and the study of the city-state constitutions, which teach what preserves and destroys states and why some are administered well and others badly.[72]

Like Hsün-tzu, Aristotle is convinced that human beings at their best are the best of all living creatures, but that without law and justice they are "the most unholy and the most savage of animals, and the most full of lust and gluttony."[73] For this reason and because most persons seem (not unreasonably) to identify happiness with pleasure, and because passion yields to force rather than argument, it is necessary to train people's character. This is difficult because hardy, temperate living is not pleasant to most of them, especially when they are young, so it is best to fix their nurture and occupation by law. Training is essential, because unlike intellectual excellence, which arises from birth and from teaching, moral excellence is the result of habit.[74] There are some thinkers, Aristotle says, who believe that we are good by nature or become so by education, but generally speaking, "most people obey necessity rather than argument, and punishments rather than the good for its own sake," so that laws are necessary to cover the whole of life.[75]

Aristotle never seems as bitter as Hsün-tzu learns to become, but their basic outlook on the need for education, habit, law, and punishment is similar—with one cardinal difference: Hsün-tzu's social ethics is highly ritualized. In his thought, the concept of ritual is changed "from an aristocratic code of conduct, a kind of *courtoisie* that distinguished gentlemen from ordinary men, into universal principles that underlay society and just government."[76] When the world observes ritual principles, says Hsün-tzu, there is order, safety, and survival; when it does not, there is anarchy, danger, and annihilation.[77] For ritual principles, he believes, not only regulate the desires and save humans from social chaos, but enhance life by giving it the form that expresses its perfect rightness. This is a view of ritual conduct that became extraordinarily effective in China.

5. *Moderation*: Hsün-tzu naturally accepts the Confucian norm that requires him to avoid extremes—his attack on immoderate, that is, onesided philosophy has been summarized. Aristotle, like Plato and other Greeks, advocates following the mean between extremes. At one point, he uses Hsün-tzu's kind of image, that of straightening bent wood, though in the rather different context of the need of each of us to counter one extreme impulse by means of another so as to "drag ourselves away from error, as people do in straightening sticks that are bent."[78] With regard to most pleasures and pains, the mean is temperance and the excess is self-indulgence. "Excellence, then, is a state concerned with choice, lying in a mean relative to us, this being determined by reason and in the way in which practical reason would determine it."[79] As usual, Aristotle is not satisfied with so general a statement and wants to apply it to individual facts. We cannot, however, follow him in his application.

It is an interesting sidelight on the feeling for moderation of both philosophers that they find danger in unregulated music. "The influence of music and sound on man is very profound," says Hsün-tzu, "and the transformations they produce in him can be very rapid." He wants music to be either balanced, to make people harmonious, or solemn and dignified, to make them orderly. He is afraid that if music seduces people toward wickedness, the people will become dissipated, indolent, and mean spirited, the army will become weak and the city walls vulnerable, and the state will become insecure and may be conquered.[80] Aristotle, who believes that "music makes our souls undergo a change," wants it to be used to educate the young and to be suited to people's age and condition; but he does not approve of vulgar, "perverted modes" and "highly strung and unnaturally colored melodies." The actual playing, he thinks, should be left to professionals, who are not freemen. He takes music in his usual analytical spirit, and shows less emotional involvement than either Hsün-tzu or his own teacher, Plato.[81]

6. *The human and philosophical ideal*: I have already given Hsün-tzu's description of the extremely pleasurable and yet resolutely moral limit of perfection that the *chün-tzu* can reach. This ideal, which Hsün-tzu praises in loving variations, is simultaneously moral, intellectual, and aesthetic. It is based on learning, perfected in ritual, embodied in the *chün-tzu's* physical being, and made visible in his activity and repose. The *chün-tzu* can be taken as a model and pattern in everything: He is easy to know but hard to be familiar with, easily apprehensive but hard to

intimidate. He is magnanimous, engages in argument, is critical, strong, flexible, respectful, cautious, but all in due measure. His moral sense fits itself to every situation, and if he speaks of the glory and beauty of his self he is not boasting idly. "How magnificently he possesses all that differentiates him from the vulgar world around him!" Hsün-tzu exclaims in enthusiasm.[82]

Although we have not exhausted the *chün-tzu's* virtues, we have heard enough of them for our purpose. It is notable that his role must be defined in moral and social terms. Whatever his pleasure in the role, his learning is never for its own sake or without reverent attention to tradition. The highest human level, that of the sage, is always seen in the guise of one of the great old kings, one of the inventors of society, who by the very resonance of his being creates joy, peace, and security.

Aristotle has a list of virtues and virtuous men and, in addition, a conception of the ideal life. The highest of the virtues, literally translated, is *great-souledness*. Its possessor must be wealthy and spend money lavishly and gladly, though not on himself but on great, honorable purposes, such as votive offerings, buildings, sacrifices, and religious worship. In accord with his merits, he thinks of himself as worthy of great things. Because he is good in the highest degree, he should not flee danger, wrong another person, or swing his arms by his side (a hint of proper external behavior so considered that it verges on the ritualistic). For what concerns the great-souled man most is great honor rightly conferred on him by good men. But he will be neither overjoyed by good fortune nor excessively pained by evil. Though not fond of danger, he will face great dangers even when his life is at stake—he knows that there are conditions under which life is not worth having. He likes to confer but not to receive favors. He bears himself proudly in company with the great and courteously toward persons of more modest standing. He should be open in his hate and love—to conceal one's feelings is a mark of timidity. Nothing to him is great, so he does not admire anything easily; and he does not gossip or speak ill or well easily. And he walks slowly and speaks in a deep, level voice.[83]

Such is Aristotle's image of the man of highest virtue. It is compatible with this image that Aristotle regards politics as the "master art" and the pursuit of the good of the city-state as even "finer and more godlike" than the pursuit of the good of the single man.[84] He goes so far as to say that "he who is unable to live in society, or who has no need because he is sufficient for himself, must either be a beast or a god: he is no part of a state."[85] Yet Aristotle is pulled toward an ideal that at least verges on the apolitical and self-sufficient. Unhesitatingly, he asserts that the ideal life is not the one pursued by the statesmanlike politician but by the God-imitating philosopher.* Aristotle's preference is likely to be a sign of changing times. Learned Chinese often changed in the same direction. I mean that, despite their inbred devotion to public service, political disappointment might lead Confucians to retire from politics to learning. It is natural to guess that the disappointment with Athenian politics experienced by Socrates, Plato, and himself led Aristotle away from Plato's ideal of the philosopher-king, an ideal that in its union of leadership, moral example, pursuit of social harmony, and profoundness of understanding is like that of the Chinese sage-ruler.

In defending the ideal of a life of philosophizing, Aristotle follows his characteristic path of reasoning by means of hierarchical analogies. Happiness, he says, is activity in accord with excellence, the intellect is the most excellent thing in us, and we are able to contemplate truth more continuously than we can anything else. Compare other good ways of life with the life of contemplation: Unlike the philosopher, the statesman, however nobly he acts, aims at something beyond these acts, whether power, honor, or his own and fellow citizens' happiness. The great-souled man needs money, to gain which he needs power; and the brave man needs power if he is to accomplish anything that corresponds to his virtue. As for the politician, he has no clear idea of what politics is and can learn it only from experience. But we, insofar as we can, must think not of mortal things but "strain every nerve to live in accordance with the best thing in us." Everything points to philosophy as the supreme human occupation:

> The activity of wisdom is admittedly the pleasantest of virtuous activities; at all events the pursuit of it is thought to offer pleasures marvelous for their purity and enduringness . . . The wise man, even by himself, can contemplate truth, and the better the wiser he is; he can perhaps do so better if he has fellow workers, but still he is the most self-sufficient. And this activity alone would seem to be loved for its own sake. (Nicomachean Ethics 1177a)[86]

---

*Although Aristotle's political and philosophical ideals appear incompatible, it is contended that Aristotle means the different accounts he gives in the Nichomachean Ethics to be complementary, not contradictory, and that—whatever Aristotle's own opinion—the passages are best considered together. Aristotle, comments Richard Kraut, gives materials to defend the thesis that "a life devoted to ethical activity is a good life, when it is properly sustained by other goods . . . Aristotle is not too distant from the truth when he sees a kinship between the philosophical and moral lives, and gives a common defense of both" (Kraut, Aristotle on the Human Good, pp. 347–48, 357 [quoted]).

Aristotle's philosopher and his God are cast, like strangely unequal twins, in one another's molds. As compared with the *chün-tzu*, Aristotle's ideal, although by nature a good man, is more concerned with the sheer pleasure he takes in his own intellection than Hsün-tzu (or perhaps even Plato) could possibly sanction. He guards the memory not of tradition but of what he cares to remember for his own individual reasons; and for all his moderation, he is unlikely to be reverent and ritualistic enough to please Hsün-tzu. However, he insists on his dignity and gives himself the full approval of his own conscience, and so he is not, after all, the psychological antithesis of the *chün-tzu*. And the accomplished *chün-tzu*, it should be remembered, has a mind that "benefits from possessing all that is in the world."

Chapter 6

✳

Early Varieties of Atomism

Democritus/Epicurus/Lucretius, "Guatama," and Nameless Buddhists

*Theme: How Innumerable Minute Beings
Replace Being as a Whole*

The idea of the atom makes possible a new kind of balance in philosophy. This is because it breaks up *being* into innumerable beings, which join, mingle, and separate in space—space which in Greece is the paradoxical inheritor of nonbeing and comes to be understood as the degree of freedom that allows the minimal beings to have changing relations with one another.

The idea of minimal, irreducible beings was invented in Greece during the fifth century B.C.E. and again in India a few centuries later. Although it is possible that the Indians got the idea from the Greeks, there is no good evidence for this conclusion, and the Greek and Indian conceptions are distinctive.

Abstractly, there should be no difficulty in accepting a world that contains both real continuity and real discontinuity, but dogma is sometimes more easily sustained or abstract analysis better supported by one or another of the two. Whichever alternative is chosen, there are mathematical models at hand, arithmetic and algebra for the atomistic approach and geometry for the continuous. Language, too, with its division of sentences into words and words into letters, gives a clue to the power of atomic analysis. Maybe the development of atomism was more natural to Greece and India because Greek and Sanskrit words break up into generally meaningless sound elements—letters or syllables—based on phonemic analysis, while Chinese characters, which are physically unchanging— uninflected and most usually monosyllabic—contain many elements of meaning along with phonetic ones.[1]

Democritus (c. 460 c.–370 B.C.E.), Epicurus (341–270 B.C.E.), Lucretius (c. 100–90—c. 55–53 B.C.E.): Atoms to Overcome the Fear of the Gods and of Death

For the sake of what historic justice we can do him, it should be said that the first Greek "to set up atoms as first principles" was Leucippus, a student of Zeno. Given the evidence we have, his atomism seems very nearly the same as that of his student, Democritus, about whom much more is known; and the atomism of Democritus resembles that of Epicurus and Lucretius enough to make it possible to describe their systems together.[2]

Democritus of Abdera was ambitious or curious enough as a philosopher to travel to Egypt to learn geometry from the priests, and (some said) to India to associate with the "naked philosophers" (gymnosophists), as well as to Persia, Babylonia, and maybe Ethiopia. He was versed in every department of philosophy—ethics, physics, mathematics, astronomy, geography, medicine, botany, music (in the wide Greek sense), and others.[3]

The third Greek atomist, Epicurus, was born in Samos. In Athens, to which he came at the age of eighteen, he founded a school, or, rather, a community of like-minded philosophical friends. Out of dislike for his philosophy, detractors ascribed voluptuous vices to him, but in actual life not only was his goodwill apparent to (almost) everyone, we are told, but he was grateful, generous, and gentle. He lived simply and frugally, content with plain bread and water. "Many friends came to him from all parts and lived with him in his garden," and his native land honored him with bronze statues.[4] This near-idyllic image is disturbed by the report that he insulted Aristotle severely, abused Socrates' pupil Phaedo, and attacked Timocrates at great length for differing with him on some philosophical point or other, and that he showed no gratitude to Democritus, from whom he took so much.[5]

The life of Lucretius, the great philosopher-poet, is essentially unknown. The one often-repeated story about him, told by Saint Jerome, is that, having become insane as the result of a love potion, he wrote his book during intervals of lucidity and finally committed suicide. No contemporary evidence exists for the story and the length and careful composition of his poem argue against it; but his strong, vividly expressed emotions, especially those on death and religious tyranny have been taken as a sign of psychological disturbance.[6] His dependence on Epicurus is open and, Epicurean fashion, very worshipful. He pays tribute to Epicurus as the first human who dared to dispute religion and as the person from whose "godlike soul" springs the philosophy that drives away the "blackness of death" and reveals that the fear of death is responsible for much of the avarice and blind craving for office that make men evil.[7]

All these atomists, the three Greeks and the Roman, declare that everything is completely made of material atoms. Aristotle explains the doctrine as a response to the older philosophers—he means Parmenides and Zeno—who thought that whatever is must necessarily be one and immovable. Aristotle continues that Leucippus constructed a theory that harmonized with the perception of change and multiplicity and yet conceded to the believers in unity that motion is not possible without a void. Leucippus did this, says Aristotle, by identifying the void with not-being and separating it absolutely from what is, which is by definition completely full, but not, Leucippus claimed, a unity. Instead, what is consists of things "infinite in number and too small to be seen. They move in the void (for there is void), and their combination causes coming-to-be, and their separation, dissolution."[8]

By this ingenious compromise, nothing that is ever comes into being or is destroyed; but the innumerable, fully full, indestructible ises join and separate in the not-being, the absolute void, where they form temporary groupings that are not true beings at all. Aristotle says that Leucippus and Democritus thought that the atoms were infinite in number and form and too small to be individually perceived. According to Aristotle, Democritus called the mixture of atoms or seeds the elements of the whole of nature, and he identified spherical atoms with the soul because their shape adapts them best to permeate everywhere and, by moving, to cause all the others to move. However, the sign of life, according to the atomists, is respiration. This is because the environment compresses the bodies of animals and forces them to expel the movement-producing atoms, which the living animal, never at rest, must replace with similar atoms from the outside.[9]

The atomists all agree that atoms (*a-tomos* means *uncuttable* or *indivisible*) must be simple and unchangeable. This is the result of the atoms' complete homogeneity and "fullness"—without parts, variations, or differences in intensity, and so without any reason or ability to change. To Democritus, the number of the atoms and the variety of their shapes is infinite—Epicurus accepts the infinity of their number but reduces the quantity of shapes to merely incomprehensibly great.[10]

Everything in nature can be explained, the atomists say, on the basis of a few properties of the atoms: their number, size, shape, order, and motion. Because of their minuteness, they escape our senses, except when they are massed. Their motion is an inherent property and, like the atoms themselves, eternal. This ability to move is purely mechanical and not, as might be supposed, a sign that they are somehow alive. Democritus says that at first the atoms moved in a random discord in which some of them rebounded and others became entangled with one another and formed various worlds. Some worlds flourished, others declined, and still others were destroyed by collisions with one another.

The atomists believe that necessity rules everything, but not in the sense that humans can predict everything by knowing the laws of necessity. This is because to the Greeks, unlike ourselves, necessity is not the "law" that links events in a cause and effect relationship, but the predictable working of the nature of particular kinds of things: fire by nature rises, a plant by nature grows, a human being by nature reasons and laughs. But with respect to the world at large, there are so many unknown possibilities that, to the ancient Greeks, it makes sense to speak even of "necessary chance."[11]

Like everything else, the soul is composed of atoms. These are of fire, Democritus says, while Epicurus says they are of fine atoms like those of wind or heat, and some finer still—atoms so fine and round that they can penetrate the whole body with great speed and influence it in each of its parts. Sensation is the reaction caused by external atoms striking the atoms of the sense organs. The sense of sight is relatively complicated. We see because objects give off successive thin films of atoms that reproduce the objects' external shapes, their "images" (eidola), which enter the eye and cause vision there. Other senses get simpler atomic explanations: a sharp taste, for example, is the effect of atoms that are sharp, angular, bent, and small. But because everyone is in a different condition, what tastes sharp to one person can taste different to another; and animals sense things differently from human beings. This leads Democritus to skepticism in relation to the senses. But he would not, I think, disagree with the belief of Epicurus that sensations are true in that, purely as sensations, they cannot be refuted. Sometimes Democritus says, in apparent discouragement, that all we know is what changes as the condition of the body changes and as what enters the body presses on it. Or he says that man must learn that he is separated from reality, or that truth is in the depths we do not know. Sensation cannot reveal its exact, atomic causes; and the testimony of sight, hearing, smell, and taste is no more than a bastard form of knowledge. Legitimate knowledge is only that of atoms and void.[12]

Less skeptical than Democritus, Lucretius offers an argument, remarkably like the modern explanation of Brownian motion, to show that sensation can indirectly image atomic movement: When tiny, jostling particles become visible in the sun's rays that enter a dark house, one sees the effect on the visible particles of the blows of the invisible ones, and therefore, ultimately, of the blows of the atoms themselves, their movement passing upward and little by little becoming perceptible to our senses.[13]

The more technically philosophical defense of atomism models itself on Zeno's way of thinking. Assume, an argument says, that things can be divided endlessly. If such division—possible only in theory—was carried out, what would remain? If what remained had any size, this remainder could continue to be divided; but if it was divided without end, divided until its size diminished to nothing, what would remain would be a mathematical point or else nothing. Because points, considered mathematically, have no size, no number of them could ever add up to any magnitude and they could in no way make up a world. How can a magnitude consist of things that have no magnitude? In a world of things without magnitude, everything would be collapsed together, nothing would be physically separable from another. Obviously, therefore, a body must contain atomic magnitudes that are indivisible. Epicurus puts it this way: If an atom was infinitely divisible, the continued division might weaken everything and grind whatever exists into nonexistence. But if each division did have *some* magnitude, the magnitude of all the infinite number of parts together would be infinite—as large, Lucretius adds, as the universe as a whole—the sort of conceptual problem that in quantum field theory is solved, so to speak, by "renormalization." Furthermore, continues Epicurus, if the atom had an infinite number of parts, whenever we moved over the atom in our imaginations, we would have traversed and—impossibly—completed an infinite in our thought:[14]

> Once one says that there are infinite parts in a body or parts of any degree of smallness, it is not possible to conceive how this should be, and indeed how could the body any longer be limited in size? And again, since the limited body has an extreme point, which is distinguishable, even though not perceptible by itself, you cannot conceive that the succeeding point to it is not similar in character, or that if you go on in this way from one point to another, it should be possible for you to proceed to infinity marking such points in your mind. (Epicurus, *Letter to Herodotus*, 57)[15]

While the physical indivisibility of atoms is the result of their minimal size, Democritus may also suppose that they are also theoretically, that is, mathematically, indivisible. Aristotle's comment on this view is that the idea of a smallest, theoretically indivisible magnitude conflicts with the science of mathematics because nothing continuous can be composed of indivisibles. A line, for example, cannot be composed of points, because the line is continuous and the points are indivisible.[16] Epicurus (amplified by Lucretius) offers interesting though obscure counterarguments to Aristotle. These say in effect that the very conception of a physical magnitude requires us to be able to distinguish in thought between what is and is not the minimal object's boundary or edge. The edge, of course, has no independent existence, so that the atom cannot be said to have parts. Because it has a boundary, the atom must have a shape. But whatever is, so to speak, inside the atom is too small to have any boundary or shape of its own.[17]

Such reasoning concerning the size of objects can be applied to time as well. Aristotle discusses and dismisses the possibility not only of indivisibles of physical magnitude but also of indivisibles of time and motion.[18] At about the same time, Diodorus Cronos attempts to conceptualize time atoms, that is, time as fundamentally jerky rather than flowing. It is possible that Epicurus and Lucretius acknowledge such a possibility, but even if they do, they refrain from exploiting it.[19]

In favor of a universe consisting of atoms and void alone, Epicurus and Lucretius stress Parmenides' principle: nothing is created out of nothing. This means to them that everything has to have its beginning in a timeless "seed." In other words, there is no spontaneous creation, which would create a completely illogical and disorderly world, not the world that we in fact know. If things originated—came to being—from nothing, every kind would be born and change quite haphazardly.*

> For little children would grow suddenly to youths, and at once trees would come forth, leaping from the earth. But . . . all things grow slowly, as is natural from a fixed seed, and as they grow preserve their kind: so that you can know that each thing grows great, and is fostered out of its own substance. (*De Rerum Natura* 1.184–91)[20]

---

*As in the nursery rhyme:
> There was a man of double deed
> Sowed his garden full of seed.
> When the seed began to grow,
> 'Twas like a garden full of snow;
> When the snow began to melt,
> 'Twas like a ship without a belt;
> When the ship began to sail,
> 'Twas like a bird without a tail.

Epicurus and Lucretius also stress a law of conservation of matter and energy, the quantity of which is always the same. No force

> can change the sum of things; for neither is there anything outside, into which any kind of matter may escape from the universe, nor whence new forces can arise and burst into the universe and change the whole nature of things and alter its motions. (*De Rerum Natura* 2.303–7)[21]

The quantity of matter must be preserved because if that which disappears was destroyed "into that which does not exist," all things would long since have perished; but the world of things has not disappeared, because all things are simply broken up into their component atoms, which rearrange themselves to comprise other things.[22]

It seems that, unlike Democritus, Epicurus believes that atoms have inherent weight and fall naturally downward. By an idea implied in his surviving works—an idea attributed to him in ancient times and explicit in the text of Lucretius—the atoms are first carried straight down the void by their own weight (as has often been observed, Lucretius does not see that the idea of an absolute direction in an infinite void, either down, up, or sideways, makes no abstract sense). Here and there, at quite undetermined times and places, Lucretius explains, the atoms push very slightly away from their straight path. Unless for this swerve (*clinamen*), they would continue falling without striking one another and would not form different compounds. Lucretius asks, rather suddenly, if motion followed motion in exactly fixed order, without any swerve that "burst the bonds of fate," what would be the source of the "will torn from the fates," the will by which each man moves to where his pleasure—not merely the mechanics of motion—leads him? There is something in us that can fight and resist external force. It is "the work of a tiny swerve of atoms at no fixed place and at no fixed time" that frees the mind from "internal necessity in performing all its acts" and allows it to escape being "overpowered and forced, as it were, to suffer and endure."[23]

This last passage says that the swerve saves the mind from internal necessity, which is the necessity, it may be supposed, of the force exerted by the body or, more narrowly, by one's initial disposition (in Epicurean psychology, this disposition is equivalent to the proportions or arrangements of the different kinds of atoms of which the person is made). The freedom granted by the swerve makes it reasonable to give moral praise and blame.[24] So to the Epicureans, belief in atomism and necessity does not contradict a substantial degree of internal freedom and self-determination. It is therefore not difficult for them to believe that training and, especially, the power of reason can for the most part lead us to live a life worthy of the gods.[25] The swerve that allows freedom was a source of ridicule in antiquity, but in our own times, of wonder, because it suggests the indeterminacy of twentieth-century physics.

We do not have a developed idea of the ethics of Democritus, although we know that he believes in a temperate life and that he thinks the gods are atomic compounds. The basic advice of Epicurus and Lucretius is to experience pleasure and avoid pain. This is a desire, Epicurus says, that is sensed and so obviously natural that it need not be proved.[26] Pleasure as Epicurus means it does not imply sensual indulgence but sober reasoning, safety, and the absence of pain. The pleasure he favors is the kind that, by his theory, produces no rough movements of the atoms of the organs of sensation and thought. To him, this is the pleasure of the absence of pain, of "untroubledness," of a calm, physical and mental, like that of a wholly calm sea.[27] "Every choice and avoidance should be referred to the health of the body and the soul's freedom from disturbance, since this is the end belonging to the blessed life."[28] Therefore, says Epicurus, the words of a philosopher are empty if they do not expel the suffering of the soul. Yet philosophy entertains at the same time as it teaches, so Epicurus gives the less obviously medical advice to "laugh, philosophize, and handle our household affairs and other personal matters, all at the same time, and never cease making the utterances which stem from correct philosophy."[29]

Epicurus' theory of pleasure as the absence of pain or as complete calm is hedonism in the style that even a Buddhist might favor. It leads him to say that glory and politics, which imprison the ambitious, are unwise, highly risky aims.* Safety from our fellow humans is more impor-

---

*The Epicurean's view of politics and public life is not as simple as it may at first seem. According to Diogenes Laertius, Epicurus says that the wise man "will engage in lawsuits and leave writings behind him, but will not deliver speeches on public occasions . . . He will be careful of his reputation . . . He will care more than other men for public spectacles, will erect statues of others, but whether he had one himself or not, he would be indifferent . . . He will be ready to make money, but only when he is in straits and by means of his philosophy. He will pay court to a king, if occasion demands . . . And he will gather together a school, but never so as to become a popular leader" (*Lives of Eminent Philosophers* 10.119–21b; trans. Bailey, *Epicurus*, p. 167).

Lucretius writes of the dispiriting, Sisyphean struggles to be elected to political power, which is never really given (3.995–1002). He finds it sweet to be safe while viewing war on the plains below him, and gladdening to look down from the heights of wisdom on those who struggle ceaselessly to rise to power and win the world. "Blind hearts!" he calls out (2.1–24). However, Lucretius, who tells us that he is writing *De Rerum Natura* for his friend Memmius, finds no inconsistency in saying that in this time of Rome's troubles he, Lucretius, cannot do his part with an untroubled mind and that Memmius cannot abandon Rome's welfare—he may be referring to Memmius' period as praetor in 58 B.C.E. or to his candidacy for consul in 54 (1.40–43). (On the attitude to politics of both Epicurus and Lucretius, see Fowler, "Lucretius and Politics.")

tant, and this is best gained by retirement, a quiet life, and, especially, friends. Our pleasure, the absence of pain, is what makes natural science valuable, because—*only* because, he says at one point—it relieves our suspicions concerning the phenomena of the sky and concerning death.[30] Natural justice in itself is nothing but the compact of men not to harm or be harmed. Thin-film images in the air show us gods, as a rule in dreams, and we regard the gods as immortal and completely happy. Being happy, they cannot be concerned with the welfare of human beings, and, having no anger or favor, they do not reward the good or punish the evil. However, to pray to the gods is a natural act; and contemplation of the gods, whose nature is blessed and eternal, is a great pleasure. Besides, a life of conformity with law and custom conduces to peace.[31] To end this account of Epicurean morality, there is a not un-Chinese or un-Indian apothegm by Epicurus: "The veneration of the wise man is a great blessing to those who venerate him."[32]

But how is the fear of death to be countered? The answer, says Epicurus, is that "all good and evil consists in sensation, but death is deprivation of sensation." Since death gives no trouble when it comes, there is no good reason to anticipate it with pain. The wise man does not fear the end of life because, while life does not offend him, life's absence seem to him no evil. A right understanding does away with the craving for immortality, so that

> death, the most terrifying of ills, is nothing to us, since so long as we exist, death is not with us; but when death comes, then we do not exist. It does not then concern either the living or the dead, since for the former it is not, and the latter are no more. (*Letter to Menoeceus*, 125)[33]

Lucretius, who is far more openly emotional than Epicurus, stresses that it is the fear of death that feeds the avarice and the blind lust for distinction that make men lawless:[34]

> Some wear out their lives for the sake of a statue and a name. And often it goes so far, that for fear of death men are seized by hatred of life and of seeing the light ... We in the light sometimes fear what is no more to be feared than the things that children in the dark hold in terror and imagine will come true. (*De Rerum Natura* 3.76–90)[35]

Absurdly, a person imagines himself alive while dead and, watching his own dead body, he infects it with his feeling of horror and deprivation. He is pitied when dead because he can no longer enjoy life; but he no longer craves anything. After all, "no one feels the want of himself and his life when both mind and body alike are quiet in sleep."[36] (When Lucretius says this, he forgets that there are people who are afraid to sleep because they are afraid they will not wake up.) Lucretius imagines nature finding her voice and addressing the fearful person. Why mourn? she asks. Either, having enjoyed life, you have had your fill of its satisfactions, or, if you have a grudge against life, why add to it? The old order is always thrust out by the new, for "matter is wanted, that the coming generations may grow." Look back and see the time before we were born and see that in time we will die. Is death "not more peaceful than any sleep?"[37]

Gautama (or Akshapada) and Nameless Buddhists: Atoms to Make Wholes Possible or to Make Selves Impossible

Simply as materialism, Greek atomism has an Indian counterpart.[38] This counterpart is known as *Lokayata*, a word that at first seems to have meant *prevalent in the world (loka)* (of ordinary people). It is not known how and when the word was accepted as the name of the school or tradition of materialism, the school that contends that *all that exists is the present world*. Such a philosophy is often attributed to Brihaspati or to Charvaka, but the existence of both is so vague that, for all we know, they are mythical figures.[39]*

The one undoubtedly authentic text that can be attributed to the Lokayatas or Charvakas is that written by Jayarashi of, perhaps, the early ninth century A.D. But although Jayarashi quotes from the basic Lokayata text, the *Brihaspati Sutra*—in Hindu philosophy a sutra is an ordered set of basic aphorisms—he seems to want to reinterpret it, and he turns out to be not a materialist but a radical skeptic. He will therefore be discussed later, along with others of his skeptical kind. But even though we lack authentic philosophical texts, the basic doctrine of materialism appears as early as the old Upanishad in which the god Indra is temporarily assailed by the fear that the *atman* takes its pleasure and suffers and dies along with the body.[40] In further evidence of early materialism, a Buddhist dia-

---

*In Kautilya's treatise on politics, the *Arthashastra*, uncertainly dated at about 300 B.C.E. (it may be several centuries later), there is the following surprising testimony to the importance of Lokayata: "Samkhya, Yoga and Lokayata—these constitute philosophy. Investigating, by means of reasoning, (what is) spiritual good and evil in the Vedic lore, material gain and loss in economics, good policy and bad policy in the science of politics, as well as the relative strength and weakness of these (three sciences) (philosophy) confers benefit on the people, keeps the mind steady in adversity and in prosperity and brings about proficiency in thought, speech and action" (*The Kauṭilya Arthaśāstra*, Part II, trans. R. P. Kangle, Bombay: University of Bombay, 1963, p. 7 (*Arthaśāstra* 1.2.10).

logue tells of one Ajita Keshakambali (Ajita of the Hair Blanket) who says bluntly that man is formed of the four elements, and that when he dies, the earth in him returns to earth, the water to water, the fire to fire, and the air to air, and the senses vanish into space. Ajita's moral is that those who preach the giving of alms or the existence of immaterial categories "speak vain and lying nonsense. When the body dies both fool and wise alike are cut off and perish. They do not survive after death."[41]

I report all this on Indian materialism simply to indicate that it exists—it was at one time widespread—and to point out that, simply as materialism, it is analogous to Greek atomism but is itself not atomistic. The origin of atomism in India is not really known.[42] The Upanishads have been suggested as a possible source. Maybe when Uddalaka teaches Shvetaketu his series of lessons, the invisible fineness of *being* that is dispersed in salt water, for example, is conceived as an invisibly fine kind of matter not unlike atoms.[43] But as far as we know, atomism was originated in India about the third century B.C.E. We find it relatively early among the Buddhists called Sarvastivadins *(those who teach that everything exists, even in the past and future)*. It also appears relatively early among the Jains and in two Hindu schools, the Nyaya *(School of Logic* or *School of Theory of Argument)* and the Vaisheshika *(School Referring to Individuality)*. Their respective founders are named as Gautama and Kanada (early commentators give the author of the Nyaya Sutras the name Akshapada, literally "eyes in his feet"). The origins of Nyaya and Vaisheshika go back more or less to the beginning of the first century A.D.—as usual in India, the dates are problematic. By somewhere close to the fourth century C.E. the teaching had taken the authoritative form in which it appears in the Nyaya Sutras (which may have been based on a preceding text supplemented by interpolations of a later date.)[44]

I will confine my account of Indian atomism to that of the Nyaya and the Buddhists. My justification is that as compared with the Vaisheshika, the Naiyayikas argue their case more philosophically from the beginning, and that the Nyaya Sutras have early commentators, which the Vaisheshika Sutras lack. As for Buddhist views, they are more widely known than the Jain, are sharp and relatively well developed, and (as far as I know) they have more philosophically interesting sequels than do the Jain views.

The context for Nyaya atomism is, if course, the Nyaya system as a whole, understanding of which is important for later chapters of this book. It is not improbable that the system began as a set of rules for debate that were extended into a study of how reasoning proceeds and what kinds of evidence it uses. This study then grew into a standard Indian philosophical system by the addition of whatever else was felt to be necessary. Much of the Nyaya Sutras shows a fairly rigorous empiricism, so that some ideas that appear in it—on purification by yoga and on liberation—may have been superimposed on the earlier, more empirical views, to our confusion and perhaps that of the Sutras' own compilers. In discussing Nyaya in the present chapter, I confine myself almost completely to the Sutras themselves and their first commentary (written by Vatsyayana in the fifth century A.D.) and omit or take special note of any of his comments that go conspicuously beyond the Sutras. I take up little except the early Nyaya view of philosophy, that is, of knowledge and its instruments, and of the self, salvation, and, of course, the atom.[45]

Nyaya is the most wholehearted exponent of the rule—adopted by other Indian schools as well—that philosophy (more exactly, *anvikshiki*, *investigative science*) is by nature the critical expression of doubts and of answers to them. The commentator's introduction to the Nyaya Sutras says that unless for the systematic use of the categories of philosophy, first among them the instruments and objects of knowledge, and then of doubt and of the other categories, philosophy, like the Upanishads, would be only the study of the *atman*, the self.[46] This remark seems directed at a less systematic, less self-questioning kind of study, probably an early form of Vedanta, the precursors of which we have met and the later exponent of which, Shankara, will be discussed along with Spinoza.[47]

Reasoning, says the commentator, is not relevant for what is either unknown or is known for certain, but only for objects concerning which there is doubt. "As said by Gautama, 'Final ascertainment is the ascertainment of an object through thesis and antithesis which result from doubt.' "[48] There are many forms of doubt, the commentator, Vatsyayana, points out, but the most important philosophically arise from contradictory statements about the same subject, for example, "the soul exists" and "the soul does not exist." Such contradictions create doubt among those who hear them because they know of no way to decide between alternatives impossible to accept together. The nature of philosophical doubt should be understood, the commentator says, because one's opponent in a critical discussion is likely to deny its existence. "Therefore, doubt, being presupposed by all forms of critical discussion, is itself critically discussed first."[49]

This resolute incorporation of doubt into philosophy (in the sense of the investigative science) is accompanied by an equally resolute, nearly commonsense realism, in the philosophical sense of belief in a material world independent of human perception and thought. We see this particularly well in the answers given to unidentified philosophers, some perhaps early Vedantists, others perhaps radically skeptical or philosophically idealistic Buddhists, both kinds disposed to deny the materiality and metaphysical independence of the world.

First comes the skeptic, who doubts the usefulness of the intellectual analysis of composite wholes. He objects that all the work of the Nyaya in setting up criteria for understanding is wasted because none of them shows an object's essential nature. The Nyaya use of analytic reason, the objecting philosopher continues, shows that a composite thing is not real but depends on its components, which depend, in turn, on their components, which when analyzed, that is, divided, in the same way eventually arrive at a point at which nothing any longer exists—everything has been analyzed away.

The Nyaya answer is by means of the conception of atoms: Atoms—with which the analysis of material things ends—are by nature imperceptible, are necessarily different from what is visible, and cannot be divided infinitely. Analytic reason cannot be curtailed: All the branches of learning, all purposive actions, and all the activities of living beings are based on the kind of means of valid knowledge that the exponents of Nyaya discuss. The thesis that "nothing exists" for reason cannot be entertained because if proof for the thesis exists, the proof refutes the view that there is nothing—because there must be at least the means of knowledge by which one arrives at the thesis. And if there is no independent way, no instrument by which to prove the thesis that nothing exists, how can it be established? And if the thesis that nothing exists for reason can be established without any independent means of valid knowledge, why not assume that the contrary thesis, "all things exist," can also be established without such means?[50]

There is also the rival to Nyaya who claims that the idea of the instruments and objects of valid cognition is mistaken because what is perceived cannot be distinguished from false perceptions, whether caused by dreams, by magicians' tricks, or by illusions such as mirages. This rival gets the answer that his comparisons are unwarranted. If he argues that the objects appearing in a dream are unreal because they are dreamed, he implies that objects experienced while awake are real. Moreover, dreams vary. Some are frightening, some pleasant, and some neutral; and sometimes one does not dream at all. If it is admitted that the false awareness of a dreamed object has a distinct cause, then these differences in dreaming must have a variety of distinct causes. Further, the memory of an object depends on its having been experienced before, and therefore the memory cannot disprove the reality of the object. Just so, the awareness of an object in a dream depends on a previous experience of the object, the reality of which the dream therefore cannot disprove. Also, when awake, the dreamer remembers what he dreamed and, being awake, knows that the dream is false. But if it is assumed that there is no difference between the states of dreaming and waking, the argument becomes useless because it denies the very existence of waking experience, with which a dream is contrasted. In the same way that a dream depends on an earlier real perception, so a mistake in ordinary perception—for example, a tree trunk taken to be a man—is determined to be a mistake only because a man was earlier perceived correctly. And the illusions a magician causes by his tricks are based on similar, real things. And the mirage of water is a phenomenon the real cause of which we understand. The cause is the flickering light that results from the intermingling of the sun's rays with the heat radiating from the earth's surface. Furthermore, the fact that the dreamer perceives his dream differently when sleeping and awake, that the magician perceives his tricks differently from the person who is fooled by them, and that the mirage is perceived differently by someone distant from someone close by cannot be explained logically if one maintains that all objects are nonexistent or without any essence of their own. Common sense must prevail.[51]

The realistic impulse of Nyaya philosophy is evidently strong. Not surprisingly, therefore, one of the main themes of the Nyaya Sutras is the explanation and defense of the *means or instruments of valid knowledge*, as the term *pramana* may be translated. According to the Sutras, there are four and only four such means: perception, inference, comparison, and verbal testimony. The evidence given by any one of them is often convincing, but that of perception—the direct contact of a sense organ with its object—is the most basic: if we know something by means of verbal testimony (we hear there is a fire), we want to know it by inference (we infer the fire from smoke), and what we know by inference, we want to perceive (the fire is here); "and when the object is ascertained through perception, the inquiry comes to its final end."[52]

Without these instruments of knowledge, nothing can be known and no act can be carried out successfully. Without them, no one knows what is worth getting or avoiding or how to carry out any activity with success, so there are no exceptions to testing by use of these instruments: "The activities of god, man and animal are maintained with the help of these instruments of valid knowledge and not otherwise."[53] A note of caution is soon struck, it is true. Nyaya is defined as "the examination of an object with the help of the instruments of valid knowledge," meaning that it makes a critical examination of what we know and makes further inferences in keeping with the rules it has determined. Of course, these inferences must not be contradicted by perception or—to strike a note of caution—by tradition, meaning, especially, the scriptures or Vedas.[54]

The occurrence of such caution here prompts me to make a brief interruption in the account of Nyaya empiricism in order to consider its attitude to tradition (*agama*) or verbal testimony (*shabda*), the word by which the translator refers to the Vedas. The Nyaya Sutras defends the Vedas' authoritative status against the charge that they contain falsehoods, self-contradictions, or mere repetitions. But the commentator's defense sounds more profane than sacred, like that of a historian who, after the usual critical examination of a source, decides that it is reliable. The Nyaya commentator (elsewhere) defines a trustworthy speaker as one who has direct and trustworthy knowledge and is able to communicate it as he knows it. The commentator adds, "This definition is equally applicable to the seer (rishi), noble (arya), and barbarian, the person without Vedic practices."[55] Then, speaking of the authoritative status of the Vedas, the commentator makes it clear that the words of the ancient, semidivine rishis, are valid for the same reasons that verbal testimony in ordinary life is valid:

> Just as statements in ordinary life, since they convey sense when properly analyzed, are regarded as sources of valid knowledge, so also the statement of the Veda, since these convey sense when properly analyzed, should be regarded as sources of valid knowledge.[56]

The declaration that there are exactly four kinds of instruments of valid knowledge lays the Nyaya open to a charge that is an exact parallel to Parmenides' charge against Plato's hypothesis of Ideas. The objector says: If we know everything by one of the instruments of knowledge, then these instruments must be made known by still other instruments. This would not only lead to the need for some instrument, some means, other than the recognized ones but also lead to a logically indefensible infinite regress. And if you suppose that it is possible to grasp a recognized means of valid knowledge without assuming still another means, you admit an instance in which such a means is unnecessary. And if one can do without a means in this instance, why do we need means of knowledge for other instances?[57]

The Nyaya answer is that one instrument or means of perception can be perceived by another. For example, the light of the lamp, an auxiliary cause of perception, is an instrument of knowledge and is apprehended by contact of the eye, which is another instrument of knowledge, that is, sense perception. Further, since we see when the lamp is present and fail to see when it is absent, we use the instrument of inference to grasp that the lamp is a cause of visual perception. And the lamp, a means of knowledge, is also made known to be such by verbal testimony, another means, when we hear the words, "In the darkness, get a lamp." In this way, as we discover, one means of knowledge is known by another analogous or different means. Similarly, by means of the perception, for example, of visible objects and sounds, we infer that we have the senses of sight and hearing, and these senses make the objects of sight and hearing known. That we see a thing when it is not obstructed and do not see when it is obstructed, as by a wall, is the logical mark in the inference according to which the senses work by coming into contact with their objects. And the knowledge that is grasped because of the peculiar relation between the conscious self and the sense (the "mind") that channels perceptions to the self is another kind of sense perception and so is itself a means of valid knowledge. Furthermore—to give another interpretation of the text being commented on—the perceived light of the lamp is the instrument for the perception of other visible objects and is therefore both object and cause of visual perception. So something can be both an object of knowledge and a producer of knowledge. It follows that we know the several instruments of knowledge by the means of these same instruments, and need no others; and we do not know them without a means of knowledge to know them with.* One individual instance of perception can grasp another. The water we perceive when it is brought to us allows us to grasp the water that still remains in the vessel from which it was taken. As in this illustration, the means and the object of knowledge cam be of the same kind although not (numerically) identical.

In the case of the mind—to Nyaya, an unconscious inner sense organ—and, equally, of the conscious self, to which the mind channels and supplies perceptual information, the object grasped and the instrument by which it is grasped are the same. This is the case when in thoughts such as *I am happy* or *I am unhappy* the conscious self grasps itself. That which grasps—the mind as an instrument—and the object that is grasped—the mind as the inferred object of the instrument—are the same. That is, the presence in our consciousness of no more than one cognition at a time leads us to infer that we have a sense organ, the mind, that channels perceptual and other cognitions, one by one, to the conscious self.

It might be argued that we have to introduce additional instruments of knowledge because there are objects unknowable to any of the recognized instruments, but no such objects are in fact known. Also, it is a mistake to argue that if the instruments of knowledge are known by instruments of knowledge, we become involved in an infinite regress. The

---

*The Nyaya position, which depends on the mutual verification of the means of evidence by one another seems to me like a contemporary philosopher's proposal that the means of belief should be understood, without any vicious circularity, to give one another mutual support. This recent "new approach to the project of ratification" is one that "is neither purely a priori nor purely empirical in character, but very modestly naturalistic, allowing the contributory relevance both of empirical considerations about human beings' cognitive capacities and limitations, and of considerations of a logical, deductive character" (S. Haack, *Evidence and Inquiry*, Oxford: Blackwell, 1993, p. 2).

argument must be mistaken because the activities of practical life are based on a correct grasp of the objects of knowledge together with the causes of knowledge. The attainment of any of the ends of life, which are virtue, wealth, pleasure, and liberation, depends on the correct grasp of the objects of knowledge and the instruments—perception, inference, comparison, and verbal testimony—by which one knows these ends.[58]

As this reasoning has implied, the Naiyayika (the exponent of Nyaya) believes in a self that is different from the sum total of the body, which includes the outer sense organs, the inner sense organ (the mind), knowledge, and feelings of pleasure and pain. Otherwise, he says, it would be impossible to understand how we experience an object through different senses, for example, sight and touch, or through one eye and, afterwards, the other, and know that it is the same object.[59] The limitation of each sense to its specific kind of object teaches us that within us that there is a conscious agent, a unitary, continuous self, able to infer from the sight of something what its previously perceived taste and smell must be. The self, that which is conscious and knows, is not a quality of the body. We infer this because the body, which never loses its color, sometimes loses consciousness. The body, then, is the locus, abode, or substratum of the self's activities; and the body "is imagined as the agent because it alone and nothing else becomes the locus of the apprehension of pleasure and pain."[60] The self, the nonbodily, unifying consciousness, the knower and enjoyer of everything, is surely eternal. Like Kant, the Naiyayika believes in an immaterial, eternal self because otherwise, he fears, morality collapses: if the self dies, the precepts of the sages become meaningless. If the self dies, the absurd result is that persons will not accumulate karma, the merit and demerit for their actions. If it dies, there is no use in the practice of celibacy to attain liberation, there is no sin in harming living things. All this is inadmissible.[61]

The Nyaya view of liberation sounds like that of the Buddhists. Pleasure is real, Nyaya says, but causes pain: We fail to get what we want, what we want is soon destroyed, or falls short of what is hoped, or needs too great an effort. Such suffering continues up to liberation, so that pleasure, the body, the senses, and so on, often mistakenly thought of as in themselves good, are to be meditated on as nothing but suffering.[62] So far, in relation to suffering (pain, *duhkha*), the Nyaya viewpoint seems familiar; but, as before, there is a check: We are told that there are no grounds, whether perception, inference, or scripture to prove that the liberated self becomes entirely blissful—on the contrary, such a result is logically impossible.

I omit the arguments to prove this and report only the explanation for why the liberated person's eternal awareness of bliss is not shared by the nonliberated person: Everything desirable is accompanied by the undesirable, so that, because selective rejection is impossible, one also rejects the desirable. Certainly, the connection with the body, the senses, and so on, is not what obstructs the nonliberated person's awareness of eternal bliss. It is the very function of the body and senses to help the self enjoy pleasure; and there is no way of showing that the self can experience either pleasure or pain when unconnected with a body. There may be a scriptural text saying that the liberated self is eternally blissful, but this is only a manner of speaking, because, as often in ordinary talk, the word *pleasure* is used in the sense of the absence of suffering. The mistaken belief that eternal bliss can be gained by means of the desire for this bliss is no more than a kind of bondage. Desire itself is bondage, "and it is not logical that one is liberated in spite of bondage." What is desired and possible is meditation on the fact that pleasure is a form of pain because it is always involved with pain. By meditation on this truth the person will become dispassionate and attain release, that is, will cease to be reborn, and all pain will disappear.[63]

The subject of God, which fits in at this point in the exposition of Nyaya, creates embarrassment for an expositor. The Vaisheshika Sutras of Kanada do not mention God at all, while in the Nyaya Sutras, God appears in three unclear sutras and plays no further role. Some scholars hold that the statement in the Nyaya Sutras that God is the cause of the universe is meant to be ascribed not to Guatama but to his opponent. If God is considered important in the Sutras, why is he not accorded more attention? And if it is Gautama, not the opponent, who holds that God created the universe, why does the subcommentary repeatedly say that the universe was never created?

As will be seen, later Nyaya philosophers defend a limited monotheism. The commentator, who accepts the idea of God, deals with it only little and inconsistently—he calls God omniscient and omnipotent but describes the omnipotence more like that of an all-knowing supervisor than a boundless creator. The commentator comments that it is God who helps a person to attain the particular result the person hopes for. When God does not help, the person's action is fruitless. God, says the commentator, must have the nature of a self from which all vice is absent. God, too, attains the result of his own action in that, being omnipotent, he creates the world at the very moment that he wills (this is a somewhat bold paraphrase).* Like a trusted

---

*To deal with the objection that God cannot create the very things (such as merit and demerit) by whose acknowledged help he creates other things, the subcommentary answers: A human being makes an ax with the help of other instruments he has made, and with the ax makes the implement with which he makes a jar, and so on. God makes the body and pleasures and pains with the help of merit and demerit, but he also brings merit and demerit into existence by means, respectively, of pure and impure intentions, and so on. It is true that God uses help at a particular time to bring particular things into existence. But God creates things in succession, at different times. As for the "beginning of creation," no such beginning is admitted and the question is therefore irrelevant (Uddyotakara's subcommentary to 4.1.21, as in Jha, *The Nyāyā Sūtras of Gautama*, vol. 4, pp. 1471–72).

friend or a father, God acts, without any self-interest, for the good of all living beings. One infers his existence as one does that of any other self, by virtue of knowledge and the like. One knows him also by the testimony of the scriptures, where he is said to be the perceiver of all, the knower of all, the omniscient.[64] But whatever God's nature, it is not clear that the commentator is very much interested in him. Certainly he is more interested in him as a powerful and fatherly friend than as someone to be adored or, to go metaphysically further, as reality in itself.

Now, finally, we return to atoms. To my mind, what is most interesting in the Nyaya (or Nyaya-Vaisheshika) theory is its view of parts—such as atoms—in relation to the wholes made of them, but made with a difference. That is, in opposition to the disintegrative preferences of Buddhism, Nyaya assumes a dimensional transition that distinguishes atoms from wholes made of atomic composites. That is, Nyaya stresses that there is a sharp dimensional transition from individual atoms, which are by nature imperceptible, to composites of atoms that are perceptible wholes.

To explain the Nyaya view: We perceive separate things, to which we can give the name *wholes*. Each whole is obviously made up of parts, which can be considered *wholes* in their own right. But the process of finding parts further divisible into wholes must come to an end in something indivisible, an atom, in India called *anu* or *paramanu*.* First, it must be realized that the atom is by nature beyond perception. Not only are the senses not adapted to sensing atoms, but an atom as such cannot have the nature and qualities of a whole, which is something that can be perceived. A single atom has only the kind of "size" *(anu)* that is minimal. The word *size* is in quotation marks because the single atom does not have size in the sense of the extensional quality called *largeness*, a quality that makes it possible to perceive whatever possesses it. A dyad—two atoms joined to form a composite—is still below the threshold of largeness. Largeness first

---

*As its use in the Upanishads indicates, the word *anu* "was a noun and an adjective in the general and ordinary sense of 'very small, very minute' *(sukshma)*. Its use in the specific sense of 'atom'— an impartite substance which is the minutest—began in the earliest Sutra-works of the various systems of philosophy . . . First, it may stand for a particular kind of magnitude *(parimana)*, which, according to the Nyaya-Vaisheshika, is a quality *(guna)*. Secondly, it may denote a substance itself . . . either an atom, the indivisible minutest substance or a dyad, the smallest and the first product out of atoms . . .

"As regards the word *paramanu* there is no scope for ambiguity, for it is exclusively used to mean an atom not only in philosophical literature but in other kinds of literature also. In fact, this specific use follows from the very etymology of the word. *Paramanu* is the combined form of *parama* (signifying 'of the highest degree') and *anu* (very minute) and therefore means what is minute to the utmost degree" (Gangopadhyaya, *Indian Atomism*, pp. 1, 3).

characterizes a triad, which is composed of three dyads. Triads are what one sees (the commentators say) when a sunbeam penetrates into a room through a window hole and illuminates motes of dust (remember Lucretius' analogous comment on sunlit motes of dust).[65]*

To be a whole is therefore necessarily to have the magnitude or extension of largeness. If so, the perceptible qualities of a whole thing cannot be those of an atom because an atom is imperceptible, nor can they be the qualities of a mere (nonwhole) conglomerate of atoms. When we perceive an object, whatever makes it perceptible must inhere in it as a distinctive whole, not in its atoms as such, nor even in its atoms as a conglomerate. How else could we perceive that "this jar is black; is one; is conjoined; is vibrating; is existing and is made of earth"?[66] Perceptibility is evidence of wholeness, of a single, distinct substance, not a mere multiplicity.[67]

Of course, this is a thesis that strikes the opponent as wrong. The argument grows too detailed for much of it to be repeated here. But one of its issues is worth retaining because it is reminiscent of a difficulty that Plato faces in the *Parmenides*. This difficulty arises when the no doubt Buddhist objector objects that the presumed whole is not real.[68] This is proved, he says, by the impossibility of logically justifying the presence of the whole within the parts or of the parts within the whole.[69] The whole cannot exist because it has no possible relationship to the parts. No individual part can by itself occupy the entire whole because of the difference between magnitudes. (In a Nyaya spirit we might ask, how could a branch be the whole tree, and, if it could, how could the other branches be related to the tree?) And if an individual part can occupy the entire whole, there can be no relation of the whole to the other individual parts. Nor can each individual part occupy an area (a segment, *ekadesha*) of the whole in the sense of "an area of the whole as

---

*Made wary by the crossfire of debate, the Indian philosopher must use concepts carefully. According to Nyaya doctrine, the smallness of the dyad must be caused by the small number of its atoms, *not* by its smallness-size. The relation of a thread to a piece of cloth or of a potsherd to a pot shows that a magnitude can give rise only to a higher degree of the same magnitude. On this principle, compounded smallness can give rise only to a higher degree of smallness, that is, to something that is still smaller. But a dyad cannot be smaller than an atom, which is as small as possible, and therefore it must depend on its small number for its smallness. I assume that this distinction is a relatively late one. Borrowing from outside their tradition, some late Naiyayikas (such as Raghunatha, c. 1500) argue that it is possible to begin with the (visible) triad as the ultimate, indivisible particle. (See Gangopadhyaya, *Indian Atomism*, pp. 20 and 250, note 27.)

a whole." For the "whole" can have no "areas" other than the individual parts.[70]*

Even with the help of a long footnote, I have not stated all of the opponent's argument, to which later commentators add complications and illustrations. One illustration, designed to refute the possibility that the whole can reside in a part is that, if it did, the perception of a single thread would lead to the perception of a whole cloth.[71]

Gautama, of course, has an answer: The opponent's arguments are based upon a semantic misunderstanding. Gautama denies the possibility that the entire whole is within the separate parts, and he denies the possibility that the whole could be present in its areas or segments even if there was place for them as well as the individual parts. For what is under discussion is a single, undifferentiated whole, the "wholeness" of which is destroyed by its division in any way or form. That is, the objections to the whole make use of irrelevant assumptions about its divisibility: The word

---

*The opponent continues: Just as the parts cannot be conceived as present within the "whole," the whole cannot be conceived as present within the parts. An entire whole cannot occupy each individual part because of the greater magnitude of the whole. And how can the whole, which is in itself a composite substance, inhere in—be entirely composed of—no more than a single substance that is one of its individual parts? Nor can the whole occupy all the individual parts by means of its "areas"—areas of the "whole" as a "whole"—because nothing but the parts of the whole can be parts of it in any sense. There is no problem, no doubt, that is worth debating—the "whole" does not exist.

Now that it is obvious, says the opponent, that the "whole" is not something different from the parts, it will be shown that it is not identical with them. Suppose that it is identical in a certain way in that the whole is a (mere) property of the parts (which possess that property). But it has already been shown that there is no logical justification for relating the whole to the parts in any way, including that of a mere property of the parts as possessors of the property. The opponent continues: Just as the parts cannot be conceived as present within the whole, the whole cannot be conceived as present within the parts. An entire whole cannot occupy each individual part because of the greater magnitude of the whole. And how can the whole, which is in itself a composite substance, inhere in—be entirely composed of—no more than a single substance that is one of its individual parts? Nor can the whole occupy all the individual parts by means of its areas—areas of the whole as a whole—because nothing but the parts of the whole can be parts of it in any sense. There is no "whole." (*Nyaya-Sutra* and *Bhashya* 4.2.8ff. Trans Gangopadhyaya, *Nyāya*, p. 346 and *Indian Atomism*, pp. 305–308.)

It should be kept in mind that this sharp but arid or arid-seeming discussion on parts and wholes reflects the difference between a solely philosophical exposition of physics and a more modern, more empirical one. To the credit of the Naiyayikas, they were trying, by their own abstract lights, to begin to explain what contemporary physicists explain by means of materials science, that is, the relations of particles or forces that give different materials their different characteristics, and by means of what, at a more complex, biological level, is accounted for by the biological sciences, beginning with genetics—for example, why is it that atoms, which have no treelike characteristics, also make up trees?

entire is used to signify the total of many entities. And the word *area* or *segment* (*ekadesha*) is used to signify any one entity among different ones. However, neither word can be used properly of an entity that is an undifferentiated whole.

If so, how can we account for the presence of the whole within the parts? The answer is that the whole is related to its constituent parts by means of the relation of inherence (as is pointed out by a later commentator), to which the whole's presumed entirety and presumed segmentation are irrelevant. To add an illustration: The inherence of a whole is just like the indivisible inherence of jarness in the parts of a jar. Whole and part are not simply conjoined. If they were, they would remain intact even when separated; but whole and part cannot exist as such if separated from one another. Gautama's commentator takes it on himself to add that Gautama means that the whole is based upon the parts; they are the (material) causes, the substratum of the whole. The "whole," which cannot represent them, is their superstratum.[72]

The discussion on the whole continues, but we turn to another aspect of the unity of things. The opponent believes that the unity is explained by no more than the massing or aggregation of atoms. He says: When we are far away, we speak of an aggregation of trees as a forest. Just so, when there is a aggregation of atoms and we cannot perceive their individual differences, we speak of the one object we do see. Not so, says Gautama. It is true that a special cause such as distance can prevent the perception of the individual trees. But there is no special cause that leads us to mistake them when aggregated for a single object. Because atoms are by nature imperceptible, their aggregations are imperceptible as well. In any case, it has not been established in a critical way that the perception of the unity of some composite object—say, a single tree—is the perception of only a mass of atoms or of something over and above the mere mass.[73]

Gautama's commentator goes on (after considerations I skip): Mere aggregations of atoms, as Gautama says, cannot have perceptible, that is, physical, magnitude and so cannot constitute the unity of a true whole. What explains the unity is the emergence of a quality called *conjunction* (*samyoga*), which inheres in a true whole. It is conjunction that causes the sound, color, and movement characteristic of a whole and not of its separate parts—at the limit, its atoms.* Unless there were true wholes, it

---

*The subcommentary (of Uddyotakara) adds that conjunction produces novelty by means of contact. For instance, when the contact of the drumstick with a drum makes the drum sound, when the contact of a jar with fire makes the jar red, and when the contact of the ground with a ball makes the ball bounce. Such sound, color, and motion would be inexplicable if not for the quality of conjunction as something distinct from the conjoined things (*The Nyāyā Sūtras of Gautama*, trans. Jha, vol. 2, p. 771 [*bhāṣya-vārtika* 2.1.36]).

would be impossible to perceive the universal (jati). And without the universal it would be impossible to explain the law that regulates knowledge and makes it possible for us to apprehend things consistently, by their universals—so that, for example, each individual cow, horse, or tree is recognized to be a cow, horse, or tree and not something else.

Why cannot the universal inhere directly in the separate parts of objects? The answer is this: Atoms themselves are beyond the reach of the senses. Of course, we do see different parts of objects at different moments. But if each of these parts by itself was the substratum of the universal, each part of a tree would be a distinct tree and each tree would contain many distinct, different trees. And so—because the universal gives an object of knowledge, a whole, that is different from a mere mass of atoms or collection of mere parts—it must be accepted that there is a whole that is something distinct in itself.[74]

Although the difference between mere parts and wholes has been explained, Nyaya must still show that the existence of atoms can be inferred by reason. The atom is regarded as that which is not a whole, because a whole is by definition divisible. The atom is defined as that which is without parts, as that than which nothing can be smaller. In the words of the Nyaya Sutra, "An absolute non-existence of all things is not possible, because an atom [the anu] remains [in the end]." The commentator explains:

> The partlessness of an atom [follows from the fact that an atom represents] an entity compared to which nothing can be smaller [and hence], in which the possibility of getting smaller and smaller due to further and further division [of the parts] is ended. [For example, the pieces of] an earth-clod (loshta), which is being divided into parts [further and further] become smaller and smaller, step by step. But such a possibility of getting smaller and smaller is ended after a piece is arrived at compared to which no other piece can be [conceived to be] smaller, i.e. which is minute to the utmost degree. Thus, what we call by the term 'atom' is an entity compared to which nothing else can be smaller. (Nyaya Sutra 4.2.16, with bhashya)[75]

If there were no indivisible atoms, the process of division would never end and everything composite would have an innumerable number of parts. As the result, the triad would lose its triad-nature. That is, instead of being the smallest perceptible substance, it could no longer be small.[76] And if there were no indivisible atoms, the unchecked separation of wholes into parts would lead to an infinite regress, which is logically unjustifiable. The commentary says that it is not logically possible to maintain that, in the process of division, the object that is divided disappears ultimately. Hence, it is illogical to claim [that the process of division] ends in an "absolute non-existence of things" (pralaya) [instead of a partless entity in the form of an atom]. (Nyaya Sutra 4.2.25, bhashya)[77]

To this conclusion, the subcommentary adds that division up to nothingness is impossible because in order to divide there must be something that is divided—the conceptions of *divide* and *something to be divided* are meaningless without each other: " 'Division' always rests upon the *divided* thing; hence it is a contradiction in terms to say that 'the divided object has ceased to exist' and 'the division is there.' " And further, if it is assumed that division of things is endless but does not lead to nothingness, both logical and empirical absurdities would result. Even a triad would have an unlimited, indeterminable magnitude, weight, and number of constituent atoms. It would follow, absurdly, that a triad would be as immeasurably great as the vast mountain Himalaya.[78]

An objection to the atom arises on the ground that the hypothetical, (vaguely) etherlike element, the substratum of sound, called *akasha*, is supposed to be all-penetrating. If so, it must penetrate into the atom, and if the atom is penetrated, it must have an inside and outside and be decomposable. The Nyaya answer is that the terms *inside* and *outside* refer to substances or to things with an extension that is produced by the combining of substances. Only substances so produced have a middle and periphery. But because an atom, being the smallest conceivable unit, can have no such extension, it has nothing that can be referred to as *inside* or *outside*.

One last objection and answer: The atom, like everything with delimited extension—not very large nor endless—and with the quality of touch, is taken to have a distinct configurations—triangular, quadrangular, uniform, or globular—implying that it has components arranged in a certain way. It must also have components in order to come into contact with other atoms. The commentary develops the question: An atom in the middle separates the two atoms on its two sides. It must therefore be conjoined with each atom on a different side and so must have at least two component parts—and parts to conjoin with atoms on other sides.

The Nyaya answer is that this is impossible because the components of atoms would have to be smaller than the smallest conceivable things. Atoms, says Nyaya, separate one another in a special way—conjunction— that gives them their ability to touch one another without any divisible extension or parts (*parts* in the sense of components). Because it has touch and position, an atom can be separated from other atoms; but the impression that it has parts is only the result of its conjunction—conjunction in its special sense—with other atoms.* The separation is by means of touch only, at what may be said to be dimensionless points. Otherwise we would have to enter into an infinite regress or accept the absurdities that would result from unlimited divisibility.[79] In modern terminology this means, I suppose, that the atoms themselves are dimensionless like mathematical points, but just as mathematical points when joined can define the boundaries of geometrical bodies, our knowledge of atoms in conjunction leads us to think of them as having boundaries or parts. Translated into modern terms, the meaning is that although an atom, having no dimensions, can be conceived, it escapes the imagination, which is based on objects that do have magnitude and can therefore be visualized.

Now to the atoms of the Buddhists.[80] As I have mentioned, atoms are part of Sarvastivada doctrine, though in a seriously developed form, as far as I know, only in that of a philosophical subgroup called the Vaibhashika.[81]** I omit much of the detail, which can grow oppressive. I say *oppressive* with a certain admiration, because if one studies the list of

---

*To Nyaya, a quality such as color pervades all of its substratum, but conjunction is the kind of quality that is not pervasive. As said before, conjunction inheres in the "whole" (*ayayavin*), which is something over and above its constituents or substratum. Ordinarily, conjunction is the result of movement, activity (*karman*). To anticipate what will in time be explained, later Nyaya argues that there is a movement that begins the process of creation by influencing atoms to move together. This movement is produced by the unseen force of *adrishta*, which is itself generated by the merit and demerit of selves or souls so that actions will gain their due fruit. But because both atoms and *adrishta* are not conscious or intelligent, God's will must also play a part (says Udayana). (See Gangopadhyaya, *Indian Atomism*, pp. 30–36.)

**The Buddhist sect of Sarvastivadins had philosophical systematists, *abhidharmikas*, who composed doctrinal summaries and treatises based on the *sutras* attributed to the Buddha. As will be seen, one of the subjects they debated was the existence of the past and future. During the first century A.D., the *Great Commentary*, the *Vibhasha*, was composed by a group of philosophical Sarvastivadins. The thinkers, Kashmiris mostly, who owed their intellectual allegiance to the *Vibhasha* were called Vaibhashikas. It was the Vaibhashikas alone who, among the Sarvastivadins, developed an atomic theory. Such, at least, is the impression that arises from Vasubandhu's *Treasury of the Abhidharma* (*Abhidharmakosha*), the fifth-century-A.D. treatise that is the indispensable source for my account of Buddhist atomism. For simplicity's sake, I will ascribe Buddhist atomism to the Sarvastivadins.

Vasubandhu bases his own thought mainly on the well-organized Vaibhashika system, but he sometimes turns to the "early masters" of Yogachara (to be described later) and not infrequently adopts the position taken by the Sautantrika school. The Sautrantikas ("those who refer to the sutras") was a later group that favored the *sutras* over the books of the Abhidharma (systematized doctrine), which they refused to regard as canonical. They were the exponents of the philosophy of point-instants, to which I will later refer. It can reasonably be assumed that they accepted any Vaibhashika idea to which they did not voice explicit objections. Vasubandhu reports disagreements among Vaibhashikas on atomic doctrine proper, but only rarely (Gangopadhyaha mistakenly says never) between them and the Sautrantikas. (See Poussin, introduction to Vasubandhu, *Abhidharmakosabhāṣyam*, trans. Pruden, vol. 1, pp. 1–4; and Gangopadhyaya, *Indian Atomism*, pp. 10–11. For the content of the *Jnanaprasthana-sutra*, on which the *Vibhasha* was a commentary, see Dutt, *Buddhist Sects in India*, pp. 152–55.)

Buddhist elements (or components or functions), among them atoms, that the Sarvastivadins assembled, one is struck with wonder at its multiplied distinctions and its order. It is as if an ingenious theoretical physicist and an attentive psychologist had collaborated in an analytical survey of the nature of human beings in their physical and perceptual world but, in surveying this world, had paid attention to polemical theory—one that separated the school from every other—and not to any empirical confirmation beyond what was furnished by analogies that must strike us now as casual. Again and again, this Buddhist analysis arrives at ideas that have a general resemblance to those of contemporary psychology or physics (or science fiction); but, except for special purposes, the detail is pursued in a temper too prosaic to have the effect of mythology and too arbitrary to have the effect of science as we now appreciate it; and one is always conscious that the Buddhists' analytic cleverness is being used to support a predetermined conclusion or, to put it in less polite words, a dogma. Yet the analysis reveals something about the bent of stubbornly philosophical minds and has aspects that remain of extreme interest.

In some respects, the Sarvastivadin atomic doctrine makes a sharp contrast with the Greek and Nyaya doctrines that have just been reviewed. The Sarvastivadins are interested in atoms because they regard them as the constituents not only of material objects in general but, in particular, of the organs of perception. Atoms must therefore be understood if human beings are to be taught how to avoid their bondage to desire and its consequence, pain.

According to Sarvastivada, atoms are composed of particles of the four primary elements, more accurately understood as energies, which are "earth," "water," "fire," and "wind." These particles or *paramanus* of the four elements are never dissociated from one another. Like the quarks of contemporary physics, they are evasive because they do not exist apart—apart, in their case, from the composite atoms they constitute. In each kind of perceptible material, each of the elements is active to the degree that fits the particular nature of the material.[82]* For example, the water we perceive is made up of composite particles, analogous to molecules, of

---

*Although they constitute primary matter, the primary particles are, so to speak, not material but premraterial—they do not have the characteristic impenetrability of matter. In addition to these primary kinds of material particles, there are four secondary (derived, composite, translucent) kinds—of color, smell, taste, and touch—that are objects of their respective sense organs. In addition to the primary and secondary kinds of material particles, there are—strangely to us—particles of thought, also secondary, which are the objects of the activity of thinking. The indivisible, "prematerial" *substance-paramanu*, the *dravya-paramanu*, is contrasted with the composite or *samghata-paramanu*, which is the most minute particle of actual, that is, impenetrable matter. Every composite particle includes five kinds of sensory particles—four, if sound particles are lacking. Each kind of sensory particle affects the corresponding particles that are the essential constituents of the sense organ, whether that of sight, hearing, smell, taste, or touch.

water, and these particles or molecules of water are themselves made up of indivisible particles of earth, water, fire, and wind.[83]

The Sarvastivada theory goes on: One knows that any given substance, whether water, wood, or any other, contains all of the primary elements because each element manifests something of the effect that is characteristic only of itself. Elemental earth is manifested by the degree of hardness that supports things—as water supports ships and wood supports buildings—elemental water by the degree of cohesion that holds things together, elemental fire by the degree of heat that matures things—as it matures wood and then rots it—and elemental wind by the degree of motion or expansion with which things have the force to grow, to be displaced, and, like a flame, to reproduce themselves in different places.[84] Briefly, everything material has some solidity (which lends resistance and support), humidity (which lends cohesion), heat (which lends ripeness, that is, accelerates development), and motion (which lends expansion, including that of growth and displacement).

Taken in its more exact sense of an indivisible monad, the *paramanu* is the smallest conceivable particle of matter—or, better, prematter—too minute to be perceived and impossible to divide either mentally or physically.* Perhaps seven of these make up an *anu*, which also cannot be perceived; seven *anus* (by one relatively elaborate scheme) make up a particle a Buddha can perceive; and so on, up by sevens (according to the same scheme), until we arrive at a complex of 1,379 (or perhaps four times that number), which is the smallest fraction of matter that can exist and be perceived independently.[85]

Vision-sensitive particles, for example, are scattered over the pupil of the eye; and sound-sensitive particles, located within the hollow of the ear, are furnished with fine hairs (the reference must be to what we know as the hair cells in the inner ear, which send impulses to the auditory nerve). Also considered an organ, of memory and reason, the mind has its own atomic receptors for particles of thought (*particles of mentation* might sound better). It should be kept in mind that all these "particles" are, in effect, energies. By a Sarvastivadin source, the total number of kinds of atoms is said to be fourteen, one kind for each of the primary elements, five for sense objects, and five for sense receptors. (See McGovern, *Manual of Buddhist Philosophy*, pp. 96–102, 119–26. For the doctrine of sensory atoms as put in a scholastic source, see Vasubandhu, *Abhidharmakośabhāṣyam*, trans. Pruden, vol. 1, pp. 123–24 (144a–b) and 184–88 (2.22). For summaries of this doctrine, see Chaudhuri, *Analytical Study of the Abhidharmakośa*, pp. 43–47, 77, 88–89, 103–104.)

*As described in a summary made from Chinese sources, the Sarvastivadin atom or *paramanu* "cannot be pierced through or picked up or thrown away. It is indivisible, unanalysable, invisible, inaudible, untastable and intangible. But yet it is not permanent, but is like a momentary flash into being . . . The organs of sense are also regarded as modifications of atomic matter. Seven such paramanus combine together to form an anu, and it is in this combined form only that they become perceptible. The combination takes place in the form of a cluster having one atom at the center and others around it" (Dasgupta, *A History of Indian Philosophy*, vol. 1, pp. 121–22, from a summary made by Yamakami Sogen).

One can be impatient of this prescientific multiplication of particles and their relative sizes and times, but to an obtusely distant ear their successive names make a rather poetic roll call, like the successions in which Walt Whitman celebrates the fertility of nature:

> *Paramanu, anu, loharajas, abrajas, shasharajas, avirajas, gorajas, chidrarajas, liksha,* that which comes out of the *liksha, yava,* and *anguliparvan,* by multiplying each time by seven; twenty-four *angulis* make one *hasta;* four *hastas* make one *dhanu;* five hundred *dhanus* make one *krosha,* the distance a hermitage should be located [from a village]. (Vasubandhu, *Abhidharma-kosha* 85–88)[86]

The Buddhist particles—which we can think of, if we please, as, in succession, subatomic particles, atoms, molecules, and macromolecules—arouse the kinds of problems we are already familiar with: If the particles that have no dimension do not touch one another, how can they, for example, produce sound; if they touch one another completely, having no size, they must coincide; but if they touch only partly, they have parts, which is contrary to the hypothesis. But if they cannot touch one another, how is it that when they are combined they do touch? Perhaps, then, a Buddhist answer goes, they are in fact juxtaposed, without space between them, but thanks to their impenetrability they remain distinct; and so on.[87] This description of Buddhist atomism leads us to its remarkable inclusion in the point-instant theory of the Buddhist Sautrantika school. Despite problems, like those of the Greek and Nyaya atoms, with infinitesimal size and structure, the Buddhist atoms as conceived by Sautrantika are different in one fundamental characteristic: Instead of being indestructible and eternal, they remain in existence, without any exception, for a time (a *kshana*) so brief that it cannot be divided into a before and an after. In their brevity these particles should therefore exceed that of the virtual particles of contemporary physics (or the modern physicist's proposed chronon, the time in which light crosses the diameter of the smallest subatomic particle).[88]* Given this

---

*There are various formulations of the speed of a *kshana*. In one of them, which resembles the chronon as a measure of time, the *kshana* is said to correspond to the time necessary for a *dharma* to arise or, rather, for a *dharma* in progress to go from one atom (*paramanu*) to another, which I interpret to mean the time necessary for one *dharma*-atom to be replaced by its successor. In terms of contemporary physics, the impression of maximal brevity is weakened and confused by a Buddhist estimate that "there are sixty-five instants in the time that it takes a healthy man to snap his fingers." In another estimate, 120 *kshanas* make a *tatkshana*, which is the time it takes a thread of medium length to touch the finger of a woman of medium age who is about to spin. No empirical grounds are given for establishing these estimates, the second of which is put with impressive care. (*Abhidharmakośabhāṣyam*, trans. Pruden, vol. 2, p. 474 [3.85]; in Poussin's translation, vol. 2, pp. 177–78, and note 488, p. 541.)

limit of temporal existence, not only atoms, but all the Buddhist monads or particles of existence, *dharmas*, are temporally dimensionless or near dimensionless.

A moment's explanation of the term *dharma*, which is of great importance: The literal meaning of *dharma* is *what holds together, what maintains, what is held to*. In the grand sense, it is *the cosmic order*. The term is used for whatever fits the social or moral norm—a principle, precept, duty, rule, or custom. To Buddhists, it has the additional meaning of *the (Buddha's) teaching*. Used at first to designate what is good *(dharma)* as against what is bad *(adharma)*, it comes to mean any basic element of existence, good or bad, that is, any element that has good or bad effects on living beings. It can mean, simply, *thing* or *phenomenon*. As used here, however, it means primarily *element of existence*, that is, anything that makes up composite things. As such a basic element, a *dharma* is separate and distinct, with its individual *own-nature (svabhava)*. Almost all the *dharmas*, which include the material elements (made up of atoms) and the nonmaterial elements, are as short-lived as conceivable. The reason is that ordinary existence in the ordinary world is always as brief as possible: "Disappearance is the very essence of existence; what does not disappear does not exist."[89] As measures of minima, "the atom *(paramanu)* properly so called, the syllable, and the instant *(kshana)* are the respective limits of matter, word, and time."[90]

These minimal reals represent the conclusion of the Buddhist practice of dividing all composite things—among which humans are the Buddhists' main concern—into "heaps" of minimal reals or elements, each of these constituting a minimal part of the stream of events—people, too, are "streams" of very small events affected or conditioned by other small and large streams.[91]

The Sarvastivadins' list of *dharmas* includes three elements that are exceptional in that they are unconditioned, that is, immutable and eternal. These three are: (1) space, the nature of which is not to impede or be impeded, that is, be displaced by any material object; (2) the extinction of what is impure in a pure understanding—complete extinction of this kind is nirvana; and (3) merely natural extinction of the impure, as when an object of sensation lapses into the past.[92] Apart from these three, there are the seventy-two kinds of *dharmas*, which are arranged in personal streams by the element of volition. All of these *dharmas* are impermanent, painful, and extremely brief, coming from we know not where and vanishing instantly. All of them are affected within the same indivisible time by the simultaneous and yet independent element forces of origination, subsistence, decay, and extinction.[93]

At this point we can turn to the everything-exists *(sarvam asti)* doctrine of the Sarvastivadins.[94] This principle means that there is a real, not simply illusory, persistence through time. As applied to the elements of existence, the doctrine is that every *dharma* in some sense exists in all three times, past, present, and future. The Sarvastivadins naturally quote the Buddha to this effect. But they also go on to reason that unless each element or moment of existence did not in some respect really exist in the past and future as well as the present, a person would not be bound by past emotions or tempted by past or future objects, and it would be impossible for past actions to affect the present and future. If so, the moral continuity of life would be lost.[95] The same conclusion is assured by our ability to make all of the three times the objects of our thought, because no true objects of thought can be totally nonexistent.

It is noticeable that the Sarvastivadin's ability to argue grows exhausted. He then takes refuge in the Buddha and says that the character of the moment, indivisible but with an infinitesimal duration, is something only the Buddha can understand; but it is sure that the moment does have some durational stability. Maybe there is a difficult distinction to be made: The own-being of an element has a conceptually quadruple character (of birth, continuance, decay, and destruction) and an existence in three different times; but the moment in which its exerts its effect, when its action is completed, is conceptually single.[96]

The sources list four different Sarvastivada interpretations of the reality of all three times: A *dharma* that goes from one period to another changes the form of its existence but keeps its nature, like a golden vase that breaks and changes shape but not color. Or, like a man attached to one woman but, because of his lust, not detached from others, a *dharma* is endowed with the character of a particular time but also retains the character of the other two times. Or, like a token placed on a square of ones, or tens, or hundreds, a *dharma* changes its condition or designation, not its substance. Or, like a woman who in time is both a daughter and a mother, a *dharma* changes its relationships with the other times.[97]*

The Sarvastivadins find themselves in a bind. In order to account for the continuity that their form of atomism threatens to break or make unintelligible, they assign the different times different qualities, but not different degrees of reality. For doctrinal reasons, they cannot adopt a theory of potentiality or of change of quality that implies belief in any lasting substance. Their *dharmas,* real in all three times, are conceptualized as different kinds of time particles moving in individual streams away from the past, into the infinitesimally brief, perpetually renewing present, and

---

*The Vaibhashikas accept only the third of these interpretations, that a *dharma* becomes different, but not in substance; the Sautrantikas, who deny that past and future exist, accept none of them (*Abhidharmakośabhāṣyam*, trans. Pruden, vol. 3, pp. 810–20 [5.26a–27d]).

toward the future—which in their sense already exists.[98] The Sarvastivadins deserve praise, it seems to me, for not shirking the difficulty of conceptualizing time as both momentary and continuous existence.

Discussion

In this chapter I have ignored one philosophically interesting variety of atomism, that of the Muslim "dialectical theologians," who attempt to strengthen the sense of dependence on God by teaching the essential discontinuity of everything, including time and causality. They will be taken up in the chapter on religio-philosophical synthesis, in the company of the Muslim and Jewish philosophers with whom they engage in disputation.

Greek and Nyaya atomism share a good deal in the way they are conceived and the intellectual problems they arouse. The atomic conception that stands out as unique is that of the Buddhists—even the time-atoms conceived by some Greeks are not equal in the boldness of their conception to the atoms created by the audacious Buddhist unification of matter (as process) with perception and time. Among Greek conceptions of time, the Stoic, with its present spread somewhat over future and past, comes relatively close to the Sarvastivadin three equally real times (analogously, Alfred North Whitehead [1861–1947] thinks that the time immediate for sense awareness is a duration with a past and future within itself).

The contrast between the Greek atomists and Aristotle proves to be lasting in Western thought. The contrast is one of mostly frontal opposition: An infinite, purposeless universe consisting of many worlds opposes a single, finite, teleologically organized universe in which nature does nothing in vain. The void and atoms oppose a continuum. The actual infinity of indivisible atoms oppose continuity and merely potential infinites. A universe in constant evolution opposes an essentially fixed universe. A material and temporary soul opposes an immaterial and perhaps partly immortal one. And many disinterested gods made of atoms oppose the god—thought thinking itself—for the love of which the world turns 'round.[99]

However, for all their differences, both the Greek atomists and Aristotle join in believing in substance, something that lasts through time and explains the nature of changing beings. To Aristotle, substance is taken to be composed of matter and form, to the atomists, of atoms alone. In conceiving substance so, the Greek atomists and Aristotle are joined by the Naiyayikas but opposed, of course, by the Buddhists. Metaphysically more moderate and eclectic than the Greek atomists, the Naiyayikas also believe in the soul and in karma. To the Naiyayikas, salvation comes by way of the analytically based convictions that expose the nature of reality and lead to the conclusion that life is pain. There is no even remotely compelling relation between their analytical methods and atomism, on the one hand, and, on the other, their somewhat ambivalent conclusion that pleasure must be considered pain. Yet Nyaya empiricism leads to an earthly method of salvation, resting on the idea, like that of Buddhism and Epicureanism, that the ideal requires absence of pain or indifference to pain.

The great difference between Epicureanism and Buddhism conceals an interesting convergence of tactics and aims. Although Buddhism theoretically rejects pleasure and Epicureanism seeks it, both define the desired state as one of calm, safety, and absence of pain. The great interest of both in analyzing the world and the mental and physical structure of human beings is meant to teach humans how to minimize their pain. That is the reason given by both Epicureans and Buddhists for making the activity of teaching a primary aim and making ignorance a primary fault. Once the structural analysis has been made, the psychophysical cure can be proposed, and, as it turns out, for both Epicureans and Buddhists the cure depends on locating reality in the minimal constituents that make up everything, including human beings. To arrive at these minimal constituents, both philosophies systematically disintegrate the human being and the world, without making a distracting distinction of kind between the self or soul and the body. The Buddhist finds the heaps of elements or reals and the Epicurean finds the complex clusters of atoms or reals, and both Buddhist and Epicurean learns to say, "I am only a temporary collection, and even when I break apart in death, the indestructible elements remain. Dying is painful only if I do not recognize it as a disintegration and only if I identify it with pain and suffering." And the Buddhist who needs them has the Buddha's mercy and the temporary paradises of Buddhism to help him on the long way to nirvana.

I am sure that Epicurus and the more creative Buddhist thinkers have a genuine intellectual interest in the physics and psychology they teach. Officially, however, their utilitarian aim turns their techniques of disintegration into no more than means to peace of mind (or, for Buddhists, something like it but indefinably better). Although both Buddhists and Epicureans believe in gods, as self-reliant physicians, they cannot leave their fates in the arbitrary or unintelligible care of gods but trust in their own sufficiently detailed descriptions of reality and their essentially secular rationales of salvation. Buddhists and Epicureans alike advise retreat from public life and secular ambition, and alike minimize the importance of sex and family in favor of a union of like-minded persons (principally men) who aim at peace of mind by the reduction of pain and trouble. For the purpose of persuading others of the truth of their doctrine and of giving their communities a human focus, both the Buddhists and Epicureans show great reverence for their teachers, especially their great originators. We see that in both philosophies, the atomism, the ethics, and the goals have an analogy that testifies to the strong relationship between intellectual analysis and practical hopes. The most general lesson may be that it is not the atomic analysis as such that helps—if it does—but the distance from appetite, pain, and fear that is created by the abstract analysis of the situation in which they occur. There is also the emotional help given by immersion in a community of like-minded believers, whether Buddhist or Epicurean.

It is hard to leave the subject of atomism without reflecting on its subsequent fate in the West, from its near eclipse to its revival and its transformation into chemistry and an increasingly complicated atomic physics.[100] Even though the subatomic particles described by physics have resisted visualization, it has now become possible to follow an object's atomic contour with a scanning tunneling microscope and, as well, to trap an individual atom in an electromagnetic cage; and a method has been invented (by Samuel Hurst, who, understandably, loves Lucretius) to detect and count individual atoms and, in principle, to identify every atom in any given object.[101] By sheer creative speculation, with no evidence we now think acceptable, the ancient Greek and Indian philosophers invented an idea, useless in practice except to support their respective philosophical aims, that has become a great, greatly useful insight into physical reality. Given time, arguments absurdly detached from physical evidence can turn out extraordinarily well.

Chapter 7

※

Hierarchical Idealism
Plotinus/Proclus, Bhartrihari

Theme: The Atomists' Tactics Are Reversed to Create Structures of Principles That Culminate in Being-as-Such

The two philosophies dealt with in this chapter are called hierarchical because they argue that the everyday world depends on a large number of vital principles, which depend on fewer principles, which depend on fewer still, up to the vital principle on the top of the pyramid, being-as-such, on which everything else depends. I have said "the top of the pyramid" because as the principles grow fewer they grow higher in the degree of their being; but because everything low in reality rests on what is higher and, eventually, on the highest, the pyramids can be seen as inverted. The two philosophies are idealistic in the philosophical sense because the principles on which each of the their structures depend have the nature of consciousness. The philosophies are also mystical in that the Being (or One) and the Word (or Brahman) in which they respectively culminate cannot be understood by reason or described in words and is knowable only by means of the wordless experience that is an intimacy or identity like that of one's experience of oneself.

The two philosophies, the one Greek and the other Indian, are near mirror images of atomism in attitude and intellectual tactics. This is certainly not intentional and stems not from borrowing in either direction but from the philosophical environment of each of the two traditions and, of course, from the similarity of the problem involved—the search for reality by means of division as against the search for reality by means of unification. In the spirit of division, the atomists begin with what they see as the relatively few, relatively complex and illusory things of the everyday world, which they divide repeatedly until, at the end of the process, there are only an innumerable number of material or other (Buddhist) atoms, all fully real, and all with the fewest characteristics possible. According to the atomists, the descent to atoms shows that the plurality of beings and qualities of the visible world is only an illusion produced by the limitations of human perception. In the contrary spirit, of unification, the hierarchical idealists reverse the atomists' reasoning and begin with what they see as the very numerous, relatively simple, illusory things of everyday experience and reduce them to a smaller and smaller number of immaterial principles until, at the end of the process, there is left only the single immaterial, fully real, absolutely indivisible atom—the absolute Being, the One or the Word that possesses all the infinitely many qualities of reality in an inseparable, indescribable union. According to the hierarchical idealists, this rise to unity shows that the plurality of beings and qualities that human beings perceive is only an illusion produced by the limitations of human perception and understanding.

In all these characteristics, the Greek and Indian forms of hierarchical idealism are alike. Whereas the atomists' atoms are completely devoid of consciousness and accessible only to analytic reason, the hierarchical idealists' being-as-such, the One or the Word, is completely devoid of matter and therefore accessible only to the self-intimacy found in consciousness. To the Indian philosophers, as we know, the highest reality had long been associated with self-intimacy, but among the Greek and Roman philosophers the unique nature of consciousness had hardly been explored until Plotinus, who characteristically insisted that "the perceiving part of the soul must turn inwards and must be made to attend there."[1]

Of course, the philosophical contexts and terminologies of the two systems are different. The most striking abstract difference is that Proclus—far more than Plotinus—uses a mathematical model of reality and Bhartrihari, a grammatical one. Proclus's model, like that of the Greek atomists, depends on the mathematical relationship between individual units and infinite quantities. In other words, this is the kind of relationship that holds between individual numbers and the total of all numbers, which is uncountable because there is no last number among them. Plotinus uses recurrent mathematical imagery that is compatible with this position but does not make use of its quasi-mathematical logic; and his references to mathematics can be elusively quick.[2] The method of proof adopted by Proclus is an open though not inherently close imitation of the method of Euclid's axiom-based geometry. In contrast, the logic used by Bhartrihari is based on grammar, which the Indians were the first to develop to a sophisticated level.

Plotinus (205–270 C.E.), Proclus (410?–485)

Goodness is unification, and unification, goodness.

The only biography of Plotinus, written by his disciple Porphyry, opens with the words, "Plotinus, the philosopher of our times, seemed ashamed of being in the body. As a result of this state of mind he could never bear to talk about his race or his parents or his native country."[3] Plotinus was twenty-eight years old when he went to Alexandria to study philosophy. After eleven years with his teacher Ammonius, he had acquired so complete a training in philosophy, says Porphyry, that he grew eager to learn Persian and Indian philosophy.[4] For this purpose, Plotinus joined the army ready to invade Persia, but the Emperor, who led the army, was killed and Plotinus, escaping with difficulty, settled in Rome, where he spent the rest of his life.

Plotinus tends to compose his writing in two rather different ways. The one way is continuous and rhetorical, with allusions to mythology and sensuous (and sensual) imagery, meant to display the world's infinite richness in unity, to teach that all there is is living thought, and to strengthen the natural yearning for the spiritual source of everything—"the true love is all things being one and never separate."[5] Plotinus' other way of writing is by a string of questions and answers, a dialectical progression meant to engage and compel the intellect. This way begins with the statement of a problem, put as a question, and is likely to continue by way of a preliminary inquiry.* But for all the effort he invested in his writing, Plotinus, we are

---

*An example of an initial question is the following: Does the faculty of sensation preexist in the divine Spirit? The answer begins with the preliminary inquiry into how one defines a human being: Is man—defined as a rational living being—a soul determined by a *logos* (a rational forming power), that is to say, by a rational Form added to the soul? If the answer is yes, it follows that the human's ability to perceive by sensing is not in the soul as such, but in the human *logos*; and because this *logos* is no more than the expression of a transcendent Form found in the divine Spirit, the possibility of sensation does preexist in the divine Spirit. Though given a solution, the initial question may arise again and require a new answer, the discussion being often circular rather than linear, maybe because Plotinus is rarely quite satisfied by the answers he gives. (The text in question is *Enneads* 6.7.4.1–5.5. See Hadot, *Plotin, Trait 38*, pp. 16–18, 216–20.)

credibly told, could not bear to hear it read more than once, and his eyesight made it hard for him to read it through at all. It was his habit first to go over a complete train of thought in his mind, and then to write it out unhesitatingly, as if copying from a book.[6] Yet his writings are filled, says Porphyry, with concealed Stoic and Aristotelian doctrines. The fact is that Plotinus was widely learned, with an excellent knowledge of geometry, arithmetic, mechanics, optics, and music.

Plotinus had many enthusiastic hearers. A gentle, helpful man, he was willing to become the guardian of the children brought to him by parents who felt themselves to be close to death. Knowing of a ruined philosophers' city, he formed the ambition of living there with his companions, according to Plato's laws. He therefore asked the Emperor and Empress, who venerated him, to revive it as the city of Platonopolis; but court intrigues prevented the city's establishment. However, Plotinus succeeded in his most profound ambition, to experience union with God. "Four times while I was with him," reports Prophyry, "he attained that goal, in an unspeakable actuality and not in potency only."[7] In a unique autobiographical passage, Plotinus himself writes:

> Many times it happened: lifted out of the body into myself;
> becoming external to all other things and self-encentered;
> beholding a marvellous beauty; then, more than ever, assured
> of community with the loftiest order . . . After that sojourn in
> the divine, I ask myself how it happens that I can now be
> descending, and how did the Soul ever enter into my body.
> (*Enneads* 8.1)[8]

Plotinus' great distant mentor is Plato. Plato, he believes, is the only philosopher who gathered the secrets of ancient wisdom, secrets Plato refused to reveal. Referring to his own sequence of metaphysical principles—the Good (or One), the Intellect, and the Soul—he says (after misquoting Plato) that this sequence, although made newly explicit, is not new, as is shown "by the evidence of the writings of Plato himself."[9] Understood correctly, Plato must always be right, he implies; but as he must be aware, he uses Plato selectively to stimulate or verify the ideas he, not Plato, wants to express. These ideas, together with similar ones of later philosophers, make a distinctive enough whole to merit the nineteenth-century name, Neoplatonism, by which it is now distinguished.

We know the life of Proclus mainly from the biography written by his disciple Marinus.[10] Sent by his father, a lawyer, to study in Alexandria, he was influenced by a revelation of the goddess Athena to study philosophy. In the then-accepted way, he prepared for initiation in the mysteries of Platonism by first studying mathematics and Aristotle. Then he moved to Athens to study in the Platonic Academy. Eventually, he was chosen as the Academy's head. When lecturing to his many disciples, it is reported, his eyes glistened remarkably and his face glowed with "divine brilliance."

The philosophical equivalent of a saint in an empire now officially Christian, Proclus remained a pagan religiously free enough to observe the sacred days of both Egyptians and Greeks.[11] He wrote on mathematics, astronomy, philosophy, literature, religion, mythology, and other subjects. He also practiced theurgy (etymologically, *divine work*), a magical form of salvation.* This made it necessary for him to know how to distinguish the different grades of gods, gods to whom he spoke in prayer and who sometimes answered him in his dreams, he believed. Read now, his philosophy is fantastic and, in keeping with his period, very credulous. But it also reflects the exactness of the commentator on Euclid who gives clear, able explanations of the differences between geometrical definitions, hypotheses, postulates, axioms, and propositions. His writing is often garrulous and concerned with enumerations of abstract gods and powers, but his *Elements of Theology* is a succinctly authoritative systematization of Neoplatonic philosophy.

Proclus's ability to join credulousness and precision are expressed in two equally original and complementary aspects of his thought. One aspect is the conviction that Plato's authentic dialogues are to be regarded as divinely inspired. The dialogues should be studied to recover their clearly or obscurely expressed but always luminous, more than natural truths. These, Proclus believed, were transmitted in secret from most ancient times, hidden by the leader of the Academy, Arcesilaus, and revealed again by Plotinus.[12] As will later be seen, Alfarabi and Maimonides read Plato in a similar light.

The second original aspect of Proclus's thought is his application of the Euclidean method to philosophy— Euclid, to him, is a member of the

---

*Although Plotinus never uses the term *theurgy*, he credits contemplation with the ability to defend the philosopher against magical attacks. Relatively speaking, however, he is a rationalist and denies that magic can affect the higher souls of either men or gods. *Ennead* 2.9, "Against the Gnostics," is a notable attack against Gnostic doctrines and magical practices. To his mind, the Gnostics pervert Plato and hate the material world and the great beauty it embodies. They refuse the traditional method of salvation through virtue and slowly acquired wisdom, he protests, and turn instead to absurd magical procedures. Nevertheless, the Neoplatonic partisans of theurgy, who include Proclus, contend that Plotinian *theoria* is only contemplative, that is, passive, while theurgic acts allow its practitioners to come into contact with divine forces. According to Proclus, theurgy, which is known by revelation, is a power higher than all human wisdom. His essay *On the Hieratic Art* expounds the idea, familiar in India, that by the principle of correspondence every part of universe mirrors every other. According to the theurgists, the manipulation of the appropriate objects brings them into contact with the gods the objects represent. (See Dodds, *The Greeks and the Irrational*, pp. 283–311; and see Wallis, *Neoplatonism*, pp. 70–72, 106–20.)

Platonic school. Like the Pythagoreans but in a more extensive, dialectical way, he fuses mathematics with ontology and for the first time demonstrates the universal harmony in the only language (he believes) that can express the harmony while proving its truth.[13]

In considering Plotinus' philosophy, we should keep in mind that the usual tension of his thought leads him to make unfamiliar uses of familiar themes and to multiply images—the inadequacy of which he stresses—in order to draw the reader deeper into his poetic yet reasoned thought.[14] Often, what he says is only a temporary fixing of his subtle, not very stable combination of many elements: Platonic Ideas (active, as Plato would never agree), Platonic themes and images drawn un-Platonically together, the Aristotelian theory of potentiality and actuality, Stoic doctrines, and much else. As one sees in the essays that constitute his *Enneads*, Plotinus thinks systematically, but his system has to be pieced together to be seen as a whole. Like systematic thinkers generally, he is sure he is right, and yet, in the tradition of Socrates, he is able to tolerate objections and discussion.[15] For what seem to me good reasons—clarity along with faithfulness to Plotinus' way of thought—my exposition will proceed along the following circuitous path:

1. A sketch of Plotinus' metaphysical hierarchy.
2. An explanation of the starting point of the hierarchy in terms of Plotinus' emotional and logical contrast between the evil nothingness of matter and the total goodness of the One.
3. An explanation of Plotinus' attempt to show how the One becomes apparently other than itself by "shining forth" into Intellect and plurality generally.
4. An exposition of the Neoplatonic proof that existence is by nature the same as oneness/goodness.
5. An explanation of why the One is ineffable, but why negation is more successful than affirmation in hinting at it.

To present Plotinus' thought in the form of a neat hierarchy is to be faithful to its immanent logic, but at the cost of misrepresenting its ambiguities and open, shifting quality. The advantages of a hierarchical presentation are the clear perception of the whole it gives and its convenient approximation to what later thinkers make of Neoplatonism.

Plotinus' hierarchy reflects the attempts of Plato and of later Platonists to decide the order of the Ideas' importance, that is, of their reality or degree of *being*. Plotinus, who gives his levels of *being* the name of *hypostases* (meaning *what stands under, what supports, what is real*), begins his hierarchy, as I have said, with the principle of the One *(hen)*, which he considers identical with the Good *(agathon)*. In the universe of Plotinus, the One dominates everything and gives its nature and direction to everything, like Aristotle's God, not by any command but by virtue of its nature, which is that of complete actuality. Again like Aristotle's God, the One is affected only by itself in relation to itself. No other "relation" is possible, because the One is everything there is. Everything that seems to be other than the One recognizes the relationship by desiring to return to what, in a sense, it has never left and still, in a sense, remains.[16] This process of going out while remaining identical is like a circle, says Plotinus, that expands and reflects in its circumference the nature of the pure, dimensionless point at its center.[17]

To continue, for the moment still descriptively and dogmatically, the *One* by its shining forth or radiation (*eklampsis*), creates all the universe—unlike Aristotle's God—without in any way growing diminished. First it radiates Intellect or Intelligence (*nous*), which differs from the absolute unity of *One* by being unity-in-plurality. Intellect remains one within the many that it includes in the same way as every mathematical theorem—and, therefore, the whole of mathematics—is contained in every mathematical theorem.[18] Intellect requires and is constituted by Forms or Ideas, which are not Plato's static pattern Ideas, but have an inherent force (*dynamis*). This is the intuitive force of Intellect by means of which the Ideas shine or radiate forth their existence and, with the help of ideal matter, give rise to the world. As "Socrates" hesitantly suggested (in the *Parmenides*), individuals, too, have their Forms.

The hierarchy continues to develop—*develop* in a logical sense; the relationships are timeless. Intellect in itself has nothing directly to do with images or time, but by means of its spontaneous radiation, it comes to be Soul. Soul is unity and, as well, plurality (understood as the failure of unity to be evident).[19] Provided with Forms and ideal matter and radiating its force of life, Soul comes to be the World Soul (*psyche tou pantos*). This, the World Soul, produces the sensible world as a hierarchy—whose nature it ordains—of diminishing unity, power, and goodness. The diminution occurs, as will be explained, because matter, which pluralizes, is "truly not being."[20]

The lower beings on the scale of existence need bodies (out of which they transmigrate into other bodies). To help themselves to survive and to recall what, as Intellect, they once knew and still know unconsciously, they also need sense organs. Unfortunately, bodies and sense organs are hindrances to higher understanding.[21] When the soul returns to intuitive contemplation, it no longer needs its lower faculties and the distinction between subject and object vanishes or nearly vanishes. Inspired by a final caution, Plotinus often says or implies that souls, although contained in the One and not really different from it, remain individual. Souls may, so to speak, see the light, or touch reality, or blend with reality, but the One remains transcendent.

So far, I have spoken for Plotinus dogmatically. Now, the dogmatic outline completed, we can take up his views in a philosophically and psychologically more natural way. To begin with Plotinus' philosophical opposition to materialism: He argues that atoms cannot exist because every body is endlessly divisible; because bodies are continuous and flexible; because individual things cannot exist without mind and soul, which cannot be made up of atoms; and because no maker would use a discontinuous material to make anything. Plotinus then ends this set of philosophical arguments impatiently, "Innumerable other objections could be, and have been, alleged against this hypothesis; so there is no need to spend more time on this question."[22]

The psychological beginning is that Plotinus simply dislikes matter and loves consciousness. He so opposes materialism that he is unwilling to think much analytically about the atomists' arguments in its favor. Instead, he points out how heavy, helpless, and cruel matter always is. The weakness of matter is such that the heavier it is, the less able it is to lift itself up when it falls; simply material bodies are the most unpleasant to fall against and hurt more than living ones, which have natural sympathy in proportion to their level of being.[23]

"This, then, is our argument," Plotinus goes on,

> against those who place real beings in the class of bodies and find their guarantee of truth in the pushings and strikings and the apparitions which come by way of sense perception; they act like people dreaming, who think that the things they see as real actually exist, when they are only dreams. (*Enneads* 3.6)[24]

Why, apart from emotion, does Plotinus speak of dreaming here? The philosophical answer is that he accepts Aristotle's definition of matter as in itself nothing but potentiality (understood by Plotinus as the ability to change from one form to anther). To Plotinus, therefore, matter is *nonbeing*, "a ghostly image of bulk, a tendency toward substantial existence . . . invisible in itself" that needs something in addition to itself in order to produce body, for its being is only apparent and "a sort of fleeting frivolity." What seems to come to be in matter is no more than phantoms, like reflections in a mirror. The mirror "seems to be filled and holds nothing; it is all seeming."[25] Maybe because Plotinus supposes matter to be what is unintelligible in nature, he finds it almost impossible to describe. Although matter is nonbeing, he says, it is not absolute nonbeing "but only something other than being," evil in that it is unmeasuredness, formlessness, neediness, "always undefined, never stable." These characteristics are "in a sort of way," the essence of matter.[26]

Since is it impossible for Plotinus to identify anything real with matter, he has to build his hierarchy on the immaterial principles he is familiar with, which are universals in the sense of Platonic Ideas. He follows clues from Plato—the clue in the *Republic* to the supremacy of the Good, the clues in the *Parmenides* to the existence of the One, and so on. Plotinus cannot help seeing reality as concentrated in oneness. He asks:

> What could anything be if it was not one? For if things are deprived of the one which is predicated of them they are not those things. For an army does not exist if it is not one, nor a chorus or a flock if they do not have their one, since the house is one and so is the ship, and if they lose it the house is no longer a house nor the ship a ship.[27] (*Enneads* 6.9.1)

Plotinus often speaks of the One with strong emotion and, helped by qualifying phrases such as "as if," brings out the perfection of the One/Good's existence as superlatively self-centered love and superlatively self-sufficient introspection:

> He [the Good] penetrates, as it were, into his own interior as if in love with himself, the "pure radiance," being himself this which he loves; this is to say that he brings himself into existence, since he is an abiding actuality . . . He in a way holds fast to himself and in a way looks towards himself, and he is not as he chanced to be but as he wills, and this will is not random nor as it happened; for the will directed to the best is not random. (*Enneads* 6.8.16)[28]

It is easy to see that the description of the indescribable One taxes the resources of Plotinus' logic and language. So does the problem of the creative transition from absolute oneness to plurality, which is first revealed in the principle of Intellect. The Intellect comes second in Plotinus' hierarchy because he cannot accept the Aristotelian view that the supreme principle is thought thinking itself. But how, then, does thought, Intellect, come into being? The answer is that the One by its activity, so to speak, generates the Intellect. It generates the Intellect because "everything has an activity belonging to its substance." For example, the substance of fire is heat, and "when fire exercises the activity innate to its substance in remaining fire," another fire comes into being from the first. Similarly, the One remains what it is, but its perfection generates activity, which is the productive power of all things. "For being is not a corpse, nor is it without life or intellection; Intellect and being are in fact the same."[29]

The difficulty that Plotinus is facing is one that has come up before: Thinking implies a subject and an object, and the Intellect's thought would be an impossible, empty activity if it did not grasp some content:

> Intellection, which sees the intelligible object and turns to-
> ward it and is, in a way, being completed by it, is itself indefinite
> like vision, but it is defined by the object of its intellection . . .
> Therefore, Intellect is not simple but many, and manifests a
> composition, though of course an intelligible one, and already
> sees many things. (*Enneads* 5.4.2)[30]

All such struggles by Plotinus to describe the indescribable and the
beginnings of the creation of a plural world do little if anything to justify
the metaphysical priority of oneness. Yet the Neoplatonists have a developed logical justification, which follows. Here I draw on the help of Proclus.
I include in the proof only what is common to both Plotinus and Proclus,
but to make the proof consecutive, I set the principles of the one in the
quasi-mathematical order of proof of the other.[31]

The proof goes this way: If you try to think of a world in which the
quality of oneness or unity is absent, you see that the world is made
possible by the metaphysical One—the One that is by nature absolutely
and indivisibly single. It is the One that makes it possible for any and all
individual things to exist. Every distinguishable thing is a *one* for itself, its
oneness accounting for its unity and identity—no being can exist unless
it is unified by the oneness that it either is or shares. So if unity or oneness
did not exist, nothing would exist, not even plurality or multiplicity, which
is made up of ones. The power of existence of everything depends on the
power of existence of the One.

Suppose the opposite. Suppose that there is no oneness but only
manyness, multiplicity. To speak of the elements of this multiplicity is
conceptually improper, because the idea of an element involves that of
oneness.[32] All the same, to go on with the assumption: A multiplicity is by
definition made up of elements, and if its elements are not ones, they must
be either nothings or multiplicities. If they are nothings, the whole, which
is the sum of its elements, is also nothing. This is absurd. But the assumption that each of the elements is a multiplicity is also absurd. The reason
is that the multiplicity with which we began is not merely infinite (uncountable) in number, but infinitely infinite. That is, each of its elements
must itself be infinite in number, and each element of these infinitely
many elements is also infinite in number. They are numerically more
infinite than the infinite, and so the infinite, the greatest quantity that can
be or be thought of, is smaller in number than the infinite number of
infinities that it contains. But a number that is infinite an infinite number
of times does not exist. Therefore the hypothesis that no ones but only
multiplicities exist leads to an absurd conclusion and is also absurd.

Consider further: If the basic reality was not *one* but plurality, numbers could not exist. The reason is that all other numbers depend on *one*,

the principle from which they are made by successive addition. If the basic reality was plural, it would be impossible to think about or know anything because every instance of knowledge is an instance of the identity of knower and known. Therefore, without unity, no such identity would be possible and all beings would be unknowable.

Therefore, as has just been proved, *one* is the basic reality, which is shared in or "participated in" by every being. This *one* of every being must be something purely one, with no admixture of anything more or different. If it was essentially both *one* and not-*one*, its unity would have to be imported into itself from another *one*, which would require the existence of another *one*, and so on, ad infinitum. If such was the case, there would be no self-sufficient source of unity.[33]

By this proof, we have in effect established not only that the One— capitalized again for its now established preeminence—is the basic reality, but also that plurality depends on unity and not vice versa. Because the One is one in more than a merely numerical sense, "it does not come within the range of number" and is "therefore not limited in relation to itself or anything else: since if it was it would be two."[34] In theological terminology, the One is transcendent and yet immanent in whatever exists, singular or plural. As such, the One is the source of everything else:

> It is because there is nothing in it that all things come from it: in order that being may exist, the One is not being, but the generator of being . . . The One, perfect because it seeks nothing, has nothing, and needs nothing, overflows, as it were, and its superabundance makes something other than itself. (*Enneads* 5.2)[35]

To grasp the hierarchy of Plotinus and Proclus, it is still necessary to prove that the One is identical with the Good. For this proof, all that is needed is to point out that everything strives to maintain its own being, whether by its physical resistance to destruction or by other means. Therefore *good* is defined as *remaining one*: "Goodness, then, is unification, and unification goodness; the Good is one, and the One is primal good."[36]*

The world that results—the apparent world—reflects the real though diminished beauty of the One from which it is descended and to which

---

*This is Proclus, speaking with a Euclidean austerity. But Plotinus is full of images for what he believes cannot be imagined or even thought. The Good he imagines as a living sphere with a multiply varied life, or as a thing made only of faces and gleaming with all these living faces. Or he imagines the Good as all the pure souls come together in one place, all without any defects, having everything that is proper to them, and the whole Intellect enthroned over them all, so that this whole place is illuminated with intellectual light (*Enneads* 7.6.15; trans. Armstrong, vol. 7, p. 137; Hadot, *Trait 38*, pp. 127–28). Is the thing made only of faces the reminiscence of a story or image of a many-faced Indian God?

it reverts. Therefore, says Plotinus, to the sensitive person the world is the sounds of all voices in a universal melody. Plotinus favors the metaphor of the sound of a voice over that of a sight because sound does not divide experience into parts but remains everywhere the same in the air, while sight, a pluralizing instrument, breaks things up and differentiates them. Yet although Plotinus makes use of the voice metaphor, he at least once denies that in the fully real, intelligible world there can be any words or speech.[37]

Proclus alters, systematizes, complicates, and fills out Plotinus' sketch of the world. One alteration is in the conception of matter—potentiality or nonbeing—which Proclus is not able to identify with evil. Instead, evil is regarded as the absence of good, or the inability to receive good as purely as it is bestowed, or a perversion of the universal aspiration upward; but matter is not evil and evil is never real.[38]

Proclus's systematizing of Neoplatonism is heavily influenced, as I have said, by mathematics. In Neoplatonism generally, mathematical beings are intermediate between the highest beings—pure forms—and merely empirical beings. Unlike pure forms, mathematical beings are divisible and extend into series and geometric figures, but, unlike empirical beings, they are exact, perfectly ordered, immutable, and can be established and related to one another by irrefutable propositions.

According to Neoplatonism, sense perception draws the mind's attention to mathematical beings and so guides us to a higher, better-unified understanding.[39] In his *Elements of Theology*, Proclus states, "proves," and links his propositions like geometrical theorems, the purpose being to construct a system of exactly ordered levels of being. His propositions tread one after the other in a brave concatenation, from the first, "Every manifold in some way participates unity," up to the last, the two hundred and eleventh, "Every particular soul, when it descends into temporal process, descends entire: there is no part of it which remains above and a part which descends."[40] The universal rationality that is represented in these propositions implies that everything has its exact level in the hierarchy of being and goodness. No level or place is empty or redundant; everything fits perfectly between what is above and below it; accidental beings or positions are ruled out. This "axiomatics of perfection" has obviously strong echoes in the philosophies of Spinoza, Leibniz, and Hegel.[41]

Perhaps Proclus's most interesting complication of Neoplatonism is his development of the idea that at each level of reality there is a movement from cause to effect and back again. This movement is the reflection of the process by which *being* "proceeds" creatively and becomes life, and life, by returning to *being*, becomes intellect. Put in other, parallel terms, the movement is from permanence (eternal sameness) to manyness (eternal difference) and back to unity (the eternal limit in which difference is overcome).[42] But for our purposes it is best to avoid such complications and the technical justifications, which have not been mentioned, often based on Aristotle. Instead, we go on to the essential Neoplatonic proof that the One/Good is by nature indescribable.

The argument is that words can describe only a world of differences and limitations. In this world, thought is possible only if the thinker is split from the object of his thought. As the Neoplatonists see it, when a person thinks of something other than himself and becomes identified with this other, the person is more nearly split into two than when thinking of himself alone. Even thinking of himself alone, the person "becomes a pair . . . while remaining one."[43] It is therefore inconceivable that the One or Good thinks at all—thinking is generated by desire and is a movement toward some good, so the Good does not think or need to think, "for the Good is not other than itself."[44]

Evidently, nothing can be predicated of the One because predication implies the distinction between subject and object and between what is and is not predicated. The consequence is that every description we give of the One is inaccurate and must be understood as though modified by the words *as if*.[45] We can speak *about* the One, but certainly not speak *it*, know it, or think of it (*Enneads* 5.3.14). Negative words, however, are less inaccurate than positive ones. This is because assertions cut up reality, while negations make them less distinct, less well defined, more indefinite. It is only by such means as negation that it is possible "to reveal the power of the One, which is incomprehensible and ungraspable and unknowable by particular intellects."[46]

Bhartrihari (c.450–510)

Grammar . . . is the door to salvation.[47]

The power of language is one of the oldest themes of Indian thought.[48] In Vedic India, speech is a great goddess and the sound of ritual chanting is essential to human welfare. In the Upanishads, Brahman, in the sense of absolute reality, is equated with language.[49] And among the orthodox, there is a universal belief in the absolute truth of Vedic words, taken to be heard and transmitted by the first sages. Given such beliefs, it is not surprising that language plays a considerable role in philosophy, as it does in Mimamsa, Nyaya, and Buddhism, each of which sees it in the light of its characteristic interests. In Bhartrihari, a grammatical view of language becomes quite central to philosophical speculation.[50]

Since nothing is really known about Bhartrihari as a person and his dates, too, are uncertain, all one can do is repeat the old story that identifies him with a court poet of the same name. This poet wrote passionately regretful poems on separation from his mistress, gnomic verses on worldly wisdom, and very ambivalent poems on renunciation. The poet Bhartrihari says that there are two worlds worth a man's devotion: the youth of beautiful women and the ascetic's forest retreat; between them, he cannot choose. While it seems psychologically improbable that the graceful, sensuous poet is the same person as the careful, not to say, pedantic philosopher, the two meet in their devotion to Brahman, unqualified reality. It has been remarked that the Chinese pilgrim, I-tsing knows of a Buddhist grammarian who seven times took a monk's vows and seven times returned to the laity. However, neither the poet nor the philosopher Bhartrihari was a Buddhist. Besides, I-tsing reports that the grammarian died about 650 C.E. This is later than is plausible to situate Bhartrihari the grammarian-philosopher, whose thought was known to the early-sixth-century Buddhist philosopher Dignaga.[51]*

Though immodest about the powers of grammar-philosophy, Bhartrihari takes little credit for his own perhaps great contribution to it. Of himself, he says merely, "This summary of the science (of grammar) was composed by my teacher [Vasurata] after learning the various other systems and our own system."[52] What at least appears to be new in his thought is the attempt to embody the grammatical point of view in a full-fledged Indian philosophy, a *darshana*, a view of reality.

Bhartrihari's chief work, *On Sentence and Word (Vakyapadiya)*, consists, Indian style, of some two thousand succinct verses distributed in three books (or cantos, *kandas*), though his own supposed commentary

---

*In India, it was fairly usual for a philosopher to be a poet as well. Shankara, for example, wrote poetry, though all on the side of renunciation. The twelfth-century skeptic, Shriharsha, who will be discussed later, wrote both his austerely philosophical text and an ornate, sexually explicit epic of love, which has (of course) been given an allegorical interpretation. In defense of the identification of the poet Bhartrihari with the grammarian, it is argued: "The poetry of Bhartrihari shares with the grammatical philosophy of Bhartrihari, as expounded in the *Vakyapadiya*, ideas with terminology drawn from traditional systems of Vedanta and Sankhya metaphysics, as well as from classical Yoga psychology. Also common to the poetry and the philosophy is a critical interest in the nature of time. In Bhartrihari's philosophy, time is a creative power that is responsible for the birth, continuity, and destruction of everything in the universe. Much of the poetry shows a pessimistic preoccupation with the beginning and end of things. The inevitability with which time is said to ravage the life of man may conceivably represent the poetic expression of the futility and dejection upon a philosopher profoundly impressed with the power of time. Good arguments are put forth to date Bhartrihari the philosopher to the fifth century C.E. The core of the collected poems attributed to Bhartrihari also probably dates to this period" (Stoller, *The Hermit and the Love Thief* [see the immediately preceding note 51], p. 23).

ends with the second book, which does not seem to demand a sequel.[53] Whoever is the author of this commentary, it is often as obscure as the main text, sometimes because of its involved, ambiguous sentences, and sometimes because of its extreme terseness.[54] There are also three later commentaries. Because my aims are general, I will not point out the differences in point of view between the text and its commentaries, and I may sometimes include their interpretations without noting the fact. Bhartrihari is more nuanced and more preoccupied with grammar than is evident from my account of him.

Here, there would be no point in more than mentioning the purely dogmatic characteristics of Bhartrihari's thought. I mean by this his conviction that the Vedas are revealed truth, inseparable from the Sanskrit, the sacred primal language in which they are embodied; that the whole, true knowledge is concentrated in a single word, the mantra *om*, "the creator of the worlds"; that the correctness of a grammatical form depends on its presence in scripture; and so on. Bhartrihari is simply a believer, though by his own grammarian's standards, who trusts that there is a Yogic ability to enter others' minds and that certain persons have what appears to us as miraculous powers of intuition.[55] Above all, he believes that "even if the different doctrines disappeared and there were no authors to compose more, humankind would not turn away from the religious law that comes from revelation and tradition" (*revelation* translates the Sanskrit *heard*, applied to directly authoritative texts; *tradition*, in contrast, applies to texts whose authority is indirect because dependent upon memory).[56]

If we omit Bhartrihari's more detailed linguistic analysis and concentrate on what remains in him of general philosophical interest, we find a group of interrelated ideas on the nature and importance of words and their organization into language:[57]

1. The "word"—a term used by Bhartrihari for language in general—has an inward meaning and an outward expression.
2. The word cannot be an unrelated fragment, such as an unrelated word, but only the expression of a unitary meaning.
3. Regardless of how many words (in the usual sense) are used to express a thought, its meaning—its inward word—is grasped as a whole by means of an intuitive act of understanding. Only after the whole is grasped can its parts, its words, be understood individually and their relationships established by analysis.
4. All thought—awareness, perception, reasoning, judgment—and therefore all knowledge are infused with language and so cannot be separated from it.

5. The world as a whole is nothing other than a structure of interrelated meanings as grasped in words (sentences), thoughts, and thought in itself. Essentially, therefore, the world is the same as the language by which it is known.

6. The relations between words express and are essentially the same as those between levels of reality. Because the structural relations between words are established by grammar, grammar is the science by which reality can be best understood.

7. The process by which our changing, material world was evolved from the unchanging, spiritual reality must have begun in and followed the process by which language was evolved.

8. In appearance, the word's power is differentiated into that of space and of time—time is the more important. Time is the regulator of the order of empirical existence, the cause of every sequence and every instance of origin, existence, or destruction.

9. Even though the world is nothing other than a structure of potential, latent, and expressed meanings, its indwelling principle, that of the word—language—is utterly beyond differentiation and expression in words.

10. Both knowledge and salvation come by way of grammar.

To go through these ideas, informally but more or less in the same order, we may begin by distinguishing between the inward sense and the outward meaning of the word (or, capitalized, the Word), in the sense of language. Word and meaning are in origin the same. To be expressed, they must take on an outward form. The outward form is, of course, the sound, the word as audible to others. Among the experts in phonetics, says Bhartrihari, there are various speculations on the cause of the audible word. Some believe that it results from the movement of the air that is set into motion by the speaker's effort and strikes the organs of articulation. Others believe that a word is made of the atoms that separate and transform themselves into shadow, light, darkness, and speech. Still other thinkers, among them Bhartrihari, are more concerned with the transition from thought to sound. They believe that a spoken word is the transformation of the subtle form that is identical with the inner knower, who transforms himself in order to reveal his form. Becoming mind (manas) and "ripened" by bodily heat, the knower enters the breath-air and "colors" it with the mind's qualities. Splitting its densities into different sounds, the breath then merges with and manifests the sounds to speech, the phonemes.[58]

Bhartrihari's conception of the process by which thought is turned into speech is, at once, psychological, physiological, and metaphysical.

By his conception, the word/meaning is at first in the mind alone. The word/meaning is itself a power (shakti), but to be externalized it needs the help of the inward principle of activity, which is the inward breath. When this breath strikes the organs of articulation, they externalize the word, which then becomes the expressive, audible word. When the word's meaning is grasped by the hearer, the circuit of communication is completed—from one mind and inmost word to another mind and inmost word.[59]

If this explanation is accepted, it is evident that the words that are actually expressed have two elements. One is their meaning, their essential cause, and the other is the sequence of sounds by which the meaning is externalized. In spite of the sequence, the meaning remains whole and enters the listener's mind whole: "From the differentiated, the undifferentiated word is born and it expresses the meaning. The word assumes the form of the meaning and enters into relation with it."[60]

Bhartrihari uses an analogy to clarify his conception: When two sticks are rubbed together, their latent fire kindles visible fire and makes both itself and other things visible. In the same way, the word in the mind causes the audibly differentiated words to manifest themselves. That is, the inner word completes its germination, is impelled by the speech organs, manifests itself in different successive sounds, and makes both itself and other things known.[61] Put otherwise, the mind searches for a pronounceable form of the word and relates the form to what the speaker intends to say. The word then seems to change into the pronounceable form that is projected onto it. But the change of the meaning into something that is divided into sequential parts is only apparent. The truth is, says the commentator, that the word in itself is neither sequential nor simultaneous but absolutely one; it seems to have parts only because of the sounds that are associated with it. In an image, the word in itself and the sound in which it is expressed are related, like the moon and the substratum of water that reflects it: the reflection is of something immobile but is perceived as if joined to the water and moving with its waves. So, too, the word in itself takes on the properties of the sound that externalizes its meaning and appears to move with the sound, whether quickly, with moderate speed, or slowly.[62]

To use a Bhartriharian image, the energy called "the word" is like the yolk in a peahen's egg: when the bird emerges from the egg, the essential uniformity of the yolk takes the form of a rich diversity. In still another image, when a painter wants to paint something made up of parts, such as the figure of a man, he scans it as a sequence of parts and then paints it sequentially, as he must. Likewise, a spoken world is at first perceived as a sequence and then, the sequence suppressed, as a partless mental unity superimposed on the sequential appearance. Just as the speaker first concentrates on the form of the word by isolating it from among other words, the hearer first tries to grasp the word's form in all the details that accompany it. Then the hearer makes out the meaning this particular spoken word has among the indefinitely many meanings that it can be given.[63]

The word *word* has been used with caution, at first in quotation marks, to indicate that it is taken in the larger grammatical and metaphysical sense of the language in which a certain thought is expressed. This caution is the result of Bhartrihari's contention that isolated words cannot be the basic units of meaning. To him, as is by now obvious, the true, unspoken word—the *sphota*, as it is called—is a whole thought and is therefore more or less equivalent to a sentence, the least linguistic form that is complete.* It is the essence or fixed meaning that underlies the articulated sounds that reveal it. Opponents of Bhartrihari claim that each word has its separate meaning, and that words or word meanings become mutually dependent in the sentence and therefore convey a meaning the words do not have when taken separately. Put more technically, the separate words are universals that, when joined with other words, are restricted and made particular.[64]

In disagreement, Bhartrihari begins with the whole sentence.[65] There are, he acknowledges, practical ways of establishing the meanings of individual words. A sentence can be analyzed into components with artificial, secondary meanings. This is possible, he says, because a sentence is primarily an expression of some action or process, so that in analyzing it we can at first isolate its main word—its main verb—to which we assign the meaning it has in that particular sentence.[66] All words that are not verbs are accessory and are assigned derivative mean-

---

*Sphota is derived from *sphut*, the literal meaning of which is *to burst forth*. *Sphota* is the idea that bursts forth in or, put less dramatically, manifests itself to the mind when one hears someone speaking. The successively larger units of spoken language are the phoneme or *varna* (the shortest articulated sound), the (ordinary) word or *pada*, and the sentence or *vakya*. Bhartrihari believes that the *sphota* can be at least vaguely revealed in any of these, but his basic contention is that the unrelated phoneme has no meaning at all (Iyer's explanation, *Vākyapadīya* 3.1, p. 2; and *Vākyapadīya* 2.210). If a single word is meaningful, Bhartrihari says, the reason is that it is the equivalent of a sentence. Therefore, the sentence should be seen as the basic linguistic unit or *shabda*. *Shabda* has a variety of meanings, including that of the uttered *sound*, to which Bhartrihari assigns the name *dhvani*. (See Coward and Raja, eds., *The Philosophy of the Grammarians*, pp. 5–6; Iyer, *Bhartṛhari*, pp. 155–61; and Iyer, *The Vākyapadīya: Some Problems*, pp. 24–29.)

ings in order to help clarify the action or process.[67]* But isolated words are indefinite, appear in many different forms, and have no fixed meaning, in the absence of which they are not only unclear but useless. Only words used together have fixed meanings; and the smallest clear, fixed meaning is that conveyed by a sentence: "The nature of all word-meaning is dependent on the meaning of the sentence."[68] It is true, Bhartrihari acknowledges, that even before a sentence is finished,. one grasps a vague meaning, not yet fit for communication; and as the later words appear, the first, vague meaning is abandoned or refined, up to the moment when the sentence ends and its full meaning can be grasped: the speaking out of the meaning and its grasping is itself a continuous process of clarification.[69]

Single words, says Bhartrihari, can be compressed sentences, clear enough in the context of their use. But the simple addition of individual words each with its supposed independent meaning, or the analysis of sentences into such words, must fail.[70] The sentence is hardly more separate from its words than its words are from the sounds, the phonemes, that make them up. "In the word there are no phonemes and in the phonemes there are no parts. Words have no existence separate from the sentence."[71] If they try, those who are drinking sherbet can taste the flavor of each separate ingredient and understand what it contributes to the taste of the whole; yet the taste is indivisible. When the indivisible sentence cannot be understood all at once, the separate and unreal word meanings are abstracted. As soon as the meaning of the sentence is grasped, the unreal meanings disappear.[72]

In order that language should fulfill its natural purpose, the conveying of meaning, the context of its use must be understood and it must be subjected to corresponding restrictions. For one, a reference to a reference

---

*In saying this, Bhartrihari is taking a position in the old argument between, among others, the grammarians and the adherents of Nyaya over the primacy of verbs. Are even nouns (or nominal stems) derived from verbs (or verbal roots)?—many Sanskrit sentences, especially those in the "nominal style," are without verbs. Of course, Bhartrihari is on the side of the grammarians and the verbs. In the last book of the *Vakyapadiya*, he makes detailed grammatical analyses to show that a sentence expresses a particular action or process, which is directly denoted by its main word, a verb. Bhartrihari thinks that the function of most nouns is to show what means or accessories the action or process requires. Analysis of a sentence is artificial, he insists, but helps to explain the indivisible word that comes to expression in the sentence. Examined with care, no two of the infinite number of sentences are alike. Individual words abstracted from a sentence by analysis of their meaning are unreal, as unreal as the stem and suffix similarly abstracted from an individual word. (See *The Vākyapadīya of Bhartṛhari*, chap. 3, part 1; trans. Iyer, pp. 1–2; Matilal, *The Word and the World*, pp. 8–10, 55–61; and Staal, "Sanskrit Philosophy of Grammar," p. 508.)

has to be restricted by the understanding of the first reference's function. To give an example: When doubt is cast on something particular and then someone casts doubt on this doubt, the doubt loses its original form. Just so, when a cognition is determining the nature of its object, "it cannot become the object of another cognition. If it did, it would lose its proper nature and become the 'object' of another cognition."[73] The purpose of cognition is to determine the nature of an external object, and it is therefore wrong to reverse its status and see it as itself the object of knowledge. Likewise:

> The sentence "all that I am saying is wrong" is not literally meant. If what it says is wrong, the point in question would not be conveyed. What is expressive cannot at the same time be the expressed. (*Vakyapadiya* 3.25–26)[74]*

All such negative self-reference is illegitimate, says Bhartrihari, because it nullifies the nature—the purpose and usefulness—of language, which it prevents from expressing anything. If "All that I am saying is wrong" is taken literally, it becomes impossible for the person who uses it to convey his intention, which is that what he said *just before* is wrong— his language is not allowed to be a means of communication. What is used to convey a certain content cannot be turned back on itself as if it is fulfilling an intention other than its own.** A function ought not take on another, reflexive one that leads to self-contradiction or infinite regress.[75]

---

*In another, more literal translation: "With 'everything I am saying is false,' that statement itself is not meant. For if its own expressing is false, one does not arrive at the point in question. For what proceeds as signifier cannot be the signified. That by which another thing is expressed, cannot be expressed in the same context." The next verse (3.27) says: "Just as 'A thesis has no proving force' does not refer to that [thesis] itself, in the same way also no property whatsoever of that [statement itself] is understood [from the statement 'everything I am saying is false']." This statement is generalized in the verse that follows (3.28): "Because there is no other (i.e. opposite) mode of functioning of a mode of functioning, therefore one should not resort to contradiction or infinite regress in all cases" (Houben, "Bhartrihari's Solution to the Liar and Some Other Paradoxes," pp. 392, 394).

**There is a clear likeness between Bhartrihari's ruling and that of Bertrand Russell in his (ramified) theory of types. By Russell's theory, too, a string of elements of a language is regarded as ill formed, rather than false, if it does not observe certain restrictions of level or form. Of course, the object is to outlaw paradoxical self-reference, so that language can be consistent. The preference of some of Russell's critics for a linguistic or semantic over a logical cure for problems of self-reference returns us to Bhartrihari, who insists on taking into account the communicative purpose in everyday language of intention, negation, reference, and self-reference (Houben, "Bhartrihari's Solution . . . ," p. 395).

In contrast to Bhartrihari, the medieval philosopher John Buridan (1300–1358) solves the paradox in a formal way: The liar paradox— *What I am saying is false*—is false. The paradox says:

When Bhartrihari says this, he probably has particular philosophical schools in mind, but it is all, in Bhartrihari's eyes, part of the explanation of how language functions. The explanation, he is sure, is that given by the school of grammar, the tradition of which has been kept by an unbroken line of learned men—to give up tradition and rely on inference alone is like running ahead on an uneven path with one's hand extended but one's eyes quite blind.[76] As a partisan of the grammatical tradition, Bhartrihari points out how fallible ordinary speech is and how limited the standard Indian instruments of knowledge. The meanings expressed in words are understood differently at different times and by different persons. Much the same is true of perception: different persons perceive the same things differently and the same persons perceive them differently at different times. "Therefore, both the comprehension and report of people who have not seen the truth (about things) are defective, unreliable, and perpetually inconsistent."[77]

The authority of sages is not enough. They perceive the true nature of things, but their perception cannot be transferred into words or put to use in ordinary life. Perception as a means of knowledge is obviously fallible, for each of us is subject to sensory illusions—we all see the sky as a surface even though logic teaches us that there is no surface there. So perception alone is inconsistent and unreliable. But logic, too, brings no certainty: clever logicians are contradicted by still cleverer ones. And when merely pragmatic persons try to understand what is beyond ordinary words, they fail (as the science of grammar does not).[78]

Yet human beings do have a spontaneous, reliable kind of knowledge. This is intuition, *pratibha*. Having the connotation of light and shining forth, it is the understanding that flashes lightlike on the mind.[79] Though essential to life, it is inexplicable:

> Having been formed from the function of one's inner self, its nature is not known even to the person. It effects the fusion of the (individual) word-meanings, without itself being logically thought out . . . In the matter of the knowledge of what to do, no one transgresses it . . . The whole world looks upon

---

If it is true it is false, if it is false it is true, if it is true it is both true and false, if it is false it is both true and false, and, finally, it is both true and false. "I maintain, briefly," Buridan responds, "that the sophism is false, because from it and a proposition expressing the case there follows something false, and yet the proposition expressing the case is taken to be true. (The 'something false' that follows is that the sophism is both true and false at once.) Now any proposition which, together with something true entails something false, is itself false" (G. E. Hughes, *John Buridan on Self-Reference*, Cambridge: Cambridge University Press, 1982, p. 58).

> it as authority (for their conduct). Even in animals the knowledge of the beginning of behavior dawns by virtue of it . . . Who alters the note of the cuckoo in the spring? By whom are creatures taught to make nests and so on? Who directs animals and birds in functions like eating, loving, hating and leaping? (*Vakyapadiya* 2.144–47, 149–50)[80]

What is translated as *intuition* evidently includes instinct. The rather miscellaneous inclusiveness of Bhartrihari's concept is evident in his enumeration of the six various kinds of *pratibha* "as obtained (1) by nature (2) by action (3) by practice (4) by meditation (5) by invisible causes and (6) as handed down by the wise."[81]

Some of the examples given by the earliest commentary may not seem fitting. Such an example, of intuition "by nature," is the intrinsic tendency of primordial matter to evolve. As examples of intuition "by practice," Bhartrihari cites the ability of experts to know where to dig for water or how to distinguish what is genuine and false in coins or diamonds. Being indefinable, this intuitive ability to assess cannot be communicated to others. It is certainly no inference; if it was, it would have an inference's ordinary grounds.[82]

I will give no further examples, because what is more immediately relevant to our subject is the intuitive ability to understand language. It is intuition that enables us to grasp a whole meant object from a word that refers to part of it, or enables us to grasp the meaning of words with missing letters.[83] But above all, intuition is the ability to make a single sense of the separate words of a sentence, and to do this even before the sentence is finished. A single heard letter may yield the sentence's whole meaning. Intuition also gives us the ability to recognize that certain kinds of sentences, such as those meant to praise or blame, have a meaning different from that indicated by their analysis into separate words.[84]

If it is conceded that thoughts are always, to begin with, latent words, then all thoughts and all forms of knowledge are inseparable from words and Word:

> All knowledge of what is to be done in this world depends upon the word . . . All knowledge is, as it were, intertwined with the word . . . It is this that is the basis of all the sciences, crafts and arts. Whatever is created due to this can be analyzed (and communicated) . . . Thanks to it, whatever is produced can be classified . . . The consciousness of all living beings . . . is of the nature of the word; it exists within and without. (*Vakyapadiya* 1.121, 123, 125, 126)[85]

Some explanation is in order. Knowing of every kind requires the ability to identify and remember. This ability is inseparable from words because it is inseparable from cognition, which is inseparable from words. Such is most obviously the case when technical distinctions are made by means of specially invented terms. The technical vocabularies distinguish what is necessary for action and might not otherwise be grasped. To understand music one must learn its science; merely listening to the different types of musical notes is not enough.[86] Even that which in some weak sense exists "is as good as non-existent as long as it does not come within the range of verbal usage."[87] Even fantasies and imaginary objects and logical impossibilities are endowed with what measure of reality they have when they are brought to mind by words. And even children understand what they do because they have understanding in a vague sense, the result of "the residual traces of words from their former births."[88]

Without words, Bhartrihari is saying, knowledge is indeterminate. For example, when one walks quickly and steps on grass and clods of earth, one has an unverbalized awareness or sensation of them. The grass is no more than tinged with awareness, the "word seed" is only latent, only ready to sprout. This not yet verbalized awareness is speech, but only in the inarticulate form that cannot denote, and the sensation has little if any effect.[89] Without determination by words, awareness is too weak to merit the name. To Bhartrihari, therefore, what has not been verbally identified is to that extent unknown or almost unknown, near to unknowable, and incommunicable and unremembered. Nothing can be grasped when there is no language. In its absence, there are no latent words, no spiritual activities, no sciences, no arts, no crafts, no communication, no consciousness, no memory, and no self.[90]

If so, the word is essentially the consciousness and self-consciousness of all beings. We can therefore dare to say that the world is indistinguishable from the words by which it is known. And if we take one more metaphysical step along with Bhartrihari, we conclude that the world is nothing other than a structure of meanings as fixed in language. Therefore,

> the power which creates and regulates this universe rests on words . . . It is the word which sees the object, it is the word which reveals the object which was lying hidden, it is on the word that this multiple world rests. (*Vakyapadiya* 1.118 and comm.)[91]

In an adventurous but reasoned sequence, it is concluded that the world is made of words, that expressed words are made of latent words or meanings, and that meanings are made of consciousness. This conclusion is the burden of the verse of invocation with which Bhartrihari's book begins: "Brahman without beginning or end, Word-Principle (shabdatattva), Immutable Phoneme (akshara), who appears as . . . the objects, from whom the world proceeds (Vakyapadiya 1.1).[92]*

The commentary goes on to say that in all its apparently different manifestations, the original material of the word remains. This is because we identify objects with the words by which they are named. And because reality, Brahman, must create the world in its own nature and because the world's nature is words, Brahman itself must be the Word of words. And because Brahman creates words in their audible form, Brahman is the phoneme as well:

> The Brahman is called phoneme (akshara) because it is the cause of the phonemes . . . What is meant by "it appears as the objects" is this—what is called appearance . . . is the assumption by the One, without losing its one-ness, through apparent diversity, of the unreal forms of others. It is like the appearances in a dream. (Vakyapadiya 1.1. comm.)[93]

The understanding of language in this metaphysical sense teaches us that latent speech is the permanent possibility of cognition and that cognition is the permanent possibility of the existence of the world. This is simpler to understand if we analyze how we know anything at all. The first source of possible knowledge is the highest universal, the Word, of which the lower universals are manifestations.[94] To know any particular thing is to know its indwelling, lower universal (jati). To know this universal is first to know the equivalent word and, by its means, the universal that dwells in whatever we are perceiving.

Take an undramatic Indian example. When we know, that is, cognize a jar and say "This is a jar," the word jar in the sentence is identified with the cognition and with the jar that is the cognition's content. And because the reality of the cognition and its object, the jar, is their indwelling universal—the jar itself is unreal—it makes sense to say that the word is the same as the jar. So the jar is derived from the word, and not the opposite—jars of clay come from verbal jars.[95] Conveying its form to an object, the word pervades and dyes it with its particular meaning, which

---

*The word akshara ordinarily means imperishable or immutable, but in the commentary to the Vakyapadiya it is given the sense of (immutable) phoneme (Iyer's note 5, p. 3 of his translation). The term shabdatattva, Word Principle or Word Essence, emphasizes that all words are transformations of the Word, while shabdabrahman, Brahman Word or Supreme Word, emphasizes that the Word is the being of everything and is subject to no limitation.

is its variety of powers to function—in the case of a pot, the powers necessary to carry water.[96]*

This raises a question: By what means does the power of the Word come to expression in the powers of the world of human experience? The answer is that time or, rather, Time is the causal agent.[97] It must be kept in mind that the many forms of the different objects of human experience do not affect the unity of the cognition that encompasses them all. They are differentiated, that is, projected as the contents of the empirical world, by Time's creative power, *kalashakti*, which is that of the Word.[98] By its power, Time regulates the Word's transformations and, by doing so, is the cause of all origins, existences, and destructions. Time pulls the wires of the world automaton (the world as robot, or perhaps as puppet show). The action of Time is by means of its two eternal aspects, the one the giving of permission for things to appear, and the other the withholding of the permission. If not for Time's aspects, things would all be born at once and chaos result. Together with its associates, the heavenly bodies, Time enables the conventional fixing of seasons, months, days, and hours. And because all things happen by their association with different times, Time is the efficient cause of all particular effects. As such, it draws real objects out of potentiality as regularly as a waterwheel draws water from a river. In a metaphor, Time brings about changes in things just as a river places and displaces grass, leaves, and creepers on its banks.[99]

Such metaphors apart, objects come into being when universals trying to find themselves an "abode"—an object to inhere in—guide potential causes into producing particular effects, which are the different particular objects. Having "prompted" the appearance of these objects, the universals manifest themselves in them "like reflections in clear water." To all appearances, they are identical with the objects and are designated by the words that identify them.[100] Bhartrihari sums up by saying, "Time is the very soul of the universe. Hence it is identified with activity itself."[101]

Brahman itself is, of course, atemporal.[102] Neither unity nor multiplicity can be attributed to it. Neither could be explained without the other, and since they are mutually dependent, disproving either would disprove the other. Clearly conceived, unity and difference are the same.

---

*According to Helaraja, Bhartrihari's tenth-century commentator, the essential nature of objects consists in their particular powers to exert effects. Their essential nature is therefore equivalent to the nature of sentences, because "a normal sentence expresses a complex meaning of which the central meaning is some action, to which the other elements contribute" (K. K. Raja, in Coward and Raja, eds., *The Philosophy of the Grammarians*, pp. 194–95).

The One Reality has no before or after even though "it shines with the divisions of time."[103]

This is the claim according to which everything in the world consists of outward appearances in which resides the one source of all transformations.[104] Therefore it is the Word, with its temporal power and transformations into words, that makes the world. Therefore, all the sciences depend upon the correct, grammatical formation of language, so that grammar is their universal basis. Corrupted forms of language have no fixed meaning and are the cause of sin.[105] "It is the word, language, that is the sole teacher."[106] The very ability to conduct a reasonable discussion depends on the immutable power of words to convey a meaning based on their primary sense, situational contexts, verbal neighbors, and grammatical use.[107*]

Grammar and grammar alone can lead us away from indefiniteness and sin. For the Word, which is Brahman,

> is endowed with all powers, which are neither identical with nor different from it; and it has two aspects, that of unity and that of [apparent] diversity . . . It is, in all states, unaffected by beginning and end, even though the manifestations appear in worldly transaction in a temporal and spatial sequence. (*Vakyapadiya* 1.1 comm.)[108]

Reality in itself is one/many. Words produce opposite effects, yet they cannot be opposed to one another because they all exist simultaneously in the same one Word or Brahman that constitutes them completely. For words can have no existence apart from the Word, and their paradoxically separate-non-separate existence-non-existence is a differentiation into forms that are unreal as dreams are unreal.[109]

The science of grammar shows how the Word (Language), the metaphysical principle of the everything, leads to salvation.[110] What is salvation? The ascent toward the Word that reverses the direction of the evolution of language and of the world. The ascent goes from articulated speech to the potential speech in the mind, to the total of word forms tinged with successiveness but going beyond it, and, finally, to the pure principle of language. Whoever aspires to this grammatical salvation must learn to see the constant Word without distinction. Such seeing requires intuition in its fullest sense, free of all differences.[111]

---

*"The meanings of words are determined from (their) syntactical connection (in the sentence), situation-context, the meaning of another word, property, place, and time, and not from their mere form. [Meanings of words are determined by] (constant) association (of two things), (their) dissociation, company, and hostility, the meaning (of another word), situation-context, evidence from another sentence, and the proximity of another word" (*Vākyapadīya* 2.314–15; trans. Pillai, p. 108).

To get to the Word in itself, one must learn to suppress sequential thinking. As hinted, to do this requires perseverance in the use of grammatically correct forms. The incorrect formation and sequencing of words obscures the light of the Word and the Vedic truth. Correct speech—Word yoga—allows the light, the truth, to shine through, allows the sequences of words and thoughts to be suppressed, allows the knots of ego to be cut and union with the Word to be consummated.[112]

Discussion

If Plotinus had gone to India, as he wanted, he would have found descendants of Uddalaka and Yajnavalkya with whom, interpreters permitting, he would have been able to find a common philosophical language. It is not likely, however, that the grammarian predecessors of Bhartrihari would have been among these discussants of the ultimacies of *being*. I say this because the grammarians' initially linguistic approach might have made them seem alien to Plotinus. The difference would have been sharpened if Proclus was substituted for Plotinus (I have not imagined Plotinus and Proclus together—psychological considerations make me doubt if Plotinus could suffer what Proclus made of his thought). Bhartrihari and Proclus would no doubt exchange accounts of their respective ancient, holy traditions, submerged for a time and then recovered. In the debate between them, it would be the semantic, grammatical order of the Indian against the Greek's mathematical translation of semantic order. The Indian, struggling with the obdurate complexities of linguistic use, would often be tentative and allow for different possibilities. The Greek, putting each statement to a "mathematical" true-false test, would claim unambiguous success at every step—in principle, his metaphysical mathematics rules out ambiguity. I do not know if the Indian would pit his mantras against the Greek's theurgic magic. But for both of them, as for us, the philosophic crux might well be the possibility of casting linguistically conveyed meanings into forms with purely mathematical modes of proof.

It is therefore all the more interesting to see how closely the two very different lines of hierarchical idealism converge. They converge, first, in the logic of hierarchy, which, for Plotinus and Proclus, is that of the hierarchical reciprocity between Ideas and, for Bhartrihari, that, ultimately, of the hierarchical reciprocity between meanings. Lines of thought also converge in the timeless *being*—Word, Brahman, One, Good—at the head of the hierarchy. To both sides, *being* is unlimited consciousness in an infinitely simple unity-in-variety beyond human conceiving and expression. There is also convergence in the idea of the creative overflow of *being* that projects and differentiates the world that, despite appearances, is identical with *being*.

How great a difference is there between saying, for Plotinus and Proclus, that reality is a structure of Ideas that proceed from and revert to their source, with which understanding humans should try to unite, and between saying, as does Bhartrihari, that reality is a structure of meanings that proceed from meaning as such, with which understanding humans should try to unite? I pose the question without answering it. I have no doubt, however, that in both philosophies there is the same belief in creative emanation from *being*, which, as best we can understand it, is a consciousness that, in false appearance, grows increasingly distant from itself as its creations grow increasingly material. Nor do I doubt the comparison of the two doctrines of causality that say that everything is related to everything by the force exerted by conscious meaning.

In the end, what is most striking in hierarchical idealism is the intellectual and emotional need to identify being-as-such, the source of everything, with the quintessence of individual consciousness and, therefore, with our nucleus as human individuals. The moral that I would draw—though differently from the Indian and the Greek hierarchical philosophers—is that what we most yearn to get close to is an inconceivably great version of ourselves.[113] This is, of course, the *atman*-Brahman theme we have met before and will meet again, in different guises.

Chapter 8

Developed Skepticism

Sextus Empiricus, Nagarjuna, Jayarashi, Shriharsha

Theme: Doubts for the Sake of (Secular) Peace of Mind, Nirvana (So to Speak), Materialism (Maybe), and (Self-Evident) Brahman

The skepticism dealt with in this chapter is well developed because, having so much previous philosophy to draw on, it has so many different positions of which to be doubtful. Its arguments show the deep symbiosis between skepticism and constructive thinking, each creating itself and the other by attack, defense, counterattack, and counterdefense. As attested by the four philosophers under consideration, the purposes of skepticism can vary widely. The weapons used by the three are often the same, but Sextus Empiricus aims only at nondogmatic peace of mind, Nagarjuna defends Buddhism against anti-Buddhists and constructive philosophers of his own, Buddhist faith, and Shriharsha demonstrates that reality, the self-illuminating Brahman, is indefinable. Jayarashi stands out as the skeptic who aims only at "the annihilation of all principles" and sees no need to ask if the skeptic's doubt is useful or not.

Skeptics, our four among them, begin with the advantage that much of what they question in philosophy is distant from common sense. But they also begin with a pair of obvious difficulties, one simply human and the other technical. The simply human difficulty is that so many people resist a drastic attack on reason because they feel that reason is essential to their survival. The technical difficulty—as expressed by Nyaya—is the one that arises when any drastic form of skepticism is proposed: If no philosophical arguments prove anything, on what grounds does the skeptic suppose that skeptical arguments prove that nothing can be proved?

Sextus Empiricus (Second or third century C.E.)

"Suspense" is a state of mental rest owing to which we neither deny nor affirm anything.

Sextus Empiricus, a doctor who hopes to cure human disquiet by means of *aporia*, a state of bafflement aroused by conflicting arguments, teaches skepticism lucidly, scrupulously, and unrelentingly.[1] He is said to have been the pupil of a pupil of Menodotus of Nicomedia, a doctor of the Empiricist school and a skeptic.[2] At one point, however, he criticizes the Empiricists for confining themselves dogmatically to what can be observed and declares that he feels closest to the Methodic school, which derives what seems beneficial from appearances.[3] Because he is reticent about skeptical predecessors of his own kind—he names only Pyrrho, Aenesedmus, and (once) Agrippa—it is hard to know what, if anything, is original in his text.[4] But as the encyclopedist of Greek skepticism, he puts it all before us. I therefore introduce his name less to speak of his own philosophy than to introduce the partisans of skepticism from whom he draws his arguments.

The fathers of the school or schools of Greek skepticism are Socrates, about whom nothing need be added, and Pyrrho of Elis (c. 360–c. 277 B.C.). As shy of writing as Socrates, Pyrrho is a powerful although vague presence. It is said that he was at first an unnoticed painter. Along with his teacher, he associated with the "naked philosophers" of India and the Magi of Persia. It was this association, we are told, that led him to introduce "the form of inapprehension *(akatalepsis)* and suspension of judgment *(epoche)*." We are also told that Pyrrho's Indian journey caused him to live in solitude because he remembered the reproach addressed by an Indian to Pyrrho's teacher, Anaxarchus, that "he would never be able to teach others what is good while he himself danced attendance on kings in their courts."[5] It is therefore possible that an Indian influence is reflected in the statement ascribed to Pyrrho "that nothing existed in reality," as well as in his Buddhist-like refusal to take sides in philosophical debates, his social detachment, and his equanimity, which seem unusual in the Greece of his time.*

Pyrrho, who lived with his sister, a midwife, would roam about with chance companions. He attracted attention and devotion by the way in which he accepted whatever life brought him, almost never abandoning his composed, non-judgmental attitude. He suspended judgment, he explained, because nothing is truly honorable or dishonorable, nothing "exists in truth," and human behavior is based on nothing but convention and habit.[6] Although he wrote nothing at all, his pupil Timon, who revered him, is reported to have summed up Pyrrho's view of the human ability to gain knowledge in the declaration (the end of which sounds conspicuously Indian)

> that things are equally indifferent, unmeasurable and inarbitrable. For this reason, neither our sensations nor our opinion tell us truths or falsehoods. Therefore for this reason we should not put our trust in them one bit, but we should be unopinionated, uncommitted and unwavering, saying concerning each individual thing that it no more is than is not, or it both is and is not, or it neither is nor is not.[7]

Pyrrho's abstention from worldly matters is said to have been emulated by many. But out of irreverent loyalty to skeptical principles, one Theodosius denied that skepticism should be called Pyrrhonism. If we can never be certain of anything, he said, we can never know what Pyrrho's real intentions were and whether or not the name is fitting.[8] Theodosius may be right. Such a connoisseur of Greek skepticism as Cicero is aware of Pyrrho only as a severe and dogmatic pursuer of virtue.[9]

---

*None of the interesting parallels between Sextus's text and Indian philosophy give decisive proof of Indian influence. His discussion of the Stoic use of sense perception and intellect as instruments of judgment recalls Indian philosophy. So does his use of two stock Indian examples, the one, doubt whether what one sees is a rope or a snake, and the other, smoke as the sign of fire. Sextus tells us that the Stoics believe in "suggestive signs"—such as smoke, which suggests fire—and "indicative signs"—such as bodily motions, which indicate the working of the soul. He says that the Stoics define an indicative sign as "an antecedent judgment, in a valid hypothetical syllogism, which serves to reveal the consequent." Sextus's rope-snake and smoke-fire examples, the Stoic way of proving the smoke-fire relation by a syllogism, and Sextus's skeptical response to all of these are reminiscent of the Indian discussion surrounding the Nyaya doctrine of inference. However, ancient Greece had its own snakes, ropes, fires, and smoke, and Stoic logic appears to have been a native growth. (See Sextus Empiricus, *Outlines of Pyrrhonism* 1.227–28 [the rope-snake example], 2.48 [sense and intellect as instrument of judgment], 2.100 [the fire-smoke example].)

When the Platonic school took its skeptical turn, in the fourth and third centuries B.C.E., Socrates became its exemplary skeptic. The members of the Academy then looked up to him as the philosopher who, lacking any doctrine or knowledge of his own, confines himself to questioning those who believe they do know something. The leader of the skeptical "New Academy," the famously persuasive Arcesilaus (315 or 316–254 B.C.E.), was a convinced Platonist and (says Cicero) someone who really wished to discover the truth.[10] Apart from the inconclusiveness of the early Platonic dialogues and Socrates' admissions of ignorance, Arcesilaus' justification of his skeptical attitude may well have been that Plato's dialogues contain only hypotheses. This justification is not unreasonable. Sometimes Plato says that he is only telling likely tales, sometimes he ends a dialogue—the *Theatetus*—in bafflement, sometimes—in the *Parmenides*—he raises harsh criticisms of Ideas and elaborates antinomies, and often enough, when he proposes a positive notion in one dialogue, he criticizes it in another.[11]

The skeptics of the New Academy live in a philosophical symbiosis with the Stoics, their chosen dogmatic opponents. The Stoics argue that it is possible to reach certainty by means of what they call *the criterion, the standard*, by which the truth of things is tested. To most of the Stoics, the criterion is the sensory impression (*phantasia*) that carries conviction because it "grasps" its object. A sensory impression of this kind occurs when a real external object—an "impressor"—gives a blow and imprints itself (so to speak) on the mind. Like light, the convincing impression reveals itself at the same time as it reveals its object. And like something the hand grasps, the convincing impression is a "grasping," a cognition (*katalepsis*), a sense perception in which, as the mind knows and assents, the object has been accurately, even if incompletely, grasped.[12]

The arguments marshalled by Arcesilaus and his successor Carneades (214?–129? B.C.) are directed in particular against the Stoic criterion. No cognition (no "grasping" impression) can exist, the two philosophers argue. This is because an impression "often deceives us and is at variance with the things which transmitted it, like incompetent messengers."[13] The Stoics, say the skeptics, contrast a true impression with a false, noncognitive one. But

> every true impression is such that a false one just like it can also occur. And where impressions are such that there is no difference between them, it cannot turn out that some are cognitive but others not. Therefore no impression is cognitive. (Cicero, *Academica* 2.41)[14]

Arcesilaus denies all proposed truths. He denies even the one truth that Socrates, as he interprets him, is sure of, that he knows that he knows nothing. Arcesilaus thinks nothing at all can be grasped with certainty by either the senses or the mind, so that anyone who makes any positive statement incurs the disgrace of agreeing to what goes beyond knowledge and perception. Refusing like Socrates to answer questions, he asks others what they think and then argues that they are wrong.[15] Without favoritism, he argues against all opinions and balances them against one another because, as he says, there are always reasons as strong against as for any view. To the charge, levelled by both Stoics and Epicureans, that his unrelenting doubt of the truth of sense perception is incompatible with staying alive, Arcesilaus answers that human action, like that of animals, is nonrational. His argument is that an impression or perception reveals its object along with itself and orients action, so that humans, too, can live by their natural impulses. To him, there is no difficulty in living while remaining aware that impressions are apt to be deceptive and that no criterion for them exists.[16]

Carneades, who was as remarkably industrious in study as he was powerful in argument, eloquence, and voice, also wrote nothing.[17] He practiced arguing both sides of a question with equal vigor and upsetting everyone else's arguments. Yet he appears to have relaxed the rigors of skepticism because, as he says, it is not possible to suspend judgment on everything.[18] That is, the skeptic answers questions *yes* or *no* without giving "actual," that is, theoretical or metaphysical, assent.[19] His provisional criterion is what is convincing or plausible (*to pithanon*). To clarify what this means, Carneades grades impressions from the apparently false to the apparently but dimly true, to those the truth of which, although only apparent, is intense. The intense impression, which admits degrees of its own, is taken to be convincing and functions in practice as the criterion of truth.

> But since an impression never stands in isolation but one depends on another like links in a chain, a second criterion will be added which is simultaneously convincing and undiverted [by an opposing impression] . . . Still more credible than the undiverted impression, and the one which makes judgment most perfect, is the impression which combines being undiverted with also being thoroughly explored.[20]

In everyday life, Carneades adds (as Sextus reports) that in small matters we question one witness, in more important matters we question several, and in crucial ones, we cross question each witness by means of the mutually corroborating evidence of the others. In the same way, "in matters of no importance we make use of the merely convincing impression as a criterion, but in weightier matters the unreversed impression, and in matters which contribute to happiness the thoroughly tested impression."[21]

In *Outlines (Hypostases)*, which summarizes skeptical doctrines, Sextus Empiricus claims that the skepticism of the Academic school is more dogmatic than that of Pyrrhonism, which he himself professes. This is because the Academy (under Carneades) accepts belief accompanied by a strong inclination and uses probability as a guide to life, while the Pyrrhonists, says Sextus, simply yield without intellectual consent to anything and live undogmatically by following their natural impulses and the local laws and customs.[22]

To Sextus, skepticism is the ability or mental attitude that opposes appearances to judgments until the equality of the propositions becomes so evident that it leads to the suspense of judgment, which leads to composure (*ataraxia*).[23] Sextus's kind of skeptic agrees neither to the formula that "all things are false" nor to the companion formula that "nothing is true"—each of these simply cancels itself out.[24] He accepts an appearance (*phainomenon*) without doubt but does not agree to what purports to be either "deep," or defining, or intrinsic concerning the appearance. Honey appears to be sweet, and this the skeptic senses and grants, but whether it is sweet by definition (as *logos* may be cautiously translated here) is doubtful because the definition is not the appearance itself but something said about it.[25] This suspension of judgment does not inhibit the skeptic from thinking the thoughts that clear appearances stimulate in reason—ideas can be grasped and inquired into without asking what underlies them.[26]

By adhering to appearances as appearances, says Sextus, the skeptic can live in undogmatic accord with the usual rules of life, without dogma, and accept the guidance of nature—of emotions, hunger, and thirst—as well as the guidance of customs, laws, the arts, and ordinary morality.[27] To believe that something is by nature bad is to be tormented by the desire to escape it. To believe that something is by nature good is to be unreasonably and immoderately elated by having it and disturbed by the thought of losing it. But to abstain from thinking that things are naturally good or bad or abstain from pursuing or avoiding anything eagerly is to remain untroubled.[28]

Humorously, Sextus explains that the skeptics managed to learn composure in the same way as Apelles, the famous painter, managed to learn how to make foam on his painting of a horse. It was when Apelles, angry at his failure, threw his sponge at the painting that the foam finally looked right. Likewise, the Skeptics, who tried and failed to attain composure by solving philosophical problems, suspended their judgment and, as if by accident, found the composure they had been searching for.[29]

The preliminaries to his *Outlines* finished, Sextus goes on to present the ten basic modes of argument of "the older skeptics" for the suspension of judgment (elsewhere he ascribes the modes to the shadowy Aenesidemus [first century B.C.]).[30] The modes begin with the those that depend, respectively, on the variety of animal species, on the differences among humans, and on the different structures of sense organs. In Sextus's exposition, one moves in a rather disorderly way (which I order somewhat) from comparative zoology (different forms of reproduction, perception, and appetite) to different human perceptual reactions and preferences: concave and convex mirrors make reflected things differ in appearance and position, and people vary in their reactions to food. From these, one moves to the differing testimony of the different senses: objects in paintings appear three dimensional to the eye but not to touch; and honey tastes pleasant but looks unpleasant. And from these one moves to the different physiological conditions, normal and abnormal, that make people perceive differently: people with jaundice see yellow rather than white and taste honey as bitter rather than sweet. And then one moves to the different testimony that results from different lighting and different optical perspectives: lamplight is dim in sunlight but bright in the dark; and the oar appears bent in the water but straight out of it. Finally—I skip some modes—one moves to the different and opposed ways of life, customs, myths, and dogmas. "For example," Sextus says,

> we oppose custom to custom like this: some of the Ethiopians tattoo their babies, while we do not. The Persians consider it becoming to wear brightly colored full-length garments, while we consider it unbecoming. Indians have sex with women in public, while most other people think this shameful . . . Custom is opposed to dogmatic supposition: with us it is the custom to ask for good things from the gods, while Epicurus says that the divinity pay no attention to us . . . We oppose lifestyle to dogmatic supposition: athletes pursue glory as a good and take on for its sake a style of life full of exertion, while many philosophers hold the dogma that glory is a bad thing.[31]

Since the general burden of this relativity is plain enough, I forbear detail or comment. Besides such modes—there are other series as well—Sextus has a rich, indiscriminate armory of skeptical arguments. Among the most interesting of them are his (or Aenesidemus') doubts concerning causality, which include comments on overconfidence, careless analogies, and arbitrary use of data. I will give an example of his attack on causality in the discussion at the end of the chapter.

Sextus ends his *Outlines* with a passage in which he answers the question of why the skeptic sometimes purposely uses arguments that he knows have little power of persuasion. The answer seems to compound his habits of medical dosage with his dry sense of humor: Because the skeptic loves humankind, he wants to use his verbal cures for dogmatism with a considerate selectivity. So, like a doctor who uses remedies to fit the severity of the disease he treats, the skeptic uses strong, stringent arguments for severe attacks of dogmatic conceit, but only mild arguments for those whose conceit is superficial and easily cured.[32]*

Nagarjuna (fl. c. 200 C.E.)

No coming, no going,
No difference, no sameness,
Pacified of elaborations, at peace.

Nagarjuna has been provided with a deeply mythical life.[33] The first part of his name, *naga*, is explained to mean *born from the ocean*. This is in turn explained to have the more profound meaning, *born from the plane of the absolute*, as well as the more picturesque meaning, *able to secure immense treasures of wisdom and achieve fiery-eyed insight*—the treasures and insight are both the properties of the serpentlike Nagas whose domain is the ocean. The *arjuna* part of Nagarjuna's name is understood to mean *he who has secured the power of the true doctrine*—the means to subdue the power of worldly sin.

In his mythical life, Nagarjuna visits the Nagas in their undersea kingdom, teaches them the Doctrine, and takes back with him the particular scriptures, the Mahayanist Perfection of Wisdom Sutras, that they have guarded for a time when humanity is ready for them. Tibetan tradition tells us that Nagarjuna performed many benevolent miracles, built many temples, and wrote books on philosophy, Buddhist practice, Tantrism, medicine, political advice for kings, and alchemy. Tradition also grants Nagarjuna a life of six hundred years, enough to accomplish all that is attributed to him. Modern scholars, less inclined to believe in such chronological miracles, would like to sort out the various possible authors that go under his name.[34]**

---

*A recent commentator finds this closing argument so "odd and silly" that he concludes, in defense of Sextus, that it is obviously "not genuine but has been tacked on by someone during the twelve long centuries between Sextus and our earliest MSS" (Mates, *The Skeptic Way*, p. 314). I prefer the explanation that it expresses a dry, patronizing humor that acts as an excuse for the zeal with which all skeptical arguments, weak or strong, are accumulated.

**"Of primary importance is the still embroiled question of the figure of Nagarjuna as a person and the author of certain works, and of the relationship between the various compositions ascribed to the masters who have borne this great name; for it is hardly to be doubted that there lived in India more than one person having this name and belonging to different periods in the history of Madhyamaka" (Ruegg, *The Literature of the Madhyamaka School of Philosophy in India*, p. 8).

Nagarjuna's aim is to strengthen the Doctrine of the Middle Way (*Madhaymaka*) within Buddhism itself. As has been described, earlier Buddhists dissolved the psychophysical human being into various "heaps" of constituents, transitory factors of existence or *dharmas*. And as described earlier, the Sarvastivadins considered the *dharmas* to be somehow existent in all three times, past, present, and future. For Nagarjuna, minimal though these constituents may be, it is a fundamental error to consider them to be real, which is to say, autonomous, with self-existence or "own-being" (*sva–bhava*). He points out that if there are things (*bhava*) that are truly autonomous, they cannot fall under the law of dependent origination, which is central to Buddhism. Immune to change, truly autonomous things would be unconditioned.

Nagarjuna's critique is designed to show the absurdity of the idea that any things—any and all *dharmas*—can be independent. They must, on the contrary, be *inter*dependent, relative to their place in the chain of causes and conditions. Their truth is no more than the surface truth of phenomena changing in accord with changing conditions. Not that the things are unreal—the adjective is too categorical. They are only "empty" (*shunya*) of self-existence (*svabhava*). Therefore we should avoid the dichotomy, suggested by our naturally dichotomizing logic, of real against unreal, which sets the surface phenomenon against the deep truth or (in Madhyamaka terms) sets unreal self-existence against real non-self-existence. The truth is only the "emptiness" (*shunyata*) or insubstantiality that expresses the union—the somethingness qualified by the nothingness—of what we, probably unlike Nagarjuna, see as the logically opposed possibilities. It is humanly impossible for the intellect alone to conceive this final truth clearly because it is impossible to separate cause from the effect, the identical from the different, and the objective from the subjective. Considering the dilemma in which reason finds itself, Nagarjuna suggests, its most reasonable employment is to analyze itself as clearly as possible in order to demonstrate its own inadequacy; for without relying on the relative truth, it is impossible to attain the absolute truth, the prerequisite for nirvana.[35]

The demonstration of reason's inadequacy is made in Nagarjuna's major work, *Fundamental Verses on the Middle (Way), Mula-Madhyamaka-karika*, which is known by several variant titles. In this book of 447 verses (excluding the two introductory ones), Nagarjuna goes through a usual Buddhist list of *dharmas*, a systematic enumeration of every kind of thing that is taken to be intrinsically real. With frequent use of the law of excluded middle, he shows that these kinds of things, though undeniable as phenomena, are in logical terms self-contradictory. This is for him the evidence that they have a kind of existence that logic cannot formulate or language put into consistent, meaningful words. To suggest their intermediate, indefinable status he uses the term *empty*, which does not commit him, he claims, to any logically

or ontologically definite description. Ordinarily, that is, if one of two contradictory alternatives is shown to be logically contradictory, the other is
accepted as true. But Nagarjuna does not mean that the opposite of what he
destroys by logic is therefore true. He means only that there is no logically
viable proof for the independent existence of anything—any proof for existence that logic offers, logic destroys.

Let me put what I have just said about Nagarjuna's logic more
slowly and carefully. It should be remembered that at this stage of the
history of Indian philosophy, logic is not yet clearly separated from its
subject matter but is still colored by metaphysics. In other words, it
contains unexpressed factual assumptions, which may or may not be
common to Nagarjuna and the opponent he is in particular addressing.
The result is that the restatement of Nagarjuna's arguments in modern
logical form shows that, if interpreted with some technical adjustments,
he manipulates his logic accurately, but that he reaches conclusions that
logic alone cannot justify. That is, his logical analysis is not enough to
bridge certain logical gaps and explain his conclusions. One critic charges
that Nagarjuna's quite crucial definition, of *own-being (svabhava)*, is either
self-contradictory or else too narrow to be effective against his opponents. Another critic charges that Nagarjuna switches from one sense of
the word translated *causal independence* (or *what is causally independent*)
to another sense, *identifying characteristic or essence* (or *what is identifiable*).
For example, Nagarjuna switches from saying that an independent thing
(svabhava) cannot by definition be born of causes and conditions to
saying—with a verbal, not logical connection—that in the absence of
an identifiable thing *(svabhava)* there can be no difference, because, to be
different, things must have identities.*

However that may be, Nagarjuna makes constant use of logic—the
logic he in principle faults but ascribes to those he opposes—in order to
show his opponents that, judged by their own standards, they always fail.
To defeat them, he uses reasoning that can be translated into syllogisms,
especially hypothetical ones. In addition, he depends very heavily on the

---

*The two critics are Richard Robinson and Richard Hayes. The former writes: "Once the
definitions and the fundamental absurdity of the concept of own-being" are taken into
account . . . "Nagarjuna's seeming paradoxes can be easily resolved" (*Early Madhyamika in
India and China*, pp. 57–58). Like Plato, says Robinson, Nagarjuna had an intuitive understanding of basic logical principles but made use of them in ways later recognized as fallacious ("Some Logical Aspects of Nāgārjuna's System," *Philosophy East and West* 6.4, summarized
in Hayes, "Nāgārjuna's Appeal," pp. 323–24). The example for the charge made by Hayes is
based on the *Fundamental Verses* 15.1–3 (ibid., pp. 317–19; for Hayes' comments on the
difficulties of translating this passage, see pp. 370–72).

In partial contradiction to both critics, it is contended (as I have said above) that Nagarjuna's
way of argument merges logic with factual assumptions, some too obvious to have escaped his

law of contradiction—he resorts to it 140 times in his 447 verses, a scholar has reckoned.[36] He feels perfectly justified in making use of the law of excluded middle against any opponent who accepts it. For example, in attacking the independent reality of motion, he asks, Apart from what goes and what does not go, what third possibility is there?[37] But what Nagarjuna most wants of the law of excluded middle is the choice it gives him. I suppose he would deny that he was really making a choice, but he is always, in effect, opting for the middle—the Buddhist middle, he is convinced—which in this case is the excluded, logically impossible, "empty" or "void" choice. He makes this choice because, to him, voidness—itself not a point of view—"is the liberation from all points of view."[38]*

To put his argument strongly, Nagarjuna also uses the Indian logical (by two-valued logic, illogical) form, the "tetralemma" (*chatushkoti* meaning, *fourfold negation*). For example, speaking of the Buddha, Nagarjuna states that the Buddha's teaching is "emptiness is suchness, not suchness, both suchness and not suchness, and neither suchness nor not suchness."[39] This quadruple proposition (so to speak) can be the following four statements: (1) Everything is suchness; (2) everything is not suchness; (3) everything is both suchness and not suchness; (4) everything is neither suchness nor not suchness. The tetralemma is all contradictions: the second statement contradicts the first; the third, which joins the first and second is self-contradictory; and the fourth contradicts the third. In logical symbols, the third statement is $a \cdot {\sim} a = 0$, a formula for the law of contradiction.

---

attention. Therefore there are gaps in his arguments that can be bridged by assuming that he transforms logical into factual dependency. This implies that attempts "to elicit relevant features of Nagarjuna's thinking by analyzing the argumentations in terms of modern propositional calculus [alone] are mistaken" (Oetke, "On the Non-Formal Aspects of the Proofs of the Madhyamikākarikās," p. 109 [note 13] quoted). In Nagarjuna's defense, it is argued that his language is sometimes only approximate and that "we should not interpret a passage in the work of a major philosopher in such a way that a crude logical error is the result" (Galloway, "Some Logical Issues in Madhyamaka Thought," p. 24).

*Richard Hayes comments: "It is quite legitimate in standard logic to predicate contradictory predicates of a given subject, provided that the subject does not name something that exists. And that, I think, is exactly what Nagarjuna tried over and over again to show in his work, namely, that there are certain subjects to which contradictory predicates can seemingly be applied, and therefore we can only conclude that the subjects themselves do not really exist" ("Nāgārjuna's Appeal," p. 350). However, according to Nagarjuna, contradictory predicates can be applied to *every* nameable subject, so it follows, it can be argued, that logic is useless except to show that it cannot be applied in all seriousness to the reality of even the everyday world. One may therefore feel impelled to believe in simple, instinctive everyday reality rather than in logical proof of any kind. In effect, this is the non-Buddhistic, non-Nagarjunian alternative that Sextus Empiricus chooses—except if one gives Nagarjuna what appears to me a misleadingly mimimalistic interpretation.

Taken intensionally, the third statement is, of course, self-contradictory; taken extensionally, it expresses that the symbolized class is empty, has no member. The fourth, last statement, which negates the previous, self-contradictory statement, is equivalent to the falsification of the law of excluded middle.

Nagarjuna's tetralemma, meant to express the four possible logical positions, is, of course, opposed to ordinary logical rules. But it serves a metaphysical and dialectical aim. That is, for him it represents the way in which the "void" and the "voiding of the void" lead to the transcendent that is beyond words and ordinary, "blind" experience. The fourth member of the tetralemma is, so to speak, the negating or emptying of the possibility of using language or logic to represent anything, including the transcendent, in a truly illuminating way.[40]*

In the *Fundamental Verses on the Middle Way*, Nagarjuna proceeds by such logical techniques to "empty" everything a philosophical Buddhist might consider real. What might be considered real includes the following (I skip many categories): the relational conditions between things (the doctrine of dependent origination); change or movement in space and time; the six internal bases of sensation (five internal bases plus "mind"); the five "heaps" or aggregates, physical and mental, that make up the human being; the fundamental elements (to the Buddhists, earth, water, fire, air, space, and consciousness); the cycle of birth and death (*samsara*); pain or suffering; self-nature or own-being (*svabhava*); the self (*atman*); time past, present, and future; and all combinations of cause and effect. For a Buddhist, the climactic deconstruction comes when Nagarjuna includes the Buddha (Tathagata), the four noble truths, and nirvana.

To show Nagarjuna's method of emptying everything of its independent existence, I now follow him, though far from completely, in a few of his beginning arguments. Because they are too brief to be understood without help, I depend on the best known of his commentators, the seventh-century Chandrakirti, whose commentary alone has preserved

---

*Interpretations of Nagarjuna's tetralemma are problematic. My own, doubtful enough, view is that Indian philosophers learned to apply negation to itself so as to work out a symmetrical scheme of possibilities. Once the scheme was fixed, the meanings given to the "self-contradictory" propositions could vary. It has been observed that Nagarjuna's interpretation of sentences of the form P · ~ P is different in different places; and his *a and non-a* can be interpreted either as contradictories or, by many-valued logic, as contraries (Ghose, "The Modality of Nagarjuna's Dialectics," pp. 296–98). An obvious use of self-contradictory propositions is to give stark expression to the mystic's coincidence of opposites. Used in a cautious, Jain kind of version, each part of a proposition might have "in a certain sense" appended to it. It would be natural for Nagarjuna to make use of contradiction to signify emptiness, and to say that all possible sentences are ill formed.

Nagarjuna's Sanskrit text. Chandrakirti finds in Nagarjuna's laconic stanzas far more than meets the eye.[41]

As I have said, Nagarjuna argues against those Buddhists who believe, some to a greater, some to a lesser degree, in the independent existence of *dharmas*. The Sarvastivadins are the most open offenders, and it is they who, among Buddhists, are Nargarjuna's most natural targets.[42] They believe not only in the reality of *dharmas* throughout all times, but believe in the real though secondary existence of a kind created by the use of words. As they see it, something fully real is unique and so its nature cannot be expressed by a common name or universal. But by referring to various unique particulars by a common name, a universal grants the particulars a common secondary existence. When such words are analyzed, it is discovered that they have no final referent. To give an instance: The word *pot* has no final referent because it consists of the quickly changing reals, *dharmas*, into which analysis decomposes it. Yet the fact that *pot* has no referent that is final does not mean that it does not, finally, have a referent. It exists in its own secondary right because it has the secondary, if artificial, unity given it by a single perception and a single word. Everything has at least a secondary unity because everything can be named—even to call something *ineffable* is to name it. And because all knowledge strengthens the possibility of liberation, everything should, in principle, be named and classified.[43]

To Nagarjuna, all such Sarvastivadin reasoning is incoherent. This is because there is nothing in the everyday world that is real (that exists independently) and, a fortiori, nothing real to serve as the substratum to whatever a word designates. The permanence that language creates is to him always spurious. That message is central to Nagarjuna's *Verses on the Middle Way*. We may choose its first chapter to represent its temper and method. The chapter is on causation or, put more carefully, the theory of how things arise in relation to their causes and conditions.

Nagarjuna begins with an argument similar, though not in contextual details, to one we have heard in Parmenides and the Greek atomists: At nowhere and no time can things ever originate from themselves, whether from other things, from both themselves and other things, or from no cause at all.[44] To Parmenides and the Greek atomists, this implies that everything that *is* always remains what it is, so that nothing new can originate. Up to a point, Nagarjuna agrees—such, to him, are the Buddhist ultimates when he distinguishes them from what is merely relative. But he wants to stress that no particular thing can possibly *be* in and for itself, meaning that nothing exists independently or exerts its own, independent causal force.

To be thorough in his argument against the possibility of independent existence or causation, Nagarjuna goes through each of the (four) conditions by which anything at all arises. The most obvious of the conditions—all of them posited by earlier Buddhist philosophers—is the primary causal condition. This is the relation between a primary cause, a seed, for example, and the plant that is produced from it. Another of the conditions of arising is the immediately preceding condition, the relation, for example, between a seed's destruction and the emergence of a new plant.

The point that Nagarjuna most wants to make is that the conditions or relations under which things appear and then disappear—giving way to their apparent results—do not lend any support to the belief in independently existing things or independent causal forces. Within the world of ordinary experience, Nagarjuna says, there is nothing at all truly independent; and so there is nothing that can act as an independent cause for anything else. The very independence of a cause would detach it from the all-encompassing chain of causes and effects. If there could be such detachment from the chain, fire might cause not light but a great darkness. Such a chaotic sequence, by which anything could arise from anything, cannot be a cause-effect relation at all. Nor can things be born from themselves, so to speak, that is, from conditions or causes that preexist in them. Nothing can in any way exist before itself. If it did, it would be observed, absurdly, before it existed and would arise to no purpose. And if there is no self-existence, there is no other-existence, that is, no extraneous existence in which a thing might possibly preexist. Briefly, in Nagarjuna's words, "If there are conditions, things are not self-existent; if there is no self-existence there is no other-existence."[45]

An objection arises: Perhaps things can be originated by the generative force (kriya) of certain conditions. An example is that of visual perception or consciousness. This perception is not produced directly by the organ of vision, by color, or by the other relevant conditions, but by the force that is inherent in them.

Nagarjuna answers the objection: "Force is not inherent in conditions; nor is it not inherent in conditions; nor are there conditions without it; conditions have no force."[46]

This answer needs to be explained: We can prove that there is no such force because it cannot be located in either the past, the present, or the future. The idea of a cause by means of a future force can be dismissed immediately. As to the past, if the force evoked by the conditions of vision appeared in the past, before the perception came into (relative) being, the force would be independent of the perception—it would be neither oriented toward nor formed in mutual relation with the result-to-be, the visual perception. And if the force appeared at exactly the same time as the perception, the moment of appearance of the force and of the perception would be identical, so that he force could not be the perception's cause. The conclusion is that since the assumed force and its assumed result cannot be related to one another in any of the three times, causal-appearing conditions cannot have any inherent force. But though generative force does not inhere in relational conditions, it does not exist in them as noninherent, that is, does not exist, absurdly, outside of the conditions. All the same, there are no conditions without the force, in the sense that we perceive that conditions do in fact give rise to new things. But the overall conclusion is that, taken in the sense that the opponent gives the term (generative) force, conditions do not have any force.[47]

An objection arises: But there really *are* conditions for visual perception and for everything else.

Nagarjuna answers: But the supposed conditions become real conditions only when their supposed effect, for example, visual perception, has already arisen. Further, nothing arises from its nonconditions, that is, from conditions not observed to have been correlated with it—there is no sesame oil that comes from grains of sand.[48]

To this it is objected: But there is the commonly observed difference between a cause, defined essentially as what brings forth something else, as compared with something defined as impossible, as without an essence, a standard example of which is the son of a barren woman.

Nagarjuna answers: As you use the words, *to bring forth* means *to produce*. But nothing existent, nonexistent, or both is really brought forth. Something that exists independently, in it own right, is not brought forth because it must already exist. What does not exist is not brought forth simply because it does not in any sense exist. And something that both exists and does not exist is not brought forth because these contradictory attributes cannot occur together in one thing. If it was assumed that they could, the result would be subject to the objections to belief in both an existent and a nonexistent thing.[49]

We are left with the idea of the cause in the sense of the immediately preceding condition, such as the destruction of the seed that precedes the appearance of the sprout. But if causes or conditions cannot arise, they cannot disappear. And there can be no exact moment in which the seed disappears just before the plant arises. And if the seed has already been destroyed, it cannot be a condition of the plant's growth.[50]

After further argument, a new kind of objection is made: Results are not separate from their conditions or causes but incorporate them. For example, a piece of cloth incorporates the threads that are its conditions.

Nagarjuna answers: Cloth and the like are not true, self-existent effects. The cloth does not exist in any one of its conditions—neither in its threads nor in the weaver's brush, loom, shuttle, and so on. We know this because the cloth is not perceived in any of them; and if they were true causes, being many, they would have many effects. Nor is the cloth the effect of all its causes or conditions taken together. We know this because, being absent from any of its individual conditions, it does not exist in all of them together.

Another, last objection is made: Yet, as you admit, there is an inherent regularity in the conditions and nonconditions of the world of ordinary experience. It is therefore right to consider the conditions to be causally effective and right to consider their effects to be real.

Nagarjuna concludes: If conditions and nonconditions existed, so would effects; and if effects existed, so would conditions and nonconditions. But our critical investigation has shown that there is no real effect, so there cannot be either real conditions or nonconditions.[51]

Because he casts doubt on the reality of the everyday world, with its objects, acts, and words, Nagarjuna feels obliged to defend himself against the charge that his attack implies belief in the very reality he doubts. How can one attack something that one claims does not exist? His defense, made in *The Averter of Arguments* or, more simply, *End to Arguments* (*Vigrahavyavartani*), is one of the more sophisticated books of Indian philosophy.* Its difficult main thesis is that Nagarjuna's Madhyamaka view is immune to refutation because it sets all assertions against all others without itself making any real assertions. As Nagarjuna says, "I have not stated any thesis (pratijna)," or, strictly speaking, "I have not *stated* any thesis"— because, though a thesis may lack its own-being or essence, it is impossible to state a thesis without an essence.[52]

Nagarjuna makes this pronouncement in spite of the many syllogism equivalents and theses in the *Verses on the Middle Way*. At its very beginning one finds the compound thesis that "at nowhere and no time can entities ever exist by originating out of themselves, from others, from both (self-other), or from lack of causes."[53] Nagarjuna's commentator, Chandrakirti, does not hesitate to identify this statement as containing four theses. The explanation for Nagarjuna's denial that he has a thesis must be that

---

*My description of Nagarjuna's philosophy is based on the *Verses on the Middle Way* and the *Averter of Arguments*, only two of the many works attributed to him. In *Nagarjuniana*, Lindtner attempts to distinguish all the authentic works, and his resulting synthesis yields a more varied picture than is drawn here. Of interpretations of Nagarjuna, a scholar remarks: "As . . . no agreement has been reached on the main issues, it seems that the textual sources themselves do not clearly attest one particular interpretation. Possibly there would remain room for significantly deviating interpretational alternatives, even if the question of the authenticity of Nagarjuna's works were settled. As interpretations in such cases and on this level might be essentially and unalterably hypothetical, it is imperative that the basis of the hypotheses and the facts they are intended to account for be precisely and explicitly stated" (Oetke, "Remarks on the Interpretation of Nagarjuna's Philosophy," p. 321).

he means, not that he has no philosophical position, including whatever theses the position requires, but that he has no thesis that rests on the assumption that anything—including any argument—has an independent existence.[54]

Nagarjuna's whole attempt to show that his own position, unlike any other, is immune to skepticism rests on the following five main points, made in conversation with an assumed Nyaya opponent. I summarize the points incompletely but in order.[55]

1. What I, Nagarjuna, say depends on much else and is therefore void of an intrinsic nature. But just as a cart has the useful function of carrying things, my statement is not void of usefulness, because it establishes the emptiness of things.

   The objection is raised that if, as Nagarjuna says, all things are empty, his statement too is empty and cannot be effective in negating.

   Nagarjuna answers: My empty statement negates only empty things, like a magic man who magically creates another such man and prevents him from doing something—both are of the same unreal, void kind. However, the transcendent truth (dharma), although itself beyond words, cannot be taught without resort to the conventional truth. My statement, which exists in the superficial, conventional sense, is consistent in its emptiness. I have no thesis. When all things are perfectly appeased and by nature perfectly isolated, their nature is, so to speak, non-nature and there can be no proposition with a nature of its own. So I cannot be charged with the logical defect of which you accuse me.[56]

2. Nagarjuna denies the objective validity of the instruments of knowledge, the *pramanas*. He argues: If I really apprehended something with the help of the instruments of knowledge—perception, inference, comparison, and verbal testimony—then I would really be affirming or denying. But since, as I say, there are no objects to apprehend, I have nothing to affirm or deny. If you believe that the existence of objects is established by the means of knowledge, then what establishes the means? If they themselves are established without the help of means of knowledge, then such means are not needed. But if you think they do have to be established by other such means, then you run into a difficulty: these other means need to be established in the same way, and so one enters into an infinite series of instruments to prove instruments. What is wrong with an infinite series? It is unacceptable because, being infinite, it has no beginning; and if there is no beginning proof, there can be no middle proof— what can it be the middle of?—nor any final proof—how can there be an end of what has no beginning or middle? Hence, there being

no final proof, there is no proof at all. If, knowing this, refuge is taken in the statement that while some objects are established by the instruments of knowledge, others are not, the exception made for these others should be defended by a special argument, but no one has offered such an argument.[57]

A further point: You may argue that the *pramanas* establish both themselves and other things, in the same way as fire illuminates both itself and other things. But the analogy is defective: A pot in darkness is illuminated by fire. The darkness having made it invisible, the light of the fire makes it visible again. But a fire itself is never invisible in darkness and so cannot be said to illuminate itself. And if fire is related to other things as it is related to itself, then fire would burn itself in the same way as it burns other things.[58]

To continue the argument: Although the instruments of knowledge cannot depend on the objects they are supposed to verify, they cannot be independent of them. This is because if they were independent, they would be useless instruments, with no objects to verify. If you admitted that they were verified by their relation to their objects, you would by this admission be verifying them again—a useless repetition of something already done. And if you think that you can use the instruments of knowledge to verify the objects of knowledge and then verify the instruments by means of the objects, you fail, because the objects used for the purpose of verification are themselves not really verified.

Such difficulties arise because an instrument of knowledge and the object it is meant to verify are relative to one another: just as there is no father without a son or son without a father, there is no instrument without an object nor object without an instrument. Each being relative to the other, both are dependent, that is, empty. So the *pramanas* are not established by themselves. Perception is not established by itself, nor is inference. Nor are the *pramanas* established by one another—perception is not verified by inference nor inference by perception. Nor are the *pramanas* established, singly or collectively, by their objects—sight is not established by what is seen.[59]

3. It is objected that if everything is empty, all Buddhist truths and practices are empty, not intrinsically good.

Nagarjuna's answer is: If you think that the good and bad nature of things is intrinsic to them, there is no point in religious practices. The Buddha's message is that the vision of the mutual dependency of things and of the origin of sorrow gives rise to the vision of *dharma* and the end of sorrow. Buddhist truths and practices teach and rest on the emptiness of all phenomena.[60]

4. It is objected that one can negate only what exists, so by negating things to prove that they are empty, Nagarjuna implies that they exist.

Nagarjuna's answer is: In arguing that I can negate only what exists, you make the assumption that what I negate is the emptiness by whose negation I prove the reality of emptiness. You assume that, by analogy with other negations, the negation of the empty or unreal establishes that the unreal is, that emptiness exists. From your standpoint, you prove that I am right in believing that things are empty. But because I do not believe that there is any negation nor anything to negate, from my standpoint, I negate nothing. You calumniate me absurdly when you say I negate. I use speech, but only to make known, to suggest. By saying that Devadatta is not at home you do not create his nonexistence but only make known that he does not exist there at the time. It is not the *saying* that things are empty that makes them so.[61]

Nagarjuna is contending that the explanatory use of words is confined to the objects of ordinary experience because both the objects and the words are unreal. Unreal as they are, words cannot describe the Buddha or emptiness but only designate and slowly lead toward them. Words can only make it known that something is nonexistent but not really negate that something—the real negation of a nonexistent thing, he agrees with his opponent, would have a real meaning.

There is a strong tinge of paradox to all these answers, because Nagarjuna is attempting to keep one foot on each of two levels of reality that are, he declares, two, but are not, he declares, two.*

---

*Among the at least apparent tensions and inconsistencies in Nagarjuna's thought, there are the following: a categorical denial of cause-effect relationships (MMK 1) as against the declaration that these relationships are empty (MMK 24.18); Nagarjuna's ostensibly rational argument as against his declaration that he himself has no propositions (VV 29); statements that certain kinds of entities and all *dharmas* do not exist—a categorical denial—as against the declaration that all *dharmas* are void (MMK 24); apparent violations of common sense as against the declaration that emptiness is compatible with the commonsense world and is even the condition for all that happens in it (MMK 24.14); nirvana described as a great ideal as against the declaration that it is identical with the everyday world (MMK 25.19,10); and, most generally, the apparent extremism of Nagarjuna's views as against his declaration that he is teaching a middle way between extremes (Oetke, "Remarks on the Interpretation of Nagarjuna's Philosophy," p. 315).

See I. Mabbett, "Is there a Devadatta in the House," an attempt to interpret Nagarjuna so as to save him from self-contradiction, in particular, the liar paradox. The opponent's charge of self-contradiction "fails because his, Nagarjuna's denial of intrinsic reality to all things does not imply an assertion of the positive existence of any intrinsic reality anywhere" (p. 316).

Toward the end of the *Verses on the Middle Way* he says, just as incomprehensibly in logical terms, that ordinary, relative existence (*samsara*) and nirvana are not at all different. Do the words "The limit of nirvana is the limit of samsara also" imply that the limit of the one state, nirvana, extends as far as the limit of the other state, of relative existence? But then why are these words on limits followed by the words, "Between them there is no difference whatever"?[62] I am not sure the question is a good one, because Nagarjuna cannot be clear, by his own standards, on the coincidence between relative and nirvanic. To him as to the Buddha, philosophical speculations about ultimate things are antinomical and not to be pursued. The Buddha taught no *dharma*, no doctrine of the factors of existence, impure or pure, to anyone at any time. Salvation comes when all perceptions, thoughts, and words are quiescent and tranquil. Chandrakirti—who may be wrong in interpreting Nagarjuna, but who probably had a better idea of him than we do—goes on to explain:

> The very coming to rest, the non-functioning, of perceptions as signs of all named things, is itself *nirvana* . . . When verbal assertions cease, named things are in repose; and the ceasing to function of discursive thought is ultimate beatitude.[63]

Jayarashi (fl. 800 C.E.)

This terrifying book, the lion of annihilation of all principles.

The *terrifying* of this quotation is probably a pun referring to the difficulty of the book it introduces and to the fear the author believes it will arouse.[64] The author, Jayarashi, is known only from his *Lion of Annihilation of Principles (Tattvopaplavasimha)*, discovered in 1926.[65] The unique manuscript, made of 176 palm leaves with sometimes blurred writing, was copied, the colophon says, on a date corresponding to C.E. 1292. The only known Indian philosophical text that is merely and unqualifiedly skeptical, it is difficult to understand because, by Indian philosophical convention, it is so laconic and is directed against various unidentified opponents.

In the context of Indian philosophy, skepticism is the rejection of all the accepted means of knowledge. Jarayashi naturally pays attention to the two most important of the means, perception and inference, and to their most sophisticated exponents, the Naiyayikas and Buddhists. Along with the surest means, he annihilates, he boasts, the other, dependent ones, which include circumstantial evidence, comparison or analogy, tradition, and verbal testimony. All the means, he says, are useless to establish the truth.

To show something of the substance of Jayarashi's argument in his own style, I follow the book for a time (simplifying and omitting on the way). Jayarashi begins with a generalization: For the means of knowledge to be established, they must be given a true (valid) definition—a point generally accepted by the Indian schools of philosophy. Only after the means are established can the objects of knowledge be established. Granted that the possibility of the means of knowledge depends on the possibility of defining them truly, if no such definition can be found, it follows that there is no way of identifying such means nor, therefore, of identifying any objects of knowledge. Lacking the definition, Jayarashi says sarcastically, "one might as well start talking about the existence of color in the soul and pleasure in a pot."[66]

To see what Jayarashi opposes, it is helpful to recall that the word *pramana* is one of a group of philosophical terms whose root has the approximate meaning of *to measure out*. *Prama* is *knowledge* or, rather, *true cognition*. As has already been explained, the word *pramana*, which applies to the means that lead to instances of *prama*, is therefore equivalent to *a means of knowledge*, that is, a means of the kind that leads to a true, valid cognition or, to put it more elaborately, to *a true knowledge-bearing awareness*.

Because perception is acknowledged to be the basic instrument of knowledge, Jayarashi begins with it. To be exact, he begins with the Nyaya definition of true perception: True perception is the nonverbal, nonerroneous cognition that arises from contact between sense and object, the determinate nature (which some affirm and others deny is invariable).[67] To make the details of Jayarashi's response clear, I summarize its general nature first: The opponent, for whom, as I have said, Jayarashi himself speaks, recognizes only two possibilities. The first is a true perception, which gives the perceiver (the cognizer) the ability to attain the object. The second possibility is a false perception, which does not give him this ability. Jayarashi adds two further possibilities, which he needs to make his case: the true perception that *fails* to let the perceiver attain the object, and the false perception that *does* let the perceiver attain it.[68]

Jayarashi may see perception and the judgment that we reach by its means as so beset by possibilities of error or misconception that there is no one who has succeeded in giving true perception a philosophical definition. It is likely that he defined his own concept of definition in an earlier work, *The Essence of Definition*, but we do not know how he did so. If we try to get closer to his way of seeing things, we see that to define something is to find or use a criterion, a characteristic sign, by which to identify it. But if a certain identifying characteristic is not confined to the things it is supposed to identify, then it is too undiscriminating and becomes useless.

Jayarashi, who intends to test all the important words in the Nyaya definition of true perception, fastens first on the most vulnerable of them, *nonerroneous*. Counting on the agreement of the opponent, Jayarashi says that nonerroneous perception depends on faultless, that is, ideal causal factors, such as perfect conditions for vision and healthy eyes. The accuracy of the perception is proved in three ways: by the absence of any contradictory perception, by the universal agreement of other persons, and by the practical success of the activity based on the perception. It is by showing that such criteria are useless in proving a perception true that Jayarashi hopes to convince his reader that it has not been possible to define valid knowledge as nonerroneous knowledge.

Consider what is implied when we require that there be no contradictory perception. It may happen, says Jayarashi, that there is no such perception because there is no cause for it to arise. For example, a faraway concentration of the sun's rays may cause a mirage of water that is not contradicted by any other perception. The truth may (or may not) become evident to someone who is close to the apparent place of the mirage, or who comes on the scene at a later time. How is it possible to specify that there should be no contradictory perception if the perceiver who sees something, say, a mirage of water, leaves the locality or dies before he has been able to have the contradictory perception, the perception that would arise if he actually visited the place where the water appeared to be? Surely, the absence of a contradictory perception is not enough to establish a perception's truth.

The opponent suggests an omniscient perceiver—many Indian philosophers believe in omniscient sages. Jayarashi's response is: The rules of valid knowledge are not established for omniscient persons only, but for everybody. At this point he recalls that one of the measures of valid knowledge is general agreement. But given all the possibilities, it is clear that illusory perceptions are not necessarily contradicted by nonillusory ones.[69] (Later, when arguing against those who claim that truth is established pragmatically, Jayarashi objects that something cannot be thought nonexistent just because it does not produce an efficient action for *all* perceivers—what of those, he asks, who have superior faculties of perception?)

The opponent then asks: What about a second criterion of nonerroneousness, the pragmatic criterion of the perception's use in practice, its fruit, in the Indian term, the success in finding water or in coming into contact with a beloved woman?

But we do not always *know*, Jayarashi answers, we are not always aware of what in us has activated our body to arrive at the pragmatic result. If we are not aware of what has activated it, how can we tell whether or not the perception is erroneous? Even if we are aware of how the perception has led to the pragmatic result, how do we know that this awareness, which is a perception, is itself not mistaken? And if we are aware of the awareness—perceive the perception—how do we know that the awareness of the awareness is not mistaken, and so on, ad infinitum?

But, says the opponent, what if one does in fact get the water one perceives?

No, answers Jayarashi, the perceiver makes repeated perceptions and cannot be sure that the water he gets is the water he saw in any particular act of perception (Heraclitus would make this point more emphatically). The water has perhaps moved about or fish or buffaloes have stirred it. Besides, if we accept the view that all water has the same form—accept that even water that has moved about, changed, and become different has the form of the same universal, *water*—we accept a standard by which we consider a perception to be true because, though false, it leads us to *any* water.

At this, the opponent makes an objection: "A false cognition does not make one obtain water connected with [exactly] that place and time, but a true cognition does; by this [one knows that] it is nonerroneous."[70]

Jayarashi answers: By such a standard of direct and immediate satisfaction, the perception of something about to vanish, or of the sun, moon, planets, constellations, and the like, which are perpetually beyond our reach, would be erroneous. Besides, the place where one perceives water, accurately or not, may be destroyed before one gets to it.

Now suppose that the opponent gives up the idea of proving the truth of a perception by the immediate usefulness of what is perceived— the actual obtaining of the object—as by the drinking of exactly the water that he perceives. Suppose the opponent is satisfied with something of the more general kind, something, for instance, quite *like* the water that had flowed away before he could actually get to it and drink it. If the opponent argues from likeness, the notion of likeness brings with it the idea of a general property or universal such as *water* that resides in all its instances and makes them all alike or essentially the same. But such a general property or universal cannot exist. The opponent asks, "How is that?" and a discussion of the possibility of universals ensues.[71]

Although this new topic is to some extent a digression, it is important enough to justify a partial summary. From Jayarashi's detailed (to me sometimes obscure) criticism I rescue a few more or less familiar ideas that emerge or can be imagined emerging in Plato's dialogues no less than in Indian philosophy. Jayarashi's main example, to which I will not refer afterward, is water. He argues: The universal must be either identical with the individual in which it is found or different from it. If different, that is, if distinct and separate, it is not a universal and is not common to many individuals, but is a distinct, separate individual in its own right. Furthermore: The recurrence of the universal in many different individuals cannot be because of a plurality in its own nature—the universal is by nature just purely itself alone. But if its recurrence in an individual is the result of identity with the nature of the individual, then the universal is not different from the individual.

Furthermore: The difference between one instance and another of the same universal cannot be accounted for by the presence of the form of the universal in one instance alone. This is because another instance would be of a different kind, that is, have the form of a different universal. And if the difference is accounted for by an additional form, a subform, there can be no reasonable end to the multiplication of forms. When a doubt arises whether or not a certain individual belongs to a certain class, if the answer is by means of the multiplication of universals, the result is an infinite regress. The only reasonable solution, says Jayarashi, is to understand that each individual has its own form, meaning that there are only individuals and no universals.[72]

At this point, I stop my account of Jayarashi's argument. His later opponents charge him with refuting himself by implying a criterion by which he decides on the impotence of the other criteria. We have already heard a Nyaya attack on skepticism, and the answer to Jayarashi is the same. In half-paraphrase it is:

> The skeptics want to prove nothing except that the means of proof are useless, and for this they need a proof, which can be nothing but a means of knowledge or an instance of its use. Otherwise the proof that all principles are annihilated would be impossible. If such an annihilation could be established without a means of knowledge, anything anyone wanted could be established in the same proofless way.[73]

A similar Nyaya response is made (in the subcommentary to the Nyaya-sutras) to the problem of the "wrangler," the debater who takes no position of his own and perhaps claims that he has no such position:

> When propounding a criticism, the critic accepts—(1) the presence of the view criticized, (2) the fact that the conception

of the other party represents a wrong idea, (3) the presence of the propounder of that other view, and (4) the presence of himself, as the person to whom the other view is propounded.[74]

Unfortunately, we do not know how Jayarashi would have answered such objections because he does not comment on the philosophical status of the arguments he makes. In the introduction to his book, he does say, with enigmatic brevity, that in attacking all principles he may seem to be contradicting the materialistic principles of Brihaspati, to whom he considers himself allied. But the basic purpose of Brihaspati's *sutra* is not, he says, to establish materialistic principles (on serious examination, they are found not to be established) but to reflect. Jayarashi appears to mean that the purpose of the *sutra* is not to affirm anything positive but to question others' views.[75]

It is noticeable that Jayarashi pays no attention to the contradiction involved when his attack on a philosophical position implies that he accepts its opposite (which he elsewhere also attacks). Together with the Buddhists, he refutes the Nyaya-Vaisheshika doctrine of universals; but he also refutes the Buddhists, by refuting their denial of universals. "Who says," he asks triumphantly, "that the universal is not perceived?"[76]

Jayarashi is just always against. But for all his detailed attacks on different, even opposite positions, in what survives of his thought he fails to show any of Sextus's or Nagarjuna's awareness of how his whole method may be subjected to criticism or of what positive beliefs may implicit in his assumption of the universal critic's role.

Shriharsha (fl. 1150 C.E.)

To that universal soul, which is one, changeless, raised
above all distinctive knowledge.

Shriharsha or Shri Harsha (*Shri* is an honorific title) was a court poet and a skeptical-believing philosopher.[77] Tradition says that his father was humiliated in debate by Udayana and therefore prayed to the goddess Durga to give him a son able to defeat this Nyaya champion. Of Shriharsha's nonphilosophical books there survive two unpublished lexicons and an epic poem—long, ornate, learned, difficult, emotional, and erotic—that retells part of the story of King Nala and his beloved Damayanti. Of his philosophy there survives the enticingly named but austerely philosophical tract, *The Sweets of Refutation* (*Khandana-khanda-khadya*), which I will call, for short, the *Refutation* (*Khandana*).[78]

Like Nagarjuna and Jayarashi, Shriharsha attacks philosophical systems from within, on their own terms. As is natural, his attack is aimed mostly at Nyaya, in particular at Udayana's version of it, with its world of real, independent beings known by reliable perception and tested inference. No less than Nagarjuna, he finds it necessary to justify taking part in debates even though he refuses to accept the means of valid knowledge. This refusal may seem to put him in a difficult, paradoxical position, but his justification is detailed and aggressive.

Shriharsha begins his argument by saying: You, our opponents, claim that there is an invariable relation between acceptance of the means of knowledge, the *pramanas*, and the holding of a formal discussion. You also claim that the means are necessary for a proper choice of the winner. But we hold, on the contrary, that there is no reason why the act of debating requires us to accept the factual existence of the means of knowledge. You are only using a formula to silence us—you argue as if the Materialists (*Charvaka*), the Madhyamikas, and Shankara, who deny means of knowledge that their opponents accept, never engaged in debate and never taught their doctrines.

But if debaters debate without referring to the means of knowledge, the opponent asks, how can they hope to prove or refute anything?

Shriharsha answers: What makes it possible to refute or prove anything is not the acceptance of the means of knowledge but of the rules of argument. The acceptance of the means of knowledge in no way guarantees the ability to prove or refute properly. Even when both sides accept the means of knowledge, they sometimes argue speciously, as is revealed in the course of the debate, and yet the debate goes on. What counts is not any prior admission made by a disputing side, but the quality of the arguments as judged by the rules. If you find no flaws in our arguments, the arguments must be granted to hold.[79]

But then how can the arguments in a debate be faulted? the opponent asks. In a debate, arguments are faulted if the speaker's intention cannot be understood. This implies the acceptance of verbal communication, which is one of the means of valid knowledge—all assertion and negation depend on the *pramanas*.[80]

Not at all! Shriharsha answers. We say that the debate can be carried on just as well by persons who, like ourselves, are indifferent to the existence of the means of knowledge. How, otherwise, would we be able to point out the mistake you have just made in construing our position to be a denial of the means' existence—we neither deny nor affirm but are indifferent to their existence. After all, you began by agreeing to debate against an opponent who, as you knew in advance, is indifferent to the means' existence or nonexistence, and their existence or nonexistence is irrelevant to the rules by which we both undertook to debate. The rules have therefore been construed broadly enough to allow for our position. If each side was to introduce restrictions, it is your side that would feel them more. Besides, you raise your present objection when the debate is already in progress. The objection is self-defeating, because you make the acceptance of the validity of the means the condition for the debate on whether or not these means are valid. Someone such as you, who does not understand even his own intentions, can hardly hope to understand what someone else means.[81]

But, the opponent answers, when you fix the conditions for carrying on a debate, you at least admit the existence of the debate. Without this admission, you would not be able to initiate the debate. And to initiate it is to give existence to something new; and to agree, as you do, that the rules oblige you to debate in conformity with the means of knowledge implies that the means have a real effect, real causal force. So the acceptance of these rules is an admission of the real existence of the various principles of reasoning and, more generally, of the means of knowledge.[82]

Not at all! Shriharsha answers again. When I agree on the rules of debate I imply no more than that I know about them. This is like knowing about the water that appears in a mirage. Two or three people can agree on something that they or others will later contradict. It is enough that the two debaters and their judge agree that they assume the existence of whatever is needed for the debate. In this limited sense, confined to a certain place and time and the few people who do not at the moment contradict one another, the essentials for debate are agreed to exist. But by agreeing to such prerequisites, we do not agree that they exist at all times and places and for all people. Debates are begun on the local and temporary assumption by a few people that the *pramanas* exist.[83]

At this point, Shriharsha feels it necessary to make a concession and says: We admit the existence of the pramanas, though only in the sense that we have knowledge of them. You may prefer to say that we agree that the knowledge itself is real and, like everything one contends is real, depends on the evidence that proves its reality. But to accept that there is such evidence does not require us to give additional evidence, and then additional evidence for the evidence already given, and so on, endlessly. A cognition may need to be verified by another—what is seen dimly at a distance is verified by approaching it. In practice, however, verification does not need to go on for more than three or four steps—there is no *final* verification. Unless the search for knowledge to verify knowledge is limited to a few steps, there is danger of falling into an infinite regress, even for those who believe in the means of knowledge.[84]

This argument on debating, the technical side of which I have minimized, goes on stubbornly, but enough of it has been recalled to show the temper of Shriharsha's skeptical defense. After this defense of his right to debate without really admitting that anything exists, he turns to the proofs that there are no acceptable definitions of the means of valid knowledge or, for that matter, of any philosophical concepts at all. Comparing his own stand with that of the Madhyamika Buddhists, he says that there is only one difference: The Buddhists hold that absolutely everything is indefinable, indescribable, and without any essential reality. He, Shriharsha, and his fellow philosophers of Brahman use different arguments to reach the analogous conclusion that nothing is either existent or nonexistent— with the one great exception that the philosophers of Brahman contend that knowledge exists, as pure, self-revealing consciousness.[85]

The Nyaya opponent now goes on the attack: You claim that the universe is indefinable, because there are difficulties in conceiving it as either real or unreal. But you have to resolve the difficulties one way or the other. If you don't, you adopt the position that things are excluded from the categories of both existence and nonexistence. This contradicts the law of logic that says that when two things are mutually opposed, there is no possibility of a third.[86]

Your argument shows, Shriharsha answers, that you don't understand your adversary's intention. How can you criticize us for not proving or defining *indefinability* when we contend that everything in the phenomenal world, including indefinability, is indefinable? After all, we who put our faith in self-established consciousness, Brahman, have gained peace of mind and have no need to think of the phenomenal universe as either existent or not; and if you reject our objections, which are made in accord with your own rules, you are in effect rejecting what you yourself have agreed to. As things are, we naturally engage in refutation, while you, to win, have to prove your point against us.[87]

Shriharsha now makes the far-reaching claim that "it is established that the phenomenal world of difference is indefinable and that Brahman alone, without a second, is absolutely real." "But what is the proof that it is without a second?" Shriharsha's imagined opponent asks. Shriharsha replies unhesitatingly with what verges, from a European standpoint, on an ontological argument: To ask for something is to have an idea of what you are asking for. How can you ask for a proof of nonduality if you have no prior idea of it? All activity is directed by knowledge and a question is an activity directed by knowledge of its aim. Otherwise actions would be undirected and chaotic.[88] So you already know the basic proof you are asking for and, by the rules of logic, your knowledge of the proof must be either valid or invalid. If it is valid, then the cause of your knowledge, your true cognition, must itself be a proof for nonduality, and you already have the proof you want. You may answer that you know the proof only generally and are unaware of the means of knowledge that establishes it. But as long as you admit that there is a proof, your request to find a particular type is as useless as the search for a crow's teeth. Anyway, the fact that you have a general knowledge of the proof implies and, with effort, eventually brings to light just the kind of proof you want. As to the exact form of the proof, we must remind you that not every individual proof can be identified. Our position is none the worse for its absence.[89]

Now consider the other possibility, Shriharsha goes on, that your knowledge of nonduality is invalid. In that case, your question about the proof contradicts itself, because an invalid means of knowledge cannot be considered a (valid) means (*pramana*) of knowing anything. If the knowledge is invalid, how can you ask by what valid means of knowledge it is known?

Perhaps, Shriharsha goes on, you will say: In *my* philosophy, the knowledge of Brahman is invalid. It is only in *your* Brahman philosophy that it is valid. I answer that since it is *you*, our opponent, who believes in the possibility of a valid proof, the proof is *your* responsibility and the self-contradiction you allege in our use of the term *pramana* does not arise.[90] To us, nonduality always holds true, but this this does not imply that our knowledge of nonduality rests on a valid means of proof. Correct knowledge can be reached by invalid means. For example, if you see fog on a mountain and think it is the smoke of a fire, even though your inference is mistaken, your conclusion that there is a fire there can be correct.[91]

To further convince his opponent, Shriharsha now takes the scriptural route to prove nonduality. In evidence, he cites the statement from the *Brihadaranyaka Upanishad*, "There is only the one, without a second, there is no multiplicity here whatsoever."[92] Shriharsha's opponent objects that the words of the Upanishad cannot be taken literally because perception shows diversity and contradicts their literal meaning.

You are wrong, Shriharsha says. The perception you consider to be contradictory is always limited to differences between a few individual objects, for example, a pot and a cloth. There is no sensory perception or inference accepted by both of us that grasps *all* the different individual things, past, present, and future. Such perception would require omniscience, something I would believe you enjoyed if you could read my mind exactly. The perception of a limited number of different objects, such as pots and cloths, does not refute the general Upanishadic statement "*all* is nondifferent." The truth is that a cognition is one with its object. That is, the awareness of the difference between pot and cloth is not distinguished from the awareness that witnesses to their difference. The unity is that of all things and their essence, consciousness.[93]

For Shriharsha, this is the great, critical point. He knows that he cannot give a direct proof for the existence of Brahman as nonduality. He can only break down his opponent's arguments and show that his own position is immune to attack. His opponent, he says, depends on perception and inference to prove the existence of a world of varied, independent objects, which are different from the consciousness that observes them. But although objects appear to be different from one another, cognition—perceptual awareness or knowledge—cannot be separated from its apparently different objects and therefore cannot be used as evidence that they are different. So there is no valid proof that things are basically different from one another. And so, to be at all effective, the series of cognitions must at some point be broken and give way to revelation.

Shriharsha now gives his argument a triumphant conclusion: It is accepted that when cognitions contradict one another, they must be supplemented by the evidence of other cognitions. This process of searching for more and more evidence is stopped by the fear of infinite regress. It is when the column of mutually negating cognitions is worn out by its march and comes to a stop that the scriptures of nonduality overtake and conquer it.[94]

In answer, the opponent, like the European devil, quotes scripture, in the form of a passage (of unknown origin) that says "all is different."[95]

Shriharsha, of course, objects. He says: "If this passage proves the difference of anything from anything else, it only proves what we already admit, which is the difference between the true and the false."* The interpretation that Shriharsha himself gives the scriptural passage is that all illusory things are different from Brahman. However, he says, if the passage is interpreted to state that all things are different from all things, the result is an absurdity, which is that all things are also different from themselves (an idea with which Plato once amused himself). To put this more technically: One cognition can be the object of another cognition, and so,

---

*This passage sounds as if Shriharsha accepts the true-false dichotomy for himself, not merely for the sake of the debate. The interpretation I have adopted—illusion, which is false, is different from Brahman, which is true—seems to contradict Shriharsha's repeated assertion that everything is the same as consciousness. Furthermore, he consistently opposes the idea that even the nonexistence of anything can be proved. The most convenient interpretation of this text is therefore that Shriharsha has agreed to the true-false distinction only temporarily, for the sake of the debate. Even to admit a "nonexistent" difference, as he does, makes enough difficulty for him. Is the statement a slip of the pen or a slip of the mind? Unable to explain how it fits Shriharsha's position, an attentive scholar is ready to suspect that it is a later addition (Granoff, *Philosophy and Argument in Late Vedānta*, pp. 54–55 and note 108, pp. 234–35).

if all cognitions are different from all others, a cognition (as object of a cognition) is different from itself (as a subject with an object of its own).[96]

After further discussion, the Nyaya opponent decides to use the language itself of the Veda as evidence for difference. He asks, no doubt ironically: How it is that the Vedic declarations of nonduality are made in language that requires differences between letters, words, case endings, and word meanings?

Shriharsha answers that difference or diversity does have existence, but only as illusion.[97] You think of ordinary causality as illusory, the opponent says to him, but if knowledge is identical with Brahman and if Brahman is without cause, how can knowledge be caused, as you contend, by Vedic texts? To this, Shriharsha answers categorically if rather mysteriously: The production of knowledge is not truly real but lies within the sphere of knowledge, so it "is in no conflict with what is the absolutely real fact . . . that knowledge is essentially 'non-producible,' i.e., eternal."[98]

Always taking care to use the arguments of his obviously changing opponent of the moment, Shriharsha now proceeds to attack all philosophical definitions. They are too broad or narrow, he finds, or suffer from circularity, infinite regress, or incompatibility with the opponent's other concepts. In other words, definitions always turn out to be useless for their declared purpose. Beginning with the concept of knowledge (prama), meaning, especially here, truly valid knowledge. Shriharsha analyzes seven of its competing definitions. The definitions propose that valid knowledge is either: (1) experience of the thatness of an object; or is (2) experience that corresponds with its object; or is (3) complete experience; or is (4) unfaltering experience; or is (5) undisputed experience; or is (6) uncontradicted experience; or is (7) experience of a particular kind of power.[99]

A simple example of Shriharsha's method is given in his first analysis of the definition of valid experience as the experience of thatness (meaning, roughly, essence). Shriharsha's overall tactic is to make a critical examination of the meanings philosophers propose for the two concepts central to the definition, the concepts of thatness (tattva) and of experience (anubhuti).*

When Shriharsha examines the proposal that valid knowledge is the experience of the thatness of an object, he remarks that the word thatness is derived from the pronoun that (tat).[100] He points out that nothing pre-

---

*Anubhuti, like its alternate, anubhava, is difficult to translate. Often translated direct knowledge, immediate apprehension, or the like, it is taken to include all states of experience in which memory plays no part. One of the objections that Shriharsha raises in his discussion of the concept is that the sharp separation between direct experience and memory is not plausible. This contradicts Nyaya reasoning, by which recollection must also be an immediate experience, and recognition must unite immediacy with memory (Granoff, Philosophy and Argument in Late Vedanta, 9–23).

cedes the definition to suggest to what the *that* refers, and he adds that since the *that* of the definition has no referent, it has no meaning. But maybe, Shriharsha concedes, the reference of *that* is to anything of which the speaker is thinking. In such a case, *thatness* refers to the natural form of a perceived object. Now, according to Nyaya, an instance of knowledge is valid when it reveals what exists in nature, which is to say, the true attribute of a perceived object. But such a definition of *thatness* is impossible to accept, says Shriharsha, because of perceptual illusion: If a shell is mistaken for silver, the object of cognition is the shell, not the natural form of silver. The cognition of silver is then invalid, as Nyaya philosophers agree. Because the proposed definition does not allow the invalid perception to be excluded from it, it is inadequate. Shriharsha asks if the definition can be modified so as to make it viable, but the opponent's efforts, though ingeniously complicated, all fail.[101]

Shriharsha goes on to ask how the opponent defines the term *experience* and faults whatever definition is suggested; and he does the same with the term *inference*. After finishing with the means of knowledge, he makes a calmly ruthless attempt to prove the incoherence of every key term in the accepted lexicon of philosophical definitions. He does so by repeating the questions, How do you define? and What is meant by? and always finding that the term he asks about is unexplained or incoherent. After he has disabled key terms from philosophical use, they disable the other terms in whose definitions they appear. For instance: No satisfactory answer is given to the question of what the opponent means by *cause*, or by the terms *before*, *after*, and *time* that the opponent invokes in trying to explain what *cause* means. To the protest that Shriharsha has shown only that the exact nature of time is doubtful, he answers, "You cannot explain the exact nature of doubt, either." And so on, in technical detail.[102]

Shriharsha destroys so much in order to shield Brahman against destructive criticism. It is to make the shield impenetrable that he leaves the perceived world an unexplained, enigmatic fact.* An admiring West-

---

*His thirteenth-century commentator, Chitsukha, does not leave it so. Although no less radically skeptical about perception and inference, Chitsukha explains the concepts of his Vedantic school, among them the arising of the illusion of independent objects. The illusion is characteristic, he says, of our own, most degenerate stage of the world cycle, a time when objects seem to be external and Brahman seems illusory. Not unlike Leibniz, he explains, for example, that time and space, which are both unreal, depend on the self and its interpretation of nontemporal, nonspatial kinds of order. He holds that temporal notions such as before and after are no more than "impressions produced by a greater or lesser quantity of solar vibrations." Spatial relations and directions, which are also only relative, are formed by the mind in reaction to the experience of bodily movements. (See Dasgupta, *A History of Indian Philosophy*, vol. 2, pp. 147–63 [156–57 quoted]; and Sinha, *A History of Indian Philosophy*, vol. 3, pp. 309–10.)

ern scholar says that Shriharsha is more consistent than Jayarashi and unique in the intensity and elaboration with which he refutes all philosophical definitions. She calls Shriharsha "the most consistent and convincing of all Indian philosophers" and adds in qualification, "if only because his task is so simplified by their inconsistencies."[103] An Indian historian of philosophy who admires Shriharsha less accuses him of sophistry and over-literal interpretation of his opponents' doctrines. By forcing his later Nyaya opponents into painstaking qualifications, he says, Shriharsha keeps them from becoming more philosophically profound and acute.[104] A contemporary Indian-English philosopher of a Nyaya cast of mind praises Shriharsha for giving his school an independent method uniquely suited to "the rational discussion of its monistic doctrine of the ineffable truth." He also counts it to Shriharsha's credit that he forces later exponents of Nyaya to defend themselves with greater philosophical sophistication and introduce "abstruse and mind-boggling technicalities" into their definitions. Considering that the compliment comes from an expert in these technicalities, it is less than enthusiastic.[105]

Shriharsha himself exudes pride. His book ends with the announcement that he has purposely introduced "hard knots" into it "so that the wicked and ignorant, thinking themselves clever, may not, through sheer audacity, read the book and dabble in its reasonings," and so that the devoted reader, whose teacher has helped him to unravel the knots, "may obtain the experience of joy arising from swimming among the waves of the essence of Reasoning and Argumentations."[106]

Discussion

I preface this discussion with a number of texts in exact quotation, translators' warts and all. Of the immediately following texts, the first two contend that if a *criterion* or *pramana* is the means of verification, it needs a like means of verification, and so on, ad infinitum. For good measure, Sextus adds the charge of circularity, which is the point Jayarashi, too, makes in the third quotation:[107]

> We do not allow them to adopt a criterion by assumption, while if they offer to judge the criterion by a criterion, we force them to a regress *ad infinitum*. And furthermore, since demonstration requires a demonstrated criterion, while the criterion requires an approved demonstration, they are forced into circular reasoning. (Sextus Empiricus, *Outlines of Pyrrhonism* 2.20)[108]

> If [you say that] the *pramanas* are established without the help
> of *pramanas*, then [your proposition] that [all] objects are es-
> tablished through *pramanas* is abandoned. If the *pramanas* are
> established through other *pramanas*, then there is an infinite
> series. (Nagarjuna, *Vigrahavyāvartani* 31–32)[109]

> The establishment of means of valid cognition depends on
> [their] true definition. And the establishment of objects of
> valid cognition depends on means of valid cognition. When
> the one (i.e., a true definition) is absent, how could one talk
> about the other two (i.e., means of valid cognition and objects
> of valid cognition) as real? (Jayaraśi, *Tattvopaplavavasimha*,
> Introduction)[110]

The skeptics all make the point that there is no absolute way to
distinguish a true from a false perception:

> Every impression is such that a false one just like it can also
> occur. And where impressions are such that there is no differ-
> ence between them, it cannot turn out that some of them are
> cognitive but others are not. Therefore no impression is cog-
> nitive. (Cicero, *Academica* 2.40–41)[111]

> [Even illusory] water does produce an efficient action charac-
> terized as cognition . . . The word "nonerroneous" is useless
> [in the definition of perception]. (Jayaraśi, *Tattvopaplavasimha*
> 1.142, 1.1baa, 1bab)[112]

> Just because someone seeing fog and thinking it to be smoke
> infers from the fog that there is a fire on a mountain where fire
> does happen to exist, does that mean that the cause of his
> inference, namely a mistaken knowledge of smoke in which
> fog is the real object, must be admitted to be a cause of valid
> knowledge? (Śriharṣa, *Khandanakhandakhādya*)[113]

The following texts claim that the temporal relation between cause
and effect is impossible:

> The cause must either (a) co-subsist with its effect, or
> (b) precede it, or come after it. But to say that a cause comes
> into existence after its own effect is laughable. But neither can
> it precede its effect, since it is said to be conceived along with
> it, and relative things, so they say, in so far as they are relative,
> co-exist and are co-conceived along with one another. Nor can

it co-exist with its effect, since if it is effect of it, and what comes to be must do so as a result of something already existing, the cause must come to be earlier and then as such produce its effect. (Sextus Empiricus, *Outlines of Pyrrhonism*, 3. 26–27)[114]

If the sensation is already produced, the energy [producing sensation] is useless . . . But if it is already produced, what has the energy to do? . . . Neither is (the existence of an energy just at the moment of) production possible, because a thing is either produced or not yet produced, there is no existence between (these two moments) . . . Since this (assumed) energy cannot be located in any of the three times (past, present and future), it does not exist altogether. (Chandrakirti's commentary on Nagarjuna *MKK* 1.4)[115]

Jayarashi, too, argues that the relation of cause and effect cannot be understood because, among other reasons, their temporal sequence makes no sense.[116] In a variant of this argument, he levels his attack on causation as understood in the Buddhist theory of point-instants:

Your established tenet is: Precisely at the time when the cause-cognition perishes the effect-cognition arises . . . And thus, the relation of cause and effect is impossible between these two [cognitions] in as much as they have arisen together. (Jayaraśi, *Tattvopaplavasimha* e.4)[117]

In his extended argument with the Naiyayikas, Shriharsha objects to their definition of *cause* as the invariable antecedent. He points out that if we accept this definition, the ants, which always come out of their nests before it rains, are to be regarded as the cause of rain. He goes on to the subject of cause in relation to time. Here is the simple beginning of what later turns into a fairly detailed discussion of the plausibility of the division of time into past, present, and future:

In the definition of *cause* it has be stated that the invariable presence of the *cause* should be *previous* to the effect; and here the word "previous" is meant to exclude the present and the future times . . . As a matter of fact however, no consideration or examination of this is possible [as there is no proof for the existence of any such divisions of time.] (Śrihaṛṣa, *Khandana-khandakhādya*).[118]

To these likenesses, there should be added the likeness between the Greek and Indian skeptics' attack on inference (and induction) as the attempt to establish the universal from particulars. The attempt must fail, Sextus Empiricus says, because "the particulars are infinite and indefinite."[119] And Sextus, like Indian skeptics, attacks philosophical definitions, the validity of which is less discussed in Greek than Indian philosophy. He says the definitions are unnecessary for apprehension, subject to infinite regress, and faulty for instruction, involving those who take them seriously in "a fog of uncertainty."[120]

All the likenesses between the Greek and Indian skeptics lead to an obvious structural comparison of the relation between Greek types of philosophers with those between Indian types: In the argument of skeptics with the upholders of criteria, the Greek skeptics are to the Stoics as the Indian skeptics are to the Naiyayikas.* What may be missed—what I may not have brought out clearly enough—is that both the Greeks and Indians distinguish the contact of sense organ with sense object from the conscious awareness of this contact. It is the awareness, including the information it contains, that is the Stoic cognition or "grasping" (katalepsis) and the Nyaya cognition or "knowledge episode" (prama). Mere sense contact may be conceded by skeptics. Their chief target is the declaration that cognitive perception—the aware certainty at the end of the process—is beyond question. It is there at the end that the skeptics' questions mostly begin.

With respect to method, Sextus and Nagarjuna test all philosophical positions for logical coherence and find them self-contradictory, circular, or otherwise deficient. For the most part, the two use philosophizing logic in order to destroy the logic's nonskeptical conclusions. Jayarashi pays relatively little attention to the formal criteria of logic—except, by constant implication, the law of (self-)identity. Instead, he tests definitions in the light of their use in the discourse of the particular philosophical systems. That is, he hunts out the misleading implications of the definitions—what goes wrong if one accepts or acts on them. He constantly asks what can be the connection between two philosophically defined and related conceptions such as universal and particular. If related to one another, he asks, are they the same or different, and if either the same or different, in what

---

*But the Academic skeptics can be close to the Naiyayikas. Despite Carneades' skepticism, an expositor says, he accepts that there can be a well-scrutinized presentation, requiring that the investigated object "(a) consistently appears such as the believable presentation p represents it to be; (b) that the conditions of light etc. under which the particular is observed consistently appear reliable; (c) that nothing is observed inconsistent with p; (d) that I, the observer, experienced consistent and consistently believable presentations such as would suggest the health of my faculties of judgment at the time of observation" (Tarrant, Skepticism or Platonism? pp. 14–15; see also Hankinson, The Sceptics, pp. 106–10; and G. Striker, "Sceptical Strategies," in Schofield, Burnyeat, and Barnes, eds., Doubt and Dogmatism).

way? If they are the same, how can they be different at all, and if different, what can the connection between them be? How can they belong to the category to which his opponent consigns them? Does anything the opponent proposes fit the linguistic-logical criteria for such a category? Can things as the philosopher defines them actually influence one another as they are supposed to? Is not the Buddhist point-instant too isolated in itself and too instantaneously, unitarily gone at its very appearance to have a causal-temporal relation with a succeeding "atom" and be part of a coherent chain? Finding the definitions ambiguous or otherwise inadequate (perhaps by assuming the criteria of a rival philosophy), Jayarashi declares them incoherent beyond redemption. To him, just as to Sextus and Nagarjuna, language fails to carry out the positive tasks that philosophers have assigned it. Shriharsha, though he has his own emphases in argument, has a similar position and uses a similar, though more consistent, less repetitive technique. When he attacks a school, he is careful to look for only such inconsistencies as it should acknowledge by its own criteria; and, unlike Jayarashi, he never uses an argument that he has elsewhere attacked against a school that he thinks is vulnerable to it.

With respect to the circularity of skeptical arguments, Sextus and Nagarjuna, who are concerned with the possible application of their doubts to their own positions, both claim that they hold no positive philosophical position at all, none being implied by their attacks on other positions. But Nagarjuna, like Shriharsha, takes care to recognize the traditional Indian levels (or apparent levels) of reality and of the adequacy of logic and language: the lowest level, simple illusion or incoherence; the next level, pragmatic everyday reality; and the next level, of higher reality as contrasted with the two lower ones; and, finally, the superlative level—or, rather, condition—the "emptiness" in which all levels are dissolved and seen to be the same. In using only other philosophers' arguments to confute these philosophers, Nagarjuna attempts a feat comparable to pulling oneself up by someone else's bootstraps and then levitating in the logical vacuum, familiar enough to Indian philosophers, of the denial of all the logical possibilities and—apparently and approximately—the denial of all the impossibilities or combinations of possibilities and impossibilities.

Nagarjuna takes what seems to me the unenviable position of believing in the relative truth of the world of ordinary experience, which he claims is logically incoherent and yet identical with the absolute truth, which is true in the sense of being false because identical with the relative truth. To put it otherwise, he wants to be ordinarily reasonable (to be samsaric) and, simultaneously, to quiet reason completely (to be nirvanic) by going, ordinarily but marvelously, beyond reason, leaving not a shade of difference between ordinary reason or experience and what is ordinarily but marvelously beyond it. The words are plain enough, but not the echo. I think the whole so strains the capacity of reason that it had best be called an immodestly modest mysticism. I doubt that Nagarjuna would mind.

Shriharsha is like Sextus and Nagarjuna in that he accepts everyday reactions for everyday purposes and yet feels justified in attacking the meaningfulness (the logical coherence and sufficiency) of all philosophical positions by their own proclaimed standards. But though Nagarjuna empties even the conceptions of nirvana and the Buddha of their explicit, conceptually grasped meanings, and though Jayarashi attacks all arguments and affirms nothing, Shriharsha is sure that reality, though indescribable in words, affirms itself. Instead of concluding, as does Nagarjuna, that everything is indiscriminately "empty," he concludes that everything is indiscriminately full. Does this difference between emptiness and fullness make more difference than calling a glass of water half empty or half full?

In contrast with Nagarjuna and Shriharsha, Sextus distinguishes only between instinctive or necessary reactions, which he accepts, and intellectually ambitious or adventurous reactions, which he rejects. In contrast with Nagarjuna, Shriharsha, and Sextus, the Academic skeptics, like modern scientists, believe that conclusions are more or less probable and have to be established in every case by a combination of experience, reason, and immediate evidence—there is no enveloping equality of doubts nor any sharp distinction between levels of certainty.

Sextus is different from Nagarjuna, Jayarashi, and Shriharsha—at least two of them limited to philosophical formalism in the service of an emotionally held certainty—by an attitude hovering between that of a comparative physiologist or ethologist and a relativistic anthropologist. With the help of his encyclopedic collection of skeptical arguments, he (or the thinker whose ideas and instances he is repeating) makes use of a wide range of empirical evidence. Satisfied with a minimally modest amplification of common "instinct," he wants to show that ambitious constructive arguments are always paralleled by equal opposite ones. Nagarjuna sets himself the philosophically and religiously more ambitious aim of showing that the contradictions to which rational thought is prone show that conceptual thinking is by nature inadequate to the tasks it sets itself. Shriharsha is as sharp as Nagarjuna (some of whose arguments he controverts) but is often less attentive to the fundamental logic of the positions he attacks than to the precise words in which they are put, words which, lacking any sense of intellectual charity toward his opponents, he always finds defective.

It might further be commented that Jayarashi and Shriharsha are taking their revenge on the Indian philosophers who presume to attempt faultless arguments. The revenge is that they demand of philosophical language the kind of exactness, consistency, and freedom from possible contradiction that we have learned to expect of mathematics alone—and not even then without severe problems.

To end this exposition of skepticism, I allow myself a critical comment on Nagarjuna, and another on skepticism in general. Not surprisingly, Nagarjuna's doctrine of the two truths inspired hostile questions and complicated though not, I think, persuasive answers.[121]* As he might well concede, to be convincing, his reasoning needs to be complemented by unreasoned experience, which is to say, meditation followed by a confirming calm and sense of insight. "*Samsara* and *nirvana* are of the same essence" to him "because they are by nature at peace."[122] It is, of course, open to Nagarjuna to define everything dependent or relative as not real. However, it seems to me more plausible to give *real* an opposite definition: Whatever affects and is affected by other things shows by virtue of this relationship that it is real, not unreal. Relationship is the clearest criterion for reality, and absence of relationship is the clearest criterion for unreality. What is fully unrelated cannot be measured, weighed, calculated, or, for that matter, thought, because measuring, weighing, calculating, and thinking are all ways of putting things into relationship with one another—as Nagarjuna so often says.

My comments on skepticism in general are Nyaya in spirit: In order to confute those who presume to be intellectually sure of something, the extreme (possibly mystical) skeptic—the Sextus, Nagarjuna, Jayarashi, Shriharsha—uses a fundamentally simple tactic of all or nothing: He demands that standards of definition and proof be applied with ideal rigor, that words be perfectly calibrated with abstract logic and with perceptual evidence, and then, having demanded impossible proofs, he concludes that nothing can be proved. But it seems ordinary common sense to hold

---

*For example, a fourteenth-century Tibetan scholastic answers: All that exists exists either as conventional or ultimate. The conventional is established in its own terms by what are valid cognitions. Valid cognitions also show that external objects and even consciousness are not ultimate. But the nonultimacy of objects shows not that they do not exist at all but that they do not exist in an ultimate sense. Their existence cannot be disproved by any cognition on the nominal level and nothing conventionally contradictory is established by "the innate apprehension of true existence," so there is no valid cognition of any kind that is enough to make us reject nominal, external objects. They must therefore be accepted nominally for what they nominally are. But the distinction between nominal and ultimate, unreal and real, is worldly alone. The system that shows this accepts the distinction and expresses and depends on worldly consciousness, something that the system itself must recognize. (See Cabezon, *A Dose of Emptiness*, pp. 357–63, 367–68, and note 1013, p. 506—appended to a different text and with a somewhat different purport. See also Patel, "The Paradox of Negation in Nagarjuna's Philosophy," pp. 22–24.)

that there is a necessary interdependence between doubting and being sure, and that the idea of universal, incorrigible doubt depends on the idea of certainty or of a high degree of probability, the expectation of which is verified by experience.* All the while he argues, the extreme skeptic uses terms and views that can only have been learned from the experience whose evidential value he doubts, and learned in ways the validity of which he refuses to concede. From an intellectual standpoint, he is left with an incorrigibly vague world, about which—in contradiction to common experience—nothing or almost nothing reliable can be learned. He can affirm the world to be inexplicably there and unfathomably effective. He can decide to be silent, mystical, or absurd—self-contradictory, antirational—while most probably living in much the same way as anyone else. We can see that the skeptic's declaration of equanimity (or, for Shriharsha, bliss) is in ironical contrast with the ardor of his contrariness. Surely, it was also ambition that drove Sextus Empiricus to compile his encyclopedia of doubts; surely it was also the un-Buddhistic pleasure of philosophical conquest that drove Nagarjuna to wield his dialectical doubts—in a witty book directed against the "arrogance" of logicians, he proposes to "grind them to dust."[123] And surely it was also small-minded, divisive pride that led Shriharsha to gloat that his detailed rejoinders were infallible in entangling "the opponent" in the labyrinth of refutations.

Whatever the radicalism of skeptics, it is possible to take a usefully skeptical but appreciative view of their doctrines. His Buddhist religion apart, it is possible to say in Nagarjuna's name that the precision of logic limits its sensitivity and scope as compared with nonlogical talk, which uses affirmation and negation with the more than logical sensitivity that experience requires.[124] Or Nagarjuna can be interpreted as teaching the moderate position that reasoning and language are by nature incapable of arriving at the full truth: the philosophical or logico-mathematical structures we create will never be exact traps for the realities they attempt to capture. If so, "to say of a set of beliefs that they correspond to reality is to pay them an empty compliment."[125] Shriharsha can be analogously interpreted as teaching that human reason, like human perception, is too

---

*Wittgenstein may serve as the representative of the many who share this view. He says: "If I make an experiment I do not doubt the existence of the apparatus before my eyes. I have plenty of doubts, but not that. If I do a calculation I believe, without any doubts, that the figures on the paper aren't switching of their own accord, and I also trust my memory the whole time, and trust it without reservation. The certainty here is the same as that of my never having been on the moon" (L. Wittgenstein, On Certainty, Oxford: Blackwell, corrected reprint, 1974, section 337, p. 43e).

restricted to grasp reality whole. Limited to a moderation that such dramatic doubters would hate to acknowledge, all four skeptics argue the conclusion that there is always something more to know about everything. This is an always pertinent lesson against intellectual arrogance of the opposite, dogmatically constructive kind.[126]

Chapter 9

Religio-Philosophical Synthesis

Udayana, Chu Hsi, Avicenna, Maimonides, Aquinas

Theme: How the Traditions Have Gained Stable Philosophical Syntheses

A philosophy is always a synthesis of some kind, but there are philosophies, like those that appear in this chapter, that embody especially notable acts of synthesis. These acts may culminate in the ordered complexity of Thomas Aquinas' *Summa theologiae*, but also in the puzzlingly unsystematic or unsystematic-seeming *Guide to the Perplexed* of Moses Maimonides, in the repetitive, often ambiguous profusion of Avicenna, in the sage informality of Chu Hsi conversing with his disciples, or in its contrary, the abstruse precision of Udayana's refutation of refutations of Nyaya-Vaisheshika doctrine. This variety shows that the force of a synthesis may come less from its visible orderliness than from its union of previously disregarded, alien, even antagonistic principles. The result of the synthesis is usually the appearance of newly refined arguments and newly stressed analogies, and always of an enlarged scope and more careful detail, or, most valuable of all, of a tighter union of reason—as formal argument or empirical or historical evidence—and faith, whether faith in Vedas, scriptures, or an ethical nature or ethical God, in whatever makes the world less alien in the proximity of human beings. Whereas philosophical analysis distinguishes between ideas and doctrines in order to

separate them—and perhaps separate the persons who hold them—philosophical synthesis joins what has been separated, in order to create a
structure varied enough to accommodate potentially contrary ideas and
thinkers. The point of a synthesis is to limit the scope of plausible but
possibly competitive ideas so that the plausibility of any one strengthens
rather than weakens that of any or all of the others.

Udayana (fl. 1050)

*Still, this logical investigation may well be called the
contemplation of God, and this is really worship . . .
Between a thing and its contradictory, there is no third way.**

It seems reasonable to take Udayana to be the author of the first full
syntheses of Nyaya with Vaisheshika, which is to say, of Nyaya's combative logical precision with Vaisheshika's strongly categorized metaphysics.[1] A sharp opponent of the Buddhist "logicians," he was revered by his
school, and he accumulated a long retinue of commentators.[2] The most
widely remembered of his seven extant books are two treatises. The first
of these, the *Discrimination of What the Self (Really) Is (Atma-tattva-viveka)*,
attacks Buddhist arguments that deny the existence of the self and the
reality of the world. The second treatise, *A Handful of Flowers of Logic
(Nyaya-kusumanjali)*, is a reasoned attack on philosophical denials of God's
existence and a both reasoned and emotional affirmation of it. As usual in
Indian philosophy, its succinct verses, arranged in five chapters or books,
are hardly intelligible without Udayana's prose commentary, which is itself
far from easy.[3]

Udayana's purpose, as he says, is to protect those on the long, deso-
late path of liberation who have grown "motionless through fear" in the
darkness of their opponents' desolating doctrines.[4] Such polemical zeal

---

*This is a composite quotation from Udayana, *Kusumāñjali* 1.3ab and 3.8ab (trans. Cowell,
Kusumāñjali, p. 3, and Matilal, *Nyāya-Vaiśeṣika*, p. 97). The first half of this quotation reads
in full: "This logical investigation of God, which may well be called reflection (or contemplation) (on him), is made (by me) as worship (of him), following immediately upon hearing
(about him in the revealed texts [*shruti*])." The word *reflection* (or *contemplation*) refers to the
three steps of understanding that, according to Vedanta, are enjoined in the Upanishads:
first, "hearing" of the truth (in the revealed texts); second, reflection on the heard truth; and
third, meditation on it. By declaring his logical investigation of God to be reflection that
follows immediately upon "hearing," Udayana is placing his (and his tradition's) doctrine
within the framework of Vedic orthodoxy. He is also saying that the Upanishadic injunction
shows that his investigation by means of reason is not superfluous (explanation courtesy of
Karin Preisendanz).

must have given the cue to a number of apocryphal stories, of which the following concerns his pride: Once, when Udayana went to the temple at Puri of his favorite god, Jagganath, he found the doors closed on all four sides. He then exclaimed, "Intoxicated with your god's pride, you disdain me, but when the Buddhists come, it is on me that your existence depends!" However, in a counterstory, he is said to have been honored by Jagganath as his incarnation.[5]

Nyaya has come up before and will come up again, so this chapter can confine itself to the Nyaya-Vaisheshika doctrine of the Supreme Soul—*Ishvara* (the Lord), who is Shiva—as presented in the *Handful of Flowers*. Udayana's sharpness is best displayed in the book's first four, primarily negative chapters. To point out flaws in others' doctrines is easier than to defend one's own; but in the context of Indian philosophy, Udayana stands out for his defense of theism in the fifth, mainly positive chapter, on which I will therefore concentrate.

Philosopher or no, Udayana accepts the argument from consensus. He begins the chapter by declaring that, in one form or another, a Supreme Being is admitted by people of all sects and schools, even by the Charvakas—what variety can he mean?—who accept Him who is established by convention.* Since the existence of this Being is universally acknowledged, how can any doubt arise? he asks, and he answers (as shown in the preceding footnote) that his "logical investigation of the Lord" is an act of reflection meant as worship to help him in the attainment of "the supreme concentration."[6]

The first of the two series of proofs for God's existence is meant to refute the refutations of Charvaka, Samkhya, Mimamsa, Buddhism, and Jainism, none of which agree that the universe needs a God to assemble it or direct its course (*to assemble* emphasizes that the Nyaya-Vaisheshika do not believe in creation ex nihilo). Udayana takes great care to state and refute the refutations because of Indian philosophical convention: If they all prove incoherent or lead to impossible consequences, his own conclusions, having survived all rational challenges, are left victorious on the field of debate.

Each of Udayana's proofs is first formulated, then shown to be free of the logical fallacies ascribed to it by opponents, and finally driven home with a confirming Vedic passage. Of the nine proofs he gives, the first two

---

*Perhaps Udayana means that the adherents of Charvaka—like Sextus Empiricus—accept worldly conventions, as is suggested by the school's alternative name, Lokayata, taken to mean *prevalent in the world (loka)* of ordinary people. Or Udayana may be referring to the kind of remark we find in a Charvaka fragment that says, ironically, that sacrifices, etc. are the Lord's way of providing a livelihood for those (no doubt brahmans) who are impotent and stupid. (Thanks for this note to Karin Preisendanz and Eli Franco.)

show that God has "created" the universe; the third, that he supports the universe in space; the fourth, that he is the destroyer of the universe; the fifth, that he is the teacher of humankind; the sixth, that he gives the Veda its authority; the seventh and eighth, that he is the author of the Veda; and the ninth, that he is the source of extension or dimensionality in the universe.

In the course of his proofs, Udayana makes frequent use of a form of reasoning that is not enough by itself, he knows, to establish a thesis but that shows what absurdities would follow if a contrary thesis were accepted. This "logical discussion" or *tarka* is reasoning by means of the negation of the consequent—the *then* of an *if-then* assumption (technically, counterfactual conditional reasoning). It is a kind of reduction to absurdity, an instance of hypothetical reasoning that shows a conclusion to be false because it contradicts experience or commits a standard logical fallacy. Using *tarka*, he shows the undesirable outcomes that would follow the rejection of his theses or the acceptance of opposite theses. For example, against someone skeptical of the relation between smoke and fire, the *tarka* would go: If smoke was not produced by fire, smoke, which cannot come from anything else, would be an effect without a cause, a conclusion whose absurdity shows that the assumption is inadmissible. (Udayana holds that Buddhists misuse *tarka* by assuming that the subject of the *tarka* does not exist. How, he asks, can you argue by formally assuming the existence of something that, in the same argument, you try to prove does not exist?)[7]

I summarize Udayana's proofs one by one, sometimes supplementing them with explanations taken from elsewhere in Udayana but skipping most of the attacks and rebuttals:[8]

1. *The proof from effect:*[9] This, the most important Nyaya proof, begins in the *Handful of Flowers of Logic* with the statement that the earth, mountains, and everything else that is produced have a maker or "creator" as their cause because they are by their nature effects: just as a jar testifies, by its nature as an effect, to its maker, so do they. Excluded from among effects is whatever is regarded as uncaused—atoms, souls, and such other eternal substances as ether, time, and space. The concept *nature of an effect* cannot be severed from the concept of *maker*. To be an effect is always to require a maker's wish, knowledge, and power. In other words, the *nature of an effect* refers to the coming into existence of what was nonexistent before, so the term *creator* is applicable to it.

   Udayana contends that it is only if the maker of the universe is eternal and omniscient that the attribute of effect can belong, as it must, to the constituents of the universe. In the absence of such a maker, they would not have come into existence. Since these constituents could not have assembled themselves, it is valid to infer that it was God, the only agent adequate to the effect, who created (assembled, ordered) the universe. Elsewhere, the argument is put in an Indian "syllogism," with its typical example. Although he does not take the trouble to say so, the thesis is meant to apply to mountains, trees, and the like—and therefore also to the universe—at whose origin no bodily person is perceived.

Thesis: That which originates independently of a body has an intelligent being as its cause.

Reason: Because it has the nature of that which has a cause (i.e., of an effect).

Example: That which has a cause has an intelligent being as cause, like a chariot.

Application: And so is this (the universe, whose origin is independent of a perceptible, bodily person).

Conclusion: So this, too, has an intelligent being as cause.[10]

Udayana must now meet an objection: Creators act by means of their bodies, but according to Nyaya doctrine, God has no body. Therefore we can say in hypothetical Indian fashion: "If God was the creator, he would have a body; but he does not have a body; therefore God is not the creator." Udayana answers that this argument suffers from the fallacy of "unproved locus." This is because the subject, God, is assumed to exist in a certain way—without a body—in order to prove that he is not the creator and therefore does not exist, an assumption that ruins the formal validity of this (counterfactual conditional) argument.[11]*

---

*The statement of this fallacy points the way to Udayana's negative ontological argument, which proves God's existence by showing the impossibility of denying it. The argument goes this way: For an inference to be valid, its terms must denote, that is, refer to something the existence of which is assumed. But when one begins an inference with "God does not exist," if the statement is true, then the concept God does not refer to anything and the full inference—in which the reason for his not existing is added—is invalid. And if the statement "God does not exist" is false, then God does exist, and the inference is invalid. So it is impossible, says Udayana, to make inferences to demonstrate that God does not exist. As Udayana would say, the locus—the logical "substratum," the subject of inference, in which the logical reason or proving property God "resides"—is unproved; and "a locus that is accepted on account of a fallacy cannot be a real locus nor can it be an object of denial." (See Chemparathy, *An Indian Rational Theology*, p. 56 [quoted], Potter, *Nyāya-Vaiśeṣika*, pp. 108–109, and Cowell's translation, pp. 67–68.)

To Udayana, the invisibility of God is no evidence against his existence because perception, he says, can judge only the existence of what is in principle perceptible; and there is no reason that a valid inference cannot be made from a visible effect to its invisible cause. After all, "it is not the fault of the post that the blind man does not see it."[12]

The invisibility of God, which follows from his bodilessness, leads Udayana to argue that God needs no body because he does not experience pleasure or pain and needs no physical instruments with which to act. Instead, he directs the causes of the universe by unmediated effort, effort not in the sense of bodily activity but of intention or endeavor. For, in Indian philosophical terms, there is no pervasion of *being an agent* by *having a body*. Besides, says Udayana, if *to be a body (be a "bodied" person)* means only *to require direction by an agent's immediate effort*, then God could be said, in a manner of speaking, to have the atoms and so on as his body—but, unlike ordinary bodies, his body would not be the substratum of the senses and of pleasure and pain. However, in keeping with widespread Indian beliefs, Udayana agrees that, for special actions, God may make use of a "body of artifice." To teach humans how to speak, even God needs vocal organs.[13]

2. *The proof from combination:*[14] By this proof, which is implied in the preceding one, an omniscient, unchangeable God can be inferred "from 'combination' (of the atoms etc.) . . . For the atoms etc. operate only when they are combined by a conscious being; because (they are) unconscious; like an axe etc."[15] That is to say, being unconscious, atoms cannot initiate or guide the movement that creates even the nonliving universe; it takes a conscious agent to set them into motion and direct and combine them. Not to admit this would be to make the origin of the effect impossible.

This proof depends on the usual though not universal Indian belief (the subject of the fourth proof) that the universe undergoes a perpetual cycle of creation and destruction. According to Nyaya, it dissolves into individual atoms, bodiless souls, and the other eternal realities (such as time, space, mind, and the categories—remember Plato!—of generality, particularity, and inherence). Recreating the universe is not a simple matter. To do it, the atoms have to be joined in order to eventually form bodies. And the omnipresent souls have to be joined with the bodies, as they are by way of bodily, atom-size "minds." Only when so joined can souls be conscious. The other eternal realities—space and time, for example—are unconscious and cannot explain the origin or the order of the universe.

Besides, at the start of a new cycle, God is the only conscious, intelligent being. Only he, knowing all causes, is able to direct them to combine into a universe that conforms to what living beings should experience in answer to the merits and demerits they have accumulated. The actions of the living beings determine their situations in life; but this relationship between actions and situations depends on the conscious activity of God.[16]

3. *The proof from failure to fall:*[17] "Although it possesses weight," the universe—all the worlds there are—"has the property of not falling down." The body of a flying bird, which possesses weight, is directly supported in space by the bird's activity, the same activity that indirectly supports the prey in the bird's claws. Just so, the universe, which possesses weight and would otherwise fall, is supported in endless space by a "command" or a "permeation" (as the scriptural words put it). The command is in this case the "embodied effort" that supports the universe. And the "permeation" is the conjunction with a being that has cognition, desire, and effort, who in this case can be only God. Because God is omnipresent, he does not conjoin the universe *with* himself but—to make a distinction —he is *in* conjunction with it, "permeates" it, and so, by his embodied effort, his knowing, desiring activity, supports it.

4. *The proof from dissolution:*[18] Apart from Mimamsa, all the Indian schools of thought believed in the cyclical destruction and regeneration of the universe. Udayana argues that destructions or dissolutions are effects and therefore require volition and effort of a kind that can be ascribed only to God. The existence of the cycles, he argues, is proved by the general periodicity of things—although rainy days follow one another during the rainy season, the first rainy day is preceded by the last sunny day and by a change in the sun's zodiacal position that leads to rain. Also, observation shows that, just as a lamp fails when it burns on, the universe is deteriorating. We see this deterioration in the declining purity of birth. Originally, creatures were produced from the mind, in the same way as Brahma bore his sons. Then they were borne by means of sexual intercourse for the sake of children, but are now borne only by means of intercourse for sake of sexual gratification. Other signs are the declining study and knowledge of the Veda, the neglect of certain rites and duties, the decline of morality, and so on—all signs of the declining physical and mental powers of human beings and the impending destruction of the world by Shiva.[19]

5. *The proof from established practices or conventions:*[20] The practices Udayana means are the usual practices of life, in particular, the

practice of using words—connected by God with various objects—
and the practice of the various crafts. A weaver's skill, like the use by
children of the letters of the alphabet, all in accord with the letters'
order, and the use by grown persons of words, depend on an independent teacher, who is the untaught teacher who long ago instructed
humans. At the start of creation, human souls no longer remember
anything they have learned—bodilessness and the pain of birth make
remembering impossible. They then need to be instructed by God, a
being who, without having to be taught, knows everything.

6. *The proof from authoritativeness:*[21] The Vedas are trusted by the great
   majority of people as altogether authoritative. This trust reveals the
   Vedas to have the nature, like perception, of a means of valid cognition. But as a means of valid cognition, the Vedas could not have
   been their own cause. Nor, lacking omniscience, could the sages
   who transmitted the Vedas have had the degree of excellence presupposed by the cause of the Vedas' authoritativeness. Only an
   omniscient author, God, could have given them their unquestionable authority.

7. *The proof from "hearing" (shruti—the Vedas):*[22] The Veda-nature of the
   Vedas is revealed by the fact that their statements are accepted by
   "the large mass of people" when no further basis for their acceptance
   can be perceived. This acceptance cannot be based on perception
   (which is unable to make out the invisible objects the Vedas speak
   of), cannot be based on other means of perception, cannot be based
   on error or deception by crafty priests (so many people cannot be
   mistaken or deceived), and cannot be based on uninterrupted tradition (every dissolution of the universe interrupts tradition). So this
   Veda-nature that distinguishes the Vedas from every other composition and that consists in their being accepted by the "large mass of
   people" can be understood only on the assumption of an author
   who immediately perceives everything of which the Vedas tell.

8: *The proof from the connection of words in sentences:*[23] "The sentences of
   the Veda are (composed) by a person; because they have the nature
   of a sentence; like the sentences by people like us." This proof is
   directed against the Mimamsa, which admits the Vedas' truth but
   denies that they had any, even divine author. If there had been so
   great an author, say the Mimamsakas, he would be remembered by
   the line of teachers descended from him. Udayana rejects this: From
   the fact that no one remembers who dug a certain unused well, he
   says, it is not concluded that nobody dug it. Just as threads cannot
   arrange themselves into a cloth, so the words of the Vedas are not
   arranged into sentences by themselves.[24]

9: *The proof from special number (that is, number above one):*[25] The existence of God, says Udayana, is proved by the existence of extended bodies. As explained in an earlier chapter, Nyaya-Vaisheshika teaches that single and double atoms have the quality of "smallness," which is "size" without extension (size is the quality that leads us to call a substance small, large, short, or long).[26] Having the quality of "smallness," single or double atoms cannot cause "largeness," which is perceptible extension or magnitude. "Largeness" is the quality or size that makes it possible for a substance to grow in magnitude in accord with the number of its constituent parts. As already explained, this size originates with triads, which are minute but perceptible combinations of three dyads.

To cut short a systematically developed, artificially complicated doctrine—something of a simulacrum of the general type of distinctions made in modern physics—one of the causes of "largeness" is the plural (at least dual) number of constituent parts of a substance. This number or numerical quality is itself dependent on the creative "relating cognition" of an omniscient person—namely, God—at the recurrent times of the formation of a world. These are times when, other than God, there are no intelligent beings in existence who might make creation possible by the knowledge that must otherwise be assigned to God. In any case, unlike God, human beings cannot perceive atoms or dyads.

So it is only God who can and does perceive directly that there are two things (two single atoms) having the number-quality *one* that together constitute something else, a pair. By means of this direct cognition God relates the two single atoms having the *one* so that the dual number arises (is actualized?) in them and produces the atomic size of the dyad. And then, by his relating cognition, God relates three dyads so that the number-quality of three arises in them and produces the size of the triad. This is the first "largeness" or perceptible dimension.[27]*

---

*The change from the "smallness" of the single atom to that of the dyad, and from the dyad's "smallness" to the triple dyads' "largeness" has something of the character of what is called, in modern physics, a (first-order, discontinuous) "phase transition." Or, if we make an adventurous comparison, by conceptually relating the atom's dyadicity and then relating the dyads to form triples of dyads, God accomplishes—in the first proof's sense of God as the creator of effect substances—the equivalent of reducing the wave packet and making a change from a basic but unvisualizable, perhaps unimaginable level of atomism, with its own strange laws, to another level, with which human beings are familiar.

Udayana concludes his book, as he began it, with a declaration of faith: God is known through the Vedas, through reason, and through Yogic intuition. Udayana prays that God will in compassion draw toward him the stony hearts of those who, despite reason and revelation, have no faith in him. He asks that believers be turned from their dissatisfaction with life to a single-minded devotion to God and in this way be saved from the torments of repeated death. Then he places his handful of flowers of logic, the *Kusumanjali*, at the feet of Ishvara, who is Shiva.[28]

Chu Hsi (1130–1200)

Nature is simply how we should be.
It is simply principle [li];
It isn't that there exists some thing.

Chu Hsi became the undisputed leader of the fellowship named *True-Way Learning (Tao-hsüeh)*.[29] Its members met in academies, where they exchanged admonitions, performed rituals, held memorial services, and fostered their version of Confucianism and one another's careers. They could be identified by the tall hats with pointed tops they wore and the conspicuous dignity with which they walked and talked. As they said in a formal claim to the emperor, they took themselves to be the inheritors of the Way transmitted by the first sages to Confucius.[30]* According to their claim, the Way was transmitted by Confucius to Mencius and from him—after a thousand-year interruption—to the brothers Ch'eng Hao (1032–1086) and Ch'eng I (1033–1107) and their disciples.[31] One can imagine with what resentment the other Confucians, those who disagreed with True-Way Learning, reacted to praise like that addressed, along with a poem, to Chu Hsi by his disciple, Ch'en Ch'un: Chu Hsi is the person who alone can be called the leader of the generation, the leader who has "wiped out the errors of over a thousand years and become the definite and unchanging standard for students of later generations."[32]

---

*The movement's modern name, Neo-Confucianism, has resulted in confusion. For Chu Hsi's period, the name is often confined to the Tao-hsüeh fellowship. But in China itself, the fellowship came to be called the Ch'eng-Chu (Ch'eng I and Chu Hsi) school and was contrasted with Lu-Wang (Lü Tsu-ch'ien and Wang Yang-ming) school. In the last, Ch'ing dynasty, Chu Hsi's school was also referred to by the thirteenth-century name, the School of Principle *(li-hsüeh)*, and Lu's, by the name the School of Mind *(hsin-hsüeh)*. (See De Bary, "The Uses of Neo-Confucianism"; *Neo-Confucian Orthodoxy and the Learning of the Mind-and-Heart*, pp. xiv–xvi, 115–19); and Tillman, *Confucian Discourse and Chu Hsi's Ascendancy*, pp. 3–4, 21, 265–66, note 1.)

Because the fellowship or faction of True-Way reformers was against peace with the "barbarian" conquerors of the Central Plain, it clashed with the influential officials who favored peace. Chu also made enemies by his sweeping denunciations of corrupt officials. Finally, he was charged with a strangely miscellaneous variety of misdeeds: plagiarism, magical practices, seduction of two Buddhist nuns, lack of filial piety (as shown by his giving his mother only the worst kind of rice), disrespect for the emperor, disloyalty, and more. Chu's partisans were charged with using secret codes to help one another pass the civil service examinations, falsifying Confucius and Mencius, and usurping the emperor's authority. In 1196, the teachings of the faction were forbidden. Two years later, fifty-nine men, including Chu Hsi, were declared to belong to the "rebel clique of false learning." However, Chu Hsi was allowed to go on studying and teaching. His troubles with the government and his death while officially under a ban raised his moral stature, and his rehabilitation began quite soon.[33]

Chu did his industrious best to edit and comment on the books he thought most valuable for tradition. His works include the True Way Learning anthology, *Reflections on Things at Hand*, compiled with a friend, which became a universally studied primer, and commentaries on the Four Books—the *Greater Learning*, Confucius' *Analects*, the *Book of Mencius*, and the *Doctrine of the Mean*. His conversations with his disciples, *Conversations of Master Chu, Arranged Topically* (or, alternatively, *Classified Conversations of Master Chu Hsi*), appeared after his death. In 1313, his commentaries were declared official and required for the civil service examinations. As a result, they were studied with great intensiveness and endowed with near scriptural authority.

Behind Chu's synthesis there lie certain political and social concerns. For one thing, he is indignant over the abandonment of North China to the Chin (Jurchen) "barbarians," and, for another, he is afraid that Buddhism, especially Ch'an (Zen) Buddhism, will prove alluring even to the intellectuals responsible for keeping the Confucian Way alive. The quietism and escape into fantasy of the Taoists—who, he says, believe in *being* as well as *nonbeing*—seem less dangerous to him than the Buddhists' destruction of human relations and, in the Ch'an sect, the wiping out of all moral principles. As he sees it, Buddhism deludes people with absurd doctrines of transmigration and karma.

Chu Hsi's hatred for Buddhism developed out of an initial attraction to it. Like many, perhaps most, of the Chinese of the time, his early teachers had been tolerant toward Buddhism. During his youth, Chu suffered the deaths of his father, his two brothers, and two of his teachers, deaths that may account for his initially profound interest in both Taoism and Ch'an. But then, as an official and a young, unusually successful scholar, he came under the influence of the orthodox Confucian, Li Tung. As he recalled in a later poem, he lost his secular worries and, learning that he did not need to live in the "empty mountain" to which Buddhism had long invited him, he perceived it as "adulterating" the truth and turned hostile to it. It is less surprising that his criticism of Buddhism is, or now appears to be, unfair, than that it is so shallow. Maybe, to make it effective, he intentionally phrases it in the black and white of caricature. As Chu Hsi says, he is trying to make clear the difference between the Confucian seedling and the Buddhist weed. What moves him is not metaphysics but his sense of the social dangers that Buddhism poses his (Buddhistically altruistic) ideals.[34]*

The only hope, Chu reiterates, is the moral regeneration of the Confucian Way. This is threatened, he feels, by those who learn merely in order to impress others. But it is threatened even more by the civil service examinations. Success in the examinations gives such prestige, power, and wealth that those who take them try to win high rank by means of careful literary style and "profound" or novel interpretations. This unfortunate concern with style, Chu says, reflects the artfulness of such poets as Su Shih, to whom style is often more important than the understanding of moral principle.[35] Book learning does have a worth of its own, he admits, but it should be used in a way that draws on the experience of the sages and on their profoundly didactic will to transmit this experience.[36] Even the increasing use of printing worries him because, with books so easily available, students no longer have to recite and memorize them or read with a disciplined penetration.[37] The right method

> is to recite a text, then ponder it over; to ponder it over, then recite it . . . For our minds then hover over the words. If it's just a matter of the mouth doing the reading but the mind

---

*Chu Hsi is familiar mainly with Ch'an and Hua-yen (the "Flower Garland" or, in Japan, Kegon school). He admires Buddhist monks who enter deep into the mountains, live there on very little, and emerge natural and charming; but they are concerned, he observes, with personal salvation alone. The Ch'an Buddhists realize what is metaphysically primordial within phenomenal forms and are able to escape control by external things; but the ultimate concern of Buddhists, Chu observes, is beyond morality. On one occasion he admits that Buddhist emptiness is not nothingness but the "mysterious [or true] emptiness" that is something real, "quite similar to what we Confucianists speak of." But usually he contrasts the "empty annihilation" of Buddhism with the Confucian belief that "all metaphysical principles are real while they say all principles are empty." He states, "Confucianism is ultimately concerned with human affairs while Buddhism is ultimately concerned with the problem of life-and-death." (The above is summarized from Wei-hsun Fu, "Chu Hsi on Buddhism." The quoted words are respectively from pp. 385–86, 381, and 401, where the references to the Chinese sources are given. See also the references in the preceding note 34.)

doing no thinking, what'll our understanding be like? (Chu Hsi, *Learning to Be a Sage*, 4.42)[38]

Chu's advice is proper to a self-confident but modest sage: "In reading, if you have no doubts, encourage them. And if you do have doubts, get rid of them . . . The problem with men is that they feel the views of others alone may be doubted, not their own" (*Learning to Be a Sage*, 5.36, 5.37).[39]

Maybe because Chu never wrote a full exposition of his philosophical views, the impression we get from the selective anthologies that take the place of a system is rather amorphous. But the vagueness of his concepts is lessened and their integrative force augmented by the simple but strong images he uses: He compares the nature that all humans possess to clear, flowing water that, if polluted, must be purified again; he says that the mind is a (polished bronze) mirror—a Buddhist image— illuminated from within, whose brightness is its humaneness; he says that the mind is like water that must be still—another Buddhist image— in order to reflect things clearly; and he identifies the life in the seed, the principle of its growth, with the principle of human growth, which is humaneness.[40]

To return to Chu's amorphousness or vagueness: If we study the metaphysical hierarchy he expounds, we discover that it has two differently named heads, which he declares to be identical. The one head, the Great Ultimate or Ultimate of Nonbeing, is taken from his eleventh-century predecessor, Chou Tun-I, and largely inspired by Taoism—this Nonbeing occurs in both Lao-tzu and Chuang-tzu. The Ch'eng brothers, on whom Chu Hsi so often relies, do not as much as mention it.[41] The "second" head of the hierarchy, Principle, comes from both Chou Tun-I and the Ch'eng brothers. Chu would be clearer, if perhaps less suggestive, if he gave up one of the two heads. It has been argued that the Great Ultimate is not well integrated into his theory. That is, although he may mean it to be the same as Principle, the complications it introduces make it an unhelpful, even alien element in his system.[42]

The common, if misleadingly hierarchical way out—suggested by some texts of Chu Hsi himself—is to assume that the Great Ultimate is the hierarchy's head. Considered to be the ultimate of Principle, it "simply means the sum total of all the principles of heaven, earth, and the ten thousand things."[43] Another possible way out is to see the Great Ultimate as the head of the hierarchy from the standpoint of metaphysical unity, and see Principle as the head from the standpoint of cognition or, in modern terms, epistemology. In accord with this solution, Principle is all that the mind embraces, the principle of seeing, of hearing, of speaking, of appearing, of thinking—the seeing clear, the hearing distinct, the speech reasonable, the appearance respectful, the thought penetrating. But the text I am paraphrasing in these words, though a possible clue to a solution, is hardly enough for the solution itself. I am afraid that we are not able to enter into the spirit of Chu Hsi effectively enough to work out the construction of a hierarchy that he himself left incompletely resolved.[44] Still, regardless of its ambiguities, the hierarchy can be described under the following five heads: The Great Ultimate—the Ultimate of Nonbeing—and Principle; the union of Principle and material force; the creative mindlessness of Heaven and Earth; the primal, constant virtues; and the need to "hold on" to mind.

The Great Ultimate (T'ai-Chi)—The Ultimate of Nonbeing (Wu-Chi)—and Principle (Li): As has been intimated, and as this heading shows, Chu Hsi's metaphysical concepts are more suitable for the logic of *both-and* than of *either-or* (or *neither-nor*): Nature is equally *being* and *nonbeing* and Principle; and, as Chu Hsi explains, Principle and principles are the same. It should be remarked that the very clear style in which he writes does not detract from the poetic resonance of even his abstract concepts. Their resonance and, within limits, even their plausibility are heightened by the antithetical nuances assumed to be implicit in them. At the very head of the metaphysical hierarchy Chu constructs, there appears—or in a sense, appear—the antithetical variety-expressing-unity of the Ultimate of Nonbeing and Great Ultimate. Growing like a tree, in Chu's image, this Ultimate divides limitlessly into branches, leaves, flowers, and in its fruit contains the principle of the ceaseless making of life.[45] Principle, another name for or mode of characterizing the one head of the hierarchy, is explained below.

Some of Chu's contemporaries find fault with his system. When criticized (in 1187, by Lu Chiu-shao) for his interpretation of Chou Tun-I's doctrine of the Great Ultimate, especially for the importance he attributes to the Ultimate of Nonbeing, Chu answers that the Ultimate of Nonbeing must be posited at the beginning together with the Great Ultimate. If not for the concept of Nonbeing, he says, the Great Ultimate would seem to be a finite, inadequate basis for all that exists; and if not for the concept of the Great Ultimate, the Ultimate of Nonbeing would seem empty and inadequate for all that exists.

Chu then turns to the charge that the concept of Nonbeing is borrowed from Lao Tzu, that it is not Confucian at all, and that it was unknown to the Ch'eng brothers (who had studied with Chou Tun-I). Chu's answer is that there was no reason for Chou not to introduce a new term. Chou, he says, had insight enough to grasp the Great Ultimate of Nonbeing in a non-Taoist way. To Chou, he continues, the Great Ultimate of Nonbeing is not empty but able to give life. Unlike Lao Tzu, who conceives Being and Nonbeing to be separate from one another, Chou conceives them to be an aspect of a single reality. But at the end of his debate with Lu, Chu grows somewhat uncertain of his interpretation of Chou Tun-I: He has just read a version, he informs Lu, of Chou's text (with possible interpolations) in which The Great Ultimate and the Ultimate of Nonbeing are conceived to be different from one another.[46]

"Principle" (Li) and "Material Force"(Ch'i):[47] The union of *li* and *ch'i* explains both the unity and the variety of nature. To avoid confusion, it should be remembered that *Li* meaning *Principle*, which is written with the radical *jade*, is different from the *li* meaning *ritual* or *rule of propriety*. *Li*, Principle, which exists before the universe, is the Great Ultimate in the sense of the pattern (the form) and the good that are inherent in everything.* It is the Way, except that the Way is wayward and is travelled on forever, while Principle is unchanging. Without physical shape, it is that which a thing ought to be, an unchanging, ideal standard, neither excessive nor deficient.[48]

All things have their own special principles and Great Ultimates.

> But all of them are completely merged without any deficiency. When they are considered separately, they become many principles [each particular piece of wood with its own particular-piece-of-wood principle], but when the ten thousand things are considered collectively, the ten thousand things are merged with one another and are only one Great Ultimate.[49]

---

*In Chu Hsi's time, this *li* was assumed, perhaps wrongly, to have the main meaning of *to work jade (according to its natural markings, its veins)* or the meaning *veins in jade*, or, by extension, *veinlike pattern*. To work jade, one has to know the structure of its veins or strata, so the word came to mean the intimate structure or essential rhythm of things by which one knows them or can work or use them. Often *pattern* is an apt translation, as is *organization* or *order*. But in Chinese philosophy, specifically in Sung philosophy, *li* is *the reason why a thing is as it is* or *a rule to which a thing should conform*, so *principle* fits in the dual sense of *principle of organization* and *moral principle*—the meanings that Chu Hsi and others want to merge in a single natural-ethical meaning. Yet A. C. Graham abandons *principle* in favor of *pattern* because "principle" suggests a truth put into words for deductive purposes, while *li* suggests a pattern running through things, even sharing their three dimensions. (See Graham, "What Was New in the Ch'eng-Chu Theory?" in Chan, ed., *Chu Hsi and Neo-Confucianism*, p. 155, note 5.)

Though it has no body, Principle never separates from material force.* However, in terms of origin, Principle (and the principles of the different things) existed first. That is, the two, Principle and material force, are entirely different in themselves; but once things exist, the two cannot be separated. Without material force, "Principle would have nothing to adhere to." And because Principle exists, "there is material force to operate everywhere and nourish and develop all things"—every change and every integration that produces life, including "what we call spirit, the heavenly and earthly aspects of the soul (hun-p'o), and consciousness are all effects of material force." Principle itself is unaffected by integration or disintegration.[50]

The mutability of the material force is what explains the difference between good and evil. What is mandated by (the principle of) Heaven is basically good, for which reason, as Mencius says, man's nature is basically good. The differences and inequalities between men are the result of their different endowments of material force, that is, of Yin's weakness, Yang's strength, Fire's dryness, Water's moistness, Metal's coldness, Wood's warmth, and Earth's heaviness and thickness. Not that these material forces are evil in themselves, but their equal or unequal division, combination, movement, and transformation result in purity and impurity, good and evil, virtue and stupidity. But the foundation is the same, and "even the most stupid can be transformed to be good," although this is very difficult.[51]

At the top of the universe, like the top of a house or the zenith of the sky, beyond which nothing more exists, is the Great Ultimate, which is the ultimate of Principle. Like a man on a horse, Principle sits inactively astride material force—passive Yin and active Yang—through which it becomes visible; and Yin and Yang produce the Five Agents—Water, Fire, Wood, Metal, and Earth—all material forces that, confined and fixed by physical nature, "are differentiated into individual things each with its own nature" and containing the Great Ultimate.[52]

---

*Material force, ch'i, is the breathlike- or fluidlike energy that is the life force in living things, as well as in the works of art and the writings that share their power of life. Since it condenses (as in living things) and rarefies or disperses (as in the dead), it is, though energy, a substance in the material sense, of which everything that exists is a permutation. It has therefore been translated material force, matter energy, energy substance, stuff/energy and, by analogy with the Greek element, ether (aer in Anaximenes and Anaximander), aither (Plato's purest aer, Aristotle's heavenly element), or pneuma (the air/fire of the Stoics). Chu Hsi and his school believe that ch'i, the power to take different material shapes, explains the physicality and physical diversity of things, as well as the moral diversity of persons. What is misleading in all the translations is that ch'i is not simply matter or energy in the impersonal sense, but also life, vigor, emotion, the cause of growth, decay, and growth again, and sometimes of vitality in a mystical sense. (See Needham, Science and Civilization in China, vol. 2, pp. 471–72, 491–93; Graham, Disputers of the Tao, pp. 351–54; and Schwartz, The World of Thought in Ancient China, pp. 179–84.)

As Chu describes it, in the beginning, when there was only material force dividing into yin and yang, the force moved, circulated, turned this way and that, gathered speed, and pushed together a mass of sediment for which there was no outlet and which therefore

> consolidated to form the earth in the center of the universe. The clear part of material force formed the sky, the sun and moon, and the stars and zodiacal spaces. It is only on the outside that the encircling movement perpetually goes on. The earth exists motionless in the center of the system, not [as some suppose] at the bottom.[53]

Heaven and Earth Have No Mind of Their Own: The Great Ultimate, the Principle of the highest good, is in each and every person and thing. *Great Ultimate* is a name that expresses all the virtues and whatever is the highest good, whether in Heaven and Earth, or man, or things (it has some kinship with Plato's Idea of the Good).[54] To the question whether or not the universe has a controlling godlike mind (heart, *hsin*), Chu Hsi gives an answer reminiscent of Hsün-tzu, which is, "No, but . . ." That is (to revert to Cheng I's words), "Heaven and Earth create and transform without having any mind of their own. The sage has a mind of his own but does not take any [unnatural] action." As Chu explains, this means that all the natural processes of Heaven and Earth run their course without having any mind of their own—whatever has consciousness, that is, a mind of its own must be a union of principle (*li*) with material force (*ch'i*). Yet the mind of Heaven and Earth—their creative reciprocity, pattern, and mind potential—is in all things; and so the sage, who does have a (conscious) mind of his own, feels in tranquil accord with everything natural, of which he is the pure expression. Unselfishly, Heaven and Earth reach all things with their order, creativity, and "mind," and when man receives it, it becomes his, human mind, just as when grass, trees, birds, and animals receive it, it becomes the mind of each of these, all being the one mind of Heaven and Earth. "Thus we must understand in what sense Heaven and Earth have mind and in what sense they have no mind. We cannot be inflexible."[55]

The Virtues: Here, just where Chu Hsi, a consummate Confucian, is sensitive and fluent, we must remain sparse and constrained. Traced to the process of creation, the Five Constant Virtues—humanity (*jen*), righteousness, propriety, wisdom, faithfulness—have the respective characters of the Five Agents; but here we need not review how this is.[56]

To Chu, as to all Confucians, the primal virtue is that of humanity or, in a perhaps better translation, humaneness (*jen*).[57] This virtue is inherent in the universe, so that when people and other things are produced by Heaven and Earth, they receive as their own mind the mind of Heaven and Earth. The virtue of the human mind can be expressed in one word, *jen*, humaneness.* Chu recalls that Mencius says, "*Jen* is man's mind" (*Mencius* 6A.11). Implanted by Heaven and Earth, humanity is the essence of the human mind, present in consciousness even before any feelings are aroused. "After feelings are aroused, its function is infinite. If we can truly practice love and preserve it, then we have in it the spring of all virtues and the roots of all good deeds."[58]

To realize *jen* we should be ready, as Confucius says, to master ourselves, return to propriety, and even sacrifice our lives. Mind, which in Heaven and Earth produces things infinitely, in human beings is the mind to love people (gently) and to benefit things; to have the four virtues; and to commiserate, have a sense of shame, of deference and compliance, and of right and wrong. Human nature and feelings must interpenetrate rather than be separated from one another. Humaneness is not love itself but the principle of love and the way of life. Humaneness is nothing other than the essence and function of the human mind.[59]

As I have said, Chu Hsi's account of virtues is too expansive to survey here. But for a reason that will be evident, I feel it necessary to mention a pair of joined virtues, the one, loyalty (*chung*), and the other, empathy or altruism (*shu*). To be loyal (to what is real and true) is to exert one's mind/heart to its center "so nothing is unreal." To be empathic is to be like-minded-hearted, to extend one's mind to others until their desires are like one's own, to stimulate filiality by filiality, and brotherliness by brotherliness. Loyalty is to empathy what form is to shadow, "for if what is harbored inside is already loyal, when it is expressed externally, it is empathy." When Confucius said,

> "Do not do to others what you do not want them to do to
> you," he was speaking about one side of the question. Actually

---

*Chu Hsi held a decade-long series of discussions, in person and by letter, with his Confucian associate, Chang Shih (Chang Nan-hsüan) (1133–1180) on the subject, among others, of *jen*. During the years of this discussion, both of them wrote and revised "treatises" on *jen*. Chu proved the dominant partner. In the course of the discussion, Chu contends that the early Confucians saw humaneness simply as love, while the disciples of Ch'eng I emphasized only empty principles. Of late, Chu says, scholars consider the mind of Heaven and Earth to be transcendental and lofty, and may therefore drown in Buddhist or Taoist emptiness and quietude. Chu warns that an emphasis—such as he finds in Chang—on the universality of humaneness may lead to self-negation, to feeding oneself, like Buddha in a former life, to a hungry tigress. All things are not the self, humaneness is not simply generosity, and love alone does not inform us how to help others. Lacking the learning that gives one "a definite idea on the meaning and content of humaneness," one is in "danger of being mired in aimless confusion." The concept of love is an aid to humaneness and humaneness is the source of love, but love can never exhaust humaneness. (See Hidoshi, "Chu Hsi's 'Treatise on *Jen*'" (see previous note 57); and Tillman, *Confucian Discourse and Chu Hsi's Ascendancy*, pp. 70–82 [p. 74 quoted].)

one should not only refrain from doing to others what one does not want others to do to him; whatever one wants others to do to him he should do to others.[60]

Holding on to Mind (Heart, Hsin): To Chu Hsi, the human mind is made of the purest *ch'i* and embraces and controls human nature and the emotions. In the beginning, the mind is in a state of equilibrium, but when the equilibrium is disturbed, to preserve the original mind, one must look for and regain this "root" and "master" of the person. Chu therefore exhorts his students to keep possession of their minds. This does not imply that they contain some principle apart from mind because "the mind is simply one mind. One doesn't control this mind with another mind. What is meant by 'preserving it,' what is meant by 'retrieving it,' is simply to awaken it."[61] His impersonal cosmic forces derived in part from Taoism but grasped as penetrating the human mind with benevolence; his doctrine of unselfish love derived from Mencius but sensitized by Buddhism, with its mercy and what he saw as its reverentially concentrated tranquility; his learning derived from his own, Confucian tradition but made more pointed by his commentaries and more urgent by his emotional commitment; and his belief in the fundamental oneness of truth, sincerity, self-discipline, hierarchy, and human service—in all this together, Chu Hsi provided China with a powerful (and arduous, often onerous) force for social and intellectual cohesion.

Avicenna (Ibn Sina) (980–1037)

Since in his [the prophet's] case the barrier between the
phenomenal and the ideal (real) has broken down,
he is identical with the Active Intellect.

Avicenna is the name that Europeans have given to Abu 'Ali l-Husain ibn Sina.[62] He lived a rather short but very full life as an Iranian physician, polymath, astronomer, courtier, and vizier.[63] Of his more than hundred genuine works, only three need to be named here: *The Canon of Medicine (Qanun), The Cure of the Soul (Shifa),* and *The Salvation of the Soul (Najat),* a widely read summary compiled by Avicenna from his own earlier works. The *Canon* is an encyclopedia of diagnosis and treatment based on Greco-Arabic medicine; translated into Latin, it was accepted by the medieval Europeans as authoritative. The *Cure* (for the soul's ignorance), Avicenna's major philosophical work, is written in the accepted order of the Aristotelian sciences, logic, physics, mathematics, and metaphysics. It is intended, says Avicenna, to be an unambiguous compendium of the fundamental principles of the ancients' philosophical sciences, as completed by the fundamental principles discovered by means of (his own) new insights.[64]

Although he grows increasingly independent of Aristotle, Avicenna regards him as the incomparable philosopher. He tells how in the course of teaching himself philosophy he reached Aristotle's *Metaphysics* and read and reread it, forty times in all, without grasping what the author was aiming at. One day, he by chance bought the book *On the Purposes of the Metaphysics*, by al-Farabi (c. 870–950), and as soon as he read it, Aristotle's aims in the *Metaphysics* became clear. Because of the reverence of both al-Farabi and Avicenna for Aristotle, they are categorized by Muslims as partisans of *falsafa*, that is, Greek, basically Aristotelian philosophy. *Falsafa* is contrasted with *kalam*, which means *(dialectical) theology*, the aim of which is to explain and defend the articles of the Muslim faith.*

In spite of al-Farabi's and Avicenna's reverence for Aristotle, their cosmos is not Aristotelian but Neoplatonic in structure (Neoplatonic as modified in the course of a complex history).[65] That is, it is proved to their satisfaction that the cosmos is radiated or emanated from the absolute One, God, in successively lower stages of *being*. For the most part, they agree, God is quite beyond human conception. Strictly speaking, Avicenna explains, God cannot even be said to think, because thinking pluralizes by distinguishing subject from object. Thinking begins in a humanly conceivable way only with the first generated Intelligence or Intellect, which generates the first cosmic sphere.

From the first, singular/plural Intelligence there emanate in succession the other "angelic" Intelligences, down (as Ptolemy's astronomy re-

---

*Like *logos*, *kalam* means *word, speech, reason*. The *dialectical* of *dialectical theologians* is meant in the Aristotelian sense of reasoning that begins with widely accepted opinions rather than with true premises. Al-Farabi classifies the dialectical theologians into two groups. One is composed of those who argue that religious opinions and postulates are known by divine revelation and go beyond and even contrary to the human intellect. The other group reconciles religion with common sense and common opinion and, when in need, falls back on the trustworthiness of the first reports, or on the limitations of the human intellect. Some dialectical theologians, says al-Farabi, go so far as to silence their opponents by shame and fear, or they ward off them off by means of falsehood or sophistry. (See al-Farabi, *The Enumeration of the Sciences*, in Lerner and Mahdi, *Medieval Political Philosophy*, pp. 27–29.)

The philosophical (Aristotelian) opponents of the theologians, who prefer to base their reasoning on the principles of Aristotelian, syllogistic logic, accuse the theologians of failing to prove anything in a basic way. But the theologians use an often subtle, nonformal logic of their own, derived from Hellenistic, especially Stoic practice. Somewhat as in India, a thesis is put by a real or pretended defender and questioned by an interrogator, who tries to trap the defender dialectically. (See J. van Ess, "The Logical Structure of Islamic Theology," in von Grunebaum, *Logic in Classical Islamic Culture*.)

quires) to the tenth level, which is that of the Active Intelligence or Active Intellect (*al- ʿaql al-fa ʿʿāl*, the Greek *nous poetikos*). This last, lowest Intelligence is the Giver of Forms, the Angel of Revelation, the angel Gabriel.[66] Its reality diminished by its distance from the first in the series of Intelligences, the Active Intellect can emanate only plurality, which is to say, the world of generation and corruption. This world includes the basic intelligibles—the basic truths—and the forms of everything in the sublunar world, including human souls. The forms are projected onto matter, which is composed of the sublunar elements, earth, air, water, and fire. It is not the Active Intellect itself that is present in the human soul, but an "absolute intellectual faculty" that resembles it closely and that emanates the forms upon the soul. Although they have souls that have descended into matter, humans can use their intellectual faculties to grasp whatever is intelligible (true, real) in the testimony of their senses.[67] If enlightened, humans strive to return to God.

The whole of this complicated Neoplatonic, Aristotelian, Muslim, pedantic, poetic structure, which I have described in such an abbreviated, merely dogmatic way, is worked out by its philosophers syllogistically and in detail, some of which follows.

God, the necessary existent: Aristotle, it will be recalled, believes that motion or change requires a first, fully actual (fully necessary, fully independent) unmoved mover. Otherwise, the cosmic spheres' motion would have to depend on an endless succession of dependent beings, and the whole would remain without any true, final cause. Avicenna at first accepts this "physicist's" proof. Later he declares it does not reflect the innermost nature of Aristotle's *Metaphysics*, which deals with the existent as such, that is, with God as the cause of all that is caused. What is caused must exclude God himself because God cannot be thought to be the cause of himself.[68]

In *The Cure*, Avicenna argues the following theses in Neoplatonic style:

1. Whatever exists does so either as necessary or as possible. That is, whatever exists is necessary if assuming its nonexistence leads to an impossibility. Correspondingly, whatever exists is possible if assuming its existence or nonexistence does *not* lead to an impossibility.

2. As we know intuitively, "that whose existence is necessary through itself does not have a cause"—to have a cause contradicts the meaning of *necessary through itself*. To suppose otherwise is to contradict oneself: If the existence being considered was necessary through itself and, simultaneously, through another, it could not exist without that other, and so its existence would not be through itself.

3. As we know intuitively, the necessity for the existence or nonexistence of what is merely possible can come only from something other

than itself. This is so because if something merely possible exists, its existence rather than nonexistence has come to it from something other. And if what is merely possible does not exist—if its essence is not enough for its existence—the attribute of nonexistence comes "from a cause which is the absence of a cause for the attribute of existence."

4. The existence or nonexistence of something merely possible "becomes necessary through a necessary cause and in relation to it." Otherwise, the merely possible something requires something more to determine its attribute of existence or nonexistence. If the chain of causes would go on without arriving at anything necessary in itself, the discussion concerning the series of causes would go on to infinity and would not ever arrive at something that determines the series' existence. But this failure to arrive at a cause necessary in itself is contrary to the assumption that existence or nonexistence is necessary through and in relation to a final, necessary cause of existence.[69]

5. If we assume that there are two coequal things necessary in themselves, then we are faced with absurdities: If both things, being coequal, are also supposed necessary when considered together, each of them is necessary both through itself and through the other. Each is then both independent and dependent, which is absurd. But if, when both are considered together, each is considered necessary only in relation to itself and merely possible in relation to the other, its existence is necessarily unrelated to the other and it is able to exist without the other. If so, the two coequal things are not coequal, which is absurd. And so on.

6. Whatever exists necessarily must necessarily be one. Otherwise it would be made up of parts each differing from the other in being different from it. This difference—by hypothesis not a difference in essence— would be merely adjoined to the part's essence. The cause of the difference could not be the necessary, self-identical essence itself. Nor could the cause of the difference be something external to it, because a necessarily existing thing is wholly uninfluenced by anything external. If the cause of the difference is neither the essence of the necessary existent nor something external to it, it can only be that of the part itself. If so, the existence of the part is the result of the "accident" (the inessential characteristic) of difference. This is self-contradictory: the part's existence would be both necessary—as assumed to begin with—and also, because dependent on an accident, merely possible. And so on.

This whole proof, which is "cosmological" in type, moves from the existence of the universe to its cause, which is *being* that necessarily exists. It is the necessity of this *being*, "superadded" to the essence of whatever is merely possible, that gives everything its power to exist. Therefore, necessary *being*, God, is eternally (nontemporally) engaged in creating everything else. Because this reasoning proceeds from the effect—the universe—to the cause—*being*—and not, as usual, from cause to effect, Avicenna sees it as less than fully demonstrative.[70]

The rational soul: Human beings are able to gain true, that is, scientific knowledge because of their faculty of the rational soul (Aristotle's *nous*), by which they grasp intelligibles. The source of knowledge is the cosmic Active Intellect, which radiates the forms of the primary intelligibles. These are the basic truths, such as that the whole is greater than the part, and the laws of contradiction and excluded middle. When reflected on and combined into definitions and syllogisms, these truths make it possible to acquire secondary truths by means of deductive reasoning.

The rational soul, which grasps such truths, is an independent substance associated with the human body during a person's life, "but this association is like the relation . . . of the wielder of an instrument to the instrument. [This substance] comes into existence together with the body, not before, but it does not perish when the body perishes and dies."[71]*

To show that there is a rational, conscious, separable soul, one can make the following thought experiment: A person supposes himself created, perfectly and instantaneously, floating in empty space with his limbs separated from one another and neither seeing or feeling anything. The person would surely affirm that he exists, but would not affirm "the reality of any of his limbs or inner organs, his bowels, or heart or brain, or any external thing. Indeed he would affirm the existence of this self of his while not affirming that it has any length, breadth or depth."[72]

In infancy, the rational soul is altogether potential, and its ability to grasp universals is unused. When the forms of the primary intelligibles are

---

*By an obscure Aristotelian explanation, which does not fit in well with other of his concepts, the passive *nous* or intellect is said to die, while the Active Intellect, "which becomes all things," is sunlike, separate, unaffected, unmixed, separable, actual, always thinking, immortal, divine—"activity" in its own essence. Alexander of Aphrodisias (fl. 200 c.e.), well known to Avicenna as a commentator on Aristotle, says plainly that the Active Intellect is not part of the human soul (the form of the body) but is the divine *Nous* "come to us from without." So Avicenna has Aristotelian conceptions to use. (See Guthrie, *History of Greek Philosophy*, vol. 6, pp. 308–30. For Avicenna's argument in outline, see Gutas, *Avicenna and the Aristotelian Tradition*, pp. 84–85; for more detail, see Davidson, *al-Farabi, Avicenna, and Averroes on Intellect*.)

imprinted on it and it is able to deduce secondary intelligibles, it is the *habitual intellect*; and when it is self-consciously engaged in rational thought, it is the *acquired intellect*. And when, having the intelligibles, it can call them up whenever it wishes, it is as close as possible to actuality. At this stage it is "like a polished mirror upon which are reflected the forms of things as they are in themselves without any distortion, and whenever it stands face to face with them having been purified through knowledge, there ensues [an automatic] practicing of the theoretical philosophical sciences."[73]

The intellect acquires rational knowledge by two means, reasoning and intellectual intuition (*hads*). Both give it the middle terms of syllogisms—by "middle term" Avicenna means, he says, "the cause which makes assent to the existence or non-existence of a thing necessary—i.e., the evidence that justifies the judgment."[74]* His idea of intellectual intuition comes from Aristotle. The use of *intellectual intuition* as a companion term not only for *self-evident knowledge* but also for *revelation* or *inspiration* helps him to close the gap between rational demonstration and religious experience.[75]**

Avicenna implies that it is intellectual intuition that explains his precocious mastery of the Koran, Ismaili theories, Indian arithmetic, dialectical disputation, Euclid, and medicine. He says that when he turned again to logic and philosophy, he examined, classified, and recorded the premises and possible conclusions of every argument he encountered, and when he was unable to work out the syllogism, he would pray to the Creator to disclose the answer. At night, he would refresh himself with wine, and when asleep, he would often solve the problems in his dreams.[76]

---

*Aristotle writes: "Let A be necessarily predicated of B, and B of C; then the conclusion that A applies to C is also necessary . . . Therefore since, if we have demonstrative knowledge of a proposition, the predicate must apply necessarily to the subject, it is obvious that the middle term upon which the proof depends must also be necessary. Otherwise we shall recognize neither the fact of the conclusion nor the reason for it as necessary" (*Posterior Analytics* 75a, trans. E. S. Forster, Cambridge: Harvard University Press, 1960, p. 31).

**Aristotle writes: "Acumen (*anchinoia*) is a talent for hitting upon (*eustochia*) the middle term in an imperceptible time; e.g. if someone sees that the moon always holds its bright side toward the sun and quickly grasps why this is—because it gets light from the sun; or he is aware that someone is talking to a rich man because he is borrowing from him . . . For seeing the extremes he becomes familiar with all the explanatory middle terms" (*Posterior Analytics* 1.34, rev. Oxford trans.). Avicenna (following Matta's Arabic translation of the *Posterior Analytics*) translates *acumen* with *dhaka* and *hitting upon* (*guessing immediately*) with *husn hadsin* (*hus* for the Greek *eu* of *eustochia* and *hads* for the remainder, *stochos*). *Hads* becomes Avicenna's term for *immediate intellectual apprehension, spontaneous understanding, intellectual intuition*, or, more economically (with Gutas), *Intuition*—always by way of the middle term of the syllogism. (See Gutas, *Avicenna and the Aristotelian Tradition*, pp. 166–68, 170–73.)

The closeness that Avicenna finds between intellectual intuition and religious inspiration gives philosophy and religion the joint flavor of the rational and the sacred. It is therefore natural that in order to find the middle term of a syllogism, Avicenna prays to God.[77] Dreams make things clear, he says, because in sleep (here he is following the Arabic version of Aristotle) the imaginative faculty is undistracted and more open to the divine effluence. In this condition, the sleeper is able to see "unknown matters" either in themselves or through their images.[78] Wine, though forbidden to Muslims, is believed by Avicenna, the physician, to balance the bodily humors and dispose the person to receive the divine effluence.[79]

The Prophet and the philosopher: To Avicenna, who in this follows al-Farabi, the prophet is a man gifted with extraordinary intellectual intuition.[80] As he explains, the imagination is a material faculty and therefore cannot grasp what is universal; but the imagination puts the images received from perception at the service of intellect. If it is strong and perfect, the imagination has psychophysical force: it makes the intelligible forms transmitted by the Active Intellect into visible symbols and impresses them on the "common sense." The "common sense" then affects the visual faculty, which transmits the symbols by means of the eyes' visual rays to the surrounding air. Returning from the air, the impressions strike the eye, enter the "common sense," and return to the imagination. Having become perceptions, the forms may be powerful enough to elicit exclamations such as, "God has overwhelming majesty!" The angel that appears to the prophet and the angel's voice he hears are such phenomena.[81] With his "angelic" intellect and blazing intuition, the prophet has knowledge of present and future facts, and, by way of symbols, of the intelligibles and the higher immaterial existents.[82] However, the intellect has its difficulties with the images that imagination associates with truth—"rational deliberation has to labor hard to cope with this faculty and its ever treacherous behavior."[83]

The prophet's sensuous symbols are indispensable to ordinary people, because they cannot understand rational demonstrations. Avicenna even insists that whoever speaks the bare philosophical truth cannot be conveying a divine message to the people, for whom sensuous symbols are literal truth.[84] To be believed, the truths "communicated to the bedouin Arabs or the crude Hebrews" had to be put in symbols and anthropomorphic images. "The Koran" itself "does not contain even a hint" of the deeper truth about the central doctrine of God's unity.[85] Avicenna does at times concede that the Koran may contain hints good for philosophers, but he believes that religions would be useless if not for the metaphors and symbols used for the sake of the multitude.* He goes on:

> How can then the external form of religion be adduced as an argument in these matters? How then can one thing (i.e. the materialistic symbols of religion) be manipulated as proof for another (i.e. the purely spiritual character of the afterlife)?[86]

Avicenna's rationalism and mysticism: Like Plotinus, Avicenna expresses mystic yearnings for God, the One, and, like him, he is literally a rationalist in that he identifies the truth with reason and the rational structure of the universe. His rationalism shows in his preference for an eternal universe rather than one created in a unique event difficult for a philosopher to rationalize. Since Avicenna's universe is pervaded by soul, united (like a Stoics') by "sympathy" and responsive to powerful ideas, he can allow miracles, magic, and the influence of (true, unmechanical) prayer. This does not contradict his preference for rational explanation over of inexplicable mystery.[87]

Avicenna contends that, to protect the public, the philosopher should use a style whose obscurity tests and trains students and keeps the full truth from those unworthy of it.[88] An example of this caution is his *Essay on the Secret of Destiny*, which deals in florid, difficult Arabic with the problem of destiny. Put very simply, the problem is this: How can God be good and just if everything is caused by his power, and yet reward and punish human beings for their conduct? Avicenna answers, in an apparently intentionally obscure way: God is not to blame, because, just as pleasure and pain are the respective outcomes of healthy and unhealthy living, the "rewards" and "punishments" of the afterlife are the inevitable outcome of the soul's behavior in the present life. After death, man is no longer under obligation or on probation, so to punish him would require anger or revenge, which are impossible to God.[89]

In spite of Avicenna's pride in seeing through symbols to the reason within them, he, too, is an allegorist. His allegories are different versions of the soul's great adventure: The soul descends into matter and

---

*In *The Salvation of the Soul* (*Najat*) Avicenna says the Koran may contain useful hints for those philosophically capable of delving into "deeper wisdom." Muslim philosophers base their opinion that part of the Koran should be interpreted allegorically on a passage (3.6) that says that the Book contains some verses that are ambiguous, their interpretation known to no one "except Allah and those firm in knowledge." The more liberal Muslim exegetes takes this passage to permit allegorical interpretation. The less liberal put a period after "Allah," to exclude "those firm in knowledge" and to delegitimize the reading of allegory into the Koran. (See Rahman, *Prophecy in Islam*, p. 77, note 39.)

forgetfulness; it becomes aware—by intuition or philosophy—of the Active Intellect and its own true identity; it undergoes the struggle between its acquired intellect and its animal faculties, which are attached to matter; and it learns to unite subtle thought with virtuous passion and see God's light and, finally—after release by death—it immerses itself in perfection.[90]

These allegories are all built on the scaffolding of Avicenna's system. Their imagery is designed for nonphilosophers and generally has a point-for-point correspondence with Avicenna's philosophical concepts.[91] Yet though committed to demonstrations and universals, Avicenna may be suspected of poetic moments in which he invents metaphorical descriptions in order to try to savor in a merely human way the perfection that even a philosopher's earthly life may miss and his syllogistic demonstrations may not convey in full.[92] In any case, although the philosopher's mind—according to Avicenna's later works—can never fully lose its identity and unite with the Necessary Existent, the philosopher's progress in knowing makes him—the mind he is—engrossingly, worshipfully, yearningly, unsensuously, nobly, contemplatively actual.[93] Going by thought through the hierarchy of existents, the philosopher comes to the vicinity of the Necessary Existent. His knowing of the Necessary Existent and return to himself take no time.

> Only a rationalist ['aqil] is permitted to enjoy the inner meanings of these words. May God, may He be exalted, grant the favor of true speech and knowledge.[94]

Maimonides (Moshe ben Maimon) (1135–1204)

Then the eyes of the blind shall be opened,
and the ears of the deaf be unstopped.

Maimonides is known in Hebrew as Rambam—an acronym for Rabbenu (Our Rabbi) Moshe ben Maimon—and in Arabic as Musa ibn Maimun.[95] When he was still young, his family fled from its native Cordoba because it had been conquered by the Almohads, then sharply puritanical (but future patrons of thinkers such as Averroes [Ibn Rushd]).[96] After years of wandering in Spain, the family settled in Fez, Morocco, also ruled by the Almohads. Arabic sources (alone) speak of the family's conversion to Islam—both Maimonides' father and Maimonides himself wrote dissertations giving advice to Jews threatened by forced conversion. Following a brief visit to what is now Israel, the family finally took root in

Fostat, Old Cairo. Maimonides made his living, precariously at first, as a physician. His growing reputation led to his choice as a court philosopher-physician. Since he was by reputation—and in old age probably by official appointment—the head of the Jews of Egypt, he was intensely busy with royal patients, lay patients, and public affairs.[97]

The first of Maimonides' two major works is the *Review of (Talmudic) Law* or, in the Hebrew original, *Mishneh Torah*. This is a codification of Jewish law, influenced by similar Islamic works, with many rationalistic interpretations, rulings by extrapolation, and other signs of independence from the traditional sources (or refusal to cite those of which Maimonides made use). The *Review* insists on a God who is predominantly of the Aristotelian/Neo-Platonic (al-Farabian/Avicennean) kind: perfectly existent, cause of all other existences, incomparably one, unqualifiedly incorporeal, and the source, by means of emanations mediated by the Active Intellect, of all human prophecy.[98] The *Review* won Maimonides enduring fame among Jews but sometimes also savage opposition. The opposition was caused by its rationalistic bias and, perhaps most of all, by its tendency to ignore others' views and substitute fixed rules for the traditional give and take of interpretation, a tendency that limited the freedom of rabbis to reach new juridical conclusions.

Maimonides' second major work, the source of the following account of his thought, is the theological, philosophical *Guide of the Perplexed*, originally published in Arabic in 1197 as *Dalalat al-ha'irin* and soon twice translated into Hebrew as *Moreh Nevukhim* (in Latin translation, it is called *Dux dubitantium*). From a letter he wrote to Samuel ibn Tibbon, one of the *Guide's* translators, we know the philosophers to whom Maimonides openly admitted his indebtedness:

> The writings [literally: words] of Aristotle's teacher Plato are in parables and hard to understand. One can dispense with them . . .
>
> The works of Aristotle are the roots and foundations of all works on the sciences. But they cannot be understood except with the help of commentaries, those of Alexander of Aphrodisias, those of Themistius, and those of Averroes.
>
> I tell you: as for works on logic, one should only study the writings of Abu Nasr al-Farabi. All his writings are faultlessly excellent . . .
>
> Though the works of [Abu] Ali Ibn Sina [Avicenna] manifest great accuracy and subtle study, they are not as [good] as the work of Abu Nasr al-Farabi.[99]

The opening of *The Guide* is very al-Farabian and Avicennian in that it turns not to ordinary people, who are incapable of understanding the true meanings of the books of prophecy, but to someone who knows the true, philosophical sciences and is, all the same, a believer in matters concerning the Law "and is perplexed as to their meaning because of the uncertain terms and the parables."[100]

In this spirit, Maimonides dematerializes God, or, rather, having accepted that God is and can be proved to be incorporeal, he takes it on himself to explain why the Bible speaks—dares to speak—of God otherwise. He also proliferates warnings that he draws from the Bible. For example, in explaining the passage "And Moses hid his face, for he was afraid to look upon God" (*Exodus* 3.6), Maimonides says that, of course, God cannot be apprehended visually, so the meaning is that Moses hid his face because he was "afraid to look upon the light manifesting itself." The reason is that Moses (as Maimonides intimates but does not say directly) had not sufficiently "achieved and acquired knowledge of the rules of logic and inference and of the various ways of preserving himself from errors of the mind"—or perhaps that Moses had not quite "killed the desires and cravings engendered in him by his imagination."[101] Likewise, Solomon, a "philosopher," gives advice to the person who is not yet prepared enough philosophically and morally, advice not to be overeager to go deeply into the truth. "Guard your foot," he says, "when going to the house of God" (*Ecclesiastes* 4.17).[102]

Like Avicenna, Maimonides holds that the truth revealed by philosophy and prophecy sometimes "flashes out to us so that we think it is day," and, like him, he holds that a prophet's flashes of insight can be so frequent that he remains "always, as it were, in unceasing light" and reaches "the degree of the great one among the prophets."[103] Maimonides' own purpose, he says, is to give a glimpse of the internal, divine meanings of the holy text, and then to allow these meanings to return to their concealment. He does not want to oppose God's purpose in hiding from ordinary people the "truths especially requisite for His apprehension."[104]

For this reason Maimonides, like al-Farabi before him, looks on himself as someone who writes quasi secrets reserved for those capable of appreciating them. Al-Farabi's view is that Aristotle was able to make things openly and flawlessly clear but sometimes had to be inconsistent so as to hide his reasoning. Aristotle's need to hide his thought, al-Farabi says, accounts for his intentional omission of a premise or a conclusion of an argument, his switching of the conclusions of a pair of syllogisms, his intentional omission of something ambiguous from an apparently exhaustive enumeration, and so on. Plato, al-Farabi goes on, used different tactics for the same end as Aristotle. Knowing through experience that habitual truthfulness endangers philosophers and city alike, Plato chose the method of concealment. Writing for a chosen few, he made use of signs, riddles, and obscurity, and only sometimes expressed himself openly and literally. Al-Farabi concludes that the philosophers of his own time can communicate with ordinary people only by means of the knowledge and arguments that they share with them. Ordinary people are "in the habit of finding what is strange to them burdensome and what is out of their reach objectionable." But the art of dialectic enables the philosopher to associate with the public and yet be looked on as engaged in an acceptable enterprise.[105]

Sharing al-Farabi's anxiety, Maimonides asks the reader to connect the separate chapters of the *Guide* with one another and to connect remarks that appear in different chapters. The reader should pay attention to a word even if does not fit the chapter's general intention, because the word was chosen "with great exactness and with exceeding precision." Some statements are to be taken literally, some not, and contradictions are apparent rather than real. Maimonides prefers, he says, to liberate a single virtuous man than to displease ten thousand ignoramuses. He then gives a fairly lengthy explanation of seven causes for apparently contradictory or contrary statements to be found in books.[106]

It is probably because Maimonides has so much to hide from ordinary eyes that for long stretches—especially in its first part—the *Guide* is no more externally than an often discontinuous piecemeal explanation of Biblical terms and Biblical "parables": the philosopher's truth is hidden behind individual exegeses of separate passages. Of the consecutive philosophical text, much is devoted to a detailed statement and refutation of the position of the dialectical theologians. These theologians, who interpret the sacred word or *kalam*, are called *men of the word, mutakallimun*. Atomists, they break space into atoms and break time into indivisible instants, all in order to deny natural causality and the existence of any substance, power, or will other than God's.* God, they insist, maintains everything in existence by the addition to it of "accidents" (in an approximately Aristotelian

---

*Apart from what Maimonides says, there is no evidence that the *mutakallimun* conceive time, too, as atomic (Dhanani, *The Physical Theory of Kalam*, p. 131). Recently recovered *kalam* texts show that, by one *kalam* doctrine, the existence of everything must be renewed by God at every (irreducible) moment, but that, by another *kalam* doctrine, atoms and other large bodies last longer when God creates the accident of "continuing to exist" in them (ibid., pp. 43–45). Some—not all—*kalam* thinkers say that atoms are conceptually indivisible but that (in a sense like that suggested by Epicurus), they occupy space. That is, atoms have magnitude and shape and somehow occupy space. Nevertheless, only two atoms together can have length, four (two above the two for length) can have breadth, and eight (four above the four for breadth) can have depth as well (ibid., p. 95).

sense). In itself, there is nothing, the *mutakallimun* claim, that has the power of continued existence. They even believe "that when a man wills a thing and, as he thinks, does it, his will is created for him, his power to do that which he wills is created for him, and his act is created for him."[107]*

Like the Muslim "Aristotelian" philosophers, Maimonides feels bound to confront the position, or rather, positions, of these theologians. In the eyes of the ("Aristotelian") philosophers, the theologians' worst trait is their refusal to accept the testimony of the senses and their subversion of reason while pretending to uphold it. To them, "everything that may be imagined is an admissible notion for the intellect." To them, a human being the size of a mountain, an elephant the size of a flea, fire that cools, and water that flames are all equally possible, because it is only habit that makes us regard as necessary what we have so far experienced.

According to Maimonides, the *mutakallimun*, who confuse imagination with intellect, defend themselves with evasive stratagems.[108] In contradiction to what is perceived, they try to prove that the world is created in time by denying that anything has a nature of its own.[109] Regardless of the nature and structure of the universe as experience and logic have shown them to be, they declare that there is no real difference between the substance of iron and of cream, both being composed of momentary atoms with momentary characteristics (accidents).[110]

In agreement with al-Farabi and Avicenna, Maimonides writes that, even when reasoning without fallacies, the theologians have learned from their Christian predecessors to begin with commonly accepted but not

---

*The *kalam* doctrine of things that vanish every moment but seem stable because they are serially replaced is developed, as we have seen, in Buddhist, especially Sautrantika thought. Furthermore, the *kalam* doctrine that a single atom has no dimensions, these being constructed, with the addition of more atoms, up to three-dimensional size, makes a more Indian than Greek impression. So does the *kalam* emphasis on the composition of bodies by means of adhesion (*ta'lif*) (Dhanani, *The Physical Theory of Kalam*, pp. 152–53), which resembles the Nyaya adhesiveness or conjunction. There is also an Indian ring to the image used in the *kalam* argument that if a mustard seed was divisible into an infinite number of parts of any size at all, it would be as large as a mountain (ibid., p. 163 and Pines, *Studies in Islamic Atomism*, pp. 15, 129–130)—equivalent Nyaya examples are of an infinitely divided grain of sand equaling a mountain in size, or a mustard seed equaling Mount Meru (but the abstract principle, that infinitely divided small things would be equal in size to great ones, is also found in Lucretius [1.615–22; see Pines, pp. 16–17]). All these likenesses, combined with the known influence of Indian on Islamic astronomy, medicine, and mathematics, strengthen the likelihood that Muslim atomism shows considerable Indian influence. Pines's conclusion (p. 140) that such influence is possible is certainly more convincing than the negative conclusion of Wolfson (*The Philosophy of the Kalam*, pp. 472–74) and of Dhanani (*The Physical Theory of Kalam*, pp. 100–101, 164–65).

necessarily true premises. Their conclusions are therefore never necessary but, at most, only possible. "According to me," says Maimonides, the correct way is to use the philosophers' methods, which

> are founded upon the doctrine of the eternity of the world. This is not because I believe in the eternity of the world or because I concede this point to the philosophers; but because it is through this method that the demonstration becomes valid and perfect certainty is obtained with regard to three things: I mean the existence of the deity, His Oneness, and His not being a body—and all this without making a judgment upon the world's being eternal or created in time. (*Guide of the Perplexed* 1.71 [96b-97a])[111]

Maimonides does not try to prove God's existence on his own but begins with twenty-five premises that philosophers—Aristotle in al-Farabian and Avicennean guise—have already proved. A necessary twenty-sixth premise, on the eternity of the world, is taken by him to be unproved and he examines it at length.[112] He states that because Aristotle, unlike his latter-day followers, taught mankind the rules of demonstration, he cannot have believed that he had really demonstrated that the world is eternal.[113] Faulting the al-Farabian/Avicennean view that necessary emanation can account for the composite world, Maimonides contends that eternal necessity would not allow God to will that anything be different from what is. If necessity ruled, then God, recognized by everyone intelligent as completely perfect, could produce nothing new in any being. "If He wished to lengthen a fly's wing or to shorten a worm's foot, He would not be able to do it."[114]

This limitation of God's power, says Maimonides, is mistaken and pernicious. God is not impelled to create or to create at any definite moment; his will is completely autonomous. It cannot be objected that, in creating, God himself changes, because change, which is the transition from potential to actual, occurs only in material things.[115] If the series of spheres and other composite beings flowed from God, who is wholly one, by necessary emanation alone, then neither the length nor the modulation of the series could account for the composite nature and plurality of the world. Necessary emanation would retain an exact correspondence between cause and effect and make the corporeality of the world unintelligible: "What relation can there be between matter and that which being separate has no matter?" Maimonides asks.[116]

There are many details of cosmology, Maimonides argues, that cannot be explained as either accidental or necessitated and so cannot be accounted for on Aristotelian principles. Everywhere we find evidence of what is called (in an old *kalam* term) *particularization (takhsis)*, which applies to particular phenomena for which there is no simply natural cause. Citing the Ptolemaic deviations from the Aristotelian cosmology, Maimonides gives examples.[117] Furthermore, he says, "the diversity of the motions of the spheres does not agree with the order of their arrangement one beneath the other, in such a way that necessity could be claimed in this field."[118] Since there is no natural law to explain them, they can be understood only by supposing that an intelligent agent "particularizes" the motions of each sphere as he wishes.[119] The distribution of the stars in the eighth sphere is irregular, Maimonides points out, and such details would be very unlikely or nearly impossible if it was believed that all the cosmos

> proceeded obligatorily and of necessity from the deity, as is the opinion of Aristotle. If, however, it is believed that all this came about in virtue of the purpose of one who . . . made this thus, that opinion would not be accompanied by a feeling of astonishment and would not be at all unlikely. (*Guide of the Perplexed* 2.19 [44a])[120]

By raising such doubts, Maimonides of course weakens the force of Aristotle's proof that the world is eternal and strengthens the hypothesis of the creation of the world in time by the agency of God. It is therefore reasonable to believe, he says, that the world did not emanate from God by eternal necessity but by an act of God's will. With the grip of necessity broken, it is easier for Maimonides to contend that prophecy is not a fully natural phenomenon but that God is able to prevent prophetic emanations from reaching unqualified persons; and, in any case, Moses was an exception. Reasoning in this way, Maimonides turns Neoplatonic Aristotelianism into a theism that remains rationalistic in temper but more easily compatible with traditional Judaism.[121]

Maimonides argues that because God "particularizes," there are many questions about the world that humans cannot answer. One who believes that necessity accounts for everything in the world, has to take recourse to answers that give the lie to and annul "all the external meanings of the Law with regard to which no intelligent man has any doubt that they are to be taken in their external meanings."[122] Intractable necessity is to be rejected because "the belief in the production [creation in time] of the world is necessarily the foundation of the entire Law."[123] Rejecting the theologians' method of proof, Maimonides insists that God can be proved only by assuming, as the philosophers do, that the world is eternal. Once its eternity has been demonstrated, he adds, "the demonstration will be perfect, both if the world is eternal and if it is created in time."[124]

By such reasoning, Maimonides turns the neo-Aristotelian system he follows into one in which God creates and makes changes by his own often inexplicable will. These changes apply, among the rest, to the doctrine of prophecy. The philosophers, says Maimonides, affirm that when a person's rational and moral qualities are perfect and "his imaginative faculty is in its most perfect state" and he has been prepared, "he will necessarily become a prophet, inasmuch as this is a perfection that belongs to us by nature.[125]

But "it may happen," Maimonides goes on, "that one who is fit for prophecy and prepared for it should not become a prophet . . . on account of the divine will. To my mind this is like all the miracles."[126] As the Bible shows and the sages have said, "God turns whom He will, whenever He wills it, into a prophet." Of all the prophets, Moses was the only one to whom speech was addressed, says Maimonides, and adds, "The term 'prophet' in my judgment is said of him in a different sense from that applied to others."[127]

This statement is less decisive than it seems. Maimonides remains rationalistic philosopher enough to claim that the ultimate perfection of a human being does not belong either to action or to moral qualities. Human perfection is intellectual. It "consists only of opinions toward which speculation has led and that investigation has rendered compulsory." Only such ultimate perfection is able to give immortality, "permanent preservation."[128] The acquisition of the intelligibles that teach the truth about divine things "is what gives the individual true perfection."[129] Maimonides repeatedly agrees with the Muslim Aristotelians that immortality depends on one's intellectual, that is, philosophical development.[130] It is therefore not improbable that one of Maimonides' concealed but implied conclusions is that even Moses, whom he exalts with such fervor, was deficient as compared with a true philosopher—as already said, he judges Moses's grasp of logic and inference, that is, philosophy, to be insufficient or his freedom from the craving, engendered by imagination, to be incomplete (although elsewhere he teaches that Moses's prophecies were all based on intellect, "without action on the part of the imaginative faculty").[131]

Maimonides' attempt to have the best of both the theologians' and philosophers' worlds makes him bewildering: The great prophet must (possibly) be the perfect philosopher who (almost certainly) does not exist, because so much is unknowable to human beings. Philosophy must be based on faultless logic, but we can prove that God exists only if we base the proof on the uncertain premise that the world is eternal. And when we prove, on this assumption, that God exists, we are free to assume the opposite, that he created the world in time.

To escape bewilderment, a thirteenth-century commentator objects that Maimonides cannot mean just what he says:

> How can one demonstrate such an important subject by means of a dubious thing, and so much more so if this thing is not true . . . and how with such premises can one form a demonstration that is not doubtful? . . . Most certainly, this could not have escaped our master, who has disposed all his words wisely.[132]

This disciple's remark shows why Maimonides is so elusive. Maimonides' radical interpreters react by assuming that Maimonides always favors the rationalistic "Aristotelian" view. That is, contrary to what he explicitly says, he does *not* believe that the world was created in time, or that the individual human soul—perhaps not even the philosopher's soul—survives. Maimonides' disciple and translator, Samuel ibn Tibbon, openly interprets Biblical creation as an allegorical version of Aristotle's teaching in the *Meteorology*.[133]*

Moderate interpreters of Maimonides believe that he aims to harmonize philosophy with traditional religion. That is, Maimonides interprets much of the Bible as allegory meant to teach philosophical truths; he justifies the commandments rationally when possible; and he accepts Aristotle's account of the sublunar world. However, say the moderate interpreters, Maimonides insists on retaining orthodox religious views on the creation of the world, on the human inability to understand God's will, on the reality of miracles, on the truth of prophecy, on the survival of the soul, and on the nature of providence.[134] In the words of a contemporary philosopher who sees Maimonides in this temperate light:

> The Rambam rejects out of hand the notion that there might be any conflict between the underlying burdens of the later and earlier revelations. The Torah, as a whole, is a dynamic unity which serves to inculcate human virtue, civil, personal, intellectual. And it does so by means which are immutable, so long as human nature does not change.[135]

---

*Like Ibn Tibbon, the contemporary scholar, Sarah Klein-Braslavy, contends that "the semantic key used by Maimonides" to interpret Biblical creation is Aristotle's *Meteorology*. He uses it exegetically to understand all its processes, which are therefore referred to the realm of "the atmosphere, and not . . . to a creation *ex nihilo* of the celestial bodies," so the Biblical term *creation* signifying any particular thing's creation applies to its functioning in its total physical context. (See Ravitsky, "The Secrets of the Guide to the Perplexed," p. 184, summarizing both Klein-Braslavy's work and his own; and see S. Klein-Braslavy, "King Solomon and Metaphysical Exotericism According to Maimonides," in Hyman, ed., *Maimonidean Studies*.)

Why, asks the philosopher, does Maimonides write his *Guide* in so apparently erratic a style? The answer is that Maimonides' intellectual situation is such that he finds it expedient to avoid writing a treatise. That is, he adopts the much more easily evasive form of the Arabic *risalah*.[136] This form, based on the literary letters of Classical antiquity, allows Maimonides to assume that the reader already knows a good deal and is committed to the writer's aim. The style of the *risalah* does not push the writer, as would that of a formal treatise, to become dangerously explicit.*

Among contemporary interpreters of Maimonides, there is one who takes an unexpected way out and denies that the text of the *Guide* is written in a manner meant to expose the truth only to those able to penetrate the *Guide's* circumspection. "In reality," says this interpreter, Maimonides "was trying to present the argument in as clear and terse a form as possible."[137]

I end my description of Maimonides with two interpretations that seem to me both interesting and relatively plausible. The one is made by Shlomo Pines, the specialist in Muslim philosophy whose translation of the *Guide* I have mostly used. Pines rests much of his interpretation on the likeness between Maimonides and al-Farabi, both of whom are intentionally secretive and inconsistent. Maimonides, al-Farabi's admirer, mentions four of his books, one of them the lost commentary on Aristotle's *Nichomachean Ethics*.[138]**

---

*This style gave Maimonides not only the ability to adopt "the legal fiction that he was not teaching metaphysics and cosmology publicly (as required by the Talmud), but also the ability to address problems without stating them. Thus, he could begin in medias res and follow the 'esoteric style' well familiar to him not only from the Aristotelian corpus but also from the Bible and the Talmud. In all of these books, one needs to read much or all before one can make use of any. And the reason is that one is not told at the outset what is at issue. Maimonides was so successful with this strategy that few readers of the Guide, including specialists, down to this day, can state correctly what the subject matter is of the bulk of Part I" (Lenn Goodman, personal communication).

**Ibn Tufayl (d. 1185), a Muslim contemporary of Maimonides, is concerned to show that al-Farabi's philosophical writings are "plagued with contradiction." He points out that in one work ("The Virtuous City") al-Farabi says that the souls of the wicked suffer eternal, infinite punishment, in another ("Political Regime"), that only virtuous and perfect souls survive death, and in a third (the *Commentary on Aristotle's [Nichomachean] Ethics*) that human happiness exists only in this life, and that, in effect, "everything mentioned beyond this is senseless jabber and tales told by old women." Ibn Tufayl adds that al-Farabi also declares that philosophy should be considered superior to prophecy. But Ibn Tufayl does not allow for the possibility that al-Farabi is interpreting Aristotle's view or is speaking only of "human" or "political happiness," which he ordinarily distinguishes from the happiness possible only in the other world. While al-Farabi is not notably consistent, would he say something in his own name so blatantly out of keeping with his other philosophical writings and so careless of the danger to the philosopher, of which he is acutely aware, of speaking too plainly? (See Mahdi, "Philosophical Literature," p. 99 [quoted]; and Pines, translator's introduction to Maimonides, *Guide of the Perplexed*, pp. lxxx.)

As Pines emphasizes, in the last pages of the *Guide*, Maimonides says that after an individual has achieved the human perfection of knowing God and, with it, "permanent perdurance," his way of life, assimilated to God's actions, "will always have in view *loving-kindness, righteousness,* and *judgment.*"[139] For an Aristotelian, these words may appear a weak conclusion, too oriented toward the social and ethical. But Maimonides does not limit the noblest ends "only to the apprehension of Him, may He be exalted."[140] He is too concerned with the welfare of the people who live in states "through the abolition of reciprocal wrongdoing and through the acquisition of a noble and excellent character."[141] The last pages of the *Guide* therefore bring to mind al-Farabi's statement that philosophers are by nature political and should "live in harmony with the public, love them, and prefer doing what is useful to them and redounds to the improvement of their condition (just as it is incumbent on them to do the same in our regard)."[142]

On reflection, we may take Maimonides' last words to be the solution to a delicate problem. To see why, it is necessary to recall that he doubts Aristotle's reasoning concerning the heavenly spheres and God. He believes that whatever the human intellect can fathom in relation to these is no more than probable or negative. For "everything that can be ascribed to God, may He be exalted, differs in every respect from our attributes." No definition of any concept is adequate to God; even the term *existence* can be applied to him only equivocally.[143] And if, in addition, the best proof of God's existence is based on a doubtful premise, to what degree can the human intellect grasp, which is to say, become identified with, God's pure intellectual immateriality? Surely, to have loving-kindness, righteousness, and judgment in view is not enough, in Maimonides' opinion, to guarantee the immortality of an individual intellect.[144] If, as Maimonides (ambiguously) intimates, perfect theoretical knowledge is not available to human beings, to them, it is practical, "political" activity that expresses the highest degree of worship. Human perfection is then identified with the imitation of God's attributes of action, with walking in the ways of the Lord as the world's governor.[145]

Such an earthly *imitatio dei* may reflect al-Farabi at his most radical. It does appear to reflect al-Farabi's view that the philosopher should engage in politics, and that he, the king, the legislator, and the imam should be one and the same person. This ideal has no equivalent in the *Guide*, but Maimonides himself lived a life not incompatible with it; and he agrees with al-Farabi in giving especial praise to a prophet who is a lawgiver and the founder of a virtuous community, like the one created by Moses, that aims at perfecting the intellects of its members.[146]

The second interpretation of Maimonides to which I have referred is that of Leo Strauss, best known as a political philosopher but also a passionate student of the *Guide* and its perplexities, which he shared. According to Strauss, the secret of the *Guide* is not its Aristotelianism, from which Maimonides deviates for religion's sake, but its identification of philosophical reasoning (as expressed in the Aristotelian sciences) with the exegesis of Biblical passages such as those that describe creation and the chariot in Ezekiel's vision.[147] The old foundation of faith having being destroyed, Maimonides is compelled to be

> passionately concerned with demonstration, with the demonstration not only of God's unity but of His very being in a sense of "being" that cannot be entirely homonymous. For he now knows that the being of God is doubtful as long as it is not established by demonstration.[148]

According to Strauss, to understand Maimonides, one must understand his perplexities.[149] The greatest is that Maimonides commits himself as deeply to divine revelation and Jewish morality as to philosophical thought. The religious and the philosophical can learn from one another only if neither surrenders its approach to truth.[150]

Thomas Aquinas (1224/5-1274)

The theology of holy teaching differs in kind from
that theology which is ranked as a part of philosophy.

Thomas Aquinas or, in Italian, Tommaso d'Aquino, was the son of one of the barons of Emperor Frederick II.[151] At the University of Naples, where he studied, the controversial views of Aristotle—those other than his logic—were already being taught. He soon joined the Dominicans, a recently founded mendicant order devoted to learning. Disturbed by this choice, his family waylaid and confined him for some two years, after which he rejoined the order. His most important posts as a teacher were at the University of Paris from 1256 to 1259 and, again, from about 1269 to 1272. He also served at the papal court as teacher and adviser. Reserved and often abstracted, Aquinas prayed with devotion and honored his commitment to poverty and austerity. In December of 1273, he underwent a crisis and abandoned his work with the complaint, "All that I have written seems like straw to me."[152] The following year he died, only forty-nine years old.

It was a great day, philosophically, when, on March 19, 1255, the writings of Aristotle, physical, metaphysical, and moral, were entered into the arts curriculum of the University of Paris and their teaching was declared mandatory (and rivalry with the faculty of theology was encouraged).[153] Aquinas himself demonstrated his preoccupation with Aristotle by writing commentaries on twelve of his works; and he accepted the commitment made by his teacher, Albert the Great, to the use of philosophical, which is to say, Aristotelian demonstration.* But like Albert, his commitment depended on the belief that the science of demonstration should not conflict with theology, the science of revelation.

Aquinas' productivity was so implausible that it inspired the report that he composed while asleep.[154] Of his many writings, the most impressive are two great *summas*, as full, well-ordered syntheses were called.[155] The first is the *Summa against the Pagans*, *Summa Contra Gentiles* (1259–64), probably meant to help Dominican missionaries persuade the Muslims of North Africa—Muslims, said Aquinas, accept neither the Old nor the New Testament, so must be persuaded by natural reason, "to which all men are forced to give their assent."[156] Therefore the *Summa Contra Gentiles* is intended to be mainly philosophical; it is only in the fourth, last book, on the trinity and incarnation, that the balance tilts clearly toward theology.

Aquinas' second great synthesis is the *Summa Theologiae* or *Summa Theologica*, its more usual name.** Begun about 1265 and left unfinished,

---

*In his *Summa Theologiae*, Albert follows Avicenna's example and paraphrases Aristotle's philosophy in its usual systematic order (Van Steenberghen, *Aristotle in the West*, pp. 177–79). But for all Albert's and Thomas's Aristotelianism, they are teachers of theology, not philosophy. Even some two centuries later, when Erasmus separates the philosophers, who claim exclusive wisdom, from the theologians, a different, "remarkably supercilious and touchy lot," Albert's and Thomas's students are regarded by Erasmus as theologians, whose "subtle refinements to subtleties are made more subtle by the different lines of scholastic argument, so that you'd extricate yourself faster from a labyrinth than from the tortuous obscurities of realists, nominalists, Thomists, Albertists, Ockhamites and Scotists" (Erasmus, *Praise of Folly* 52, 53; trans. A. H. T. Levi, Harmondsworth: Penguin Books, 1971, pp. 151, 152–53, 156).

**It is divided into three main parts, the second of them divided into two. The subdivision of a part is a *question* (*questio*), whose further subdivision is an *article* (*articulus*). In all, the *Summa* contains 512 questions divided into 2,669 articles. Part Three, which breaks off unfinished, has a supplement pieced together from Aquinas's other writings. Disregarding the *Summa's* more narrowly theological content, its "Prima Pars" (1a) takes up God's existence and attributes—unity, perfection, goodness, infinity, immutability, and eternity; God's knowledge, will, love, justice, mercy, providence, and power; the emanation of all created things from God; the union in humans of body and soul, and the powers of the intellect; and God's government of the world. The "Prima Secundae" (1a2ae) takes up happiness as the human goal; human acts (voluntary and involuntary); the functioning of the human will (good and malicious); habits, virtues, and sins; and law (eternal, natural, and human). The "Secunda Secundae" (2a2ae) takes up faith, hope, charity, religion, and the virtues. The "Tertia Pars" (3a), on Christ, is entirely theological.

it was meant for students of theology. This *summa* has often been compared to a cathedral. To see the comparison, one must remember that, for Aquinas, sacred doctrine uses human reasoning not to prove the faith—to prove it would detract from the merit of believing—but to make the doctrine's implications manifest *(manifestare)*.[157] This is to make visible the scheme of reasoned faith by the enumeration of its principles, parts, and details, and by the articulation of their arrangement, that is, the symmetrically repeated divisions and subdivisions that clarify the levels and interrelations of the truth that they manifest. What in this resembles a cathedral? The answer is that a cathedral of the High Gothic period is an attempt to embody all Christian knowledge in a well-articulated structure that balances traditional elements, uniformly divided and subdivided, in a complex structure made of homologous subunits, not unlike the complex structure of a cathedral, with its nave, transept, and chevet, and their homologous internal divisions.[158]

In the *Summa Theologiae*, each question is worked out in a sequence of units and subunits. The question with which the *Summa Theologiae* opens is "On what sort of teaching Christian theology is and what it covers." Aquinas answers by defending the position that what human reasoning can discover by itself must be supplemented by what God reveals.[159] As an example of the logical relationship of units, I choose the beginning of the second question of the *Summa*. The question is whether there is a God. Then comes a subquestion or "article" (Is it self-evident that there is a God?). Then comes a first objection (It seems self-evident that there is a God). The objection is supported by an authoritative quotation (from St. John of Damascus, saying, "the awareness that God exists is implanted by nature in everybody"). The point of the objection is supported by a second objection (that a proposition is self-evident if we perceive its truth immediately upon perceiving the meaning of its terms—as when we understand the meaning of the word *God*). The point is supported by a third objection (Even in denying the truth we admit it—if there was no truth it would be true that there is no truth) and backed by a quotation ("I am the way, the truth and the life").

The objections are followed by the statement of the author's position on the question (On the contrary, he says: Although it is impossible to think the opposite of a self-evident proposition, it is possible to think the opposite of "God exists"). The statement of the answer is supported by an authoritative quotation ("The fool said in his heart, there is no God"). There follows the writer's reply (saying in general that an intrinsically self-evident proposition is not always self-evident to human beings). This reply is supported by an authoritative quotation and by rational argument ("God exists" is inherently self-evident, yet not self-evident to us, because to us it is not self-evident what it is to be God). Then come answers to the three initial objections (The awareness of God's existence is not clearly or specifically implanted in us; some people have believed God to be a body; and it is self-evident that there is truth in general but not that there is a First Truth).[160]

This first article of the second question, whose structure I have just described, is soon followed by what is probably the best-known passage of the whole *Summa*, the statement of five different ways of proving that God exists. In summary:[161]

1. The first, most obvious way (Aquinas says), is based on change, change understood in the Aristotelian sense of "motion" from potentiality to actuality. Such change or motion is caused by something other than what moves: it is something actually hot that changes something else from potentially to actually hot. The process by which one thing is changed by another, which is changed by another, and so on, can begin only in some first cause—which alone (who alone, Aquinas says) can cause change without being changed by anything. "And this is what everybody understands by God."

2. The second way is based on the nature of causation. In the world we observe, Aquinas states, causes come in series. Nothing can cause itself. To cause itself it would have to precede itself, which is impossible. But a series of causes must have a first member. If there was no first cause, there would be no intermediate cause, nor any last effect. So one must believe in a first cause, "to which everyone gives the name *God*."

3. The third way is based on the difference between what need not exist and what exists necessarily. Not everything can spring into existence and die away. The reason is that whatever does not necessarily exist goes out of existence at some time or other. Given enough time, there would come a time when nothing was in existence. But what does not exist can be brought into existence only by something that does exist. So if there ever was a time when nothing existed, nothing would now be in existence. This contradicts what we in fact observe. One is therefore forced to assume that something must exist that owes its existence to nothing else and is itself the cause for the necessity of the existence of other things. "And this everyone calls *God*."*

---

*This proof is a near repetition of one by Maimonides (*Guide* 2.1; trans. Pines, pp. 247–48). Maimonides' proof depends on Avicenna's contrast between the possibly existent and the necessarily existent. According to Avicenna, to avoid an infinite regress, a first cause must exist necessarily and by virtue of itself, and it must therefore have the attributes assigned to God. Maimonides puts this proof in terms of potentiality and actuality (*Guide* 2.1; trans. Pines, p. 249). Variants are stated by Albert the Great and Aquinas (*Summa Contra Gentiles* 1.15). Whatever its direct source, the proof turns up in cosmological and ontological variations used by later philosophers, among them Leibniz and Spinoza. (See Davidson, *Proofs for Eternity, Creation and the Existence of God*, pp. 378–406.)

4. The fourth way is based on the gradation we observe in things. Some things, as we find, are better, truer, or more noble than others. All such comparative terms describe the degree to which an absolute is approximated: *hotter* implies *hottest*, that which (Aristotle says) causes everything else to be hot. Something therefore exists that is the truest, best, and most noble of things and causes the being, goodness, or other perfection in everything else, "to which everyone gives the name *God*."

5. The fifth way is based on the government that the natural world reveals. All bodies, even those with no awareness, that obey natural laws show regularity of action. Their action varies very little and almost always turns out well. This shows that they tend to a goal and do not reach it by accident. But nothing that lacks awareness tends to a goal except if directed—like an arrow by an archer—by someone who is aware and understands. Therefore, everything in nature is directed toward its goal by someone with understanding. "And this we call God."

These five proofs, which I have represented fairly, are clear, but they do not show Aquinas at his painstaking, subdividing best.* What they do show is how dependent he is here on Aristotle and how little original he wants to be in offering the proofs. As they demonstrate, his views are basically those of a Neoplatonizing Aristotelian like Albert the Great. Often they sound like a more conservative, more theistic version of al-Farabi or Avicenna and may therefore be close to Maimonides' overt position.[162]

Aquinas cites Avicenna about 450 times, sometimes to agree with him and sometimes to disagree.** His disagreements should not lead us

---

*Aquinas goes through these proofs in much greater detail in the *Summa Contra Gentiles*, mostly with the help of Aristotle. In stating the first way, Aquinas summarizes Aristotle's proofs from motion: Everything moved is moved by another, and so on, making it necessary to believe that an unmoved mover must be posited (*Physics* 241b, 234b, 254b). Aquinas also cites Aristotle's argument, derived from his conception of potentiality and actuality, that nothing moves itself (*Physics* 257a, 201a), to which he adds Plato's argument—compatible with Aristotle's, he says—that the first mover does move himself, but only in the sense of knowing and willing or loving himself (*Phaedrus* 247c). For the second way, Aquinas goes through Aristotelian proofs that there can be no infinite regress among movers and things moved (*Physics* 241b, 234b, 241b, 247b, 256a; *Metaphysics* 994a, 993b).

**To enumerate the major points of disagreement: Avicenna believes that, except for God, *being* is added to give existence to merely possible things; Aquinas believes things have their own intrinsic being. Avicenna thinks of the intelligences or souls of the spheres as "angels," each of which creates the sphere just below, down to the last sphere, the soul of which is the Active Intellect, the Giver of Forms, the Angel of Revelation. Aquinas, on the contrary, to minimize the influence of Muslim and Jewish philosophy on him. The extent to which he draws on or (because of his intellectual situation) comes to argue like Avicenna, Averroes (Ibn Rushd), and Maimonides can be followed in his writings.[163]* Of these philosophers, the most radicalizing was Averroes, whose commentaries on Aristotle were translated between about 1220 and 1230. It was not long before the more adventurous masters contended that philosophy—as Aristotle had taught and as their Muslim teachers had repeated—is the highest of callings. One of these masters, Siger de Brabant, said plainly that those who comment on the Philosopher's books should note "that his opinion is not to be concealed, even though it be contrary to the truth."[164]

What was most disturbing in Averroes was his doctrine, more radical than Avicenna's, that a separate transcendent intellect—in which both

---

sees the creative ability assigned to the spheres as a limitation on God's omnipotence. So, too, he sees the necessity of the emanation of spheres as a limitation on God's freedom. Necessary emanation also implies, he says, that human beings cannot have free will, because, if such necessity prevails, it follows not only that the movements of the heavenly bodies rule human bodies but that the movements of the heavenly souls rule human souls. Instead of an Active Intellect from which truth emanates to human potential intellects (which are also emanations), every human soul has its own active intellect and potential intellect, which is illuminated by God. Aquinas also refuses to accept Avicenna's opinion that God knows individual things only by means of universals, or that the ability to prophesy can be simply natural, or that there can be no resurrection of bodies. (See Avicenne, *La Métaphysique du Shifa*, trans. G. C. Anawati, Introduction, vol. 1, pp. 67-73; and, on Avicenna's influence on Scholasticism in general, Davidson, *al-Farabi, Avicenna, and Averroes on Intellect*, pp. 209–17.)

*Consider the following examples of arguments in Aquinas that resemble those of Avicenna, Averroes, or Maimonides: 1. Avicenna and Averroes contend "that the underlying matter of the universe must be eternal since matter could have only have come into existence from an already existing, prior matter." Maimonides, Albert the Great, and Aquinas all record this argument and all say that it is not conclusive (Davidson, *Proofs for Eternity, Creation and the Existence of God*, p. 13). 2. Avicenna holds that matter cannot come into being from nothing because, before it comes into actual existence, it must first be possible, and this possibility or potentiality must in a sense be existent. This argument, too, is cited by Averroes, Maimonides, Albert the Great, and Aquinas (Davidson, *Proofs*, pp. 16–17). 3. Against the arguments for the world's eternity, Maimonides contends (*Guide* 2.17) that the nature of anything that comes into existence is different from both the nature of that from which it comes into existence and from its own nature during the process of coming into existence. Because of these differences, no inference can be drawn from the nature of an already existent thing to its earlier nature or natures. So "the nature of the stable, perfected, actual universe" cannot prove that the universe must always have existed. Those who believe in the creation of the world from nothing—creation after nonexistence—do not believe that it came into existence in accord with the present laws of nature. This reasoning is repeated in Albert the Great. Similarly, Aquinas argues that the laws that relate to the realm of nature do not necessarily relate to the realm of divine nature (*Summa Theologiae* 1.45.2, ad. 2; 1.46.1, ad 3). (See Davidson, *Proofs*, pp. 31–35.)

philosophers believed—is directly and identically present in all human souls. What disturbed was the conclusion that if the immortal principle of human souls is the one eternal intellect, immortality cannot be personal.[165] It is against this doctrine, as taught by Siger, that Aquinas directs the arguments of his treatise *On the Unity of the Intellect* (*De Unitate Intellectus*) in 1269.[166]* In this treatise, Aquinas argues that even if we accept, on Aristotelian principles, the existence of a single active intellect, each human soul (as the commentator Themistius explains) has its own active intellect that, illuminated by the transcendent intellect, illuminates the souls' potential intellect. Aquinas contends that Averroes perverts Aristotle and that, on Averroes' theory, the individual persons' actual thinking cannot be explained.[167]

The emphasis in Aquinas' polemical treatise is different from that in the earlier, much fuller account, in the *Summa Theologiae*.[168] In the *Summa*, Aquinas adopts the general definition of the soul or *anima* as that which animates, gives life. He says that a human soul is not merely nutritive and sensory, but also rational; being rational, it must also be incorporeal; and, being incorporeal, it "subsists," meaning that, as a substance in its own right, it acts independently.

Aquinas explains: There are four internal senses or sensory powers, the common sense, the imagination, the cogitative power, and the memory. Of these, it is the common sense that gives awareness of the impressions made on the external senses, and it is the imagination (phantasia) that stores the images or "phantasms" of the objects that have made the impressions. These stored images retain the individuating details of their external source. But although color, for example, is always individuated in a colored body, it is not mistaken to consider color and its properties apart from a colored apple. "This is to consider the nature of the species apart

---

*Because of his attempt to be faithful to Aristotle, Averroes in time gives up the idea that the universe is the result of successive emanations. He holds, instead, that each cosmic intelligence or intellect exists in its own right. The Active Intellect does not emanate natural forms. Its function is to illuminate the eternal material intellect and the images in each human imagination. By this unusual conception, the material intellect is a species intellect that is only potential in individuals. "The material intellect, acting as a medium, permits individual imaginative faculties to acquire individual intelligible thoughts . . . And now that the material intellect is immortal merely because it is an incorporeal substance from the start, no shred whatsoever of the individual man will be able to survive the body's demise" (Davidson, *al-Farabi, Avicenna, and Averroes on Intellect*, pp. 228–31, 355–56 [quoted]). This later view of Averroes was available to Siger and Aquinas in Averroes' Long Commentary on *De Anima*, translated into Latin about 1230 (ibid., p. 300). Averroes' commentary is reflected, it seems, in Aquinas' refutations and is the source of much of Siger's *Quaestiones in Librum Tertium de Anima*, which is dated before 1270 (ibid. p. 305). (See also E. P. Mahoney, "Sense, Intellect, and Imagination in Albert, Thomas, and Siger," in N. Kretzmann, A. Kenny, and J. Pinborg, eds., *The Cambridge History of Later Medieval Philosophy*.)

from the particular, or the intelligible species apart from the phantasm."[169] And so, from a stored image (of, perhaps, a colored apple), the active or agent intellect abstracts the nature, form, quiddity ("whatness"), or intelligible species of what is being perceived (the apple's color, perhaps). The intelligible species is then stored in the potential intellect. It is only the active intellect—which can become and make all things—that can abstract the species from the individuating matter that the phantasms represent; and yet it knows these natures as they are *in* the phantasms.[170]

Obviously—at least in this life—the intellectual soul needs the body to supply it with objects. Every act of perception must therefore be an act of the soul compounded with the body. Aristotle has said that understanding is an act of the soul—the only such act—that takes place without a physical organ. But the soul is only part of human nature and no more a whole person than is a hand or foot.[171] Yet because it is a principle that cannot *not* be, the human soul must be immortal.[172]

So to Aquinas the human being is a single substance whose soul (as intellect) is the subsisting, immaterial, imperishable form of the human body. Speaking of the soul's creation theologically, as he must, he states that it is created by God each time a new human individual is born.[173] He also recalls that Aristotle says that the soul is not merely added to the body as its motor but belongs to the body as closely as the shape of a piece of wax belongs to the wax.[174] When the body dies, powers such as sensation and nutrition, the subject of which is the body-soul compound, survive only in a virtual form. But the intellectual powers remain in the soul when the body dies.[175] After death, the nature of the soul remains the same. Even though its union with the body was in keeping with its character, it must now have another mode of being. Now it no longer understands as it did when united with the body but "by means of participated species [or 'likenesses' (*similitudenes*)] resulting from the influence of the divine light."[176]

As has been noted, Aquinas' doctrine of the soul is in part a response to the belief of Avicenna and Averroes in a transcendent active intellect, and of Averroes in the unity of all human intellects. Aquinas also feels it necessary to respond to these philosophers' argument that the world must be eternal. Like Maimonides and Albert the Great before him, Aquinas' response is that the eternity of the world is both unprovable and irrefutable.[177] He agrees that the world was created necessarily, but only in the sense of complete dependence on God, not in the sense that it was brought into existence at a particular time. This solution, which Aquinas proposes in his brief treatise, written in 1270 or 1271, *On the Eternity of the World* (*De Aeternitae Mundi*), permits the world to be both created, as the Bible has it, and eternal, as the philosophers prefer.[178]

Aquinas begins the treatise by stating that it would be an intolerable error against both faith and philosophy to claim that anything eternal (other than God himself) was not created by him. But if the claim is only that there is something that always existed but is wholly created by God, the claim merits examination.[179] Aquinas asks: Is the creation of something that always existed a logical impossibility? He answers: Some thinkers hold that God can do the impossible, or hold that he cannot do it "because of its nonentity" and because his power is "to do what is real." But although I am convinced, he says, that it is wrong to hold that God can do the impossible, this opinion is not heretical.[180] However, as is not impossible, God can produce an instantaneous effect, and so "he does not have to precede his effects in duration." Analogously, a fire begins to heat at the very moment that it comes into existence and the sun radiates light—produces the form of light—instantaneously. As these analogies prove, it is not impossible that an efficient cause should *not* precede its effect in time.[181] Furthermore, even if one takes the statement that something was made from nothing to mean that something was made after nothing, the term *after* is used very abstractly and may just as well indicate priority in nature as priority in time. This is not to say that nothing and *being* exist simultaneously—nothing did not precede *being* in time. "Thus, therefore, it is clear that in the statement—for something to be made by God and never to have existed—there is not anything unintelligible."[182]

At the end of his treatise, Aquinas recalls an old problem: Souls survive the death of the body, so their number keeps increasing. If the world is eternal, there is a paradoxically infinite number of surviving souls in existence. Aquinas' solution is that God could have made the world without human beings or made them after the world had already been in existence for a long time. "And furthermore it has yet to be demonstrated that God cannot make an actually infinite multitude."[183]

In 1270, the year when Aquinas wrote his treatise on the eternity of the world, the bishop of Paris, disturbed by philosophers' radicalism, made an ineffectual condemnation of four propositions: that the soul is one, that the human will is determined, that the world is eternal, and that there is no divine providence. Seven years later, on the authority of the same bishop, 219 propositions, a number of Aquinas' among them, were declared heretical. One of the social roots of the condemnation is revealed by the condemned propositions "that the philosophers alone are the wise men of the world."[184] The condemnation encouraged the conservatives and intimidated the others. However, by weakening the scholastics' tie to Aristotle, it stimulated them to consider alternatives to his natural philosophy.*

---

*For instance: The condemnation of the view that God could not produce more than one world led to the speculation that God could create many worlds each with its own center and circumference. This gave a many-world alternative to Aristotle's single, closed world. Likewise, the condemnation of the view that God could not move the world in a straight line because a vacuum would be left behind led to the speculation that there was empty space

In the context of his times, Aquinas proved a resourceful synthesizer of different currents of thought. More systematically and less ambiguously than Maimonides, he created a union of rational, that is, Neoplatonic Aristotelian "science," a metaphysically infinite God free to act as he willed, and belief in the truth, literal or metaphorical, of the scriptures.[185] He is notable mainly for the breadth, seriousness, cohesion, and viability of his synthesis. In his praise, a Thomist scholar says (and emphasizes with italics) that his is *"the first really original [Christian] philosophy produced by the thirteenth century and, even, by Christian civilization in general."*[186]

Discussion

Philosophical synthesis is the attempt to make different philosophical techniques, themes, and approaches intellectually and therefore also socially cohesive. As described here, the Indian synthesis is primarily of (Nyaya) theory of knowledge with (Vaisheshika) metaphysics and cosmology and with (Vedic) religion; the Chinese synthesis is primarily of (Confucian) hierarchical ethics with (Buddhist) selfless altruism and (Buddhist and Taoist) tranquility, and with (partly Taoist) cosmology; and the European synthesis is primarily of ("Aristotelian") philosophy with scriptural dogma (Muslim, Jewish, or Christian).

Although these syntheses are perhaps even more beset by philosophical problems than other, less openly synthesizing philosophies, this does not prevent them from serving—briefly in the Muslim case—as stabilizing centers of their respective traditions or subtraditions.* Of the

---

beyond the world into which the world could be moved. And if God could create an (anti-Aristotelian) vacuum outside of the world, why not inside it as well? "Analyses of these and similar 'thought experiments' were often made in terms of Aristotelian principles even though the conditions imagined were 'contrary to fact' and impossible within Aristotelian natural philosophy" (Grant, "The Effect of the Condemnation of 1277," pp. 538–39).

*The institutional basis for philosophy among the Muslims and Jews was weak. It is usually said that philosophy in the "Aristotelian" sense soon died out among them. But the relevant history has not been much explored, and the generalization may reflect prejudices concerning the nature of philosophy. The fourteenth century was perhaps the most flourishing period of Jewish "Aristotelianism" (Sirat, *A History of Jewish Philosophy in the Middle Ages*, p. 342). The last considerable philosophers in the medieval Jewish tradition were Gersonides (Levi ben Gershom [1288–1344]) and Hasdai Crescas (1340–1412).

In Islam, theology overbore ("Aristotelian") philosophy. Sharp, socially effective criticism was leveled against it by al-Ghazali (1058–1111) and Ibn Taymiyah (1263–1328), a traditionalist who argues that Aristotelian logic can give knowledge only of universals, not of existing things. In reviewing the sciences, including philosophy, the sociologist and historian Ibn Khaldun (1332–1406) "refutes" philosophy as "wrong in all its aspects" because it deals with completely unknown essences. Philosophers, he says, fail to understand that intellectual speculation cannot give us joy like that of direct mystical experience (Ibn Khaldun, *The Muqaddimah*, pp. 398–405 [401 quoted]). However, Avicenna's philosophy continued to influence theology for a time. It lingered most openly in Persian-speaking territories, among "illuminists" such as al-Suhrawardi (c. 1155–1191). The last considerable illuminist was Mulla Sadra (Sadr ad-Din ash-Shirazi [c. 1571–1640]).

group of five philosophers, Chu Hsi, a moral teacher more than a metaphysician, does not engage in sharply logical debate. The technically sharpest critic among the five is clearly Udayana, the most architectonically developed is clearly Aquinas, and the most down-to-human is clearly Chu Hsi; but they and Avicenna and Maimonides are all masters of their specific forms of argument, with which they support but often transcend literal interpretation of their scriptures. Yet even Udayana, so expert in exposing weaknesses, leaves the impression that everything critical and constructive he says is designed to support a preexisting system, which therefore acts as a dogma to be defended—the technical resourcefulness accentuates the fundamental dogmatism.

The group of Neoplatonizing Aristotelians: The two Muslims, al-Farabi and Avicenna, the Jew, Maimonides, and the Christian, Aquinas, share much of their scriptural heritage, although in different, mutually rather hostile ways. All depend on the same philosophical background, a Greek tradition in which Plato (little known directly) and Aristotle (recast by commentators) are presumed to be expressing the same Neoplatonically structured truth. For the two Muslims, the Jew, and the Christian, Aristotle is the paradigmatic philosopher, the "medium through which the ancient philosophers . . . benefit the future ones."[187] Plotinus and Proclus are not known to them by name but are present by proxy in their thought, especially in the doctrine that it is the unknowable One, *being* in itself, from which everything emanates and toward which everything tries to return.

The Neoplatonic doctrine so providentially readied for the philosophical theology of Muslims, Jews, and Christians is, of course, adapted by the four philosophers to the needs of their respective religions.[188] Neoplatonism is doctrinally difficult for them because its scheme of natural and eternal emanation excludes God's individuating will, his personal concern, and his unique act of creation of the world. Each of the four philosophers feels bound to resolve such difficulties, at the cost, if necessary, of ambiguity or ambivalence. Al-Farabi, Avicenna, and Maimonides often come close to declaring that scripture is nothing more than philosophical truth vulgarized to appeal to the ignorant, literal-minded majority. Yet each begins with a faith he accepts, as far as we can tell, sincerely and, in any case, cannot deviate from very much without paying too heavy a price.[189] The result is that each of these philosophers appeals strongly enough to reason to put him in religious danger and strongly enough to faith to put him in philosophical danger—a socially unequal balance but, to the philosopher, a poignant one.

The desire, difficulty, and danger in attempting the balance are illustrated by the Parisian prohibitions of 1270 and 1277 and their sequels. Another illustration is that comprised by the legal and philosophical arguments of al-Ghazali, the theologian, jurist, and Sufi mystic, and the counterarguments of Averroes—in this Muslim context, to be called Ibn Rushd—the doctor, jurist, judge, and Aristotelian commentator and philosopher.* Al-Ghazali raises a question of Muslim law: What allegorical interpretations of scripture (the Koran and sanctified tradition) go beyond the learned Muslims' legally binding consensus (ijma) and deserve to be stigmatized as disbelief, that is, apostasy. Though sometimes unfortunately trivialized, al-Ghazali says, the charge of disbelief "is a legal pronouncement that involves confiscation of property, capital punishment, and the sentence to eternal punishment in hellfire."[190] Thinking juridically, he finds that two doctrines of al-Farabi and Ibn Sina, God's ignorance of particulars and the impossibility of bodily resurrection, contradict the Koran, imply that Mohammed was a liar, and constitute disbelief. In his philosophical book, he adds, as a third instance of disbelief, the doctrine that the world is eternal.[191]

Ibn Rushd gives an elaborate answer. In its course, he says that al-Ghazali himself shows that one must be tentative in calling people disbelievers for violating the consensus of the learned. So when al-Ghazali calls al-Farabi and Ibn Sina disbelievers, he does not mean to be categorical. In such questions, there cannot be any unanimity of the learned. Historically, this is because many early believers and others showed they accepted allegorical interpretation. Their acceptance is evident because they caution "that there are allegorical interpretations which ought not to be expressed except to those who are qualified to receive allegory."[192]

I cannot go into the arguments with which Ibn Rushd harmonizes philosophy with religion by explaining, explaining away, or softening the three of his doctrines that al-Ghazali stigmatizes. Ibn Rushd's pragmatic and legal argument takes the following line: Like legal theorists, philosophers need a great deal of time, much cooperation, and intensive study to arrive at satisfactory results. Without geometry and astronomy, which were

---

*The more legalistic side of the debate, continued by Ibn Rushd over a divide of some eighty years, is the subject of al-Ghazali's *The Decisive Criterion for Distinguishing between Islam and Unbelief (Kitab Faysal al-Tafriqah . . .)*, written between 1096 and 1106, and then of Ibn Rushd's brief work, *The Decisive Treatise, Determining the Nature of the Connection between Religion and Philosophy (Kitab Fasl al-Maqal . . .)*, written about 1179. Ibn Rushd states that the purpose of his *Decisive Treatise* is "to examine, from the standpoint of the Law, whether the study of philosophy and logic is allowed by the Law, or prohibited, or commanded—either by way of recommendation or as obligatory" (Averroes, *On the Harmony of Religion and Philosophy*, p. 44 [of the translation]). The purely philosophical side of the debate is found in al-Ghazali's *The Incoherence (or Disintegration) of the Philosophers (Tahafut al-Falasifah)*, finished in 1095, and Ibn Rushd's *The Incoherence of the Incoherence (Tahafut al-Tahafut)*, dated about 1180.

perfected over long periods of time by many men, how could anyone learn the sizes, shapes, and distances from one another of the heavenly bodies?[193] Ibn Rushd's conclusion is that the Law obliges us to study the science developed by the ancients

> since their aim and purpose in their books is just the purpose to which the Law has urged us, and that whoever forbids the study of them to anyone who is fit to study them [fit by natural intelligence, religious integrity, and moral virtue] is blocking people from the door by which the Law summons them to knowledge of God, the door of theoretical study which leads to the truest knowledge of him.[194]

Ibn Rushd then says, with telling brevity, "Truth does not oppose truth but accords with it and bears witness to it."[195] He explains: The lawyer must use reason in order to infer a decision that scripture implies rather than states explicitly. In much the same way, the philosopher must use reason to solve an apparent discrepancy between scripture and demonstrative science. The aim of his interpretation is to make evident how the inner meaning of scripture agrees with the demonstrative truth.[196] This need for interpretation makes it evident that those who are fit to study philosophy are obliged to do so. However, the allegorical meanings given should be recorded only in "demonstrative books," where only persons "of the demonstrative class" encounter them.[197]

Toward the end of his discussion of the legal status of philosophy, Ibn Rushd recalls, emotionally and somberly, the sorrow and pain that was caused him

> at the hands of people who claim an affinity with philosophy. For injuries from a friend are more severe than injuries from an enemy. I refer to the fact that philosophy is the friend and milk-sister of religion; thus injuries related to philosophy are the severest injuries [to religion].[198]

Rationalism, universality, and tolerance: The very attempt at synthesis is bound to make the synthesizing philosophers acutely aware of the bounds set by scriptural dogma. But avid for truth, the *Nyaya-sutra* favors its discovery by means of doubt and debate, and Udayana certainly shares the usual tolerance of Indian philosophers to arguments they are barred by faith from accepting. Indian philosophers such as Udayana give usually rational answers (salted, maybe, by sarcasm they cannot resist) to even Veda-denying arguments. Denunciations, if any, may precede or follow the arguments but do not ordinarily replace them. However, I do not know what degree of social tolerance Udayana advocates or whether, apart from his commitment to reasoned argument, he sees it as a problem for his philosophy.

Chu Hsi I have described as growing intolerant because of the social threat he perceived in Buddhism and Taoism. He is unfair, I have argued, in his presentation of Buddhist doctrines. But he continues to admire certain Buddhist and Taoist qualities. His resulting emulation of those for whom he has little tolerance allows him to recommend selfless altruism (like that of Buddhists) even outside the family, and to try to make such altruism compatible with the Confucian emphasis on family and hierarchy. This emphasis explains why the altruism he recommends comes into typical play in the relations between superiors and inferiors. Chu Hsi also tries to combine Confucian activity (i fa) with Buddhist-Taoist tranquility (wei fa) and achieve the ideal state of activity in tranquility. In sum, Chu Hsi is not at all intolerant when a Buddhist or Taoist value appears useful for the synthesis he is creating.[199]

Al-Farabi, Avicenna, Averroes, and Maimonides are very special instances of tolerance that stems from the conclusion that their scriptures should be understood philosophically rather than literally. Because they are sure that ordinary people have no philosophical understanding, they contend that the prophets had to provide the people with imaginative symbols and anthropomorphic images. As reported earlier, Avicenna dares to say (somewhat inconsistently with his other, less extreme remarks he makes) that ordinary people depend so much on anthropomorphism that the Koran contains not "even a hint" of the truth about the unity of God.[200] Al-Farabi remarks that some religious symbols are more adequate than others, nearer to the essence. But they can vary considerably from one another, so that

> the religions of even good societies and states come to differ, even though they all believe in an identical type of salvation (or happiness), since religion is only the imaginative symbols in the minds of a people . . . These things are thus allegorized for every nation or people in terms familiar to them, and it is possible that what is familiar to one people is foreign to another.[201]*

---

*"Al-Farabi and Averroes, while maintaining the superiority of Islam in religious symbolism, do not, to my knowledge, derogate any other religion by name. Avicenna, however, has attacked Magianism and Manicheaism . . . and Christianity . . . The former are accused of producing an unintelligible symbolism (light and darkness). Against Christianity it is urged that its symbolism is ineffective. The question concerns the resurrection of the body. If, Avicenna says, you regard the body as man or as part of man, then, of course, you must believe in the resurrection of the body; but then why not speak of bodily happiness and unhappiness? If, on the other hand, happiness and unhappiness are purely spiritual, what is the sense in affirming bodily resurrection?" (Rahman, *Prophecy in Islam*, p. 78, note 41).

Like al-Farabi, Avicenna, and Averroes, Maimonides agrees that a prophet need not be of the religion the philosopher accepts as best, even though the prophet must be perfect in every way—physiologically, morally, psychologically, and intellectually.[202] A non-Jew who is sufficiently moral (in the sense of the Jewish Bible) and is on a high enough philosophical level is no less capable of achieving immortality than a Jew.[203] The Messianic era, Maimonides predicts, will be without famine, war, jealousy, or strife. In this era, the Christians and Muslims will recant their errors and will return to the true, original monotheism, that of Judaism.[204]

Seers, sages, prophets, philosophers: Each of the synthesizing philosophers comes to be looked on as a sage and may perhaps think of himself as one. But in keeping with the conservative side of his nature, the sage philosopher thinks it imperative that he be a spiritual descendant of earlier sages—of the sages of the Upanishads and those responsible for the Nyaya and Vaisheshika Sutras; or of Yao, Shun, Confucius, and Mencius; or of Plato, Aristotle, and—depending on the faith in question—Moses, Muhammad, or the Church Fathers.

In India there does not appear to have been any decisive distinction between the sage and the philosopher, nor was there such a distinction in China (except in a sort of divinizing of Yao and Shun and Lao-tzu and Chuang-tzu). However, among the Muslims, Jews, and Christians the issue of the likeness or difference between the prophet and the philosopher was a matter for detailed controversy.

To begin with Udayana, as an observant Hindu, he is committed to belief in the Veda, created—he thinks he proves—by God. He is also committed to belief in the truth of the doctrines of sages known to be truthful, reliable, and selfless. As an adherent of Nyaya-Vaisheshika, he accepts the typical Indian belief in yogic perception, "which apprehends all objects, subtle, hidden, remote, past, future."[205] The yogalike perception of the sages responsible for the scriptures is the result of "the contact of the *manas* [mind organ] with the self and a peculiar *dharma* or power born of austerities." Such intuitive cognition, unrelated to the sense organs, is a distinct, vivid perception free of doubt and illusion. Never vacillating between alternatives, it is found to be in actual agreement with the facts.[206]

Chu Hsi gives a purely naturalistic explanation of sagehood. Take, for example, the great sages Yao and Shun. According to him, it is because they "received the clearest and the purest material force" that they were "intelligent, spiritlike, and sagely." Confucius, too, "received the clearest and purest material force, and was born with knowledge from the start." By his time, however, the material force of the universe was weak, and his own force was not long lasting, so he was not effective enough politically—he failed to be appointed to office—and he lived only a moderately long time.[207]

The explanations of sagehood and prophecy given by al-Farabi, Avicenna, and Maimonides are also naturalistic, in the sense that they depend on the unvarying nature ascribed to the universe.[208] As we have seen, the explanation accepted by al-Farabi, Avicenna, and Maimonides is that the higher forms of prophecy, like veridical dreams, are emanated by God by way of the Active Intellect. These philosophers make the immodest equation of the superlative prophet's inspiration with the philosopher's intellectual intuition. Therefore, prophets such as Muhammad (for Avicenna) and Moses (for Maimonides) are philosophers who have the ability, lacking in ordinary philosophers, to put philosophic understanding into symbolic form. Just how al-Farabi, Avicenna, and Maimonides conceive the tie between imagination, intellect, and the different levels of prophecy need not occupy us here.[209] Maimonides, who follows the Muslims' lead, declares that it is natural for everyone with the right, adequate disposition to become a prophet, though in accord with the free will of God—in this conclusion, he breaks with al-Farabi and Avicenna.[210]

Along with al-Farabi, Avicenna, and Maimonides, Aquinas recognizes that pagan prophecies are natural. He, too, agrees that prophecy requires intellect along with imagination. However, having deprived the Active Intellect of its cosmic position, it is easy for him to consider prophecy to be the gift of God, which he may grant even to those who are not, to begin with, attuned to it. God can will to strengthen the imagination of the person he wants to make a prophet—the prophecy itself goes from God to a (metaphysically real) angel and from the angel to the prophet.[211]

The different ways that medieval philosophers conceive prophecy are critical points of their synthesis of reason with faith. The ways represent strategies for either identifying or distinguishing between philosophy and prophecy, and for deciding whether or not the philosopher knows the ultimate truth as well as or perhaps better than the prophet.

Synthesis and physics: The philosophical synthesizers discussed here have an incautiously comprehensive vision. Comprehensiveness is needed because the syntheses would remain radically incomplete if the philosophers did not set their leading abstractions in the context of the universe as a whole. Even so predominantly an ethical philosopher as Chu Hsi feels that synthesis requires cosmology: If one preaches moral reform, one wants to know how morality relates to the nonhuman world and what in the world can be expected of the pursuit of morality. To Chu Hsi, it is essential that although Heaven and Earth have no conscious mind, it is their mind that is the humaneness inherent in every human mind, and that it is the original equilibrium of the human mind that must be retained and preserved. Aided by the doctrine of Principle and material energy, Chu Hsi counters the Buddhist disintegration of persons, things, and moral tradition.

As has been described, Udayana makes use of Nyaya analysis and Vaisheshika metaphysics to establish the characteristics of the world. His cosmology supports his realism (in the philosophical sense) and his belief in God. That is, his realism depends on his belief in matter, which depends on his proof that there are atoms. And the nature of the atoms is such that a visible material universe can never be constructed unless a cosmic intelligence, God, gives the atoms special characteristics that make possible the three dimensions and the order that the world in fact exhibits.

To generalize, all the syntheses discussed here require the reality of substance—to Udayana, al-Farabi, Avicenna, Maimonides, and Aquinas, common observation and morality require substance in things and persons. And for all four, common observation and morality also require a superlative or at least (for Udayana) a supervising God. Udayana's position is nullified by the Buddhist dissolution of the substance of things and persons, especially selves, and by the Buddhist substitution of a law of causality for God. Analogously, the positions of the four medieval philosophers is nullified by the Kalam dissolution of things and souls. While Udayana uses atoms to prove God's existence, inherently insubstantial atoms are the instrument that enables the Muslim dialectical theologians to conceive of a universe that depends wholly on God's repeated acts of will. In contradiction to these theologians, al-Farabi, Avicenna, Maimonides, and Aquinas conceive an Aristotelian universe, one in which atoms are a logical impossibility—a universe different not only from that of the conservative Muslim and Jewish atomists but from that of the faithless, materialistic atomists of ancient Greece and Rome. To each kind of atomist his own doctrinal habitation.

Chapter 10

✳

Logic-Sensitized, Methodological Metaphysics

Gangesha, Descartes, Leibniz

Theme: How to Pursue Certainty, Metaphysical and Empirical, by Means of a Methodically Applied Logic

Each of the three philosophers, Gangesha, Descartes, and Leibniz, is a logician. He is a logician in the sense that he wants to understand the world by isolating the methods by which we reason from the particular subjects they are applied to, in the hope that this will enable him to improve the methods and apply them more successfully. Gangesha does his best to perfect an existing logical technique for ensuring the soundness of induction, the most dependable means of knowledge, he is sure. Descartes has the ambition to substitute mathematics for syllogistic logic, because syllogistic logic, he says, is helpless to solve real problems.[1] Leibniz, who is a genuinely creative logician, loves, uses, invents, and imagines logic, whether of a known or still-unknown variety.[2] All three philosophers are committed to acutely formal care in reasoning. Their logical methods are intended not to dismiss the empirical world but to grasp it in its complexities, to apply not only to philosophy but to life as well, in Descartes's case even to medicine, and in Leibniz's, to law. Gangesha's preoccupation with the problems of valid induction and parsimonious explanation is in spirit like that of contemporary philosophers of science. Descartes and Leibniz are themselves active scientists with an extraordinary range of interests. Descartes's own scientific and philosophical practice is too intuitive to make a convincing illustration for the method he advocates, but he resembles Gangesha and Leibniz in attempting to create a metaphysically unquestionable basis for an understanding of the world that joins the empirical and theoretical and secular and sacred.

Gangesha (fl. 1320 A.D.): Certainty by "Invariable Concomitance"

Gangesha was a villager who settled in Mithila.[3] It is said that he was illiterate as a youth—a story not in itself implausible but of a kind told to the greater glory of those to whom it is ascribed.[4] There in Mithila, his followers, beginning with his son, established their own philosophical tradition or, rather, subtradition. His most famous book, *A Thought-Jewel of Truth (Tattva-chintamani)*, is meant, Gangesha says, to ornament scholars and to deprive opponents of their proofs; it earned him the name The Jeweler.[5] Comprehensive, concise, and acute, it is much the most successful philosophical text of its era. Its three hundred or so pages (in modern printed editions) were responsible, it is estimated, for over a million pages of commentary.[6] Gangesha's position was thought different enough to be called the "New Nyaya"—Navya-Nyaya—that is, to translate clumsily, the school of the newly logicized epistemic ontology. Its style of philosophizing came to dominate Nyaya and relegate old works of the Logic School to obscurity.

Gangesha makes philosophy the unmistakable preserve of those who have mastered a specialized language. He and his followers compose definitions that stretch the mind and invite exact criticism, but only of those who have become adept at manipulating the relevant technical terms and modes of reasoning. Because much of his philosophy is an elaboration of Udayana's, on whom I therefore draw here, Gangesha's originality is exhibited more in his dialectics, in the care and acuteness with which he reasons—splits hairs, it is easy to say—than in fundamental theory.*

---

*Udayana may well be the more original of the two. Greater originality has also been ascribed to Raghunatha (fl. 1500 C.E.), Gangesha's successor, commentator, and critic. A later Navya-Nyaya philosopher praised for depth and originality is Gadadhara, the seventeenth-century commentator of both Gangesha and Raghunatha. Writing of Navya-Nyaya, the late Bimal Matilal says: "The masters of Navya-nyaya did not lay down conclusions first and justify them later with theory. They were seriously engaged in following reality wherever it might lead them, imposing as softly as possible their own prejudices . . . It is precisely the same trait that

Gangesha's *Thought-Jewel of Truth* is organized into four parts—perception, inference, comparison, and verbal testimony—corresponding to the four Nyaya means of valid knowledge. The first part or book, on perception, contains a notable discussion of *pramanya-vada*, that is, of the theory of the instruments of valid knowledge or, to put it somewhat differently, the means of veridical awareness.[7] The second book, on inference, contains a long section, to which I will return, called *Inference of God*. Gangesha's discussion of inference was so influential, it is said, that for some three or four centuries Navya-Nyaya philosophy flowed through channels cut by its single sentences or phrases.[8]

Gangesha is committed to the Nyaya belief in a real, external world, in a real, nonmaterial self, and in the especial ability of perception and inference, each aiding the other, to reach certainty. To explain how Gangesha understands perception, I begin with the Nyaya view of the mind and the self. As already explained, in Nyaya doctrine the mind is an unconscious internal ("sense") organ or cause that channels to the conscious self the successive sensations that come from the external sense organs. By doing so, the mind "contributes" the event of perceptual knowing, which is the particular perceptual awareness or instance of perceptual cognition that the conscious self, so to speak, "possesses."

Because we can become particularly aware of only one kind of perceptual object at a time, we infer that the mind is not present everywhere. If it was, it could be connected with several senses at once. It is therefore reasonable to conclude that the mind can be connected with only one sense at a time. This limitation is taken to imply that the mind is of an absolutely minimal size, that of a single atom, and is therefore below the threshold that confers actual dimensions—extension—on composite structures.[9] It is only after the mind comes into contact with a particular sense that it connects with the self; and the self, which, unlike the mind, is conscious, synthesizes the testimony of the different sense organs.

It is the self that accounts for memory, as (Nyaya contends) Buddhist theory cannot. The Naiyayika asks: If there was no conscious, lasting, mediating self, how could a past perception of blue account for the later memory of this selfsame blue? If not for the self and the memories it

---

I find admirable among the creative workers of modern science and philosophy" (*The Navya-nyaya Doctrine of Negation*, p. x).

While I have great respect for Matilal, his words are not always applicable to Gangesha. When Gangesha conducts the discussion, described later in this chapter, on the existence of God, he is thorough and vigorous in reporting objections to his own view—maybe he sometimes even invents an opposing view in order to show how neatly he can overcome it. But his conclusions, on God at least, are the preordained expressions of Nyaya doctrine.

preserves, how could anyone explain that something I once saw with my left eye is later recognized by my right eye, and that I know that I am seeing what I saw before? If not for the self, the memories it preserves, and its mastery over the different senses, how could anyone explain that my sense of taste is affected and my mouth begins to water when I see a color or smell an odor that reminds me of a sour fruit I once tasted.[10] Besides, the self is the only possible seat of consciousness. Our self cannot be a property of our body—the body is something that, to consciousness, is *mine*—nor be a property of the senses nor of the "mind," which, like the senses, is only an unconscious instrument of the self. So the only possible substrate of consciousness is a real, stable, permanent, and independent self, that for which the body exists.[11]

The mind and the self described, we can go on to perception and awareness. Gangesha develops the Nyaya view that a perception can be partly valid knowledge (*prama*) even when it is in part untrue. For example, even when a rope is mistaken for a snake, there is *some* true knowledge, knowledge of the "thisness" of the object lying on the ground. The false part of the perceptual awareness rests on the partial or full identification of what is in fact seen, with a different kind of object: I am unquestionably aware of something curved and long on the ground, which I misidentify as a snake. The evidence that proves my perceptual awareness as a whole to be right or wrong is the success or failure of the actions that follow from the awareness: only a snake, not a rope, actually bites.

In making this point, Gangesha follows Udayana and other Naiyayikas with the help of a distinction between initial awareness or cognition, which cannot be mistaken, and later awareness or cognition, in which mistakes are possible.* Gangesha's is perhaps the first elaborate Nyaya explanation of the differences between the two kinds of awareness. It is only by reflecting on the nature of perception, he repeats, that we come

---

*The word translated here as *awareness* or *cognition* is *jnana*. Some expositors prefer *knowledge*, *apprehension*, or *judgment*. In any case, *jnana* refers to an instance of awareness or cognition of something, a (particular case of) knowledge. In Nyaya, there is no pure consciousness. "The conscious subject, or self, is analyzed as the subject that *has* cognition or *jnana*, the obvious conclusion being that a *jnana* or cognition-particular is a quality (*guna*) or a qualifier (*dharma*) of the self . . . something belonging to the self . . . which is its substrate or locus. A *jnana* is a particular just as a color spot or a tone is a particular." A *jnana* is *of* or *about* something that is its object. Acts of perceiving, inferring, knowing, doubting, wondering, guessing, remembering, and dreaming are all instances of *jnana*. Emotional or volitional states are not instances of it, their relation to objects being supposed to depend on or result from a *jnana*. The implicit argument for the distinction may be that to want, hate, or love something, one must first have an idea of what it is. (See Matilal, *The Navya-nyāya Doctrine of Negation*, pp. 6–8.)

to understand the necessity for distinguishing between the two. To know what something is, we have to be able to recognize it, and to be able to recognize it, we have to be aware *what* it is, what *kind* of thing it is, that is, to know by what property or "real" or universal it is qualified. For what initially comes into awareness must be a particular indeterminate something or "this" that is joined with a property—such as *cowness*—that inheres in or accompanies it. But neither the subject appearing in the awareness, the particular something-possibly-cow, nor the generic property are in the beginning conceptually joined with one another, so that there is still nothing the perceiver can make out clearly, name, or report.*

Therefore, when we analyze awareness, we find that it begins unstructured, unrelational, unqualified. This awareness without conceptualization (*nirvikalpaka jnana*) is the kind that "is not conjoined with a name, a universal, etc.," that "does not apprehend anything as qualified and which is devoid of any qualifier whatsoever."[12] What succeeds it is the kind of awareness that is structured, relational, qualified—awareness with conceptualization (*savikalpaka jnana*).[13] We fully know what we perceive only when we become aware of it as the complex composed of the generic with the particular, or, more fully, of the qualifier, the qualified, and the relation between them, and we are able to say—triumphantly!—*pot*, or *this is a pot*.

It is only after we have already become aware of something that awareness of awareness becomes possible. Often, we are too affected by the content of a thought to think that we are thinking it. But simple awareness may be followed by self-reflective awareness or aftercognition,

---

*An object is known by means of its general properties, among them the generic property or universal that accounts for its sameness with others of its kind. The qualifier in awareness is a common property of what is qualified, the qualificand. The terms for universal, *jati* or *samanya*, are sometimes considered synonymous, sometimes not; but their possible distinction is not relevant here. According to Nyaya, a universal is eternal and is real (though not in the same way as substances, qualities, and movements are real). The universal is also fully *one* even though it is fully resident in each particular. It can be grasped, that is, observed or perceived, only when it inheres in a particular. There are times—the most drastic being the dissolution of the world—when there may be no particulars in which a certain universal inheres; but a universal is possible only if the particulars in which it inheres are possible. A universal reveals itself directly in awareness; a particular is recognized—identified—only by means of its inherent universal. If one thinks of these (Nyaya) generic properties or universals as having instances rather than as inhering in particulars, one is making a Platonic or Aristotelian translation of a view that is neither.

A qualifier or distinguishing mark is called a *visheshana*. What is qualified, the qualificand, is a *visheshya* or *dharmin* (the possessor of a property, *dharma*). When one is aware of a pot, the universal *potness* is the qualifier, the *visheshana*; the qualificand, is the *visheshya* or *dharmin*.

expressed in words such as "*I am aware of this.*" Gangesha, of course, allows his philosophical opponent, the objector, to voice his objections to all these conclusions, and objections and answers to them go on in the usual contentious way of Indian argument.[14]

Perception is the basis for inference, to which Gangesha now turns. He begins by answering an objector who argues that, unlike perception, inference is not a reliable instrument of knowledge—things that have occurred together a hundred times may not occur together afterward.

To this, Gangesha answers: Your argument against inference depends on an inference. When you say that inference is not an instrument of knowledge you mean that it is doubtful or false to state that it is such an instrument. But that it is doubtful or false cannot be known by means of perception. So when you say that inference is not an instrument of knowledge, you contradict yourself by using an inference. In any case, because there is doubt of the validity of perception, its validity cannot be intrinsic but must be proved by inference, so that if inference is invalid, perception, too, is invalid, because then there is no proof of its validity.[15]

To explain the nature of inference, Gangesha turns to the subject of pervasion. As we already know, according to Nyaya, a sound inference—an error-free (deductively formulated) induction—depends on pervasion (*vyapti*), which is helpfully but imperfectly translated *invariable comcomitance*. The philosophical term *vyapti* comes from a verb meaning *to reach or spread through completely* or *to pervade*. Examples are the way that salt pervades the sea, that a large circle pervades—includes—the small circle inside it, and that two coinciding circles pervade each other. In the stock Indian example we have encountered, the possessor of fire pervades that of smoke; but smokiness (or, to use a better but nonstandard word, smokeness) does not pervade fieriness (or fireness). This we see by the example of red-hot metal, which is fiery but gives off no smoke: the relation between smokiness and fieriness is not reversible because there can be fire without smoke.

To Gangesha, pervasion is the unconditional relation produced by the very nature of a reason or cause, such as the unfailing relation of smokiness with fieriness, which is the relation that in this case can be explained by the nature of fire and the nature of smoke as the product of fire. To call the knowledge unfailing is also to say that we do not know anything that shows the relation to be accidental. This seems clear enough. But before Gangesha gets to a definition of pervasion that satisfies him, he discards twenty-one proposals and arrives at a result too intricate to discuss here.[16] Based on the terms of the Indian "syllogism," the definitions he discusses are probed by him to see if they withstand criticism. That is, he tests each definition to see whether or not it covers all types of pervasion between properties (such as fieriness (or "fireness") and smokiness (or "smokeness") that allow correct inferences to be made, that is, allow only cases that fall under the definition of pervasion. In other words, the definitions he tests are hypotheses, attempts to formulate the state of affairs by means of which to characterize an adequate pervasion or invariable concomitance. In modern European terms, an adequate pervasion is the relation responsible for guaranteeing a fully adequate induction. Though Gangesha's solution cannot be put both completely and simply, much simplified it is:

> There is pervasion of A by B if, and only if, A has a common locus with B in such a way that B is none of the things that qua class are completely absent from some locus of A.[17]*

If one has doubts, says Gangesha, they can be cleared away by a careful consideration of the nature of the particular concomitance. For example, we can test the invariability of the concomitance of fire with smoke—that there is fire wherever there is smoke—by analyzing the kinds of possible doubts, setting aside each one in turn, and convincing ourselves that there is an absence of instances of smokiness without fieriness. We test the concomitance by setting out the possibilities: If we doubt that smoke is invariably caused by fire, then it is either *always* caused by something other than fire, or it is *sometimes* caused by something other than fire, or—if not caused by fire or anything else—it must appear without any cause at all. What we know about fire and about the causal conditions of smoke does not support any doubt that fieriness pervades smokiness.[18] The inference is very well founded.

---

*If, for the sake of comparison and logical convenience, one takes the conceptual risk of translating common properties, as Indians see them, into Western class relations, then the explanation of pervasion that follows is this: "Pervasion is conceived as a relation between two classes in the sense that one class pervades the other (e.g., 'fire pervades smoke' means that the class of fires pervades the class of smokes), in the same way as inclusion, or implication, is thought of as a relation between two classes in the sense that the one includes, or implies, the other" (Goekoop, *The Logic of Invariable Concomitance in the Tattvacintāmaṇi*, p. 116).

If, to remain faithful to the Indian idea of common properties, one avoids the language of class relations, then Gangesha's final, twenty-second definition can be translated as follows: "Invariable concomitance is the coexistence of the property x (i.e., a probans) with the property y (i.e., a probandum) which is not what is qualified by the delimitor of the counterpositiveness of an absolute absence which does not have a common locus with its counterpositive and which has a common locus with the property x" (Wada, *Invariable Concomitance in Navya-Nyāya*, pp. 127–28). Gangesha's definition turns out to be imperfect because it "suffers from the defect of narrow-application" (p. 155). Wada also translates the later, more complex and satisfactory definition by Raghunatha (p. 136).

What about errors? In a familiar context, we have considerable ability to avoid or correct them. To return to Udayana for the moment, consider the case of a man whose eye disease makes him see the moon double. Even the repeated experience of this doubling will not be enough to convince him that what he sees is really double. He knows that the perception of the double moon resembles the false kinds of perception of which he has learned, and he knows that it contradicts the answers he got when he was first struck by the disease and asked others if he was seeing rightly. Human behavior also shows that in practice there often is no doubt as to the correctness of a cognition or certainty of a concomitance, and this certainty in practice contradicts and ends the doubt that theory raises. The pragmatic nature of certainty and doubt is enough—as Gangesha agrees with Udayana—to show that the removal of one's justified doubt need not be followed by other doubts in an infinite series.[19]

The skeptic (Shriharsha) is unimpressed by Udayana's solution. He points out that Udayana depends on the contradiction between theoretical doubt and the action that contradicts that doubt. But to assume such a contradiction is to assume that that particular doubt and action are necessarily and universally opposed to one another (or, technically, do not occur in the same substratum). Where there is activity, then, there is no doubt, and where there is doubt, there is no activity. This negative relation is just as clearly an instance of universal concomitance as is a positive relation. In appealing to contradiction, so the skeptic objects, Udayana merely exchanges one difficulty— the possibility of doubting that universal concomitance can be reached—for another—the possibility of doubting the assumption that activity is universally related to the absence of doubt. And if Udayana defends himself with another inference, that is, by appealing to some other concomitance, it, too, will be subject to doubt. It is impossible to establish that two phenomena observed to occur together in a limited number of cases must continue to occur together at distant times and places.

To this criticism Gangesha, as always, has an answer: His predecessor, Udayana, says that he does not imply that contradiction involves a universal concomitance. He states only that it is obviously absurd for someone who doubts the connection of smoke with fire to light a fire whenever he wants to produce smoke. By noticing this absurdity and pointing it out as self-evident—a procedure that does not have to be justified by reasoning that involves a universal concomitance—we are able to reason our way out of our doubts concerning the basis of the inference, the universal concomitance.

Furthermore, it is a fact that we get rid of doubts. If someone is unsure whether what he sees at a distance is a tree or a man, it is enough for him to come closer and make out whether the ambiguous object has branches and leaves or hands and feet. Such certainty, such knowledge of universal concomitance, does not arise from the mere repeated observation but from experience, that is, from the reasoning that removes possible doubts about universal concomitance. Once we have such knowledge, we usually act without reflecting on the knowledge by which we act. We need to overcome a doubt about the status of this knowledge only when the doubt in fact arises. The reasoning that ends the doubt may lead us beyond mere knowledge into the awareness that we know. But simple knowledge or awareness is usually enough for action.[20]

Recalling an old Nyaya view, Gangesha adds that there are certain convictions so deeply ingrained in human thought that it is impossible to doubt them. On reflection, therefore, it is also impossible to doubt the universal comcomitance that underlies these convictions or what is logically derived from them. According to this old view, there is no need to enter into a regress of doubts, because such convictions cannot be assailed by doubt.

No number of observations, however great, shows concomitance to be certain. Knowledge of the concomitance comes all at once: Seeing a particular instance of smoke is the result of a particular contact of smoke with the visual organ. In the awareness that results, the previously cognized qualifier (such as the generic or universal property, the universal) is *smokeness* and the object of the qualification is the particular occurrence of smoke. As a universal, smokeness gives general awareness of all occurrences of smoke at all times and places—its loci are all the particular occurrences of smoke everywhere. And so the awareness of the universal cannot be the result of its own contact with the visual sense. Instead, it results from the contact of the visual sense with the particular occurrences of smoke in which the universal inheres. The presence of this universal in all the particulars that belong to it makes knowledge of universal concomitance possible.[21]*

---

*There is a clear analogy here with Aristotle's theory of induction, in which a single sense experience can give an intuition of the universal common to all its instances of the same nature. But the Naiyayikas do not say that the universal (the qualifier, the generic property that serves as a qualifier) such as smokeness is instantiated in a particular smoke, but that the universal occurs in a particular locus of smoke. A "real" universal is one that, among other conditions, has at least one locus in which to occur (Matilal, *The Navya-nyāya Doctrine of Negation*, pp. 16, 17). Some Nyaya philosophers use the term *samanya* synonymously with *jati* for a generic property or "real" universal; some use *samanya* more broadly, to include *all* common properties, every property that can serve as a qualifier. (See Ingalls, *Materials . . .* , p. 42.)

The mere observation of two things happening together a few times is not enough to justify the assumption of a universal concomitance. Nor is the agreement of many persons. Gangesha consistently denies the (Mimamsa and older Nyaya) argument that the universality of a belief—the length of time it has been held or the number of those who hold it—establishes the belief's truth. If widely applied, such an assumption would make belief the criterion for inference and make recourse to inference impossible. Why? Gangesha asks. Because, he answers, the assumption would lead us to accept all often-observed associations—and only such associations—as necessary ones. But these past associations, observed for subjects different from the present subject of inference, have not yet been shown to be relevant to it—the association must be observed in the case of the present subject as well. Simply to assume the relevance of the past observations to the case we are concerned with would have an absurd result: The past observations would give us knowledge of the universal concomitance of the property to be proved and of that which is *different* from the present subject.[22]

There remains the skeptic. But he is less than he seems:

> He invariably lights up a fire if he wants to produce smoke . . .
> The skeptic's own action stultifies the doubt. Hence there is no infinite regress [of hypothetical reasoning to overcome doubt about the universality of the concomitance, because, by acting as he does, the skeptic has obviated the need to use further hypothetical reasoning to overcome further doubt].[23]

After ending his defense of inference as an instrument of knowledge, Gangesha goes on to use inference to prove God's existence. Even though Buddhism has by his time almost vanished from India, he sees the Buddhists, who argue that such a proof is impossible, as his most persistent opponents. The arguments Gangesha depends on are elaborated variants of some of those made by Udayana. Gangesha proceeds by first considering and eliminating invalid inferences, that is, inferences that are invalid because their constituent parts cannot be defined properly. The process by which he eliminates these inferences and replaces them with his own, demands the technical precision and ingenuity—not well enough reflected in my account—in which Gangesha excels.[24*]

---

*"Gangeśa surpasses even Udayana in this sense that the former takes up only the philosophically most important inference to establish the existence of God and discusses and defends it thoroughly. Further, he formulates the establishing inference itself so carefully that it meets the objections of the Buddhists and the Mimamsakas . . . In particular, Gangeśa's treatment of the faults of the presence of additional condition and counter-thesis in the reason of the establishing inference shows considerable acumen, dialectical skill and even originality. Not even Udayana treats these problems with such thoroughness and skill" (Vattanky, *Gangeśa's Philosophy of God*, p. 150).

In relation to God, Gangesha's basic problem, inherited from his Nyaya forebears, is to show that the world has the nature of an effect the only possible producer of which is the eternal God, an omniscient self without a body. In other words, he intends to prove that, just as a pot has the nature or property of *being an effect* pervaded by *having a maker*—the potter—so the world has the nature of *being an effect* pervaded by *having a maker*—God.[25] In Indian logic, it is wrong to take something that is doubted or regarded as unproved as the subject of an inference. Therefore its subject is, in the one case, the jar and, in the other, the world. From the existence of pot and world, both of which we perceive as being effects, we infer their having their respective makers.

But a pot is not a world and a potter is not God. What does the inference concerning the pot show? That when the inferred maker, a human craftsman, makes anything, he must have immediate, perceptual knowledge of the material he uses, must have the desire to produce what he does, and must carry out an act of striving, in other words, make the effort that activates his body. But what humans can know immediately is not enough for creating worlds, and the God therefore postulated as the world's creator raises the question of what can be done by an eternal, omniscient person who has no body to activate. In formulating his inference, Gangesha must take account of all the objections he is willing to concede to his opponents.*

The Buddhists had long proliferated objections to a creator-god. Dharmakirti, for instance, had asked, How can one make an empirically supported inference that there is a God of the Nyaya kind if there is no known example of anything created by an omniscient being? We know that the structure of a pot—the parts and the way they fit together—is the

---

*After rejecting a number of formulations of the subject of his inference, Gangesha settles on three. These three exclude all that can be made by human beings directly or, by Buddhist ' or Mimamsa doctrine, indirectly, that is, by the "unseen" results of their good and evil acts. What the exclusions leave unexcluded is the universe, presumed to be made directly by the only being who, by Nyaya-Vaisheshika doctrine, can know its material cause (the atoms as material causes). To produce the universe, God must be omniscient and eternal. Gangesha defends his complete inference (subject, property to be proved to qualify it, and reason) as a faultless induction by means of an invariable concomitance of *having a maker* with *being an effect*. (See Vattanky, *Gangeśa's Philosophy of God*, p. 138.)

Paraphrased, the first formulation of the subject (*paksha*) of the inference reads: "All things which are produced, which are not due to the merit or demerit of individual selves, which are not produced by bodily movements which are themselves effects of volition, and which inhere in something are created by a self which has effort, desire to infer, and immediate awareness"— and so on, more technically." The property to be proved to qualify the subject, its predicate, is this: "Created by a self which has effort, desire to act, and immediate awareness (all three) concerning the appropriate material, (these three) not being counter-positives to any prior absence pervaded by a prior absence of merit and demerit" (Potter and Bhattacharyya, eds., *Nyaya-Vaiśeṣika from Gaṅgeśa . . .* , p. 215; compare Vattanky, pp. 183–84.)

work of an intelligent maker because we have seen potters making pots. But does this knowledge require us to infer that an intelligent being made a tree? Or to infer that it was a potter who made something of a quite different kind, an anthill? The identity of the words used—words such as *the parts and the way they fit together*—does not mean that what the words signify plays a logically identical role. If they did, the words *transformation of clay* would be enough to lead us to infer that an anthill and a pot, both a "transformation of clay," played exactly the same role. And if God, an active maker, is eternal, as Nyaya assumes, a change must have occurred in him, from noncause to cause, at the time he created the world. But something eternal cannot change and so cannot act. Besides, things become transformed and made productive by their mutual interaction. We see this when a seed grows, its growth being caused and further affected by a change in the nature of the ground and the other factors that cause and affect it. The causation of the plant and the interaction of the ground and other factors show that no God need be postulated to account for the world.[26]

In the past, Udyana had shown by his arguments that he was well aware of Buddhist objections to Nyaya theology. Since there is no need to repeat Udayana's proofs, in expounding Gangesha on God, I will do no more than suggest the spirit in which he argues. To this end, I will summarize some objections cited and answered by him that relate to two Nyaya doctrines. The one doctrine is that God, though bodiless, is a creator—in this argument Gangesha parallels Udayana. The other doctrine is that the world has only one creator—in this Gangesha makes explicit what Udayana leaves implicit.[27]

With respect to God's bodilessness, an objector to Gangesha's Nyaya doctrine says: When a person wants to produce anything, desire causes an effort, and the effort causes the needed bodily movements. The object to be proved by your inference is God, or is, more exactly, "having a maker" who can be no one but God. But only human beings, a potter for example, are observed to be makers, and the knowledge, desire to act, and effort of such humans or agents, unlike those assumed for God, are always noneternal. Neither God nor the knowledge ascribed to him are yet established. And in human experience, the ability to make something always implies having a body. So the only inference we can make is that, having no body, God cannot produce anything.

Gangesha answers: Your assumption that only persons with bodies can create—because having no body contradicts being a creator—does not hold between all persons and all acts of creation. In our particular argument you cannot invoke experience. True, there is no visible case of the coexistence of bodilessness with the ability to create, but what holds for one, perceived kind of subject, a human being, does not necessarily hold for another, unperceived kind, God. Different subjects, which are different substrata, allow the coexistence in themselves of different properties. For example, the property *being a part* is opposed to the property *being eternal*—except in atoms, which are both parts of dyads and eternal. There is much that can be explained only on the hypothesis of a bodiless creator.[28]

With respect to the number of inferred agents of creation, an objector says: There is no inference to establish that the world was created by only one person. Logically, the proving property of the inference, the world's *being an effect*, is not pervaded by the property to be proved, *having (only) one creator*.

Counterobjector (speaking for Gangesha): The view that only one self was the agent of creation should be accepted because it is the simplest, most parsimonious explanation that can be given.[29]

Objector: Simplicity—parsimony—is not recognized as an instrument of valid knowledge.

Counterobjector: An instrument of knowledge establishes the inference with simplicity as an auxiliary. The world can be proved to have *at least one* creator. Because the proving property, the world's *being an effect*, is pervaded by *having at least one creator*, it allows the existence of more than one creator. But simplicity helps to establish that the world-as-effect has *only one* creator.[30]

Objector: The awareness of simplicity is not a usual supporting concomitant of inference. Inferences are based directly on the inferential mark, preceded by other considerations. Inferences are not postponed by a consideration of simplicity. If they were, the postponement would prove that simplicity is actually used to support inference.

Counterobjector: The awareness of simplicity is a concomitant cause when the inference is simple, that is, when it deals with something conceived to be simple.[31]

Objector: This is only circular thinking, which amounts to saying that the awareness of something conceived as simple, that is, the awareness of simplicity, can be considered to be caused by the awareness of simplicity. (This amounts to the fallacy of self-dependence.)

Counterobjector: Simplicity is a concomitant cause when the inference is concerned with particular individuals.[32]

Objector: If a simple inference made in these cases would be adequate, all the other characteristics of what was inferred would be conceived as simple and, as simple, they would be beyond any doubt. But that is not the case. Doubt persists.

Counterobjector: But only one creator is established, because there is no means of knowledge that proves that there are many creators.[33]

Objector: One could equally well say that because there is no means of knowledge that proves only one creator, many creators are proved.

Counterobjector: *Oneness* is not the explicit object of the inference. But in this case, reason (by force of its relation to the specific subject of the inference) establishes one creator. And the fact that the inference does not have a second creator as its object proves that there are not many creators. If not for the inference of *a* creator, no inference at all could be made about the number of creators. So it is only *one* creator whose existence is established.[34]

Objector: The inference proves nothing about number. The object of the inference is not the oneness of the agent but an agent as such. Therefore we can know about *being an agent* without also knowing about *being one*—number is irrelevant.

Counterobjector: Yet it is by the nature of things that only a single creator is established, not by the knowledge of oneness.[35]

Objector: But even if, by the nature of things, the agent inferred is established as only one, the knowledge obtained is not firm. A firm knowledge that God is one, not many, has not been reached and is impossible when oneness is not established by an inference.

Counterobjector: When we infer the creator, oneness is the qualifier. In order for oneness to become the object of awareness, simplicity must be a concomitant. If the evidence allows, it is the awareness of this simplicity that makes it possible to become aware of oneness, such as the oneness of God. When a means of knowledge in general can cause either a complex or a simple instance of knowledge, the principle of simplicity becomes relevant. It is by means of this principle that we become directly aware of unifying, simplifying concepts such as *being a cause* and *pervasion*. It is by means of this principle that we learn to confine a concept to its most directly pertinent form. For example, when we consider that sticks are used to make pots, in other words, that a stick is a cause of pots, the *causeness* in question is limited only by the property of *being a stick*, that is, applies only to what is a stick. We are not aware of the many other less immediately pertinent or useful properties or characteristics of a stick—such as *being substance* and *being existent*—that are present in other things as well; and *causeness* does not apply to them when we think most economically and pertinently. The principle of simplicity also restricts our knowledge of the denotations of words to the most useful, defining characteristics of things: When we infer the denotative power of the word *jar*, we cognize it as limited by the property of jarness, not the property of having a round neck. If not for the principle of parsimony, human conversation and the related social usages would be impossible. We would be unable to infer the restriction of denotative power to the most pertinent property or characteristic of words, for there is no other factor that would decide between the alternatives. Parsimony is a concomitant of all the means of knowledge. And since we accept the principle of simplicity in general, we should accept it in the inference of God and establish that he is one.[36]

Objector: If this is so, then in the case of a pot, though it may have been made by several potters, simplicity should lead us to establish that the potter, its inferred maker, is only one. But this does not lead to the conclusion you are aiming at. For this case of the potter does not, as you assume, set our doubts to rest for the inference of God as qualified by oneness. On the contrary.

Counterobjector: Even in this case of the potters, oneness is established because of simplicity. But the principle of simplicity can lead to a mistake. The principle of simplicity would first lead to the conclusion that there was only one potter; but then doubt would arise as to the validity of the conclusion, and, by the use of other instruments of knowledge, it would be proved that there had been many potters, and the inference that there was only one maker would be nullified.[37]

Objector: But when the inference of one God as the creator of the earth, etc., is made, there remains the ineradicable doubt whether he is *only* one or there are many.

Counterobjector: The inference of the potter as one was nullified by the later inference of many potters. But the inference of God as one is shown to be valid because the oneness is not nullified by a later inference of many gods. And one should not argue that the absence of a proof of his oneness nullifies his oneness, because in such a case, the (auxiliary) principle of simplicity is decisive, and the inference of one God stands.[38]

Descartes (1596–1650):
Certainty by Method and by Self-certainty

René Descartes spent his life from about the age of ten to eighteen in a Jesuit secondary school, studied law for a time, and twice served briefly as a gentleman-volunteer in an army.[39] After years of travelling, in 1622 he settled in Holland, where he created his philosophical system, a combination of physics, physiology, and philosophy. A great deal of his time was devoted to the practice of anatomy and not a little to the search for a diet to prolong life. The *Discourse on the Method of Rightly Conducting One's Reason and Seeking the Truth in the Sciences* (1637), which first made him famous, was written in French, not the conventional Latin, in order, as he said, to reach people who use their natural reason rather than books.

The *Discourse* was published as an introduction to three "essays," on optics, on meteorology, and on geometry, demonstrating the use of the proposed method. Descartes's second very famous book was the *Meditations on First Philosophy* (1641), written in Latin but soon translated, retouched by him, into French. It was later published with six (and then seven) sets of objections solicited and answered by Descartes. The neatest and fullest integration of his thought was in *The Principles of Philosophy* (1644 in Latin, 1647 in French).

Descartes is as much the mathematician, physicist, and physiologist as the philosopher. These sides of his thought cannot be dealt with in this account, but it must be noted how thoroughgoing a mechanist he is in constructing a world machine. This is, as he conceives it, a space-filling geometry, everywhere in local motion, its laws imparted to it by God at the moment of creation. Descartes is also a mechanist in biology. To him, the human body is a machine made by God. Descartes compares it to the hydraulic machines in the royal garden, where the force of the water is great enough to move different machines and even "make them play certain instruments or utter certain words depending on the various arrangements of the pipes through which the water is conducted."[40] Descartes explains that the body's muscles and tendons are like the devices and springs that set the machines in motion, the "animal spirits" of the body are like the water that drives the machines, the heart is like the sources of the water, and the cavities of the brain are like the storage tanks.* Breathing and other normal activities that depend on the flow of the spirits are like the movements of a water clock or water mill.

> And finally, when a *rational soul* is present in this machine it will have its principal seat in the brain, and reside there like the fountain-keeper who must be stationed at the tanks to which the fountain's pipes return if he want to produce, or prevent, or change their movements in some way.[41]

---

*Compare this view with Aristotle's: "The movement of animals is like that of automatic puppets, which are set moving when a small motion occurs: the cables are released and the pegs strike against one another . . . When, under the influence of heat or cold or some other similar affection, an alteration is produced in the region of the heart . . . it produces a considerable difference in the body, causing blushing and pallor" (Aristotle, *De motu animalium* 701b, trans. M. C. Nussbaum, Princeton: Princeton University Press, p. 42, 44). In *De motu*, Aristotle turns against his earlier proto-Cartesian position (p. 278). Medieval physiology, too, can be mechanistic. For example, Henry of Langenstein (d. 1397), writes: "If not a clock-like machine, the human body is certainly analogous to a steam or internal-combustion engine that is driven on by vital and sensitive spirits flowing through its nerves and arteries" (N. H. Steneck, *Science and Creation in the Middle Ages*, Notre Dame: University of Notre Dame, 1976, p. 127).

Summarizing toward the end of the *Principles of Philosophy*, Descartes claims that there is no phenomenon of nature he has not considered in his treatise, and that he has explained everything by the various sizes, shapes, and motions found in all bodies. Like Democritus, he says, he explains by means of invisible particles, but these particles are divisible and move, not in a vacuum, but in a plenum, and they have no gravity but are moved as a function of the position and motion of other bodies. So although he uses no principles "not accepted by Aristotle and all other philosophers of every age," he rejects practically all the suppositions of Democritus and the other philosophers—Descartes apparently takes principles and suppositions to be different.[42]

Descartes had great influence as a physicist and biologist. He surely helped drive out the Aristotelian concepts of form and matter and potentiality and actuality in favor of concepts that fitted the more aggressively mechanistic sciences that were developing in his time. However, for students of philosophy his persistent attraction seems to rest on his *Discourse* and, even more, on the thought sequence of the *Meditations*.

In the *Discourse*, Descartes describes how he discovered the inconclusiveness of earlier philosophy. He then proposes to himself to begin science and philosophy again, but to begin it like a man walking in the dark, so slowly and carefully that he will at least not fall.[43] The method he finds (quite like that of Francis Bacon, whom he does not mention) is comprised of four rules: Not to accept anything that is not so clear and distinct that he cannot doubt it; to divide difficulties into as many parts as possible and as required to resolve them better; to proceed in an orderly way from the simplest and most easily known to the complex; and to make repeated reviews to make sure that nothing is left out.[44] This program is an ideal rather than a method that Descartes actually practices. In spite of the impression he usually makes, he most often regards deduction not as a justification of knowledge but as a way of displaying knowledge systematically. As he writes in a letter, his purpose in the *Discourse* was not to teach the whole of his method but only to show that the views in his scientific books were not random and deserved to be examined.[45]*

---

*Elsewhere, Descartes says that his account of the rainbow in the *Meteorology* is the best example of how the use of his method can lead to new knowledge. But the *Meteorology* does not begin from first principles and what he says in it about the rainbow is a mixture of experiment and geometry. To explain the phenomenon of the rainbow, Descartes takes a large glass sphere filled with water—his model raindrop—and moves it in the sunlight to make rainbow colors appear. Using the refractive index of rainwater, he then makes a geometrical analysis of the angles of refraction that produce the colors. This is far from the Euclidean kind of axiomatic, deductive proof one might expect of a scientific "rationalist." Descartes in fact argues that the "synthetic" method of axiomatic construction is not a way of discovery but of presenting what is already known by connecting it with first principles. (See Gaukroger, "Descartes: Methodology," pp. 179–89.)

The *Meditations* begins in a dramatic rehearsal of doubts, like those of the Greek skeptics: Perhaps, says Descartes, his senses are deceiving him so that what they show—extended, bodily things and, along with them, every science that assumes them—is illusory. Perhaps he is dreaming and, if so, perhaps his real body is different from the way he experiences it in what may be his dream. Perhaps the sky, air, earth, colors, shapes, sounds, and all external things are delusions caused by some malicious, omnipotent demon.* But even if there is such a supreme deceiver, and even if I am deceived, it is necessarily true that whenever I think that *I am, I exist*, that I really do exist. I can still not be sure I have a body or senses, but I am real, I am something as long as I am thinking: I am a thing that thinks, that doubts, understands, affirms, denies, wills, imagines, and has sensory perceptions. Furthermore, from the pliable wax I hold in my (apparent) hands I can understand the space-filling nature of extended bodies.

Descartes continues meditating: For the moment, he says to himself, I believe nothing except that I am a thing that thinks. I am quite certain of this because I have a clear and distinct perception of what I am asserting. From this certainty I learn the universal rule that whatever I perceive very clearly and distinctly is true.

Now the thought of God comes to mind (a God, it may be added parenthetically, of a Neoplatonic medieval kind). We know by our natural light, Descartes continues, that nothing can arise from nothing, that what is more perfect cannot arise from what is less perfect, that there must be at least as much reality in a cause as in its effect, and that there cannot be an infinite regress in the realities that are the objects of my thought. I become aware that most of the ideas I entertain can come from within

---

*As a rule, an Indian or Chinese philosopher prefers, even when original, to attach himself to an ancestor, but Descartes, even when imitative, prefers to ignore his sources. However, in the second set of replies he excuses himself for reheating and serving the material precooked by the Academics and skeptics (Cottingham, Stoothoff, and Murdoch, *The Philosophical Writings of Descartes*, vol. 2, p. 94). The deceptive demon may be borrowed from Cicero (*Academica* 2.15), where it is said to be possible that the deity who sends dreams has the power to make false presentations just like true ones. In *On the Trinity* 12.15, Augustine— the probable source of Descartes's *cogito ergo sum*—writes of persons who, though awake, had experiences caused by "malignant and deceitful spirits." The illusion-creating demon is mentioned by sixteenth-century religious writers such as St. Teresa of Avila and the Cardinal de Bérule, the cleric who urged Descartes to publish the *Meditations*. For other predecessors of Descartes's demon—perhaps beginning with the suggestion in Plato's *Republic* (381e) that a god might wish to deceive by presenting in word or action what is only appearance—see R. Spaemann, "Genius malignus," in J. Ritter, ed., *Historisches Wrterbuch der Philosophie*, vol. 3, Basel and Stuttgart: Schwabe, 1974, p. 310. Rodis-Lewis, *L'anthropologie cartésienne*, chap. 4, discusses the resemblances and differences between Augustinianism and Cartesianism.

me—the ideas of duration, number, shape, position, and movement may well be modes of myself as a substance.* But my idea of God is such that it could not have originated from me alone. A finite substance cannot think an infinite one. All that can account for my idea of the infinite substance is that it comes from an existing infinite substance. Therefore a supremely perfect and infinite being must actually exist. Since I am a thinking thing that has within me some idea of God, what causes me to think it is itself a thinking thing with the perfection that I attribute to it. It exists in its own right, and I exist by virtue of it. If its existence was supposed to be derived from something else, the result would be an impossible infinite regress of one existence derived from another derived from another, and so on. So from the fact that I exist and have within me an idea of the most perfect being, God, it is proved that God really exists. And since I cannot have invented the idea, it must be innate in me, placed there by God like the mark of a craftsman on his work. And God being who he is, it is clearly and distinctly evident that God cannot deceive me.

I now understand, continues Descartes, that I am, so to speak, midway between God and nothingness, between the supreme being and nonbeing, and I go wrong not because of anything he created in me but only to the degree that I participate in nothingness or nonbeing. I err because my faculty of choice or freedom of will, given to me by God, has a scope

---

*In Descartes, the term *idea* (*idée*) is very often degraded from its Platonic and Neoplatonic status. By Descartes's time, it had already taken on increasingly non-Platonic nuances and meanings. It was in use for *species* (in the more or less medieval sense), for the image that perception "stamps on the mind," and for *phantasm* (mental image); and Montaigne and others had used it with a then modern imprecision. Yet the breadth of meaning that Descartes gives it—as "the form of any given thought, immediate perception of which makes me aware of the thought"—is taken to be quite new even by his contemporaries ("Author's Replies to the Second Set of Objections" in *The Philosophical Writings of Descartes*, vol. 2, trans. Cottingham, Stoothoff, and Murdoch, p. 113).

In answer to Hobbes, who objects that *idea* means only *image*, Descartes writes: "I am taking the word "idea" to refer to whatever is immediately perceived by the mind. For example, when I want something, or am afraid of something, I simultaneously perceive that I want, or am afraid; and this is why I count volition and fear among my ideas. I used the word "idea" because it was the standard philosophical term used to refer to the forms of perception belonging to the divine mind, even though we recognize that God does not possess any corporeal imagination. And besides, there was not any more appropriate term at my disposal" ("Third Set of Objections (by Hobbes) with the Author's Replies," in *The Philosophical Writings of Descartes*, vol. 2, pp. 127–28).

On the history of the term *idea* see See K. Neumann, *idee*, in Ritter and Gründer, eds, *Historisches Wrterbuch der Philosophie*, Schwabe, esp. pp. 103–105.

wider than that of my intellect; and my will leads me to extend my
intellect to matters I do not understand and in this way leads me to error
and sin. If I restrain my will and pay enough attention to what I understand perfectly, avoiding whatever is confused and obscure, I will surely
reach the truth.

In this spirit, Descartes goes on: I consider my ideas of the sizes,
shapes, positions, and durations of things, all of which I can distinctly
imagine. It is clear from their geometrical natures and necessary relations
that they cannot have been invented by me. Considering the laws of
geometry, I understand that I can no more think of God as nonexistent
than I can think of a mountain without a valley; but while I know that the
valley does not necessarily exist, I cannot think of God except as existing.
And I know that I am incapable of error whenever my understanding is
transparently clear. All the certainty and truth of all my knowledge depends uniquely on my knowledge of the true God.

We already know, Descartes goes on, that material things can exist
as the subject matter of pure mathematics, by means of which I perceive
these things clearly and distinctly. I probe my mathematical imagination
and notice that it requires a peculiar effort of mind not needed for understanding, so I conclude that imagination is not necessary to my essence,
that is, to the essence of my mind, because, even if I lacked my imagination, I would still remain the same individual I now am. I also see it was
not unreasonable to think that what the senses show me is distinct from
me, because what they show is too vivid and unrelated to my will to be
formed by me. Besides, I am not able to explain my appetites, pains,
pleasures, and emotions except as something that nature has taught me.
Knowing that I exist and am a thinking thing, I know I can exist without
my body. But my imagination and sensory perception depend both on me
as a thinking thing and on corporeal, extended substance, which is free of
intellect. Corporeal things exist because God has given me a strong propensity to believe that my ideas are produced by corporeal things. So
corporeal things do exist.

> Nature teaches me by the sensations of pain, hunger, thirst,
> and so on, that I am not merely present in my body as a sailor
> is present in a ship, but that I am very closely joined and, as
> it were, intermingled with it, so that I and my body form a
> unit. (Sixth Meditation)[46]

Nature also teaches me, says Descartes, that there are other bodies
near my body, some of which I should seek out and others avoid. I
understand that my body is by nature divisible and my mind by nature
indivisible. This is because as a thinking thing I have no parts but am

single and complete. Even though my whole mind seems to be joined to my whole body, I know that if I lost an arm or foot, as a thinking thing I would have lost nothing. Mentally, I can divide any corporeal thing—any extended, that is, space-filling thing—into parts; it is by its nature divisible. This is enough to show me that mind and body are altogether different, as I understand for other reasons as well.

At this point, I—the author of this history—break in again. The meditation sequence I have just briefly paraphrased is probably the most famous passage in the history of modern European philosophy. I include it only because its absence would leave too conspicuous a gap here. The sequence, a well-written collection of old arguments in a new philosophical context, convinced relatively few of its professional readers. I forbear analysis but remind the reader, as Descartes would want, that his famous proof beginning from his existence as a thinking thing is not meant to be a syllogism or a logical inference but an intuition. The text in the *Meditations* does not read *cogito ergo sum* but *Ego cogito, ergo sum*, and in the *Discourse* it reads *Ego cogito, ergo sum, sive existo*. The emphasis is not on formal logic, but on how absurd it would be for the *I* who is speaking to deny that it exists. Descartes wants to avoid the appearance of the syllogism, *Everything that thinks exists; I think; therefore I exist*, because the unquestionable truth he begins with cannot reasonably be a conclusion derived from two other premises. The awareness that we are thinking things, says Descartes, is a primary notion, something that is self-evident by a simple intuition of the mind that is the result of the individual's personal experience.[47]*

Some eleven years after the publication of the *Meditations*, Descartes admitted to Frans Burman, who interviewed him, that the connection between soul and body, whose natures are completely different, is "very difficult to explain; but here our experience is sufficient, since it is so clear on this point that it just cannot be gainsaid."[48] Not without pride, he also told Burman that now that he, Descartes, had established the certainty of

---

*It is the undeniable self-evidence of intuition that makes deduction possible, because it is by intuition that we grasp single propositions and are certain that a proposition necessarily follows from those that precede it (for example, that from 2 and 2, which make 4, and from 3 and 1, which make 4, it necessarily follows that 2 and 2 are equal to 3 and 1). And since memory is fallible, our confidence in the correctness of a long chain of inferences depends on our ability to run through the chain in a quick, continuous movement of thought that intuits one relation after another so quickly that we hardly need to rely on our memories and we seem to intuit the whole chain at once (Descartes, *Rules for the Direction of the Mind*, rules 2, 7; Cottingham. Stoothoff, and Murdoch, *The Philosophical Writings of Descartes*, vol. 1, pp. 14–15, 25. See Gaukroger, *Descartes*, pp. 115–24).

metaphysical questions against the skeptics, it was not necessary for every-one to spend time and trouble considering these questions. He, Descartes, had gone quite deep enough. Attempts to pursue the questions deeply "draw the mind too far away from physical and observable things, and make it unfit to study them. Yet it is just these physical studies that it is most desirable for men to pursue, since they would yield abundant benefits for life."[49]

Descartes, like Leibniz, has the ideal of a universal language so clear and rational that whoever uses it will find it nearly impossible to make a mistake. He has often been called a rationalist and contrasted with the empiricists of his time, especially Locke. But his rationalism, such as it is, has its obvious limits. Astonishing as it may seem, on one important issue he takes the position typical of medieval nonrationalists, including many of the Muslim theologians. Because they conceive God to be unique, self-sufficient, infinitely powerful, and incomprehensible, these nonrationalists believe that all truths are created by God. Every truth is therefore depen-dent for its truthfulness, they say, on God's existence and will. In Descartes's words, God "was free to make it not true that all the radii of the circle are equal—just as free as he was not to create the world."[50] Like the Muslim theologians, Descartes does not believe in the even relative ability of sub-stances to exist of their own power or because of apparent causes. Nothing but God exerts any real causal effect. He insists that

> from the fact that we now exist, it does not follow that we shall exist a moment from now, unless there is some cause—the same cause which originally produced us—which continu-ally reproduces us, as it were, that is to say, keeps us in existence.[51]

As not infrequently happens, the new, radical views—Descartes's dualistic separation of matter and mind; his axiomatic, mechanistic phys-ics; his mechanistic biology and largely mechanistic psychology; and his fervent rationalism—had their energizing, radicalizing effects, while his antirationalism (if that is the proper name for his unqualified dependence on God), although so important to himself, made no lasting difference to the history of European thought.[52]

Many subsequent criticisms of Descartes's thought are prefigured in the objections that, to this credit, he himself gathered. But despite the criticisms made of him, his influence was very strong, even on a scientific enemy such as Newton and on a more openly emotional, religious enemy such as Pascal, who wrote of him:

In general terms one must say: "That is the result of figure and motion," because it is true, but to name them and assemble the machine is quite ridiculous. It is pointless, uncertain and arduous. Even if it were true we do not think that the whole of philosophy would be worth an hour's effort.[53]

Each succeeding philosophical generation measured its thought against that of Descartes. Leibniz's criticisms are summarized below, in the account of Leibniz's thought.* In the nineteenth century, Hegel regards him as the inaugurator of modern philosophy. "*Cogito ergo sum*," he says, "are the first words in his system; and it is precisely these words which express modern philosophy's difference from all its predecessors."[54] Nietzsche objects that the awakened, knowing person says "body am I, and nothing else; and soul is only a word for something about the body," that is, about the self, the ruler and sage, which is the body.[55] More prosaically, Nietzsche objects that the notion that thinking measures actuality and that what cannot be thought cannot be, "is itself a mad assumption, which experience contradicts every moment."[56]

Of the important twentieth-century philosophers, the one most obviously influenced by Descartes is Edmund Husserl, who complains of the current state of philosophy and writes, in nostalgia for Descartes's defiance of philosophical convention:

Must not the only fruitful renaissance be the one that awakens the impulse of the Cartesian *Meditations*: not to adopt their content but, in *not* doing so, to renew with greater intensity the radicalness of their spirit, the radicalness of self-responsibility, to make that radicalness true for the first time by enhancing it to the last degree, to uncover thereby for the first time the genuine sense of the necessary regress to the ego, and consequently to overcome the hidden but already felt naiveté of earlier philosophizing?[57]

---

*Among Descartes's earlier critics, the Abbé Simon Foucher (1644–1696) is particularly damaging. Foucher argues that Descartes begs the main questions. We cannot know that our sensations (or ideas) resemble the external things that we suppose cause the sensations because our souls cannot leave themselves and enter directly into external things. Besides, Descartes wants an idea, which has no extension or figure, to represent material things, which does have them. How, by Cartesian principles, can the knowing mind be like material things? Finally, Descartes must be wrong, because he himself describes the interaction, in the pineal gland, between mind and matter, an interaction that he declares is impossible.

    Although Foucher's book was not read much, its arguments were passed on by the learned Pierre-Daniel Huet (1630–1721), in *Censura philosophae cartesianae*, which was read by Pierre Bayle, whose *Dictionnaire historique et critique* was read by Locke, Berkeley, Hume, and the other philosophers of their time. (See Watson, *The Downfall of Cartesianism*, esp. pp. 24–28.)

Karl Jaspers, who has a strong dislike for Descartes, says that he reaches no more than a wonderful pseudoclarity. According to him, Descartes's thought gives real satisfaction only to those who suffer from an inner dualism or pluralism and are therefore not purely anything. The very different views he inspires all tend to dogmatism, even fanaticism. He particularly stimulates those who want to become simply rational, who believe in a mathematical-positivistic world and live on polemics and resentment. Using pure reason ruthlessly, Descartes attempts to legislate for the whole world.[58]

In sharp contrast to Jasper's evaluation, the French scholar Roger Lefèvre, who is exceptionally familiar with Descartes's works, concedes that Descartes's method has proved to be too simple and rigid, his physics to be merely transient, and his metaphysics to be based on an arbitrary doubt and an insupportable dualism. What survives is the spirit of his doctrine: Descartes teaches us to resist blind feelings while remaining independent and reasonable, to respect and study our internal world without despising the external world, in which we play out our destiny, to promote rational demands, to hold the will to be free and responsible, and yet to recognize the impenetrable mystery of the world. It is not a minor virtue for us to follow Descartes and repeat, if only for a moment, "I am a thing that thinks."[59]

I end my account of Descartes with an estimate of "Descartes's error" by the neuropsychologist A. R. Damasio. This error is "the abyssal separation between body and mind." Damasio observes that the current metaphor by which mind is a software program may well have been caused by "the Cartesian idea of a disembodied mind." If we believe that mind can be separated from body, Damasio says, we may try to understand it "without any need to be influenced by knowledge of neuroanatomy, neurophysiology, and neurochemistry."[60] The mind surely comes from the brain, but the brain alone, in the absence of the rest of the organism and the whole human environment, is not enough to explain the mind. The critical issue is to consider the "reasons why the brain's neurons behave in such a thoughtful manner." Unfortunately, "versions of Descartes' error obscure the roots of the human mind in a biologically complex but fragile, finite, and unique organism; they obscure the tragedy implicit in the knowledge of that fragility, finiteness, and uniqueness."[61]

Leibniz (1646–1716):
Certainty by the Logical Principle of Individuation

It was early in life, at the age of thirteen, that Leibniz—Gottfried Wilhelm Leibniz, to give him his full name—discovered logic and was stirred by its wonderful ability to classify and give order.[62] He recalls his discovery in the words:

> My greatest pleasure lay in the categories, which seemed to be
> but a standard roll of everything in the world, and I examined
> many logics to see where the best and most exhaustive lists
> could be found. (Letter to Gabriel Wagner, 1696)[63]

Leibniz, who became a living, usually good-tempered encyclopedia,
was an extraordinarily curious and fertile thinker. He wrote on so many
subjects that he was said to be equal to several savants at once. Apart from
mathematics, logic, linguistics, and physics, he wrote on law (he hoped to
standardize it), on religion (he hoped to reunite Catholics and Protes-
tants), on politics (he hoped to establish peace in Europe, perhaps by a
joint attack on the Turks), and on learned academies (he hoped to help
establish them).

One of Leibniz's favorite projects was a universal language by which
all peoples could learn to communicate. For a while he thought that
Chinese might serve the purpose, but he discovered that Chinese characters, too, were ambiguous. However, he remained sure that there were
marks that could be substituted for words and produce the same knowledge as they do:

> The characters of the Chinese show this. And we could intro-
> duce a Universal Symbolism—a very popular one, better than
> theirs—if in place of words we used little diagrams which
> represented visible things pictorially and invisible things by
> means of the visible one which go with them, also bringing in
> certain additional marks suitable for conveying inflections and
> particles.[64]

Leibniz agrees with those who believe that there once was a universal, "Adamitic," language. The nature of Chinese strengthens his and others' conviction that such a universal language could be reinvented. This
language would be "a kind of *truly philosophic writing*, in which ideas were
reduced to a kind of *alphabet of human thought*." On the assumption (like
that of Proclus) that reality has a rational structure, he hopes that the
language he and others would create would assign every elementary idea
a symbol, such as a letter of the alphabet. These letters could then be
manipulated like the symbols of algebra. Once a dictionary of all fundamental ideas was completed, he thinks, it would be possible to substitute
calculation for argument.[65]

Leibniz is also encouraged to find that the hexagrams of the *Book of
Changes (I Ching)* can be interpreted as a binary notation like that of the
arithmetic he was proposing. "Reverend Father Bouvet and I," he writes,
"have discovered the meaning, apparently truest to the text, of the characters of Fohi [Fu Hsi], founder of the Empire, which consists simply of

combinations of unbroken and broken lines." Despite later interpretations, says Leibniz, "the 64 figures represent a Binary Arithmetic which apparently this great legislator possesses, and which I have rediscovered some thousands of years later."[66]

Leibniz published no more than a single philosophical book, the *Theodicy*. As a result, his contemporaries knew far less of his work than we do; and even now, some of it remains unpublished. He never stops thinking, but exactly what he means remains elusive. His meaning is hard to fix because most of his writing is in the form of letters to learned correspondents in which he treats the same problems with nuances that keep varying. It helps to follow his thought as it develops, but this requires a more elaborate exposition than is possible here.

Leibniz is proud of his ability, furthered by a basically Neoplatonic mode of thinking, to reconcile the ideas of different philosophers. Like Aristotle and the Neoplatonists, he sees the desire to know everything as a way of approaching God and God's universal harmony. But harmony loving as he is, his good will fails him when he faces great scientific rivals like Newton and great philosophical ones like Spinoza and Descartes.

Leibniz's criticisms of the two philosophers are a convenient preface to his thought. His interest in Spinoza was deep, but Spinoza was rightly, I suppose, suspicious of his sometimes two-faced visitor. After Spinoza's death, Leibniz tried to buy his manuscripts, and he was for a while tempted by his thought and able to praise him; but his antagonism grew. When he first read the *Ethics*, he found faulty proofs; but what in the long run is far worse to Leibniz is the determinism the *Ethics* teaches, along with the moral indifference of God and the subjectivity of good and evil—all ideas deadly to religion, Leibniz is sure.[67]

Against Descartes, Leibniz is less bitter, but his list of complaints is longer and more detailed. He comes to regard Descartes as a great man gone wrong, ungrateful to the many philosophers and scientists he pillages for ideas and too eager to appear novel and create a sect, one, moreover, that refuses to work cooperatively for the good of science. Leibniz's criticisms—in which his jealousy is sometimes transparent—include Descartes's mathematics, physics, and theology.

I must omit Leibniz's longer or more technical criticisms, such as his attacks on Descartes's geometrical approach to physics, and limit myself to his less technical ones.[68] The first of these is on Descartes's four rules of the *Discourse on Method*, of which Leibniz says: These are unoriginal chemist's rules: take what you need, operate as you should, and you will get the result you hope for. This is much too vague. We need an exact inventory of what is known and reasoning formalized like algebra.

On *ego cogito, ergo sum*, Leibniz says: To feel that one cannot doubt is an obscure, highly capricious reason for certainty. It would be better to say that one was unable to find reasons for doubting, but even this statement would yield "only a conjecture or presumption." Given the usual idea of reason, "the appearances of our reason are often as deceptive as those of the senses." The demonstration and linking of truths must be based on the principle of contradiction; otherwise it is impossible to reach certainty.[69]

On *clear and distinct*, Leibniz says: Distinct knowledge has degrees—usually the concepts entering into the definition themselves need definition. When everything that enters a definition, down to the primitive concepts, is known distinctly, there is adequate and intuitive knowledge. But this is very rare; most human knowledge is confused or requires suppositions.[70]

On the proof of God, Leibniz says: The idea of the greatest of all numbers is self-contradictory. Before the idea of God as the greatest of all beings is used, it must be proved not to be not similarly self-contradictory. Descartes says he conceives of the most perfect of all beings because he conceives his own imperfection, but the ability to conceive something *more* perfect is not that to conceive something *most* perfect, infinitely perfect. I can conceive of a number greater than any particular number, but not of a greatest or infinite number.[71]*

On the distinction between soul and body, Leibniz says: This is not entirely proved. Descartes admits that we do not conceive distinctly what thought is. It can therefore be said that "perhaps it is only our ignorance which distinguishes them and that in some way unknown to us thought includes extension."[72]

On biological mechanisms, Leibniz says: Descartes does not distinguish between the machines that human beings construct and natural machines. "The machines of nature have a truly infinite number of organs . . . A natural machine remains a machine even in its smallest parts." In natural machines, "the soul or form creates a true unity corresponding

---

*In Leibniz's versions of the ontological argument, as in its usual medieval versions, absolute perfection is something quite apart from relative perfection and alone ensures existence. Leibniz also urges a proof for God's existence based on the principle of sufficient reason. He asks, dramatically, why there is something rather than nothing. The premise of the argument is that if anything exists there must be a sufficient reason for its existence. Because the world is a series of contingent beings, the sufficient reason must be a necessary being outside the series. (Leibniz, *Philosophical Papers and Letters*, p. 369 ["The Principles of Nature and Grace, Based on Reason, sections 7–8]. See Blumenfeld, "Leibniz's Ontological and Cosmological Arguments," pp. 354–55, 362–63. 367–68) This argument is found, worded differently, in Descartes as well. As hardly needs to be pointed out, Descartes's and Leibniz's proofs are variants of earlier, medieval ones.

to what is called 'I' in us. Such a unity could not occur in artificial machines or in a simple mass of matter."[73]

On the union of soul and body, Leibniz says: "So far as we can tell from his writings, Descartes gave up the struggle over this problem . . . His disciples concluded that we sense the qualities of bodies because God causes thoughts to arise in our soul on the occasion of material movements and that when our soul in its turn wishes to move the body, God moves the body for it."[74]

These objections show us, first, that Leibniz depends for certainty on logical principles and, second, that he wants to retain the old intimacy of body and mind. He begins with the principle that is, he says, enough by itself to demonstrate every part of mathematics. This is "the principle of contradiction, or identity, that is, the principle that a proposition cannot be true and false at the same time; and that therefore A is A, and cannot be not A."[75] But all metaphysics except that of the Materialists, Leibniz believes, also needs "the principle of a sufficient reason, viz. that nothing happens without a reason why it should be so, rather than otherwise."[76] This principle is enough, says Leibniz, to demonstrate everything in metaphysics or natural theology and, in physics, the principles of force.

How does Leibniz think the demonstration can be made? In nature, he holds, there are never any two identical individuals. "Two drops of water, or milk, viewed with a microscope, will appear distinguishable from each other. This is an argument against atoms."[77] So to the great principle of a *sufficient reason* we can add the subprinciple of the *identity of indiscernibles*. By this principle we mean that when we suppose that two things cannot be distinguished from one another, we refer by two names to the same one thing. Why so? Because of the axiom that "*there is nothing without a reason, or no effect without a cause.*" From this there follows the axiom that "*there cannot be two individual things in nature which differ only numerically.*"[78] There *must* be some intrinsic way to distinguish between any two individuals or individual events. Otherwise, there is no reason for their difference and the world becomes arbitrary instead of intelligible. That is why it is merely an impossible fiction to imagine that in the beginning the universe had a position different from the one it really had or to imagine that God created the universe some millions of years before he in fact did—with no particular reason for doing so.

To put it otherwise, everything must be individual; and because everything exists in a universe for which everything has a cause for being exactly what it is, the complete concept of an individual includes all its characteristics and all its past, present, and future. It includes everything that individuates it and fits it in with all the other individuals into whose company it must fit.[79] All this requires a God who orders the universe and chooses what he does knowing how things will work out. When he freely creates a particular Adam, he also freely chooses his exact posterity. So the full individual concept of a particular Adam includes the particular individual conditions that distinguish him from others, no matter what their similarity to him.[80]

Understood in this way, the principle of the identity of indiscernibles has important metaphysical results. To begin with, it makes it impossible to accept the ordinary conceptions of space, time, and atoms, that is, of absolute space, absolute time, and atoms identical except for their positions in time and space. Leibniz does accept the before-and-after of subjective experience, which he calls *duration*, and the perceived relationships between bodies, which have *extension*, he says. Duration and extension are the attributes of substances, so that "to coexist and to exist before and after is something real."[81] But pure, empty, absolute, indifferent time and space, apart from events and from bodies, are creatures of abstract reason. Time and space cannot be substances, something absolutely uniform in which every point is identical with every other. In such time and space, what reason could there be for the world to be created at one year rather than another or with an orientation one way rather than another? So the reality of space and time is only secondary; they are relations, and their reality is like that of an army or a society.[82]

The subject of space brings us to that of atoms and to Leibniz's substitute for them, which he calls *monads* (from the Greek *monas, one* or *unit*). Monads appear in his thought relatively late. As he explains, in the beginning he was an Aristotelian, and after freeing himself from Aristotle, he accepted the void and the atoms, because they satisfy the imagination. But then he saw that such an infinite collection of parts is a multitude without any true unities. Also, a material being cannot be perfectly indivisible, and the continuum of space cannot be made up of mere points. He therefore had recourse to a concept of primitive, soullike forces. He saw, he says, that these nonmaterial forms or souls or forces have a true unity-in-variety, even if they are incomparably less perfect than rational souls, and that, like atoms, they cannot in any natural way be destroyed. Their unity is not that of artificial machines but is like that of the 'I' in us. They are *metaphysical points*; they have no parts; and they are "the sources of action and the absolute first principles of which things are compounded."[83]*

---

*Leibniz describes a substance somewhat as the Sarvastivadin Buddhist does a *dharma*. What is true of a substance, he says, must be so because of its own nature, not the nature of something other. A substance is a spontaneous, causally independent, unique principle of force. This force is not the medieval philosophers' potentiality for action. Instead, "it is carried into action by itself and needs no help but only the removal of an impediment . . . I say that this power of action inheres in all substance and some action always arises from it" (Leibniz, "On the Improvement of First Philosophy, and on the Notion of Substance"; quoted in Rutherford, "Metaphysics: The Late Period," p. 127; also [under a somewhat different title]), in Leibniz, *Philosophical Papers and Letters*, p. 433).

Except for one interesting deviation, the rest of Leibniz's conception of monads and their relationships is fundamentally that of a Neoplatonic hierarchy: All things are in some sense animate and spiritual, and all fit together in a graded, infinitely rich and harmonious whole. God is the primary unity of which all monads are, so to speak, born by "continual fulgurations of the divinity from moment to moment."[84] In its own way, every monad, having to fit into the entire universe, is a mirror of the whole. The one interesting point of deviation from the Neoplatonic conception is that the monads, their natures and futures unalterably fixed in advance, cannot be affected by anything. "Monads have no windows through which anything could enter or depart."[85] In this quality, they resemble the atoms of the ancient Greek atomists.

The one further characteristic of the Leibnizian world I want to bring out is its continuity. This continuity, which resembles that of the calculus, involves both the theory of monads and the principle that no transition is ever made by means of a leap. This principle we learn from experience and from the order that analysis reveals to our intellect: the more we analyze things the more they satisfy our intellects, which do not suffer gaps, and which keep insisting on further and further explanations, as the law of sufficient reason demands.[86]

The beauty of nature requires apparent jumps; but in principle there is continuity, and the different forms and states and classes of being are continuous with others. There are no vacuums among forms, even though these appear in particular places, and even though the most stupid man is far more rational than the most intellectual of all the beasts.[87] The orders of natural beings are links that clasp one another as if they made up a chain. This means that there is no sharp break between the living and the dead, the perceiving and the unperceiving, the conscious and the unconscious. Even in conscious life many perceptions are confused. In sleep, we have feeble, confused sensations, and even the loudest noise awakens us because it has a small start. Our minute perceptions "constitute that *je ne sais quoi*, those flavors, those images of sensible qualities, vivid in the aggregate but confused in the parts."[88]

> These insensible perceptions also indicate and constitute the individual, who is characterized by the vestiges or expressions which the perceptions preserve from the individual's former states, thereby connecting these with his present state. Even when the individual has no sense of the previous states, i.e. no longer has any explicit memory of them, they could be known by a superior mind. But those perceptions provide the means for recovering this memory at need.[89]

Minute insensible perceptions often determine how we act even when do not think of them.[90] We are driven by insensible perceptions that could be called sufferings if we were aware of them. "This is the true character of that disquiet which we sense without taking cognizance of it," which may degenerate into conscious suffering but which is also essential to the variability we need for our happiness.[91] Our actual, complete volitions are produced by the conflict among various perceptions and inclinations.[92]

Given his emphasis on order and logic, Leibniz has to wrestle with the problem of free will, most notably that of God. For God, the solution is that it is by his goodness and free will that he chooses the best among equally possible universes. Whether or not God can be said to be logically constrained to pick the best is a Leibnizian crux. Leibniz defends his position in subtly different, always problematic ways, only rarely stated in satisfying detail.[93] One of his favorite defenses depends on his mathematical doctrine of infinite analysis: The proposition that a particular world is the best is a certain proposition. But in the sense that it cannot be demonstrated by a finite analysis, it is not a *necessary* proposition. Relative to the finite human ability of humans, the proposition is therefore contingent, and therefore God's choice should be considered to be free.[94] Another favorite defense rests on what seems to me an amusing distinction that in less logically adroit hands would constitute a clear begging of the question. Of all logically possible worlds, Leibniz says, God freely chooses one, but once it is chosen, all its individual details follow necessarily.[95] So when God creates the best of all possible worlds, what occurs must be logically possible in its own nature—it cannot be self-contradictory—but its *non*occurrence does not imply a self-contradiction. Having been chosen, this world is completely necessary; but it is also not a necessary world, in the sense that its noncreation does not imply a self-contradiction. The world *not* chosen by God

> remains possible in its own nature, even if it is not possible
> with respect to the divine will, because we define as possible
> in its own nature what in itself does not imply a contradiction,
> even if its coexistence with God can be said in some way to
> imply a contradiction.[96]

It is interesting to note that Voltaire, whose Pangloss parodies a Leibnizian addicted to optimism—and who praises Leibniz in public but in letters calls him a charlatan—seems unable to escape the butt of his own parody. That is, he often, if inconsistently, agrees with Leibniz's position, and he ends with a belief in God's goodness like enough to Leibniz's.[97] But eighteenth-century French thinkers were much less impressed by Leibniz than were German thinkers of the same period. Classifying him with Christian Wolff (1679–1754)—the two corresponded and shared a good deal philosophically, though far from everything—the Germans spoke of a Leibniz-Wolffian doctrine, which dominated German intellectual life for a generation, at least until the time when Wolff died. Wolff's system, influenced, rather like Spinoza's, by the ideal of "mathematical" proof, is the most orderly, detailed, expansive, and erudite of his time.[98]*

Leibniz himself, endlessly curious, seems to refuse to believe that there is anything that cannot in principle be explained: The more closely we analyze things, the more we learn about them and the better they (have to) satisfy the understanding and demonstrate their organic (nonmechanical) union. In order to explain, Leibniz varies and synthesizes the explanations he has learned from others: all the European tradition is grist to his philosophical mill. He insists that literally everything must fit into a whole, the coherence of which he again and again tries to recreate in logical form.

> But though Leibniz had to struggle to achieve overall coherence, in the process he made major contributions to philosophical thought about the issues he discussed; his theories of substance, identity, causality, space and time, and innate ideas are illuminating and historically influential. For all its internal tensions and unresolved problems, his system in its various forms remains one of the most impressive examples of speculative metaphysics.[99]

---

*Like his mentor, Leibniz, Wolff was an admirer of Chinese civilization. His knowledge of China stemmed from Jesuit reports and translations or summaries of Confucian classics, including a précis of Confucianism by Chu Hsi. In 1721, in a soon famous lecture at the University of Halle, Wolff made the point that Confucianism is a moral philosophy based on nature and reason rather than divine revelation. To the assembled faculty and students, he "proclaimed the virtues of the Chinese and the harmony of the Confucian teachings with his own moral philosophy." After a bitter two-year controversy, the King of Prussia expelled Wolff from the university and from Prussian territory. Wolff moved to University of Marburg, situated in the more tolerant land of Hesse. "It has been estimated that Wolff's dismissal from Halle inspired the writing of two hundred polemical tracts, one hundred and thirty against Wolff and seventy for him." In a lecture at Marburg, Wolff extolled Confucian government, organized on the model of the family, he said, and exemplified by the first [mythical] Chinese emperors—in Wolff's eyes, philosophical kings or kingly philosophers. In the meanwhile, the Crown Prince of Prussia, the future Frederick the Great, was studying Wolff's system and writing a book, *Anti-Machiavel*, in which he expounded his own version of enlightened despotism. After Frederick became king, Wolff returned to Halle, where he continued to work on his system (and, with reasonable reservations) to praise China. (See D. F. Lach, "The Sinophilism of Christian Wolff [1679–1754], in Ching and Oxtoby, eds., *Discovering China.* The quotations are from pp. 119 and 123.)

I end my account of Leibniz by returning to his interest in Chinese thought. This interest is strong enough to suggest that it had an influence on his own philosophy. In sharp contrast to Descartes and Locke, whose emphasis is on mechanism or materialistic atomism, he is an organicist. His hierarchy of harmoniously integrated, mutually mirroring monads has some resemblance to the Neoconfucian hierarchy of Li and lis.

> When he says "Every portion of matter may be conceived of as a garden full of plants or a pond full of fish; but every stem of a plant, every limb of an animal, and every drop of sap or blood is also such a garden," we feel that here is Buddhist speculation seen through a Neoconfucian glass, yet meeting (*mirabile dictu*) with the experimental verifications through the microscope by Leewenhoek and Swammerdam, verifications of which Leibniz knew and to which he admiringly refers.[100]

Leibniz has a fairly accurate conception of Neoconfucian philosophy, which he judges to be a natural theology and, as such, compatible with Christianity—the question of this compatibility was of the greatest interest to the missionaries of his time. Leibniz's *Discourse on the Natural Theology of the Chinese* gives evidence of his knowledge. But despite his interest in Neoconfucianism and his sense of the harmonious integration of all things, an analysis of his intellectual development shows that his thought is not basically indebted to the Chinese. Sometimes he is critical of their intellectual shortcomings; they are ignorant of formal deduction, he remarks. But in response to the testimony of the Jesuit missionaries he is willing to say that the Chinese surpass the Europeans "in comprehending the precepts of civil life." To the Russian Tsar he writes that unless "we"—the Europeans—promote understanding with the Chinese, "when they have learned from us what they wish to know they will then close their doors to us."[101]

Discussion

I have explained Gangesha at greater length than Descartes or Leibniz. This is not because I think him a more important philosopher but because his importance lies in the careful persistence of his argument. I have insisted on rather than explored the technical virtuosity he deploys, but in compensation have tried give some sense of his tenacity. Because his thought is unfamiliar in the West and because I have aimed to explain clearly, I was unable to be as brief in his case as in that of the others.

The mind-matter or self-matter distinction: To continue, we must remember that we are comparing the European conception of mind or soul with the Indian conception of *atman* or self, and not with the "mind" (*manas*) in the Indian sense of a specialized "sense organ." This granted, the mind-matter or self-matter distinction is made by all the philosophers involved. However, an absolute distinction of the kind is possible only to the two Nyaya philosophers, Udayana and Gangesha, and to Descartes (who complicates things by saying that the soul and the body are surely one even though the human mind cannot simultaneously conceive of their union and distinction).[102] For the Indian philosopher Shankara, the distinction is illusory, and for the European, Leibniz, one of different degrees of spiritual reality and of the illusoriness of spatial masses. So in terms of the mind-matter distinction, the Naiyayikas and Descartes are on one side and Shankara and Leibniz on the other.*

The self: There are both Indian and European philosophers who believe that the self/soul is pure conscious intelligence and is intuited as such. In contrast, there are philosophers, Indian and European, who place more stress on indirect or inferential knowledge of the soul. Shankara, who plays no part in this chapter, joins Descartes as a representative of the first point of view. The heir of Yajnavalkya, he says, "Every one is conscious of the existence of (his) Self, and never thinks, 'I am not.'" With a more Cartesian explicitness, he goes on:

> Just because it is the Self, it is impossible for us to entertain the idea even of its being capable of refutation. For the (knowledge of) Self is not, in any person's case, adventitious, not established through the so-called right means of knowledge; it is rather self-established . . . for it is the essential nature of him who refutes. The heat of a fire is not refuted by the fire itself.[103]

This undoubtedly resembles Descartes's *ego cogito, ergo sum*, which Descartes, like Shankara, takes to be an intuition.** Leibniz does not

---

*To Leibniz, the world contains only simple substances, which perceive and have appetites. "Matter and motion are not so much substances as they are phenomena of percipient beings, whose reality is located in the harmony of the percipient within himself (at different times) and with other percipient beings." (Letter of June 30, 1704; Leibniz, *Philosophical Papers and Letters*, pp. 536, 537 [quoted].) This appears to mean that bodies or corporeal masses are "well-founded phenomena" based on the only realities or substances, the monads (Rutherford, "Metaphysics: Late Period," pp. 143–53).

**One sometimes gets the impression that nothing is ever said first. Something like Descartes's proof is attributed by Sextus Empiricus to the "dogmatic" philosophers: "The soul, they assert, exists, seeing that even he who says that the soul does not exist makes this statement by employing it" (Sextus Empiricus, *Against the Physicists* 1.197; in *Sextus Empiricus*, trans. R. G. Bury, vol. 3, Cambridge: Harvard University Press, rev. 1953, p. 101).

reject the intuition but thinks it is too subjective and prefers his more logical and metaphysical approach. He contends that by separating body completely from mind and soul, Descartes and Locke deprive the mind of the sensory material needed for thought, make thought inexplicable and remote from anything we know, and give an opening to professed free-thinkers.[104] Instead of a Cartesian machine inhabited by a human soul, he sees a full, unique individual, part of God's plan as such, a conscious substance with a continuous gradation of experience from the highest degree of consciousness to the unconscious.[105]

Udayana and Gangesha, unlike some others of their school, acknowledge that the self is the object of *I*-consciousness or *I*-awareness; but the self is also inferred from desire, aversion, effort, pleasure, pain, and cognition. The Nyaya view of the self is developed in contradiction to the self-less, discontinuous Buddhist conception. There is, then, a real if qualified equation: Descartes is to Leibniz as Shankara is to Udayana and Gangesha. But while the Cartesian self is all just conscious intellect, the Shankaran soul has a magical-metaphysical fullness. In contrast to both these philosophers, Leibniz and the Naiyayikas have a developed sense of soul/self as forming a complex though temporary unity with its body. And the Naiyayikas, contending with a long, self-denying Buddhist tradition, are subtly analytical, while Leibniz's subtlety and sense of gradation come from the Neoplatonic tradition.

God: For the most part, Gangesha confines himself to the proof from the conscious purposefulness by which the universe must have been produced. Because he acknowledges that human merit and demerit affect the functioning of the cosmos, God's role in creation—which cannot be creation from nothing—must be distinguished from the human role. Descartes, who still sees God with Neoplatonic eyes, chooses ontological or similar proofs, such as that the conception itself of an infinitely perfect being makes the existence of the being undeniable.

The part played by God in Udayana's and Gangesha's world is less striking than in Descartes's and Leibniz's world, which would simply vanish in God's (unimaginable) absence. Yet there is a point of resemblance between the one kind of God and the other: In Descartes's physics, the role of God is to impart motion and physical law to the particles in which the universe begins, while for Gangesha God is essential to make the atomic combinations and essential, after humans are in existence, to direct the effort by which the results of human merit and demerit are implemented. Gangesha's argument, the result of hundreds of years of debate against acute opponents, is far more thorough and philosophically professional than Descartes's—his professionalism is at the level of that of the late European scholastics.

Gangesha argues from perceptual evidence—the strongest kind of evidence, he thinks—that the world is such that God must exist and be good (though he implies his goodness rather than makes an issue of it). While his contention is made with the persistent help of a formalized logic, this logic remains inductive. In contrast, Descartes guarantees the basic veracity of ordinary experience by arguing that it is logically impossible—in the strict, deductive sense of *impossible*—for a perfect God to deceive us.*

Unlike Descartes and Leibniz, Gangesha allows the atheist to argue at length and with logical acumen. The actual or merely invented atheistic arguments he states and refutes are most usually those of the Buddhists, who are deeply religious, in contrast to European atheists. Gangesha's arguments for God are made quite without emotion, an example of the philosopher's hard-learned craft as such. Yet he invokes two holy texts in final evidence.[106]

Relation to modern science and philosophy of science: Both Descartes and Leibniz combined their interest in the theory of science with an interest in scientific practice. Mathematics apart, Descartes's strongest influence on practice was the result, I think, of his advocacy of a lawful, wholly material world inhabited by living machines, animal and human, created by God—in the case of the human machines, inhabited by immaterial souls. Leibniz's strongest influence on practice was, perhaps, the result of his emphasis on a universe in which everything at all knowable could be known by, investigated as, and argued to a practical conclusion in terms of a universal calculus. What influence Gangesha, that is, Navya-Nyaya, may have had on Indian science I do not know, but some of the ideas he expresses are paralleled in twentieth-century science or philosophy of science. Consider, for instance, Gangesha's idea that perceptual awareness

---

*William of Ockham, to whom this argument is already well known, refutes the view that there is any such logical impossibility: God cannot be under any obligation and so cannot act wrongly even if he deceives (M. M. Adams, *William Ockham*, Notre Dame: University of Notre Dame Press, 2 vols., 1987, vol. 1, p. 627). Ockham takes the position of the objector in Gangesha's argument on the possibility of proving that there is only one God. Ockham argues, on nominalistic grounds, against Duns Scotus, that it cannot be proved that there is only one God, or even that there is a God at all. Like Descartes and Leibniz, Scotus relies on deduction. But Ockham, while acknowledging that faith proves that there is only one God, contends that the proposition that God exists cannot "be proved from things that are known per se, since in every argument for that conclusion something will be accepted that is either doubtful or [merely] believed; nor, it is clear, is the proposition in question known through experience." Even if we accept that God's existence can be proved strictly, says Ockham, the proofs of his unity from his infinite intellect, infinite power, and so on, cannot be demonstrated but only believed (William of Ockham, *Quodlibetal Questions*, 2 vols., trans. A. J. Freddoso and F. E. Kelley, New Haven: Yale University Press, 1991, vol. 1, p. 6).

is made up of successive acts, the first act vague and unrelated to intellect (to conceptualization) and the second act clear, intellectual, and verbal. The separation Gangesha makes between nonverbal perception and verbally determined recognition proves to be well founded. We know (from the evidence of psychiatric illnesses) that the names of objects can become lost for use even though the objects for which the words stand continue to be recognized in a practical sense. And we know that a quick, emotional, intellectually unformulated awareness (or, to Nyaya and, often, to Western psychiatry, a non- or subawareness) such as that of fear, comes before a later conscious or verbal one and is mediated by a different brain mechanism, that is, first by the amygdala and only afterward by the cortex. A contemporary researcher, who gives the Indian kind of example of the perception of a possible snake, adds that the reason for the first quick, unverified response is that the cost of treating a stick as a snake is in the long run lower than that of treating a snake as a stick. In his words:

> The sight of a slender curved shape lying flat on the path ahead of us is sufficient to elicit defensive fear responses. We do not need to go through a detailed analysis of whether or not what we are seeing is a snake . . . The brain simply needs to be able to store primitive cues and detect them. Later, coordination of this basic information with the cortex permits verification (yes, this is a snake) or brings the response (screaming, hyperventilation or sprinting) to a stop.[107]

Gangesha's interest in careful simplicity—the simplest hypothesis adequate to a problem—and in careful induction are close to the interests of present-day philosophers of science. What to him is the auxiliary instrument of simplicity is to us Ockham's razor, which an expositor of Ockham puts as the principle that "it is futile to do with more what can be done with fewer" and that "plurality should not be assumed without necessity."[108]*

I am not aware of any explicit comment by Descartes on Ockham's razor. Leibniz writes about it openly and favorably. He compares hypotheses to expenditures, because, he says, "reason demands that we avoid multiplying hypotheses or principles, somewhat as the simplest system is always preferred in astronomy."[109] As for the process of induction, Descartes,

---

*Ockham's formulations are sometimes reminiscent of Gangesha's. Thinking of how to establish that things belong to the same genus, he arrives (as paraphrased) at the following definition: "X and y are co-generic if and only if some essential part of x is maximally similar to some essential part of y and some essential part of x is somehow dissimilar to some essential part of y" (Adams, *William Ockham*, vol. 1, p. 118).

of course, gives rules for it, and he and Leibniz use induction freely, but the need for induction seems to them to reflect human weakness, and—despite their practice—they believe in principle that it is best to grasp the world in terms of abstract principles and deductions from them. The Nyaya-Vaisheshika philosophers—who do not engage in scientific experiments, inductive or other—have a very different emphasis. Since they lack the Euclidean model and the Neoplatonic faith in pure abstraction, their logic is made up of decision procedures for induction and is therefore comparable in purpose to Descartes's (or Bacon's) method, although worked out in more formal terms.

Yet from the standpoint of the more exact sciences, the Indian philosophers' lack of a mathematical-deductive or even experimental-mathematical ideal is striking and marks their thought as, in that respect, prescientific. Descartes and Leibniz, for all their empirical practice of science, are enthusiastic partisans of the deductive ideal. For they believe that the universe has an abstract structure created by God according to his superlative logic, so that it is in principle clear that human beings can arrive by logical means at accurate universal generalizations, even though humans are subject to the constraints of their ignorance (in saying this I ignore Descartes's belief that God can change the laws of logic). Udayana and Gangesha, pressed by their opponents' doubt of the possibility of a reliable criterion, take a view of induction (concomitance) more modern than that of both Descartes and Leibniz. They analyze the conditions needed for accurate empirical generalizations and recognize that exceptions are always theoretically possible; but they recognize as well that both reason and practice set practical limits to skepticism. For this reason they propose (as, in a later time, do Charles Peirce and William James) that only living doubts be entertained with full seriousness.

Chapter 11

Immanent-Transcendent Holism

Shankara, Spinoza

Theme: The Identification of Oneself with Reality as Such

Small things, including philosophers, can feel lost in the great world. Not so with philosophers such as Shankara and Spinoza. As their doctrines show, they are confident they coincide with or blessedly share in its incalculable greatness. Their confidence is not enough to make them a congruous pair. Although Shankara was an ascetic and Spinoza tended toward asceticism, the two led quite different lives in quite different physical and intellectual surroundings. Shankara was conventionally and devoutly religious, while Spinoza was unconventionally and devoutly, so to speak, irreligious. Shankara was a commentator preoccupied with exegetic details more than with system or with proofs of what he was sure that only personal more-than-personal consciousness could demonstrate. Spinoza, though also a commentator of scriptures, was preoccupied with objectively incontrovertible demonstrations, with the objective, inescapable nature of causality, and with the inescapable parallelism of body with mind. The one philosophical and, no doubt, emotional trait that justifies joining the two thinkers in this account is their particular kind of interest in the relation of the individual human being to reality as a whole. Taken abstractly, this is the relationship, touched on earlier, of part with whole, or, as the two philosophers see it, of the minute, apparently individual, human part with the inclusive reality that Shankara calls Atman and Brahman and Spinoza calls God, Nature, and Substance.

Neither the Indian nor the European conceives the whole of everything to be the mere sum of its parts. To the Indian, every part is an illusorily small, illusorily separate manifestation of reality as an unqualified whole; and to the European, every finite part is a relative nothing within the infinitely infinite whole. Each of the two philosophers calls on the seemingly separate individual to strive for liberation. The Indian is sure that the individual's consciousness can be liberated by realizing its identity with the limitless consciousness that is Brahman. The European is sure that the human intellect can be liberated by realizing that it is a finite mode of thinking determined by another such mode, and so on, and that all the modes are parts of the eternal, infinite intellect of God or Nature. For the Indian, to realize the self/Self, atman/Atman identity is to be ultimately clear and experience *moksha*. For the European, to realize the intellect/Intellect's (mediated) identity is to experience the clarification and strengthen the noble tenacity with which one should act for one's own advantage and be blessed in God's infinite love for himself.

Shankara (700–750)

My paean is but a rite of salutation made
to the ocean with its own waters.

Shankara lived considerably earlier than Shriharsha, a partisan of the same general view, but exactly how much earlier is unclear.[1] All considered, an estimate of about C.E. 700 to 750 seems reasonable, though not in the least certain.* Quoted fragments remain of early biographies, but the full biographies of Shankara are from the fourteenth to the eighteenth centuries.[2] Written in a style like that of epic poetry, these biographies look

---

*This is the date favored by Hajime Nakamura, who makes a detailed review of the evidence (see his *History of Early Vedanta Philosophy*, p. 89). Tilmann Vetter holds that it is not yet possible to set a date more exact than 650 to 800 (*Studien zur Lehre und Entwicklung Śankaras*, p. 11). Govind Chandra Pande's opinion is that Shankara lived between 650 and 775, within which he prefers 650 to 700 because of Shankara's supposed meeting with Kumarila and his contemporaneity with Mandana (*Life and Thought of Śankarācārya*, p. 52).

The long-accepted date of C.E. 788 to 820 is based on manuscripts that do not precede the sixteenth century and is difficult to reconcile with the facts that must be taken into account. The sixth to fifth centuries B.C., suggested by the monastic heirs of Shankara's tradition, appear to be impossible. The Shankarite monasteries at Kanchi and at Shringeri have long disputed which is the more ancient one. The absence of critically edited texts with a history of the manuscripts used makes an assessment of the conflicting biographies difficult (Pande, ibid., pp. 41–45, 35).

on Shankara as the incarnation of the God Shiva, come to earth to rescue the Vedic faith from heterodoxy and sin.

With mythology and detail reduced to a still picturesque minimum, what tradition tells us of Shankara is roughly this: He is born in a village in the state of Kerala, in the southwest of India. His father dies when he is still a small child. In school, he masters the Vedas, their related studies, and the orthodox systems of philosophy, with extraordinary ease. At the age of eight he returns home for a time and either he or, by another version, some sages impressed by his ability, persuade his mother to allow him to become a homeless ascetic, a *sannaysin*. In the usual, embellished versions of his life this persuasion gets the help of a perhaps supernatural crocodile, which releases its grip on him only after he cries out to his mother, whose agreement releases him from ordinary life and allows to be symbolically reborn in renunciation.[3] Years later, to fulfill his promise to his mother, he defies the behavior prescribed for a *sannyasin* and performs her funeral rites. His kinsmen and fellow villagers are said to ostracize him in punishment.[4]

To return to Shankara as a boy, having become a *sannyasin*, he undertakes a long journey northward, to his destined *guru*, Govinda. From the age of nine to twelve, he studies with Govinda, who is acknowledged as his teacher in colophons to his books. Govinda is the disciple of Gaudapada, of whom nothing is known; but Gaudapada's extant book is one of the sources of Shankara's philosophy. This is acknowledged, it appears, by Shankara himself when he says that he bows to his teacher's teacher, his *paramaguru*, who, in accord with custom, is unnamed. Shankara also quotes Gaudapada, without naming him, as a master of tradition.[5] On his teacher's request, Shankara goes to the holy city of Kashi (Varanasi, that is, Banaras), where he begins to accept disciples and to work on his commentaries (to be described later). Credibly or not, he is said to finish them all by the age of sixteen.[6]

Shankara not only writes a great deal, including poetry, but becomes an energetic religious reformer. This aim involves him in many debates. The most notable, against the philosopher Mandana, is described as having lasted for fifteen days. The credibility of this story is lessened by the fact that the arguments assigned to Mandana by Shankara's biographers are incompatible with Mandana's surviving works.[7]* Debating with invariable

---

*An imaginary episode pits Shankara against Mandana's wife, Ubhayabharati, who is an incarnation of the goddess of learning. After Shankara defeats Mandana, Ubhayabharati silences him with questions on the science of erotics. Allowed a month's delay, Shankara enters the body of King Amaru, who has just died of a hunting accident. Preserving his ascetic dispassion, he engages the king's body in erotic encounters with the king's hundred wives. Returning in his own body to the debate, Shankara is able to prove his understanding of erotics, is acknowledged the victor, and wins the philosopher and his goddess-wife as disciples. "His" erotic experience allows him to write the erotic book ascribed by the ignorant to Amaru. This myth fits in well with the erotic poetry and Tantric works ascribed to Shankara. (See Siegel, *Fires of Love, Waters of Peace*, pp. 4–5, 11; and Isayeva, *Shankara and Indian Philosophy*, pp. 79–80.)

success, his biographers say, Shankara travels through much of India, defeating partisans of other views and suppressing bloody sacrifices and orgiastic rites.[8] He also goes on pilgrimages and establishes monasteries (*matha*) for his disciples. Buddhism is still flourishing in some areas of India, especially in the east.[9] Shankara's monasteries, no doubt meant to be centers of practice and learning like the Buddhists', prove to be successful in accomplishing this aim. Shankara also undertakes to reorganize the ascetic orders of Vedanta into ten groups, each headed by a disciple.[10]

The events in Shankara's later life are described in different sources in quite different, inconsistent, often unbelievable ways.[11] His death occurs when he is only thirty-two years old.

Shankara's clear, even graceful philosophical writing is enlivened by sometimes homely examples and occasional invective. His name is attached to more than three hundred works, not all of which he wrote. The confusion has most probably been created by the practice of assigning the name Shankaracharya to the successive heads of the monasteries at Shringeri and Kanchi: the works of all of them are by one Shankara or another.[12] The question of how, in so brief a lifetime, Shankara—the primary one—wrote as much as is plausibly attributed to him is answered with the reminder that his works are mostly commentaries, that he is often rather repetitive, and that he is acute and intense rather than widely learned.[13]

Shankara's most important writings are his commentaries on the sacred works that comprise the Vedanta (the *end of the Veda, end* referring to the Upanishads in relation to the Vedas that preceded them). The sacred works on which he comments include the old Upanishads, the Brahma Sutra(s) (or Vedanta Sutra(s)), and the *Bhagavad Gita*. His main doctrine is the teaching of Uddalaka (as he interprets him) and Yajnavalkya: Reality is nothing but Brahman, which is identical with the individual self or *atman*. In his commentaries, Shankara above all tries to show that this is the message the scriptures invariably intend. Such an effort is essential to his case because the "scriptures" do not lend themselves easily to a uniform interpretation of this or any other kind.*

---

*Shankara's nondualism (*advaita*) or absolute nondualism (*kevala vidya*), which teaches the absolute identity of self and Brahman, is often taken to be less true to the Brahma Sutra's intention than is the interpretation by Ramanuja (traditionally, 1017–1137), which teaches identity-in-difference (*bheda-bheda*) or qualified nondualism (*vishishta-advaita*). By Ramanuja's interpretation, selves and universe are inseparable from Brahman and yet related to him— the supreme self—as his inseparable qualities. None is either like him or different from or external to him. He is the one who wills to become many, of which he remains the harmonizing unity. For the interpretations of Bhaskara (fl. tenth century), Nimbarka (fl. twelfth or thirteenth century), and Madhva (traditionally 1238–1317), and others see the books under *Competing Interpretations of Vedanta* in note 1.

To Shankara, the object of all of the Vedas is expressed in a single sentence, the nine times repeated lesson that Uddalaka teaches Shvetaketu: *Tat tvam asi*, That is you![14] Since he is convinced beforehand of the truth of the doctrine he takes these words to express, Shankara uses interpretive tactics identified with theology rather than philosophy. For example, in the *Brihadaranyaka Upanishad* (3.2.13) Shankara encounters a passage that declares that "one becomes good through good work," *good work* meaning the right performance of ritual. According to Shankara, this applies only to the visible universe. He can make this claim because, to him, bondage is ignorance, to which work is irrelevant, while it is knowledge that destroys bondage and reveals what is eternal and beyond name and form (3.3.1).[15]

Shankara's principle of exegesis is clear and drastic: the Vedas *must* be interpreted in his monistic, nondual sense. Not that the authority of the Vedas can be violated, but only a Vedantic exegete of his, Shankara's persuasion knows how to test its passages so as to establish their consistently monistic intent.* Shankara respects reasoning, but it leads, he says, to conflicting results. All the assembled logicians of the past, present, and future could not agree to regard anything as perfectly well known. This is because the true nature of the cause of the world is beyond reason, as it is beyond perception. Only with the help of the holy texts is it possible to know this cause and end the conflict of opinions. Because it stems from the suprarational, reason, to be reasonable, ought to serve the suprarational.[16]**

---

*To Shankara, once the words of a Vedantic text have been "determined to refer to Brahman, and their purport is understood thereby, it would be improper to assume them to have a different sense" (*Commentary on the Vedānta Sūtras* 1.1.4; trans. Thibaut, vol. 1, p. 22). The concept of purport or intent (*tatparya*) was essential to Vedic exegesis. Attribution of Vedic intent came to be based on a number of criteria: knowledge enabling the selection of significant sentences; correlation of sentences to discover their dominant theme; use of the theme to introduce order into the various Vedic sentences; ignoring of sentences irrelevant to Brahman; skipping of sentences that convey only empirical information; rejection of merely apparent meanings; and the inner core of truth (Murty, *Revelation and Reason in Advaita Vedānta*, pp. 76, 80).

**In his commentary on Gaudapada, Shankara summarizes that "both the falsity of plurality and the truth of nonduality are first presented through authoritative tradition as a 'mere thesis' and then supported by 'examples,' 'reasons,' and 'logical reflection' (*drishanta, hetu, tarka*), so that they are finally established 'by scripture and reason' (*shatrayuktibhyam*)" (Halbfass, *Tradition and Reflection*, p. 140). In other words, given the alternative of regarding the Vedas as an instrument of knowledge and therefore subject to rules of verification, or as revealed, unfalsifiable truth—which nonbelievers can reject as a whole—Shankara defines the Vedas as both an instrument of knowledge and as revealed, unfalsifiable truth (Biderman, *Reality and Illusion in the Philosophy of Śaṅkara*, pp. 96–103).

To see the philosopher in Shankara, it is necessary to piece together the philosophical reasoning that lies behind his interpretive maneuvers, explanations, and defensive attacks. For this purpose, the best of his works is his masterpiece, the commentary to the Brahma Sutra, often given the later name, the Vedanta Sutra.[17]* Structured in accord with the Sutra, his commentary (bhashya) consists of four books (adhyaya), each divided into four chapters (pada). It has for a long time been the most widely read and explicated work in Indian philosophy. Its favorite part, called the *Four Sutras* (Chatuhsutri) is made up of its introduction and first four *sutras*.[18]

Shankara's commentary begins with the declaration that everything we know appears to be divided into ego and non–ego. No proof is needed to show that all non–ego—the object (vishaya) of knowledge, the *that*—is different from the (universal) Ego—the subject (vishayin) of knowledge, the *you*. The two, as opposite as darkness and light, cannot be identified with one another. Whatever applies to the object and the subject of knowledge applies to their attributes, which therefore cannot be identified with one another. It is therefore wrong to superimpose the subject or the subject's attributes onto the object, that is, to mistake the subject for the object or the subject's attributes for those of the object.[19]

However, because of mistaken knowledge, there is an eternal tendency of human beings to fail to distinguish object from subject, and therefore to couple the real (self) and unreal (object) and superimpose the nature and attributes of the unreal on the real. So a person naturally but mistakenly says, "I (my self) am that (my body)," and, "That (the object) is mine (belongs to my self)." This error is like the perceptual illusion that mistakes mother-of-pearl for silver by superimposing the nature of silver on that of mother-of-pearl. However, the subject is not a nonobject in an absolute sense: insofar as it is merely an *individual* soul (jiva), conditioned to be such by (the fundamentally unreal) senses, internal organ (manas), and so on, the subject appears to be limited.[20]

Knowledge (vidya) shows superimposition (adhyasa) to be (primal) ignorance (nescience, avidya). Yet it is only natural to assume that it is right for the nonself to be superimposed on the internal self. All the practical distinctions made in ordinary life, including the ritual distinctions made in the Veda, are based on the mutual superimposition of nonself and self. Without the fundamentally erroneous but practically necessary

---

*The Brahma Sutra, attributed to Badarayana, is meant to systematize the philosophic doctrines of the Upanishads. Its date is hard to fix, though the first century c.e. is hazarded. The Sutra's 555 often fragmentary aphorisms need a commentary. The early commentaries, whose authors' names are preserved, were eclipsed by that of Shankara. His is therefore the earliest commentary still extant.

idea of the body, the senses, and so on, we could not perceive anything nor make any use of the other means of knowledge.* In this respect, humans are like animals, who act in accord with their perceptions and what they learn from them—a cow draws back from a man with a raised stick but comes up to a man with fresh grass in his hand, just as human beings run from men with drawn swords and a threatening appearance and approach those who look and act benign.

It is natural for states such as desire, intention, doubt, and determination, all attributes of the internal organ (manas), to be superimposed on the self. Our ability to select what we want to pay attention to can be explained only if we assume that there is such is an internal organ, whose function it is to modify the self.** What happens is that the internal organ—the organ of selective attention and producer of the notion of the ego—and "the interior Self, which is the witness of everything," superimpose themselves on one another.[21]

The study of Vedantic texts, Shankara declares, aims to help attain knowledge of the absolute unity of the Self and so to free the individual self from the erroneous idea that causes all evil.[22] But before the study begins, there is a preliminary question to settle: If the study's point is to know Brahman, and if Brahman is known in advance of any inquiry into its nature, why undertake the enquiry at all? Shankara answers, first, that the existence of Brahman is beyond question. This is because Brahman is everyone's Self, as everyone one is conscious. No one ever thinks "I am not."[23]

---

*Although Shankara has no general discussion of the means of knowledge, he refers to perception, inference, and scriptural testimony. His school regards knowledge as valid when functionally useful and uncontradicted. As put by Dharmaraja in the seventeenth century: To be uncontradicted "means 'not contradicted during mundane existence (samsara)' and therefore the definition of valid knowledge is proper in respect of the jar, etc." Dharmaraja means that ordinary empirical knowledge is correct—up to the realization of the Ultimate Reality. (See Solomon, Avidya, pp. 495–96; and, for Dharmaraja's view, J. Sinha, Indian Psychology, vol. 1, Calcutta: Sinha Publishing Co., 1958, pp. 128–36.)

**This organ is called, Shankara says, by names such as manas ("mind"), buddhi (intellect), vijnana (intelligence), or chitta (thought) (Commentary 2.3.34; trans. Thibaut, vol. 2, p. 48). Elsewhere he says that it is manas that is given different names, names of which he makes sometimes indiscriminate use. Once he speaks of the modifier of the atman as twofold, referring perhaps to buddhi and manas. He also describes a sequence of superimposing organs: By reflecting and limiting the self's intelligence (vijnana), the intellect (buddhi) transmits the reflection to the mind (manas), which transmits it to the organs of action, which transmit it to the body. At every step there is mutual superimposition. All people therefore identify themselves, in accord with their discriminations, with the body and the organs and their modifications (Commentary on the Brihadaranyaka Upanishad 4.3.7; trans. Madhavananda, p. 612; and see Mayeda, "The Advaita Theory of Perception," pp. 223–28; and Vetter, Studien zur Lehre und Entwicklung Śaṅkaras, p. 113).

In a later passage, Shankara puts this insistence, that we know the Self (the universal Self, which is the true personal self), in a more detailed, persuasive way, which may bring Augustine and Descartes to mind. The self is such, he argues, that it is impossible even to entertain the idea that its existence can be refuted: the self is self-established. It does, of course, make use of perception and other means of knowledge. But the energy that acts through the means of knowledge dwells in and presupposes the existence of the self; and it is impossible to refute the existence of such a self-established entity. In Shankara's own words (which have been quoted in the account of Descartes), something extrinsic can be refuted, "but not that which is the essential nature (of him who attempts the refutation); for it is the essential nature of him who refutes. The heat of a fire is not refuted (i.e. sublated) by the fire itself" (Commentary 2.3.7).[24]

Consider, Shankara goes on, how the object of knowledge changes when we say that we at present know (something), knew in the recent past, knew in the more remote past, and will know in the near and in the more distant future. Through all these changes, "the knowing agent does not change, since its nature is eternal presence" and "we cannot even conceive that it ever should become something different from what it is."[25] But although the self (the Self), which is Brahman, knows itself by itself, its particular nature is subject to dispute. Ordinary, unlearned people and materialists (Lokayata) suppose that it is solely the body that has the intelligence identified with the self. Others ascribe intelligence to the body's organs of action or to the internal organ. Others (Sarvastivada Buddhists) say that the self is only a momentary idea, and still others (Madhyamika Buddhists) that it is the void. And there are those (Naiyayikas) who, depending on the Veda, maintain that there is a transmigrating being, different from the body, that is both the agent and enjoyer of the fruits of action. Others (exponents of Yoga) believe that there are both individual souls and an all-knowing, all-powerful Lord. Finally, there are the Vedantins such as myself, who hold that the Lord is the self. Because of these many opinions, people may thoughtlessly embrace one or another view that will keep them from the highest blessedness. Hence the need to inquire into Brahman, with the help of the texts of the Vedanta and with fitting arguments.[26]

Brahman in the absolute sense is beyond inquiry, but we can assign attributes to him in the sense of the Lord and creator of the empirical world and define him, in this sense, as "that which is . . . which originated the entire creation."[27] We can be sure that Brahman has not sprung from anything. This is because "the relation of cause and effect cannot exist without a certain superiority" of the cause, and nothing is superior to Brahman. Besides, Brahman cannot spring from anything particular. This is because "we observe that particular forms of existence are produced from what is general— for instance, jars and pots from clay—but not that the general is produced from particulars." Brahman, which is *being* (*sat*), cannot spring, as some believe, from *nonbeing* (*asat*). The reason is that a cause is the self of its effects, and nonbeing has no self to enable it to be a cause. Effects spring from other effects, but Brahman is no effect; unless we admit an uncaused causal substance, we fall into an infinite regression of causes.[28]

In the absolute sense Brahman is eternal, omnipresent, within everything, the self of everything, and without parts, without action, unborn, undying, fearless, and, because of the inadequacy of all epithets, best described negatively, by *no! no!* Everything—Vedic texts, tradition, and reasoning—tells us that the highest Self has no differences that depend on time, space, or anything else.[29] It is therefore impossible to explain how indescribable, unchanging Brahman produces effects, an ability that in gods and other intelligent creatures requires organs of action, which Brahman lacks: "The transcendent highest Brahman can be fathomed by means of Scripture only, not by mere reasoning."[30]

The world cannot have originated, as some argue, from nonintelligent primal matter, nor from atoms, nor sprung up spontaneously. Furthermore, we have the evidence of the Vedas, whose "quality of omniscience cannot be sought elsewhere but in omniscience itself."[31] The explanation of the changing influence, so to speak, of Brahman on the world is that he is grasped in two seemingly different forms. The one form is Brahman without qualities or attributes (*nirguna* Brahman). The other, Brahman with qualities or attributes (*saguna* Brahman), is qualified by the limiting conditions of the world of name and form. As created by this Brahman, the world "reveals itself in a graduated series of beings, and so appears in forms of varying dignity and power."[32]

Brahman's functioning as the world's all-pervading Lord is not the result of any insufficiency or extraneous purpose. As natural as breathing, which follows the law of its nature, the Lord's activity "may be supposed to be mere sport *[lila]*, proceeding from his own nature, without reference to any purpose." To the Lord, the creation of this world "is mere play."[33]*

---

*God's ability to create without extraneous means is compared by Shankara to that of intelligent beings of great power, such as gods and rishis, who create various object—chariots, palaces, etc.—"by mere intention"; to the spider, who "emits out of itself the threads of its web"; to the female crane, "who conceives without a male"; and to the lotus, which "wanders from one pond to another without any means of conveyance" (Śaṅkara, *Commentary on the Vedānta Sūtras* 2.1.26; trans. Thibaut, vol. 1, pp. 347–48). In *De ludo globi* (1463), Nicholas of Cusa, too, uses the analogy between playing, which involves nothing extraneous, and creation (P. M. Watts, *Nicolaus Cusanus*, Leiden: Brill, 1982, p. 195).

But if Brahman is absolutely one, you may ask, how is all this apparent activity possible? How (as the Neoplatonists ask) does the partless, unmoving, unqualifiedly one become the divisible, moving, qualified many? "Listen how," answers Shankara, and proceeds, not unmysteriously:

> Belonging to the Self, as it were, of the omniscient Lord, there are name and form, the figments of Nescience [avidya], not to be defined either as being (i.e. Brahman), nor as different from it, the germs of the entire expanse of the phenomenal world, called . . . the illusion (maya), power (shakti), or nature (prakriti) of the omniscient Lord. Different from them is the omniscient Lord himself. (Commentary 2.1.14)[34]

How does Shankara understand terms such as nescience (avidya) and illusion (maya)?[35] The particular sense he gives them is the relatively new one they acquired in Mahayana Buddhism. Only in this Buddhism are avidya and maya consistently evoked to explain why humans experience the world of phenomena as if it was real. In Shankara, avidya is not only the ignorance that causes the continued empirical existence of individual humans but also the lack of insight— a potent lack—responsible for the illusory existence of the entire empirical world.[36*]

A willing purveyor of this meaning, Shankara's predecessor, Gaudapada, uses Brahmanical sources in the light of Mahayana Bud-

---

*The terms avidya and maya have a varied history: In the Vedic hymns, avidya is ignorance and, later, a positive hindrance to knowledge or to nonspiritual knowledge. Maya is a synonym of intelligence or mental power (prajna) and its realization in practice. In the Atharvaveda, maya generally means mysterious power or intelligence and its result. A power or shakti of creation, it is not illusion. In the Upanishads, vidya may mean true, adequate knowledge (as of atman and Brahman). Avidya is lack of such knowledge, or (in the Maitri Upanishad) false knowledge, or (in the Brihadaranyaka Upanishad) the tendency to imagine something where it does not exist, for example, to identify atman with the body. Maya continues to mean mysterious power, and also gets the meaning of guile. In a late Upanishad (the Maitri), maya is the insubstantial manifestation of a magician's power. By making the Brahman-atman equivalence and associating avidya with the self's ability to conjure up appearances in a dream, Yajnavalkya (Brihadaranyaka Upanishad 4) preceded Gaudapada and Shankara, but it is not sure that he saw the world as illusory appearance (Solomon, Avidyā, p. 39; and chaps. 1, 2. See also Gonda on maya [note 36]).

In Sarvastivada (Vaibhashika) and Sautrantika Buddhism, ignorance (avidya) is the first link in the process of dependent origination and leads to the illusion of a permanent self (ibid., pp. 127, 131). The word avidya does not appear in the Vedanta Sutra. Maya there refers to dream states (thought to be prophetic). The Vedanta Sutra says nothing about the reality of the objective world (ibid., pp. 117–18).

dhism and the analogy it draws between dreams and waking experience. The cosmic power of *maya* is now regarded as the material or auxiliary cause of the appearance of the world, of the appearance of separateness of individual souls, and even of the apparent attributes of Brahman as the Lord. Expressed in an image, *maya* exists in the same way as an illusory serpent exists in a rope. Grasped without imagery, *maya* refers to the inexplicable relationship between Brahman and the perceived, plural, illusory world.[37]

A question arises: Is the cosmic ignorance, *avidya*, a projection of Atman/Brahman and so, in a sense, Atman/Brahman itself? Shankara answers the question, but ambiguously. When true knowledge springs up, he agrees, perception and the like are no longer valid. When this happens, the Vedas themselves are no longer valid: "In this state a father is no father, a mother no mother, the worlds no worlds, the Vedas no Vedas."[38]

But if there is nothing separate, nothing truly in particular, the questioner asks, Who then is characterized by the absence of true knowledge? The answer is, You yourself who ask this question! The questioner, not satisfied, asks how this can be if, as scripture says, he, the questioner, is identical with the Lord?* "If you have arrived at that knowledge," answers Shankara, "then there is nobody who does not possess such knowledge"—the Self itself is not necessarily affected with duality by ignorance, *avidya*.[39] Accepting the doctrine of *avidya* does not introduce plurality— *avidya* is not something added to Brahman.[40] So the elimination of *avidya* would not deprive Brahman of its nature as the sun would be deprived if its light and heat were eliminated.[41]

In such ways, Shankara both hypostatizes *avidya* to account for the material world and denies the reality it would gain as a projection of

---

*In Shankara's *A Thousand (Verses of) Teachings (Upadeśasāhasrī)*, a student asks a similar question: If *avidya* is the mutual superimposition between Atman and non-Atman, then just as the non-Atman does not really exist in the Atman, the Atman does not really exist in the non-Atman. If so, "neither the body nor Atman exists." This is unacceptable, so the conclusion is that the "body and *Atman* are not superimposed upon each other through *avidya*." The teacher answers only indirectly: The Atman is not composite and cannot be connected with anything. However, in the same way as things have space even though space is not connected with anything, the body and other things have Atman. (Mayeda, *A Thousand Teachings* 2.2.55, 58; trans. 82–83.)

Shankara probably does not feel obligated to explain *avidya*, which is assumed in order to explain the false plurality of the empirical world. To avoid an infinite regress, Shankara must begin with something unexplained. (See Biderman, *Reality and Illusion in the Philosophy of Sankara*, pp. 124–28.)

Brahman. Its nature is simply indeterminable.* This indetermination, which seems not to trouble Shankara much, leaves his disciples a stimulating difficulty. Each does his best to find his way between interpretations that are negative, positive, both, or neither.[42]

Given his insistence on the illusoriness of the empirical world, Shankara, like the Buddhists, is faced with the question of how the use of illusory means can help anyone to get beyond them. After all, the texts of the Vedas, with their injunctions and prohibitions, depend on ultimately illusory distinctions. Even the doctrine of release depends on a distinction, which, simply as a distinction, must be illusory. Shankara answers by way of an analogy: You may say that a rope imagined to be a snake does not bite, but the imagined or dreamed bite of a cobra can be fatal; and dreams can foretell good and bad fortune in waking life. The moral is that real effects can result from illusory causes.[43] A person's knowledge of Brahman is vouched for by his heart's conviction and cannot be denied by anyone else.[44]

Against the Buddhists, on whose ideas he draws, Shankara is relentless. The reason is probably the historical situation, which encourages him to adapt Buddhist ideas to help fortify the reaction against Buddhism.[45]** He classifies the Buddhists into "those who maintain the reality of everything" (the Sarvastivadins), "those who maintain that thought [vijnana] only is real" (the Vijnanavadins, to be discussed later), and "those who maintain that everything is void" (the Madhyamikas).

---

*For Shankara, avidya is only rarely synonymous with maya. To him, maya, meaning illusory appearance, is as a rule produced by avidya. Sometimes maya gets the old sense of the power to project illusions (Commentary 1.3.19; trans. Thibaut, vol. 1, p. 190). Shankara says that the omniscience and omnipotence of the Lord (Ishvara) depend on avidya. Later, he adds that if one accepts the truth that Brahman is the cause of the world, Brahman must be "all-knowing, all-powerful, and possessing the great power of Maya" (Commentary 2.1.14,37; Thibaut, vol. 1, pp. 329, 362; and see Solomon, Avidyā, pp. 233–40).

In Shankara's use, avidya has at least five distinguishable meanings: (1) wrong knowledge, including lack of knowledge, doubt, and indecision; (2) erroneous mutual superimposition of atman (self) and anatman (nonself), which results in the illusion of the empirical world; (3) the eternal, prenatal disposition to err, which can be dispelled by right knowledge; (4) the cosmic principle of the phenomenal world, which conditions Brahman and results in individuation; and (5) the material causal potency out of which the world emerges, and which is identified with maya, prakriti, akasha, and other forces (Solomon, Avidyā, p. 240).

**"The age of the happy coexistence of Buddhism and Hinduism had already passed when he was born, and his age was marked by a Hindu revival. Although he tried to Vedanticize the Gaudapadiyakarika," Shankara adapted its Buddhist elements to his own system. "Thus the Vedanta in the Brahmasutra, which may be characterized as realistic monism, was transformed into illusionistic monism, which regards everything but Brahman as unreal. At the same time the difference between the individual atman and Brahman is looked upon as due to nescience (avidya) and therefore unreal" (Mayeda, A Thousand Teachings, pp. 13–14).

Of the Sarvastivada doctrine of aggregates (*skandhas*), shared by Buddhists generally, Shankara observes that the aggregation of the aggregates cannot be explained on Buddhist principles. Composed of atoms, the material aggregates have no intelligence; and Buddhists do not accept either a permanent soul or a ruling Lord that could cause the atoms' aggregation. And if atoms and aggregates were spontaneously active, their activity would never end and release would be impossible.[46]

Shankara goes on: Buddhists argue that the aggregates succeed one another in a self-renewing series that begins with ignorance (nescience, *avidya*). This argument explains the aggregates' succession but not their initial formation. Ignorance cannot be the explanation because, to exist, it needs the aggregates. And if we assume, with certain Buddhists, that atoms are momentary and unconnected with souls or with the potency (*adrishta*) in souls that generates the outcome of merit and demerit, what can cause the aggregation of the aggregates? If it is assumed that one aggregate necessarily produces another, there are two possibilities: If one aggregate produces only another like itself, then transmigration—contrary to Buddhism—would always be from like to like: once a human being, always a human being. But if there is no settled rule and like can produce either like or unlike, a man could suddenly become an elephant or a god and again become a man (the argument used by Lucretius). And by Buddhist doctrine, there is no permanent enjoying soul, so there is no one to desire anything—enjoyment serves only itself, just as final release, nirvana, serves only itself.[47]

Shankara even argues that the Buddhist view of causality makes cessation, nirvana, impossible: To the Buddhists, cessation has no positive characteristics. But then cessation cannot interrupt the causal chain of events the Buddhists postulate or annihilate any of its moments. The annihilation would interrupt the continuity of the existence—from past to future—of the things we observe. If the cessation is assumed to be the result of perfect knowledge, then—in violation of Buddhist doctrine—cessation has a cause. And if cessation takes place of its own accord, it is useless to Buddhist doctrine.[48]

Shankara continues: Whoever maintains that all things are momentary cannot explain how a momentary perception is retained in memory. The memory belongs to the perceiver. No one confuses who it is, himself or someone else, who has a memory. No one thinks, "I remember; another person made the observation." What grasps the similarity of successive moments must itself be the one permanent subject.[49] The general principle to keep in mind, Shankara says, is that

> whenever . . . something perfectly well known from ordinary experience is not admitted by philosophers, they may indeed

establish their own view and demolish the contrary opinion by means of words, but they thereby neither convince others nor even themselves (*Commentary* 2.2.25).[50]

Shankara says that the thinkers who declare that "only cognitions (*vijnana*) exist" claim that they resemble the Vedantists. They resemble them, they say, because they believe that perception is a solely internal process "whose constituting members are the act of knowledge, the object of knowledge, and the result of knowledge."[51] Unwilling to accept such a philosophical kinship, Shankara answers in a brisk commonsense tone that there is no need to pay attention to the words of someone who denies being conscious of outward things. The very nature of consciousness requires us to believe that the outward object exists apart from consciousness. All those who perceive a post or a wall are conscious not only of perception but of "posts, walls, and the like as objects of their perceptions."[52] The very attempt of the Buddhists to distinguish internal from external is, at bottom, an acknowledgment that the external exists.[53]

With Madhyamaka, Shankara is impatient. Philosophically speaking, this is strange, because Shankara knowingly echoes some of Gaudapada's ideas and Gaudapada knowingly echoes Madhyamaka ideas.[54]* Yet Shankara says only that Madhyamaka needs no special refutation because all the means of valid knowledge contradict it.[55] He ends his discussion of Buddhist philosophy harshly. However you test the Buddhist system, he says, it has no foundation to rest on and "gives way on all sides, like the walls of a well dug in sandy soil." It is folly to use it as a guide in daily life. "By propounding the three mutually contradictory systems," the Buddha "has made it clear that he was a man given to making incoherent assertions, or else that hatred of all beings induced him to propound absurd doctrine by accepting that they would become thoroughly confused" (*Commentary* 2.2.32).[56]

---

*Gaudapada writes: "Nothing whatsoever is originated either from itself or from something else; nothing whatsoever existent, non-existent, or both existent and non-existent is originated." Imitating Nagarjuna but substituting the sense of *reality* for that of *emptiness*, he writes: "There is neither cessation nor origination; no one in bondage, no one aspiring, no one desirous of liberation, no one who is emancipated—This is the Highest Truth" (*Gaudapadakarika [Agamasastra, Mandukya-karika]* 4.22, 2.31, from King, "Śūnyata and Ajati," pp. 387, 400).

The commentary on the *Gaudapada-karika*, traditionally attributed to Shankara, is summarized in Potter, ed., *Advaita Vedanta up to Śaṁkara and His Pupils*, pp. 308–17. According to Mayeda, in this commentary Shankara "intentionally misinterprets Buddhist terms so as to give Advaita readings to passages on which he comments, but...he needed to know Buddhism to do that" (ibid., p. 309).

In criticizing Buddhism, Shankara makes an astonishing omission: He shows no sign of recognizing that all the Buddhist philosophies he criticizes accept a dual standard of truth, that of the lower, empirical truth, by which ordinary perception and inference are valid, and that of the absolute, by which ordinary perception is misleading.* Shankara's attack on Buddhism and the Buddha suggests that the motive for the omission is polemical.

While Shankara stigmatizes the Buddhists as nihilists, Shankara's later theistic rival, Ramanuja (traditionally 1017–1137), stigmatizes Shankara and his followers as surreptitious Buddhists "who take shelter under a pretended Vedic theory."[57] He prefaces his long hostile analysis with a denunciation: Their entire theory "rests on a fictitious foundation of altogether hollow and vicious arguments, incapable of being stated in logical alternatives." It is a theory, Ramanuja says, devised by men with darkened intellects.[58]

Shankara is mainly a commentator and does not have a finished, philosophically coherent system.[59] The coherence he does achieve is created by his overriding principle and the forensic vigor with which he subordinates the Vedas' variety to this principle. In making reason the servant of the suprarational as revealed in sacred texts, Shankara is nothing but a theologian.[60] But in requiring the texts to yield only his own, nondual interpretation and in attacking rival philosophies with unmistakably philosophical arguments, he is a distinctly philosophical theologian. All the same, he seems not to care that his commonsense criticisms against the mentalistic variety of Buddhism (Vijnanavada) can also be used against his philosophy of nondualism. He leaves it to his followers to turn this nondualism into a well-articulated system or, rather, group of systems.

It is a serious mistake to regard Shankara as the very archetype of Indian philosophical preceptors, but he has for a long time been the most widely revered among them. Perhaps his thought can be reworked into a viable contemporary form.[61] An Indian philosopher has given Shankara a

---

*In his dialogues, the Buddha sometimes speaks conventionally without drawing attention to the fact; but often he protests that conventional language is made up only of mere names. Buddhist commentaries formalize a distinction between conventional and absolute truth: "The Blessed One proclaimed the Four Noble Truths, but he also declared Two Truths, relative truth (samvritisatya) and absolute truth (paramarthasatya) . . . If the idea of a thing disappears when this thing is dissipated, or broken to pieces, by the mind, this thing would be regarded as having a relative existence; for example water. If we grasp and remember the dharmas, such as color, etc., in the water, then the idea of water will disappear . . . Thus if one says, from the relative point of view, "There is a jug, there is water," one is speaking truly, and one is not speaking falsely. Consequently this is relatively true." But atoms, sensations, and dharmas in general exist absolutely, and so the idea of them is absolutely true. (Vasubandhu, Abhidharmakośabhāṣyam 6.2.D; trans. L. M. Pruden, Berkeley: Asian Humanities Press, 1989, vol. 3, pp. 910–11).

logical, linguistic, Wittgensteinian turn, according to which Shankara is not trying to redirect our way of seeing things but to show how concepts are applied to—superimposed upon—reality, which is nonconceptual.*

Spinoza (1632–1677)

The wise man . . . never ceases to be.

His given name was Baruch in Hebrew, Bento in Portuguese, and Benedictus in Latin, and his surname was Spinoza, de Spinoza, or Despinoza.[62] His mother died when he was six, his stepmother when he was twenty-one, and his father, when he was twenty-two. On his father's death, he and his brother Gabriel took over the family import-export business.[63] Like other Spanish and Portuguese Jews, the family had fled to Amsterdam because of religious persecution. Not all Dutch cities accepted Jews, and even in Amsterdam, where they were given the then extraordinary privilege of living outside of a ghetto, the government obliged them to declare that they were faithful to the law of Moses and believed in God and a future life.[64]

The influence of persecution on Jewish life in Europe helps to explain both the boldness of Spinoza's thought and the formal ostracism that cut him off from the Jewish community—as death had cut him off from his parents. Death and ostracism released him from most of the social limits on his freedom to philosophize. His creative response makes his life no less exemplary than the trial and death of Socrates. Hence the following relatively detailed account.

Forced to choose between emigration and conversion, many Spanish-Portuguese Jews had converted to Catholicism. Unsure of their sincerity and maybe jealous of their success, inquisitors worked with inquisitorial zeal to unmask those who remained crypto-Jews or, as they were called, Marranos. By threat and torture, the inquisitors forced some crypto-Jews to inform on others. To further their work, they sent spies

---

*I am referring to Ganeśwar Miśra (1914–1985), who writes: "A concept . . . has no occurrence except in the judgment. A judgment . . . is not found in the world . . . It is co-extensive with human nature. To know is to judge and to judge is to apply a concept, a non-illusory unreal entity in a beginningless manner. This is technically called *avidya* or *ajnana* in the Vedantic literature. It does not signify a psychological state or absence of knowledge. It only signifies a beginningless process of applying concepts in judgmental knowledge . . . A particular case of judging couples a real and an unreal because it shares in the general nature of judgment which cannot escape the method of applying a concept to an existent" (Ganeśwar Miśra, *Language, Reality, and Analysis*, ed. J. N. Mohanty, Leiden: Brill, 1990, p. 8).

to Amsterdam to discover which crypto-Jews had thrown off their disguise, so that their property in Spain and Portugal could be seized and their relatives there punished for remaining, the inquisitors assumed, secret Jews. Such victims of the inquisition were hailed by the Jews of Amsterdam as martyrs.[65]

In Spinoza's time, Amsterdam was a flourishing metropolis of about 180,000 inhabitants, with a Jewish community of about 5000 members. Because the community was so largely made up of refugees or their immediate descendants, including many formerly Spanish or Portuguese crypto-Jews, it was subject to strong social tensions. Among the newly revealed Jews there were those who had studied theology and medicine in Iberian universities and preferred a desacralized Biblical faith with a universal morality. Sometimes they also mocked the rabbis and the prevailing orthodox beliefs.[66]

The community's religious, civil, and economic life was administered by an elected council of six respected men, mostly businessmen. The council appointed its rabbis. Officially responsible for the conduct of the Jews it administered, it had to be careful not to offend Christian sensibilities.* Its rules were enforced, even against prominent members, by fines and the threat of ostracism from the community. Its records show that an excommunication might last only a day; its average duration was several months. Punishment by excommunication was normally revoked when the accused person made a public declaration of repentance. Spinoza's case was very exceptional in that his excommunication had no time limit and was marked by such bitter language.[67]

During the two weeks before Spinoza's excommunication, the council was preoccupied with resettling hundreds of Jewish refugees from southern Germany.[68] The edict of excommunication was read out in the synagogue on July 27, 1656. Spinoza was then twenty-four years old. The edict declared that the council had tried

> by various means and promises [apparently including an offer
> of a regular subsidy], to turn him from his evil ways. But
> having failed to make him mend his wicked ways, and, on the

---

*Christians were likely to suppose that unbelieving Jews would undermine Christianity too. Calvinist theologians had earlier charged that many unbelievers were being produced by the Portuguese-Jewish community. Dutch theologians attempting to convert the Jews were sometimes answered without much restraint. Therefore the Christian preachers of Leiden turned to the States General of Holland to demand that steps be taken against blasphemers of Christianity. In 1677 the Portuguese-Jewish congregation of Leiden forbade its members to engage in discussions on matters of faith with Christians. This prohibition was ineffective. (See Kaplan, *From Christianity to Judaism*, pp. 136, 272–73.)

contrary, daily receiving more and more serious information about the abominable heresies which he practiced and taught and about his monstrous deeds, and having for this numerous trustworthy witnesses who have deposed and born witness to this effect in the presence of the said Espinoza, they became convinced of the truth of this matter.[69]

It is not known exactly to what ideas and acts this excommunication refers. There are clues, however. The first is a ban, whose justification we know, pronounced against Juan de Prado in February of 1658.* Another clue is a letter sent in April, 1657, by William Ames, the head of the Quaker mission to Amsterdam. It describes a conversation with an unnamed person, almost certainly Spinoza, who, it seems, translated Quaker missionary pamphlets into Hebrew. Ames describes "a Jew at amsterdam that by the Jews is Cast out (as he himself and others sayeth) because he owneth no other teacher but the light."[70]

Other clues are furnished by two reports made in 1659, before Spinoza had left Amsterdam, to the inquisitional tribunal of Madrid. The philosophically more informative report, made by an Augustinian friar, speaks of Dr. Prado and

> of someone whose family name was de Espinosa . . . who had studied at Leiden and was a good philosopher . . . They themselves told him that they had received circumcision and had observed the laws of the Jews, but that they had changed their view . . . and that God exists in a philosophical sense only; and they had consequently been expelled from the synagogue.[71]

---

*Juan de Prado was a crypto-Jew who had studied philosophy, medicine, and theology in Spain. He held a kind of deism, according to which Judaism, Islam, and Christianity have the same aim, based on natural law, and can all lead to salvation. He and his wife escaped Spain and the inquisition. When he got to Amsterdam, he joined a synagogue and practiced medicine, but remained so poor that he often had to depend on the community's charity. A little before Spinoza's excommunication, Prado made a public confession of remorse for causing scandal in word and deed. In February 1658, he was excommunicated for persevering "in his evil and false opinions" and being instrumental "in disaffecting a number of young students." De Prado tried to have the excommunication revoked, but four of his students testified that he had said that "these absurd Jews seem to want to set up an inquisition here," that it would make sense to kill the rabbis who made the rules, and that the Jews were fools to believe in salvation by means of synagogue attendance and the like. He had also said that it was best to act in accord with one's own understanding and natural morality and not what others told one, and said that the world must be older than 5000 years, as proved by Chinese tradition. A student also reported that Prado had asked him "what cause we have to believe in the Law of Moses more than in the teaching of the various other sects?" (Kaplan, *From Christianity to Judaism*, pp. 122–42 [135, 139 quoted].)

While the businessmen who dominated the Jewish council were probably less interested in individuals' beliefs than in communal solidarity and in safety in a potentially hostile environment, Spinoza made it clear that, to him, the critical issue was freedom of speech. Not only is the attempt to limit it futile, he says, but those who suffer in its behalf are heroes, who think it is "a glorious thing to die for freedom . . . The only lesson to be drawn from their death is to emulate them, or at least to revere them."[72]

Cut off from the Jewish community, Spinoza became friendly with relatively freethinking Christian groups. Apart from Quakers, they included Mennonites and also Collegiants, who reacted to Calvinist persecution by dispensing with clergy and worshiping in small groups or *collegia*. While in Amsterdam, Spinoza took part in a philosophical circle of such men, some of whom remained his correspondents.[73] In relation to them, Spinoza can be described as "a semi-Quaker, semi-creedless Collegiant."[74]

Spinoza moved from Amsterdam to the village of Rijnsburg, near Leiden, then, in 1663, to another village, Voorburg, where he worked on his philosophical writings, including a preliminary version of his *Ethics*. By the middle of 1665, well before the *Ethics* was finished, he began to write the *Tractatus Theologico-Politicus*. As he explained in a letter, it has several purposes: to interpret the Bible in order to expose the prejudices of theologians, which prevent men from thinking philosophically; to counter the opinion of the common people, who accuse him falsely of atheism; and to vindicate the freedom to philosophize, which is suppressed by "the excessive authority and impudence of the preachers."[75] The *Tractatus*, published in 1670 and soon translated into Dutch, was anonymous, but Spinoza was soon identified as its author. Scandal was aroused throughout Europe, not only by the its call for philosophical freedom, but also by its view of ordinary religion as no more than superstition based on fear and greed; by its ridicule of belief in miracles; by its separation of reason, aimed at truth, from faith, aimed at obedience; by its subjection of religion to the laws of the state; and by its opposition to the letter of the Bible in favor of the "universal divine law," which demands justice, charity, decency, and obedience to morality.[76]*

---

*The *Tractatus Theologico-Politicus* shows the influence of a number of contemporary thinkers. One of them is Isaac La Peyrère, whose *Men Before Adam* argues that mankind developed in more than one place, in China, for instance; that Moses could not have been the author of the whole Bible; and that some books of the Bible were copies, though its essential passages are clear enough and teach the truth of millenarism. Another influence on both the political and religious views of the *Tractatus* is Hobbes's *Leviathan*. In chapter 33, "Of the

In 1670, Spinoza moved to Leiden (The Hague), where he died in 1677, at the age of forty-four, presumably of tuberculosis. In the preface to his posthumous works, his friend Jarig Jelles speaks of his interest in optics, in which he might have been outstanding, and continues:

> He spent most of his time in investigating the nature of things, in reducing discoveries to order, and in communicating them to his friends . . . Such ardor for the pursuit of truth was burning within him that, according to the testimony of those with whom he lodged, for three successive months he would not go out into the open.[77]

The only work Spinoza published under his own name (in 1663) was his attempt to demonstrate Descartes's *Principles of Philosophy* by the use of the mathematical, that is, Euclidean method. This work was accompanied by a short, independent appendix, *Metaphysical Thoughts* (*Cogitata Metaphysica*). Spinoza's posthumous works include the *Short Treatise on God, Man, and His Well-being* (*Korte Verhandlung van God, de Mensch en deszelfs Welstand*), an unfinished *Tractatus Politicus*, a *Compendium of Hebrew Grammar*, Spinoza's learned correspondence, the *Treatise on the Correction of the Intellect* (*Tractatus de Intellectus Emendatione*)—first published in the late eighteenth century—and, above all, as the title page puts it, the *Ethics Demonstrated in Geometric Order and Divided into Five Parts, which Treat*

I. Of God
II. Of the Origin and Nature of the Mind
III. Of the Origin and Nature of the Affects
IV. Of Human Bondage, *or* of the Power of the Affects
V. Of the Power of the Intellect, *or* of Human Freedom

It is to the *Ethics* (*Ethica Ordine Geometrico Demonstrata*) that all the following pages on Spinoza are devoted. Although its full title says that it will be demonstrated in geometrical order, there is no prior explanation to

---

Number, Antiquity, Scope, Authority, and Interpreters of the Books of the Holy *Scripture*," Hobbes writes that other history had not made evident who originally wrote the several books of the Bible. "The light therefore that must guide us in the question, must be that which is held out to us from the Bookes themselves" (*Leviathan*, Oxford: Oxford University Press, 1909 [1651], p. 292). Furthermore, in a book published in 1660, the Quaker Samuel Fisher—whose words the *Tractatus* reflects—argues that it cannot now be ascertained to what extent the human version of God's message coincides with God's, but it is the inner light of the word of God that is important, not the reputed word. (See Popkin, *The Third Force in Seventeenth-Century Thought*, pp. 129–30.)

soften the abruptness with which the eight definitions and six axioms of the first book are introduced. Then come thirty-six propositions, each followed by a demonstration. The demonstration draws on the beginning definitions, on previously demonstrated propositions, or on both. It ends, as in Euclidean geometry, with Q.E.D. This structure—definition, axiom, proposition, demonstration—is continued, with variations and informal interpolations, throughout the *Ethics*. Sometimes postulates are added, or lemmas (subsidiary propositions), or scholia (a scholium is an amplifying note); and a demonstration may have corollaries.

Spinoza is no doubt taking the idea of demonstrative rigor in philosophy in accord with the standards of his time. It should not be expected that, any more than Proclus, he should be faithful to present-day standards of formal rigor.[78]* It is therefore not surprising that he does not succeed in being rigorous or even very clear about the kind of rigor he is aiming at. The only earlier example encountered here of attempted rigor, mathematical and metaphysical, is that of Proclus; but such attempts have a relatively long and complicated history.**

Spinoza is flexible enough about his method to assume that it can give a very exact presentation of Descartes's philosophy, with nothing foreign to Descartes, even though he thinks that many of Descartes's doctrines are false. Although Spinoza does not say so, the cost may be that (he supposes) the premises of his formalization of Descartes are faulty.[79] Spinoza knows that his kind of deduction—that of a variety of things from an

---

*Writing in 1978, J. I. Friedman reports that, using only a minimum of modal logic and metalogic, he has succeeded in showing that Spinoza's deductions can be formalized if one supplies a number of suppressed premises, none foreign to Spinoza's system. The number of extra premises for Part I of the *Ethics* turns out to be 165, some 32 of them nonanalytic ("Spinoza's Denial of Free Will in Man and God," pp. 52, 82 [note 19]). Friedman reports that it is ironic that, of his two formalizations of Spinoza's ontological argument, one "is indeed deductively valid, but then its premises are not logically necessary. The other version has logically necessary premises, but alas, it is invalid" (p. 53).

**The Greek physician Galen (second century C.E.) prefers the linear, geometric method to the syllogistic one because of its demonstrative clarity and ability to advance without contradiction from the given to the previously unknown. The sixteenth and early seventeenth theoreticians who prefer the geometrical method for the nonmathematical sciences depend mostly on Galen (Schühling, *Die Geschichte der axiomatischen Methode* . . . , p. 11).

Proclus's *Elements of Physics*, a closer imitation of the Euclidean method than his *Elements of Theology*, is divided into two books, each with a list of definitions in the Euclidean style and followed by propositions that have demonstrations and corollaries on often geometrical principles. The whole is said to organize Aristotle's points into a strict, often clarified and supplemented sequence. (See O'Meara, *Pythagoras Revived*, pp. 177–78.) The *Book of Causes (Liber de Causis)*, translated from Arabic into Latin in the twelfth century, is mostly excerpted from Proclus's *Elements of Theology* and served as a model of rigor for certain medieval theological and philosophical works. The translation in 1533 of Proclus's commentary on the first book of Euclid's geometry also stimulated attempts to axiomatize thought.

isolated concept—is not the same as mathematical deduction: To a correspondent, he readily concedes that from the definition alone of a geometrical figure, such as a circle, only one property can be deduced before the circle has been related to other things, for example, the radii drawn from its center. To deduce more from its definition, Spinoza holds, extension "must be defined by an attribute which expresses eternal and infinite essence. But perhaps," he adds, "if life lasts, I will discuss this question with you some other time more clearly."[80]

Evidently, Spinoza's attitude toward deduction is metaphysical (in this, he is like Proclus and Avicenna). His deduction is meant to be formal, but it requires the metaphysical definition of the essences of things, from which their properties are then deduced.[81] His letters have repeated expressions of confidence in the a priori certainty of his kind of deduction. A believer in inmost essences, he writes that we do not need experience to define things whose existence, identical with their essence, "follows from their definition.* Indeed," he goes on, "no experience will ever be able to teach us this: for experience does not teach us the essence of things."[82] To a correspondent who asks about the possibility of a perfect method, Spinoza answers that "the understanding is not, like the body, subject to accidents," and that the true method consists "only in the knowledge of the pure understanding, and of its nature and laws."[83]

Spinoza's method allows him to consider "human actions and appetites just as if they were a question of lines, planes, and bodies," and it frees him from appealing to any authority but that of reason.[84] In its praise, Spinoza's translator says, "Spinoza's choice of the axiomatic method represents nothing more, and nothing less, than an awesome commitment to intellectual honesty and clarity."[85] I reject the *awesome*, agree to the *honesty*, and add orderliness, self-containment, strenuous faith in reason, and, along with these, a strong defense against controversy and socially inflicted pain (like an armadillo rolled up into itself, the *Ethics* presents a surface that is armored at every point).

Except at the moments when Spinoza explains informally, his text is dense with a staccato of sententious truths moving forward, backward,

---

*"To be called perfect, a definition will have to explain the inmost essence of the thing . . . The properties of things are not understood so long as their essences are not known." An essence "is to be sought only from the fixed and eternal things"(*The Emendation of the Intellect*, sections 95, 101; *The Collected Works* . . . , trans. Curley, vol. 1, pp. 39, 41). Such rather enigmatic explanations have a Neoplatonic resonance. *The Emendation of the Intellect*, an unfinished early work, is Spinoza's equivalent to a treatise on method. The careful, though unfinished, commentary by Joachim (*Spinoza's* Tractatus de Intellectus Emendatione) makes an unfavorable judgment of the book's clarity and persuasiveness. On the tension between Spinoza's deductive thinking and his nominalism, see Hubbeling, *Spinoza's Methodology*, pp. 20–26.

and forward again. This denseness, with its air of the incontrovertible, has an imposing effect, which we may identify as Spinoza's rhetoric, rhetoric informally heightened with a biting scorn. If one suspends one's own beliefs and follows the argument in detail, it is easy to fall into the rhythm of Spinoza's thought. The strong effect he can make does not carry over into summaries (including my own, and maybe even Spinoza's). He would feel betrayed by my failure to give his thought its self-verifying continuity.

Before explaining the major concepts of Spinoza's *Ethics*, I summarize its content in its own usually bare, declarative style. Especially because what follows is a summary, the sequence of ideas is likely to be too rapid to follow easily, so for someone who is not already acquainted with Spinoza, it is probably best at first reading not to try to grasp it in detail but to get a general impression—the conclusion of the sequence will show toward what it all tends. In accord with his conception of proof, Spinoza begins with definitions. His first definition is of *cause of itself (causa sui)*. Such a cause, he says, is one whose essence involves existence, by which he means that it is impossible to conceive the cause except as existing. In keeping with tradition, he identifies this cause with substance; but he adds, untraditionally, that substance is conceived *through* itself, by which he means that the concept of substance is not formed from—not based on, not subordinate to—the concept of anything else.[86] Then he defines *attribute*. An attribute, he says, is whatever the intellect perceives as the essence of substance. Then he defines the term *mode* (used by Descartes as an equivalent of the traditional *accident*) as a modification ("affection") of substance. The mode, says Spinoza, is unlike substance because it exists in something else, or is in something else through which it is also conceived. Then comes the definition of God—later proved to be the only possible substance—as an absolutely infinite being. To Spinoza this means that God is infinite in all possible ways, that is to say, in an infinite number of ways: he is a substance that consists of an infinity of attributes, each of which expresses a different, infinite aspect of God's eternal and infinite essence.

Acording to Spinoza, by (true) definition nothing can in any way influence or compel substance to be or do anything; so substance, determined by its own nature alone, is rightly called free. What is not free is called necessary or compelled, which means that its existence and effects are determined by something other than itself. By definition, the existence of anything that follows necessarily from its definition (for example, substance, or a triangle) is unaffected by time and unexplained by time, but is eternal.

These definitions are followed by axioms, some of which (like some definitions) I omit. The first axiom says that everything that is, is either in itself or in something else (a traditional truism that goes back to the Aristotelian distinction between what is and what is not a substance).[87] There is an axiom that says that a given "determinate" (limited, particular) cause has a necessary effect, and if there is no such cause, there can be no effect. Another axiom says that the knowledge of an effect depends on and involves the knowledge of its cause. And still another axiom says, conventionally, that a true idea must agree with the idea's object.

Given his definitions and axioms, Spinoza proceeds, proposition after proposition, to prove (he is sure) that there is nothing in nature whose existence and characteristic effects have not been determined by the necessity of God's nature (part 1, prop. 29).* God no more acts out of freedom of will than out of freedom of motion and rest. Will does not pertain to God's nature (1.32, corollary 2). Things could not have been produced by God in any other way or order (1.33).

At the end of the first part of the *Ethics*, Spinoza, writing informally, says that human beings think they are free because they are conscious of their volitions and appetites but ignorant of the causes of their wanting and willing. By analogy with their own activity in making things for themselves, they inferred that the universe had a ruler or rulers endowed with freedom like their own. They therefore thought up different ways of worshiping God in order that he might love them in particular and direct nature for their insatiably greedy benefit. But "nature had no fixed aim in view" and "all final causes are merely fabrications of men."[88]

In the second part of the *Ethics*, Spinoza continues his bold restoration of the uniformity of nature. He proves, in his sense of proving, that thought and matter are not opposites, as ordinarily supposed, but are parallel aspects of God or Nature. Individual thoughts, he begins, are modes that express God's nature in a limited, particular way, and modes are modifications of substance, that is, of God. So God must have an infinite attribute of thought that individual thoughts (ideas) involve and are conceived through: God is a thinking thing (2.1). Likewise, individual bodies are modes that express God's nature in a limited, particular way. So

---

*In the *Short Treatise*, Spinoza uses *God* and *Nature* as unqualified synonyms (e.g., in the first dialogue following part 1, chap. 2). But elsewhere in the *Short Treatise* (1.8, 9) he makes the same distinction as in the *Ethics* (1.29, scholium), between nature conceived as independent (*Natura naturans*) and as dependent (*Natura naturata*). *Natura naturans* is God considered as a free cause, while *Natura naturata* is nature in the lesser sense of the (infinite) modes that follow from the necessity of God's nature or from any of his attributes. The two terms were in common use, though not in a uniform sense, in the scholastic philosophy of Spinoza's time. (See Wolfson, *The Philosophy of Spinoza*, vol. 1, pp. 253–55; and Gueroult, *Spinoza*, vol. 1, pp. 564–68.)

God must have an infinite attribute of extension: God is an extended thing (2.2).[89]

Because thought and extension are attributes of the same substance, the order and connection of thoughts or ideas is the same as that of extended things (2.6, 7). This order and connection are also the same in human beings, who, unlike God, are metaphysically dependent (2.20). A human being's mind is constituted by the idea of the human body (2.13). The interdependence of mind and body is such that the mind does not know itself except to the extent that it perceives the ideas of the modifications of the body (2.23). But so far as these ideas of the body are related to the human mind alone, they are confused and inadequate (2.28). Ideas can be clear and adequate only to the extent that they are related to the infinite whole, to God. Fortunately, whoever has a true idea knows and cannot doubt that it is true: just as the light shows both itself and the darkness (an Indian-sounding analogy), truth is the standard both of itself and the false (2,28; 2.43 and schol.).

Spinoza now turns to the affects or emotions—hate, anger, envy, and so on.* Unsparingly deterministic, he insists that man, the human being, never has absolute power over himself. Because the laws of nature are always and everywhere the same, the emotions "follow from the same necessity and virtue (power) of nature as other particular things." Like other particular things, the emotions depend on causes, through which alone they are understood.[90] The emotions are the modifications (affections) of the body that either increase or diminish its power to act; and they are, as well, the ideas of these modifications (book 3, def. 3). Ideas of affects can be adequate and effective only if the affects' causes are clearly understood. And it must be understood that even though the mind's object is the body, the body cannot determine the mind to think, nor the mind determine the body to move or rest. Only a body influences a body (3.2).

Everything, including a human being, is inherently a striving (conatus) to remain in existence (a Stoic idea, renewed by Hobbes). In Spinoza's terminology, this striving is a thing's actual essence. Nothing destroys itself—only external, contrary causes can force humans to harm or destroy

---

*The translation of the Latin term *affectus* by *emotion* is usually natural, though not every "modification" of the mind that Spinoza calls an *affectus* would be classified by us as an emotion. Spinoza also uses *affectus* for a "modification" of the body. Although influenced at this point by Descartes, he gives non-Cartesian meanings to an *action*—to him, an emotion of which we are the adequate cause—and a *passion*—an emotion of which we are the inadequate, that is, partial cause. Spinoza reacts with scorn to Descartes's opinion that the soul or mind can by acts of will affect the brain, that is, the pineal gland, a material organ (*Ethics* part 5, preface). (See the glossary-index in *The Collected Works of Spinoza*, trans. Curley, vol. 1; and Wolfson, *The Philosophy of Spinoza*, vol. 2, pp. 185–95.)

themselves (3.4–7). Striving of the mind alone is called will. When the striving is related to both mind and body, it is called appetite and, when conscious, it is called desire. This striving, the essence of man, determines what we judge to be good or bad (3.9 and schol.).

Striving of the body is paralleled by striving of the mind. It follows that if anything increases or diminishes our body's power body to act, the idea of this thing increases or diminishes our mind's power to think effectively (3.10, 11). When the mind, paralleling the body, changes to a greater perfection, its emotion is that of joy (or, for body and mind together, pleasure or cheerfulness). When, on the contrary, it changes to a lesser perfection, its emotion is that of sadness (or, for body and mind together, pain or melancholy).

As far as it can, the mind tries to imagine whatever will increase the body's power of action and to recollect whatever will exclude the existence of things that diminish the body's power (3.12, 13). This explains the nature of love and hate: love is pleasure accompanied by the idea of an external cause that we want to preserve because we believe that it helps us; and hate is pain accompanied by the idea of an external cause we want to remove and destroy because we believe it harms us (3.13 and note).

Love and hate are aroused by anything we associate with their causes, that is, by incidental or accidental associations and by resemblances (3.14–16). When something causes us both pain and pleasure, either in itself or by association or resemblance, we both love and hate it (3.17). We are sad when we imagine (that is, think) that what we love is destroyed, and are joyful when we imagine it is preserved; and, on the contrary, we are joyful when we imagine that something hated is destroyed and sad when something loved is preserved (3.19, 20). Emotional identification with other persons affects us in accord with the emotion we imagine them to have: We are sad when we imagine someone (*something*, Spinoza says) we love is sad or someone we hate is happy, and we are joyful, happy, or pleased when we imagine someone we hate is sad; and so on. And we hate someone that, we imagine, makes someone we hate happy; and we love someone we imagine makes that person sad (3.21–24). Even when we are indifferent to a thing (Spinoza means a person) we imagine to be like us, we are affected by the same emotion that we suppose affects that thing. When the emotion is related to sadness, it is what we call pity. That is why we can't hate a thing we pity but try, instead, to free it from suffering and destroy what causes the suffering. The will to do good, which is the desire born of pity, is benevolence (3.27 and schols.).

Everyone is naturally affected by benevolence, so in the absence of hatred and even of love, we strive to do what we imagine makes people happy and avoid what we imagine makes them sad. Such "imitation of emotion" leads us to love or hate things simply because others love or hate them; and when such love or hate coincide with our previous love or hate, the emotion becomes more fixed or constant. But if the emotions we imagine other people to have are opposite to ours, our emotions are inconstant (3.31). By this dialectic of emotions, we hate those we imagine hate us, even without cause, and love those who love us, even without cause, the result being reciprocal hatred or love (3.40, 41).

Now come propositions that are critical to the whole of Spinoza's moral position:

> Hate is increased by being returned, but can be destroyed by Love . . . Hate completely conquered by Love passes into Love, and the Love is therefore greater than if Hate had not preceded it [because the joy of love as such is increased by the striving to remove the sadness of hate and by the idea, which accompanies the striving, of the once hated person as a cause of joy] . . . The Joy which arises from our imagining that a thing we hate is destroyed, or affected by some other evil, does not occur without some Sadness of mind. (3.43, 44, 47)[91]

How, Spinoza asks, can we restrain our emotions? Spinoza answers by pointing out that an emotion that affects the body— the body's power to act—simultaneously and similarly affects the mind. We should understand that, just as an affection of the body cannot be restrained or removed except by an opposite and stronger bodily cause, so an emotion cannot be restrained except by a stronger, opposite emotion (4.7). And we should understand that an emotion directed toward something we imagine (think of) as existing in the distant future is much less intense than one directed toward something in the present. For this reason, the desire arising from the (emotional equivalent of) knowledge of good and evil can be restrained by other, more violent desires arising from other emotions, including those for pleasures of the moment (4.8, 14–16).

The human striving to exist, the essence of man, is stronger when it arises from joy than from sadness. When it arises from joy, it is defined both by human power and the power of the external cause of the joy (4.18). Therefore, reason, which demands only what is compatible with nature, demands that all persons should love themselves. This means that they should seek their own advantage, act from the laws of their own natures (4.18 and schol.). When ruled by the laws of one's own nature, says Spinoza, everyone necessarily desires what he judges to be good, which is what increases his ability to be, to act, to live, to actually exist. Everyone is necessarily repelled by what he judges to be evil, which diminishes this ability (4.19, 21).* As experience shows and philosophy proves, the reasonable way to preserve oneself is to act in a reasonable, virtuous way (4.24). There is nothing we know to be surely good or evil except what leads to or prevents understanding (4.27).

Human beings disagree only insofar as they lack knowledge and are torn by negative emotions (4.32, 33). To the extent that they are guided by reason, meaning, by what follows from human nature as reason defines it, they always necessarily agree among themselves. So humans are of most use to one another when each of them acts in the most reasonably selfish way (4.35 and cor. 2).

Emotions, we know, can help or hinder the body's power of acting. That is why joy and cheerfulness are good and sadness is evil (4.41,42). But although pleasure, a kind of joy, is in itself good, and pain, a kind of sadness, is in itself evil, when the pleasure is such that it stubbornly limits the body's ability to react, it is evil, and when the pain restricts an evil pleasure, it is good (4.43). Hate for other humans is always evil, as are the related emotions of envy, mockery, disdain, anger, and vengeance. This is because to hate is to want to do the hated person some evil, and to do evil is painful and limits our ability to survive (4.45 and cors.). Hate makes the hater miserable, whereas the person who tries to overcome hate by love is joyous. When the love succeeds in overcoming the hate, those conquered by the love yield with joy and are strengthened by their submission.

For a person guided by reason, pity, which is a kind of sadness, is evil and useless.** Instead of pitying, one should try to act as well as possible

---

*The belief that all natural things aim at conserving themselves was a commonplace often repeated by medieval and Renaissance thinkers (Wolfson, *The Philosophy of Spinoza*, vol. 1, pp. 195–99). In the course of an attack on the Darwinian idea of the "struggle for existence," Nietzsche refers sarcastically to the scholars who claim that self-preservation is basic. He believes it is a limitation of "the really fundamental instinct of life which aims at *the expansion of power* and, wishing for that, frequently risks and even sacrifices self-preservation. It should be considered symptomatic when some philosophers—for example, Spinoza, who was consumptive— considered the instinct of self-preservation decisive and *had* to see it that way; for they were individuals in conditions of distress" (F. Nietzsche, *The Gay Science*, section 349, trans. W. Kaufmann, New York: Random House, 1974, pp. 291–92).

**Nietzsche paraphrases this passage without acknowledging its source, which he knows— his earlier discovery of Spinoza amazed and delighted him. Suffering, Nietzsche adds, may sometimes be reduced because of pity, but this usually insignificant result does not justify the essentially harmful nature of pity. "Supposing it was dominant even for a single day, mankind would immediately perish of it" (Nietzsche, *Daybreak*, section 134, trans. R. J. Hollingdale, Cambridge: Cambridge University Press, 1982, p. 85). On Nietzsche's discovery of Spinoza, see his letter of July 30, to Franz Overbeck (C. Middleton, trans., *Selected Letters of Friedrich Nietzsche*, Chicago: University of Chicago Press, 1969, p. 177).

and do so with joy (4.50 and schol.). Self-esteem, if it arises out of reason, helps one's power of acting, whereas humility—the sadness by which one considers one's own lack of power—hinders it (4.52, 53). Repentance, which is the evil of sadness following an evil desire, does not arise from reason (4.54). As for the fear of death, a free man is led not by fear but by the reasonable desire for self-preservation. "A free man thinks of nothing less than of death, and his wisdom is a meditation on life, not death" (4.67).[92]

If an emotion, an affect, is not attributed to an external cause but is joined with other thoughts and is understood within the necessary sequence of cause and effect, the love or hate for the external cause is destroyed (5.2). The affect then ceases to be an inadequate, confused idea and becomes an adequate, clear, distinct idea, separated from the thought of an external cause. The more the mind understands that all things are necessary, the greater the power it exerts over the affects (4.6) The mind undestands best by relating all the body's affects or images of things to the idea of God (5.14). To understand God is to understand the causes of all things, so that no one can hate God (5.18). Nor can anyone who loves God strive to make God love him in return. To strive for God's love would be to strive, absurdly, that God should not be God (5.19).

In God, there necessarily exists an idea "that expresses the essence of this or that human body under a species of eternity" (5.22).[93] The existence of the mind is limited in time only insofar as the mind expresses the actual existence of the body. But the mind conceives things "with a certain eternal necessity, through God's essence," and what it conceives in this way must be eternal. So "the human mind cannot be absolutely destroyed with the body" (5.23).[94]

Whatever we know by the highest kind of knowledge is a source of the greatest possible joy, accompanied by the idea of oneself, and therefore of God, as its cause (5.32 and cor.). Directed toward God as eternal, the love that arises by the highest kind of knowledge is the eternal intellectual love of God (5.33 and cor.). Because his infinite perfection is accompanied by an idea of himself as its cause, God "loves himself with an infinite intellectual love" (5.35).[95] Although the ability of the human mind to love God intellectually is limited by the mind's nature, this love is part of God's infinite love for himself (5.36). "From this it follows that insofar as God loves himself, he loves men, and consequently that God's love of men and the Mind's intellectual Love of God are one and the same" (5.36 cor.).[96]

What perishes is the imagination. What remains, which is the intellect, is more perfect (5.39 and cor.). Finally—this is the last proposition of the *Ethics*—"Blessedness is not the reward of virtue, but virtue itself; nor do we enjoy it because we restrain our lusts; on the contrary, because we enjoy it, we are able to restrain them" (4.42).[97]

So far, I have only summarized or, rather, severely contracted the *Ethics*, with a minimum of interpretation. Looked at closely, the *Ethics* is at times unclear or possibly inconsistent. I therefore add some considerations on a number of Spinoza's puzzling concepts, which I explain as best I can in keeping with what I take to be his position.

Substance, attributes, modes:[98] Everything whatsoever is in Spinoza's God or Substance. Here, the word *in* means metaphysically dependent on. In other words, God/Substance is "prior in nature" to its "affections," which are its modes. It transcends the sum of its modes, just as the Neoplatonic God transcends the sum of its emanations.[99] In contradiction to most traditional European thought, Spinoza insists on confining the conception of substance to what is absolutely unlimited and perfect— namely, God—and refuses it to anything finite.[100] Spinoza also insists that the modes of substance are not accidents in the traditional sense but real beings.[101] And he insists that God's essence reveals itself in extension, that is, matter, no less than in thought.

There has been much debate over whether or not Spinoza takes the attributes to have an objective existence. When he defines them as "what the intellect perceives of substance as constituting its essence," does his *if* mean *as if*? Does he mean that human limitations cause us to perceive God *as if* he was infinite matter and infinite thought rather than as simply Substance, without real attributes because not subject to qualification. The question obviously suggests the medieval debate on whether or not the ascription of objective attributes to God is false to his unity.

All things considered, Spinoza's text seems to me to favor the objective interpretation; but no interpretation is without its difficulties. He does say that the distinction between the two attributes expresses no real difference. But he also says that only God's infinite intellect is able to perceive that thought and extended substance are one and the same (*Ethics* 2.7 schol.). In contrast, the human mind is capable of knowing only what the idea of a limited, actual body involves or what can be inferred from its idea.[102] Since to think of something is to think of its attributes, to think of substance is to think of it from the only two (attributive) points of view known to us. That only two of the infinite number are known is an unexplained fact—Spinoza does not hesitate to answer questions, but his answers are not necessarily clear to those who study him.*

---

*In a letter, Spinoza answers the question how one and the same thing, substance and attribute, can be called by two different names. He answers: *Israel* means the third patriarch, and so does *Jacob*, the name given him because he seized his brother's heel (*The Correspon-*

The attributes belong to a metaphysical hierarchy. Each attribute being infinite of its kind, it must be related to a corresponding (immediate) infinite mode. *Must* because an attribute, being infinite, can be the direct cause only of something infinite (1.29). The infinite mode of the attribute of thought—the immutable act of thinking—is given several names, including *God's idea* or *God's infinite idea* (1.21; 2.3, 4, 8), and the *absolutely infinite intellect*.[103] The equivalent (immediate) infinite mode of extension is *motion-and-rest* (*Ethics* 1.32, cor. 2), or just *motion*. In the *Ethics* Spinoza also speaks of a necessarily existing, infinite mode that follows from an attribute of God "by some mediating modification" that exists necessarily and is infinite (1.23). In a letter, Spinoza gives the example of *the face of the whole universe,* "which, although it varies in infinite ways, yet remains always the same." Maybe this "mediate infinite mode" is a principle of order of both extension and thought.[104]

Particular, finite things, whose essences do not involve existence, are determinate modifications of God's attributes (2.25, and cor.). As noted, a finite thing cannot be directly produced by anything infinite but can follow from it only if the infinite is modified by a finite modification. This finite modification is modified by another finite one, and so on, to infinity. Therefore God is only the mediate cause of finite things; but everything that is, is in God and cannot be or be conceived without him (1.28, and schols.).

Evidently, Spinoza's hierarchy has the following members: Substance or God, two known and an infinite number of unknown attributes, two (of no doubt an infinite number) of "immediate" infinite modes, and two (known) "mediate" infinite modes. From the mediate infinite modes there follow their finite modifications, the endless series of finite things that are the effects and causes of other finite things. This whole hierarchy is rather simple, and its intermediate levels are hardly explained—in the *Ethics*, some are not even named. But Spinoza evidently

---

dence of Spinoza, trans. Wolf, letter 9, p. 108). If the distinction between substance and attribute is only verbal, is that between extension and thought more than verbally different?

The argument of Wolfson, in favor of subjectivity (*The Philosophy of Spinoza*, vol. 1, pp. 142–57) may be compared with that of Curley (*Spinoza's Metaphysics*, pp. 28–36). Gueroult (*Spinoza*, vol. 1, pp. 237–39, 428–61), who decides in favor of objectivity, says that the opposite position is "the summit of a pyramid of misinterpretation." Curley, Spinoza's exemplary translator, asks why attributes should not be supposed to constitute many substances, and complains that Spinoza gives no real answer. Curley then himself answers that the attributes are "very special elements" of "this particular complex." He explains: "The existence of each one of the attributes implies the existence of all the others . . . Since each of them, considered separately, exists in itself and is conceived through itself, they always *had* to be in it (substance) together" (*Behind the Geometrical Method*, pp. 29–30).

feels the need to sketch out what resembles a system of emanations.[105] He faces a conceptual problem like that which faces a Neoplatonist: How is the transition made from the perfect, transcendent One to the imperfect, temporal many? For Spinoza, the equivalent problem is: How is the transition made from the transcendent, infinite Substance to the dependent, finite modes?*

Determinism:[106] Rather like Aristotle, Spinoza defines the will not as desire and avoidance but as affirmation and negation of what is true or false: will is judgment that precedes and informs desire (which undergoes irrational attractions and repulsions).[107] To Spinoza, the will is only a certain mode of thinking, which, as a mode, cannot be the free cause of its own actions, but is determined by a particular cause, which is determined by another cause, and so on (2.48 and schol.). The idea of a general faculty of willing is a fiction, a merely universal entity (2.48, schol.). There are only individual acts of affirmation and negation—for example, the act of the mind that affirms that a triangle's three angles are equal to two right angles (2.49). As this example shows, acts of thinking and acts of willing are the same, which shows that the will and the intellect are the same (ibid., cor.).

Spinoza is an unrelenting determinist with respect to God as well as man. God's will and intellect are infinite, he is sure, but they are no more free than are motion and rest, modes of the attribute of extension (1.31; 1.32 and cors.). If God was free and if, as the result, things were produced in some other way or order than they have been, God's nature would have to be different from what it is. This difference would mean that God is imperfect and (by changing himself or his mind) is subject to time. It would also imply that his will is fallible. God's essence is neither his will nor his intellect but his power. From his power everything follows by necessity, even God—he is his own unchanging cause (1.33, 34). What

---

*Spinoza "was interpreted by some as a Kabbalist, and his metaphysics may reflect a synthesis of Cartesianism and Kabbalism. Our received view of Spinoza's thought as growing out of the Cartesian ferment has dulled us to the much richer, more exciting intellectual world in which he flourished. If we can see him as some of his contemporaries did, we may discover that in spite of all the difficulties that dogged his intellectual career, and in spite of his ongoing polemical attacks on Judaism and the Jewish community in which he was reared, Spinoza may have still derived a central part of his philosophy from a vital part of his heritage—the Kabbalism then being studied in Holland. Perhaps he was trying to utilize the Neoplatonized Kabbalism of [Abraham Cohen] Herrera as a way of integrating the new sciences and the rational/spiritual mysticism of his time. If we can suspend disbelief in Spinoza as a Kabbalist, we may find him a much more exciting and excited thinker" (R. Popkin, "Spinoza, Neoplatonic Kabbalist?" in Goodman, ed., *Neoplatonism and Jewish Thought*, pp. 402–403).

could God need that he should want to act for the sake of some particular end? (part 1 appendix)[108]*

Although, to Spinoza, human beings have no free will, his repeated advice to us to learn to become more effective in our own behalf implies an ability that can reasonably be accounted a freedom.

The three kinds of knowledge:[109] We form universal notions, Spinoza says, of three different kinds. The first, most primitive kind is gained from common or universal notions. Many images formed at the same time confuse the senses, so the mind, unable to "imagine" (perceive) the sensed bodies as definite individuals, "imagines" them in a confused way, as if they were general. The mind then expresses itself in common notions— "transcendental" terms such as *being* or *something*, or universals such as *man*, *horse*, and *dog* (*Ethics* 2.40, schol. 1). Spinoza calls such "confused" knowledge *opinion* or *imagination*. The term *imagination* is used by him broadly, to include sensory perception, conditioning by repeated perception, knowledge of past events, and, most generally, knowledge from vague experience (2.17., and cor.; 2.40, schol. 1, 2).

Knowledge of the second kind—reason, *ratio*—joins universal notions with adequate ideas of the properties of things. By understanding in what several things agree, differ, and contradict, the mind can know what is common to them, can contemplate things clearly and distinctly, and can determine itself internally in the sense of having ideas that resemble those of God (that is, true ideas) (2.40, schol. 2; 2.29, schol.). Having true ideas, the mind follows its own deductive, nontemporal lines of thought and sees things "under the aspect of eternity."[110]

Knowledge of the third kind—intuitive knowledge, *scientia intuitiva*—proceeds from an adequate idea of the formal essence of an attribute of God to the adequate knowledge of the essence of things. The difference between the three kinds of knowledge is that between finding the unknown, fourth term of a proportion by a rote method, or by a mathematically proved method, or by direct insight. Direct insight is the kind by which we immediately see—without referring to a rule—that the numbers 1 and 2 are to each other as 3 (the third given number) is to 6 (2.40, schol. 2). Only knowledge of the first kind can cause falsity. The other two

---

*On the problem of good and evil, Spinoza gives the answer, given before him by Maimonides, that something is good or evil or perfect or imperfect not in itself, but in relation to the desire of a particular being. Good and evil are notions we form by comparing different things, which are taken differently by different people (4, preface). Spinoza gives the Neoplatonic (and Cartesian) answer that God produced everything an infinite intellect can conceive, from the highest to the lowest grade of perfection. Spinoza indignantly denies Aristotle's claim that nature does nothing in vain (not of use to human beings) (part 1, appendix, section 3). (See Wolfson, *The Philosophy of Spinoza*, vol. 1, pp. 436–40.)

kinds are necessarily true (2.42). But it is only the third kind, not restricted to generalizations, that results in the "intellectual love of God."

All this shows how much more knowledge of the third, intuitive kind can accomplish "and how much more powerful it is than the universal knowledge I have called knowledge of the second kind" (5.36, schol).[111]

The immortality of the mind:[112] To Spinoza, we know, the human mind is the idea of an actually existing human body (2.11, 13). When the body dies, the ordinary, confused, inadequate ideas we have of changes in the human body disappear. Yet Spinoza does not believe that the body and the mind are the same in relation to eternity: While the body is destroyed, something eternal of the mind remains (5.23), as an eternal truth, unrelated to the passage of time. The truths that the mind knows about the body cannot die. In proclaiming these truths eternal, Spinoza is thinking of them as reflexive, self-conscious ideas. In other words, adequate ideas—those known by the intuitive form of reason—are self-known, conscious of themselves (it is not clear if the whole mode of infinite intellect is conscious). These ideas are retained eternally in the infinite intellect, as the eternal essence of each particular body (5.21, 23, 38). The essence of "this or that human body" remains in God as an idea, "under the form of eternity" (5.21).

According to Spinoza's difficult concept of the eternal persistence of part of the mind, immortality is in one sense personal—the complex idea or "formal essence" that remains is that of a particular individual necessarily related to a particular body, which no longer exists (2.8). In another sense, Spinoza's concept is impersonal, confined to abstract knowledge (I suppose) of the mind-body relation, both in general and with respect to a particular body. There is no longer any possibility of imagining or remembering anything (5.21).

It seems unreasonable to try very hard to clarify what Spinoza himself left so unclear. But it is worth pointing out that Maimonides and, before him, Alfarabi and Avicenna (and Aristotle) had an analogous, analogously unclear, conception of the immortality of the intellectual part of the soul (the active intellect, or the acquired active intellect). Avicenna even speaks of different grades or qualities of immortality.*

In the beginning, Spinoza was attacked as a covert, dangerous atheist.[113] The most influential early attack on his philosophy was that made

---

*To Avicenna, all human souls are immortal but only a soul with a perfectly developed intellect will enjoy "supreme eudaemonia." "Simple," unintellectual souls are like a "formless 'material substratum'" and reside in "a kind of peace" (H. A. Davidson, *Alfarabi, Avicenna, and Averroes on Intellect,* New York: Oxford University Press, 1992, pp. 54–57, 103–107, 200–102 [quoted: pp. 106, 109–10, 111]). Maimonides, rather like Spinoza, writes that because by Pierre Bayle (1647–1706). Bayle praises Spinoza's personal decency but blames his philosophy as absurd and, perhaps insincerely, as dangerous. Spinoza's philosophy arouses so many objections, he writes, that "his poison carries with it his own antidote." According to Bayle, Spinoza's basic failure is his principle that there is only one substance, with an infinity of attributes, of which all existing bodies and souls are modifications. But God's immutability, says Bayle, is incompatible with the nature of extension, which allows for the division of its parts.[114]

Spinoza's philosophical radicalism and his unrancorous steadfastness made him an underground hero to the more radical European thinkers. He was accorded the status of a philosophical saint even by many of those who denounced his philosophy. One of the complimentary denouncers was Voltaire. But after Voltaire read Spinoza carefully, he hesitated to call him an atheist, and he soaked in much of what Spinoza said about the Bible and morality, and even proposed a God from whom everything flows.[115] Other thinkers more impressed by Spinoza's character than by his philosophical acumen include—I make a meager, near-random choice— Moses Mendelssohn, Friedrich Schleiermacher, Bertrand Russell, and Karl Popper.

During the German Enlightenment, Spinozism was at the center of the "pantheism controversy" that involved Moses Mendelssohn, Jacobi, Lessing, Herder, Goethe, and then Kant. After a time, Kant came to charge that Spinoza denied God intelligence, purpose, and causality, and made him into a blind, lifeless, primordial substance.[116] Novalis, however, honored Spinoza as the God-intoxicated man, and Schelling prescribed initia-

---

the soul needs the body, the soul perishes with the body, but "the form of the soul [i.e., the acquired intellect] is not destroyed . . . but of its own nature knows and comprehends ideas apart from bodies and knows the Creator of the universe" and exists eternally (*Mishneh Torah* [*Review of Law*] 4.9, as cited in Wolfson, *The Philosophy of Spinoza*, vol. 2, pp. 290–91).

It is possible to argue that Spinoza does not imply that any part of the mind can exist without the body in the sense of having temporal properties (such as existing *after the body dies*). Not surprisingly, the commentator who says this confesses "that in spite of many years of study, I still do not feel that I understand this part of the *Ethics* at all adequately . . . I also believe that no one else understands it adequately either" (Curley, *Behind the Geometrical Method*, pp. 85, 84).

L. Lermond, who claims she has arrived at a consistent interpretation, concedes that it is not one that Spinoza expresses "explicitly and unambiguously." Lermond argues that Spinoza cannot be a nominalist, as usually supposed, even though he explicitly denies that abstract universals are real. According to Lermond, "There remain elements of genuine universality without which his philosophy becomes unintelligible. The attributes are concrete universals, as are the infinite modes . . . Like Plato, Spinoza is talking about causes . . . He was likewise a realist." By this interpretation, the essences of both individuals and of man are real beings, "concrete essences" (Lermond, *The Form of Man*, pp. 59, 68–69).

tion into Spinozism as the condition for approaching the philosophical truth. Even now, Spinoza retains the ability to inspire.*

Despite the comparisons I will make, Spinoza does not fit easily into any philosophical lineage. Brave as a man and bold as a philosopher, he was the first European thinker after Epicurus, Democritus, and Lucretius—favorites of his—to conceptualize a universe without any purpose or any miracles. He was also the first since them and the Stoics to refuse to consign matter to an inferior position. Stubbornly, he insisted that the only object of the mind is the body, by which he meant that the mind cannot be separated from physiological responses, a conclusion we might now prefer to refine in neuropsychological terms but not repudiate. Almost in the vein of an evolutionary biologist (such as E. H. Hamilton), Spinoza worked out an objective ethics, tied to no religion, in which intelligent self-interest is equated with virtuousness and the social interest.[117]

To speak for myself, what remains most impressive in Spinoza is his dialectical psychology—the identity, difference, and interplay of body and mind, the augmentation and diminution of emotions by one another, and the therapy by which one frees oneself as much as possible and makes oneself more effective and more content—a therapy by objective understanding. But like the God he envisions, Spinoza is self-contained, and he projects little human warmth and, scorn apart, little humor. It cannot be denied that his reach, like that of so many other philosophers, exceeds his grasp. Maybe his uniqueness as a philosopher is his ability to embrace so much—a mystic's identification with nature, a scientist's objectivity, and a systematist's unification of everything scattered and unexplained, and to join all these into a densely causal system.

---

*See, for example, the articles and discussions in Bloch, ed., *Spinoza au XXe siècle*. Among the views discussed, those of Jean Caivailles and Emmanuel Levinas are particularly interesting: "I am a Spinozist," said the philosopher-mathematician and resistance fighter Cavailles. "We find necessity everywhere. The chainlike sequences of mathematics are necessary, even the stages of the science of mathematics are necessary, and this struggle we lead is necessary too" (pp. 71, 72). The notion of structure is the model that allows us to think the "self-illumination of the scientific movement . . . a revelation that is not different from what is revealed. Structure speaks of itself" [p. 86] [B. Huisman's interpretation]).

For the philosopher Emmanuel Levinas, there is in Spinoza some treason against Judaism. But though Spinoza chooses to think *sub specie aeterni*, Spinoza also remains anti-Spinozist, like the lived Talmudic intuitions he opposes. That is, he justifies the existence of the prophet by the complexity of things; and he needs the third kind of knowledge, like the prophet's light, to achieve the intellectual love of God. What is sacred is the conduct of human beings inspired by justice and love—the word of God is obligation to one's neighbor. As Spinoza shows, ethics is not reducible to adequate ideas (pp. 225–35, A. Negri's interpretation).

Discussion

As the history of philosophy grows longer, it offers increasing possibilities of classifying philosophers and of trying to assemble them, no doubt too mechanically, out of fragments of their predecessors—a kind of historical game of who makes up whom. In the case of Shankara and Spinoza, I would first classify Shankara as a post-Buddhistic, Bramanistic hierarchical mystic, and Spinoza as a postmedieval, naturalistic hierarchical mystic. Then I would construct Shankara out of predecessors such as Uddalaka/Yajnavalkya and Dignaga/Dharmakirti.* Spinoza I would construct out of Epicurus/Lucretius, Avicenna (and the Proclus in him), and, for some purposes, Maimonides, and Descartes. I would construct the two philosophers approximately so in spite of the fact that Shankara castigates Buddhism in bitterly unphilosophical terms and Spinoza disapproves of Platonism and scornfully controverts Maimonides.

To explain briefly: Shankara is faithful to the Upanishads' frequent identification of *atman* with Brahman, but he understands this identity in accord with Buddhist idealism, to which the perceived world is an illusion constructed by the human mind. As for Spinoza, he is post-medieval because he reacts strongly against medieval philosophy but retains much of its reverence, conceptual vocabulary, ways of arguing, and focuses of interest. Because he is so opposed to the medieval Aristo-Platonizing and its allegorical interpretation of the Bible, it is striking that he argues, like Alfarabi, Avicenna, and Maimonides, that the prophets' revelations were produced not by their intellects but their imaginations. This accounts, he says, for their imaginative words, images, parables, and allegories, as contrasted with the philosophers' intellectual principles and axioms.[118]

The basis, the be-all, of Spinoza's thought is God/Substance, which he conceptualizes and proves (like most of his philosophical contemporaries) in still medieval terms. To give a striking example: When Spinoza proves that there can be no more than one God, he does so in the same

---

*Surendranath Dasgupta, the historian of Indian philosophy, constructs Shankara more elaborately. He states (referring to schools not dealt with here) that Shankara's philosophy is closely related to Samkhya and Yoga. He goes on: "Shankara and his followers borrowed much of their dialectic form of criticism from the Buddhists. His Brahman was very much like the shunya of Nagarjuna. It is difficult indeed to distinguish between pure being and pure non-being as a category. The debts of Shankara to the self-luminosity of the Vijnanavada Buddhism [to be discussed here in the following chapter] can hardly be overestimated. There seems to be much truth in the accusation against Shankara by Vijnana Bhikshu and others that he was a hidden Buddhist himself. I am led to think that Shankara's philosophy is largely a compound of Vijnanavada and Shunyavada Buddhism with the Upanishad notion of the permanence of self superadded" (Dasgupta, *A History of Indian Philosophy*, vol. 1, p. 494).

way, essentially, as Alfarabi, Avicenna, and Maimonides: it is impossible that there should be two (necessary, absolutely infinite) substances because two assumed Gods would have to be either related or unrelated to one another, but both possibilities contradict the conception of God.[119] To give a second example: When Spinoza argues that all things proceed from God's power in an eternal, necessary way, he is repeating the reasoning of Alfarabi and Avicenna. Even when Spinoza compares the necessity of God's action with the necessity that the angles of a triangle are equal to two right angles, his illustration, though characteristic of a seventeenth-century radical such as Descartes, is not alien to Proclus (see the *Ethics* 1.16). And as I have pointed out, the intellectual immortality taught by Spinoza resembles that taught by Alfarabi, Avicenna, and Maimonides. Certainly, in believing in the possibility of eternal intellectual closeness to God, all three are rational mystics in much the same sense as Spinoza: to them, it is the intellectual in human beings that is immortal and close to or, in a sense, in God.[120]

This derivation of Spinoza's thought from medieval Neoplatonism helps to show his likeness to Shankara, whose resemblance to the Neoplatonists is more obvious. It is the greatness of the distance between Shankara and Spinoza that makes the great likeness between them impressive. The distance is Spinoza's method and his slow, systematic deployment of arguments, which has no counterpart in Shankara. The distance is also the equality, on which Spinoza insists, between extension and thought.

In what, then, do the similarities lie? In the metaphysical infinity and atemporality of Brahman and of God/Substance. In the total unity (in total variety) of Brahman and God/Substance. And in the total dependence of everything on both, because everything follows from or emanates from them. The similarities lie in the complete impersonality of both Brahman and Spinoza's God. Neither has any purpose. Correspondingly, Shankara's attitude toward karma is, in principle, lawlike and without exception. And both Brahman and God/Substance are conscious and, as such, experience themselves in some more than human way.

This is not all: To both philosophers, the difference between the metaphysical infinite and the finite objects and persons that are its manifestations or that follow from it, is absolute; but this absolute difference is in fact conceptually bridged. The Spinozistic bridge is constructed by means of the attributes of thought and extension and their infinite modes, not to speak of God's causal power, which infuses everything. The Shankaran bridge, like the Spinozistic one, is by hierarchical stages: Brahman, in which/whom there are no (discernibly separate) qualities, first becomes— nontemporally appears to be—Brahman with qualities or attributes. Belonging to this Brahman, there are name and form, which are figments of nescience not to be defined either as the same as or as different from Brahman; and there is "illusion," *maya*, the power or nature of Brahman with attributes. Shankara's cosmic nescience (*avidya*) is, among other things, the cosmic principle that conditions Brahman and results in individuation. The reality or irreality of this principle, which both is and is not Brahman, was to be (as I have said) a great problem to Shankara's philosophical successors.

Given the descriptions I have made of the two philosophies, there are many possible ways of reading their resemblances and differences.* Both philosophies accept three levels of knowledge, the intermediate level one of well-attested empirical knowledge, and the final, intuitive one that goes beyond the merely empirical. The two philosophers are obvious worlds apart. All the same, it is reasonable to stress what is common to them because they give so basically similar an answer to the existential lesson they have both learned. The lesson is the sense of imperviousness, the steadily tranquil frame of mind, that comes with success in identifying oneself with the unfathomable reality that constitutes us and, if we are enough like Shankara or Spinoza, consoles and enraptures.

---

*A Neo-Vedantist who compares Spinoza with Shankara says, among the rest: In Spinoza, "divine causation should not be regarded as real transformation [of God], but only as appearance or *vivarta* . . . The purpose of introducing the conception of Attribute in the philosophy of Spinoza is the same as that of *Ishvara* in the Vedanta . . . a dynamic principle is needed . . . Substance and *Natura Naturans* are related in the same way as Brahman and Ishvara; the two are two only connotatively, but not denotatively . . . Spinoza identifies self-love in the highest sense with the intellectual love of God. This shows that for him the real self of man is God, and intuition is nothing but the discovery of this real self. He uses the term 'love' which suggests the duality of the lover and the beloved. But as is clear from the nature of self-love, duality is not necessary for love . . . True love is true unity" (Tripathi, *Spinoza in the Light of the Vedānta*, pp. 318, 319, 321).

Chapter 12

❈

Perceptual Analysis, Realistic and Idealistic

Asanga/Vasubandhu, Locke, Berkeley, Hume

Theme: Does Consciousness Refer to Anything Outside Itself?

The thinker who denies that there is anything external to individual consciousness does so mainly, I suppose, in order to deny that there is anything totally alien to human beings and therefore totally impervious to the efforts that humans make to improve their condition. Such a thinker is ready to pay a double price, social and philosophical. The social price is the incredulity of many philosophers and, in the West, the almost certain scorn of nonphilosophers. The philosophical price is the difficulty of explaining why the supposed illusion of externality is universal and almost universally persuasive. Why should nature be so perverse?

The three idealistic philosophers dealt with in this chapter—Asanga, Vasubandhu, and Berkeley—internalize or dematerialize the world. They do this by identifying consciousness, the medium of all that anyone knows about the world, with all that there is, at least in the human sense. In other words, the medium itself of knowledge is the essential nature of everything to which it bears witness. In both India and Europe, this view leads to a contrast between the philosophical points of view called "realism" and "idealism." The kind of idealism called subjective, meaning, concerned

407

primarily with the minds of individuals, is rare in European philosophy—
Berkeley is its only prominent advocate. Both in India and in Europe, it
seems to be unstable, by which I mean that it transforms itself easily into
something grander and more encompassing, objective idealism, which is
itself a variant of what I earlier called hierarchical idealism.

This chapter shows that the background of both subjective and
objective idealism is the methodical analysis of the activity and contents
of the mind or, as the Buddhists call it, *chitta* or *vijnana*.* On the Indian
side, the analysis is into momentary cognitions, acts of knowing regarded
as identical with their content. On the European side, the analysis is into
what the Europeans call ideas. In both India and Europe, such an analysis
is most natural, I assume, to persons with an introspective tendency who
think about how and what they think. In the case of the Indian philosophers, the analysis is accompanied and validated by meditation, which is
practiced intently and often. Berkeley, like Plotinus, shows that the sheer
dislike of matter may also help to stimulate idealism.

As used here, *idealism* is the term invented in the early eighteenth
century to contrast with materialism and, somewhat later, with realism—
the belief that thought has external, nonmental objects. For example, Leibniz
contrasts Epicurus the materialist with Plato the idealist, and considers
Descartes, too, an idealist.[1] Thomas Reid (1710–1996), the Scottish
commonsense philosopher, argues against what he calls the Ideal System,
which he attributes to Descartes, Locke, Berkeley, and Hume.

A number of definitions of the term *idea* may be helpful at this point.
To begin with Plato, an idea is "an eternally existing pattern of any class, of
which the individual members are imperfect copies." Ages later, Descartes
and Locke take *idea* to be—not unlike the equivalent Buddhist concepts—
"whatever is in the mind and directly present to cognitive consciousness,"
or whatever is "the immediate object of thought or mental perception."
Then, in the earlier nineteenth century, Hegel uses *idea* to refer to "the
absolute truth of which all phenomenal existence is the expression."[2]

As these definitions imply, the term *idea* has a complicated history,
to which I will return. But the theme pursued here is the refusal of some
philosophers to separate the objects of perception from the consciousness

---

Chitta (*citta*) is derived from a verbal root meaning to observe, perceive, think. *Vijnana* is
from a verbal root meaning to know. A third associated term, *Manas,* is cognate to the Latin
mens and akin to the English *mind*. Taken in a general sense, the three terms are synonymous
in Buddhist thought, but each has specialized uses, some of which have been or will be
mentioned. (See A. Bareau and J. May in Auroux, ed., *Les notions philosophiques,* vol. 2, under
the words' respective entries; Griffiths, *On Being Mindless,* pp. 55, 169 [notes 30, 31], 182
[note 46]; and Suzuki, *Studies in the Laṅkāvatāra Sūtra,* pp. 179–99, 398–402 [*citta*], 430–
31 [*manas*], 441 [*vijnana*]).

that perceives the objects. A helpful if incomplete analogy might be the web of computer networks, Internet, or, to use a more comprehensive term, cyberspace, with its extraordinary complexity and clusters and constellations of data "ranged in the nonspace of the mind."[3] So for science fiction, God can be a superlative computer whose "mind" or essence is the information, direct and self-referring, that the computer contains.*

Such an analogy is too weak because everyone in fact lives outside of computers and information networks, but never, that we are aware of, outside of consciousness. It's impossible for us to get out of our minds. Common sense says that the mind, in the sense of consciousness, is an instrument whose main purpose is to refer to what is outside itself, so it can help the person whose mind it is to live in and with all that lies outside. But the uncommon sense that strives for a certain simplicity, purity, and self-containment says that the reference to what is outside is unnecessary and misleading. This is the basic philosophical reason for the idealistic philosophizing that follows.

Asanga and Vasubandhu (fl. 350)

Nirvana is where one understands that everything is merely that which is seen in (of) one's own mind only.[4]

Asanga was the oldest and Vasubandhu the middle son of a brahman, a court priest, who lived in what is now called Peshawar.[5] Both brothers became Sarvastivada monks. Though freed by meditation from desires,

---

*To someone who is always exchanging computer messages with people whose existence is, in electronic practice, confined to the messages they send, the world may appear to be composed of the indefinite complex of electronically coded information that the messages convey from one point to another and back again. Since to have absolutely full knowledge is to have the key to reality, mastery of cyberspace can be said to give this key and, in this sense, to be the essence or the reality of reality. If so, to be real is to exist in cyberspace. For hints bearing on this ambition, see "Networks," *Scientific American*, special issue, 1995, and *Time*, special issue on cyberspace, spring 1995.

"Discorporation [divorce of mind from body]... is not uncommon in cyberculture," a recent book says, "where growing numbers spend their days in 'static observation mode,' scrolling through screenfuls of data. Bit by digital bit, we are becoming alienated from our increasingly irrelevant bodies, a sense of discorporation captured in the performance artist Laurie Anderson's quip, 'I am in my body the way most people drive their cars.' With this alienation comes a *body loathing*, a combination of mistrust and contempt for the cumbersome flesh that accounts for the drag coefficient in technological environments" (M. Dery, *Escape Velocity*, New York: Grove/Atlantic, 1996, pp. 234–35; see also S. Turkle, *Life on the Screen*, New York: Son & Schuster, 1995).

Asanga was desperate to grasp the doctrine of emptiness. About to commit suicide, he was deterred by the explanation given by a Hinayana monk. But though Asanga grasped and experienced emptiness, he was so intent on understanding it, tradition says, that he used the power given him by meditation to rise to the Tushita heaven, where the bodhisattva Maitreya, "the kind one," taught him the Mahayana doctrine of emptiness. Back on earth, Asanga found himself unable to overcome his listeners' skepticism, so he prayed to Maitreya to descend and himself teach Mahayana. Maitreya did as he was asked, and every night for four months he recited the sutra of what would be Asanga's great work, *Stages of Spiritual Practice (Yogachara-bhumi)*, the truth of which Asanga expounded during the day.[6]*

In the meanwhile, Vasubandhu had been writing Hinayana works, and Asanga, afraid that his younger brother might harm Mahayana, pretended to be sick. Vasubandhu came to console him. When he asked Asanga why he was sick, Asanga answered that it was because of the harm that Vasubandhu's writings were doing to the Great Teaching. "This," said Asanga, "is a hateful crime." Vadubandhu answered, "If so, it is a crime of the tongue, so the tongue must be cut off." Asanga answered, "That's not necessary. Instead, you should compose Mahayana works, so that the Great Teaching may be known more widely." So Vasubandhu composed five hundred Mahayana works and the people called him the Master of the Thousand Manuals.[7]

A Tibetan biographer of the fourteenth century, who depends on older sources, says that when religious questions were debated, "the younger brother had quick and sudden flashes of ideas, whereas the elder required some time in order to give a good answer." As Asanga explained,

---

*Though he is all mercy, Maitreya continues to trouble researchers. When Asanga attributes five of the books he comments on to Maitreyanatha, the researchers ask if he means to refer to a human teacher who was later confused with the like-named Bodhisattva. Perhaps he means to refer, some say, to the Bodhisattva that he believes, or wants others to believe, gave him inspiration. To explain the opening of a book (the *Madhyanta-vibhanga*) attributed to Maitreya and commented on by Asanga, Vasubandhu says: Asanga, "having received the blessing of Saint Maitreya and entering with his help (the trance called) 'Intuition of the stream of the Elements of Existence' he discovered this treatise and explained it" (*Mādhyanta-vibhanga Discourse*, trans. Stcherbatsky, p. 9). But Asanga seems not to have written the books he attributes to Maitreya, which are different from those he surely wrote (Frauwallner, *Die Philosophie des Buddhismus*, p. 296; Keenan in Griffiths, Hakayama, Keenan, and Swanson, *The Realm of Awakening*, pp. 30–33). Maybe Asanga decided to declare writings that he came upon, revised, or even invented to be inspired and said so in the religiously accepted style. It is amusing that the Italian scholar, Giuseppe Tucci, who wrote a good defense (*On Some Aspects . . .*) of the actual existence of a human author called Maitreya was later convinced by the French Buddhologist, Paul Demiéville, that there had in fact not been any such person (G. Tucci, *Minor Buddhist Texts, Part I*, Serie Orientale Roma IX, Rome: Instituto Italiano per il Medio ed Estremo Oriente, 1956, p. 14, note 1).

Vasubandhu had been a scholar for five hundred births and had had time to acquire analytic wisdom, while he, Asanga, was able to answer only after he questioned his tutelary deity.[8] A present-day scholar feels that both thinkers demonstrate genius but have complementary temperaments: "Asanga is more the creator, more spiritual, sometimes confused; Vasubandhu is more intellectual, with a methodical, systematic mind."[9]

Implausibly many books are ascribed to Asanga and Vasubandhu, and the more liberal one is in accepting their authorship, the vaguer they become as thinkers. In the case of Vasubandhu, I depend mainly on his concise *Proof in Twenty (Verses) of Representation Only (Vimshatika Vijnapti-matrata-siddhi)*. His later *Proof in Thirty (Verses) of Representation Only (Trimshika Vijnapti-matrata-siddhi)* is doctrinal rather than philosophical.* When limited to these two works and a number of commentaries, Vasubandhu becomes a less scattered, more plausibly individual, philosopher than he otherwise appears to be.** To Maitreya/Asanga and/or Asanga, who is less philosophical than Vasubandhu, I will refer only in passing.

The doctrine taught by Asanga and Vasubandhu is given a number of different names: Yoga Practice *(Yogachara)*; Doctrine of Consciousness, or Doctrine of Cognition *(Vijnana-vada)*; and Doctrine of Consciousness Only, or of Mind Only, Cognition Only, or Representation Only (the Sanskrit terms include *Vijnana-matra-vada, Vijnapti-matra-vada,* and *Chitta-matra-vada*—a predominantly Tibetan term).

---

*The translation *representation only* is less usual than *mind only*. Other possible translations are: *perception only, consciousness only, cognition only, ideation only, mere consciousness,* and *mere ideation*. *Vijnapti* is translated *information* by Jacques May because—like *vijnana* in the old tradition—it is the apprehension or perception of objects, of whose identity it informs the perceiver (J. May, "Vasubandhu," in Matti, ed., *Les Oeuvres philosophiques,* vol. 2, p. 3985). Griffiths et al. translate *vijnapti* as *conscious construction* and explain that in its technical use in this philosophy "it means that which causes conscious knowing to occur, and thus signifies the conscious construction of concepts and words that mediate understanding. The fact that such conscious constructs are not impressed upon the mind in virtue of the causal action of external essences is emphasized by the term *matra*, 'only,' and the associated abstract nominal form *matrata*" (Griffiths et al., trans., *The Realm of Awakening,* p. 13).

**In his monograph *On the Date of the Buddhist Master of the Law Vasubandhu,* Frauwallner argues that there were two Vasubandhus. The one, who lived, he estimates, C.E. 400 to 480, wrote the Hinayana epitome, the *Abhidharmakoshabhashya* (hereafter, *AKB)*. The other, earlier Vasubandhu, dated 320 to 380, is Asanga's brother. Assuming two of Vasubandhu, should the various Mahayana works ascribed to Vasubandhu also be divided between them, and if so, how? Of recent writers, Griffiths *(On Being Mindless,* pp. 164–65) opts provisionally for a Vasubandhu who is the author of the *AKB* and a substantial number of Mahayana works (which he does not name), and who is probably the half-brother of Asanga. Williams *(Mahayana Buddhism,* p. 279, note 1) is open to the suggestion that there were two Vasubandhus, each converted to Mahayana. Wood *(Mind Only,* p. 199) is noncommittal. Writing in 1992, Schmithausen ("A Note on Vasubandhu . . . ," p. 396) regards the question as still unsolved.

This doctrine did not spring up all at once. The unending Buddhist emphasis on the fluctuations of consciousness and on the nonexistence of the self did not restrain some of the faithful from trying to arrive at a more immediately plausible understanding of the continuity of consciousness. As they were taught, consciousness is the last factor to disappear before death and the first to reappear at rebirth, with memories in principle cumulative and intact. And if the world of apparently stable objects and lasting selves is an illusion created by thought, why should some Buddhist not borrow from the old Indian belief in the power of consciousness to create not only dreams but also the waking world?

In answer to this question, hints from the older Buddhist literature were amplified and set within newly invented sutras (conversations of the Buddha). The effect was to accentuate the positive or the continuous more than the older Buddhism allowed.* *Emptiness, shunya,* was now given the quasi-positive meaning—so to speak—of a superlatively featureless insight considered to be the very perfection of wisdom. In the light of such an understanding of perfection it could be said, for example, that the ultimate is "to abide in nonabidance as Buddhas do, and dwell securely in ultimate quiescence, the inconceivable state."[10] For this ideal, "perfect wisdom is by its own-being empty" because "that is its essential nature." The expressively willful paradox created is that to have an essential nature is to exist, so that perfect wisdom is said to exist in the sense that it does not exist, and vice versa.[11]

To make this idea of emptiness clear—clear, so to speak—emptiness, which is indefinable, is given twenty definitions. As an instance, to the question, What is the emptiness of ultimate reality? the answer is given:

> "Ultimate reality" means Nirvana. And that Nirvana is empty of Nirvana ["Nirvana" is not an objective entity but only the disconnection from all phenomenal elements], on account of its being neither unmoved nor destroyed. For such is its essential nature.[12]

Consciousness (*chitta*) is also accorded a superlative. When quite pure, it is declared to be beyond both existence and nonexistence, because "suchness, emptiness, the limit, Nirvana, Dharmadhatu [all possible worlds],

---

*Hints from the older literature: The Pali canon appears to accept the view that consciousness (*vijnana*) is what collects the impressions of karma and, by doing so, creates the continuity of a life with the lives that succeed it. Many passages make it clear that consciousness ends with liberation, but many others say that consciousness continues, although "without attribute, endless and radiating all round," or without "support" or "resting place" (Waldron, "How Innovative Is the *Ālayavijñāna*?" pp. 224, 225–26, notes 10, 12). In scholastic Hinayana, it is said that the latent dispositions (*anuśaya*) make it possible for actions to accumulate and give rise to a new existence (Waldron, ibid., p. 211).

variety of will-bodies—they are nothing but Mind, I say."[13] This quite pure consciousness is described in necessarily paradoxical language and is glorified rather as if it was *brahman/atman*.[14] The Great Jewel-Heap Sutra (*Maharatnakuta Sutra*)—really a group of forty-nine sutras—says that consciousness, like a puppeteer out of sight, operates things by intelligence and supports the existence of every being in the realm of dharmas. Though residing in impure beings, consciousness is not tainted by them. At death, it combines with memory and is the seed of the next life. If there would be no consciousness, there would be no world.

To illustrate the power of consciousness, the sutra uses an image from the lesson Uddalaka taught Shvetaketu. "Consider," says the text,

> the seeds of the banyan and udumbara. Though small, these seeds can engender huge trees, which will in turn produce seeds. These new seeds will leave the old trees to produce new trees . . . Similarly, after leaving its small body, the consciousness of a small sentient being may take on a big body of some kind, according to its karmas.[15]

These eloquent descriptions of the indescribable are not given any developed philosophical defense. However, they serve as prelude to the thought of Vasubandhu and Asanga, and Vasubandhu, at least, builds up a genuinely philosophical defense for them. To show how he does so, I go on to his *Twenty Verses* (actually twenty-two), accompanied by his own commentary. Because the book is short, the paraphrase that follows is able to convey much of its structure and argument.[16]

After a quite brief introduction, Vasubandhu declares (verse 1): Everything is mind or representation [or conscious construction] only, because nonexistent (*asat*) objects appear, just as they do to a person suffering from an eye disorder, who sees things that do not exist, such as hair, the moon, and so on.*

---

*At the very start of *Twenty Verses* Vasubandhu is kind enough to relieve the translator of considerable difficulty when he says that *chitta, manas, vijnana,* and *vijnapti* are synonymous. But though the translator has a choice of terms with which to translate, none is really satisfactory. Anacker translates Vasubandhu's *vijnapti-matram-avaitat* with *perception-only;* Chatterjee with *mere ideation;* Kochumuttom with *mere representation of consciousness;* Wood with *mind or representation only;* and Frauwallner with *Erkenntniss,* the relevant English translation of which is *cognition.* It is too difficult to attempt exact termininological consistency, but, to begin with, I have chosen *representation,* because it suggests relationship to an assumed object and because it allows a natural use of the verb *to represent. Cognition* is better in that it carries a stronger implication of conscious scrutiny than *representation. Conscious construction* may be best though too long for comfort. *Ideation,* by which I am tempted, is avoided because its use would imply a likeness with the idea philosophies of Locke, Berkeley, and Hume and would therefore prejudice the comparison that follows.

Vasubandhu then says, in the name of an objector (verse 2): If representation had no (external) object, there would be no restriction to place 'and time, no nonrestriction of personal streams of consciousness, and no correspondence of effects with actions.

What does this mean? asks the objector, and, explaining his question, continues: If the representation of a form and so on arises in the absence of an external object, why is the representation restricted to a particular place? Why is it restricted to this place at a particular time? Why does it arise in the minds—the streams of consciousness—of all those situated at this time at this place, instead of being restricted to one person, as are the appearances of hairs and so on that arise only in the mind of someone with an eye disorder? Why is it that the hairs, bees, and so on seen by someone with an eye disorder do not have the same effect as the (nonimaginary) hairs and so on that others see? Why is it that the food, drink, clothing, poison, weapons, and so on that we see in a dream do not have the effect they do in waking life? If the object of such a representation does not exist, then, as with nonexistent things, there should be no restriction to place and time, no nonrestriction of streams of consciousness, and no correspondence of effect to action. Yet different individuals in fact see the same sights, and effects in fact correspond to the actions that precede them.

Vasubandhu answers (verse 3): Place and so on are restricted in the same way as in a dream. How? In a dream, one sees particular things, such as bees, gardens, women, men, and so on, in a particular place and time, even though no external object exists. To show that effects can correspond to actions even though no external object exists (verse 4), Vasubandhu then cites examples, such as that of a man who, without sexual intercourse, emits semen in his sleep.

Another, to us exotic, example is that of the ghosts of the dead who, because they were evildoers, live in hell. Vasubandhu gives this example to show that no external objects are needed to explain either restriction to place and time, or nonrestriction of streams of consciousness, or correspondence of effects to actions. The evildoers in hell see (or hallucinate) hell guards, dogs, crows, iron mountains, and so on, all at a particular place and time.* The evildoers appear to be tormented by the hell guards,

---

*By Buddhist doctrine, living beings transmigrate through different states of being. One such state is that of ghosts (pretas), who wander over the earth, tormented by hunger and thirst. Because the ghosts of the dead have all earned the same karma, they all suffer from the same hell deception. Sarvastivadins take them to be shapes, made of lifeless elements, called up by the power of karma. Sautrantika, with whose teaching in this matter Vasubandhu agrees, says that the hell guards are only the product of the evildoers' minds—a simpler theory, he says. (See Wei-shih-er-shih-lun, trans. Hamilton, notes pp. 29–30; and Frauwallner, Die Philosophie des Buddhismus, pp. 357–58.)

who are not real. They are all tormented at the same time because of the similar time of ripening of their evil deeds—they all have an equivalent karmic history.

Speaking for an objector, Vasubandhu asks himself: Why not admit that the hell guards are living beings, who have an external existence? (comm. verse 4c). Because it is not possible that they have an external existence, he answers. They cannot be true inhabitants of hell because, unlike the evildoers, they do not experience its torments. If the evildoers and the hell guards tormented one another, it would be impossible to distinguish between them. And if the guards are not evildoers, how can their karma cause them to be reborn in hell?

An objection arises (comm. verse 5). It is that of a realist, a Sarvastivadin. He asks: Why not admit that the actions of the evildoers result in the arising of shapes composed of elements that have the color, form, size, and power that cause them to be called hell guards?

Vasubandhu answers (verses 6, 7): If you say that elements arise and change themselves so because of the evildoers' actions, why not accept the simpler view that the changes are only changes of consciousness? Why imagine elements? According to you, Vasubandhu goes on, an action's impression—which, as you agree, clings to consciousness—is in one, internal place, while its effect, its fruit, is in another, external place. But why not accept the simpler view that the effect of the action is in the same place, the stream of consciousness, as its impression?

The objector objects (comm. verse 7): My reason is the Buddha's teaching on the senses' fields of operation. The teaching implies that the senses have external objects.

Vasubandhu answers (verses 8–10, much simplified): This teaching of the Buddha is meant to help persons who are not yet able to grasp the full truth. He does not mean that there is an external world. But for the sake of those whose understanding is undeveloped, he says that what is perceived is no more than an interaction between the sense organs and an object (a *dharma* or element of experience). Trust in this partial truth leads to its inner meaning, which is that there is no self, no one who sees or hears. To realize this is to be closer to the truth that the *dharmas* of form that arise in the mind are all without self, without substance.

The objector retorts (comm. verse 10b): But if this is so, representation only—perception without an external object—does not exist either. How can you maintain the doctrine?

Vasubandhu's answer is to agree, though in a qualified way. He says (comm. verse 10b–c): To understand that there is nothing more than representation is not to mean that nothing in any way exists. It means only that it is wrong to imagine, as fools do, that there is a distinction between subject and object. We ordinary humans are unable to express the selfless nature—the absence of own-being—of the elements of experience, and no one but the Buddha is able to cognize these elements. But our inability should not be taken to mean that the elements do not in some humanly inconceivable sense exist. The selflessness of a representation is understood when the object constructed by a previous representation is understood to be empty. Otherwise, a representation would have the previous representation as its object. This object would exist apart from consciousness, and, if so, the doctrine of representation only would be invalid.*

Another question follows: How can you know that in referring to the existence of the fields of vision and so on, the Buddha did not really mean to teach that there are external elements that become the objects of the sense organs?

Vasubandhu answers with a summary of his objections to a material, external world (verse 11). His argument, which seems original with him, is basically as follows: If there is something external to consciousness, it is, of course, material. The most plausible hypothesis to explain the existence of a material world is that of atomism. This is because material objects, being spatially extended, are divisible into parts, which are divisible, at the limit, into indivisible atoms. However, reason demonstrates that atoms are not possible—or that their existence cannot be demonstrated. If there can be no atoms, there can be no matter and, therefore, no external world.**

---

*In a note to his translation of Hsüan Tsang's translation of the *Twenty Verses*, Hamilton explains: "In the perfect intuition of the Buddha the true nature of elements as representation-only is apprehended in its real existence. This, Vasubandhu contends, is not denied by the doctrine of the insubstantiality (lit. egolessness) of elements." Hamilton continues (with an interpretation different from that reflected in my text) that "ordinary mortals, even philosophers like Vasubandhu, may think about representation-only as an object, but such knowledge does not transcend the subject-object relation and hence is void. All representations of representation-only must therefore fail, but this is not to say that its true nature as immediately known to Buddha does not exist" (*Wei-shih-er-shih-lun*, trans. Hamilton, p. 43, notes 53, 54).

**To put the argument more as Vasubandhu does: There are three possible ways in which the perceptual object can exist: as a whole made up of atoms but distinct from them (the Nyaya-Vaisheshika view); as a mere collection of atoms; or as combinations or conjunctions of atoms. None of these possibilities makes sense: There cannot be a unity different from its atoms because no whole is actually perceived that is different from its parts. Nor can the object of perception be a mere collection of atoms, because, as is acknowledged, individual atoms cannot be perceived. Nor can the object be a combination (a conjunction or composite) of atoms, because the existence of the individual atom *(paramanu)* cannot be demonstrated.

Vasubandhu explains (verse 12ab): An atom is assumed to be in the middle of six others—one for each direction—and to come into contact with them all. It must therefore have six distinguishable places of contact, because each atom excludes the other atoms from

Whether or not the combination of atoms is accepted, Vasubandhu continues, nothing in which spatial distinctions can be made is a unity (verse 14ab). If one admits that an atom has spatial distinctions, then one admits the distinction of *front* for an atom that faces another, as well as the distinction of *bottom* for an atom that is above another. How, then, can the atom be a true unity?

But if, on the contrary, it is claimed that an atom has no spatial distinctions, there is no explanation for shadows and the blocking of light (14c). If the atom has no spatial distinctions, that is, physical dimensions, then how is it that at sunrise the light of the sun is not everywhere at once, but that there are shadows on one side and light on the other? And just as the nondimensional atom has no other part, no further surface, that light can fail to strike—if struck at all by light, all of it must be struck at once—it has nowhere—no extended surface—to keep the light from being visible elsewhere. And if the atom, having no spatial distinctions, has no further side to resist the impact of another atom, all the atoms that combine have the dimension of a single atom. But what is the use of discussing atoms or combinations of atoms if their character as merely visual and other representations is not refuted?

Vasubandhu now changes course and says: What remains for discussion is the question if the objects of visual and other representations are many, as they seem to be, or only one. Why discuss this? Because the error in assuming them to be many—to be atoms or combinations of atoms—has been demonstrated, leaving us with the logical alternative that they are only one.

In considering this alternative, which is on its face absurd (though Parmenides had his reason for thinking it true), Vasubandhu does not flinch. Like a more metaphysical Lewis Carroll, he tries to conceive the visual consequences of a condition that he cannot imagine. First he gives

---

its own place. If it is assumed, on the contrary, that the place of the one atom is identical with that of the other six, the combination would in effect be one atom, because whatever occupies a place excludes everything else from that place (verse 12c–d). (But quantum mechanics violates such commonsense logic. It recognizes a state of matter, called a Bose-Einstein condensate, that results from extremely cold temperatures. In this state, the speed of particles is close to zero and a large system forms made of atoms with identical wave properties. Then it is impossible to distinguish any atom's position or identity from that of any other.)

It can be objected that the Vaibhashikas of Kashmir say that (prematerial) atoms (*paramanus*) can combine only when they are associated (in an *anu* or more). However, says Vasubandhu, there is no reason to suppose that an association of atoms is different from the atoms in it. He continues (verse 13) that a combination of atoms cannot combine because its individual atoms cannot combine.

an abstract summary of the absurdities that result (verse 15): If everything is a unity, it is impossible to move gradually, or to grasp and not grasp simultaneously, or to be separate and varied, or to be minute and unseen. To explain what he means: If one assumes that the object of vision is unbroken and represents something that is one and the same, gradual motion is impossible because there is no separation or distance between anything.* Everywhere is all the same place and is reached everywhere all at once. So a single step goes everywhere. Because nothing has a closer or further part, it is not possible to grasp anything close by and not simultaneously grasp what is further away. Thinking apparently of an unbroken spatial field that, by force of imagination, suggests a field in which animals graze, Vasubandhu says: In a unity there cannot be separate, disconnected things such as elephants, horses, and so on. How can two things be separate from one another? How can one place be both occupied and unoccupied by them, with an intervening space in which they are not present? Finally, even if we assume that it is possible to distinguish between different things, there are no particular spatial distinctions to mark differences in size, so that what is minute—water animalcules, for example—and what is less minute are equally visible, which is absurd.**

---

*Compare this with Aristotle's discussion of Leucippus: "For some of the ancients thought that what is must necessarily be one and motionless, since the void is non-existent and there could be no motion without a separately existing void, and again there could not be a plurality without something to separate them. And if anyone thinks the universe is not continuous but consists of divided pieces in contact with each other, this is no different, they held, from saying that it is many, not one, and is void. For if it is divisible everywhere, there is no unity, and therefore not many, and the whole is void. If on the other hand it is divisible in one place and not another, this seems like piece of fiction" (Aristotle, *Physics* 187a1; Kirk, Raven, and Schofield, *The Presocratic Philosophers* [bib. chap. 2, note 24], p. 407).

Also, compare what Vasubandhu says with the argument of Sextus Empiricus: To exist, the existent must be either one or many, but neither is possible. "A one of any kind is not a one, because it is divisible; but if there is no one, there cannot be many." And "even if anything exists it is unknowable and inconceivable by man" (Sextus Empiricus, *Against the Logicians* 1.73–75; in *Sextus Empiricus*, trans. Bury [bib. chap. 8, note 1], vol. 2, pp. 39, 41).

**Perhaps Vasubandhu means (as Frauwallner says) that if we assume that the things are different only because of different kinds of distinguishing features, the very minute water creatures would be visible along with the less minute ones because they are constructed in the same way. As I understand Chatterjee, he thinks the meaning is that all creatures, from the imperceptible or barely perceptible to the large, should have the same perceptibility, because each of them is one, and to be one is to be perceptible. According to Hsüan-tsang's Chinese version of *Twenty Verses*, the meaning is this: "Moreover there should also be no such scarcely perceptible tiny things as water animalcules, because being in the same single space as the coarse things they should be of equal measure"—each occupying object fills the whole of the place occupied, so in a body of water, each animalcule is equal to the whole. Therefore large and small would be the same in size, which is absurd (*Wei-shih-er-shih-lun*, trans. Hamilton, p. 57).

Assuming that the hypothesis of unity has failed, Vasubandhu continues: Because of such absurdities, one has no alternative but to accept that things are divided into atoms. The atomic theory has not been demonstrated, but neither has it been demonstrated that everything is representation only.

The objector then asks: Existence and nonexistence are determined by the evidence given by the means of knowledge. Of all these means, perception is the most important. If no external object exists, why is it that I have the consciousness of having perceived something?

Vasubandhu answers (verse 16): Perception discriminates as it does in dreams. When a perception takes place, the object of the perception is nonexistent. It is not perceived at the moment that my consciousness is "I perceive this"— by the time that there is consciousness of the perception, the visual impression—transmitted to consciousness by way of the mind organ (manas)—is already gone. How, then, can the object be considered to be perceived, especially by someone who accepts the teaching that everything is momentary?

The Objector asks: How could consciousness alone remember something that was not earlier perceived by the senses? There must be direct sensory perception of the remembered (external) object. It is this sensory perception that allows us to remember the form and other perceived characteristics that represent the object.

Vasubandhu answers that he has already discussed how the appearance of an object is nothing but a representation, from which memory arises (verse 17ab). He then turns to the objection that if waking representations were like those in dreams, people would understand by themselves that the objects did not exist.

Vasubandhu responds (17c): As long as people are not awake, they do not realize that the objects they see in a dream are nonexistent. When they are asleep and sunk in the false mental constructions with which habit has impregnated them, they cannot recognize that the objects they see are unreal. It is not until they awaken that they realize the truth that the objects are nonexistent. When they are awakened by supermundane, construction-free knowledge—the antidote to mental construction—they gain pure mundane knowledge and realize the nonexistence of the objects of sense perception. Both awakenings are alike (and together, we may add, recall what Chuang-tzu said about the great awakening).[17]

The objector says: Suppose that an image of some object arises in the mind because of some change in the individual's stream of consciousness and not because of some external object. But if no one and nothing exists outside of one's stream of consciousness, how do you explain the differences in understanding that result from friendship with good or evil persons or from the hearing of true or false doctrines?

Vasubandhu answers (verse 18a): What consciousness represents is subject to the ruling effect (the "ruling cause," *adhipatitva*) that the mind of one sentient being exerts on that of another. A particular representation in one stream of consciousness determines the arising of a particular representation in another stream. If you ask why actions in a dream state do not have the beneficial or harmful effects for the future that a waking state does, the answer is that in sleep the mind (*chitta*) is weakened by its inertness, so the future consequences are different—the difference is not because of the presence or absence of an object (18b).

This answer leads to a more dramatic question: But if there are only representations and no one really has either a body or a voice, how is it that sheep and so on die when slaughtered by shepherds? If the death of the sheep and so on is not caused by the shepherds, why are they held responsible for the sin of the taking of life?

Killing, answers Vasubandhu, is the modification of someone else's mental representations by a hostile representation of these representations (verse 19)—death, so to speak, is a fatal meeting of minds. As Vasubandhu explains: This is like the loss of memory, or like the dreams and so on, caused by possession by spirits and demons. The force of a certain representation of another person can modify this other person's stream of consciousness. It does this by counteracting the person's life force and leading to the break in the stream's homogeneity that we call death. That is why the Buddha regarded the mental harm done to others as a crime greater than bodily or verbal harm, which are easier than mental harm to accept with forbearance (verse 20).

To this, the objector says: But if there is only mind or representation, does the knowledge of another's mind (*chitta*) really know it or not? What difference does this make? you ask. The difference is that if it is impossible to know other minds directly, there is a contradiction with the scriptures, according to which certain enlightened persons do have direct knowledge of other minds (*para-chitta-vijnana*). But if they know them as direct objects of thought, the doctrine of mind only is mistaken.

Vasubandhu answers (verse 21): The knowledge of those who know other minds does not correspond to things are they really are. Why? Their knowledge is like the knowledge one has of one's own mind (*sva-chitta*). Even this is concealed by ignorance (*ajnana*), the ignorant distinction between subject and object.

Vasubandhu then concludes (with verse 22, which must have once been verse 20):[18] The *Proof in Twenty Verses of Representation Only* has been finished to the best of my abilities. But full understanding of representation cannot be grasped by (merely human) thought. Persons such as myself cannot grasp it in any form, because it is not the object of logical thought. In whose domain is the whole of it? In the domain of the exalted Buddhas, whose wisdom, which encompasses everything knowable in every form, is subject to no impediments.

In spite of the difficulty in understanding how a mind grasped by another might not be an object of thought, Vasubandhu is quite sure that other minds exist, at least in terms of human understanding. Hsüan-tsang, his seventh-century translator and interpreter, is very emphatic in upholding the existence of other minds. A thought, he says, does not directly grasp an external object the way a hand does, but rather the way a mirror reflects it. When the objector asks whether the mind-only doctrine is not contradicted by the existence of other minds as objects of thought, Hshüan Tsang answers:

> What a persistent skeptic! The doctrine of consciousness only does not teach the existence of a single consciousness (vijnana), my own. If only my consciousness existed, the variety of ordinary persons and of Aryas (noble persons), of good and evil, of the causes and fruits of the ten cardinal directions, would all disappear. What Buddha would teach me? What doctrine (dharma) would he teach for the sake of what fruit?[19]*

I turn now to a dialogue attributed to Dharmakirti, a seventh-century philosopher of a later, logical tradition, who will be discussed in the next chapter.[20] The dialogue, written from the standpoint of the mind-only school, defends the existence of other minds. Its basic idea is that the mind-only philosophy is superior to realistic philosophy because it gives a simpler explanation of human experience—the doctrine of the existence of many minds (mental "streams") with nothing external to them avoids solipsism and is both necessary and sufficient for the explanation. In other words, the belief in external, nonmental, material things is an unnecessary and therefore useless philosophical complication.

---

*The mind-only philosopher Ratnakirti (fl. 1070) flatly contradicts Hsüan Tsang's view. "The Buddha," he says, "never asserted the existence of another mind in any fashion." In partial but probably not final opposition to Dharmakirti, whose dialogue I summarize just below, Ratnakirti argues that because neither external objects nor external minds are directly perceptible, there is no more reason to infer the existence of the minds than of the objects. Although his argument is, on the worldly level, that of a solipsist, Ratnakirti is a partisan of ultimate nondualism (Wood, Mind Only, pp. 149–59, 205–6, 223–30 [229 quoted]). More exactly, Ratnakirti thinks that "in ultimate reality the cognizing subject, its act of awareness, and the cognized object coalesce—all are fabrications superimposed on what is really an indivisible evanescent now (svalakshana)" (McDermott, An Eleventh-Century Buddhist Logic of 'Exists,' p. 1).

The dialogue that follows is a free, telescoped version of Dharmakirti's original. It takes the form of a debate between Buddhist idealists, with whom Dharmakirti identifies himself, and realists. So far as most of Dharmakirti's own text goes, the realists might be partisans of Nyaya, but the two commentaries say that Dharmakiriti is referring to the Sautrantika Buddhists (sutras 34 through 39, which I omit, dispute the view of the Vaibhashika Buddhists).[21] To make the dialogue more natural, I have often substituted the singular *I* for the plural *we* (in "we answer," and so on).

The dialogue goes so:

Realist: I infer the existence of other minds by analogy with my own. My inward desire to move or speak precedes the actual movements I make or words I speak. So I infer that the movements I see someone else making or the words I hear someone else speaking are preceded in that person's mind by the desire to move or speak.* But you, the idealist, don't believe in the existence of external, bodily actions or of speech outside of a mind, and you can't directly perceive the desire in another person's mind. How, then, can you infer the other mind's existence?

Idealist: The other mind surely does exist. You wouldn't see other persons or hear what they said if there was no other mind, or if the other mind had no conscious processes, no motives, to make this other person move and speak. It is true that our doctrine does not hold that we directly perceive the other's mind, but you face the same kind of difficulty because you cannot directly perceive the activity of the other consciousness that, by your doctrine, must precede the other's bodily actions and speech.[22]

Realist: I have another reason for inferring the existence of the other's mind. The reason is the inability of *my* mind to be the cause of the other person's movements and speech. I mean, I don't experience in myself the intentions that would precede such movements if it was me who was making them. If the movements had resulted from *my* mind, I would have perceived them as my own. Instead, I see the other as an object in external space, as a body different from mine.

Idealist: The internal and the apparently bodily or external both depend on consciousness. Like you, I see movements and hear speech that are caused, as I am conscious, by my own mind, and I see other movements and hear other speech that I perceive to be externally caused. If I believed that these external movements were not caused by a mind, I

---

*Compare Wittgenstein: "I know consciousness only from myself, I don't *know* whether anybody else has consciousness, but it makes *sense* to assume it, and I do make the assumption in a class of cases" ("Notes for Lectures on 'Private Experience' and 'Sense Data,'" in L. Wittgenstein, *Philosophical Occasions 1912–1951*, ed. J. C. Klagge and A. Nordmann, Indianapolis: Hackett, 1993, p. 279).

would have to admit that my movements, too, were not necessarily caused by a mind. When an arrow I shoot goes up into the air, its flight is not my movement—it is not *my* body that moves—and when *I* swing somebody else, it's the other person I see moving. Such representations appear to me to be outside of my body even though it is my will that causes them. I add the example of hypnosis (or the magical influence of someone else), because actions carried out under such influence are involuntary. And when somebody rocks or whirls me, the movement is mine even though it is not by my will that I move. Briefly, both you and I often perceive actions without being conscious of any motives in ourselves that correspond to them. So both you, the realist, and I, the idealist, have to infer that the motivations are those of another mind. The general weakness of your position is that it's unnecessarily complicated. From what you see and hear—the representations in your mind—you infer the bodily movements and speech of someone else, and from this inference you infer the existence of another mind. I need only one inference, from the representations to the other mind.[23]*

Realist: You say that another mind causes the representations of the movements and speech in which another person appears. Why don't you say the same of the movements and speech in dreams?

Idealist: Representations in dreams are explained on the same principles as those we see when awake. But I think, just as you do, that when a person is overcome by sleep, representations of another person's movements and speech appear without the direct influence of any other mind—the consciousness of a dreaming person may be empty of the support of another person's mental activity.[24] Illusions may appear in dreams, when consciousness is weakened by sleep and the like. Among the special conditions or causes there are the predisposition to see pleased faces or, on the contrary, bloody visions. Other minds influence ours: Dreams can sometimes be true because of the interference of the gods. The activity of another mind can have a ruling influence on the representations that appear our minds. Subconscious impressions made by the activity of another

---

*What my paraphrase above says of the greater simplicity of the idealist's position is more strongly emphasized—as it is in Wood—than in the translations I am using, one of which says, "the Realist thinks that he perceived real actions of the other [person] and not noticing the corresponding motivations in himself, infers the existence of the other mind. The Idealist infers the same, considering however, that it is not real movements of the other but only their images that are perceived" (*Establishment of the Existence of Other Minds*, trans. Stcherbatsky, pp. 92–93, sutra 23). The other translation (Kitagawa's) ends (pp. 413–14) with a different point: "[Therefore, you have] the same [fault which you have pointed out in the method of our reasoning]."

mind can have deferred results. So even dreams can give evidence of the existence of another mind.[25]

Realist: The movements that appear in dreams are not the movements of someone else but only ideas of movement.* We don't infer the existence of another mind from illusions or mere representations. But real physical movements give indications of the existence of another mind.

Idealist: By what right do you decide that some representations do have external objects and others, as in dreams, do not? If you admit that some representations have no objects, why not admit that none of them have them?[26]

Realist: I can't. If someone who hears and sees me has representations in which my speech and actions appear, how, on your view, can the represented speech and actions be indications of the existence of *my* mind, which has no effect on the other's? There is no direct causal relation between what arises in the listener's mind—his mental stream—and the thoughts—the mental stream—of the speaker.

Idealist: I don't argue that the representations you have of the other's movements and speech are directly related to the other's mind. I argue only that there is a causal relation of some sort between them. Only those representations of the movements and speech that result from the willed acts of our own consciousness are real marks of mind. Another person's movements and speech are marks of mind in a weaker sense, that of convention and analogy.** In ordinary experience, one mind-stream "regulates" another, or is its "collateral" or indirect cause, in the sense that one can infer from its representations that the other has similar representations, marks, we say, of the other's mind. When two persons make out the same object in a clear and distinct representation, their experience is independent and the likeness coincidental. The cause (in each case) consists in the experiences that take place in previous existence and give consciousness its special force. This is a causal process that creates representations that convince different people that they are perceiving the same external objects. The representations and actions of the two different persons come from the same source. Two persons suffering from the same eye

---

*Compare Wittgenstein: "People say sometimes 'We only believe in the reality of physical objects, we don't know it.' Or again someone might say 'we don't even believe in them': he might say they are *fictions*. But what is meant by this? A centaur is a fiction. King Lear is a fiction. But what would it be like to invent 'physical objects'?" ("Notes for Lectures on 'Private Experience' and 'Sense Data,'" in L. Wittgenstein, op. cit. [see footnote before last], p. 204).

**Compare Wittgenstein: "It is as though, if/although/you can't tell me exactly what happens inside you, you can nevertheless tell me something general about it. By saying e.g. that you are having an impression which can't be further described" (Wittgenstein, op. cit., p. 317).

disease may both see two moons and point this out to one another. Each of them experiences only his private perception—there is no corresponding external object. But our phenomenal life is timeless and repetitive, and so, in a habitual, conventional sense the perceptions of the two persons can be considered to be related and sufficient marks of mind.[27]

Realist: If you have no direct knowledge of the other's mind and if the other's mind is not an external object, how can you affirm that the other mind exists and has cognitions? You can't establish the existence of another mind unless you know its own-being (svabhava, independent existence).

Idealist: The same objection can be turned against you. You say that the perception of movements and speech allow you to infer that some other mind exists. But if its real existence was the object of your knowledge, its forms would have to be represented in your consciousness just as clearly as are your own movements and speech. Otherwise, why assume that you grasp its own-being (svabhava)?

Realist: To the extent that one grasps another mind not by knowing its own-being but only by some mark or other, what is grasped is only a general concept.

Idealist: If it is only the general concept of mind that you grasp, you don't grasp, don't cognize the other mind itself. Inference—the instrument of rational thought—can't cognize the exact forms or own-being of things. Inference is a source of valid knowledge, and we base our practical activity on it. Having inferred that there is another person nearby, we greet him, invite him into our home, and entertain him with food and drinks, prepare his bed, give him water for washing his feet, clean and massage his feet, and so on. The practical outcome of this inference of another mind— the person's response to our friendly acts—is the result we expect from the activity of the mind whose existence we have inferred. We live in a world that is all purposive activity, our own and that of the others whose existence we infer. But unlike perception, the validity of inference does not consist in the capture of the real individual existence (svabhava) of things. When smoke leads us to infer the existence of fire, the inferred fire is not the same as fire that we perceive. If it was, inference wouldn't be able to direct us to a nonexistent fire, to fire in the past and future, and to imaginary fire. Inferred fire doesn't burn. A mind inferred is not a mind the particular forms of which we know by direct cognition.[28]

Realist: What about the ability of a yogi to have direct knowledge of the mind of another person? If he can directly perceive the own-being of another person's mind, the other's mind must be an external object to him. You assume that this ability of the yogi is a kind of direct perception, and you contend that direct perception grasps the own-being of things. But if the yogi does not perceive the own-being of the other's mind, you are contradicting your belief in perception as a unique source of knowledge.

Idealist: As long as the yogi is no Buddha, he cannot completely release himself from the tendency to distinguish between subject and object. His knowledge of the other's consciousness is only good enough for practical guidance. We see our body and identify it with ourselves, but this knowledge, though it serves us, is not knowledge of our real independent nature. By means of yoga, the yogi can have representations so clear that they seem to be almost those of the specific forms of the mind of another person. His forms are the same as the other's forms; but they remain in his mind, and so he does not grasp the other's mind, his basic consciousness, directly. It's convenient to call the yogi's ability "perception," but it's like inference, because it is valid only insofar as it does not betray him. It's therefore not enough to raise the contradiction of which you accuse us.

To conclude: A Buddha is quite free of the tendency to distinguish between subject and object. If a Buddha can know another mind in itself, then something exists that is external to the knowing subject. But if a Buddha does not have this ability, his knowledge is not perfect. The answer to this dilemma is that the Buddha knows everything but that his knowledge cannot be grasped by analytical thinking, because he is in every way beyond our thought and words.[29]

Two doctrines of great importance to the mind-only school have not yet been discussed. One is the doctrine of the three transformations of consciousness, of which the first and most important is the *alaya* consciousness, the store consciousness. Described simply, it is the doctrine that this consciousness, which is hidden, holds the imprints of past experiences and is therefore the latent cause of all other kinds of consciousness. The other is the doctrine of the Dharma Body *(dharma-kaya)*, which is the absolute.

The doctrine of the transformations of consciousness is the main subject of Vasubandhu's *Thirty Verses* and is prominent in the works attributed to Maitreya and Asanga.* In keeping with its idealism, the *Thirty*

---

*The term is translated variously as store consciousness, storehouse consciousness, receptacle consciousness, and container consciousness. These all have the psychological flaw that they make one think of a large three-dimensional object that contains other objects. I therefore often use *alaya* consciousness. A traditional name that does not suggest something three dimensional is *appropriating consciousness (adana-vijnana)*. An unorthodox translation I have considered is *adhesive consciousness*. The term *alaya* "is a nominal form composed of the prefix '*a*,' 'near to, towards' with the verbal root '*li*,' 'to cling or press closely, stick or adhere to, to lie, recline, alight or settle upon, hide or cower down in, disappear, vanish.' 'Alaya' thus means 'that which is clung to, adhered to, dwelled in, etc.,' thus 'dwelling, receptacle, house, etc.' as well as an older meaning found within the early Pali materials of 'clinging, attachment or grasping'" (Waldron, "How Innovative Is the Ālayavijñāna?" Part II, p. 34, note 154).

Verses begins with the statement that the terms *self (atman)* and *elements (dharmas)* refer to the transformations of consciousness (verse 1).[30] The transformation is threefold: the first is that of fruition, the second, that of thinking, and the third, that of the representation of objects. The first, the *alaya* or store consciousness—the only transformation to be described here—is the fruition of all potentialities or "seeds" (verses 1, 2). It is the perception that abides in what is unperceived and grasps it. It is always associated with the contact between the object, the sense organ *(manas)*, and consciousness; with attention; with sensation or feeling tone—pleasant, painful, and neutral; with conception; and with volition (verse 3). And it is characterized by moral indifference, is undefiled and undefiling, and is always evolving like a torrent (verse 4).

The torrentlike evolution suggested by this last verse prompts Hsüantsang to say that the *alaya* consciousness is neither permanent nor impermanent. From beginningless time, he says, it has been an uninterrupted, homogeneous sequence that is born and perishes every moment.

> It (carries along) sentient beings, sometimes floating, sometimes sinking, without allowing them to leave (the cycle of existence) . . . It is like a violent torrent which, though beaten by the wind into waves, flows onward without interruption.[31]

The defense of this doctrine is implicit in Vasubandhu and, at least at one point, explicit in Asanga. The defense is that the *alaya* consciousness is essential to explain birth, development, death, and rebirth.[32]* Because this view, which is a scholastic elaboration of earlier ideas, incorporates so much that is arbitrarily precise, not to say dogmatic, a history of philosophy is not the place to go into its details. But its relative rationality and its psychological depth make it worth serious attention. By relative rationality I mean that once basic Buddhist ideas are granted, the defense of the *alaya* consciousness is not unlike a defense that one might now make of a hypothetical set of related psychobiological processes, the object of the extremely ambitious hypothesis being to integrate all these processes as they develop in the embryo, persist throughout life, and are transmitted by heredity.

The conception of the *alaya* consciousness is psychologically deep because it is the attempt to formulate the development of a complex

---

*A commentator on Asanga's *Summary of Metaphysics (Abhidharma-samuchchaya)* gives eight arguments for the existence of the store consciousness. Without it, he claims, there could be no development of a new body, no origination or simultaneous functioning of the sense consciousnesses, no clear "mental" consciousness, no mutual "seeding," no action, no physical experience, no attainment of mindless meditation, and no death. (See Griffiths, *On Being Mindless*, pp. 129–43.)

function of the mind that interrelates everything that is under the threshold of consciousness—including preconscious processes, inborn dispositions, acquired habits, and hidden and available memories—with everything that is above it, including desires, perceptions, and abstract thoughts. The doctrine creates the sense of a living process by using metaphors of seeds and ripening, of "perfuming," and of growth, accumulation, and dispersal. A scholar pays the concept a not unemotional tribute when he writes:

> The *alayavijnana* expresses deep truths about the human condition, about our capacity to understand and work with what we are—and what we are not. It indicates that the real obstacles to self-understanding and self-control, and the concerted efforts to develop them within our deeply implicated relationships with others, depend upon an appreciation of the continuing influence of past experiences without reference to which even the most mundane activity is ultimately unintelligible.[33]

Yet in the eyes of the idealistic Buddhists, who inherit the idea of emptiness, the *alaya* consciousness, like everything else nameable, is metaphysically empty, because it, too, is interdependent, changing, and ultimately inexplicable. So this consciousness turns out to be an extended metaphor—more Lamarckian and Freudian than Darwinian—for the complex continuity of life and, as well, for the impenetrability of the ultimate truth about life. Impenetrability except for the perfectly certain way of escape, we are told, from pain and uncertainty.[34]

The impersonal breadth of the description of the *alaya* consciousness suggests something well beyond the individual streams of consciousness that dominate Vasubandhu's *Twenty Verses*. Even if "empty," the *alaya* consciousness is an imposing nonreality. In *The Discrimination between the Middle and the Extremes (Madhyanta-vibhaga)*, the text of which is ascribed to Maitreya/Asanga, emptiness is assigned an essence *(shunyam)*, and the essence is said to be the nonexistence of duality and the existence of this nonexistence. And the synonyms of emptiness are declared to be suchness *(tathata)*, the reality limit, the signless, the absolute reality, and the fundamental reality *(dharma-dhatu)*.[35] Clearly, emptiness in this text refers to absolute reality. The commentator on the text (Sthiramati) explains that this position is midway between the skeptical extreme of Madhyamika and the realistic extreme of those who believe in the reality of both subject and object. For if one says, with the Sarvastivadins, that every element exists, then both subject and object exist, and one denies the middle way of emptiness, that of abolition of the divide between subject and object.[36]

Toward the end of the *Thirty Verses* Vasubandhu states and restates his "empty" ideal and says that "the true nature of mind only *(vijnapti-*

matrata) is the true nature *(paramartha)* of all *dharmas*, because, remaining as it is at all times . . . it is suchness *(tathata)*" (verse 25). These thoughts are in tone and content so different from the *Twenty Verses* that one supposes either that Vasubandhu's views have changed and he is now less modest than earlier, or, as seems more likely, that the *Twenty Verses* were intended to apply to the everyday, worldly level alone.

Vasubandhu now makes it clear that the problem of human knowledge, which is illusive, is the distinction between subject and object. In ideal knowledge, it vanishes: "The mind is established in the nature of consciousness only *(vijnana-matra-tva)*" when the mind no longer seizes on any object at all. "When there is nothing that is grasped, that is mind only . . . That is the supreme, world-transcending knowledge *(jnana)*, without mind *(achitta)* and without support or object" (verses 25, 28, 29). Finally: "That alone is the pure realm *(dhatu)*, unthinkable, good, unchanging, blissful, the liberation body, the *dharma*-body *(dharma-kaya)*, of the great sage (verse 30).[37]

At least on their verbal surface, these passages contain open contradictions: that of paradoxically mindless knowledge—in Asanga "thought without thought" *(chittam achittam)*—and that of thought that is paradoxically without an object.[38] But such contradictions are common among mystics and may even be taken to define their philosophical position.[39] Though often cautiously "emptied" by paradoxical qualification, Asanga's terms for the final knowledge, truth, or reality—terms like *suchness* and *dharma* body (essence body, truth body)—express a kind of objective idealism. In the vein of this idealism, Asanga affirms that the visible body of every historical Buddha depends on the *dharma* body, so that in the "pure realm" one cannot speak of either the unity or the plurality of bodies—in essence, Buddhas have no physical bodies.* For just as space

---

*Asanga accepts and teaches the doctrine of the three bodies *(tri-kaya)* of the Buddha—the Buddha's historical "appearance body" or "transformation body" *(nirmana-kaya)*, his "enjoyment body" *(sambhoga-kaya)*, and his (and other Buddhas') essence body or truth body *(dharma-kaya)*. The transformation body is so named because the essence body limits and transforms itself to appear as an actual human being. The enjoyment body is visible where Buddhism is preached, in the sense that it is seen there intellectually and emotionally. Both the appearance body, or transformation body, and the enjoyment body emerge from and are "supported" by the *dharma* body. As Asanga says, Buddha is essentially one because he embraces all beings equally and, like space, is bodiless. But he is not one, because innumerable beings have realized the *dharma* body, and because to rescue all individual beings in endless time there have been and will be different bodhisattvas, with different resources and practices, all of them supported by the *dharma* body. None of this plurality can be in vain. (On one and many Buddhas, see *The Realm of Awakening*, pp. 85–89, the commentaries on *Mahayanasamgraha* 10.3b–d. For a careful exposition of Asanga's version of the three-body doctrine, see Keenan's introduction to *The Realm of Awakening*, pp. 23–26. See also Nagao, *Mādhyamika and Yogācāra*, chap. 10.)

is universal in all forms, Buddhahood (*Buddhata*) is universal in all beings, which share suchness without any discrimination.[40]

I go no further into this mystical suchness but note that it aroused the opposition of the Madhyamikas, Nagarjuna's successors. I have described Madhyamaka thought as possibly culminating in an experiential "reality" to which neither positive nor negative terms can be applied. But Madhyamaka circumspection was too great to accept the mindless world-transcending consciousness of the mind-only school, or even the school's devaluation of the relative reality of external objects as contrasted with consciousness. Buddhists choose the middle between extremes, but they interpret the extremes differently. To the mind-only philosopher, the extremes are, or come in time to be, realism and Madhyamika skepticism, a skepticism that is nihilistic. To the philosopher of Madhyamika, the extremes are, or come to be, realism and mind-only skepticism, which is the idealism of the Buddhists who reduce all conventional reality to consciousness. What is even worse in Madhyamika opinion, the idealists are also extremists in contending that emptiness—the absence of duality—in some sense exists.[41] The philosopher Bhavaviveka (c. 490–570) summarizes his Madhyamaka objections in a sweeping anti-idealistic sentence: "There is no nature (*svahaba*), no ideation (*vijnapti*), no entity (*vastu*), and no storehouse (*alaya*). They are imagined by foolish dunces . . . who are themselves no more than corpses."[42]

As said in an earlier chapter, the Naiyayika objects to the idealist's analogy of waking experience with dream experience. We know that dreams are unreal, the Naiyayika says, only because we contrast dreaming with waking.* In developing this argument, the Nyaya philosopher points out that there are two different senses of nonexistence, one of them temporal, the other not. The temporal sense applies to what does not exist at a given time. This sense is different from the timeless nonexistence of an impossibility, a sky flower. It is easy for the idealist to show that dreamed objects do not exist in the temporal sense, but this is not relevant to the nontemporal one: When the idealist says that a dreamed object does not exist, he means that waking experience fails to demonstrate its existence. But to assume that the nonexistence of the dreamed object is demonstrated by the failure to perceive it when one is awake is also to assume the converse—that the existence of the object is demonstrated by the success in perceiving it

---

*Compare Wittgenstein's argument against both solipsists and idealists: Solipsists and idealists would say (Wittgenstein is reported to have said) that "they 'couldn't imagine it otherwise,' and that, in reply to this, he would say, 'if so, your statement has no sense' since 'nothing can characterize reality, except as opposed to something else that is not the case'" (G. E. Moore, "Wittgenstein's Lectures in 1930–33," in L. Wittgenstein, *Philosophical Occasions 1921–1951*, ed. J. Klagge and A. Nordmann, Indianapolis: Hackett, 1993, p. 103).

when one is awake. So the dream proof of nonexistence depends on accepting waking experience as proof of existence. So the proof does not support but refutes the idealist.*

John Locke (1632–1704), George Berkeley (1685–1716), David Hume (1711–1776)

No man's knowledge here can go beyond his experience.

As a student at Oxford, Locke learned to dislike the obscurity and, as he saw it, the uselessness of the Scholastic philosophy taught there.[43] At the age of twenty-seven, when his father died, he became a tutor at Oxford. His view of human understanding was largely based on the "corpuscularian Hypothesis" of his friend, Robert Boyle, which of all theories, he insists, gives the best explanation of the qualities and powers of bodies.[44]** Locke's

---

*The Naiyayika adds: Objects as they appear in dreams are errors of cognition. How can we be sure of this? By contrasting dreamed objects with what we know to be correct. Having a generic knowledge of snakes—the snake universal—we may in a certain context wrongly ascribe it to the rope we mistake for a snake. The error depends on the correct knowledge that makes it possible. As for dreams, if a dream object was only a form of consciousness, it would be purely internal and could not be communicated—we cannot share another person's consciousness. But we can tell someone else about our dreams. This ability to share the knowledge of a dream object must be based on the features—the generic nature or universal—it has in common with the external objects that people experience. Furthermore, the conditions for erroneous perception are generally known, and so are the causes that explain the nature of many dreams. Unlike the person who believes in the existence of external objects, the idealist can give no convincing explanation of the difference between cognitions that appear to him to be internal as against those that appear external. Cognition is by nature about external objects. (See Vatsyayana's commentary on the Nyaya Sutra 4.2.31–37. Translated in Matilal, "A Critique of Buddhist Idealism," pp. 160–63, and, especially, Uddyotakara, *Nyāyavārtikka* [c. 650], as summarized pp. 147–50 and translated pp. 163–68. See also Kher, *Buddhism as Presented by the Brahmanical Systems*, chaps. 2–4.)

**Boyle prefers the word *corpuscle* to *atom* because, he says, no material particle is literally or logically indivisible—God might be able to divide the smallest naturally existing particles. He argues that with only the principles of matter and motion, both closely related to experience, his theory gives the most comprehensive possible explanation of material phenomena. Just as one can make up all the words in all the books of all the poets by putting together the letters of the alphabet, so the few basic properties of matter should eventually be enough to explain an enormous range of material phenomena. Sensed qualities such as color, sound, odor, and taste, Boyle says, are the effects on us mainly of the corpuscles' "texture" or patterns of organization (Alexander, *Ideas, Qualities and Corpuscles*, pp. 61–63, 76). Boyle's theory is of course a variant of the atomism of Epicurus and Lucretius, revived and reconciled with Christianity by Pierre Gassendi (1592–1655). Locke owned a copy of Lucretius, of Diogenes Laertius' *Lives of Eminent Philosophers*, of Gassendi's responses to Descartes's *Meditations*, and a book-length abridgement of Gassendi's philosophy. Not surprisingly, he echoes Gassendi rather often. (See Aaron, *John Locke*, pp. 32–35; Ayers, *Locke*, vol. 1, pp. 15, 35; and Joy, *Gassendi the Atomist*, pp. 220–25, and p. 300, note 99, who emphasizes the differences between Gassendi and Locke.)

medical mentor, the great physician Thomas Sydenham, impressed him deeply by his method, which required careful attention to the facts and acceptance of hypotheses only if suggested by meticulously careful observation.[45] Locke was also much impressed by Newton, but Newton's influence was too late to affect the *Essay* more than slightly.* As for philosophy, it was only when Locke came to read Descartes that his earlier dislike of the subject was replaced by a strong attraction.[46] Although his *Essay* is highly critical of the speculative, a priori character of Descartes's thought, Descartes's influence on him remains evident.[47]

There was a decisive turn in Locke's fortunes when he made friends with Lord Ashley, the future Earl of Shaftesbury. Ashley invited Locke to live with him as his physician, and when Locke saved his life (by draining a cyst of the liver), he gratefully encouraged Locke to develop his talents. In politics, both men were convinced by the example of Holland that prosperity depends on religious tolerance, which they preferred, however, to deny to atheists and, for political reasons, to Roman Catholics.[48]

Locke participated in Shaftesbury's discussions with his political friends and was entrusted with his "secretest negotiations"—for Locke was not only measured, pious, practical, and affectionate to friends and children, but also by nature suspicious and secretive (he often wrote in code and he cut signatures from letters he kept).[49] After the failure of his intrigues against the future king had forced Shaftesbury to flee to Holland, where he died, Locke, too, fled there. During his more than five years in Holland, he wrote prolifically. In 1689, William of Orange having taken the throne, Locke, then fifty-six years old, returned to England. Soon, within the year, his principal works, the *Essay Concerning Human Understanding*, the *Two Treatises of Government*, and the *First Letter on Toleration* were all in press. *Some Thoughts Concerning Education* appeared in 1693. It argues in favor of an education that sets a personal example, creates a good character, and encourages and rewards rather than preaches and punishes. Locke wants children to be healthy, know God, and be virtuous, free, and spirited. A practical man, he discourages serious teaching of art and doubts that poetry has any use— there is no gold or silver in Parnassus, he says.[50]

---

*The *Principia Mathematica* was published in 1687, before Newton and Locke had struck up their friendship, and two years before Locke's *Essay* was sent to the printer, but Newton's view of space may have influenced Locke's even before the *Principia's* publication (Ayers, *Locke*, vol. 1, pp. 233–36). Locke tried for years, with help from Newton himself, to master the *Principia*, but finally took its mathematical proofs on Huygen's word. He reviewed the *Principia*, clearly and at length. His close study of the *Principia* led to a few changes in the *Essay's* third and fourth editions. (See Alexander, *Ideas, Qualities and Corpuscles*, p. 164; and Axtell, "Locke, Newton and the Two Cultures," in Yolton, ed., *John Locke*.)

During Locke's last years, he was mostly preoccupied with religion. In *The Reasonableness of Christianity*, which was published in 1695, he preaches a simple Christianity based on belief in Christ as the Messiah and on the morality, in accord with reason, that follows from this belief. Particularly in ethics and politics, his tendency to make compromises between opposed principles, neither of which he gives up, is responsible for both the effectiveness and the unclarity of his solutions.[51]

Though by nature moderate, Locke was in his time an effective participant in a philosophical revolution, which in France breached the limits of the religious faith and philosophical dualism that Locke himself teaches. To speak only of his *Essay*, our subject here, he proposes what was in his time a bold, boldly modest theory of knowledge, an ontology, compatible with the new science, in which the fundamental substance is matter, a tolerant religious attitude, and the ideal of an exactly rational ethics. Locke's desire to write as if conversing with his readers, of whom he won many, makes it easy for him to forget how often he repeats himself and hedges his views, though hedging, too, exhibits the virtue of moderation. Often he devotes less space to reasoning than to the human examples that, like an anthropologist, he enjoys reporting (and the reader, reading). His *Essay*, though rhetorically inviting, does not trade on emotion or eloquence, spin out webs of logic, or take its readers on metaphysical adventures, so it has lost its philosophical glamor; but it remains the type of an honest, careful, not unsubtle moderation.[52]

An Essay Concerning Human Understanding is divided into four books: (1) Of Innate Notions; (2) Of Ideas; (3) Of Words; and (4) Of Knowledge and Opinion. The account here will be confined to the first book, parts of the second, and some themes from the fourth.

In his introduction, Locke explains that his purpose is to give a plain description of how our "notions of things" develop, and to consider how much certainty our knowledge has and what the reasons are for the great, often contradictory variety of human views (*Essay* 1.1.2). Before he actually begins, he asks the reader's pardon for the frequent use he makes of the word *idea*. This word is the best, he says, for anything that is the object of human understanding, so he has "used it to express whatever is meant by *Phantasm, Notion, Species*, or whatever it is, which the Mind can be employ'd about in thinking" (1.1.8).[53] *Phantasm*, to Locke, means *mental image* or *representation* (of a present or a remembered object); *notion* means *concept*; and *species* means *form* (as a technical term, *species* suggests the old view, opposed by Descartes and Locke, that an object is perceived by means of the form that it emits).[54]

The accommodating breadth of this conception of *idea* leads to inconsistencies and ambiguities, but these are absorbed into Locke's generalizing rhetoric. They do his argument no conspicuous harm but sometimes make it hard to state just what his position is. As he sees it, to have an idea is to perceive or think of something; to have an idea with the words ("names") usually attached to it is to have a concept; and to have a concept is to be able to think or conceive of whatever it is of which the idea is the concept. The persistent use of *have* is natural here because, as Locke believes, to think of something is to have the corresponding idea within one's mind as the object of one's thought. Once the mind *has* the idea, the mind is able to "manipulate" it, and then, making its manipulation of the idea the object of its thought, to manipulate the manipulation, and so on.[55]

Locke asks the reader to suppose that the mind is white paper with no characters, no ideas, on it yet (in Plato's *Theatetus* [191d] the equivalent image is a block of wax with no imprinted perceptions or ideas). How does it happen, Locke asks, that the paper becomes filled with all that "the busy and boundless Fancy of Man has painted on it, with an almost endless variety? Whence has it all the materials of Reason and Knowledge?" (2.1.2).[56]

Locke answers, "in one word, From *Experience*: In that, all our Knowledge is founded; and from that it ultimately derives it self." Experience, he goes on, has two great sources, that is, sources of ideas. The one source is sensation, which conveys the effects of particular sensible objects into the mind. The other source is reflection, which, by perceiving the operations of our own minds as they deal with ideas, has ideas as distinct as those that follow from the sensing of material things. As the soul reflects on the mind's operations, the operations furnish the understanding with ideas such as perception, thinking, doubting, believing, reasoning, knowing, willing, and all the other actions of our minds of which we are conscious. *Operations* is a broad term and includes not only the actions of the mind in relation to its ideas but also the emotions ("passions"), such as satisfaction or uneasiness, that thoughts arouse (2.1.4).[57]

Locke states that if we make a full survey of all the modes, combinations, and relations of the ideas of sensible qualities and of the ideas the mind has of its own operations, we discover that our minds contain nothing at all that does not enter them in one of the two ways, sensation and reflection, that he has described. However one searches one's understanding, and however great the mass of knowledge one imagines lodged in one's mind, every idea it contains has been imprinted there by either sensation or reflection—"though, perhaps, with infinite variety, compounded and enlarged by the Understanding, as we shall see hereafter" (2.1.5).[58]

In defense of this empiricism, most of the first book of Locke's *Essay* is devoted to a pleasantly rambling, occasionally witty polemic against the doctrine of innate ideas. Although not named during the course of the polemic, Descartes is clearly its main target. No principles, Locke says, are universally accepted (1.2.2–3). Take the two basic principles of demonstration: Whatever is, is; and, It is impossible for the same thing to be and not to be. Children and mentally deficient persons ("idiots") have no idea of these principles; and it is very nearly a contradiction to say that there are truths imprinted on the soul that the soul neither perceives nor understands (1.2.4–5).* Locke takes up the claim of Descartes (who is not named) that the soul always thinks. This is no more plausible, Locke says, than that the body always moves. Descartes is mistaken because consciousness, the perception of ideas, is to the soul as motion is to the body—not its essence but only one of its operations (2.1.10). Suppose that even when a person was asleep and unconscious the soul was thinking. While the body of Socrates was asleep, his soul would have its own thoughts, concerns, and pleasures and pains, and Socrates awake, knowing no more of these experiences than of some unknown person in the Indies, would be a different person from Socrates asleep (2.1.11). No one who sleeps without dreaming can ever be convinced that the soul is always thinking (2.1.12).**

The innateness and universality of moral principles is even more doubtful than that of the "speculative maxims" so far discussed (1.3.1). What most humans seem to agree on is justice and the keeping of contracts. But a highwayman who acts fairly with his fellow highwaymen does so only by a rule of convenience and may plunder or kill the next honest man he meets. It may be urged that those who live by fraud and plunder agree tacitly to what their practice contradicts. This is not plausible, but, in any case, there is no universal assent to moral principles, which most persons'

---

*Locke is not satisfied with the answer that the principles must be innate because all humans know and accept them as soon as they attain the use of reason. Why, he asks, should a truth be considered innate if it requires reason to discover it? And if there are innate propositions, why do they have to be proposed before they are accepted? Does the act of proposing them print them in the mind more clearly than nature did? If so, a person knows them better after having learned them, and they can have little authority in themselves and are unfit to be the foundations of all our other knowledge (1.2.21).

If the partisans of innateness mean only that we accept the supposedly innate principles as soon as we begin to reason, they are wrong. A child does not know that three and four are equal to seven until it can count to seven and understands what *equal* means. And it is only after a child understands that a rod and a cherry are not the same thing that, given time and observation, the child can get to know that it is impossible for the same thing to be and not to be. Even truths supposed to be innate have to be learned (1.2.12–17).

**There is something that suggests present-day dream research in Locke's challenge to Descartes's notion of an always–thinking soul: "Wake a Man out of a sound sleep, and ask him, What he was at that moment thinking on, he must be a notable Diviner of Thoughts, that can assure him, he was thinking: May he not with more reason assure him, he was not asleep?" It is revelation rather than philosophy to disclose to someone else that there are thoughts in my mind when I myself cannot find any there (2.1.19; *Essay*, ed. Nidditch, p. 115).

conduct and some persons' open admission has questioned or denied (1.3.2–3). Furthermore, no moral rule can be proposed for which one cannot rightly demand a reason—a ridiculous demand if the rule was innate or self-evident (1.3.4). Whole civilized nations have practiced the custom of abandoning unwanted children. Except for the internal rules absolutely necessary to keep a society together—rules generally broken in relation to other societies—there is hardly a principle of morality that is not, somewhere or other, slighted and condemned by whole societies (1.3.10–11).

Of all ideas, Locke goes on, that of God can most plausibly be thought innate. But not only are atheists recorded in ancient history, but discoverers have found whole nations, for example, in Brazil and the Caribbean Islands, that have no notion of God and have no religion (1.4.7–8). And the missionaries to China, even the Jesuits, all agree "that the Sect of the *Litterati*, or *Learned*, keeping to the old Religion of *China*, and the ruling Party there, are all of them *Atheist*" (1.4.8).[59]

Having refuted the belief in innate ideas, Locke turns to the distinction, essential to his philosophy, between simple ideas and complex ideas. With the help of the assumed relationship between the two kinds of ideas, he can develop his theory of the nature and limits of knowledge. The complex ideas, he says, do not obscure the differences between the simple ideas that make them up: We can both see and touch the same object, or, at the same time, see both its motion and its color, or feel both its softness and its warmth; but each of these simple ideas, though united in the same subject, is clear and distinct and contains within itself "nothing but *one uniform Appearance*, or Conception in the mind, and is not distinguishable into different *Ideas*" (2.2.1).[60]*

Once simple ideas are stored in the mind, the mind can repeat, compare, and unite them into an almost infinite variety of new, complex ideas. However, just as in the visible world we can only compound and divide the available materials, not one atom of which a human can create or destroy, in the inner world of the understanding, we can only use and

---

*To serve as the basis of an unquestionable judgment, Descartes says, a perception must be both clear and distinct. It is clear if it is strong and immediately accessible to the attentive mind, and it is distinct if (unlike many pains) it is sharply separated from all other perceptions (*Principles of Philosophy* 1.43–46, 65–75). Locke (like a Greek Stoic or a Naiyayika) explains that an idea is clear if it is one of which the mind has a full and evident perception of the kind received from an outward object affecting a healthy sense organ. A distinct idea is one that the mind perceives as different from all others (2.29.4).

Descartes prefers a perception to be clear and distinct so that it can serve judgment adequately, whereas Locke prefers an idea or perception (whether of sense or of reflection) to represent its object adequately so that it can be given a name that is unambiguous enough to fix the name's reference (2.29, 6–12). To instruct or convince, one should always use the same word in the same sense (3.11.26). Such consistency (as Hsün-tzu would agree) is needed because speech is the great bond that holds society together and allows the transfer of knowledge from person to person and generation to generation (3.11, 1, 5). For this reason people should take care to use their words in commonly accepted ways (3.11.11).

compound, but never create, a simple idea, the only source of which is the senses or the mind's reflection on its own operations. But maybe in other parts of the universe there are intelligent beings of whose faculties a human being knows as little "as a Worm shut up in one drawer of a Cabinet" knows of human senses or understanding (2.3.3).[61]

In Locke's terminology, the power of a subject to produce an idea in our mind is a quality of the subject. The qualities of a snowball are to produce in us ideas of white, cold, and round. The qualities that are completely inseparable from all bodies, from every particle of matter under all conditions, are solidity, extension, figure, and mobility (2.8.8–9). The primary qualities must come from the objects that, in the process of perception, reach our eyes and convey some motion to the brain, which produces the ideas we have of these bodies. It is plausible to think that it is the effect of imperceptible particles on our sense organs that also produces the ideas of such secondary qualities as color, smell, taste, and sound (2.8.12–14). But while it is easy to assume that the ideas of the primary qualities resemble the objects that cause them—the qualities' patterns as they really exist in the bodies themselves—the ideas produced by the secondary qualities do not resemble the bodies at all. The sensations of sweet, blue, or warm are no more in bodies than sickness or pain is in manna (2.8.15–17).

Locke continues his empiricistic account of knowledge—a kind of mechanics of the formation of knowledge from ideas—in much more detail than can be reported here.*

The last book of Locke's *Essay,* "Of Knowledge in General," illustrates his characteristic mixture of metaphysical doubt and certainty, and religious and moral rationalism. Empiricist or not, he now stresses intuitive knowledge, to him an unquestionable direct "seeing," whether by sense perception or by the faculty of intelligence. Locke in effect argues that such intuition is not the same as knowledge by means of implanted innate ideas; it is knowledge by the evidence of perception.[62] By intuition the

---

*Locke discusses various faculties of the mind, among them the ability to distinguish ideas from one another, to compare them with one another, to compose or put simple ideas together, to use verbal signs (words), and to abstract—to use ideas and their names to represent others of their kind (2.11). He goes on to discuss the activity of the mind in combining, relating, and abstracting ideas, and the three possible types of combinations of ideas—modes, substances, and relations. Modes he defines as complex ideas that are assumed to subsist only in dependence on substances. The ideas of substances, Locke contends, are nothing but combinations of the simple ideas that represent particular things that subsist by themselves: *man* or *a sheep,* or an *army* of men, or *flock* of sheep. Ideas of relation are those of the comparison of ideas with one another (2.12). Among simple modes— modifications of a simple idea—Locke takes up those of space, duration, expansion (of space and duration into determinate lengths), number, and of infinity (2.13–14). He also sketches a psychology, which he recognizes to be undeveloped, but which he most likely wants to rival that of Descartes (2.19–20). Locke then goes on to the complex ideas of substance, relation, and identity and diversity (2.23–27).

mind perceives that white is not black or that a circle is not a triangle, as immediately and easily as the eye sees the light at which it is directed (4.2.1). When such agreement or disagreement of ideas is plainly, that is, intuitively perceived by means of intervening ideas, we have *proofs* or *demonstration* (4.2.2–4). Each step in a demonstration must be intuitive; otherwise that step would itself need a proof (4.2.7). Our failure to extend the certainty of demonstration to fields other than mathematics may be the result of our failure to use the right method (4.2.9). There is good reason to believe that the idea of a supreme being and the idea of ourselves as rational beings can yield rules of morality that can be demonstrated by propositions as self-evident as those of mathematics (4.3.17–18, 47).

Although Descartes is wrong in supposing that we have an innate idea of God, God has given us what means we need to discover him and prove his existence, prove it with a certainty equal to that of mathematics (4.10.1). Locke disdains the sheerly logical proof, by Descartes among others, from the idea of a most perfect being. This argument, says Locke, is arrogant—it forbids us to use other, less neat or overbearing proofs— and is implausible, because some people have no idea at all of God, and because the ideas of God are so various (4.10.7).

Locke wants a deductive, unquestionable proof, which he presents only informally. He does not begin with an empirical generalization, such as that the world shows evidence of order. Instead, he begins with an unquestionable perception, followed by, in his sense, an intuition: First, we all clearly perceive our own existence and know beyond doubt that we exist. Second, we have an intuitive certainty that no real being can be produced by nothing, so there must be some real being. Third (I break the argument into more steps than Locke does), a real being cannot be produced by nothing, so there must have been something from eternity. Fourth, since what does not exist from eternity must have a beginning, it must be produced by something else. Fifth, it is evident that what has its being and beginning from something else must have all its powers from the same eternal source, which (by ancient principle, I add) must therefore be the more powerful (Locke says, "the most powerful"). Sixth, because man finds in himself perception and knowledge, we are certain that the being that exists is a knowing, intelligent being—it cannot have been unthinking matter, operating blindly and without perception, that produced a knowing being (4.10. 2–5).[63]*

---

*Though he says he believes in revelation, Locke is very cautious about it. No one who has had a revelation, he says, can communicate to others simple ideas they have not themselves had—words are only sounds that revive the latent ideas we already have. God may reveal some truths that reason, too, can discover, but no revelation is needed for self-evident ideas. Our assurance of the truth of anything else that is revealed cannot be any greater than our

There follow some entertaining passages, only part of which I summarize: Granted there is a God, there are those who might argue that the eternal thinking being is material. Suppose that, in their name, we make the implausible assumption that matter as such can think. On this assumption, it would follow that there would be as many eternal thinking beings, as many gods, as there are particles of matter. But this conclusion would be rejected by the believers in a material God; and if it is not the essential nature of material particles to think, it can hardly be argued that a thinking being can be made out of nonthinking particles. And if it assumed that there is a single God-atom that by its powerful thought made all the rest of matter, and if the making of the rest of matter was by the only possible means, those of thought, the believers in a material God would have to give up their beloved maxim (from Lucretius and his predecessors), *Ex nihilo nil fit*. And if it is argued that the eternal thinking being is a certain organization of matter—maybe this is the ordinary person's conception of God—we have the absurd fantasy of an eternal thinking being made only of particles of matter each of which is void of thought. If the parts of this organized material that cause thought are all at rest, this "God" is only an ordinary lump of matter. But if the parts on which thinking depends are in motion, all the thoughts must be accidental and limited, because each of the particles that by its motion causes thought is without thought. Being without thought, the particle cannot regulate its own motions, which of course cannot be regulated by the thought of the whole, because the whole is the consequence, not the cause, of the motions (4.10.14–17).*

What of skepticism? Our own being we know by intuition; God's existence we know by reason; the existence of other things we know by

---

assurance that the revelation really comes from God. Nothing called a revelation can rationally convince anyone if it is in direct contradiction to the clear evidence of that person's understanding. Since no evidence of our faculties by which we receive a revelation "can exceed, if equal, the certainty of our intuitive Knowledge, we can never receive for a Truth any thing, that is directly contrary to our clear and distinct Knowledge" (4.16.14, 4.18.3–5 [5 quoted, from *Essay*, ed. Nidditch, pp. 691–92]).

*In spite of these arguments against a material God, Locke aroused the criticism, among others, of Leibniz and the Bishop Stillingfleet, by stating that our knowledge is so limited that we may never be able to know whether or not any simply material being thinks. We are unable to discover "whether Omnipotency has not given to some Systems of Matter fitly disposed, a power to perceive and think, or else joined and fixed to Matter so disposed, a thinking immaterial Substance" (4.3.6; ed. Nidditch, pp. 540–41). Leibniz, reluctant to accept such an argument, supposed that Locke meant that thought might be miraculously added to matter. But Locke was most probably thinking of the human ignorance of the essence or "substance" of matter, which God may (or might) have made so that it can (or could) also think. Locke, who believes that God created matter and chose the laws of mechanics, does not seem particularly fond of miraculous interference with the course of already created nature. (See Ayer, *Locke*, vol. 2, chap. 12.)

sensation. I can no more deny that something really exists that causes me to see white and black than that I write or move my hand (4.11.1–2). Anyone who doubts the existence of the things he sees and feels will have no controversy with me, says Locke sarcastically, because he can never be sure that I say anything to contradict his opinion. God has given me assurance of the existence of external things; this assurance I have because by using the things differently I can cause myself pleasure and pain (4.11.3). I am sure that perceptions are produced by external causes that affect the senses, because no one who lacks the organs of any sense can have the ideas belonging to that sense (4.11.4).

Even when my eyes are closed, I can call up the ideas of light or of the sun, which sensation earlier lodged in my mind; or I can at will recall the idea of the smell or a rose or the taste of sugar. Yet there is an evident difference between recalling these ideas and having the equivalent direct perceptions, which force themselves on me as only an external cause is able to (4.11.5). And unless we believe in the existence of sensible things outside of us, how can we explain that our senses bear witness to the truth of each other's reports? Or explain that one can actually burn one's hand in a fire, as one cannot burn it in an imaginary one (4.11.7).

What, then, if someone affirms that all we experience is nothing but a long, deluding dream? The answer to this skeptic is as follows: If everything is a dream, he who is questioning me is dreaming, and so it is of little importance that the answer be given by someone who is awake. But if he pleases, the questioner may dream that I give him this answer, that the testimony given by our senses of the existence of things in external nature is as great as humans can attain and as much as human beings need. And if our dreamer wants to test whether or not the heat of a furnace for making glass is only a figment of a drowsing man's imagination, he need only make the test of putting his hand into the furnace, which may waken him into a certainty greater than that possible to bare imagination (11.4.8).

In 1707, when Berkeley was twenty-two, he became a Junior Fellow at Trinity College, Dublin.[64] Living in relatively undistracted leisure, he decided to write his Fellowship thesis on the subject that so interested him: Does matter exist? For the sake of his thesis, he read current philosophy and science—mathematics, physics, optics, and theories of vision.

Berkeley inherits his empiricism and much of his philosophical vocabulary from Locke, but his immaterialism, the doctrine of the nonexistence of matter, is suggested by Malebranche, then widely read by English thinkers, including Dubliners with whom Berkeley was familiar.[65] It is from Malebranche, whom Berkeley often names in the *Philosophical*

Commentaries, that he gets the view that none of the qualities we perceive are inherently those of matter. From Malebranche, too, comes the view that unthinking, that is, material things are passive, that only minds are active, and that God is the true, all-inclusive cause: God, and not matter, is the direct source of our sensory perceptions or ideas, and God's will alone maintains the regular connections—those of apparent cause and effect —between the ideas.* Pierre Bayle, whose skepticism shook Berkeley's faith in much of Malebranche's position, is another source of arguments against the reality of matter, especially of the argument that whatever can be said against the reality of "secondary" qualities like color can be said against the reality of "primary" qualities like extension.

Stimulated to agree and disagree by these philosophers, Berkeley set out eagerly to develop his own kind of immaterialism. By the age of twenty-eight, he had already published the three books that are responsible for his place in the history of philosophy: *An Essay towards a New Theory of Vision* (1709), *A Treatise Concerning the Principles of Human Knowledge* (1710), and *Three Dialogues between Hylas and Philonous* (1713).

I will not summarize Berkeley's later career as an enthusiast for a college in Bermuda, meant to make it possible for planters' sons to become educated pastors and young mainland Indians to get a higher education. The shattering of this dream seemed to age him, and an old illness became chronic. In his last public role, as the Bishop of Cloyne, he displayed, among his other admirable qualities, a great concern for the poor of Ireland.

Berkeley's literary style is clear, economical, and attractive. But the pleasure it gives can obscure the thinness of his argument at times; his words *evident* or *obvious* sometimes introduce reasoning that is neither. What is always evident is his horror of atheism and fatalism and his

---

*The general aim of Nicolas Malebranche (1638–1715) is to synthesize Descartes with Augustine, that is, with a Christian Platonism. It is possible that Malebranche was indirectly stimulated by the doctrines of the Muslim dialectical theologians, available to him in the works of Maimonides, Aquinas, and Francesco Suarez (1548–1617). Like the Muslim theologians, Malebranche believes that God unceasingly creates everything and coordinates the relations between perceptions and their objects. Hume, who read Malebranche, may also echo the Muslims. To stretch the possibilities of historical connection further, the Muslim theologians—as I have said before—are likely to have depended in part on Buddhist or Hindu atomic theories. (See Weinberg, *Ockham, Descartes, and Hume,* 1977, p. 122; and Smith, *The Philosophy of David Hume,* p. 89 and note pp. 89–90.)

Malebranche is likely to have had another source as well, the writings of Ockhamites such as Pierry d'Ailly (1350–1421), which he probably encountered in Suarez. D'Ailly argues that although God acts in accord with logic, he need not follow the laws of nature. God can cause a nonexistent object to be perceived (or, rather, cognized) or maintain the vision of an object that is no longer in existence. Knowing this, we realize that sensory perception is inherently fallible.

antagonism to the belief in matter and the skepticism that foster them, he is sure.

Berkeley's later books often have an interest independent of their defense of religion. For example, his brief *De Motu* (1721) is an insightful positivistic analysis of the concepts of physics.* In *De Motu* he argues that only metaphysical abstraction allows us to assume that the force of gravity is different from motion and rest, which are the source of the assumption that gravity is present.[66] Terms such as *force, gravity, attraction*, he says, are very useful for reasoning about and computing motions, but they do not help us to understand the nature itself of motion. Likewise, Newton's *attraction* is not a true physical quality but only a mathematical hypothesis.[67] "The physicist studies the series of successions of sensible things" and the laws by which they are connected, but it is only by metaphysical reasoning that it is possible to rescue "truly active causes... from the surrounding darkness" and make them known to some extent.[68]

Siris (1744), Berkeley's last book, which praises the healing powers of tar water, repeats Berkeley's earlier teachings. It also attests to the instability of his kind of idealism because, in keeping with a Neoplatonic attitude, it takes the universe to be a chain or scale that rises from minimal beings to the metaphysically infinite being, God.

Berkeley begins to philosophize with great optimism. His notebooks show him working on the problems of his immaterialism, the doctrine that there is no matter and only conscious things—persons, "spirits"—really exist.[69] Put with formulaic brevity, immaterialism is expressed in the principle: To be is to be perceived, *esse est percipi*. But if to be perceived is enough, Berkeley asks himself, why do things appear to continue to exist even when unperceived? Is it possible that, unperceived, they lapse out of existence?** He cautions himself (with abbreviations meant for himself):

---

*As Karl Popper points out, Berkeley's philosophy of physics is surprisingly similar to that of Ernst Mach, which had so powerful an influence on modern physics, especially the theory of relativity. "Berkeley and Mach, both great admirers of Newton . . . are both convinced that there is no physical world (of primary qualities, or of atoms . . .) behind the world of physical appearances . . . the view that physical things are bundles, or complexes, or constructs of phenomenal *qualities*, of particular experienced colors, noises, etc. . . . The difference is that for Berkeley, these are directly caused by God. For Mach, they are just there" (K. H. Popper, *Conjectures and Refutations*, London: Routledge and Kegan Paul, 1963, pp. 171–72, 173).

**Descartes, Malebranche, and Locke all precede Berkeley in the conviction that it is by God's unceasing creation that all creatures are conserved. Descartes writes that we continue to exist only if God continues to reproduce us (*Principles* 1.21). Malebranche agrees, and so does Locke, who writes: "If I have just seen the collection of simple ideas that is usually called *a man* and I am now alone, I cannot be sure that the man still exists. Strictly speaking, it is highly probable that millions of men now exist, but while I am writing this, I do not have the certainty of this knowledge, though I, of course, do not actually doubt it" (*Essay* 4.11.9).

"I must be very particular in explaining w^t is meant by things existing in Houses, chambers, fields, caves etc w^n not perceiv'd as well as w^n perceiv'd" (*Philosophical Commentaries*, entry no. 408 [in part]). Hesitating, he thinks of various possibilities—when not perceived, maybe they exist as powers, or maybe they do exist but not absolutely (entries no. 52, 293a, 185). He divides things into the active kind—spirits—which perceive, understand, and will, and the inactive kind—ideas—whose nature it is to be perceived (no. 673).[70] And he extends his principle and says, "To exist is to be perceived or to perceive," or, more exactly, "Existence is percipi or percipere." To this sentence, he adds, "The horse is in the stable, the Books are in the study as before" (no 429). They are there because, given the continued existence of the active perceiver, it is possible to understand why the idea or succession of ideas, though unperceived for a time, is succeeded by other ideas that are the "same." He also enters the note, which seems already essential to complete his theory, "The propertys of all things are in God i.e., there is in the Deity Understanding as well as Will" (no. 812). With his revised principle and his conception of God, his case, he is sure, is impregnable.[71]

I have begun with Berkeley's principle in order to emphasize that it represents a philosophical boldness the originality of which may not seem evident in retrospect. As he says in a note, "I wonder not at my sagacity in discovering this obvious tho' amazing truth, I rather wonder at my stupid inadvertency in not finding it out before" (no. 279). He is right to wonder, because his sources had put his immaterialism almost in his grasp, like a searched-for word at the tip of his tongue. His bold stroke is hardly more or less than the union of Locke's ideas and faith in experience with Malebranche's barely restrained immaterialism and unrestrained faith in God as the place of ideas.

To make the simplicity and boldness of Berkeley's principle the clearer, let me spell out its relation to the thought of his immediate predecessors. We know that Locke is a predecessor also in that he takes the link between ideas and matter to be largely unclear—for secondary qualities, the link is a simply arbitrary fact, and for primary qualities, a relation understood in no more than tenuous detail. With respect to Malebranche, I will dwell on two philosophical traits alone, the doubt as to the existence of bodies, and the certainty that all ideas exist in God.[72]

After giving examples familiar from Greek and Cartesian skepticism, Malebranche summarizes: There is no necessary connection between the presence of an idea in a person's mind and the existence of what this idea appears to represent. This is proved well enough by dreaming and delirium.[73] The ideas that human beings have of purely intelligible things, such as the existence of God and the nature of his decrees, are much clearer than those they have of perceptible things. This is so because the union of the human mind with God is immediate, direct, and necessary. It teaches us what God thinks and even what he wants, teaches us necessary truths and eternal laws, not a few of which we cannot doubt that we know with certainty. God, says Malebranche elsewhere, is the intelligible world or the place of mind, just as the material world is the place of bodies. It is by God's power that bodies receive all their modifications, by his wisdom that they receive all their ideas, and by his love that they are moved in all their regulated movements.[74]

In contrast with our ideas of intelligible things, Malebranche insists, our ideas of the bodies around us never give us completely accurate information and are often quite false. For this reason it is more difficult than one might think to give a positive proof that the bodies of whose existence our senses inform us do in fact exist.[75] If we accept the report of our senses, we believe that color is really on the surfaces of bodies, heat really in fire, sweetness really in sugar, and odor really in musk. But as has been proved, none of these qualities is outside the soul that senses them. Why then, on no more than the report of our very often deceptive senses, should we conclude that there are in fact external bodies and even that these bodies resemble those that our senses represent to us? The sharpest of all our feelings, with the apparently most necessary relation to an actually existing body, is that of pain. But it often happens that persons who have lost an arm feel extremely violent pains in it, even long after the loss. They know very well that they no longer have the arm, but the feeling of pain deceives them. The insane, who believe they see themselves as they in fact are, may think they have horns on their heads, or that they are made of butter or glass, or that their bodies are shaped like a rooster, a wolf, or an ox. Their souls deceive them, just as the reports of the senses can deceive other, sane persons. It is clear that a person passes for mad not because he sees what is not there but because what he sees is contrary to what others see, whether or not the others are mistaken. If a peasant would see the moon with one of the new telescopes and cry out in admiration at the mountains, valleys, oceans, and lakes he saw, his companions would be likely to think that he had been injured by the malign influences of the planet he was observing.[76]

Malebranche continues: When I judge by means of my senses, I am not sure of anything, certainly not of Descartes's explanation of how the brain is affected by external bodies. The workings of my body, of which I am unsure, and the existence of the bodies around me, of which I still more unsure, compel me to believe in a superior intelligence that works within us and can cause us to represent bodies outside of ourselves. In any case, why is it necessary that there be external bodies so that movements in our brain should be excited? Sleep, the emotions, madness—do they not produce such movements without the help of external bodies? To be assured that there are external bodies, it is absolutely necessary to know God, who gives us the feeling of them, and to know that, being infinitely perfect, he cannot deceive us. Because if the superior intelligence, which gives us the ideas of all things, wanted, so to speak, to divert itself by representing nonexisting bodies to us as if they existed, it would surely not find it difficult to do so.[77]

Everything considered, Malebranche concludes, we cannot question that there are bodies external to us. Yet it is evident that what really exists is not external. The material body that we move is not the one that we see with our bodily eyes. The body that we see is in itself an intelligible body, with intelligible spaces separating it from other bodies. I see these, with their sensed secondary qualities, by means of the purely intelligible ideas God has of them. God does not see the material world except in the intelligible world he contains and in the knowledge he has of his decrees, which give actual existence and movement to all things. The scripture speaks of bodies, so I have faith in their existence. But the evidence for their existence is not full, and we are not absolutely compelled to believe that there is anything in addition to God and our minds.[78]

Now to Berkeley and Bayle (a relation I report only in part): In his article on Pyrrho, Bayle puts into the mouth of an unnamed "philosophical abbé," a defender of Pyrrhonism, the view held by the scientist Simon Foucher (1644–1696). The abbé says: If "heats, smells, colors, and the like, are not the objects of our senses" but modifications of the soul, why cannot the objects of the senses "appear extended and shaped, in rest and in motion, although they are not so?"* Like the real Foucher, the abbé falls back on the argument, accepted by Malebranche, that there must be an external world because God is not a deceiver. But Bayle, who is tough when he wants to be, is not satisfied. He adds (in the name of the same unnamed abbé): The argument that external bodies must exist because God would not deceive us is very weak. This is because it proves too much:

---

*Foucher's criticisms of the first volume of Malebranche's *Recherche* were answered in the second. Although Malebranche does not give this particular criticism a direct answer, in his "clarification," we have seen, he agrees that it is extremely difficult to prove the existence of external objects, and, like Foucher, he falls back on faith in God's truthfulness. Foucher criticizes both Descartes and Malebranche on the ground that if mind and matter differ in their essence, they can have no similarity—no modification of the mind can represent anything extended or material because it cannot resemble it. To Malebranche's answer that ideas are *not* modifications of the mind, Foucher answers that, if so, ideas are no less difficult for the mind to know than material objects (Watson, "Simon Foucher," p. 213). (See also Rodis-Lewis, *Malebranche*, esp. chap. 5.)

Ever since the beginning of the world, all mankind, except perhaps one out of two hundred millions, has firmly believed that bodies are colored, and this is an error. I ask, does God deceive mankind with regard to colors? If he deceives them about this, what prevents him from doing so with regard to extension?[79]

Of course, the abbé goes on, God forces no one to deny that colors or extension do not exist outside of the mind, but only that their existence outside it is doubtful. But faith does not allow religion the criterion of evident truth (on which the historical Foucher depends). We base our syllogisms on the truth that things that are not different from a third thing are not different from each other. And yet, the revelation of the mystery of the Trinity assures us that this axiom is false. Invent as many distinctions as you please, you will never be able to show that this maxim of logic is not denied by this great mystery.[80]

This argument against the proof from faith in God's truthfulness teaches Berkeley that Malebranche's way leads to a measureless skepticism. So Berkeley needs to show that it is unnecessary to believe that matter exists, and that materialism and atheism are wholly implausible.[81]

Berkeley's boldness and debts made clear, I summarize a number of his doctrines under the following heads: (1) the irrelevance to experience of the notion of matter; (2) the misleading character of abstract language; (3) pragmatism; (4) objects as connected sequences of ideas; and (5) "spirits" and God.

The irrelevance to experience of the notion of matter: It seems absurd to say that we eat and drink ideas and are dressed in them. According to Berkeley, this is because in ordinary speech we call the combinations of sensible qualities *things*, not ideas. It remains true, however, that we are fed and clothed with what we immediately perceive:

The hardness or softness, the colour, taste, warmth, figure, and such like qualities, which combined together constitute the several sorts of victuals and apparel, have been shewn to exist only in the mind that perceives them; and this is all that is meant by calling them *ideas*; which word, if it was as ordinarily used as *thing*, would sound no harsher nor more ridiculous than it. (*Principles*, section 38)

Nothing I say here, says Berkeley, is meant to detract from the reality of things. We agree that the objects perceived by sense are only a combination of sensible qualities and so cannot exist by themselves. All we mean is that the unthinking beings that sense perceives exist only in being perceived and, for this reason, only in "those unextended, indivisible substance, or *spirits*, which act, think, and perceive them" (sec. 91).

The misleading character of abstract language: The doctrine of abstract ideas makes the best known things in the world, such as particular instances of time, place, and motion, the most incomprehensible (*Principles*, sec. 97). The attempt to think of abstract time, of time abstracted from the uniform succession of ideas in a person's mind, leads to inextricable difficulties. The same happens when we try to abstract extension and motion from all other sensible qualities, even from perception. In the same way, we only cause intellectual difficulties when we try to frame an abstract idea of happiness divorced from all particular examples of pleasure, or frame an abstract idea of goodness divorced from everything that is good (secs. 98–100). The mistaken opinion that sensible objects exist apart from being perceived depends at bottom on the doctrine of abstract ideas (sec. 5). Words must be used with great care so that they do not impose on the understanding. Therefore, says Berkeley, I will stay clear of all purely verbal controversies.[82]

Pragmatism: As William James and Charles Peirce were to notice, Berkeley is their kind of pragmatist, in the sense that he substitutes sequences of ideas, that is, of sensations or perceptions, for underlying substances and then equates the sensation sequences with the expectations they serve and mean.[83]* The experience of the succession of ideas in our minds, Berkeley says, often allows us to make well-grounded predictions, which are based on no more than regularity of succession:[84]

> The connexion of ideas does not imply the relation of *cause* and *effect*, but only of a mark or *sign* with the thing *signified*. The fire which I see is not the cause of the pain I suffer upon my approaching it, but the mark that forewarns me of it. (*Principles*, sec. 65)

---

*William James writes: "Berkeley's criticism of 'matter' was . . . absolutely pragmatistic. Matter is known as our sensations of colour, figure, hardness and the like. They are the cash-value of the term. The difference matter makes to us by truly being is that we then get such sensations. . . . These sensations then are its sole meaning. Berkeley doesn't deny matter, then; he simply tells us what it consists of. It is a true name for just so much in the way of sensations" (W. James, *Pragmatism*, lecture 3; in *William James: Writings 1902–1910*, New York: Library of America (Literary Classics of the United States), 1987, p. 525).

When the sequences of ideas are regular enough, we call them laws of nature. The laws are learned by experience, which teaches us that such and such ideas are attended with such and such other ideas, in the ordinary course of things. This gives us a sort of foresight, which enables us to regulate our actions for the benefit of life. (*Principles*, secs. 30–31)

Objects as connected sequences of ideas: In the third of the *Three Dialogues between Hylas and Philonous,* Berkeley is led by his respect for perceptions to a position that is hard to identify with the kind of common sense he favors. In the dialogue, Philonous, who represents Berkeley, says: I want to be represented as someone who trusts the senses and who knows that things exist only as perceptions, without any material substratum.[85]

Hylas, the persistent questioner, asks: But what about sensory illusions? If you are right, how is it possible for a man to think that the moon is a smooth, bright surface, or that an oar with one end in water is crooked?[86]

Philonous answers: The man is not mistaken about the ideas he actually perceives but in the inferences he makes from them. He is mistaken if he thinks that the crooked oar—the crooked-oar idea—will look crooked or feel crooked when he takes the oar out of the water, and mistaken if he thinks that if he came closer to the moon it would still look the same. When circumstances change, so do ideas. We do not perceive any motion of the earth, but that does not mean that if we were as far from the earth as from the other planets we would not see its motion.[87]

After further conversation, Hylas asks: If the true nature of a thing is what the senses discover, why should all perceptions not agree? If when we look at something we perceive its true nature, why should we use a microscope to perceive it?

In response, Philonous says:

Strictly speaking, Hylas, we do not see the same object that we feel; neither is the same object perceived by the microscope, which was by the naked eye. But in case every variation was thought sufficient to constitute a new kind or individual, the endless number or confusion of names would render language impracticable. Therefore to avoid this as well as other inconveniencies which are obvious upon a little thought, we combine together several ideas, apprehended by divers senses, or by the same sense at different times, or in different circumstances, but observed however to have some connexion in Nature, either with respect to co-existence or succession; all which they refer to one name, and consider as one thing . . . When I look through a microscope, it is not that I may perceive more clearly what I perceived already with my bare eyes, the object perceived by the glass being quite different from the former. But in both cases my aim is only to know what ideas are connected together; and the more a man knows of the connexion of ideas, the more he is said to know of the nature of things.[88]

A further interchange, and Hylas says: But the same idea that is in my mind cannot be in your mind or anyone else's. Your principles would lead to the absurd conclusion that no two people can see the same thing.

Philonous answers: In the usual sense of the word *same*, they do see the same thing, that is, the same idea does exist in different minds. The word *same* is used for instances in which one does not perceive any distinction or variety. Philosophers, who debate the abstract notion of identity, may not agree, but this is of little importance. If several men in the same place, with the same faculties and similarly affected by their senses, had never known how to speak, their perceptions would certainly agree, and if they learned to speak, they might call what they saw the *same* thing. Because of the diversity of the people involved, others who began to speak might use different names. But the dispute is about a word—whether or not *same* is applicable. If the exterior of a building was not changed but its interior completely rebuilt, what difference would it make if you said it was the same house and I said it was not? "Men can dispute about identity and diversity, without any real differences in their thoughts and opinions."[89]

"Spirits" and God: A spirit, says Berkeley, which is the only substance or support in which ideas can exist, cannot itself be an idea or be like an idea (*Principles*, sec. 135). I denote what I myself am by the term *soul* or *spiritual substance*, but to prevent confusion, it is best to distinguish between *spirit* and *idea*, though if we do say that we have an idea of spirits, this usage is of no more than verbal interest (sec. 142). However, unlike my knowledge of ideas, our knowledge of other spirits is only by means of

> their operations, or the ideas by them excited in us. I perceive several motions, changes, and combinations of ideas, that inform me there are certain particular agents like myself, which accompany them, and concur in their production. Hence the knowledge I have of other spirits is not immediate, as is the knowledge of my ideas; but depending on the intervention of ideas, by me referred to agents or spirit distinct from myself, as effects or concomitant signs. (sec. 145)

The works of nature—most of the ideas or sensations we perceive—are not produced by human beings, so there must be some other, nonhuman spirit that produces them. Because the effects of nature are so much more numerous and impressive than those ascribed to humans, we perceive God's existence far more evidently than that of human beings (sec. 147). God is intimately present to our minds and produces in them all the variety of ideas or sensations present in them, the ideas on which we entirely depend, so it is in him that *"we live, and move, and have our being"* (sec. 149).*

In *Three Dialogues between Hylas and Philonous*, Berkeley disagrees with Malebranche's belief that humans see things in the essence of God. Yet he accepts that sensible things are independent of his own mind and must have an existence outside of it. It is plain, Berkeley says,

> that these ideas or things by me perceived, either themselves or their archetypes, exist independently of my mind, since I know myself not to be their author, it being out of my power to determine at pleasure, what particular ideas I shall be affected with upon opening my eyes or ears. They must therefore exist in some other mind, whose will it is that they should be exhibited to me.[90]**

A brief word on Berkeley's reputation. Hard as he tried to make himself clear, almost everyone who reacted publicly understood him to deny the existence of a sensible world and made him the unworldly butt of their jokes. Hume responded with the psychologically devastating remark: "That all his arguments, though otherwise intended, are, in reality, merely sceptical, appears from this, *that they admit of no answer and produce*

---

*In *An Essay towards a New Theory of Vision*, which precedes the *Principles*, Berkeley writes: "I think we may fairly conclude that the proper objects of vision constitute an universal language of the Author of Nature, whereby we are instructed how to regulate our actions" (sec. 147). In the *Dialogues*, Berkeley writes that God perceives nothing by sense (ed. Luce and Jessop, vol. 2, pp. 241–42). In *Siris*, he writes in a Malebranchian vein: "God knoweth all things as pure mind or intellect; but nothing by sense, nor in nor through a sensory" (sec. 289).

**At this point it is hard to refrain from a criticism like that of Foucher against Malebranche: When Berkeley argues that the ideas or things he perceives exist independently of the human mind, so that as "either themselves or their archetypes" they must be in God's mind, he gives up the ideas' particular immediacy. Usually, he seems to maintain that an idea appears in and is limited to the mind of a particular person at a particular time; but here, he tends to make ideas external to the human minds that perceive them. Later in the dialogue (see note 90 just above), he says that ideas exist not only when he is not perceiving them, but before he is born and after his supposed death. This means that a person's ideas can also be external to his own mind. Berkeley's solution must lie in supposing that every spirit and every idea held by every spirit are internal to God. He is trying to create a difficult union between his "commonsense" idea-empiricism and a Neoplatonic or, at least, Malebranchian conception of the world.

no conviction."[91] Kant, who probably read nothing of Berkeley in the original, was anxious to dissociate himself from him, no doubt because, to his great discomfort, critics had identified his philosophy with Berkeley's.[92] In America, in the New England colonies, Berkeley's fate was much better, for largely theological reasons; and later American idealists were also naturally interested in him.[93] Now, he is praised for having understood how arbitrary it can be to elevate scientific abstractions into metaphysical realities. The tributes paid him by William James, Charles Peirce, and Edmund Husserl testify how much they appreciated his investigation of the phenomenology of perception.[94]

When David Hume, the last of the three English philosophers taken up here, reviews his life, he writes that his father's early death left him, his sister, and his elder brother in the devoted care of their mother.[95] "I . . . was seized very early," he says, "with a passion for Literature which has been the ruling Passion of my Life, and the great source of my Enjoyments." His family hoped that he would study law, but he had an intense dislike for everything but philosophy and "general Learning," and so, instead of poring over law books, he spent his time secretly devouring Cicero and Vergil.[96]

To judge by Hume's own testimony, he thought about what was to become *A Treatise of Human Nature*, his first and most influential book of philosophy, before he was fifteen, planned it before he was twenty-one, and wrote it before he was twenty-five.[97] When the *Treatise* was published some years later, in 1739–40, it "fell *dead-born from the press*, without reaching such distinction, as even to excite a murmur among the zealots."* Supposing that the difficulty lay more in its style than its substance, he recast its first part in *Philosophical Essays concerning Human Understanding* (1748) (later renamed *An Enquiry of Human Understanding*), but this, too, "was entirely overlooked and neglected," in favor of a Dr. Middleton's *Free Enquiry.*

---

*Some two to three hundred copies of each of the *Treatise's* three volumes were later auctioned off cheaply, but "the actual evidence is that from the time of the publication of *A Treatise of Human Nature*, Book I . . . Hume was regarded as an important thinker by the several reviewers of his work." The immediate influence of the *Treatise* was on the intellectual atmosphere of the Scottish Enlightenment. His views were soon discussed and refuted, but "it took quite a while to see Hume as a key member of the British empirical tradition, one who had raised a fundamental problem of metaphysics and epistemology. It is probably Kant who gave Hume such a status" (Popkin, *The High Road to Pyrrhonism*, pp. 197, 212; also Kemp Smith, *The Philosophy of David Hume*, pp. 519–23).

A Treatise of Human Nature was the product of strong hopes, a good deal of work, and much emotional turmoil. During the period he conceived it, Hume wrote a manuscript, which he later burned, on the subject of religion. It reflected, he tells a correspondent, "a perpetual Struggle of a restless Imagination against Inclination, perhaps against Reason."[98] Much of the creative turmoil in which the *Treatise* was conceived is described in a letter Hume wrote in 1734, when he was twenty-three, to an anonymous physician. He writes that he was disinclined to submit to philosophical or literary authority and hoped to discover a way of establishing the truth. At about the age of eighteen, he says, he was transported "beyond Measure" and inspired to "throw up every other Pleasure or Business to apply entirely to it."[99] But he was struck by a profound depression, much of which passed when he allowed himself some indulgences. For three years, he writes, he has "collected the rude Materials for many Volumes." But his spirits are low and he cannot write them attractively enough to draw the world's attention to him. "I wou'd rather live & dye in Obscurity," he says with author's proud resolve, "than produce them maim'd & imperfect."[100]

The *Treatise* was actually composed somewhat later at La Fleche, in France, where he could recollect his emotions in tranquillity. Yet the *Treatise* has passages that say, for example, that "the wretched condition, weakness, and disorder of the faculties, I must employ in my enquries, encrease my apprehensions."* Hume is afraid of the "forelorn solitude" in which his philosophy puts him, and of the enmity, to which he exposes himself, "of all metaphysicians, logicians, mathematicians, and even theologians."[101]

Hume's later publications include *An Enquiry concerning the Principles of Morals* (1752), *The Natural History of Religion* (1757)—to him, incomparably the best of all his writings—and *Dialogues concerning Natural Religion*, written about 1751 but published, as Hume preferred, after his death. Of all his books, it was the six-volume *History of England* (1754–

---

*Hume read widely. Soon after he left La Fleche he wrote a letter telling a friend which philosophical books he thinks are most relevant to the *Treatise*. Hume says in the letter that his philosophy depends so little on earlier systems of philosophy that it can be judged by his friend's natural good sense alone. But he would like the friend to prepare for the *Treatise* by reading "La Recherche de la Vérité of Pere Malebranche, the Principles of Human Knowledge by Dr Berkeley, some of the more metaphysical Articles of Bailes Dictionary; such as those [. . . of] Zeno, & Spinoza, Des-Cartes Meditations would also be useful" (Popkin, *The High Road to Pyrrhonism* [Letter of August 26–31, to Michael Ramsey], p. 291).

1762) that gave him the readers and the great reputation he wanted.* Unfortunately, he lent his reputation to the prejudice that there had never been "a civilized nation of any other complexion other than white, nor even any individual eminent either in action or speculation."[102]

He never married, he traveled widely and he filled many different posts, from caretaker of a mad young nobleman to aide-de-camp to a military ambassador, librarian of the Faculty of Advocates, and secretary of the English embassy in Paris, where he was lionized. Having won the literary fame he had so long wooed, he spent his last years in Edinburgh, where he surprised the learned world with the example of a decent, even-tempered, eloquent, happy pagan.

A Treatise of Human Nature was published in three volumes, the first, *Of the Understanding*, the second, *Of the Passions*, and the third, *Of Morals*. Each has its own interest, but the discussion here will be limited to the first volume and, for the most part, to the subjects of causality and personal identity. This is the choice encouraged by tradition. Hume's own choice for emphasis was causality—his preference is made clear by the anonymous *Abstract of a Treatise of Human Nature* that he wrote to arouse interest in the work's first two volumes, whose reception had disappointed him badly.[103]**

In the introduction to the *Treatise*, Hume maintains that all sciences to some extent depend on the science of man, because they are all subject to human awareness and relative to human abilities. If we were thoroughly acquainted with the extent and power of human understanding and with

---

*Hume's intentions were, as always, "critical and revisionist . . . Most disturbing of all, he made a point of showing how the Church had succeeded in corrupting politics at nearly every important period of British history. Overall the history of England as told by Hume could hardly have been less glorious . . . Not surprisingly, the History created a furor" (N. Phillipson, *Hume*, London: Weidenfeld & Nicolson, 1989, pp. 11–12).

**Of the thirty-two pages of the *Abstract*, Hume devotes thirteen to causation. The *Abstract* concludes with the boast that the author of the *Treatise* is a true inventor because "of the use he makes of the principle of the association of ideas, which enters into most of his philosophy." It should be noted that Hume came to regard his *Enquiry* as far better than the *Treatise*. Late in life, he appended a complaint to his collected essays that the critics, who directed their attacks at his anonymous "juvenile work," were acting "very contrary to all rules of candour and fair dealing" (*Enquiries*, ed. Selby-Bigge, p. 2). In defiance of Hume, it is fairly generally agreed that the *Enquiry* is better written and more coherent, but that the *Treatise*, with all its vagueness, detail, repetition, and vacillation is the philosophically more intense and important work. (See Selby-Bigge's introduction to the *Enquiries*, followed by a comparative table of contents; and Kemp Smith, *The Philosophy of David Hume*, pp. 530–40, who concludes that, in preferring the *Enquiry*, Hume was his own best critic.)

the nature of the ideas we use and how we reason with them, the sciences might be greatly improved. This is true even of mathematics, and natural philosophy (natural science), natural religion (religion based on natural belief, religion without revelation).[104]* And it must be all the more true of logic, Hume says, the purpose of which is to explain how we reason and what our ideas are; of morality and criticism, which express our preferences and feelings; and of politics, which considers the mutual dependence of humans:

> There is no question of importance, whose decision is not compris'd in the science of man; and there is none, which can be decided with any certainty, before we become acquainted with that science . . . And as the science of man is the only solid foundation for the other sciences, so the only solid foundation we can give to that science itself must be laid on experience and observation.[105]

The *Treatise* opens with a few definitions that depart conspicuously from Locke's.[106] "All the perceptions of the human mind," says Hume, resolve themselves into two distinct kinds, which I shall call IMPRESSIONS and IDEAS." The perceptions that strike on the mind most forcibly are named *impressions*. They include "all our sensations, passions and emotions, as they make their first appearance in the soul." *Ideas* are "the faint images of these in thinking and reasoning." Of course, the force of impressions, too, may be relatively faint; and in sleep, fever, madness, or violent emotion, the force of ideas may approach that of impressions. But impressions and ideas are in general very different and deserve different names (Hume notes that he perhaps restores the word *idea* "to its original sense, from which Mr. *Locke* had perverted it, in making it stand for all our perceptions").[107] Simple impressions and ideas all correspond with one another, so that many perceptions of the mind appear both as impressions and ideas. However, says Hume, many complex ideas—such as an imagined New Jerusalem, with gold pavements and ruby walls—have never

---

*Hume makes skeptical analyses of proofs for God's existence and tends to detach morality from religion. (The best theologian he ever met, he used to say, was the old Edinburgh fishwife who, having recognized him as Hume the atheist, refused to pull him out of the bog into which he had fallen until he declared he was a Christian and repeated the Lord's prayer.) Yet he professes belief in an omnipotent mind and will (e.g., in a note to the *Treatise*'s appendix; ed. Selby-Bigge, p. 633). His own belief may be expressed in a note to a final revision of his *Dialogues concerning Natural Religion*. He there suggests that natural theology resolves itself into the simple, somewhat ambiguous proposition *"that the cause or causes of order in the universe probably bear some remote analogy to human intelligence"* (*Dialogues concerning Natural Religion*, ed. Kemp Smith, p. 227).

had a corresponding impression, while complex impressions—Paris, which I have seen—has no perfect representation in an idea (*Treatise*, book 1, part 1, section 1).[108]

The first proposition to be established is this: All our simple ideas are at first derived from corresponding simple impressions. Because every simple impression is attended by a corresponding idea, and because the impression always precedes the idea, which is less forceful and lively, we can be sure that our impressions are the causes of our ideas and not the opposite. This is also proved by the fact that people born blind or deaf have, respectively, neither visual nor aural impressions nor ideas. We can't form an accurate idea of a pineapple without having actually tasted it. However, we can use our imagination and interpolate a never-seen shade of a color between shades of it that we have seen, or interpolate a gradation of a never-heard sound between sounds that we have heard (1.1.1).[109]

Impressions are of two kinds, of sensation and of reflection. Those of sensation, which arise in the soul from unknown causes, make us perceive some kind of heat or cold, thirst or hunger, or pleasure or pain. Impressions of reflection are largely derived from ideas. That is, a sensory impression is copied by the mind, and this copy, which remains after the sensation is gone, is called an idea. Such an idea, of pleasure or pain for example, makes "new impressions of desire and aversion, hope and fear." Being derived from reflection, these may properly be called impressions of reflection. These impressions are, in turn, "copied by the memory and imagination, and become ideas; which perhaps in their turn give rise to other impressions and ideas" (1.1.2).[110]

An impression that reappears in the mind still relatively vivid—somewhat between an impression and an idea—is ascribed to the faculty of memory. But if the impression that reappears is faint and unsteady, it is ascribed to the faculty of imagination. Of the two faculties, only the imagination has the freedom to transpose and change its ideas (1.1.3). But the imagination, which joins simple ideas into complex ones, operates in accord with the uniting principle. This principle does not create inseparable connections, which are excluded from the imagination, but is a gentle force of association. For example, languages correspond so nearly to one another because nature, so to speak, points out to everyone the simple ideas that fit most properly into complex ones. The relations or qualities from which such an association of ideas arises are three in number: resemblance, contiguity in time or place, and cause and effect. The relations by which the imagination unites our simple ideas have effects that are much clearer than their causes and much more rewarding for the philosopher to investigate. The complex ideas that arise from a principle of union among our simple ideas may be divided into relations, modes, and substances (1.1.4). Relations, in turn, may be divided into those of identity, of space and time, of quantity or number, and of quality or degree (1.1.5). Substances are much more problematic. Not being colors, sounds, or tastes, they cannot be derived from impressions of sensation. And not being resolvable, like most impressions of reflection, into passions and emotions, they cannot be derived from impressions of reflection. Therefore, we have no idea of substances other than as collections of particular qualities, and no idea of the modes of substance except as qualities referred to an unknown something in which they are supposed to inhere (1.1.6).

As to abstract ideas, we know that all ideas are derived from impressions and can differ from them only in degree of vividness, so all ideas must have a particular quantity and quality. There is no triangle in general, one without particular sides and angles. What happens is that a particular idea is made general by joining it to a general term. A general term is a term that has been related to many other particular ideas and recalls them easily to the imagination. With its admirable ability to collect ideas, the imagination is nothing less than "a magical faculty in the soul," a faculty that human understanding is completely unable to explain. But we must understand the artificiality and dependence on custom of abstract ideas (1.1.7).[111]

Take, for example, our ideas of space and time. I acquire the idea of space or extension in the following way: I open my eyes, turn them and perceive many visible bodies, and then, when I shut my eyes again, consider the distance between the bodies. I borrow the idea of the extension of the table before me from the impressions I get of colored points arranged in a particular way. Together, sight and touch create compound but indivisible impressions of space (1.2.3). All this shows how abstract ideas are based on particular ones and joined to general terms to represent a great variety of particular ones that are alike in some respect and different in others. The abstract idea of time includes a variety even greater than that of space. It is derived from the succession of our perceptions—ideas and impressions of all kinds (1.2.3).[112] The conclusion is that "the ideas of space and time are therefore not separate or distinct ideas, but merely those of the manner or order, in which objects exist" (1.2.4).[113]

Hume's empiricism having been made explicit, we can go on to his view of causality. Of causality, he says firmly that every demonstration ever made for the necessity of a cause is fallacious and sophistical (1.3.3).[114] We may begin with a further statement, which, if true, makes induction an arbitrary or, at the least, quite doubtful prodecure, supported not by plausible argument but by habit alone:

> The supposition, *that the future resembles the past*, is not founded on arguments of any kind, but is deriv'd entirely from habit, by which we are determin'd to expect for the future the same train of objects, to which we have been accustom'd. (1.3.12)[115]

Hume sets out, he says, to find a philosophical explanation of "the secret force and energy of causes." He refers us to "Father *Malebranche*, Book VI, Part ii, chap. 3, and the illustrations upon it." In this chapter we find Malebranche's own conclusion that there are no bodies, large or small, that one can conceive to have the force to move themselves or, as is obvious, to move other bodies. Bodies are essentially extension and, as such, have no actual motion, no force of their own: When a moving ball strikes and moves another, it does not communicate anything it has.* It is only an "occasional cause," determined by the will of God, of the motion of the second ball.[116]

Hume, of course, rejects the function Malebranche assigns to God, but he accepts his view that matter in itself has no causal force. It is impossible, he says, to show any instance of the exertion of causal force.[117]** He concludes, "Upon the whole, necessity is something that exists in the mind, not in objects," and he defines a cause as an object that precedes and is contiguous with another, when all the objects that resemble the former (the preceding one) are in the same relations of preceding and contiguity with objects that resemble the latter (following one) (1.3.14).[118]

---

*In the *Abstract*, Hume turns Malebranche's balls into billiard balls: When the first ball strikes the second and the second, formerly at rest, moves, "this is as perfect an instance of the relation of cause and effect as we know, either by sensation or reflection." But nothing in the shock of the two balls can explain the result but two suppositions, based on nothing more than experience: Like causes in like circumstances produce like results, and, the future must conform to the past. "This conformity is a *matter of fact*, and...will admit of no proof but from experience. But our experience in the past can be a proof of nothing in the future, but upon a supposition, that there is a resemblance betwixt them. This therefore is a point, which can admit of no proof at all, and which we take for granted without any proof" (*Abstract of a Treatise of Human Nature*, pp. 11–15).

**Yet Hume gives eight rules by which to judge what are causes and effects: 1. Cause and effect must be contiguous in space and time. 2. The cause must be prior to the effect. 3. Cause and effect must be in constant union. 4. The same cause must always produce the same effect and the same effect rise only from the same cause. 5. If different objects produce the same effect, it must be because of some common quality. 6. If two objects that resemble one another have different results, the difference must be from the trait in which they differ. 7. If an object increases or diminishes as its cause increases or diminishes, the effect must be from the union of several effects, which arise from several different parts of the cause. 8. If an object exists for some time "in its full perfection" without any effect, the effect must be participated in by some other principle (1.3.14; ed. Nidditch, pp. 173–75).

Having adopted the doubts of Malebranche and Bayle (and Berkeley) but no certainties from anyone, Hume goes these philosophers one great doubt better: He doubts "the nature of the uniting principle, which constitutes a person" (1.4.2).[119] "When I enter most intimate into what I call *myself*," he says, he always stumbles on particular perceptions, "of heat or cold, light or shade, love or hate, pain or pleasure," but, he says, "I never catch *myself* at any time without a perception, and never can observe any thing but the perception." For everyone except the metaphysician who claims to perceive something simple and unchanging that he calls *himself*, Hume makes the famous declaration:

> I may venture or affirm of the rest of mankind, that they are nothing but a bundle or collection of different perceptions, which succeed one another with an inconceivable rapidity, and are in a perpetual flux and movement . . . The mind is a kind of theatre, where several perceptions successively make their appearance; pass, re-pass, glide away, and mingle in an infinite variety of postures and situations. There is properly no *simplicity* in it at one time, nor *identity* in different; whatever natural propension we may have to imagine that simplicity and identity. The comparison of the theatre must not mislead us. They are the successive perceptions only, that constitute the mind; nor have we the most distant notion of the place, where these scenes are represented, or of the materials, of which it is compos'd. (1.4.6)[120]

When we reflect on a succession of related objects, says Hume, it is natural for the mind to move smoothly from one object to the other as if it was contemplating a single persisting object. Therefore we make the mistake of substituting the notion of identity for that of related objects, and therefore, to get rid of interruptions, we "run into the notion of a *soul*, and *self*, and *substance*, to disguise the variation." When we attribute identity for this reason, our mistake is usually accompanied by "a fiction, either of something invariable and uninterrupted, or of something mysterious and inexplicable, or at least with some propensity to such fictions" (1.4.6).[121] The human mind is

> a system of different perceptions or different existences, which are link'd together by the relation of cause and effect, and mutually produce, destroy, influence, and modify each other. Our impressions give rise to their correspondent ideas; and these ideas in their turn produce other impressions. One thought chaces another, and draws after it a third, by which it is expell'd in its turn. In this respect, I cannot compare the

soul more properly to any thing than to a republic or common wealth, in which the several members are united by the reciprocal ties of government and subordination, and give rise to other persons, who propagate the same republic in the incessant changes of its parts. (1.4.6)[122]

The Hume of the *Treatise* regards himself as an antimetaphysician, in the sense that he objects to facile abstract solutions to problems that need detailed analysis and research.[123] We should begin, he says, with the detailed study of human nature (an idea he takes less formally but no less determinedly than Kant). His deep interest in the psychology of perception, emotion, and imagination is evident everywhere. From the standpoint of psychology today, his basic definitions may be too simply additive, as when he speaks of simple ideas as the parts of complex ideas; but in spite of what may now strike us as based on crudely spatial analogies, the direction of his thought can still be stimulating—he is interested in the small details of perception, and when he fails to explain them, acknowledges his failure.*

---

*The present-day psychology of perception is still often additive, though with better evidence than Hume had. For example, different retinal neurons have different sensitivities— to lines with different orientations, edges, colors, and so on. Hume tends to fall back on imagination to explain what is now regarded as a function of the central nervous system (visual constancy, for example). In a way reminiscent of modern research, he relates emotion with perception, even of space and number: "Every part . . . of extension of number has a separate emotion attending it, when conceiv'd by the mind" (2.2.8; ed. Nidditch, p. 373).

Granted his interests, I think that Hume would welcome modern research into the physiology of the nervous system, on which, he complains, his contemporaries merely speculate. I think he would also welcome—though insist on further interpreting—the research of a psychologist such as Michotte, which on its face contradicts his view of causality. That is, Michotte's experiments show that under certain conditions we actually see a kind of causality, the transmission of motion from body to body, just as surely and consistently as we see anything else (so that in Hume's terms the transmission of motion can be a visual impression, and not, as he argues, a natural but merely superstitious belief). Hume would also be interested in the apparent motion (stroboscopic motion, phi-phenomenon) that results when pictures projected in quick enough succession are perceived to move even though the image on the retina does not move. (See A. Michotte, *La Perception de la causalité*, Louvain: Presses Universitaires, 1954.)

For a contemporary discussion based on experimental data, see D. Sperber, D. Premack, and A. J. Premack, eds., *Causal Cognition: A Multidisciplinary Debate,* New York: Oxford University Press, 1995. The Afterword to this symposium contrasts "the **arbitrary** tradition of Hume (in which causality is learned)" with "the **natural** tradition of Michotte (in which causality is directly perceived." Hume's case is represented by the experimental animal that learns the arbitrary relation between pressing a bar and getting food, while Michotte's case is represented by the human who sees an object striking and, by a natural relation, launching the movement of another object. To the question "Is the representation of causality the same in the two cases?" the answer given is "apparently 'no,' " as shown by further experiments (p. 653).

In keeping with his general position, Hume turns over most of the work of understanding to its faculty of imagination, which ranges far beyond the immediate present and makes full use, for better or worse, of the association of ideas. To him, often, the mind is hardly other than the imagination.[124] Where Malebranche, doubtful of everything, falls back on the always supporting, always creating God, Hume falls back on the always mysteriously creative power of the imagination, which bridges the gaps between impressions and, using memory, gives force to the propensity to suppose that existences are continuous (1.4.2).[125] The imagination can be loosely, wildly, madly associative, but when guided by the more stable, persistent, irresistible, universal relation of cause and effect, persuades us by the feeling that something is real and by the belief that distinguishes what probably exists from what is (almost) surely fictitious— "an idea assented to *feels* different from a fictitious idea, that the fancy alone presents to us."[126]

Hume is a skeptic who generally believes in experience and generally trusts habit, though he expresses the doubtfulness of habit at length and with some pathos. He generally accepts his habitual ways and thoughts not because they are beyond doubt but because, having no sane alternative, he is skeptical of his doubts as well as of his convictions. The details of his struggle to arrive at this conclusion reflect his psychological difficulties (1.4.7).[127] It is perhaps his struggle for his own unity and equanimity that influences him to attribute so much more importance to parts, to individual perceptions and fragments of experience, than to the wholes they constitute—why, I ask, must a skeptic regard every fragment of every whole with less suspicion than the whole they make up? But Hume's struggle lends eloquence to his description of the human mind as a republic made up of different, possibly changing members and laws—a conception that fits the views of contemporary researchers far better than that of a unitary mind.

I have put some emphasis on Hume's relation to contemporary psychology because, with all his skepticism, he is a partisan of progress, especially in the science of man, to which he wants to contribute his share. Under the circumstances of his time, his refusal to speculate about ultimate principles was to his honor. So, too, were and are his conclusions that nothing can be proved beyond the possibility of doubt, that belief is natural to us all, that it is natural to philosophize on problems that cannot be settled, that there is a great difference between probable beliefs and superstitions, and that human beings are not fundamentally rational creatures. His ambivalence enables him to defend both doubt and certainty, and to side more with the Academic skeptics of Greece, who accept probabilities, than with the Pyrrhonists, who do not.[128] His humane temperament, his intellectual excitement, his literary skill, his philosophical minimalism, his constant demand for perceptual evidence, and his deep yet hopeful skepticism, combine to keep him philosophically alive.

Discussion

Think of two small constellations of philosophers, an Indian Buddhist and a European, mostly empiricist constellation, shining on the dark sky, of truth, maybe. In the center of each constellation is a double star, one star small, the other large. I have imagined this double star to be central because, as the star of idealism, it is now our center of interest. In the Indian constellation, the smaller central star is named Vasubandhu, and the larger one has the compound name Asanga/Vasubandhu. In the European constellation, the smaller central star is named Berkeley, and the larger one, Malebranche/Berkeley. From where we stand, we see to the left of each central star, a star that blinks on and off. This is the star of skepticism. In the Indian constellation its name is Nagarjuna, and in the European, where it blinks less regularly and severely, its name is Hume; and close by Hume there is a skeptical companion star, named Bayle. To the right of each central star, of idealism, there is a star of realism. The European realism star is named Locke; not far off there is Descartes, a star of a different realism family. The Indian realism star has only a class name, Sarvastivada; and rather far to its right there is a star, of a different realism family, with the class name of Nyaya. An attentive further look shows that between Nagarjuna and Asanga/Vasubandhu-Vasubandhu, which are close to one another, there is the star called Dharmakirti. The order of the whole, almost linear Indian constellation—from its skeptical leftmost star to its realistic rightmost—is this: Nagarjuna, Dharmakirti, the double Asanga/Vasubandhu-Vasubandhu, then Sarvastivada, and then Nyaya. The order of the counterpart, European constellation is, from left to right: Hume and Bayle, the double Malebranche/Berkeley-Berkeley, then Locke, and then Descartes.

It turns out that, on analysis, the light of the corresponding stars of each constellation has different spectral components—some of these differences will be described in a moment. The purpose of the constellation image, however, is not to point out the spectral differences but to show that philosophy casts its light on the world from a naturally complementary set of positions that, taken together, make up something like the whole light that philosophical thought can cast on the world at a given time. In nonmetaphorical terms, the human situation—or the sociology of philosophical speculation—is such that it tends to create an analogous range of responses in different intellectual traditions.

Now a word on the double stars. I make the star of idealism a double one because I believe that the subjective idealist cannot or does not want to be separated from an encompassing immaterial reality. Berkeley remains a subjective idealist in that he regards the tie of one human mind with another as an indirect one, grasped by analogical inference; but he is an objective idealist in that he believes that everything that exists does so within the immaterial God. Like Berkeley, Malebranche refuses to believe that any human mind participates directly in another. He thinks, instead, that the knowledge in each human mind necessarily refers to the same pure, godly archetypes. And he also thinks that each mind exists by grace of God's sustaining power, its existence located, so to speak, within God's existence. So on the European side, there is, in the final synthesis, God the omniscient creator, sustainer, and container; and, on the Indian side, in the final synthesis, the omniscient Buddha, suchness, and the truth body (the *dharma* body)—for Buddhahood, universal in all beings, is the beings' essence. The Vasubandhu of *Thirty Verses* expresses the Mahayana (and Advaita Vedanta) ideal of the abolition of the difference between subject and object. This is also the Neoplatonic ideal, which has some place in the genealogy of Berkeley's thought, though I assume it would appear to him too arrogant to entertain with respect to any human beings.

There are, of course, differences between the analogous philosophers. I take up the differences in the order of the three English philosophers: Locke, with his realism, belief in corpuscularian atomism, unitary soul, and God, is most like a Nyaya philosopher. Among the Buddhists, he most resembles the Sarvastivadins (of the Vaibhashika type), because he, like them, is a realist and atomist; but his belief in God and in the soul distinguish him from Buddhists of every type.

Berkeley, as is evident, most nearly resembles Vasubandhu. Both identify what is real in the world with the individual's perceptual awareness, and both deny that the existence of matter can be proved and that it is necessary to believe that there is a reality external to an individual's consciousness.* Naturally, both also deny (as does Dharmakirti in his dialogue) that the existence of matter would in any way help to explain

---

*Such a view may well have a prephilosophical basis. This may be suggested by a vague but interesting anthropological example: The Jivaros or, more exactly, the Achuar, who live in Ecuadorian Amazonia, are not philosophical in the sense adopted here, yet they are relatively close to "the immaterialism of a thinker such as Berkeley" in that "they appear to found the existence of cognizant entities and the elements of their environment more or less upon the act of perception." To them, as to Berkeley, "it is the perceptive qualities that…constitute at once things themselves and the subject that perceives them…It seems to me that the Achuar structure their world on the basis of the type of exchange that they can establish with all its diverse inhabitants" (P. Descola, *The Spears of Twilight*, London: HarperCollins, 1996).

our experience—all that experience really gives us is sequences of ideas or acts of awareness.[129] Therefore Berkeley and Vasubandhu both have to answer questions such as: Is the food we eat only a figment of consciousness? And such as: If there are only individual minds and mental representations or ideas, how does it happen that different persons see the same place at the same time, as if it was objectively there for them all? Because Berkeley differs from Buddhists in believing in God and the soul, his and Buddhist answers usually fall back on different dogmas: Vasubandhu's answer to the second of the two questions just asked is that different persons appear to see the same place at the same time because they are in a similar karmic state.[130] Berkeley, who does not believe in identical ideas, answers that the place and time are only similar, but similar enough to be spoken of as the "same." Another, in this place, implicit answer given by Berkeley is that God coordinates the ideas that different persons have. To distinguish further, unlike Berkeley, Vasubandhu uses the analogy between ideas (representations) and dreams to strengthen his case: dreams, too, he says, have actual effects (I doubt if Berkeley would care for this line of argument, because to him ideas are passive; in any case, the example of the emission of semen while dreaming would not earn his ecclesiastical approval). Vasubandhu gives his human mind sequences the special power to enter into, even terminate, that is, kill, another mind sequence.[131] I am not aware that Berkeley ever deals with such mutual enmity and the at least apparent lethal powers of minds over one another. Though only sequences of representation, Vasubandhu's minds therefore seem more robust and mysteriously active than Berkeley's minds or souls.* However, at its simplest, most obviously logical level, Vasubandhu's and Berkeley's defense of subjective idealism is the same: the subjective experience is what you are sure of, and you don't need anything beyond it.

---

*A. K. Chatterjee, who thinks that it is very unjust to Yogachara to compare it with Berkeley's idealism, writes: "Berkeley distinguishes between an idea and a creative act for which alone the idea exists. For the Yogachara the idea itself is the creative act . . . The ideas are precipitated in this creative act and they can have no separate existence than that of being posited. Their apparent otherness is itself ideal . . . Any form of idealism which is not an absolutism cannot be a consistent idealism" (*The Yogācāra Idealism*, Delhi: Banarsidass, 2d rev. ed., 1975, pp. 210, 215).

My answer is: Vasubandhu's *Twenty Verses* and Dharmakirti's dialogue do represent a Yogachara doctrine comparable to Berkeley's subjective idealism, even though Berkeley does not aim to overcome the subject-object split (a Neoplatonic aim). Berkeley's God does the creative and communicative work that Berkeley's philosophy demands of him and is by implication more or less Malebranche's incessantly creative divine consciousness—with a philosophically functional likeness to Buddha's *dharma* body. Chatterjee is right, however, in saying that Berkeley's idealism is not fully worked out.

Hume is clearly the most Buddhistic of the three English philosophers.[132] This is in part because he is doubtful of the existence of God, but mainly because he denies—in rational theory though, quite un-Buddhistically, not in living emotion—the existence of the self. Using the equivalent of the Buddhist term *heaps*, (*skandhas*), Hume ventures that human beings are only bundles or collections of different perceptions that succeed one another in a rapid, perpetual flux. His general equivalent to the Buddhist law of dependent origination is defined by the set of rules by which we recognize and anticipate cause and effect. When he speaks of causal relations, Hume is thinking mainly of the laws of individual psychology, especially of association, and of laws such as those that Newton proposed. When the Buddhists speak of causal relations, they are thinking mainly of the cycle of birth, development, death, and rebirth.

A few last similarities: The philosophers, English and Buddhist, are all analytical, in the sense that they break up experience into its theoretically final factors, including atoms. Even Nagarjuna accepts *dharmas* as the analytic basis for understanding the world of ordinary experience; even Berkeley accepts perceptions of atoms as valid ones; and even Vasubandhu, who argues that the hypothesis of atoms is self-contradictory, accepts atoms, though only because the contradictory hypothesis, that everything is spatially one and the same, has such absurd consequences. In addition, the English and the Buddhist philosophers are all empiricists in that they base their thought on the experience of individual perceivers and perceptions, in that they deny the metaphysical reality of abstract terms—there are no true substances but only experienced sequences of perceptions—and in that they regard sensory perception not as a way of establishing or exemplifying fixed truths but as a way of making approximate generalizations to help human survival.[133]

Whatever arrogance these philosophers display in their analytic fragmentation of human experience, they retain an acute sense of the complex, the unknown, and the unknowable. In Buddhism this is expressed in the humanly impossible knowledge of the Buddha, which is able to solve problems too difficult for even the devoted, superlatively intelligent philosopher. The Buddhist idealist's understanding of the world's complexity is also expressed in belief in the store consciousness, which conceptualizes the mysteriously complex continuities of life and the impenetrability of the ultimate truth about it (except for the truth of pain and the escape from pain). The idealist's synthesis of human bafflement and certainty is formulated in the Yogachara declaration that, in essence, the truth is the nonexistence of duality and the existence of nonexistence.

The European empiricists we have described use other terms to express their synthesis of uncertainty and certainty, whether about scientific hypotheses, such as those concerning atoms, about the physiology of the brain, or about the sources of subjective experience. The language in which they express their doubts is not fitted to twentieth-century science and technology. But the doubts are justified if they are reduced to the truth that, as science itself demonstrates, the more we learn, the more aspects of our ignorance we reveal: Our intellectual progress demonstrates more exactly how profoundly limited our now extensive knowledge is. As a contemporary mathematician points out, the earlier, simpler images of nature and science are giving way to others, in which everything becomes in principle more complicated, and in which the reasons for the human inability to grasp the world in detail and predict its future become clearer:

> The universe does not go *directly* from simple laws, like the laws of motion, to simple patterns, like the elliptical orbits of the planets. Instead, it passes through an enormous tree of ramified complexity, which somehow collapses out again into relatively simply patterns on appropriate scales . . . Nature's patterns are "emergent phenomena." They emerge from an ocean of complexity, like Botticell's Venus from her half shell—unheralded, transcending their origins.[134]

To the kinds of idealism discussed here, there remain two powerful deterrents, the one "common sense" and the other the theory of evolution. Common sense is exemplified by the reactions of Nyaya, which I have summarized earlier. For users of English (maybe especially for Scots), common sense is exemplified by Thomas Reid. Having studied Hume with care and initial affection, Reid insists, without any of Hume's philosophical doubts, that the natural principles or habits of thought must be accepted. Why, he asks, should convictions that are in themselves evident need to be justified by reason? Not the result of reasoning, these convictions cannot be tested by means of impressions and ideas, which are too impoverished to explain what we think and believe even about impressions and ideas. Anyone who allows philosophical arguments to reason him out of the principles of common sense suffers from "*metaphysical lunacy*," an intermittent malady "apt to seize the patient in solitary and speculative moments."[135]

The objection from the theory of biological evolution is neither to empiricism nor to Buddhism, which is itself a theory of psychobiological evolution, but to idealism in whatever guise. By evolutionary theory, everything develops from simple to complex, which is to say, develops from the nonliving, nonsocial, nonconscious, nonspiritual, and nonreligious, that is, from the most elementary forms of matter or "concretions" of energy. However, such a theory does not in itself answer the question whether an independent reality can be separated from the process by means of which this reality is perceived or thought.

Chapter 13

✖

Fideistic Neo-Skepticism

Dignaga/Dharmakirti, Kant

*Theme: Because Human Reason Imposes Its Structure
on the Real, The Real as Such Is Inaccessible to It*

The evidence of European and Indian philosophy shows that there is an intellectually attractive compromise between dogmatic rationalism and extreme skepticism. By this compromise, which, of course, takes different forms, the power of the human mind is both affirmed and limited. It is affirmed by assigning it the rule over all that lies within our ordinary conscious experience, the structure of which is said to be created by our acts of intellectual synthesis. This intellectual synthesis implies logical principles that we cannot deny because it is with them that we structure the world and conduct our thinking: The structures of perception and the structuring rules of thought are the conditions by which there is a world at all, a world for *us*. As Kant said: thoughts (concepts) without sensory contents are empty, and "intuitions"—sensory contents—without concepts are blind.[1] The experienced world is the union of both.

Given such a view, we can be assured of the stability of the usual world and, as empiricists or scientists, can pursue our research without any disabling skepticism. However, when we ask what lies behind everything, what it is that causes our instruments of perception and abstract thought to react as they do, we run into insuperable difficulties. This is because we can analyze *how* we sense and reason but cannot detach ourselves from our sensing and reasoning so as to discover what the world is like, what it is in itself, before being processed by sense and reason, our basic instruments of knowledge. The demand we make to know the world, before it is (possibly) changed by the acts by which we know it, is impossible because the instruments by which we first perceive and think it are the only ones we have. How can we use our eyes to see how the world would look without them, or think, with the necessary help of the law of contradiction, how the world is in the absence of such a law, or infer what causes something if we have no idea of causation? This drastic (to me, meaningless) question is: How would the world be to us if we had no sense organs or logic, or if we could think them away temporarily, or could look at our situation from the vantage point of creatures unlimited by the need to sense and to structure? The question is meaningless because it requires us to exist in a way that negates the possibility of existence of such sensing, thinking beings as we are.

There are persuasive modern analogies to drive the problem home. Suppose we were imprisoned in a windowless room with a television set and wanted to know how accurately it showed us the world that we assumed existed outside. What could we do in order to know? We could examine the set, and if we had good enough understanding of electronics, could grasp the basic principles on which it worked. However, without the chance to compare the images on the television screen with the reality we supposed it to picture, we could never be sure that what we saw on the screen—its degrees of clarity, its contrasts of light and dark, its framing and angling of pictures, its color balances, its sequences, maybe even its subject matter—was the result of the nature of the television set, the nature of the assumed reality outside, or the result of the union of both. In principle, the technique called "virtual reality," though still quite imperfect, makes a more realistic analogy than a television screen because the helmet and the glove or suit immerse one in a world composed of sights generated by computer but responsive to changes of the viewer's position—the aim of the developers of virtual reality is to create a simulated environment that cannot be distinguished from the real one.[2]*

---

*Italo Calvino's meditative character, Mr Palomar, who seems to have Indian ancestors, maybe dissident Naiyayikas, has combined something like Kantianism with anti-Kantianism. Thinking of his ego as someone peering out of his own eyes as if leaning on a windowsill, he, or Calvino, asks if Mr Palomar "is not a piece of the world that is looking at another piece of the world? Or else, given that there is world that side of the window and world this side, perhaps the I, the ego, is simply the window through which the world looks at the world. To look at itself the world needs the eyes (and the eyeglasses) of Mr Palomar" (*Mr Palomar*, London: Minerva, 1994, p. 102).

In a philosophically realistic system, the world that is perceived is, for the most part, the true world. In a hierarchical system, there are analogies by which to guide ourselves to understand the different levels—maybe, even slightly the highest—to all of which a single reality is common. In a skeptic's world, nothing of any kind is sure, so we live by instinct or intuition. In philosophy of the kind we are considering, Dignagian or Kantian, the human mind is a prisoner in a prison constructed by the paradoxical agency of its own instruments of knowledge. As a result, this philosophy is able to accept ordinary and scientific thought and also to open the way to the nonrational and maybe contrarational (though all three philosophers are clearly opposed to self-contradiction, Kant, I suppose, most explicitly).

Standing between what it sees as excessive dogmatism and excessive skepticism, Dignagian-Kantian philosophy feels obliged to explain itself by constructing a theory of perception, of reasoning, and of the interaction of the two. But it also feels obliged to demonstrate the limits, absolute or verging on absolute, of this interaction. Drawing, therefore, on the thought of those it accuses of unjustified dogmatism and of excessive skepticism, it is impelled to make subtle distinctions, which—given the joint use of presumptions of certainty and presumptions of doubt—may be self-defeating.

As usual, the exposition that follows is simplified in the interests of clarity; but given the unavoidable nuances of the subject, the simplification may be greater than usual. Besides, the interpretation of Dignaga and Dharmakirti is only now being developed in the West. A clear-minded expositor remarks of Dignaga that "trying to piece together his thought on the basis of the Tibetan translations is like looking at a human skull and trying to imagine what the person's face looked like when alive."[3]

Dignaga (c. 480–540), Dharmakirti (c. 600–660)

Saluting him, who has become the means of cognition, who seeks the benefit of living beings.

Born a Brahman, Tibetan tradition says, Dignaga became a Buddhist of the school that believed (exceptionally for Buddhists) in an indescribable egolike "person" (*pudgala*), indescribable because neither the same as nor different from the groups of elements that constitute the human being.[4] As a Tibetan historian of Buddhism tells the no doubt legendary story, Dignaga meditated on this "person" but could not find it. He then kindled "four great fires at the four directions and stripped

his body of its clothing" and opened his eyes as wide as possible and
searched everywhere in the sky but still could not find a person.[5] This
failure, which surely implies skepticism, led Dignaga's teacher to dismiss
him. He then studied with Vasubandhu (the modern historian may think
the chronology impossible) and became especially well versed in logic
and in both the earlier and later philosophy of the great Vasubandhu.

The traditional story says that Dignaga was so outstanding that he
won miraculous help. He had no more than written the auspicious salutation to his *Compendium of the Means of Knowledge* when "the earth
trembled, a light blazed forth, a tremendous sound of thunder was heard,
and the legs of the heretical teachers became stiff like wood."[6] A jealous
heretic engaged him in debate and, although defeated three times, refused
to become a convert and emitted defiant flames from his mouth so furious
that they almost burned Dignaga. In despair at his inability to save even
this single heretic, Dignaga was about to give up his holy work. However,
Manjushri, the Bodhisattva of Wisdom, appeared before him, promised to
protect him, and prophesied that his work would become the authority for
all scientific treatises.

Dignaga's most inclusive book, probably his last, is the *Compendium
of the Means of Knowledge* (*Pramana-samuchchaya*). It consists of some two
hundred verses accompanied by Dignaga's own laconic comments in prose.
Neither his verse nor his prose is intelligible by itself. Much of the difficulty
in understanding him, whether in verse or prose, comes from his practice
of anticipating objections and stating counterpositions that he may or may
not agree with in the end. At present, his *Compendium* is known by means
of two Tibetan translations, one perhaps less mechanical and unreliable
than the other, by Sanskrit fragments, and by a subcommentary written by
Jinendrabuddhi.[7]

We come now to Dharmakirti.[8] Dharmakirti, who adopted much of
Dignaga's philosophy, is said to have studied his *Compendium* with one of
Dignaga's students but to have proved to understand it better than his
teacher. As described in the first chapter of the present book, Dharmakirti
won famous if legendary victories over Hindu philosophers, including the
great Kumarila and the great Shankara. After travelling "through many
countries and cities," he accepted a king's invitation to reside with him and
composed his works, the most inclusive and influential of which, comprised of 1,452 stanzas, is the *Commentary on the Means of Knowledge*
(*Pramana-varttika*)—short, probably, for *Commentary on Dignaga's Compendium of the Means of Knowledge.*[9] Among Dharmakirti's other extant works
there are the brief *Summary* ("*Drop*") *of Logic* (*Nyaya-bindu*), which has
been translated into English, and *The Definitive Theory of the Means of*

Knowledge (Pramana-vinishchaya), the first two chapters of which have been translated into German.

Dharmakirti's subtle distinctions and the fertile variety with which he argues make him difficult to understand. Unfortunately for those who want to know his thought as a coherent whole, his books are loosely organized.[10] His *Commentary* is perhaps sharper and certainly more detailed than Dignaga's *Compendium*, on which it bases itself, though it suffers—and gains interest from—its frequent ambiguity. The four chapters of the *Commentary*—only the first with his own explanation—deal respectively with inference, with the validity of Buddha (as compared with God or the Vedas) as a means of cognition or authority, with sense perception, and with the syllogism.[11]

Dharmakirti says piously that the venerable Dignaga has faultless insight, but that because "this dull-witted world does not understand his difficult words correctly" they should be explained out of compassion for those who stupidly reproach him.[12] But he does not, in fact, always agree with Dignaga, and although the two philosophers used to be discussed as if they were almost one, there are obvious differences between them. I will therefore supplement Dignaga's thought with Dharmakirti's and distinguish between them when it is clear that Dharmakirti disagrees with Dignaga or goes far beyond him on some important point. Their logic, despite its historic importance, will not be dealt with technically.

It is hard to leave Dharmakirti as a person without noting that he shows pride of a kind doctrinally denied to Buddhists and sometimes supposed to be foreign to Indian philosophers. In the next to last stanza of his *Commentary* he writes that no one in the world will be able to grasp its deep sayings easily: "It will be absorbed by, and perish in, my own person," as a river is lost in the ocean. Even those whose force of reason is great, he says, or whose thought is exceptionally brave cannot fathom its depth or see its highest truth.[13] Pride, doubt, and bitterness mingle here. Dharmakirti seems to be reacting to lack of appreciation. Does he have only Buddhists in mind? Maybe he also wants but fails to impress the other Indian, non-Buddhist philosophers—later, at least, they rejected him, unlike Dignaga, as too polemical and too merely Buddhist.[14]

To return from a philosopher's pride to philosophy proper, the first of the six chapters of Dignaga's *Compendium*, the chapter we will be mostly concerned with, deals with perception, in the sense of direct awareness. The second chapter deals with the logic of inference for oneself, which Dignaga contends is different in nature from the logic of inference for the sake of others, the subject of third chapter. The fourth chapter is on true and false examples of inference.* The fifth is "on the question of what verbal symbols make known," that is, on word meaning as inference by means of exclusion (apoha). And the sixth, last chapter surveys different kinds of futile refutations and counterarguments.

Dignaga opens his discussion by distinguishing between the two possible means of acquiring knowledge. He takes these to be perception and inference; the others he includes in these two. The word usually translated perception (pratyaksha) is explained by him etymologically (in a different work) as that which "occurs in connection with [prati] each sense faculty [aksha]."[15] To translate this perception can easily be misleading when it applies to an unstructured awareness. Pratyaksha is evidently immediate awareness of all kinds, and so it is often best translated, with varying degrees of naturalness, as sensation, sensory awareness, or perceptual awareness. Somewhat unwillingly, I will allow myself to use whichever translation seems best in a particular passage and hope that the context will prevent any confusion—the critical issue is here always the absence or presence of structure. Of the term translated inference (anumana), it is enough to note that it is often used in the general sense of reasoning.

After distinguishing between sensation (or perceptual awareness) and reasoning (or inference), Dignaga declares that every knowable object has only two aspects, the one particular and the other universal. Apart from these, there is no aspect to be known. I will prove, he says, that sensation has as its object the particular aspect alone, and that reasoning has as its object the universal alone. It is only when the operation of the mind (manas) relates the particular (such as a pure sensation of color) to the universal (such as color[ness] or being-a-color) that we can know (infer, judge) that we are seeing something colored. There is a temptation to assume separate means of knowing by means of which to recognize or

---

*As a logician, Dignaga is notable for creating a scheme to clarify when a "reason" (hetu) is valid, invalid, or doubtful. His scheme is the table or "wheel" of reasons (hetuchakra) that shows nine possible relations between the "reason" and predicate of the thesis under examination. A specialist in Buddhist logic contends that Dignaga's way of classifying would be helpful in improving modern logic. As he explains it: Whitehead and Russell's Principia Mathematica lacks an overall system, for example, a systematic treatment of constants such as truth functions. According to Emil Post, the logic of the Principia could be simplified by a process of tabulation in which not one but a few primitive concepts were involved. This suggestion recalls Dignaga's way of classifying propositions. "Post's theory, with Dinnaga's Hetuchakra as its avant-garde . . . would provide us with a 'logic of logic,' or 'meta-logic,' by which various factors in logic: the constants (functions), the variables (arguments) and rules of inference, would be introduced in an orderly way" (R. S. Y. Chi, "Dinnaga and Post-Russell Logic," p. 114). Unfortunately, I am not able to estimate the plausibility of Chi's rather grand claim.

want already known objects. But to assume such additional means of knowing would risk multiplying them infinitely.

Dignaga says, "Sensation is free of structure," that is, of conceptual structure (*kalpana*). Then he gives examples of the five different ways in which words construct conceptually:

> In the case of arbitrary words, a thing is expressed as distinguished by a name, for instance, "*Dittha.*" In the case of genus-words, a thing is expressed as distinguished by a genus, for instance, "cow." In the case of quality-words, a thing is distinguished by a quality, for instance, "white." In the case of action-words, a thing is distinguished by an action, for instance, "a cook" [a verbal noun]. In the case of substance-words, a thing is distinguished by a substance, for instance, "a staff bearer," "a horn bearer." (*Pramana-samuchchaya* 1.3cd, with commentary)[16]

For our purposes it is not necessary to interpret this passage in detail. We need only note that Dignaga is using his understanding of grammatical theory to indicate how he thinks language imposes structures by its modes of categorization. He goes on to complicate the doctrine by saying that awareness is not only sensory but also "mental," by which he means carried out by awareness, but in a way that is still preconceptual and therefore still free of error. One kind of "mental perception" (*manasa-pratyaksha*) is awareness of external objects. Another is the awareness (always a self-awareness) of desire, anger, ignorance, pleasure, pain, and the like, which Dignaga considers to be mental perception (or perceptual awareness) because it does not depend on any of the five sense organs (here, *pratyaksha* cannot be translated *sensation*).[17] The essential point is that a pure, that is, unstructured, perceptual awareness cannot be expressed in words and cannot be in error.[18] In itself, it is present, real, and self-aware.

Unlike Dignaga, Dharmakirti believes that unstructured awareness can be regarded as free of error only if it is stipulated that the awareness is not illusory. Otherwise, its freedom from error would be contradicted by the illusion caused by color blindness—the cause of the illusion being an eye disease—or by the illusion of a fiery circle created by a firebrand swung quickly, or by the illusion of moving trees created by travel on a ship. Bodily diseases can also cause deceptive images to arise, and so can strong blows to certain parts of the body.[19] Dignaga's answer would surely be that the awareness itself of motion is without error and that only the mind's interpretation of the motion is mistaken.

To continue with Dignaga: A sensation, a perceptual awareness—of color, sound, smell, and so on—is the causal condition of the perception or cognition that follows. That is to say, pure sensation "supports" the thought that, helped by a sense faculty, grasps some object. The sensation itself, although it is direct knowledge in its own right, is never a direct reflection of its assumed physical object. As inference shows, this is because all atoms are round and identical. But since atoms are never sensed by us, the presumed atoms have no intelligible relation to the particular sensory nature of a sensation or to the forms of what is perceived. Visual appearances no more resemble atoms than they resemble the eyes that see the appearances:

> Even if atoms are the material causes of the sensory phenom-
> enon, the atoms are not its field of operation, because the
> phenomenon no more has the appearance of atoms than it has
> the appearance of the sense-faculty. (Alambanapariksha)[20]*

Perceptually inaccessible to awareness, atoms, as they are conceived to be, resemble nothing but themselves, so that, alone or aggregated, they are not the "supports" of perceptual awareness:

> Difference in shape occurs only in what is conventionally real,
> but it does not exist in the atoms themselves [which are real

---

*Dignaga's *Examination of the Object of Knowledge* (Ālambana-parīkṣā), which consists of eight verses with Dignaga's commentary, is directed against the pretensions of atomists. It contends that no external objects—atoms or aggregations of atoms—can be known to support sensory cognition. But it does not deny the existence itself of atoms, nor (as seen above) deny that they are in some mysterious way a cause of sensation. However, they cannot be the support or the object of sensory cognition because they do not provide any cognition form, that is, they cannot support any representation. And even if an atomic aggregate caused some representation, atoms, being all identically spherical, could not cause representations that had other forms or forms different from one another—for example, the form of a cup and that of some other vessel, whose diversity as forms does not exist in the atoms. Tola and Dragonetti, "Dignaga's Ālambanaparīkṣāvṛtti," interpret this work of Dignaga as expressing the idealism of the Yogachara (Vijnanavada) kind (against such an interpretation see Hayes, p. 217, note 4).

In the *Compendium* (Pramana-samuchchaya) 1.4, Dignaga accepts the Sarvastivadin (Vaibhashika) theory that the initial objects of perceptual awareness are aggregates of atoms (as variegated wholes not yet distinguished from the individual atoms that make them up). There is no conceptual construction yet involved, says Dignaga (Hattori, *Dignaga on Perception*, pp. 26–27, with notes). This seems to contradict the *Alambanapariksha* and PS 2d–e; Dharmakirti PV 3.194–230 makes use of a Sautrantika distinction to fit: "Individual atoms, which are imperceptible, come to possess, when they gather together, a pre-eminent quality...which enables them to present a certain form in a cognition" (Hattori, p. 90). See also Matilal, *Perception*, pp. 365–66.

in the rigorous sense]. The water-jug and so forth are conventionally real *because if the atoms are taken away, the awareness of their form is destroyed.* In the case of what is [in a different way] rigorously real, such as color and so forth, even when one has taken away what is connected with it, there is no removal of the awareness of the color itself. Therefore it follows that the field of operation of the sensory awareness is not an external object.[21]

Sensations as such are rigorously real. Although they and the perception or cognition they support seem to be external, they are internal to us. So we are perceptually aware only of appearances or phenomena, which are related inductively to their unperceivable external causes. Even granted that there may be such causes, there can be no intelligible idea of the resemblance between them and the perceptions believed to follow from them. In theory, without atoms there would be no awareness of any forms, but we are nevertheless aware of phenomena alone:

> The support [the awareness of the real] is just that which occurs internally, appearing to be external in the absence of an external object, because it has the characteristic of awareness itself, and because it is the causal condition of awareness.[22]

Now we go on to Dignaga's conception of inference. This, too, is knowledge, but of the necessarily erroneous kind. As compared with perceptual awareness, which is vivid, exact, particular, and in itself impossible to express in words, inference is vague, inexact, general, and expressible in words. The particular, grasped by perceptual awareness, is by nature nonverbal. But perceptual awareness, though exact, can give us no general knowledge. General knowledge pertains not only to the smoke, for instance, that we see but to the fire that we do not see but associate with the smoke, and, as well, to other instances of the association of smoke with fire. Such general, inferential knowledge (reasoning) allows us to name the particular by means of a word or universal. But a word or universal, though useful, has no reality of its own. This is because there cannot be anything real that, like a universal, is both indivisible and present in many individuals. That is to say, it is not possible for us to know individuals completely enough to be sure what qualifies them to be put under the same universal. The most we can do is to use an inferential sign (*linga*), a reason or an evidence (*hetu*) by which it can be known that smoke, for example, generally indicates a fiery place. The inference is based, of course, on rules of association: the inferential sign must mark whatever is being argued over (smoke must mark the place where, it is argued, there is fire); the inferential sign must be *known* to be at or be associated with at least one place with the property being argued (there must be at least one acknowleged instance of the association of smoke with a fiery place); and the inferential sign must *not* be known to be associated with any place where the property being argued over is absent (there must not be an acknowledged instance of the association of smoke with a place from which fire is absent)—this Indian way of formulating the problem of induction has already been described, but we should remember that Dignaga preceded Udayana and Gangesha by centuries.*

According to Dignaga's scheme, a single positive association is enough for an inference, because as long as all instances of smoke are produced by *some* fire, it does not matter if some fires do not produce smoke. The negative criterion (the nonoccurrence of smoke in the absence of fire) is more difficult to meet, but it is essential, Dignaga emphasizes, both in making judgments for oneself and in proving things to others.[23] Obviously, the criterion of nonperception (doesn't it require still another inference?) cannot be fully met because there is an endless number of possible instances of lack of association between the inferential sign and the "arguable property." In emphasizing it, does Dignaga mean only to show that the process of inference, though so useful, has practical limits, which fall short of certainty? Or does his account, by showing how fallible inference must be, have a skeptical intention?[24] In relation to Dignaga's account, the first answer seems more likely to me.[25] But I do not think that the contrast needs to be drawn, because such pragmatism and skepticism are two faces of the usual Buddhist coin.

To Dignaga, the process of acquiring knowledge by means of inference and by means of words is the same. The analogy between inferring and making use of words (and the universals they signify) is this: When I apply the same word, such as *fire*, to the particular instances of the fire that I perceive, I know that the instances belong to the same group: the linguistic sign *fire* produces general knowledge just as an inferential sign does. What we know about something when we hear a word applied to it is essentially the same as what we infer about it by other means.[26]

---

*In paraphrase, Dignaga's position is that a reliable judgment requires that "1. The inferential sign must be a property of the subject of the inference. That is, there exists in the subject of the inference a property, which is different from the inferable property and which is furthermore evident to the person drawing the inference . . . 2. The inferential sign must be known to occur in at least one locus, other than the subject of inference, in which the inferable property occurs. 3. The inferential sign must not be known to occur in *any* other loci in which the inferable property is absent" (Hayes, *Dignaga on the Interpretation of Signs,* p. 153; see also Franco, "Valid Reason, True Sign").

In agreement with Bhartrihari, whose work he knows, Dignaga says that an isolated word has no meaning in itself. The true bearer of meaning is the entire sentence; an individual word is a conceptual entity abstracted from the sentence.[27] But to Dignaga, unlike Bhartrihari, the knowledge that words give is not different from what is learned by means of inference. This is because a word, having a broad range of meanings, is by nature ambiguous, and also because it by nature signifies nothing positive.

Why nothing positive? With words as with inference, says Dignaga, exclusion is the key. A word gets all of its meaning by excluding everything to which it is not meant to refer. Take, for example, the word *blue*, which, in accord with its conceptual structure, signifies only the exclusion of everything that is not blue. As Bhartrihari, anticipating Dignaga, puts it: When we perceive similarities in nonidentical objects, we give them abstract, identical names. This unity-by-name depends on the process of exclusion (*apoha*) of the objects' differences, that is, on the disregard of what is distinctive in them.[28] Luckily, in order to know something, as we do, by means of exclusion, it is not necessary for us to go through *all* the instances that could be excluded. This doctrine of definition by exclusion leaves—as we, not Bhartrihari, may add—a certain aura of incompleteness or a priorism, because the process by which we identify or name things is most usually incomplete.

At this point, the partial similarity between Bhartrihari and Dignaga ends. This is because, as a Buddhist, Dignaga is committed to believe in the fundamental inability of words to represent reality, whereas Bhartrihari insists that it is the reality of language that lends reality to everything else. While Bhartrihari is the ultimate "realist" with respect to language, the Buddhists are convinced nominalists or, at most, conceptualists. Dignaga points out that names (nouns) are necessarily inexact because it is impossible to verify whether all the instances characterized by a name do, in fact, fit it. A word cannot do simultaneous justice, he says, to a preconceived idea and to different actual individuals. Bhartrihari's preestablished similarity requires the metaphysical fitness of words to what they designate. Dignaga finds this to be implausible, even ridiculous.[29]

Dharmakirti softens Dignaga's conception of the process of knowing by declaring that negation must be supplemented by affirmation. He also thinks that it is wrong to confine inference to the observation of instances of copresence (association) and coabsence (dissociation). He writes as if he accepts the criteria proposed by Dignaga, but he goes well beyond him and says categorically that invariable comcomitance "is neither due to the observation [of two things together] nor to the non-observation [of two things together]."[30]

By so restricting the relation, Dharmakirti moves from Dignaga's noncommittal, correlational view of sequences of events to a metaphysically more committed view. This shift, meant to ensure that concomitances are really necessary, is made in terms of the Sautrantika doctrine of point-instants, which Dharmakirti accepts and develops. Both philosophers are interested in what is or might in some sense be a precursor to what is conceptually structured and external: Dignaga explores the consequences of belief in perceptually inaccessible atoms without (I think) either accepting or denying their existence. Dharmakirti feels it necessary to believe in point-instants (atoms, if they exist, are among them) because, unless they are posited, we cannot understand what causes anything or why things appear, change, and vanish. But our explicit ways of grasping or describing the point-instants are no more than relative.

In explaining views in which Dharmakirti goes considerably beyond Dignaga, I begin with the conception of the (point-)instant or *kshana*, which is the instantaneous particular or *svalakshana*. I then go on to Dharmakirti's inference that establishes the nature of the causal tie, to his explanation of ordinary, continuous perception, and to his pragmatism, by which I mean, his view that universals, words, and inferences are primarily aids to purposeful human action.

The point-instant: To exist, Dharmakirti believes, is also to be effective. He accepts the Sautrantika conception of the point-instant, a self-contained particular that perishes immediately because it exists and exists because it perishes immediately. Endowment with existence, Dharmakirti repeats, is identical with instant perishability. In identifying existence with efficacy and efficacy with instantaneous appearance/vanishing, Dharmakirti lays an axiomatic basis for the Buddhist belief that nothing ever endures (except in the sense that nirvana is out of time) or is ever, if more than a *dharma* or point-instant, a true unity. But although the point-instant is all there really is in the world, it is, in a sense, out of this world, or, more accurately, out because it is so deep within. This is because it resembles nothing at all and has neither temporal nor spatial dimensions. As a point of pure existence, an existence-point, each *svalakshana* is unique. It must be unique because to exist is to be independent, meaning, to have no dependence on or relations with anything else at all (unless otherness counts as a relation). And since to exist is also to be effective, each existence-point is also an efficacy-point or causality-point. Outside of time, space, and comparison, the point-instant is of course described as indescribable, despite all the terms, positive and negative, by which it is described.[31]

Following Dignaga, Dharmakirti makes the claim that it is possible for everyone to experience that perceptual awareness can precede naming and so be free of concepts and unattached to memory. To show this, he suggests an experiment in introspection:

> When I withdraw my thought from everything, though I still every inward motion, my eye nevertheless sees a color. This is a [pure, indeterminate] perception. When afterwards I perceive again, [because the perception was not determinate] I do not consciously think, "I had a similar perception." (Dharmakirti, *Pramāṇavārttika*, 3.123-25)[32]

Pure, indeterminate awareness is vivid (error, too, can be so). When awareness is not pure, when one not merely senses something but thinks of it, the reflection of the object in awareness is vague. This vagueness or blurring is evidence that the object of awareness is now constructed by thought. Only the pure, vivid perceptual awareness has a unique particular as its object.[33]

As Buddhism teaches, everything in our ordinary world is impermanent and perishes. This empirical observation is explained, says Dharmakirti, by what we cannot observe but must assume—the invariably immediate perishing of the point-instant. We see this if we ask ourselves what the reason can be for the perishability of the objects of ordinary experience. If the perishability of a jar, for instance, is not inherent in the jar itself, the reason for its perishability must be either the jar's cause or its effect. If it is the jar's cause, it must, like all causes, exist immediately before its effect. But how can a jar's perishability—its breakage, perhaps, by falling—exist before the jar does? And if the jar's perishability—its breaking by someone—is regarded as the effect of the jar's existence, this breaking is not a natural, sufficient cause. For the jar to be broken by someone there must be other contributory conditions—a weak grasp, a slippery hand, a hard floor—so that the breaking is not a *necessary* cause of the jar's perishability. That is, one cannot infer from the nature of the pot as a pot that it is necessarily breakable. But as everyone admits, pots, like other products, are inherently perishable, so the perishability must be inherent in the pot not simply because it is a pot but simply because it exists.

Ordinary people are not aware that, in a philosophical sense, a jar does not persist in time. Instead, it is a temporal succession of jars, that is, of jar-instants; and the jar's natural perishability can be explained only by the constant perishing of the point-instants that are the jar's reality. The basis of the inference that the jar must perish is the identity of nature, which is to say, the identity of the jar's existence with that of point-instants, whose very existence is their perishing.[34]

Inferring the nature of the causal tie: As we see, the conclusion that perishability is inherent in things depends on the inference that the point-instants are their causes. This brings us to the subject of causality in general, or, rather, to the inference by which we establish what the nature of the causal tie must be. Dharmakirti recalls Dignaga's triple test for inference (he himself has a five-stage test). In relation to the stock smoke-fire example the test is: (1) that smoke is generally known to be a property of fire, (2) that smoke is perceived to occur where fire occurs, and (3) that smoke is perceived not to occur where fire does not occur (as in a lake).[35] Dignaga's test is satisfied by the inference that fire is the cause of smoke, Dharmakirti says. Continuing with this example, he repeats various objections and gives them all answers.

An established causality is a stable relationship. Random departures from it are implausible. Even if smoke is observed rising from some anthill (used in Vedic fire sacrifices), it is unreasonable to claim that an anthill produces smoke (or we must conclude that the anthill has the nature of fire). This is because smoke does *not* not arise—or does *also* not arise—in the anthill's absence. Because the anthill is not by nature capable of producing smoke, any smoke that (in the absence of fire) would arise from it would be causeless. But maybe, says the objector, there could be an effect similar to smoke with a cause qualitatively different from that of fire. A Buddhist, intimates the objector, does not regard smoke as one and the same but as a series of similar smoke-moments.

Dharmakirti answers: Whatever the differences between different kinds or moments of smoke, the cause of all smoke is always fire, so, in principle, nothing but smoke can be genuinely similar to smoke and nothing but fire can be its cause. What springs from a qualitatively different cause must be different. If similar effects could spring from dissimilar causes, causal effectiveness would be impossible to determine and none of the many forms and varieties of things in the world would have their own particular causes. Then "all things might come into existence from all things."[36]

Dharmakirti goes on, slowly, carefully, laboriously: If something was uncaused, it would be independent of all influences or conditions. It would exist perpetually or arise spontaneously, without a cause, or would not exist at all. The fact that things go in and out of existence is the result, we know, of their dependence on circumstances. Therefore, the occurrence of smoke in a particular way at a particular place and time, and its absence even a single time—because of insufficient conditions—shows an exact, that is, causal, dependence. If the tie to conditions was not so close, the fire would not occur there even once. Smoke is that which has its specific character determined by certain specific conditions. And, conversely,

> the cause must also be possessed of the character of producing
> the effect of such description. If the smoke were to be gener-

ated in any other condition (than fire), it (fire) would not be possessed of the character of being cause. (And consequently) it would not be able to produce smoke even for once. Nor again would the effect be smoke. (Dharmakirti, *Pramāṇavārttika*, verse 1.35, comm.)[37]

So it is the nature of fire to serve as the cause of smoke. "If smoke was brought into existence by what is not the cause of smoke, it (smoke) would be tantamount to an uncaused event."[38] Of course, there are many conditions that contribute to the appearance of smoke or any other effect. Only the combined total, the whole causal complex, of all the relevant conditions or subcauses has causal capacity. The combination of conditions varies and accounts, for example, for the qualitative differences between plants of the same species.[39]

Concomitance in agreement and in difference shows that one thing is the necessary consequent of another or, in other words, that no effect can derive its being from anything other than the cause. The conclusion is that the necessity of the causal relation or concomitance is established by as little as

a single instance of observation and non-observation (as set forth in the five stages) . . . It cannot be determined by the empirical knowledge of co-presence and co-absence, because that would require the observation of concomitance in agreement and concomitance in difference in each and all cases (which is humanly impossible). (Dharmakirti, *Pramāṇavārttika*, verse 38, comm.)[40]

Ordinary, continuous perception: Our sense of the continuing identity of the things we perceive is the result of the illusion of continuity produced by the corresponding sequences of point-instants. Perhaps there is an intermediate between the point-instant and the named sequence, with its apparent continuity in space and time. As has been said, Dignaga speaks, though without explaining much, of "mental perception." Taking the cue from Dharmakirti, Dignaga's commentator explains "mental perception" as the mind's still preconceptual awareness whose object is derived from the object—such as the unnamed, unlocated blue—of the just-preceding sensory awareness.

Having explained, this commentator is faced with an objection: If the sound mind of a blind person can by "mental perception" bypass the sense of sight, why is the blind man not aware of the same object, the color, of which the seeing man is aware? The answer is that a mental perception is conditioned by the just-preceding sensory perception, for which reason the blind and deaf have neither sensory nor mental perception. The presumed process is this: A purely sensory awareness disappears and gives rise to a "mental perception." This second awareness, itself too brief to admit error or be described, evokes the image of its object, for example, a blue patch of color. A prominent commentator insists that there are no facts to prove that there really is such a mental awareness. It is only a postulate of Dharmakirti's system.[41] But obviously, it would not be useful as a postulate unless it suggested how the unbridgeable chasm between sensory awareness and conceptual construction could be crossed.

Whatever the unbridgeable chasm that precedes it, a perception of a nameable kind is composed of an ordered sequence of moments of perceptual awareness. Each of these moments is the effect of all the cooperating factors of the preceding moment: of previous knowledge, of senses, of the object of the perception, of the quality of attention directed at the object, and of the condition of the perceptual medium or mediums—light, sound, odor, and so on.[42] Since nothing real endures, no moment in a perceptual series overlaps any earlier or later moment. Therefore the cause of the emergence of, say, a sprout from a seed cannot be the seed as a persisting entity or even the sequence of seed-moments. All but the last of the moments have vanished. Therefore the cause can be only the immediately preceding moment, the last, just-vanishing/vanished seed-moment, with all its attendant conditions—momentary earth, momentary water, momentary heat, and so on (everything equally momentary).[43] The perception that results must resemble its object, that is, "possess" the object's form. Therefore, in agreement with Dignaga, Dharmakirti gives the object of knowledge the following definition: The object of knowledge is the cause of knowledge that is capable of projecting its image into knowledge (Dignaga uses the definition to show that nothing, including atoms, can really be such a cause).[44]

Universals, words, inferences, and the empirical world: In itself, perception grasps every object in its distinctive individuality. This individuality is the reflection of the uniqueness of each of the moments of the perceived sequence, a uniqueness sustained by a particular local constellation of attendant circumstances. So the objects or entities we perceive cannot be identical with one another and cannot assimilate mutual identity into their uniqueness.

Nyaya-Vaisheshika philosophers contend that entities are the same by virtue of the class character common to them. This class character—such as cowness—is inherently inseparable from all the individuals of the same kind and is the ontological entity that distinguishes them from individuals of all other kinds. That is, it makes the individuals be of the kind they are, and its existence cannot be distinguished from theirs. But, asks

Dharmakirti, if the entities are identical with a common universal, they have no other identity, no identity of their own, and they lose their distinctiveness. If it is argued that the universal, although one, appears to be different because of the individuality of the individuals in which it inheres, the answer is that, if so, the universal is not identical with them but different. And if it is argued that each universal has its own self-character, it cannot have the character of the individuals in which it is supposed to inhere.[45] The argument continues, all rather as in the medieval European debates on universals.

From Dharmakirti's standpoint, what follows is that entities are by their own nature different from one another, and because they are different, they themselves can in no way be the source of the similarity of things—of fires to fires, pots to pots, cows to cows. The source of the similarity is conceptual construction:

> Our understanding appears to take stock of the universal by connecting the individuals . . . It never cognizes the individuals as related to one common entity. . . As the relation of inherence is too subtle, it escapes notice and so the universal appears as identical with the individual. And this (apparent perception of identity) is downright error. (Dharmakirti, *Pramāṇavārttika*, 1.42, comm.)[46]

The universal, says Dharmakirti, is not perceived as such and is not numerically different from the individual object. It misleads by its uniformity, because what is real cannot be comprehended by a single word or single judgment: There is always some other aspect left to be comprehended by another word or judgment.[47] However, each of the specific properties of the object is grasped in its general form by the conceptual judgment that follows a perceptual awareness. The perceptual awareness is the core of the encountered reality and the conceptual construction is the unreal image of that awareness. The reality, the object-moment, evokes the appearance of universals and the judgment that this that we see is a seed and that this something else we see is of the same kind, also a seed.

By judging that what we are aware of belongs to the seed-kind, or pot-kind, or fire-kind, we form an expectation based on experience. The expectation is that the seed, like all seeds, can produce a plant, the pot, like all pots, can contain milk, and the fire, like all fires, can cook a meal. So in judging what things are of what kinds, we determine what human purposes a particular sensed continuum can serve. When the image is identified with the perceptual awareness, we make the perceptual judgment, the determination (*adhyavayasa*) that "this is a pot." The word *this* refers to the unique, unnameable awareness; and the word *pot* gives the perception a class name or universal that is applicable to all pots and relevant to all actions involving pots. By such judgments, we construct the world of objects in which we conventionally live.[48] The judgment, which grasps an object in terms of its universal properties, is inherently indirect, partial, and essentially misleading; and yet it is only by its means that we are enabled to get what we want and avoid what we do not want.[49]

Knowing this, we can refine our understanding of the common aim, the difference, and the mutuality of the two means of knowledge, perception and inference. To begin with, we can give a double characterization of *means of knowledge (pramana)*: First, it is noncontradictory knowledge. Second, it is what reveals a previously unknown object.[50] The noncontradictoriness of the knowledge is its ability to fulfill a human purpose. That is, a means of knowledge promotes an action the results of which do not contradict the perception or the inference on which the action is based. The knowledge of the location of water by means of sound perceptual awareness or by means of adequate inference leads us to the water, and real water—unlike mirage water—satisfies our thirst.[51]*

Dharmakirti's characterization of *pramana* as "that which reveals what was not known before" excludes mere recognition and memory, that is, it excludes perceptual judgment. To know, as perceptual judgment makes known, that something is a pot is to use memory to identify what has been identified before. Perceptual judgment gives no new information. Perceptual awareness, however, is of a momentary, unique particular. It can reveal *only* what is new; and because what such awareness reveals is accurate, it gives us essential pragmatic guidance.

Perceptual awareness is by nature free of error (Dharmakirti accepts this only, as said before, if it is not illusory). In contrast, inference is always susceptible to error. Inference is said to be contradictory when we make a misjudgment, such as mistaking a shell's glitter for the glitter of silver, and are led to a result that contradicts what we anticipated. Perceptual judgment identifies the abstract class to which an object belongs. The

---

*With Dharmakirti and like-minded Buddhists, Nietzsche believes that we are able to get along in a practical sense only by making the essentially misleading but conventional judgment that things are identical. "There is in every judgment," Nietzsche writes, "the avowal of having encountered an 'identical case'; it therefore presupposes comparison with the aid of memory. The judgment does not produce the appearance of an identical case. Rather it believes one: it works under the presupposition that identical cases exist" (Nietzsche, *The Will to Power*, trans. W. Kaufman, New York: Random House, 1967, p. 289, [section 532]).

Again essentially like Dharmakirti, Nietzche says: "The utility of preservation—not some abstract-theoretical need not to be deceived—stands as the motive behind the development of the organs of knowledge—they develop in such a way that their observations suffice for our preservation" (ibid., *The Will to Power*, section 480, Kaufman, 1967, pp. 266–67).

process of inference does far more. From a sign, the smoke perceived somewhere, we call up the memory of the invariable connection of smoke with fire, and then we infer a fire at that particular site. This process combines perceptual and conceptual knowledge to satisfy an expectation: If we go to the site, we will find a fire previously unknown to us, a fire that produces just the kind of smoke by which we inferred its presence. The inference misleads us by the generalization it involves, but it is based on real smoke (smoke-moments) and leads to a real, particular fire.[52] So what is in a deep sense misleading can be the source of mundane truth, and, in the end, perhaps lead beyond it.

I return from these philosophical details to a general characterization of Dignaga and Dharmakirti. All told, Dignaga makes the impression that he is more interested in understanding than in winning victories. Maybe he is as a whole skeptical, although less completely and much less obtrusively than Nagarjuna. In the same way as Vasubandhu, his Idealistic predecessor, Dignaga says (though not invariably) that sensation gives knowledge of phenomena but not of the external objects, such as atoms, that we conceive to be their causes. Logic, which corrects logical errors, provides no independent constructive truths. As Dignaga holds, only perception and inference are reliable means of knowledge, and, of these, inference is by nature erroneous and, even so, must often be incomplete. It should follow that both unwritten tradition, based on a succession of witnesses, and scriptures are also fallible.

It is unlikely that Dignaga ever says anything of this kind about Buddhist tradition and scriptures. However, what he says of non-Buddhists (the Samkhya) makes it at least possible that he believes that the correctness of statements concerning metaphysical, religious, and moral doctrines can be judged only by means of experience or of rightly constructed arguments.[53] The basic standards always remain those of experience and reason.

But even if we assume Dignaga to be close to skepticism with respect to religious dogma, we can ask whether he was a skeptic of a believing kind (as I have taken Nagarjuna to be) or a skeptic like Sextus Empiricus. A skeptic like Sextus would be a Buddhist to whom nirvana is only the overcoming, in the present life, of the absurd certainties and appetites that cause suffering and keep us from the peace of understanding.[54] This hypothetically skeptical Dignaga is a doctrinally modest, contemporary one to match a similarly doctrinally modest, contemporary Nagarjuna. But how then is one to take Dignaga's opening invocation to the Compendium of the Means of Knowledge and his following explanation? Are the traditional honorific epithets he applies to Buddha only a convention he feels he has to follow? Or does he, or does Dharmakirti in expounding him, try to use the traditional epithets and their relationships to hint at a Buddha who is not more than a powerfully humane and immaculately reasonable but still human person? True, by calling the Buddha "the personification of the means of cognition," Dignaga justifies his own kind of philosophizing. But what, other than convention, may he be referring to when he recalls the Buddha's perfections, the Buddha's purpose to benefit all living beings, the Buddha's perfect distance from the phenomenal world, and the Buddha's nature as a protector who saves the world?

Dharmakirti is willing to accept the authority of scriptures, at least Buddhist scriptures, when they give information on doctrines that cannot be confirmed by direct induction. He argues the matter in the second chapter of his *Commentary*, where he expands on Dignaga's praise of the Buddha as the personification of the means of cognition or authority (*pramana-bhuta*). For the words to be considered reliable, it must be shown that their speaker has consistently spoken the truth and has something to teach that goes beyond direct experience, the teaching's truthfulness being guaranteed by the teacher's freedom from egoistic goals. Omniscience is important to us in that it teaches us what is necessary in order to release beings from their suffering, not in that it informs us of facts irrelevant to release, such as the number of all the worms in the world.[55]

Only someone who has experienced the causes of suffering can teach how to be liberated from suffering. And the deepest knowledge and deepest compassion are the same. To Dharmakirti, compassion is therefore the virtue that provides the motivation for practicing all the other virtues. The Buddha was able to reach perfection in this trait only through practice in many methods during innumerable lives. And so, the Buddha's teaching stems from someone who by the changes he underwent shows that he does not lie and shows by his message that he knows the saving truth supremely well.[56]*

---

*In the beginning of his commentary to the *Compendium*, Dignaga, the confirmed logician, puts five epithets of the Buddha into relation with one another. To explain Dignaga's scheme, Dharmakirti (or perhaps another Buddhist commentator) tries to show that each of the last four is a necessary condition for the following one. This enables him to infer the epithets from each other in the following order: Because the Buddha is a protector, as is evident from his revelation of the four noble truths, he is a knower. This is expressed in the epithet *sugata*—its root *gam*, *to know,* and its prefix *su, well*—which has three meanings. These three meanings show that the Buddha's knowledge is true, lasting, and complete. Because he has far more knowledge than is necessary for an ordinary *arhat*, the Buddha is a "teacher." And because he is a teacher, that is, one who exerts himself for the sake of others, he is full of compassion, that is, seeks the benefit of all living beings, something he is able to do, no doubt, because he has gained a full understanding of the causes of their suffering, which is to say, a full understanding of causality. And because of all four epithets taken together, the Buddha is a means of valid cognition or authority. (See Franco, "Was the Buddha a Buddha?" p. 83; and "Yet Another Look . . ."; and *Dharmakīrti on Compassion and Rebirth*.)

Kant (1724–1804)

*If appearances are things in themselves,
then freedom cannot be saved.*

Immanuel Kant was the son of poor parents whom he remembered all his life as paragons of decency.[57] During his years as a private tutor and as a *Privatdozent* at the University of Königsberg, with no salary but only his own students' fees, he remained oppressively poor. In 1770 he was appointed professor of logic and metaphysics at the university, where he remained all his academic life. As was then required, he lectured on a variety of subjects other than his own specialties, and his interests remained very wide. His early philosophical project was to create a scientific compromise between a Leibnizian and a Newtonian point of view. By his own account, he was awakened by two philosophers: Hume, whom he opposed, and Rousseau, over whom he was enthusiastic. It was Newton, he said, who laid bare the order and regularity of the external world, and Rousseau who discovered the hidden nature of man.[58]

In his physical prime, Kant was described as serene, lively, and witty, but he grew increasingly, even obsessively, rigid and distinctly misanthropic. His early publications, mostly on science, include *The General Natural History and Theory of the Heavens*, in which he argues that the solar system originated in a nebula and that our galaxy is only one of an infinite number of others. Years of intensive silent work were reflected in his *Critique of Pure Reason*, which came out first in 1781 and was republished, in part rewritten, in 1787. In Germany, after a few years of indifference, it gained him enormous if puzzled fame, only increased by his many later publications. These include two further "critiques"—*Critique of Practical Reason* (1788) and *Critique of Judgment* (1790)—and *Religion within the Bounds of Pure Reason* (1793). The last of these aroused the King of Prussia to forbid Kant to publish anything more on religion on the grounds that he was undermining the Scriptures and Christianity. Kant's later books include *On Eternal Peace* (1795) and the *Metaphysic of Morals* (1797). He also left behind disordered fragments of an ambitious work that his editors call *Opus Postumum*.

Kant is surely a great philosopher, but, as he acknowledges, his greatest book, *The Critique of Pure Reason*, is often obscure. He excuses himself by saying that he worked out his ideas painstakingly for twelve successive years but composed his book quickly. To have achieved clarity, Kant writes in a letter,

> I would have needed a few more years instead of the four or five months I took to complete the book out of fear that such

an extensive project would finally become a burden, were I to linger any more, and that my advancing years (I am already sixty) would perhaps make it impossible to finish the whole system that I still have in my mind. And I am now actually satisfied with my decision, as the work stands, to such an extent that I should not wish it unwritten for any price, though neither would I want to take on again for any price the labors that it took to produce it. People will get over the initial numbness caused unavoidably by a mass of unfamiliar concepts and an even more unfamiliar language (which new language is nonetheless indispensable).[59]

Because Kant's use of terminology is inconsistent, interpreters find it relatively easy to support contrary interpretations. However, he makes his basic intentions quite clear. This is especially true of the preface to the second edition, meant to clear up the misunderstandings that had greeted the book's first publication. In this preface he says that philosophers have so far assumed that our knowledge must conform to objects. But metaphysics is an isolated kind of speculation that has not yet found itself the secure path of a science; it is a battleground well suited for those who prefer to engage in mock combats in which there is never any lasting victory. This is because philosophy extends its concepts beyond all possible experience and fails to arrive at any acceptable proofs.[60]

Metaphysics may be more successful, Kant says, if we try out a Copernican idea and shift our interest from the objects we observe to the spectator who makes the observations. His own Copernican hypothesis is that we human beings know the nature of objects a priori, prior to experience, because objects must conform to the faculty by which we intuit them. And because intuitions need concepts to become knowable, Kant goes on, he assumes that our experience of objects also conforms to our concepts, and not, as previously assumed, that the concepts conform to the objects.[61]

This hypothesis makes use of a new method of thought, Kant declares, which is modeled on the scientist's method—the search for elements of pure reason that allows confirmation or refutation by experiment. Kant has long come to prefer the Newtonian way of beginning with evident knowledge and working back from it to its principles.[62] However, unlike a scientist's experiment, this philosophical experiment cannot be made with the objects of experience, because pure reason goes beyond all possibility of experiential proof. Instead, the experiment singles out and explains the concepts that precede experience and make experience at all possible. The experiment also singles out and explains the principles that isolated reason uses in order to arrive at objects that, by transcending the limits of experience, are nothing more than thought.[63]

One viewpoint is that of the concepts that, together with sensation, make experience possible. The other viewpoint is that of the principles by which reason tries to go beyond possible experience. If the distinction between the two viewpoints yields a consistent, reasonable philosophy, and if, when the distinction is ignored, a single viewpoint involves reason in unavoidable conflict with itself, "the experiment decides in favor of the correctness of this distinction."[64]

Kant continues: My proposal is, therefore, to limit philosophy to what does not transcend the limits of possible experience and

> leave the thing in itself as indeed real *per se*, but as not known by us. For what necessarily forces us to transcend the limits of experience and of all appearances is the *unconditioned*, which reason, by necessity and by right, demands in things in themselves, as required to complete the series of conditions. (*Critique of Pure Reason* Bxx)[65]

Kant goes on: If we learn to assume that it is *we* whose intuitions present the world and *we* whose concepts form the world, we can allow pure speculative reason latitude in choosing the objects of its thought. We will then be able to turn metaphysics into a science, on condition that we assign pure reason the task of measuring itself and discovering the a priori powers the thinking subject derives from himself. This is possible because metaphysics is based on logic and therefore deals only with abstract principles. Therefore metaphysics can study itself and learn its limits without drawing on empirical experience. The advantage of a definitive, critically purified science of metaphysics is, first of all, negative, because it warns us never to speculate beyond the limits of experience. But this narrowing of the role of pure speculative reason will give freedom to "the absolutely necessary *practical* employment of pure reason—the *moral*—in which it inevitably goes beyond the limits of sensibility."[66]

In defense of his philosophy, Kant declares that the *Critique* has a positive effect: When it is clear to us that we cannot *know* things in themselves by proving their possibility in either an empirical or a priori way, we are freed to *think* whatever we like about them, provided only that we keep our concepts possible by not contradicting ourselves. When we get to understand that the object of experience can be taken in a double sense, as appearance and as thing in itself, we can accept the principle of causality as true of appearances and, at the same time, accept freedom as true of the thing in itself. It will then be clear that there is no contradiction in supposing that the will is necessarily subject to the laws of nature in its visible acts and, in that sense, is "*not free*, while yet, as belonging to a thing in itself, it is not subject to that law, and is therefore *free* . . . Though I cannot *know*, I can yet *think* freedom."[67]

The ability to think human freedom is of the utmost practical importance in Kant's eyes. It is so important, he says, because it does not have to be proved but has only to be thinkable—not contradict itself—and put no obstacles in the way of a free act. Freed of impossible proofs, we can think (in our critical, nonmetaphysical way) of God, freedom, and immortality. These three ideas are hard to resist because they are natural: The idea of a wise, great Creator is natural because it comes from the order, beauty, and providential care that all nature displays. The idea of freedom is natural because it comes from the duties we impose on ourselves—in opposition to our inclinations. And the hope of a future life is natural because it comes from our inability to be satisfied with what is temporal. Dogmatic, uncritical metaphysics, which tries to prove what it cannot, has no room for such unproved but necessary beliefs. The very effort of metaphysics to prove something and its repeated failure to do so lead to radical and destructive philosophical views—materialism, fatalism, atheism, and fanaticism. The effort and failure also cause the philosophies of what Kant calls idealism and skepticism (idealism is exemplified by Descartes's *I am* and Berkeley's view that spatial objects are imaginary; and skepticism is exemplified by Hume's skeptical censorship of reason). "I have therefore found it necessary," says Kant, "to deny *knowledge*, in order to make room for *faith*."[68]

It is faith that allows us to use pure (unempirical) reason to give us beliefs beyond empirical validation. Hence the ideas of soul, world, and God, which are neither innate nor learned from experience but pure, "transcendental" (unempirical) ideas resulting from pure (unempirical) reasons that drive us to complete the synthesis our understanding has begun. So reason drives us, beyond what we can prove, to the belief that each of us has an *I*, a thinking nature or soul that is associated with other real things outside it. And reason drives us to believe that all things have a purposive unity. Science itself exists by virtue of the belief that things fit together and have, in the large and small, reasons for being *what* they are and *as* they are. "The assumption of a supreme intelligence, as the one and only cause of the universe, though in the idea alone, can therefore always benefit reason and never injure it."[69]

And so we see, Kant argues, that pure reason, which in unlimited metaphysics tries and fails to extend our knowledge beyond the limits of experience, can be understood as giving us purely regulative principles. These principles prescribe greater unity to experience than we can prove by our empirical understanding, and they place the goal of understanding so high that it can "carry its agreement with itself, by means of systematic unity, to the highest possible degree."[70]

It is at this conclusion that the *Critique of Pure Reason* is aimed. But even if its conclusion is not accepted, its mode of analysis and synthesis remains of great interest. To show this, I turn to its first part. In this part, Kant distinguishes (as will be explained) between knowledge that is "pure" or a priori and knowledge that is empirical or a posteriori, and then between knowledge that is analytic and knowledge that is synthetic. He then takes up what he calls *transcendental aesthetic* (*transcendental* meaning *beyond possible experience*, and *aesthetic* meaning *concerning perception or sensation*). Under this heading he deals with the two (he thinks) preconceptual forms of perception, space and time. Then he turns to the *transcendental logic*, by which he means the understanding and its pure concepts. The twofold distinction between transcendental aesthetic and transcendental logic corresponds to the basic distinction on which Kant, as he says, bases his whole "experiment" in reasoning.*

To begin at the beginning: Kant defines a priori knowledge as knowledge absolutely independent of all experience. The surest criterion of a priori knowledge is that it is necessary and universal. Any of the propositions of mathematics is a good example. Another is the proposition "Every effect must have a cause." In this case, the relationship between the subject of the proposition, *effect*, and its object, *cause*, is necessary because the meaning of *effect* includes that of relation to a *cause*—that is, analysis of the concept of *effect* reveals that it is determined by relation to *cause*. Such an a priori judgment is therefore called *analytic*. In contrast, in the similar-sounding judgment "Everything that happens has its cause," the cognition of the subject, *everything*, includes nothing about cause, so what follows—that it (everything) must have its cause—joins an additional meaning to that of *everything* and creates a synthesis of two independent concepts. Such a judgment is therefore *synthetic*, or, more completely, *synthetic a priori*.[71] These distinctions are needed because all of speculative metaphysics is made up of synthetic a priori judgments, so that our inquiry can be concentrated in the single question, How are a priori synthetic judgments possible?[72]

---

*It may not be helpful to begin by paying much attention to the formal structure of the *Critique of Pure Reason*. Its two basic divisions correspond to the twofold distinction on which Kant basis his "experiment." The two divisions are the Transcendental Doctrine of Elements and the Transcendental Dialectic. The Transcendental Doctrine of Elements has two parts: the Transcendental Aesthetic, which is divided into two sections—space, and time—and the Transcendental Logic, which is divided into four subjects (for some reason, Kant does not call them *sections*), the names of which I refrain from repeating.

Kant continues: To further our inquiry concerning the a priori, we should investigate how we make the a priori synthetic judgments of mathematics, exact science, and philosophy. We should ask how—by what apparatus and laws of thought—pure mathematics and the pure science of nature is possible and, with the greatest pertinence to philosophy, how metaphysics is possible, whether as a natural human disposition or as a science.[73]

As a natural disposition, metaphysics has always become dogmatic and self-contradictory. Knowing this, we should turn away from dogmatism, which leads to contradictions and, by these contradictions, to skepticism. Instead of dogmatizing, we should study how metaphysics is possible as a critical science, that is, how it is limited by our possible experience. From all this, says Kant, we are led to the idea of a special science that can be called *Critique of Pure Reason*.[74] By examining all *transcendental* knowledge—knowledge occupied with the possibility of knowing objects a priori—this science can limit and clarify our reason and keep it free of errors.

Kant now goes on to the *transcendental aesthetic*, in which he takes up the nature and effects of "intuition." By *intuition* he means the immediacy, the directness and vividness, through which all modes of knowledge are related (in a particular, not a general way) to their objects.* He makes the cardinal point that everything we "intuit," that is, everything we sense, is grasped as occurring in space and in time. How so? With respect to space, we grasp things as spatial by means of the *outer sense*, which represents objects as outside ourselves, in other words, as out in space, where they have shapes, sizes, and relative positions, the invariable characteristics of all spatial things. Space cannot be a concept learned from experience, because in order for an experience to be of something outside myself it must be attributed to a location outside, so that my prior ability to represent it in space is what makes it at all possible for me to experience

---

*Translating terms from Kant's German is not necessarily easier than translating philosophical terms from Sanskrit or Chinese. The term *intuition*—like the word it translates, *Anschauung*—is by etymology *looking*, and now most usually means *knowing without reasoning*. This match of English to German is therefore rather good. But the English word *intuition* is strange where Kant uses *Anschauung* to mean *sensation* (as a faculty, or with the meaning of *sense datum*). Nonetheless, Kant takes care to distinguish *intuition* from *sensation* (*Empfindung*): sensation "does not *contain* space and time, even though it posits the object corresponding to itself in both" (*Prolegomena*, para. 24). Intuition as Kant uses it usually refers to that which makes sensation or sensations possible and contains them as its "matter." Perception (*Wahrnehmung*) is defined by Kant (at one point) as a kind of sensation (a sensation that is "referred to an object in general but not determining it") (*Critique of Pure Reason* A374).

The difficulty in matching connotations in the two languages is compounded by Kant's linguistically natural but quite personal use of the term and by his inconsistent veering from one connotation or term to another. The exact meaning, I am afraid, has to be left to intuition in its more usual English sense. (See the essays by M. S. Gram and H. H. Rudnick in Gram, *Interpreting Kant*.)

it out there where I find it. Furthermore, while we can easily think of space as empty of objects, we cannot think of space as absent: the intuition of space precedes that of the objects we locate in it. Therefore space must be regarded as the condition of the possibility of all appearances, not as something learned from them. We can be sure that space is an intuition rather than a concept because we represent it to ourselves as infinite, with all its infinite number of parts coexisting *within* itself. As such, it is grasped scientifically by means of geometry.[75]

Now to time: Time, the form of the *inner sense*, is not derived from experience. We could not experience things either at one time or at successive times if not for our prior ability to sense things as already being in time. And while it is easy for us to think of time as empty of appearances, we cannot think away time, the condition of the possibility of their appearing. So time, too, is a priori and an invariable condition for experience rather than something acquired from it. And time is an intuition rather than a concept because different times are all parts of one and the same infinite time, which cannot be grasped as such by concepts. And it is only by intuition that we grasp that different times cannot be simultaneous. Therefore concepts relating to time must rest on the intuition of time. Pure arithmetic, with its succession of numbers, is related to time somewhat as geometry is related to space.

Now to "transcendental logic." In this logic we isolate the understanding from all sensation and dissect out the a priori concepts needed for knowledge. It is essential that the concepts we dissect should be pure—not learned—and fundamental—not derived from other concepts. It is also essential that their number is complete and their order established. Only then will we be able to appreciate their interrelations and see how, when they are taken together, the unity of experience becomes possible. For these pure concepts of the understanding, the *categories*, connect or synthesize the otherwise disunited a priori testimony given by intuition alone.*

---

*Like Dignaga and Dharmakirti, Kant has to work out transitions from an initial condition to another with a different nature. One such initial condition is the multifariousness (*mannigfaltigkeit*) or undifferentiated awareness of "intuition" that in translations of Kant is called *the manifold*. This initial multifariousness cannot be represented even as such until it is unified ("synthesized") into a single representation. Before the force of imagination synthesizes the multifariousness of "intuition" into an image, it must draw the multifariousness into its own activity by means of what Kant calls the synthesis of apprehension. No memory is yet involved, nor any recognition or concept. What follows is the synthesis of recognition in a concept. This synthesis requires memory and the consciousness that what we now think is the same as what we thought a moment earlier. To recognize that the earlier and later representations are of the same object, concepts or rules are needed—the concept of the object that is recognized and concepts of number, quality, and modality. Evidently, Kant's *synthesis of apprehension* plays a bridging role rather like that of Dharmakirti's *mental perception*, and his *synthesis of recognition*, rather like that of Dharmakirti's *perceptual judgment*. (For Kant see the *Critique of Pure Reason* A99–100, A103–105, A120–21; and Brook, *Kant and the Mind*, pp. 124–30.)

To discover the fundamental categories, Kant observes the common logic by which he himself thinks. In logic, he claims, the understanding has only itself and its own form to deal with. For this reason, it has not advanced a single step beyond Aristotle.[76] Kant begins by making a systematic list of the most fundamental kinds of thoughts we formulate or, in Kant's terms, the (synthesizing) judgments we make in relation to objects. Each form of judgment has a corresponding concept or category that acts as a rule for its use. Since judging is a single intellectual function, it has a single integrated table. It was Aristotle, Kant recalls, who first searched for the categories. But Aristotle searched haphazardly, while he, Kant, develops them systematically and completely from the faculty of judgment, which is the faculty of thought. He is the first, he claims, to classify the categories and show that no others are possible.[77] The connection of these concepts supplies a rule, he explains, by which each of them is assigned its place and by which their systematic completeness can be determined.[78]

By Kant's definition, the categories are the pure concepts that give knowledge its a priori synthetic unity. He finds four groups of them, two "mathematical" and two "dynamic." Each group contains three "moments," the third arising from the combination of the second moment with the first. The table of categories, representing the whole system of the elementary concepts of the human understanding, is as follows:

1. *Categories of quantity:* unity, plurality, totality.
2. *Categories of quality:* reality, negation, limitation.
3. *Categories of relation:* of inherence and subsistence (substance and accident), of causality and dependence (cause and effect), of community (reciprocity between agent and patient).
4. *Categories of modality:* possibility—impossibility, existence—nonexistence, necessity—contingency.[79]

I will not comment on these categories except to point out that the importance for thought of the first group—unity, plurality, totality—was noted earlier, in the exposition of Neoplatonic philosophy. Because the categories belong to understanding alone, they are not enough, Kant says, to unify experience. "Synthesis in general," results from "the power of imagination, a blind but indispensable function of the soul, without which we should have no knowledge whatsoever, but of which we are scarcely ever conscious (*Critique of Pure Reason*, A78, B103)."[80]

The a priori synthesis of imagination is related to another kind of a priori "transcendental" synthesis. This (last) kind—the necessary unity of the self in consciousness—is the *transcendental synthesis of apperception.*

Imagination, Kant says, gives the content of intuition the form of an image; but our experience must also be ascribed a priori to "an abiding and unchanging *I* that is

> the correlate of all our representations in so far as it is to be at all possible that we should become conscious of them . . . The unity of apperception is thus the transcendental ground of the necessary conformity to law of all appearances in one experience. (*Critique of Pure Reason*, A123, A127)[81]

In a final Kantian summary:

> However exaggerated and absurd it may sound, to say that the understanding is itself the source of the laws of nature, and so of its formal unity, such an assertion is none the less correct, and is in keeping with the object to which it refers, namely, experience. (*Critique of Pure Reason*, A127)[82]

There is one more Kantian problem that I think must be mentioned. It is the problem of the antinomies of pure reason, which, Kant says, was decisive in turning him to critical philosophy.[83] Antinomies are the contradictions that reason runs into when it tries to extend cosmology beyond possible experience to what escapes all conditions. This effort causes reason to be trapped in natural antitheses, the result of a natural, unavoidable illusion, an illusion that can be made harmless by analysis but never eradicated.[84] Such natural antitheses show that "*nothing whatever* can be thought" by means of the affected concepts.[85] Antinomies, Kant insists, arise in a priori cosmology but not in the pure, formal sciences of logic and mathematics, or in the empirical sciences.[86]

The four antinomies are: 1. The world has a beginning in time and is limited in space; the world has no beginning in time and is unlimited in space. 2. Everything either is or is made up of absolutely simple parts; nothing is or is made up of absolutely simple parts. 3. To explain the world one needs both the causality of nature and the causality of freedom; everything takes place by the laws of nature alone. 4. There is an absolutely necessary being that belongs in the world or outside it as its cause; there is no absolutely necessary being in or outside the world as its cause.

In these antinomies, Kant concentrates in skeptical opposition many of the conflicts that have been considered in earlier chapters. The only antinomy confined basically to the West is that concerning necessity and freedom (suggested, however, by fatalists of the Buddha's time). The first antinomy is obviously the same as the first and second "unanswerable" questions the Buddha refuses to answer on grounds possibly like those of Kant. Taken in terms of later Buddhist philosophy, Kant's solution, that things in space and time are in themselves nothing and so are neither finite nor infinite, is akin to the solution of "emptiness" with respect to space and time (and also with respect to everything else logical and verbal). The interpretation of philosophy as consisting of antinomies is, of course, native to most of the skeptics who have been described here.

In the foregoing almost bare outline of the main themes of *The Critique of Pure Reason,* I have not gone into any difficulties or showed that Kant not infrequently vacillates or is incautious. Usually (not invariably) he is careful to use the (not invariably) synonymous terms *thing in itself, noumenon,* and *transcendental object* in a purely negative sense.* Yet he makes it obvious that he cannot avoid thinking that the thing in itself exists:

> Appearance can be nothing by itself, outside our mode of representation. Unless, therefore, we are to move constantly in a circle, the word appearance must be recognized as already indicating a relation to something, the immediate representation of which is, indeed, sensible, but which, even apart from the constitution of our sensibility . . . must be something in itself, that is, an object independent of sensibility. (*Critique of Pure Reason* A251–52)[87]

There are difficulties: I know of no persuasive reason why Kant's something in itself should be knowably different from the phenomenon, nor, I add in Buddhistic style, *not* knowably the same as the phenomenon. As has been noted above, Kant once relates to this problem by saying no more than that we view things from "two different points of view." Elsewhere, he says that "nothing whatever can be asserted of the thing in itself" that may underlie particular appearances.[88] Yet in other texts Kant shows himself to be sure—that he cannot help believing—that the thing

---

*By the transcendental object "is meant a something = X, of which we know, and with the present constitution of our understanding can know, nothing whatsoever, but which, as a correlate of the unity of apperception, can serve only for the unity of the manifold in sensible intuition" (A250, trans. Smith p. 268). In A366 Kant identifies the thing in itself with the transcendental object. In A252 he says that the concept of the noumenon is purely negative and signifies only the thought of something in general. Soon after, in A253, he denies that the transcendental object, the completely indeterminate thought of something in general, can be the noumenon (taken in a positive sense). In A287–89/B342–45 he allows the transcendental object, considered to be the cause of appearance, to be called "noumenon," the term then making only negative sense. The second edition of the *Critique of Pure Reason* distinguishes (B307) between *noumenon* in the positive sense—as the (impossible) object of a nonsensible intuition—and the only sense usable for Kant, a negative one. In the rewritten passages of the second edition, says Allison (p. 246), the term *transcendental object,* which has become unnecessary, vanishes. (See Allison, *Kant's Transcendental Idealism,* pp. 242–46.)

in itself and the phenomenon are different.* The reason he gives that there can be no exception to the principle that everything that happens in the perceived world is subject to the unchangeable laws of nature. Therefore, "if appearances are things in themselves, freedom cannot be upheld. Nature will then be the complete and sufficient determinant of every event" (A536/B564).[89] Kant also argues (though not in *The Critique of Pure Reason*) that if space and time were forms of things in themselves, that is, if they were a priori conditions of existence that would persist even if there were no ordinary things, "they would also have to be conditions of the existence of God." Then, because of their infinity and necessity, space and time "would even have to be made into divine properties."[90] This objection sounds as if Kant has in mind the dangerous philosophy of Newton or of Spinoza.

Incautiously, Kant often speaks of the thing in itself or the transcendental object as the cause or ground (but never the matter) of appearances. It would seem, strictly speaking, that the thing in itself cannot be the cause of the phenomenon—according to Kant, causality belongs, of course, to the world of phenomena. To put it more cautiously, the thing in itself cannot be either *known* or *represented* as a cause. Nor can the thing in itself either be or be represented as a noncause. The Buddhist notion of emptiness might be helpful at this point, but Kant has no equivalent. To say, as Kant does, that something is only given to or only affects the mind makes the terms involved sound softer and vaguer but does nothing to solve the problem.

A generous, exegetically difficult solution is that Kant does not make any illicit claims but only points out that the analysis of the concept of an object requires the supersensible or transcendental to be assumed as its ground. By this solution, the categories—including causality—can be used in a purely logical way in relation to things in themselves. So used, they do not imply that transcendental things have any (even inaccessible) reality of their own—Kant does say clearly that the categories can "serve to determine the transcendental object, which is the concept of something in general."[91] I admire this solution. The inconsistency of Kant's language does not conceal his undoubted desire to be consistent, and he deserves a reasonable degree of interpretive help. But this help should not obscure his often genuine ambivalence. Like so many others, he wants things (as

---

*"Surely the epistemologically interesting but metaphysically neutral fact that we can know objects only if they conform to certain conditions does not imply that those objects or any other objects do *not* in themselves conform to those conditions, even if for some reason the fact of their conformity can or should even be omitted from certain *conceptions* of those objects" (Guyer, *Kant and the Claims of Knowledge*, p. 338).

he says) more than one way. Made as modern and as close to consistent as possible, he is no longer Kant but a post-Kantian.[92]

To go on: Kant holds that our knowledge can be abstractly exact and comprehensively logical but cannot be basic. We are able to discover what abilities, what faculties, are necessary for knowledge and how they fit together, but their existence and coexistence is an otherwise unexplained fact. The basic reasons for the order in our experience are unknown; we have no idea why we experience things in space and time. If it was not so, our empirical imagination would have nothing appropriate on which to exercise its powers. And then the empirical imagination would "remain concealed within the mind as a dead and to us unknown faculty."[93]

By proxy for his reader, Kant is for a moment surprised that nature's conformity to laws should depend on our ways of perceiving it. But then, speaking for himself, he responds that there is no reason for surprise if we consider that the nature we know is not a thing in itself but "merely an aggregate of appearances" united a priori by "the radical factor of all our knowledge," which is transcendental apperception.[94] But the radical unity itself remains unexplained. As he says elsewhere (in the *Anthropology*), the association between the laws of sensibility and the imagination "is carried on *in conformity with* understanding, though it is not derived *from* understanding." When understanding combines ideas in this way, says Kant, it acts like the different physical elements that together produce something else:

> Understanding and sensibility, for all their dissimilarity, join together spontaneously to produce knowledge, as intimately as if one had its source in the other, or both originated from a common root. But this cannot be—at least we cannot conceive how heterogeneous things could sprout from one and the same root. (*Anthropology* parag. 31)[95]

It does not take long to see that the price that Kant pays for making everything that is experienced lawful and, in this sense, comprehensible is that nothing at all can be understood basically: the root is always hidden, always empirically indemonstrable and theoretically lacking in evidence. Then there is the enigmatic *I* we must presuppose, with its power of uniting by apperception and of making free decisions on the basis of rational principles. In a lecture, Kant asks if he possesses such absolute liberty and answers:

> The "I" proves that I myself act; I am a principle, not something that is principled ... When I say "I think, I act" etc., then either the word "I" is inappropriate or I am free ... All practically objective demands would make no sense, if man was not free.[96]

Much of Kant's time was occupied in the defense of his system. His opponents ranged from empiricists influenced by English philosophy, to skeptics, to defenders of the Leibniz-Wollfian position. One prominent skeptic was Gottlob Ernst Schulze, who argues in his *Aenesidemus* that Kant's *Critique of Pure Reason* simply assumes propositions that Hume has already shown to be doubtful. According to Schulze, Kant's notion of a power or faculty does nothing at all to explain a phenomenon; and to think up a faculty that may underlie representations is no proof that such a faculty in fact exists. Kant reasons circularly: How can he deny that the concept of causality applies to things in themselves and yet claim that the objects of experience are appearances whose content is derived from outside us?[97] Another skeptic was Solomon Maimon, whose philosophy is a "coalition system" in which Hume and Kant predominate, but in which Maimonides, Leibniz, and Spinoza also play their parts. Maimon accepts as plausible only the negative conclusions of Kant's critical philosophy. As Maimon sees it, Kant does not prove that human experience is in fact subsumed under valid scientific laws, such as the law of causation. Kant's philosophy is self-consistent but remains separated from the particular— it cannot go beyond its transcendental frontiers. And the idea of things in themselves, instead of explaining anything, only drives us into an infinite regress of explanations—what causes the things in themselves to cause just these sensations, and what is it that causes these other causes to have just such effects, and so on? To relieve his Kantian doubts, which are doubled by Humean ones, Maimon falls back on an inclination to believe in an infinite creative mind, rather like the Active Intellect of Maimonides. With the help of this mind, Maimon solves the dilemma he finds in the relation of a priori forms to sensuous objects.*

The leader of the Wolffians was Johann August Eberhard, who, in a magazine established for the purpose, made widely publicized, potentially

---

*According to Maimon we face the following dilemma: We can be conscious of the form of a thought only if the thought has some content, but to have ideal completeness, the thought can in no way be given by facts, which are always deficient. The thing in itself should therefore be understood as a limit-concept, present in consciousness alone, of that which our thought is still ignorant in relation to some object or other. The notion of the thing in itself is unavoidable because appearance, which implies something given from the outside, is always incomplete for a human consciousness. A complete concept of a real, determinate object is theoretically possible, but only to an infinite mind—which can be known only a posteriori. This mind is not God himself (Maimon says defensively) but resembles the Active Intellect of Maimonides and the God/Nature of Spinoza. Neither analytic nor synthetic, the activity of such a mind creates ex nihilo both the real object and its complete concept. (Atlas, "Maimon"; Bergman, *The Philosophy of Solomon Maimon*, chaps. 1, 4, 10, 11; Bransen, *The Antinomy of Thought*, pp. 62–66, 76–78, 88–95, 109–16; and Giovanni and Harris, pp. 32–36.)

dangerous attacks on Kant's philosophy. Eberhard contends that Kant has only taken over Leibniz's a priori, to which he has added the false thesis that knowledge is limited to appearances. Furthermore, says Eberhard, on Kant's view, empirical knowledge lacks any foundation, either within us or outside of us, because, in either case, the only possible foundation is the thing in itself. So all that Kant really says is that the foundation of knowledge cannot be known, and that the a priori knowledge of the categories comes to us, as does empirical knowledge, in an occult way. In defense of his own, Wolffian position, Eberhard declares that any chain of reasoning must be anchored in a first truth, which is our consciousness that nothing contradictory can be thought. Therefore we must accept the objective truth of conclusions based on the "transcendentally valid" principles of the *form* of our knowledge—the principles of contradiction and sufficient reason—and on the valid syllogistic logic by which the principles are extended. Reason, the only basis for distinguishing between truth and falsity, cannot be a source of illusion.*

Especially painful to Kant was the clumsiness, as he saw it, or, even worse, the apostasy of his defenders. Herder went over to those who preferred the language of poetry and metaphor to that of critical analysis. Apostasy began in the perhaps innocent desire to strengthen or complete Kant's system—especially in what concerned the thing in itself—in ways that Kant considered damaging to the fabric of his thought. He especially resented Fichte's claim that the critical philosophy was no more than a preface to a complete system of transcendental philosophy (something Kant himself had often said) and repeated the proverb "May God protect us from our friends, and we shall watch out for our enemies ourselves."[98] But despite his resentments and his pride in his system, Kant kept developing—perhaps in directions his apostates had suggested—as is shown, certainly though unclearly, by the fragments preserved in his *Opus Postumum*.[99]

Discussion

The philosophical woods we name Dignaga/Dharmakirti and Kant contain many trees that draw attention to themselves. Suppose we look

---

*Eberhard often ignores Kant's basic contention that we confuse our concepts of things with the things themselves. In his answer, which is not free of bitterness and polemical misrepresentation, Kant tries to show that Leibniz's views—on sufficient reason, monadology, and the preestablished harmony—are only anticipations of his own, better-developed views. He also clarifies some of his doctrines and makes a significant restatement of his distinction between analytic and synthetic judgments. (See Allison, *The Kant-Eberhard Controversy*; and Vleeschauwer, *The Development of Kantian Thought*, pp. 138–51.)

at the woods first, which are fairly symmetrical with one another: The problem of Dignaga, Dharmakirti, and Kant—two of them faithful if rationalistic Buddhists and one a faithful if rationalistic Christian—is to affirm the ordinary sense of objectivity but to thin it enough to encourage the attempt to transcend its assumed superficiality. In other words, the problem for these philosophers is to preserve their faith and, along with it, to find a way between a plausible, well-analyzed conception of reality, which accepts careful standards of theoretical and empirical proof, and a rationally plausible skepticism.

Dignaga, Dharmakirti, and Kant begin to find the way by analyzing all ordinary experience into two constitutive factors: perception/"intuition" and inference/concepts. According to this analysis, perception results, mysteriously but vividly, from the "outside," but is in itself nameless, structureless, unlocated in time and space, unconnected with anything else. As Kant says, the perception is blind (of structure and meaning) and the conception is empty (of perceptual content). It is only when perception is given its rational structure by means of concepts that it is transformed into ordinary, identifiable, usable reality, subject to the laws and constraints of ordinary life.

Let me document at least this elementary likeness, philosopher by philosopher:

Apart from the particular and the universal there is no other object to be cognized, and we shall prove that perception (*pratyaksha*) has only the particular for its object and inference (*anumana*) only the universal . . . Among these [two means of cognition] perception is free from conceptual construction (*kalpana*). (Dignaga, *Pramāṇa-samuccya* 1.B, C)[100]

Right knowledge is twofold. Direct and indirect (perceptive and inferential). Direct knowledge means here neither construction (judgment) nor illusion. Construction (or judgment) implies a distinct cognition of a mental reflex which is capable of coalescing with a verbal designation. (Dharmakirti, *Nyâya-Bindu* 1.3–5)[101]

Intuition (*Anschauung*) and concepts (*Begriffe*) constitute . . . the elements of all knowledge. . . .These two powers cannot exchange their functions. The understanding can intuit nothing, the senses can think nothing. Only through their union can knowledge arise. (Kant, *Critique of Pure Reason* A50–51/B74–75)[102]

As I have said, the positions of the three philosophers are complex compromises. In the case of Dignaga and Dharmakirti, on one side there stand philosophers such as the Nyaiyayikas, who believe (some more, some less) in perception and inference as mutually supportive criteria that reveal the real world, and who believe, as well, in the direct perception of real universals. On the same side, that of metaphysical certainty, stands the quite different figure of Bhartrihari, who furnishes Dignaga and Dharmakirti with clues to the nature of language. Dharmakirti goes further in agreement with him, but Bhartrihari's hierarchy, in which "words" are metaphysical realities, contradicts Buddhism and is indefensibly dogmatic in both Buddhists' eyes.

On the other side of Dignaga and Dharmakirti stand the skeptics, especially, as they see things, Nagarjuna and his Madhyamaka successors—to whom, it must be admitted, they show no open antagonism. They navigate between the two sides, not quite steadily. Sometimes they veer toward phenomenalism: apart from the Buddhist absolutes, only phenomena—metaphysically empty surfaces—are said to exist, exist within (self-)consciousness. But sometimes they veer toward a belief in the primal reality of sensation in itself, and, quite explicitly in Dharmakirti's case, in the unknowable point-instant causes of sensation. Whatever their ambivalence or, sometimes, lack of definiteness, Dignaga and Dharmakirti always insist on the two contrasted factors of knowledge that together, and only together, produce full empirical experience. They show themselves to be empiricists in requiring the truth of inferences to be tested by their practical results. Since they are Buddhist empiricists, they cannot accept universals as metaphysical realities. They see them as necessary but necessarily vague, never fitting any individual, and never real in themselves.

Kant, too, is faced by opposite philosophical positions. On the one side is the metaphysically Leibnizian position, represented in Kant's philosophical vicinity by Christian Wolff—Kant writes that in the execution of the plan prescribed by his critique for a critically limited system of metaphysics it will be necessary "to follow the strict method of the celebrated Wolff, the greatest of all the dogmatic philosophers."[103] On the same side, in terms of what he considers dogmatism, is Leibniz's great scientific rival, Newton. On the other, skeptical side is Hume. In a well-known passage, Kant writes, "I freely admit: it was David Hume's remark that first, many years ago, interrupted my dogmatic slumber and gave a completely different direction to my enquiries in the field of speculative philosophy."[104] Where Hume's tendency is toward phenomenalism and toward a theory of natural sympathy, Kant finds his middle way between the rational order and deterministic certainty of science and the guiding, hope-giving "transcendental" ideas—to which nothing objectively provable corresponds—of God, freedom, and immortality. To him, these ideas would have been as intellectually fragile or distant in a deterministic world as nirvana to a Buddhist in the world of the fully real objects, real universals, and accurate perceptions of the Nyaya, or worse still, the gross world of the materialists. The problem of Dignaga, Dharmakirti, and Kant is to keep the opposite possibilities in a viable, even symbiotic relationship.

One more point involving Dignaga, Dharmakirti, and Kant: As the result of close study of the two Buddhists, it has been argued that much of Dharmakirti's divergence from Dignaga is by means of an idea borrowed from Bhartrihari: Each of the particular things we experience—each fire, each lotus, each cow—has an ideal linguistic object—of fire, of lotus, of cow—as its essential nature (*svabhava*). This resembles and is borrowed from Bhartrihari's theory of universals but is metaphysically more modest, because the "essences" themselves are taken to be unreal. Dharmakirti's reals, we know, are point-instants, whose singularity is reflected in pure perceptual awarenesses. Only the point-instants have a real effect; without them we would not be able to satisfy our desires. But the "essences," a priori linguistic objects latent in understanding and language, are necessary for understanding what anything is. Projected onto the reals, they make perceptual judgments possible.

To spell this theory out a little: Dharmakirti holds that every object of our thought, even if a fictitious "sky flower," has an essential, defining property or ideal structure. This property—fire, perhaps—is the same as the collocation of properties—redness, heat, smoke, impermanence—that are essential to the object's identity. The ideal object, the property fire as a group of properties, is the identity—though not the reality—of all fires. Such an essential property, "essence," or *svabhava*, is not something that can be established by inference from perception because, as we have learned, to perceive similarities and absence of similarities is never enough to prove a causal tie: "Perception is not the conclusive proof of anything."[105]

Opposed, as a Buddhist, to realism, Dharmakirti prefers to avoid the usual explanation of a universal as an expression of the identity or similarity of objects with others of the same kind. Instead, he understands an essential nature to be something identical with its defining properties and incompatible with foreign ones, as fire is incompatible with cold. An essential nature also includes the relation of causality (but not causal effectiveness), like that of producing smoke.[106] Such an essential nature or ideal linguistic object is elicited from the mind, where it lies latent, by perceptual experience. For example, the mother's breast elicits the equivalent ideal object in the baby's mind, followed by the baby's recognition that "this is there."[107]

According to Dharmakirti, an ideal linguistic object springs from a beginningless habit-energy. It relates either to what exists—such as, perhaps, cloth—to what does not exist—perhaps a "sky flower"—or to what supports both existence and nonexistence—perhaps God. This is obscure, but the sources do not allow greater exactness. All the same, the symbiosis of perception with ideal linguistic objects is clear: "Truth, in Dharmakirti's system, has two components of equal importance; an a priori component, which resides in language, and an a posteriori component, present in language and the understanding through beginningless time."[108]

Dharmakirti turns out to be more explicitly Kant-like than Dignaga because he believes in a priori concepts that are devoid of reality, are beyond empirical confirmation, and yet are essential to human understanding. But whichever Buddhist is in whatever way closer to Kant, it has by now become evident that a detailed comparison of the three would be complicated and might lead in many directions. For the present, it may be enough to sharpen contrasts and give a formulaic summary of what I take to be philosophically natural antagonisms: Dignaga/Dharmakirti are to Bhartrihari and (implicitly) Nagarjuna as Kant is to Leibniz/Wolff and Hume.

To complete this formulaic summary, we should recall the analogous points of tension in Kant and the Buddhists. In Kant, they are most evident in his remarks, which strain consistency, on the thing in itself, and in his hesitations and struggles over the nature and reach of the human I: the I as it combines representation by means of the inherently limiting categories in which it thinks; the I as it unites all experience in its relation to its subjective self; the I as it spontaneously pays attention, abstracts, and forms concepts; and the I as it grasps and experiences the autonomy of reason and the spontaneity of the will.[109] The bridgelike tension in Kant between the world that is merely thought and the unthinkable world beyond, the source of all morality and all hope, is parallel to the tension evident in the Buddhist philosophers between the truth of the conventional world grasped by thought, and the truth, the source of all wisdom and hope, that lies beyond the conventional world. One might say that the ambivalently grasped but central I in Kant plays a bridging role analogous to the self-conscious consciousness in Buddhist philosophy, which, by knowing its empirical limitations, makes it possible to transcend them philosophically and experientially.

The formulaic summary explained, we can go on to test it and elaborate on some of its points. The comparison between Buddhist and Kantian philosophy has a brief but enlightening history, which begins, I think, in the comparison of Nagarjuna with Kant. As long as Nagarjuna, like Buddhist philosophers generally, was considered to be a nihilist, the comparison with Kant remained unattractive. However, the Russian Buddhologist Th. Stcherbatsky (1866–1942)—whose views resemble those I am expressing—interpreted Nagarjuna as a believer and affirmed the Kant-Nagarjuna comparison. Human thought, Stcherbatsky believed, tends to develop in an analogous way even under quite different historical circumstances.[110] The comparison was then adopted by others, notably the Indian philosopher, T. R. V. Murti, who wrote that, for both the Madhyamika and Kant, philosophy is nothing other than criticism. Speculation, both hold, gives us not knowledge, but illusion.

> Neither the Madhyamika nor Kant has any doctrine or theory of their own. The Madhyamika is more decided and consistent. The critical philosophy of Kant led to the rise of the great Idealist and Absolutist systems of Fichte, Hegel and Schopenhauer. Likewise, the two great absolutist systems of India, Vijnanavada and Vedanta, although they did not accept the Śunyata of the Madhyamika, are still the direct outcome of the Madhyamika dialectic.[111]

For all the great differences between Kant and Nagarjuna, the comparison between them seems to me still defensible.* This is because, as I have argued, every attempt to compare requires its suitable degree of latitude, from complete abstraction to a saturation with detail so great that any comparison violates the contextual integrity of the objects of the attempt. But even though the Nagarjuna-Kant comparison is defensible, it is

---

*Buddhologists such as Stanislaw Schayer and Jan de Jong rejected Stcherbatsky's comparison (Hayes, "Nagarjuna's Appeal," pp. 332–33). Writing in 1948, de Jong declared that Stcherbatsky's search for analogies with Western thinking often leads to a distortion of Buddhist thought. For example, the translation of *shunya* (emptiness) by *relative* plays on two meanings of *relative: being in relation with* and *the opposite of absolute.* "Because of this initial error all his [Stcherbatsky's] subsequent interpretations of Nagarjunian thinking are false." This is an excessive verdict. *The New Shorter Oxford English Dictionary* defines *relative* (in a central sense, used by Stcherbatsky) as *existing only by relation to something else; not absolute or independent.* In accord with such a definition, Stcherbatsky (for want of a better solution, he says) uses *relative,* meaning *contingent* (Stcherbatsky, *The Conception of Buddhist Nirvana,* p. 42). Since he explains his use carefully enough, I find nothing in it seriously misleading. De Jong continues: When, in 1934, Stcherbatsky takes the Buddhist absolute or body of doctrine *(dharmakaya)* to be the "absolute truth," he identifies Buddhism with Kantianism. "The attempt to elucidate the absolute of the Madhyamakas by means of the transcendental dialectics of the critique of pure reason, seems to indicate a lack of understanding of the mystical and soteriological character of the philosophy of the Madhyamakas" ("The Problem of the Absolute in the Madhyamika School," *JIP* 2 [1972]; reprinted in de Jong, *Buddhist Studies,* pp. 53–58 [57–58 quoted]). To this charge, the present discussion is a partial answer.

less rewarding than the one, to which I now proceed, of Kant with Dignaga and Dharmakirti.

I have suggested a parallel between Kant's relation to Hume and Dignaga's to Nagarjuna, but, as I have said, there is no external sign that Dignaga's thought is directed against Nagarjuna. For a historian, it is natural to analyze Dignaga's thought as a construction that grows out of earlier Buddhist philosophy, including Nagarjuna's. Besides, Stcherbatsky has been shown to be mistaken in attributing to Dignaga doctrines that become explicit only in Dharmakirti. Among the doctrines he attributes to Dignaga without explicit evidence there are three of Dharmakirti: a version of the Sautrantika point-instant theory; the idea that point-instants, which alone are real, alone have causal power; and the idea that the truth of judgments and inferences is tested by their practical results.[112]

The development of Buddhist philosophy from Nagarjuna to Dharmakirti may be put in the following, too categorical, way: Nagarjuna extends Buddha's view that it is unprofitable to engage in philosophical debate on final matters. He extends it by arguing that everything is empty, that is to say, dependent or relative, and cannot be proved either to exist or not to exist. The phenomenalists or idealists, such as Asanga and Vasubandhu, carry on the belief that the existence of external things can neither be proved nor disproved. But they argue that mind or consciousness, which is internal to us, not only exists but can be shown to comprise everything apparently different from it. According to them, when consciousness is pure—not split by the distinction between subject and object—it leads to nirvana, or is itself nirvanic.

At least to begin with, Dignaga and Dharmakirti are phenomenalists or idealists of this kind.* However, they come to value the possible tie of

---

*Dignaga's and Dharmakirti's ambiguous idealism or phenomenalism invites comparison with the real but still ambiguous tendency to idealism of Kant in his old age. Although an opponent of Berkeley's idealism, Kant was, of course, the chief precursor of the German idealists. In the notes that constitute the *Opus Postumum*, Kant explains in his transcendental way "how physics is possible." He there says that the subject posits itself, including the representation of its own activity, makes itself into an object, and posits space and time as pure manifolds, as "products of our imagination, hence self-created intuitions."

Kant's notes lack continuity and a clear philosophical context. But it is clear that there is idealism, not unlike that of the Buddhists, in passages such as this: "The appearance of appearances (that is, how the subject is mediately affected) is metaphysically [the same] as how the subject makes itself into an object (is conscious of itself as determinable in intuition). It contains the principle of the combination of the moving forces in space, in order to realize space through empirical representation, according to its form—not through experience, but for the sake of experience as a system of the subject's empirical representations . . . It is we who first provide the data out of which cognitions can be woven (into the cognitions possible from them) . . . *He who would know the world must first manufacture it*—in his own self, indeed [with reference to the aphorist] Lichtenberg" (Kant, *Opus Postumum*, trans. Förster and Rosen, pp. xlii, 109, 240).

the mind with something other than mind. Although contained within consciousness, this tie implies something outside it—it is, one might say, an outward-pointing vector. So the tie, pure sensation or sensory awareness, is excepted by the two philosophers from Nagarjuna's verdict of emptiness. As they see it, pure sensation is the pure particular, about which little (strictly speaking, nothing) more can be said because it is still unshaped by the falsifying constructs of the human mind. According to one of Dignaga's formulations, whatever is continuous in space and time is constructed on the basis of realities—pure sensations—and is therefore neither completely real nor completely unreal.[113] Dharmakirti agrees and elaborates, but as compared with Dignaga, he tends more to philosophical realism—even though he agrees that the nonconceptual tie to external reality is always within self-consciousness. Probably more than Dignaga, he is always inside consciousness, but he cannot help always looking outside it.

Dignaga and Dharmakirti seem to be apter than Nagarjuna for comparison with Kant because, like him and unlike Nagarjuna, they devote so much of their effort to an understanding of the logic and structure of the world of phenomena, which they take to be unreality supported by indescribable reality.* All the same, the likeness of Buddhist thinkers to Kant is often denied. It is said that Kant has the un-Buddhistic purpose of confining science to phenomena in order to preserve morality and the disinterested will. It is said, as well, that Kant's insight is into the tension created between traditional values and natural science, a tension quite unknown in Indian thought, to which Kant has no relevance.[114] Another objection is put in terms of Kant's distance from the reality he acknowledged:

> [Kant] was able to accept the notion that we never are knowingly in touch with reality as such in any way. The Buddhist logician on the other hand, as long as he remains a progress philosopher, is bound to allow that there is a way in which humans can mount to knowledge which is not invalidated through infection by concepts.[115]

Or it is said, in relation to Nagarjuna, that "the Kantian dialectic is the play of the powerlessness of reason . . . On the contrary, the Madhyamika

---

*The comparison may be furthered by Dharmakirti's strong interest in the pragmatic pursuit of human ends, an interest sometimes not distant from Kant's interest in the power of human sensibility to construct forms and make associations, and in foresight and the use of symbolic signs. Kant deals with such subjects in his *Anthropology from a Pragmatic Point of View*, although Kant's use of *pragmatic* there does not often fit our modern understanding of the word.

dialectic is truly constitutive of reality, which it completes by way of abolishing it."[116]

An objection of another kind is that Kant is not relevant to contemporary, post-Nietzschean interests, so that to choose him for the exegesis of a Buddhist philosopher is the surest way to isolate the Buddhist "in a quaint Asian backwater." On the principle that to treat a text in purely historical, philological terms is to deny its truth, the comparison with Kant is said to imply that the Buddhist has "nothing of importance to say to a culture that is struggling to free itself from a Kantian epistemology that has not led to any new or interesting insights for some time."[117]

I summarize these and similar objections in the following four statements:

1. Kant directed his thought against the skeptic, Hume, but Dignaga's thought is not directed against Nagarjuna and therefore not against skepticism.
2. Kant's basic problem—the relation of morality and religious belief to the universal assumptions made by science—is foreign to India.
3. Unlike Kant, the Buddhist philosophers believe that humans are able to arrive at nonconceptual knowledge.
4. Because contemporary thinkers are trying to free themselves from Kant's influence, comparison with Kant makes the Buddhist philosophers irrelevant to our own times.

Answer to objection 1. It is true that Dignaga shows no open sign of antagonism to Nagarjuna's position. As he sees things, perhaps he is only developing themes that he finds in earlier Buddhism, including Madhyamaka.[118] If one takes this position, one might say that Nagarjuna generalizes and logicizes the traditional Buddhist skepticism of abstract thought, while Dignaga qualifies Nagarjuna's skepticism by retaining a conceptually uninformative, purely sensory tie with "reality." In his formalized logic of induction, Dignaga works out the extreme conditions a justified induction has to meet and shows—here is Buddhist skepticism again—that perfect induction is in practice impossible.[119] So whatever Dignaga's exact purposes, it is not hard to construe him as varying and qualifying Nagarjuna rather than clashing with him. It is somewhat as if Kant were to say that Hume's skepticism was basically right but that he, Kant, would compensate for Hume's lack of interest in the formal structures of knowledge and in the need to keep a minimal tie with reality.

Nevertheless, it remains true that Dignaga is in implicit disagreement with Nagarjuna. Although he himself may not have wanted to dwell on his differences with Nagarjuna, a forceful, not always polite debate opens between those who inherit their respective points of view. The debate is prominent in Chandrakirti's commentary to Nagarjuna. In this commentary, Chandrakirti reasserts the doctrines of emptiness and of the two truths (one "truth" only relative and indeterminate). He in particular wants to avoid any positive viewpoint, avoid any proposition with a positive subject, and avoid the independent use of inference.[120] Of course, he opposes realism, whether Buddhist or non–Buddhist, the Buddhist being exemplified by Buddhist atomism and point-instant theory, and the non–Buddhist by materialism, that is, Charvaka, and Nyaya dualism. Most relevant here is his accusation that Dignaga (whom Chandrakirti does not name) or, more generally, the "logico-epistemological school," adopts a position that makes no sense and forgets that Nagarjuna has subverted the reliability of all means of knowledge.

Chandrakirti argues in his usual either-or manner: You—Dignaga or Dignaga's partisan—maintain that there are no more than two means of knowledge, which conform to an ultimate particular (sva-lakshana) and a universal (samanya-lakshana). But we can ask what subject the two characterize and whether or not this subject exists. If it does exist, the question asked makes it the object of a third kind of knowledge, different from the two that you have assumed. If the subject does not exist, then both the sensory particular and the mentally added universal, having nothing to characterize, do not exist either. In both cases, the duality of knowledge you assume makes no sense. As Nagarjuna says, a thing that has no characteristics is unintelligible; and if no subject that can be characterized is proved to exist, the characteristics that require this subject's existence do not exist either.[121]

In defense, the partisan of Dignaga theorizes that the underlying reality is an absolute, self-characterizing particular. Chandrakirti naturally argues that nothing of the kind makes any sense. We leave this argument without following it into further detail. Later in the debate, Chandrakirti also objects to the unusual sense Dignaga gives the word *perception* (pratyaksha). To use it to mean pure perceptual awareness distorts the everyday meaning of the word. Even granted such a general meaning, says Chandrakirti, it is misleading to apply it to isolated instants of perceptual awareness, and certainly misleading to apply it to analyze perceptual awareness and its object as they occur in everyday life.[122]

I bring in this debate only to show that philosophical antagonism does in fact develop between the Madhyamikas and the partisans of the Dignaga/Dharmakirti position. It is therefore reasonable to keep the parallel between, on the one hand, Dignaga/Dharmakirti and Nagarjuna, and, on the other hand, Kant and Hume.

Answer to objection 2: It is true that Kant, unlike the Indian philosophers, is concerned with the relation of morality and religion to the universal assumptions made by science. Although he believes that Newtonian science should have its principles clarified by transcendental philosophy, "it is quite clear that Newton's *Principia* serves as the model for scientific achievement during the whole of Kant's long career." And the law of universal gravitation remains his paradigm of a well-established physical law.[123] To Kant, causality according to natural laws allows no exceptions.

Since this commitment to determined causes and effects leaves no possibility of free choice nor, therefore, of morality, Kant finds it necessary to believe in freedom in the sense of the human ability to begin an internal state spontaneously, from itself. But freedom in this sense is a transcendental Idea, the kind that can in no way be derived from experience or applied to any object given in experience. Understood practically, freedom is simply the sense of the will's ability to choose its actions on the basis of principles whose rationality makes the will able to resist sensuous impulses.

The great problem is that if absolute, transcendental freedom is denied and eliminated, practical freedom is eliminated along with it (*Critique of Pure Reason* A534/B562). Kant goes so far as to say—perhaps incautiously from his standpoint—that "through experience we know practical freedom to be one of the causes in nature" (A803/B831). That is, we are in fact able to resist inclination and act on the basis of rational moral imperatives. Sometimes Kant appears to be saying that the reality of practical freedom demands the reality of transcendental freedom; but sometimes he appears to be saying that the concept of practical freedom demands only the Idea of transcendental freedom.[124] Depending on which passage in Kant we read, the noumenal is or is not known to be joined or contiguous with the phenomenal appearance, of which, Kant is capable of saying, it is the ground.

The closeness, the hint of the joining, is made by way of man's "pure apperception," through which man has inward knowledge of himself as something that cannot be explained by natural law:

> Man . . . who knows all the rest of nature solely through the senses, knows himself also through pure apperception . . . He is thus to himself, on the one hand phenomenon, and on the other hand, in respect of certain faculties, the action of which cannot be ascribed to the receptivity of sensibility, a purely intelligible object. (*Critique of Pure Reason* A546/B575).[125]

Given Kant's general position, the joining of the empirical and transcendental is impossible in intuition and cannot, in the usual sense, be known at all. But in the quoted passage there is a suggestion of the copresence of the empirical and transcendental, in the absence of which practical freedom would be impossible. Kant does have a defense for their presence together. It appears in the quoted words and elsewhere. The defense is, very simply: "I am conscious of myself, not as I appear to myself, but only that I am" (*Critique of Pure Reason* B157). The word *only* is the key. As Kant explains, self-consciousness is undoubtedly of the self, but it is too indeterminate to be self-knowledge. Self-consciousness shows that one's existence is not mere "appearance (still less illusion)." But to know one's self in a determinate way, one's existence must conform with the inner sense, of time, and to know one's self in time is to know not one's self but only how one appears to one's self.[126] Evidently, Kant does not hesitate to say that we have a consciousness of the noumenon as self; but consciousness is less to him than knowledge.[127]

Kant completes his explanation of the unity of reason in the *Critique of Judgment*. He there plays with the fire of the noumenon, draws back protesting his ontological innocence, and, though innocent, is drawn to the fire again. While trying to solve "the antinomy of taste," he suggests that the two apparently conflicting propositions may both be true because the judgment rests not on a determinate but on an indeterminate concept, that of the "supersensible substrate of the phenomenal." He continues:

> The subjective principle—that is to say, the indeterminate idea of the supersensible within us—can only be indicated as the unique key to the riddle of this faculty, itself concealed from us in its sources; and there is no means of making it any more intelligible. (*Critique of Judgment*, para. 57)[128]*

The impossible connection is created by the human necessity of thinking of the noumenal and phenomenal as one. In a metaphor that may be unfair, this is the leakage of the noumenon into the phenomenon, comparable to the "tunneling" of electrons through a barrier that classical physics makes impermeable but that quantum physics allows them to cross—a solution that appeals more to a (Zen?) sense of impossible reality than to a world that obeys the rules of standard logic.

---

*Referring especially to the *Critique of Judgment*, a commentator explains the relation of Kant to his idealistic successors: "Kant recognized that the most important matters about the ultimate reality of the universe and about man himself were beyond the limits of mere cognitive judgment, but that not only the urgency of practical life but the most rigorous pursuit of this strictly cognitive function compelled man to recognize his membership in that ultimate reality and hence to transcend the limitations of his understanding. For Kant that realization took on a religious dimension. For his successors it remained a philosophical one ... What Kant had locked away in an inaccessible transcendence, they retrieved as a transfiguring immanence" (Zammato, *The Genesis of Kant's Critique of Judgment*, p. 345).

It is easy to admit that Dignaga and Dharmakirti have no equivalent to Newtonian science. But they do know about and formalize induction, and they do believe strongly in their law of causality, to which there are no exceptions in the empirical world. And while they cannot believe in the apperception of a real self, they believe that the phenomenal world, rightly understood and experienced, leads toward nirvana; and they believe that, by way of intellectual and nonintellectual meditation, there can be earlier intimations of nirvana. While they are not explicitly concerned with the freedom of the will, they everywhere imply the possibility of slow, conscious self-determination in spite of the destructive pull of desire. Instead of the noumenon leaking into the phenomenon or electrons tunneling through apparently absolute barriers, we have two truths declared to be different but pulling toward identity, which is to say that phenomena (*samasara*), although radically different from the noumenon—the point-instant and, ultimately, also or only nirvana—are supported by the noumenon and (unintelligibly) constituted by it.

Answer to objection 3. As has been shown, it is reasonable to hold that Kant doubts but in some sense also believes that humans are able to arrive at more than merely conceptual knowledge. His religious beliefs are not as organized or detailed as those of the Buddhist philosophers; but although his beliefs are regulatory rather than explanatory, he takes them to exert a powerful effect on human beings and to be essential to their welfare. Like the Buddhists, he does not want to confuse the worldly forms and concepts of religion with the conceptually unknowable (nirvanic?) noumenon; but, like them, he never forgets the noumenon, because that is all there really is. Though the noumenon is absent from sensory intuition and is conceptually indescribable, it remains hidden behind all that appears. To use a metaphor, it is as full to the free will as the vacuum is full to quantum mechanics. For in Kant's eyes, deliberative rationality includes an ineradicable component thought of practical spontaneity, and practical spontaneity is allied—ineradicably—with true spontaneity.

What is the analogy with Buddhism? As Dignaga and Dharmakirti see it, Buddhism is based on an ineradicable sense of the way in which one can absolve oneself of desire, the way that is allied—ineradicably—with the faith in the Buddha and the "truth" beyond concepts. Comparably, Kant says that reason, which is always and under all circumstances present in the actions of men, "is not itself in time, and does not fall into any new state in which it was not before. In respect to new states, it is *determining*, not *determinable*" (A556/B584).[129] This passage is not innocent of a suggestion of the Kantianly impossible juncture of noumenon and phenomenon, as if Kant was almost willing to say, "freedom, which is necessarily incompatible with determinism, is necessarily compatible with it," or, "for the will, the noumenon is the phenomenon and the phenomenon the noumenon, and there is not a shadow of difference between them."* Yet Kant will not translate his acknowledgment of human spontaneity into the claim that there can be a reasoned, more than critical system of philosophy. Late in life, he speaks of "God, the world, and I: the thinking being in the world who connects them." But then he insists that, when made formally explicit, this conception is empty of existence:

> God and the world are the two objects of transcendental philosophy; thinking *man* is the subject, predicate and copula. The subject who combines them in one proposition. These are logical relations in a proposition, not dealing with the existence of subjects, but merely bringing what is formal in their relations of these objects to synthetic unity: God, the world, and I, man, a world-being myself, who combines the two.[130]

Although they have a different conception of spontaneity and freedom, Dignaga and Dharmakirti believe, as does Kant, that a hidden, inexplicable reality lies within the external pseudoreality: The absolutely real is, so to speak, the reality "within" the intellectual construction that falsifies it (though falsifies it usefully). As a Buddhist and idealist, Dharmakirti contends that all our awareness of objects contains an element of self-awareness.[131] But he pushes his idealism in the external direction because he sees—with calmly unmoralizing eyes—that mundane human life is directed by desire. Objects of awareness, he says, are objects of desire and repulsion and, as such, cannot be detached from an external cause: one desires what one does not have. If there was no external cause, neither desire, nor karma, nor perception would make any sense, because these all imply an external object. Nor could we understand, in the absence of different external causes, why different people have different experiences.

---

*A scholarly interpreter writes: "With respect to the main concern of this study, it makes possible to avoid attributing to Kant the view (suggested by much of his language) that free agency occurs in a distinct 'intelligible world' or that distinct noumenal activities somehow intervene in (without interfering with) the causal order of the phenomenal world. It offers instead the more appealing contrast between two 'points of view' of descriptions under which a single occurrence (a human action) can be considered . . . We are left with the very real problem of reconciling the presupposition of freedom . . . with the causal determinism governing human actions, considered as natural occurrences. For all its obscurity, verging at times on incoherence, Kant's theory of freedom is, in my judgment at least, the most profound and sustained attempt to deal with this problem in the history of Western philosophy . . . I have emphasized throughout Kant's incompatibilism or, better, his unique attempt to establish the compatibility of compatibilism and incompatibilism" (Allison, *Kant's Theory of Freedom*, pp. 4, 249).

Something that comes into being, Dharmakirti says, does so as either desired or not desired,

> so the [cognized] object has a cause in consciousness and this [desire-laden consciousness] affects the experience . . . If one experiences oneself as desirous or otherwise [i.e., as averse to whatever], then [any] object is known as desired [only a Buddha does not experience in this way]. Although it is an external object that is being known, it is such that it accords with the nature of the [desire-infected] experience . . . If it is not an external object that is cognized, of what could there be awareness? If without comprehension of an external thing as such, what else could we believe? If the experience of two [people] were not [differing] through a difference in what is [regarded as] expedient, [then there could not be variations in experience]. If it is thought that this is under the control of [karma] the unseen force, then there would not be understanding that is under the control of the object . . . If thought manifesting what is desired and what is not were not perceptual (akshadhi), that which is seen would be unconnected to what is undesired, etc. [and this is obviously false]. (Pramāṇavārttika 2.338–41a, 342–43, 345).[132]

Evidently Dharmakirti thinks that the basic characteristics of the world, including the great causal law of karma, require the existence of, or the belief in the existence of, external objects. Otherwise, he says, the world we experience makes no sense. As a Buddhist, Dharmakirti must believe that it is possible for a human being to at least approximate a desire-free consciousness. But (like the translator of the quotation just above) he excepts a Buddha and only a Buddha from the need to posit external objects.* When Dharmakirti makes the exception, is he saying

---

*Both Dignaga and Dharmakirti accept the traditional belief in yogic intuition, which is less than a Buddha's. They interpret this intuition as a perceptual awareness (yogi-pratyaksha). In the highest stage of deep meditation, what the yogin sees is so vividly perceptual that it no longer has anything of the past or of intellectual construction. The yogin's direct (not constructed) knowledge "is not contradicted by experience, since (the object of meditation) which is being apprehended represents the 'pure' object (the point-instants of efficiency that are elicited) by logical (analysis). Hence it is direct knowledge, just as (sensation) and other varieties of direct cognition are" (Dharmakirti, Nyāya-bindu 11.18–12.9 [12.8 quoted]; Stcherbatsky, Buddhist Logic, vol. 2, pp. 30–33). See Shah, Akalaṅka's Criticism of Dharmakīrti's Philosophy, pp. 217–18, summarizing PV 2.281–86). The yogin's conscious, purely perceptual grasp of point-instants would be as clear a validation of their existence as is a contemporary method of identifying and so validating the existence of individual atoms. I suppose the comparison should be carried further, to subatomic and virtual particles.

anything very different from or more or less orthodox than Kant when Kant declares (puzzlingly) that "original intuition," the nonspatial and nontemporal intuition that "can give us the existence of its object," is "a mode of intuition which, so far as we can judge, can belong only to the primordial being" (*Critique of Pure Reason* B72).[133]*

Answer to objection 4: The objection is that comparison with Kant makes Buddhist philosophers irrelevant to contemporary philosophical needs, which are no longer those of Kant. While everyone is welcome to make the comparisons that seem the most enlightening, I cannot agree that Kant has ceased to be an interesting philosopher or that a Buddhist who is compared with him becomes irrelevant to us because of the comparison itself.** Nor can I agree, as the objector contends, that the concept of *objectivity* is obsolete or simply mistaken, or that it is necessarily falsifying to attempt to be faithful to a text or use a text-critical or philological method. I have certainly felt safer in interpreting Indian, Greek, or Chinese philosophers—even Kant, who is so much closer in time and culture—when I have been able to draw on competent linguistic analyses. In any case, if the gist of the objection is that no objectivity is in any way possible, it is self-defeating, as has been argued in these pages by philosophers of each of the three great philosophical traditions.[134]

---

*Despite the quotation just above, Kant is concerned not with God as a being capable of "intellectual intuition" but as "a highest moral being under which all world-beings stand. Which cannot be the *dabile* (intuition) but only the *cogitabile* (thinkable)—the moral-practical. There is a God: for there is in moral-practical reason a categorical imperative, which extends to all rational world-beings and through which all world-beings are united." Yet Kant remains doubtful to the end whether God in fact exists. In the *Opus Postumum*, from which I have just quoted, he defines God as "a being, which has unrestricted power over nature under laws of reason." Then he qualifies the definition with the words, "However, there still seems to be the question as to whether this idea, the product of our reason, has a reality or is a mere thought" (Kant, *Opus Postumum*, trans. Förster and Rosen, pp. 198, 200–201; Akademie ed. 22.117, 105).

**Which philosophers are just now or should just now be regarded as most pertinent to our concerns is a contentious question. In direct contradiction to the view I have just cited, I have come across another that claims that the influence of Kant and the close reading of Kantian texts helped to make possible "the reception of Continental hermeneutics and poststructuralist thought, as well as the more radical critiques of realism they espouse." The study of Kant now shows, it is said, that we ought "to wonder whether the postmodernist and Habermassian critiques of subjectivity are perhaps historically naive and poorly grounded" (R. R. Velkley, in Henrich, *The Unity of Reason*, p. 2). The history of philosophy is endlessly volatile.

Afterword

❄

I start this page with a feeling almost of nostalgia for the years of work that I am about to end with the words I set down now. It takes an effort to dismiss the idea that now that I have finished I know enough to begin again. I also dismiss the idea that I should end with suggestions for research. These I have left implicit in the first, introductory chapter. What I most want to do here is to learn how the writing of this history has affected the way in which I think of philosophy. What follows is therefore a coda meant to make clear—to myself, too—the attitudes that I have either developed or reaffirmed as I worked.

The first of these attitudes is that comparative philosophy ought to set an example of fairness of exposition and decency of appraisal. Unfortunately, as I have come to see, such fairness and decency are not entirely helpful to the effort to philosophize. Why say this? Because such qualities can easily discourage creative thought by the limits they impose on its freedom. Creative thought struggles loose of scruples. It nourishes itself by begging, borrowing, stealing, distorting, and reworking others' ideas, and by encouraging the vain but invigorating hope that the result will prove itself forever superior to the thought of all rivals. (If I know myself, I will quote more than once from that very human skeptic, Montaigne, who says in his unfairly but eloquently dismissive vein, "Trust in your philosophy now! Boast that you are the one who has found the lucky bean in your festive pudding!")[1]

The ideal of fairness makes the amoral intensity of creative thought more difficult to sustain. In any case, the ideal is put into play for a purpose that is rather different from philosophizing per se. Given the ideal, whoever studies the history of philosophy gets to play the role of what anthropologists and sociologists call a participant observer, someone who studies a group by participating in its activities but who remains in the end detached from it. In the case of philosophy, the historian's effort to understand, which is to place, define, explicate, compare, and react, is in temper detached from

517

the philosophical issues under discussion. This is because, ideally, the historian should understand a philosophy as it was understood by its partisans, its opponents, its successors, and its successors' opponents. So to be fair, the historian first has to show how a philosophical position can once have been and may even remain persuasive. This the historian can do only by withdrawing for the while from every other position and acting as a temporary partisan. It is only after this partisanship has displayed the position to its best advantage that the historian's critical remarks are allowable—they are, after all, only natural, they bring the historian's own views to light, and they make it easier to judge his work. But they are allowable only on condition that they are identified as criticisms, do not (at least, not consciously) contaminate the exposition itself, and do obey the rules of fair play. Put negatively, the historian who, for the sake of fairness, identifies with a position while it is being expounded is unable to identify with it fully or for long, and therefore unable to identify fully with any position at all. How else can the historian be equally fair to its opponents and successors? One result is that such a participant observer, whose attitude is by nature unstable, may arouse misgivings among philosophers, a feeling shaded with disrespect for the outsider, who, unable to experience philosophizing in its full intensity, is not able to understand it from within. This historian, the philosophers are apt to think, is to the true philosopher as the actor is to the historical figure whose role he takes. How can the historian pretend to stand impossibly above the fray and judge the philosopher, who takes philosophical risks, is engaged in difficult, deeply felt argument, and is truly creative? The conclusion may be that the history of philosophy is secondary to the creation of philosophy and parasitic on it. The response may be that the life of these parasites and these hosts has come to be symbiotic and, when perspectives are exchanged, it can be difficult to decide which is the parasite and which the host.

This is not to say that the historians of philosophy are all subject to the reproach that they take the easy way out by remaining fundamentally detached from philosophical problems. The Tibetan historians of Buddhism, Buston in the fourteenth century and Taranatha in the sixteenth, are both exultantly partisan.* What of Indian and Chinese his-

---

*There was a special genre of historical writing in Tibet called *Origin of Buddhism* (*Chos 'byung*). "It is possible that with the proliferation of various doctrinal cycles a need was felt to place these in historical perspective and thereby legitimate them. In any case, we find, starting with the twelfth century, an enormous upsurge of interest in Indo-Tibetan religious history in particular. Unfortunately, only a fraction of the potentially available literary corpus of such texts has been located and published to date . . . The thirteenth century, too, knew of a considerable number of such treatises, the sole information concerning which is owed to a very brief remark by Bu ston as well as potentially to a number of quotations in his own *chos 'byung*" (L. W. J. Van der Kuijp, "Tibetan Historiography," in J. I. Cabezon and R. R. Jackson, eds., *Tibetan Literature*, Ithaca: Snow Lion, 1996, p. 46).

torians? Unlike the Tibetans, the Indians have an only rudimentary interest in history, including the history of philosophy. Their histories of philosophy are confined to genealogical lists of teachers and disciples, legends of heroic thinkers, and doxographies, that is, simple collections of opinions or doctrines. All the Indian schools wanted, of course, to understand their rivals. The Buddhists are prominent among the earlier Indian doxographers, but the doxographic literature as a whole seems dominated by the Jains and Advaita Vedantins. For the Jains, the reason for compiling such a record is that they believe that all points of view have some truth, all the truths being joined in their own philosophy of perspectives. Like the Jains, the Advaita Vedantins are drawn to doxography in order to show that their position includes and transcends all the others, which are presented in the order of their increasing likeness to their own doctrine.* Yet though the ancient Indians have little interest in history, they have their own way of remaining aware of the philosophical context of their thought. This is the eminently technical care they have learned to exercise in repeating and answering their rivals' questions. By means of such care, they remain integrated into their tradition as a whole: the systematic asking and answering creates a web of argument that imposes a coherence on the classical philosophy of India probably more complex than that of medieval Europe and certainly more careful than that of modern Europe (I am referring to the philosophers' arguments with one another, not to late nineteenth- and twentieth-century philosophical scholarship).[2]

In contrast, early Chinese thought is by nature historical, but it tends to merge philosophy, as the West distinguishes it, with culture in general. Chinese literature, including the literature we count as philosophical, is preserved in anthologies. The most extensive of these, meant for official use, are considered to be encyclopedias. Their extracts from

---

*Two of the Indian doxographies are relatively well known in the West. One is the eighth-century *Compendium of the Six Systems* (*Shaddarshana-samuchchaya*) written by Haribhadra, a Brahman converted to Jainism, who was so full of learning "that he laid gold bands around his body to prevent his bursting," and so confident that he wore an inscription saying that he would become the pupil of whoever cited a philosophical sentence he could not understand. The second doxography is the fourteenth-century *Summary of All Doctrines* (*Sarvadarshana-samgraha*) by Madhava-Vidyarana, a follower of Shankara. The Advaita Vedanta's arrangement of views can be illustrated by a doxographical work attributed to Shankara himself. The order is as follows: "Lokayata, Arhata (i.e, Jainism), Bauddha (Buddhism, divided into four types), Vaisheshika, Nyaya, the Mimamsa of the schools of Prabhakara, Samkhya, Yoga, the doctrine of 'Vedavyasa' (essentially that of the *Mahabharata*), and the Advaita Vedanta." (See Halbfass, *India and Europe*, chap. 19; the quotation is from pp. 351-52. The stories about Haribhadra are from M. Winternitz, *History of Indian Literature*, vol. 2, Delhi: Banarsidass, 1983, p. 461.)

past literature are examples of literary or moral excellence and deal, among the rest, with "human affairs," broadly interpreted.[3] The earliest historical picture of Chinese philosophy, that which ends the *Chuang-tzu* book, is an exception. Relatively comprehensive, it shows its partisanship in the sadness it expresses over the departure of most thinkers from the true Way and in the words in which it ends, with a lament for Hui Shih: How sad, it says, that the logician Hui Shih dissipated his talents in distinctions and analyses that kept him from achieving anything a Taoist valued. The greatest of Chinese historians, Ssu-ma Ch'ien, narrates history in political terms, but he also composes biographies, grouped by categories that include philosophers. His biographies of Confucius and Chuang-tzu, both of which have been cited here, are the earliest we have. Ssu-ma means both to be objective and, like Plutarch, to draw moral lessons from the biographies. He shows his interest in morality and his historian's nature in his attitude, for example, to the "seventy disciples" of Confucius. He refuses, he says, to praise or to disparage too much, as did those who never knew the persons they were talking about. The words that follow express his usual desire to be objective:

> There is a register of the disciples preserved by the K'ung family and written in archaic characters which I believe to be generally accurate. I have used this list of names and surnames of the disciples, combining it with the questions and answers of these men found in the *Analects*, and arranged the material in this chapter. Material that seemed doubtful I have omitted.[4]

Greek philosophy first takes on a self-consciously historical aspect in Aristotle. His *Metaphysics* opens with the often-cited words, "All men by nature desire to know," and goes on to the sequence of speculative philosophers from Thales to Plato. How accurate Aristotle may be, even in relation to Plato, is a matter for dispute. As a creator of philosophy, not the participant observer I earlier identified with the historian, his interest in the history of philosophy is mainly to improve and exploit previous thought.[5]

Not surprisingly, the most important of the early Greek doxographers is Aristotle's student and successor, Theophrastus; but most of his topical summaries of the opinions of the pre-Socratic "physicists" have been lost. The only complete surviving doxography, Diogenes Laertius' *Doctrines of Eminent Philosophers*, long remained the most influential model for the history of philosophy.[6] Diogenes has no purpose beyond an orderly, entertaining, and impartial record—Pyrrhonists and Epicureans meet with equal treatment and sympathy.*

The history—historiography—of European philosophy turns modern when it turns self-reflective, not unlike Aristotle in the distant past. It has two outstanding early representatives, one toward the middle of the eighteenth century, and another toward its end. The earlier of the two is Johann Jacob Brucker, whose massive five-volume *Critical History of Philosophy* was studied by Diderot, Goethe, and Kant, and was still referred to by Hegel and Schopenhauer.[7] Brucker attempts to be exhaustive and to capture doctrines in exact numbered propositions (of which Aristotle, according to Brucker, professes 210). Brucker insists that a philosophy remains obscure if one does not take account of its author's life, temperament, and human and philosophical surroundings. As a self-conscious historian, he holds that "one must avoid substituting one's own opinions for those of the philosophers" and that "ancient philosophy should not be reduced to ours."[8] He is confident that the history of philosophy is that of the errors, discoveries, and still unfulfilled needs of the human understanding as a whole.

The other outstanding historian of philosophy is Dietrich Tiedemann, whose six volumes of the *Spirit of Speculative Philosophy* were published between 1791 and 1797.[9] What is most striking in Tiedemann is his conviction that the history of philosophy shows that reason advances endlessly. The historian of philosophy therefore "ought to examine with care what each philosophy has brought that is proper to itself and new" and "in what measure each philosopher has given science new concepts or clarified or improved the definition of old ones." To demonstrate the progress of reason, Tiedemann begins with Thales and goes on to his own times, finding progress in each phase, and refusing to see an end to the progress, because, he says, there is no one criterion for truth nor any final definition of philosophy.[10]

Much in Tiedemann anticipates Hegel's lectures on the history of philosophy, first published in 1833, after Hegel's death. Hegel believes that "the history of philosophy is not a collection of arbitrary opinions, but a necessary interconnection from its first beginning to its rich development."[11]

---

*A translator of his work writes, "The impression left upon the unprejudiced reader by close acquaintance with our author is that he is dealing with a Dryasdust, vain and credulous, of multifarious reading, amazing industry, and insatiable curiosity" (R. D. Hicks, introduction to Diogenes Laertius, *Lives of Eminent Philosophers*, Cambridge: Harvard University Press, 1925, vol. 1, p. xiv). The "Dryasdust" seems to me an unmerited description of a writer so full of curious stories.

But quite unlike Tiedemann, Hegel is sure that the progress is toward an absolute goal. In spite of "perverse" instances, he claims, the history of philosophy is a series of increasing approximations of his own "philosophy of the present." Hegel's is the highest of all philosophies, he claims, because, in annulling the earlier ones, it preserves what is of value in them and is able to reflect both on them and on itself—this is the kind of claim made, *mutatis mutandis*, by Jainism, Advaita Vedanta, and Hua-yen (the Flower Garland school of Chinese Buddhism), each of which assimilates other philosophies as partial or lower truths into its own, supposedly complete, final truth. In Hegel's scheme, it should be recalled, Chinese and Indian religion and philosophy occupy a low place: There is no self-consciously free individual in the Orient, which has been "superseded" by the Occident, Hegel is sure. Yet he holds that Indian thought is able to correct the subjectivism and anthropocentrism of modern Western thought, and in time he corrects himself and concludes that India did have "real philosophy," philosophy distinct from religion. But he seems to have held fast to his view that "no inherent morality is bound up with the Chinese religion, no immanent rationality through which human beings might have internal value and dignity."[12]

Having allowed these historians to pose the question of progress, I find myself reluctant to take it up. In one way, the answer to it is self-evident and in another, acutely subjective. What is self-evident is that every tradition of philosophy has progressed in its own terms, for its own ends. Its progress depends, as I have said, on its necessary elaboration. This in turn depends on the answers given in the course of debate within the tradition itself and debate with external opponents, not to speak of the assimilation of useful fragments of other philosophies. If its historical continuity is unbroken, each philosophy is provided with successively better answers to its rivals and goes on building its structure higher, more firmly, and more elaborately. Given time, philosophical structures become fully elaborated, that is, worked out in the full detail that enriches and individualizes their culture. They then become summary expressions of these cultures, like the great Christian cathedrals, or the great Muslim mosques, or the great Hindu or Chinese temples or Buddhist stupas.

Although modern Western philosophy has had a relatively short unbroken history, it too has progressed, not only in the elaboration of which I have been speaking but in a clear special sense. I am referring to Western philosophy's recent assimilation of much of the evidence given by the sciences, whether more or less exact—in either case generally superior to whatever existed before—and by the broader, exacter knowledge that has become available to everyone. In the West, even the Heideggerian or other opponent of modern thought can feel (sad) progress in that philosophical evil has now shown its reductive, mathematical, technocratic face so much more clearly and can be the more persuasively exposed and confuted. The real or purported victims of this reductive technocracy, imprisoned (its opponents say) by mechanization and by concepts that by their nature as concepts always miss what is really real or really valuable, can turn its weapons against it and grow famous by virtue of the lectures, books, broadcasts, and sundry honors that technocratic evil, as they see it, has put at their disposal.

Each philosophy or philosophical school and each tradition has therefore progressed. But this progress has been limited in two not unimportant ways: First, although it has progressed, it appears no closer to victory over its rivals, which have also progressed; and, second, its fundamental attitudes may not be superior to what they were to begin with. There is much still to doubt and not a little to hope for. While continued argument leads to a philosophy's greater and greater elaboration, why regard elaboration in itself as the final measure of philosophical success? Why not, instead, self-doubt or self-restraint, the ability to be philosophically modest and to say, along with Montaigne, that even on stilts, we can walk only on our legs? Montaigne would surely extend to philosophers and their subtleties the skeptical admiration with which he views lawyers and legal subtleties (so I take the liberty of substituting the word *philosophers* for his *lawyers* in the quotation that follows). Montaigne begins with the question, Have you ever seen children making attempts to arrange

> a pile of quicksilver into a set number of segments? The more they press and knead it and try to make it do what they want the more they exasperate the taste for liberty in that noble metal: it resists their art and proceeds to scatter and break into innumerable parts. It is just the same here: for by subdividing those subtle statements philosophers teach people to increase matters of doubt; they start us off extending and varying our difficulties, stretching them out and spreading them about. By sowing doubts and then pruning them back they make the world produce abundant crops of uncertainties and quarrels, just as the soil is made more fertile when it is broken up and dug deep: "It is learning which creates the difficulty." (Montaigne, *On Experience*)[13]

When he says this, how distant is Montaigne from Wittgenstein's disabused statement that "a philosopher is a man who has to cure many intellectual diseases in himself before he can arrive at the nothings of common sense?" Or from Montaigne's own minimalizing directness that says, "When I dance, I dance. When I sleep, I sleep."[14]

To go on, why value philosophical elaboration as such over openness of imagination or sympathy, or fantastic humor, like that of Chuang-tzu, or even the uncommon quality that is called common sense—don't Confucius and the equable older Hume have it? When Chuang-tzu, like Montaigne, wants to teach the absurdity of acting against nature, he does so in many ways, some of them explicitly philosophical by the characterization we have adopted, but also by fantastically humorous stories such as one that is based on the myth of Hun Tun, a god whose face has no features, that is, no apertures:

> The god of the south sea was Shu [Brief], the god of the north sea was Hu [Sudden], and the god of the center was Hun Tun [Formless]. Shu and Hu occasionally used to go together to Hun Tun's land, and Hun Tun received them very cordially. Shu and Hu planned how to replay his generosity. They said, "All humans have seven openings with which to see, hear, eat, and breathe. Only this one has not yet got any." So they tried chiseling him. Each day they chiseled one opening. On the seventh day, Hun Tun died. (*Chuang Tzu* 7.7)[15]

Nor, to go on, has there surely been progress if one judges philosophy from an esthetic standpoint, as a creative effort the value of which lies in the transforming, individualizing power of the effort itself: each of us starts as the raw material that, by accident and prolonged effort, can transform itself into an intellectually more complex, more deeply understanding creature. Like ancient Indian gods, we can be born intellectually out of our longing to be born so (desire, the *Rigveda* says, evolved in the beginning, which was the first seed of thought—desire then gave birth to thought, or thought to desire, or maybe, Indian fashion, each gave birth to the other).[16] Maybe the transformation that a person undergoes in creating or assimilating a philosophy is more important than the abstract truth that is attributed to it. One makes oneself by making one's philosophy that fits oneself, and, considered in detail, no one else. Witness, again, Montaigne, who says, "Since philosophy has not been able to discover any good general method for tranquillity, everyone should search for it as an individual"; and witness again Wittgenstein, who says, "No one can think a thought for me in the way no one can don my hat for me."[17] I hear you, maybe, but only I can philosophize for *me*.

The remark about the transforming power of philosophy leads to the view, which I favor, that philosophers should be seen also (I mean, not exclusively) as artists whose medium is abstract thought. From this standpoint, philosophy is the art of telling the abstract truth as fully, exactly, and affectingly as possible, or, alternatively, of drawing, with affecting exactness or convincingly rational rhetoric, the exact limits to the ability to tell the abstract truth. Philosophy can then be characterized as the art by which the individual philosopher tries—never, of course, with more than relative success—to surpass the limits of time, place, and individuality, but perhaps gives this relative failure an aura of success by hinting at what has evaded the effort and so helping others to go further.

We praise artists for their originality or individuality, but if we are not skeptics or relativists, we seem to assume that philosophers should all ideally reach the same general conclusions and be in this respect like exact scientists. Yet the evidence is that every uncoerced philosopher is persuaded by an at least subtly unique set of reasons and reaches conclusions that, closely observed, are unique as well. My reasons are as generally human as my person, but they are spoken in what can be only my own unmistakably individual voice and are, perceived from close by, as individual as my face. As the history of philosophy makes clear, such an individualistic view of philosophy does not fit traditional views and is not very usual, but I take it to be accurate at a fundamental level.

Some artists claim to express the truth, but they do so, judged from an ordinary philosophical standpoint, indirectly, by the equivalence of their perceptual means and expressive structures to the more purely intellectual means that philosophers use. Philosophers, like other writers, rely on all the means that rhetoric gives them, but granted their usual passion for verbal exactness and logical consistency and transparency, they cannot rely too openly on the means that other kinds of artists use. In a way, therefore, the uniqueness of the philosophical art is the more focused, narrow, and striking—it is, or seems to be, exclusively about some philosophical end, most often, the philosophers say, about truth. That they generally aim at truth has made them at times hardly if at all distinguishable from scientists. But we have learned by now to separate between science, especially when exact, and philosophy. We have or should have come to agree that when philosophy contradicts exact science or what we seriously believe to be fact, we have little choice except to consider philosophy to be mistaken. However, even when mistaken, its mistakes and the intellectual effort they represent can lead to interesting and possibly fruitful ideas. And in what philosophy is not mistaken, it can persuade us of what it cannot prove. Its persuasiveness does not answer to the strict standards of evidence that the exact sciences require, and what it persuades us of therefore remains vague, that is, not capable of being declared either right or wrong by such strict standards.

The failure of philosophy to be provably right or wrong has turned out to be a reason that it does not become superfluous. That is, the prescientific, parascientific, nonscientific, or extrascientific nature of philosophy remains necessary, even for the sake of science, for the ambiance in which science can flourish. The reason is that the more exact a science becomes or the more exactly it is interpreted, the more it is limited to ideal, sheerly abstract circumstances and to conditions so exactly defined that they, too, are ideal and not, very strictly speaking, repeatable. An exact science or an exact fraction of a less exact one is therefore incomplete and not exactly coherent with any other exact science or fraction of science and—as we at present know the sciences—cannot be a coherently fitting part of an encompassing exact science.[18] Then who but the philosopher, together with the scientist in a philosophical role, is to determine by what exact standards a science may be considered exact? What, if anything, the philosopher asks, is *the* scientific notion of *a* scientific method? What general conclusions, if any, can be drawn from exact science? None of this discussion is itself exactly exact. So philosophy helps to provide an indispensable intellectual context for clarifying the nature and limits of science, and in doing so it enlarges, deepens, and helps to complete our intellectual grasp of the world. Without it, we cannot attempt to think carefully beyond and between the more or less exact sciences. So, in our own times, philosophy and science make a dissimilar but complementary pair; and they pair as well with other creative activities, literature in particular and art in general. To the extent that these activities are distinguishable from one another, they flow in and out of one another like streams that join, mingle their waters for a time, then diverge, and then mingle again. In human thought and in the real—not analytically divided—world, their stringent separation is artificial.

I have said that philosophy is like art because philosophers aim not only at the truth but are concerned, like artists (and maybe more openly than scientists) with having an effect on others. They want to lodge in the minds of as many persons as they can. This view of philosophers influences the relative skepticism and the strong social emphasis with which I have learned to judge the possibilities of comparative philosophy, along with philosophy in general, and the answers I give to the questions that follow.

There are two questions that I cannot escape. The first is this: Does the comparative history of philosophy that has just been concluded lead to any final reckoning? The history has been constructed as a series of variations on common themes. Whoever continues it in a similar spirit may change the themes or variations or increase their number, and should, in any case, make them more exact, the degree of their exactness having no clear limit. But none of this more varied or exact research will in itself answer the question. It should by now be self-evident that my answer is that this history cannot lead to a final reckoning—not unless one counts as final the evidence that philosophers, regardless of their convictions, have always been remote from anything that can plausibly be called a final reckoning. What history does that is so valuable is to extend our memories. The decisions that our judgment reaches with the help of these memories remain most usually subjective. Yet the similarities between the basic concerns of philosophers and the limited number of basic answers they give can be documented, and so can the small and large reasons for their disagreements. If perceptively gathered and analyzed, such documentation is certainly illuminating. But the very proliferation of the philosophers' points of view justifies the verdict that they have all been subjective, by which I mean, unable to prove anything of importance in an unmistakably compelling way. This inability of philosophers to achieve an unquestionable position—and of the skeptics among them to achieve an unquestionable array of doubts—characterizes both the traditions that the philosophers express and the doctrines they invent or adapt to their individual purposes.

As a second, final question I ask, Does this inescapable doubtfulness show that philosophies have all been invented in vain? Surely not, I answer. This is because traditions, or, rather, many of the individuals who comprise each tradition, need philosophy to give their lives an overriding intellectual pattern. It is impossible to live a merely nebulous life, with nothing in particular to do and nowhere exactly to go. Everybody needs a structure of habits and goals. These develop as if by themselves, but the structure has its architects, some well known, some obscure. In the sense of implicit philosophy, there always is an underlying architecture. For a tradition must embody a view of life, a view that is more various, tangled, deep, and subtle, I suppose, than reasoning can fully articulate. Yet the ability to put a prolonged succession of thoughts in *explicitly* rational ways—to give their structures an explicitly rational defense and subject them to explicitly rational analyses—is a great historical accomplishment.

In any case, everybody has to live in some definite intellectual neighborhood, to which philosophy of the explicit kind I mean helps to give a structure with openly exhibited abstract girders. Human beings are everywhere domiciled in locally made houses, local communities, and localized traditions with localized philosophical modes of expression. They have had little choice except to live according to the meanings that they perceive in their own vicinity and (as Dignaga, Dharmakirti, and Kant would say) the perceptions they create by their humanity and—we have to add—their acquired habits of thought.

The result is that philosophy is the abstract yet always local shape that those who need it give to their thought. But the local shape cannot be *merely* local. Just because there is no philosophy divorced from a location, none that is nothing but general, it always turns out to be a variant of what tradition has given the susceptible individuals. For a more than primitive philosophy, one has only the materials—the terms, concepts, beliefs, and intentions—that tradition has already provided, and one is able to build the whole structure only by varying the plans that tradition has already drawn. Even when conservative, the early philosophers we know in each tradition are (or appear to us to be) strikingly individual, while those who follow them, whether in India, China, or Greece, become associated with subtraditions or schools, which they defend, with sometimes subversive methods.

To put it somewhat differently: Philosophy is an initially optional sublanguage or jargon, growing, in time, increasingly technical, that is practiced so that its vocabulary and syntactic structure help one to express oneself in certain modes of generalizing, self-justifying thought. For anyone who has learned such a language, the importance of a philosophic tradition or subtradition is that it defines the group of those who understand the individual philosopher's generalizing talk more exactly and, the philosopher must hope, more sympathetically. In India and China, we know, there have been many philosophical languages and dialects. So, too, in the West, the philosopher has talked the necessary local dialect of one or more of the philosophical languages, ranging from the Platonic, Aristotelic, Epicuric, and Stoic languages, in the distant Greek past, up to Heideggeric and Wittgensteinic in the present. A language identifies the philosopher who speaks it as the member of a certain community of thought and perhaps of action and style of life. Having learned the language, a philosopher continues to take part in the engrossing pursuit of "truth," "higher life," "authenticity," "clarification," or other goal, mostly within the community and mostly, of course, by the rules it sets. Of course, the history of philosophy, especially if comparative, tends to go beyond the local community's bounds, break the authority of its rules, and maybe create broader though vaguer communities of its own.

As we have witnessed, philosophical reasoning varies greatly; but within the variety of the reasons that philosophers give, there remain, we have also witnessed, many immediate and potential similarities. A philosopher cannot be merely individual, and Indian, Chinese, Greek, or other traditions or subtraditions cannot belong solely to their own geographical, temporal, or human limits. Even though every individual human being, philosophy, and philosophical subtradition and tradition is bound to a particular local context, every individual, philosophy, subtradition, and tradition is also bound to humanity at large. This is obviously because human thought everywhere, like human perception, exhibits similar capacities and is responsive to similar needs. Since we are creatures that are built alike and breathe, eat, excrete, talk, love, generate, fight, and socialize, we cannot avoid many similarities in the ways we think.

To be similar, it must be repeated, is *never* to be just the same. *Every* philosopher is an unrepeatable individual who reasons within a unique subtradition at a distinct moment of its historical development. Yet ideas presented in a philosophical, that is, abstract form are relatively easy— easier than works of art—to divest of their conspicuous local traits and put in a different or more general language. When ideas are presented so, it becomes natural to ask how many general reasons can be given for being, for instance, a skeptic, an atomist, or a mystic? And how many for trusting or distrusting perception, reason, testimony, or sacred texts? Or for complying or not with social demands? Or for accepting or disowning a tradition or subtradition of thought? In every case, the answer is "not many."

If to be similar is never to be quite the same but never quite different, one needs careful eyes to see the nuances of similarity and difference, which are the analogies and failures of analogy by means of which we create so much of our thought. If it lacked the power to make analogies, our thought would become helpless. No one event could teach us how to anticipate that another event would, in practical or theoretical effect, repeat it. Even the same words and even the anonymous *x* of abstract thought could not stand for effectively identical instances (Nietzsche, who wants to discredit all language because it assumes identity, does not take into account—as Chuang-tzu does—that the general failure of language would invalidate the antilinguistic argument he uses language to make). As I have said earlier, China has had enormous internal variety of every kind, has had variable boundaries, and has not always been politically united. That we take it be one rather than many Chinas is so by virtue of a succession of analogies that show us what is internal to it, and failures of analogy that show us what is external. In the same way, India is one and Europe is one by virtue of analogical and disanalogical acts of classification.

Unless we take great care in viewing others' ideas, we see in them only reflections of ourselves: a self-indulgent choice of texts, a twist of meaning here, the shift of a word there, the minimizing of an inconvenient belief, and we once more experience the thought—our own—on which we set so high a value. Among the archetypes of the philosopher there are both Narcissus, unknowingly in love with his own reflection, and Echo, able only to repeat the words in which Narcissus expresses his self-love and frustration. We may want to decide what is particular to Chinese, Indian, or European thought, or, at the usually unhelpful limit of abstraction, to Eastern as compared with Western thought. The decision may come intuitively, as if by itself. But it shows us only our own faces, unless we make it with care, revise it as often as we learn more, and grant it a full spectrum of possibilities.

Implicitly, so I think, we have learned that each human being needs the emotional closeness given by a particular community, language, poetry, pictorial expression, and—in what concerns us most in this history—a set of abstract reasons. Abstract reasons, too, articulate and strengthen or weaken our emotional affinities. Philosophy spends itself in elaborating these reasons. In a sense that is sometimes personal and always social, when our intellectual surroundings stimulate us to reason with sustained explicitness, the elaboration of the reasoning is simply necessary, in the long run almost as necessary as food, shelter, and companionship.

In the end, we see: All the world's a forum, and all the thinkers who appear in it are full of strange ideas, jealous in honor, seeking a fragile reputation in exchange for the gift of their thought. Do you have any philosophy in you? they ask, and, usually without waiting for an answer, go on, We do (or, I do) and you have to listen to us (or, to me). In spite of their narcissism, their gift is valuable. Whoever learns to take in what the philosophers have reasoned is so much the richer and sometimes even the wiser. Their voices are invigorating because they are, after all, intermittently persuasive, but also because they so persistently argue with one another. To testify for myself, I am happy to have lived in their demanding, discordant company. Their discord is part of the evidence that no philosophy they have ever invented is simply right or grasps human experience fully—remember Montaigne's image of the children trying to divide a lump of quicksilver into equal parts. Yet when I think of how I myself try to philosophize, I sense that many of the philosophers have been more or less unconsciously assimilated into my thought. They live in the study that I and you make of them, and their presence within us makes it possible for us to be more generally human in a more individual way. Such a cacophany of fathers, to depend on and measure oneself against! Such a great, creative turmoil and babble of thought!

This history ought to end so, with an exclamation of gratitude. When I make the exclamation, I of course feel the impulse to elaborate; but why add to the surfeit of words and reasons? Philosophy will not be concluded by any reasons I can add to those that have already been given. I therefore refuse to allow my own explicit philosophy the victory that, as the author, I could give it here, at least verbally—I cannot play the master in the forum where so many others have to have their say.

Notes

✳

Chapter 1. The Three Philosophical Traditions

1. B.-A. Scharfstein, ed., *Philosophy East/Philosophy West*, Oxford: Blackwell and New York: Oxford University Press, 1978, chaps. 1, 2 ("Three Philosophical Civilizations: A Preliminary Comparison").

2. **Mesopotamian thought**: J. Bottéro, *Mesopotamia: Writing, Reasoning, and the Gods*, Chicago: University of Chicago Press, 1992 (esp. for "The Dialogue of Pessimism"). S. Dalley, *Myths from Mesopotamia*, Oxford: Oxford University Press, 1989, (esp. for the probable moral of the Gilgamesh epic) p. 150. P. Garelli, "La Pensée préphilosophique en Mésopotamie," in B. Parain, ed., *Histoire de la Philosophie*, vol. 1, Paris: Gallimard, 1969, pp. 24–49. T. Jacobsen, *The Treasures of Darkness*, New Haven: Yale University Press, 1976, chaps. 7 and 8, and epilogue. H. McCall, *Mesopotamian Myths*, London/Austin: British Museum Publications/University of Texas Press, 1990. J. B. Pritchard, ed., *Ancient Near Eastern Texts Relating to the Old Testament*, 2d ed. Princeton: Princeton University Press, 1955, pp. 600–601 ("The Dialogue of Pessimism").

3. **Egyptian thought**: J. Assmann, *Maat, l'Egypte pharaonique et l'idée de justice sociale*, Paris: Julliard, 1989. H. Brunner, "Die Lehren," in *Ägyptologie: Literatur*, vol. 1.2 of B. Spuler, ed., *Handbuch der Orientalistik: Der Nahe und der Mittlere Osten*, Leiden: Brill, 1970. E. Hornung, *Conceptions of God in Ancient Egypt*, London: Routledge & Kegan Paul, 1983, esp. "Conclusion." A. Loprieno, ed., *Ancient Egyptian Literature: History and Forms*, Leiden: Brill, 1996 (see chaps. on didactic literature, theology and literature [in French], and myth and literature; the index of topics does not contain the entry *philosophy*). J. Yoyotte, "La Pensée préphilosophique en Egypte," in B. Parin, ed., *Histoire de la Philosophie*, vol. 1, pp. 1–23.

4. **Eskimo thought**: K. Rasmussen, *Intellectual Culture of the Iglulik Eskimos*, Copenhagen: *Report of the Fifth Thule Expedition 1921–24*, 1929, vol. 7(1), pp. 54–56. See Rasmussen's other books.

5. C. Leslau and W. Leslau, *African Proverbs*, Mount Vernon, N.Y.: Peter Pauper Press, 1962, pp. 8, 9, 19, 48, 51.

6. **African thought**: Dilemma Tales: W. Bascom, "African Dilemma Tales: An Introduction," in R. M. Dorson, ed., *African Folklore*, New York: Anchor Books (Doubleday), 1972, pp. 148–49. R. D. Abrams, *African Folktales*, New York: Pantheon Books, 1983, part 2.

The character and rationality of traditional African thoughts: D. Forde, ed., *African Worlds*, London: Oxford University Press, 1954. R. Horton, *Patterns of Thought in Africa and the West*, Cambridge: Cambridge University Press, 1993 (Horton finds "features of cognitive life that were common to both Africa and the West" and argues that contextual explanation is also needed for the ideas that Westerners consider rationally founded (pp. 12, 14). J. S. Mbiti, *African Religions and Philosophies*, Garden City: (Doubleday), 1970. Two (among many) monographic studies: J. W. Fernandez, *Bwiti: An Ethnography of the Religious Imagination in Africa*, Princeton: Princeton University Press, 1982 (shows how the Fang (of Gabon) have tried "to recapture the totality of the old way of life" (p. 9). W. MacGaffey, *Religion and Society in Central Africa*, Chicago: University of Chicago Press, 1986 (Kongo [Zaire] life as it reflects the tension between religious, political, and economic values and leads to the "speculative and explanatory thought" that religion makes possible (p. 250).

Argument over the existence of African philosophy: In general: V. Y. Mudimbe, *The Invention of Africa: Gnosis, Philosophy, and the Order of Knowledge*, Bloomington: Indiana University Press, 1988, chap 5, (surveys the debates of anthropologists and of contemporary African philosophers). P. Radin, *Primitive Man as Philosopher*, New York: Appleton, 1927 (defends the implicitly rational character of so-called "primitive thought"; in contrast to Horton [above], philosophically unsophisticated).

Specific constructions or denials: P. K. Gyekye, *An Essay on African Philosophical Thought: The Akan Conceptual Scheme*, Cambridge: Cambridge University Press, 1987. M. Griaule, *Conversations with Ogotemmeli*, London: Oxford University Press. P. Hountondji, *African Philosophy*, London; Hutchinson, 1983. P. Ikunobe, "The Parochial Universalist Conception of 'Philosophy' and 'African Philosophy,' " *Philosophy East and West* 47.2 (April 1997). A. Kagame, *La philosophie bantu-rwandaise de l'Être*, Brussels: Académie Royale des Sciences Coloniales (Mémoires, Nouvelle série, Vol. xii, fasc. 1), 1956. H. O. Oruka, ed., *Sage Philosophy*, Leiden: Brill, 1990. P. Tempels *Bantu Philosophy*, Paris: Présence Africaine, 1959. K. Wiredu, *Philosophy and an African Culture*, Cambridge: Cambridge University Press, 1980. I have not seen two recent books, *Postcolonial African Philosophy*, a textbook, and *African Philosophy*, an anthology, both edited by E. C. Eze and published in Oxford by Blackwell. The books' respective dates are 1996 and 1997.

7. **Indian philosophy**: S. Dasgupta, *Indian Idealism*, Cambridge: Cambridge University Press, 1933 (a series of lucid, relatively concentrated lectures). E. Frauwallner, *History of Indian Philosophy*, 2 vols., Delhi: Banarsidass, 1973 (a not particularly elegant but generally reliable translation of the German original, an unfinished work of original scholarship that tempts fate by trying to work out the historical development of early Indian philosophy). B. K. Matilal, *Perception: An Essay on Classical Indian Theories of Knowledge*, Oxford: Oxford University Press,

1988; *Logical and Ethical Issues of Religious Belief*, Calcutta; University of Calcutta, 1982; *Logic, Language and Reality*, Delhi: Banarsidass, 1985; *The Word and the World: India's Contribution to the Study of Language*, Delhi: Oxford University Press, 1990 (Matilal was a noteworthy mediator between Indian and Western, especially analytical, philosophy). J. N. Mohanty, *Reason and Tradition in Indian Thought*, Oxford: Oxford University Press, 1992. K. H. Potter, *Presuppositions of India's Philosophy*, New Delhi: Prentice-Hall, 1965. K. N. Tiwari, *Suffering: Indian Perspectives*, Delhi: Banarsidass, 1986 (especially the essays by K. H. Potter, B. K. Matilal, and A. Sharma).

Relations between Indian and European philosophy: H. von Glasenapp, *Das Indienbild deutscher Denker*, Stuttgart: Koehler Verlag, 1960. W. Halbfass, *India and Europe*, Albany: State University of New York Press, 1988 (a clear-minded, very knowledgeable account of the intellectual relationship). S. S. Rama Rao Pappu and R. Puligandla, *Indian Philosophy: Past and Future*, Delhi: Banarsidass, 1983 (contemporary Indian philosophers assessing the present status of their tradition). E. J. Sharpe, *The Universal Gītā: Western Images of the Bhagavadgītā*, London: Duckworth, 1985. S. Sommerfeld, *Indienschau und Indiendeutung romantischer Philosophen*, Zürich: Rascher Verlag, 1943.

Chinese philosophy: R. E. Allinson, ed., *Understanding the Chinese Mind*, Hong Kong: Oxford University Press, 1989. Fung Yu-lan (in Chinese order, last name first), *A History of Chinese Philosophy*, 2d ed., 2 vols., Princeton: Princeton University Press, 1952, 1953 (a standard work that, unlike the other histories of Chinese philosophy mentioned here, continues up to the twentieth century); *A Short History of Chinese Philosophy*, New York: Macmillan, 1948. Qi Gong, "The Relationships between Poetry, Calligraphy, and Painting," in A. Murck and W. C. Fong, eds., *Words and Images: Chinese Poetry, Calligraphy, and Painting*, New York/ Princeton: Metropolitan Museum of Art/Princeton University Press, 1991, pp. 11– 20. A. C. Graham, *Disputers of the Tao: Philosophical Argument in Ancient China*, La Salle: Open Court, 1989 (philosophically sharp). H. Lenk and G. Paul, *Epistemological Issues in Classical Chinese Philosophy*, Buffalo: State University of New York Press, 1993. F. W. Mote, *Intellectual Foundations of China*, 2d ed., New York: Knopf, 1989 (brief, clear, and intelligent), B. Schwartz, *The World of Thought in Ancient China*, Cambridge: Harvard University Press, 1985 (in particular, alert to the relation between Chinese and world culture).

Relations between Chinese and European philosophy: J. Ching and W. Oxtoby, eds., *Discovering China: European Interpretations in the Enlightenment*, Rochester: University of Rochester Press, 1992. J. Gernet, *China and the Christian Impact*, Cambridge: Cambridge University Press, 1982. D. E. Mungello, *Curious Land: Jesuit Accommodation and the Origins of Sinology*, Honolulu: University of Hawaii Press, 1989.

Japanese philosophy: L. Brüll, *Die Japanische Philosophie*, Darmstadt: Wissenschaftliche Buchgesellschaft, 1989.

European philosophy: I include Europe for the sake of the symmetry I am trying to preserve, but to keep the bibliography manageable, confine it to a few recent books on the history of the history of Western philosophy. L. Braun, *Histoire* *de l'histoire de la philosophie*, Paris: Ophrys, 1973. L. Goldsetzer, *Die Philosophie der Philosophiegeschichte im 19. Jahrhundert*, Mannheim: Hain, 1968. T. Z. Lavine and V. Tejera, eds., *History and Anti-History in Philosophy*, Dordrecht: Kluwer, 1989. R. Rorty, J. B. Schneewind, and Q. Skinner, eds., *Philosophy in History*, Cambridge: Cambridge University Press, 1981. U. J. Schneider, *Die Vergangenheit des Geistes: Eine Archäologie der Philosophiegeschichte*, Frankfurt: Suhrkamp, 1990.

8. W.-t. Chan, trans., *A Source Book in Chinese Philosophy*, Princeton: Princeton University Press, 1963, p. 128. I. Kant, *Anthropology from a Pragmatic Point of View*, The Hague: Nijhoff, 1974, p. 185.

9. **Comparative philosophy and "interpreting across boundaries"**: E. Deutsch, ed., *Culture and Modernity: East-West Philosophical Perspectives*, Honolulu: University of Hawaii Press, 1991. G. J. Larson and E. Deutsch, eds., *Interpreting across Boundaries*, Princeton: Princeton University Press, 1988. B. Lewis, E. Leites, and M. Case, eds., *As Others See Us: Mutual Perception, East and West*, New York: International Society for the Comparative Study of Civilizations, 1985. B.-A. Scharfstein, ed., *Philosophy East/ Philosophy West*, chap. 1 ("Cultures, Contexts, and Comparisons").

10. K. Jaspers, *Einführung in die Philosophie*, Zürich: Artemis, 1949, pp. 91ff.

11. S. N. Eisenstadt, ed., *The Origins and Diversity of Axial Age Civilizations*, Albany: State University of New York Press, 1986. K. Jaspers, *Vom Ursprung and Ziel der Geschichte*, Munich: Piper Verlag, 1949. G. Fohrer, *History of Israelite Religion*, London: S.P.C.K., 1972.

12. **India and the Muslim and British conquests**: A. Ahmad, *Studies in Islamic Culture in the Indian Environment*, Oxford: Oxford University Press, 1964 (especially part 2, chaps. 1, 2). A. L. Basham, *A Cultural History of India*, London: Oxford University Press, 1975 (parts 3 and 4). R. Thapar, *A History of India*, vol. 1, Harmondsworth: Penguin, 1966, chaps. 12–14. S. Hay, ed., *Sources of Indian Tradition*, vol. 2, New York: Columbia University Press, 1988. K. W. Jones, *Socio-religious Reform Movements in British India*, Cambridge: Cambridge University Press, 1989. A. Sharma, ed., *Neo-Hindu Views of Christianity*, Leiden: Brill, 1988.

By implication, I deny the basic *philosophical* creativity of the new or renewed theistic cults, but the Kashmiri Abhinavagupta (c. 1000 C.E.) is an impressive figure and, at the least, a great esthetician. On his thought see P. E. Muller-Ortega, *The Triadic Heart of Śiva*, Albany: State University of New York Press, 1989. For the continued development of Navya-Nyaya see D. H. H. Ingalls, *Materials for the Study of Navya-Nyāya Logic*, Cambridge: Harvard University Press, 1951, pp. 4–27 (a clear, sympathetic description of the main personalities of the school). For a fuller account, see K. H. Potter and S. Bhattacharyya, eds., *Indian Philosophical Analysis: Nyāya-Vaiśeṣika from Gaṅgeśa to Raghunātha Śiromaṇi*, Delhi: Banarsidass, 1993.

13. **China and Buddhism**: K. K. S. Ch'en, *Buddhism in China: A Historical Survey*, Princeton: Princeton University Press, 1964; *The Chinese Transformation of Buddhism*, Princeton: Princeton University Press, 1973. A. F. Wright, *Buddhism in*

Chinese History, Stanford: Stanford University Press, 1959. E. Zürcher, *The Buddhist Conquest of China*. 2 vols., Leiden: Brill, 1972.

14. The quoted words, used to describe Hinduism alone, are from Halbfass, *India and Europe*, p. 187.

15. **Recent Chinese philosophy under Western influence**: O. Brière, *Fifty Years of Chinese Philosophy: 1898–1948*, New York: Praeger, 1965. W.-t. Chan, ed. and trans., *A Source Book in Chinese Philosophy*, chaps. 36–44. Wm. De Bary, W.-t. Chan, and B. Watson, eds., *Sources of Chinese Tradition*, New York: Columbia University Press, 1960, chaps. 22–29. B. A. Elman, *From Philosophy to Philology: Intellectual and Social Aspects of Change in Late Imperial China*, Cambridge: Council on East Asian Studies, Harvard University, 1984. J. K. Fairbank, *China: A New History*, Harvard: Harvard University Press, 1992, esp. chaps. 9–13. J. Gernet, *China and the Christian Impact*, Cambridge: Cambridge University Press, 1982. J. R. Levenson, *Confucian China and Its Modern Fate: A Trilogy*, Berkeley: University of California Press, 1968. Yuan Weishi, "A Few Problems Related to Nineteenth Century Chinese and Western Philosophies and Their Cultural Interaction," *Journal of Chinese Philosophy* 22.2 (June 1995).

On recent Japanese thought under Western influence: C. Gluck, *Japan's Modern Myths: Ideology in the Late Meiji Period*, Princeton: Princeton University Press, 1986. Tominaga Nakamoto, *Emerging from Meditation*, trans. M. Pye, Honolulu: University of Hawaii Press, 1990. R. Tsunuda, Wm. T. de Bary, and D. Keene, *Sources of Japanese Tradition*, New York: Columbia University Press, 1958, chaps. 15–29.

Recent Indian thought under Western influence: A. Bharati, *Great Traditions and Little Traditions*, Varanasi: Chowkhamba, 1978; *Hindu Views and Ways and the Hindu-Muslim Interface*, Santa Barbara: Ross-Erikson, 1982; "The Hindu Renaissance and Its Apologetic Patterns," *Journal of Asian Studies* 29.2 (February 1970). R. Lipsey, *Coomaraswamy: His Life and Work*, Princeton: Princeton University Press, 1977 (the same editor and publisher have put out two volumes of Coomarawamy's selected papers). T. Organ, *Radhakrishnan and the Ways of Oneness of East and West*, Athens (Ohio): Ohio University Press, 1989. S. S. Rama Rao Pappu and R. Puligandla, eds., *Indian Philosophy: Past and Future* (essays by contemporary Indian philosophers). A. Sharma, *Neo-Hindu Views of Christianity*, Leiden: Brill, 1988.

16. H. Nakamura, "The Meaning of the Terms 'Philosophy' and 'Religion' in Various Traditions," in G. J. Larson and E. Deutsch, eds, *Interpreting across Boundaries*.

17. D. Snellgrove, *Indo-Tibetan Buddhism*, 2 vols, Boston: Shambala, 1987, vol. 2, p. 442.

18. F. E. Peters, *Greek Philosophical Terms: A Historical Lexicon*, New York/ London: New York University Press, University of London Press, 1967.

19. W. Halbfass, *India and Europe*, chaps. 15 ("*Darśana, Ānvīkṣikī*, Philosophy"), 16 ("The Adoption of the Concept Philosophy in Modern Hinduism"), 21

("The Concept of Experience in the Encounter Between India and the West"). For a less intensive but wider discussion, see R. Pannikar, "Śatapathaprajñā: Should We Speak of Philosophy in Classical India?—A Case of Homeomorphic Equivalents," in *Contemporary Philosophy*, edited by Guttorm Fløistad, vol. 7, *Asian Philosophy*, Dordrecht: Kluwer, 1993.

20. Halbfass, "*Darśana, Ānvīkṣikī*, Philosophy," pp. 273–86 (p. 275 quoted).

21. Ibid., "*Darśana, Ānvīkṣikī*, Philosophy," pp. 263–73.

22. **China and Japan**: T. Grimm, *Sinologische Anmerkungen zum europäischen Philosophiebegriff*, Heidelberg: Karl Winter Universitätsverlag, 1981. J. Hamada, *Japanische Philosophie nach 1868*, Leiden: Brill, 1994. Lao Sze-kwang (Lao Yung-wei), "On Understanding Chinese Philosophy," in R. E. Allinson, ed., *Understanding the Chinese Mind*, Hong Kong: Oxford University Press, 1989. G. K. Piovesana, *Recent Japanese Philosophical Thought 1862–1962*, rev. ed. Tokyo: Enderle Bookstore, 1968. N. Sivin, "Ruminations on the Tao and Its Disputers," in *Philosophy East and West* 42.1 (January 1992), pp. 21–29.

23. On Nishi, see Hamada, *Japanische Philosophie nach 1868*, pp. 17–22; and Piovesana, *Recent Japanese Philosophical Thought 1862–1962*, pp. 5–18

24. On the need to escape and its difficulty see B.-A. Scharfstein, *The Dilemma of Context*, New York: New York University Press, 1989. See also: S. Dasgupta, *A History of Indian Philosophy*, vol. 1, Cambridge; Cambridge University Press, 1922, chap. 4 ("General Observations on the Systems of Indian Philosophy"). N. Sivin, "Ruminations on the Tao and Its Disputers," in *Philosophy East and West* 42.1 (January 1992), pp. 21–29.

25. **Competing philosophical conceptions of rationality**: S. Biderman and B.-A. Scharfstein, eds., *Rationality in Question: On Eastern and Western Views of Rationality*, Leiden: Brill, 1989. See also *Philosophy East and West* 52.4 (October 1992), an issue largely devoted to the subject of "culture and rationality."

26. **Logic in India**: S. Bagchi, *Inductive Reasoning*, Calcutta, 1933 (no publisher recorded). S. Bhattacharyya, *Gadadhāra's Theory of Objectivity*. 2 vols., Delhi: Indian Council of Philosophical Research in association with Banarsidass, 1990 (vol. 1, a general introduction to Navya-Nyāya concepts, relates them carefully to symbolic logic). J. Ganeri, "The Hindu Syllogism: Nineteenth-Century Perceptions of Indian Logical Thought," *Philosophy East and West* 46.1 (January 1996). C. Goekoop, *The Logic of Invariable Concomitance in the Tattvacintāmaṇi*, Dordrecht: Reidel, 1967 (consistently translates Navya-Nyaya logic into symbolic logic). R. Hayes, *Dignaga on the Interpretation of Signs*, Dordrecht: Kluwer, 1988. D. H. H. Ingalls, *Materials for the Study of Navya-nyāya Logic*, Cambridge: Harvard University Press, 1951. B. K. Matilal, *The Navya-nyāya Doctrine of Negation*, Cambridge: Harvard University Press, 1968. K. H. Potter, ed., *Indian Metaphysics and Epistemology: The Tradition of Nyāya-Vaiśeṣika up to Gaṅgeśa*, Delhi; Banarsidass, 1977. C. Oetke, "Ancient Indian Logic as a Theory of Non-Monotonic Reasoning," *Journal of Indian Philosophy* 24.5 (October 1996) (an extended, rather technical attempt to show

that Indian logic should not be equated with Western classical logic(s), especially not the Aristotelian doctrine of the syllogism, but with recent doctrines of "commonsense inference" considered as examples of so-called Non-monotonic Logic[s]). K. H. Potter and S. Bhattacharyya, eds., *Indian Philosophical Analysis: Nyāya-Vaiśeṣika from Gaṅgeśa to Raghunātha Śiromaṇi*, Delhi: Banarsidass, 1993. F. Staal, *Universals: Studies in Indian Logic and Linguistics*, Chicago: University of Chicago Press, 1988 (for the use of *vipratiṣedha* see p. 110). T. Wada, *Invariable Comcomitance in Navya-Nyāya*, Delhi: Sri Satguru Publications (Indian Books Centre), 1990.

27. Staal, *Universals*, pp. 110, 125–26. There is relevant material in all of the first five chapters of the book.

28. Mohanty, *Reason and Tradition in Indian Thought*, pp. 120–21. Mohanty quotes Udayana's *Nyāyakusumāñjali* 3.8.

29. **Chinese logic (or its absence)**: D. Bodde, *Chinese Thought, Society, and Language*, Honolulu: University of Hawaii Press, 1991. A. C. Graham, *Disputers of the Tao*, La Salle: Open Court, 1989; *Later Mohist Logic, Ethics and Science*, Hong Kong: Chinese University of Hong Kong; and London: School of Oriental and African Studies, 1978; *Studies in Chinese Philosophy and Philosophical Literature*, Buffalo: State University of New York Press, 1986. C. Hansen, *Language and Logic in Ancient China*, Ann Arbor, University of Michigan Press, 1983; "Language in the Heart-Mind," in R. E. Allinson, ed., *Understanding the Chinese Mind*, Hong Kong: Oxford University Press, 1989; "Term-Belief in Action: Sentences and Terms in Early Chinese Philosophy," in H. Lenk and G. Paul, *Epistemological Issues in Classical Chinese Philosophy*, Buffalo: State University of New York Press, 1993; "Should the Ancient Masters Value Reason," in H. Rosemont, ed., *Chinese Texts and Philosophical Contexts*, La Salle, Open Court, 1991; *A Daoist Theory of Chinese Thought*, New York: Oxford University Press, 1992, chaps. 1, 2. C. Harbsmeier, "Conceptions of Knowledge in Ancient China," in Lenk and Paul, eds., *Epistemological Issues in Classical Chinese Philosophy*; "Marginalia Sino-Logica," in Allinson, ed., *The Chinese Mind*. Yameng Liu, "Three Issues in the Argumentative Conception of Early Chinese Philosophy," *Philosophy East and West* 46.1 (January 1996) (too late for me to take account of). J.-P. Reding, "La pensée rationelle en Chine ancienne," in G. Fløistad, *Contemporary Philosophy*, vol. 7, *Asiatic Philosophy*, Dordrecht: Kluwer, 1993. R. P. Peerenboom, *Law and Morality in Ancient China*, Buffalo: State University of New York Press, 1993.

30. Graham, *Later Mohist Logic, Ethics and Science*, pp. 25, 38–39, 199–200 (quoted). For further examples see Graham's index under *contradiction*. Despite the difficulty of conceiving abstractly of a sentence, the ancient Chinese have a near equivalent, *tz'u*, which refers to a deliberately composed verbal utterance (pp. 208–209). The exceptional text I mention is interpreted as using *tz'u*, the usual meaning of which is *phrase*, as having the meaning *sentence*; and it conceives of the sentence as having a parallel structure and, perhaps, an organic unity (pp. 480–83). Graham later repented of having considered the *tz'u* to be the equivalent of a proposition. Hansen, who rejects the meaning of *sentence,* prefers that of a string or unit of words made up of functional parts. See Hansen, *A Daoist Theory of Chinese Thought*, p. 45.

31. Harbsmeier, "Marginalia Sino-logic" p. 132. The quotation is from *Chuang Tzu* 17.21.

32. C. Harbsmeier, "Marginalia Sino-logica," pp. 126–30. Harbsmeier's essay is a rebuttal of Chad Hansen and others who make sweeping statements such as that "Chinese philosophy has no concept of truth" (*Language and Logic in Ancient China*, p. 492).

33. G. Paul, "Equivalent Axioms of Aristotelian, or Traditional European, and later Mohist Logic: An Argument in Favor of the Universality of Logic and Rationality," in Lenk and Paul, *Epistemological Issues in Classical Chinese Philosophy*. See also Reding, "La penseé rationnelle en Chine ancienne" (note 28, above).

34. Chuang Tzu, *The Complete Works of Chuang Tzu*, trans. Watson, New York: Columbia University Press, 1968, p. 376 (Chuang Tzu 33).

35. Graham, *Later Mohist Logic, Ethics and Science*, p. 174–75.

36. The anecdote is from Harbsmeier, "Marginalia Sino-logica," p. 152. Chad Hansen uses the white-horse paradox to exemplify his thesis that the Chinese language uses mass nouns. Graham agrees, but with qualifications, while Harbsmeier resists in what seems to me convincing detail—see his article "The Mass Noun Hypothesis and the Part-Whole Analysis of the White Horse Dialogue," in Rosemont, ed., *Chinese Texts and Philosophical Contexts*. To follow the white-horse controversy as reflected in the work of a single scholar, see Graham's three articles written at different times and reaching different conclusions in Graham, *Studies in Chinese Philosophy and Philosophical Literature*. The last of the articles contains a complete translation of Kung-sun Lung's authentic essays. K. O. Thompson, "When 'White Horse' Is Not a 'Horse,'" *Philosophy East and West* 45.4 (October 1995) contains a translation of two treatises by Kung-sun Lung. According to Thompson, Kung-sun Lung shows that it is the logician's narrowness, which misses the communicative function of words in human life, that leads to absurdities such as the white-horse paradox.

37. Bodde, *Chinese Thought, Society and Science*, chap. 2, "The Dynamics of Written Chinese," gives a fair description of the factors that make for ambiguity as against those that make for clarity. He quotes opinions (pp. 91–96) of those who think that any idea at all can be well enough expressed in Chinese. To this view he objects, as he does to the opposite, that the influence of the language on ideas is all-encompassing.

38. Nakamura, *Ways of Thinking of Eastern Peoples*, pp. 191–93.

39. Aristotle, *Complete Works*, ed. Barnes, 2 vols., Princeton: Princeton University Press, 1984, vol. 1, p. 48 (*Anal. Pr.* 29b).

40. Matilal, *Logic, Language and Reality*, pp. 166–70; and Mohanty, *Reason and Tradition in Indian Thought*, pp. 125–31.

41. Mohanty, *Reason and Tradition in Indian Thought*, pp. 113–15, 117–18, 46–47.

42. Ibid., pp. 112–15.

43. See Bhattacharyya, *Gadādhara's Theory of Objectivity*, vol. 1, pp. 47–49; Mohanty, *Reason and Tradition in Indian Thought*, pp. 122–25; and Staal, *Universals*, chap. 7.

44. Guthrie, *Aristotle*, pp. 187–90. E.g., in *Prior Analytics* 68b, Aristotle speaks of "the syllogism that originates an induction," taking *induction* here in the sense of *perfect induction*.

45. The following characterization of Dignaga's logic is based on Hayes, *Dignaga on the Interpretation of Signs*, chap. 4.

46. Ibid., pp. 161–67.

47. Goekoop, *The Logic of Invariable Concomitance in the Tattvacintāmaṇi* (contains extensive translations of Navya-Nyaya logic into symbolic logic); Ingalls, *Materials for the Study of Navya-nyāya Logic*; Matilal, *Logic, Language and Reality*, chaps. 1–3, and *The Navya-nyāya Doctrine of Negation*; Mohanty, *Reason and Tradition in Indian Thought*, pp. 116–17; Staal, *Universals*, chaps. 2, 3. My statement on the subtleties that remain untranslated echoes Ingalls as quoted in Matilal, *Logic, Language, and Reality*, p. 155. See also Bhattacharyya, *Gadādhara's Theory of Objectivity*, vol. 1, which makes both a formal and philosophical comparison of Nyaya with Aristotelian logic.

48. Potter and Bhattacharyya, eds., *Indian Philosophical Analysis: Nyāya-Vaiśeṣika from Gaṅgeśa to Raghunātha Śiromaṇi*, pp. 71–75, 79–81. Mohanty, *Reason and Tradition in Indian Thought*, pp. 118–22, 125–31. K. K. Chakrabarti, *Definition and Induction*, Honolulu: University of Hawaii Press, 1995, which came to my attention too late for me to make use of it, is a comparative study of Greek and Nyaya views of definition and induction. Chapter 9 is on the "Carvaka-Humean Critique of Induction."

49. **History of logic in Europe**: W. and M. Kneale, *The Development of Logic*, London: Oxford University Press, 1962. See also C. L. Hamblin, *Fallacies*, London: Methuen, 1970, chaps. 2, 3 (on Aristotle and the Aristotelians), 5 (on the Indian tradition).
   On the early history of the axiomatic method in Europe: D. J. O'Meara, *Pythagoras Revived: Mathematics and Philosophy in Late Antiquity*, Oxford: Oxford University Press, 1989. H. Schüling, Die Geschichte der axiomatischen Methode im 16. und beginnenden 17. Jahrhundert, Hildesheim: Olms, 1969.
   Spinoza's logical method: J. Bennett, *A Study of Spinoza's Ethics*, Cambridge: Cambridge University Press, 1984, esp. chap. 1. E. Curley, *Behind the Geometrical Method: A Reading of Spinoza's Ethics*, Princeton: Princeton University Press, 1988. G. H. R. Parkinson, *Spinoza's Theory of Knowledge*, London: Oxford University Press, 1954. H. A. Wolfson, *The Philosophy of Spinoza: Unfolding the Latent Processes of His Reasoning*, 2 vols., Harvard: Harvard University Press, 1934, esp. vol. 1, chaps. 1, 2.

50. See J. Hintikka, "The Role of Logic in Argumentation," *The Monist* Jan. 1989, vol. 72, no. 1, for an attempt to rehabilitate the importance of logic and

deduction in philosophical and scientific argument. He believes in the dovetailing of deductive and interrogative strategies.

51. **Debate in China**: E. Balasz, *Chinese Civilization and Bureaucracy*, New Haven: Yale University Press, 1964, chap 14 (on pure talk). P. Demiéville, "Philosophy and Religion from Han to Sui," in D. Twitchett and M. Loewe, *The Cambridge History of China*, vol. 1, Cambridge: Cambridge University Press, 1986, esp. pp. 828–46. Graham, *Later Mohist Logic, Ethics and Science*, introduction, part 1.1. R. G. Henricks, *Philosophy and Argumentation in Third-Century China*, Princeton: Princeton University Press, 1983, a translation of debates in essay form between the poet, musician, and essayist, Hsi K'ang and others; I have paraphrased from it.

52. D. Holzman, *Poetry and Politics: The Life and Works of Juan Chi* A.D. *210–263*, Cambridge: Cambridge University Press, 1976, pp. 170–71.

53. **Debate in Greece**: P. Cartlett, P. Millett, and S. Todd, eds., *Nomos*, Cambridge: Cambridge University Press, 1990. W. K. C. Guthrie, *A History of Greek Philosophy*, vol. 3, pp. 41–44 (sophists); vol. 6, pp. 150–55 (Aristotle's *Topics*), Cambridge: Cambridge University Press, 1969, 1981. H. Hansen, *Athenian Democracy in the Age of Demosthenes*, Oxford: Blackwell, 1991, chaps. 6 (the Assembly), 8 (the People's Court). S. Hornblower, *Thucydides*, London: Duckworth, 1987, chap. 3. G. B. Kerford, *The Sophistic Movement*, Cambridge: Cambridge University Press, 1981, chap. 6. G. E. R. Lloyd, *Magic, Reason and Experience*, Cambridge: Cambridge University Press, 1979 (chap. 2, on dialectic and demonstration in Greece). J. De Romilly, *The Great Sophists in Periclean Athens*, Oxford: Oxford University Press, 1992, chap. 3.

Debate in medieval Europe: G. Leff, *Paris and Oxford in the Thirteenth and Fourteenth Centuries*, New York: Wiley, 1968, pp. 137–84. Peter Abelard, *A Dialogue of a Philosopher with a Jew, and a Christian*, trans. P. J. Payer, Toronto: Pontifical Institute of Mediaeval Studies, 1979.

54. Kerford, *The Sophistic Movement*, pp. 60–67. For Plato's remark on eristic as young men's play, see the *Republic* 539b.

55. See Aristotle, *Topics*, book 8.

56. *Topics* 163b, 164b.

57. **Debate in India**: Matilal, *Logic, Language and Reality*, chap. 1, pp. 9–29; *Perception: An Essay on Classical Indian Theories of Knowledge*, Oxford: Oxford University Press, 1986, chap. 3. E. A. Solomon, *Indian Dialectics*, 2 vols., Ahmedabad: B. J. Institute of Learning and Research, 1976, 1978.

58. Lama Chimpa and A. Chattopadhyaya, trans., *Tāranātha's History of Buddhism in India*, Delhi: Banarsidass, 1970, pp. 230–37 (237 quoted).

59. The parable of the blind men and the elephant is from E. W. Burlingame, *Buddhist Parables*, [1922] reprint Delhi: Banarsidass, 1991, pp. 75–77.

60. **On cultural relativism**: For a refutation of extreme cultural relativism see Scharfstein, *The Dilemma of Context*. There are relevant essays in B. Lewis, E. Leites,

and M. Case, eds., *As Others See Us: Mutual Perceptions, East and West*, International Society for the Comparative Study of Civilizations, 1985. M. Dascal, ed., *Cultural Relativism and Philosophy*, Leiden: Brill, 1991, suggests philosophic ways of reacting to relativism. On relativism with respect to comparative philosophy, see E. Deutsch, ed., *Culture and Modernity: East-West Philosophic Perspectives*, Honolulu: University of Hawaii Press, 1991; and J. Larson and E. Deutsch, *Interpreting across Boundaries*.

61. A. S. Cua, *Ethical Argumentation: A Study in Hsün Tzu's Moral Epistemology*, Honolulu: University of Hawaii Press, 1985, p. 85.

62. D. L. Hall and R. T. Ames, *Thinking Through Confucius*, Albany: State University of New York Press, 1987, pp. 324–25.

63. C. Hansen, *A Daoist Theory of Chinese Thought*, p. 3.

64. Ibid, p. 53.

65. For Talmudic thinking, characterized as "the non-propositional logic of fixed association" and dialectical argument—argument developed by means of questions and answers—see J. Neusner, *Introduction to Rabbinic Literature*, New York: Doubleday, 1994, chaps. 1, 3, 4.

66. Aristotle, *Nichomachean Ethics* 1181b15 (quoted), 1094b, 1095a5–6 (quoted) (quotations from *The Complete Works of Aristotle*, ed. Barnes, vol. 2, pp. 1866, 1730). See the account in W. K. C. Guthrie, *A History of Greek Philosophy*, vol. 6, *Aristotle*, Cambridge: Cambridge University Press, 1981, chap. 15.

67. See, e.g., Basham, *History and Doctrines of the Ājīvikas*, London; Luzac, 1951. D. Chattopadhyaya, in collaboration with M. K. Gangopadhyaya, eds., *Cāravāka/Lokāyata*, New Delhi: Indian Council of Philosophical Research, in collaboration with Ṛddhi-India, Calcutta, 1990. J.-P. Reding, *Les fondements philosophiques de la rhétorique chez les sophistes grecs et chez les sophistes chinois*, Berne: Lang, 1985.

68. A. T. Embree, ed., *Sources of Indian Tradition*, 2d ed., vol. 1, pp. 80–82 (a Jain argument against a creator-god). E. Lott, *Vedantic Approaches to God*, London: Macmillan, 1950. S. Radhakrishnan and C. A. Moore, eds., *A Source Book in Indian Philosophy*, Princeton: Princeton University Press, 1957, pp. 498–505 (Mimamsa arguments against god as creator). J. Sinha, *A History of Indian Philosophy*, vol. 1, Calcutta: Sinha Publishing House, 1956 (see entries under "Īśvara (God)" in index).

69. W. D. O'Flaherty, ed., *Karma and Rebirth in Classical Indian Traditions*, Berkeley: University of California Press, 1980. B. R. Reichenbach, *The Law of Karma: A Philosophical Study*, Honolulu: University of Hawaii Press, 1990.

70. The complex origins of the belief in Heaven, T'ien, are described in R. Eno. *The Confucian Creation of Heaven*, Albany: State University of New York Press, 1990. For early times, see also M. Loewe, "The Concept of Sovereignty," in D. Twitchett and M. Loewe, *The Cambridge History of China*, vol. 1, Cambridge: Cambridge University Press, 1986.

71. Genesis 1.14, *The Holy Bible*, revised standard version, ed. H. G. May and B. M. Metzger, New York: Oxford University Press, 1973. For a detailed characterization of Chinese thought as organicistic and lacking the idea of natural laws, see J. Needham, *Science and Civilization in China*, vol. 2, Cambridge: Cambridge University Press, 1956, chap. 18.

72. Mo-tzu 27, as translated in Bodde, *Chinese Thought, Society, and Science*, p. 335.

73. Bodde, *Chinese Thought, Society, and Language*, pp. 342–43.

74. I. Kant, *Immanuel Kant's Critique of Pure Reason*, trans. N. K. Smith, London: Macmillan, 1933, p. 33 (B xxvii–xxviii).

75. In the last paragraph I draw on the article "Organicism," by G. N. G. Arsine, in P. P. Wiener, ed., *Dictionary of the History of Ideas*, New York: Scribners, 1973. Apart from Needham (note 67, above), and Bodde, *Chinese Thought, Society, and Science*, pp. 332–55, see Peerenboom, *Law and Morality in Ancient China*, pp. 81–84. Like Bodde, Peerenboom thinks that Needham's discussion of laws of nature is too strongly polarized. To this I add that the organicism discussed is limited in early Chinese thought and fully developed only in Neo-Confucianism.

76. This kind of statement has been repeated too often to document, but one can find a variant in S. Radhakrishnan's *History of Indian Philosophy*, 2 vols., London: Allen and Unwin, 1923, 1927 (see the introductory pages of vol. 1). My representation of the view I think mistaken is paraphrased in part from P. T. Raju, "The Western and the Indian Philosophical Traditions," in S. S. Rama Rao Pappu and R. Puligandla, eds., *Indian Philosophy: Past and Future*, pp. 69–71, 79.

77. E. W. Burlingame, *Buddhist Parables*, pp. 92–94.

78. H. Lenk, introduction to Lenk and Paul, eds., *Epistemological Issues in Classical Chinese Philosophy*, p. 6.

79. D. Krishna, M. P. Rege, R. C. Dwivedi, and M. Lath, eds., *Saṃvāda*, Delhi: Indian Council of Philosophical Research, in association with Banarsidass, 1991. For a broader description see D. Krishna, "Emerging New Approaches in the Study of Classical Indian Philosophy," in G. Fløistad, ed, *Contemporary Philosophy*, vol. 7, *Asian Philosophy*, Dordrecht: Kluwer, 1993. The quotation is from p. 73.

80. Krishna, "Emerging New Approaches in the Study of Classical Indian Philosophy," p. 75.

81. W. Halbfass, *On Being and What There Is*, Albany: State University of New York Press, 1992, pp. 248–55. The translation is of a passage from the commentary of Vyomaśiva, of perhaps the ninth century C.E., on the standard Vaiśeṣika treatise written by Praśastapāda, of perhaps the sixth century C.E.

82. See the attempts made by J. N. Mohanty in his *Reason and Tradition in Indian Thought* or those made by a variety of Indian philosophers in S. S. Rama Rao

Pappu and R. Puligandla, eds., *Indian Philosophy: Past and Future*, Delhi: Banarsidass, 1983.

83. This list has been mostly drawn from the tables of contents of J. Sinha, *Indian Psychology*, 2 vols., Calcutta: Sinha Publishing House, 1958, 1961.

84. The passage is from Hsün Tzu 23, as translated word for word in Bodde, *Chinese Thought, Society, and Science*, p. 51, and normally in B. Watson, trans., *Hsün Tzu: Basic Writings*, New York: Columbia University Press, 1963, p. 162.

85. Lao Tzu, *Tao Te Ching* 1.2, trans. D. C. Lau, Hong Kong: Chinese University Press, 1982, p. 5 (the same translation appears in Penguin Books).

86. Bodde, *Chinese Thought, Society, and Science*, pp. 74–80.

Chapter 2. The Beginnings of Metaphysical Philosophy

1. B.-A. Scharfstein, *The Dilemma of Context*, New York: New York University Press, 1989, pp. 59–137.

2. For detail and references, see Mookerji, *Ancient Indian Education*, pp. 119–22, 124, 128–30. See also Gonda, *Vedic Literature*, pp. 352–53, and the accounts of Uddalaka and Yajnavalkya in Barua, *History of Pre-Buddhistic Indian Philosophy*.

3. **Translations of the Upanishads**: I have consulted three translations: P. Deussen, *Sechzig Upaniṣad's des Veda*, 1897, 1905, 1921; trans. into English by V. M. Bedekar and G. B. Palsule as *Sixty Upaniṣads of the Veda*, 2 vols., Delhi: Banarsidass, 1987 (with the largest index and most helpful notes); F. Edgerton, *The Beginnings of Indian Philosophy*, Cambridge: Harvard University Press, 1965 (the translation on which I have most relied); and R. E. Hume, *The Thirteen Principal Upaniṣads*, 2d ed. London: Oxford University Press, 1934. P. Olivelle's translation into contemporary English, *Upaniṣads*, Oxford: Oxford University Press, 1996 (with a good introduction, good notes, and a good index), was published too late for use here, except in one footnote.
General background: R. Gopal, *India of Vedic Kalpasūtras*, Delhi: National Publishing House, 1959. R. K. Mookerji, *Ancient Indian Education*, London: Macmillan, 1947. E. J. Rapson, ed., *Cambridge History of India*, vol. 1, Cambridge: Cambridge University Press, 1922, chap 5. See also note 46, below.
Philosophical and religious background and interpretation: B. M. Barua, *A History of Pre-Buddhistic Indian Philosophy*, Delhi: Banarsidass, 1921 (an adventurous account of Upanishadic philosophers person by person). P. Deussen, *The Philosophy of the Upaniṣads*, reprint New York: Dover, 1966 [1906]. E. Frauwallner, *History of Indian Philosophy*, vol. 1, trans. V. M. Bedekar, Delhi: Banarsidass, 1973 (generally accurate but not very elegant translation). J. Gonda, *Vedic Literature*,

Wiesbaden: Harrassowitz, 1975, chap. 8 ("The Brāhmaṇas"). J. M. Winternitz, *A History of Indian Literature*, vol. 1, trans. V. S. Sarma, Delhi: Banarsidass, 1981 (trans. from the German of 1906), pp. 209–88. R. T. Vyas, *Bṛhadāraṇyaka Upaniṣad— A Critical Study*, Vadodara: Oriental Institute, 1987. See also note 46, below.

For *Upanishad*, see the index to Deussen, *Sixty Upaniṣads of the Veda*. See Deussen, *Philosophy of the Upaniṣads*, pp. 10–22, for the meaning and pp. 22–38 for the history of the Upanishads. The relative dates of many can be plausibly established, but discussions of their absolute dates are quite inconclusive. See Keith, *Religion and Philosophy of the Veda*, vol. 2, pp. 498–505; and Gonda, *Vedic Literature*, pp. 357–60. Prof. Preisendanz (see acknowledgments) tells me that there is a convenient modern summary of different scholarly interpretations of the term in H. Falk, *Zeitschrift der deutschen Morgenländischen Gesellschaft* 136 (1986), pp. 90–97.

4. *The Mahābhārata*, trans. J. A. B. van Buitenen, vol. 1, Chicago: Chicago University Press, 1973, p. 45 (Mahābhārata 1.3.25–27).

5. My paraphrases and quotations of Uddalaka's words are from the *Chāndogya Upaniṣad*, chapter or section 6, as translated in Edgerton, *Beginnings of Indian Philosophy*, pp. 170–78.

6. Ibid., p. 170 (*Chāndogya Upaniṣad* 6.1).

7. Ibid. (*Chāndogya Upaniṣad* 6.2).

8. Ibid., pp. 171–72 (*Chāndogya Upaniṣad* 6.2–4).

9. Ibid., p. 173 (*Chāndogya Upaniṣad* 6.7).

10. Ibid., pp. 173–74 (*Chāndogya Upaniṣad* 6.8).

11. Ibid., pp. 175–76 (*Chāndogya Upaniṣad* 6.9–10).

12. Ibid., p. 176 (*Chāndogya Upaniṣad* 6.11).

13. Ibid., p. 176 (*Chāndogya Upaniṣad* 6.11).

14. Ibid., pp. 176–77 (*Chāndogya Upaniṣad* 6.12–13).

15. Ibid., pp. 177–78 (*Chāndogya Upaniṣad* 6.15–16).

16. The following paraphrases and quotations are from the *Bṛhadāraṇyaka Upaniṣad*, book 4, sections 3 and 5, as translated by Edgerton in *The Beginnings of Indian Philosophy*. Here and there I may have used a phrase from R. C. Zaehner, *Hindu Scriptures*, London: Dent, Everyman's Library, 1996. For a full translation, see Deussen, *Sixty Upaniṣads of the Veda*, vol. 1, or Hume, *The Thirteen Principal Upaniṣads*. See also Barua, *History of Pre-Buddhistic Indian Philosophy*, chap. 11, on Yajnavalkya (a spirited but not very cautious interpretation); and Vyas, *Bṛhadāraṇyaka Upaniṣad—A Critical Study*. Nakamura, *A Comparative History of Ideas*, pp. 103–23, undertakes comparisons of Uddalaka with Plato, Xenophanes, Parmenides, and Anaxagoras, and compares Yajnavalkya with Lao Tzu and Plato.

17. Edgerton, *Beginnings of Indian Philosophy,* pp. 153–55 (*Bṛhadāraṇyaka Upaniṣad* (4.3.1–10).

18. Ibid., p. 155 (*Bṛhadāraṇyaka Upaniṣad* 4.3.10–14).

19. Ibid., pp. 156–57 (*Bṛhadāraṇyaka Upaniṣad* 4.3.20–32).

20. See A Fort, *The Self and Its States,* Delhi: Barnarsidass, 1990 (suggestion of Prof. Presendanz).

21. For dreaming in Homer, see E. R. Dodds, *The Greeks and the Irrational,* Berkeley: University of California Press, pp. 104–105; and B. Simon, *Mind and Madness in Ancient Greece,* Ithaca: Cornell University Press, 1978, p. 58. See also J. Bremmer, *The Early Greek Concept of the Soul,* Princeton: Princeton University Press, 1983. For a concentrated account of Indian theories of dreaming, see J. Sinha, *Indian Psychology,* vol. 1, 2d ed., Calcutta: Sinha Publishing House, 1958, chap 15. See also note 46, below.

22. Edgerton, *The Beginnings of Indian Philosophy,* pp. 159–62 (*Bṛhadāraṇyaka Upaniṣad* 4.4.1–9).

23. Ibid., pp. 164–65 (*Bṛhadāraṇyaka Upaniṣad* 4.4.24–28). I have been following Edgerton's translation, without commenting on the differences between the two recensions of the text, the Kanva and the Madhamdina—differences that are often interesting but not, I think, important for our purposes.

24. Ibid., p. 168, footnote, on the interpretation of this passage.

25. Ibid., pp. 166–69 (*Bṛhadāraṇyaka Upaniṣad* 4.5).

26. M. Detienne, *The Masters of Truth in Archaic Greece,* New York: Zone Books, 1996 (on the conception of truth, *aletheia,* and its double source—magical-religious thought and logical discourse—clearly evident in Parmenides). Diogenes Laertius, *Lives of Eminent Philosophers,* vol. 2, trans. R. D. Hicks, Cambridge: Harvard University Press, 1941, pp. 408–25. H. Fränkel, *Early Greek Poetry and Philosophy,* Oxford: Blackwell, 1975, pp. 370–97. W. K. C. Guthrie, *A History of Greek Philosophy,* vol. 1, Cambridge: Cambridge University Press, pp. 303–92. E. Hussey, *The Presocratics,* London: Duckworth, 1972. C. H. Kahn, *The Art and Thought of Heraclitus,* Cambridge: Cambridge University Press, 1979. (So as not to compound confusion, I have generally followed Kahn's translation and interpretation, including his "old-fashioned" understanding of the cosmic fire.) G. S. Kirk, J. E. Raven, and M. Schofield, *The Presocratic Philosophers,* 2d ed., Cambridge: Cambridge University Press, 1983.

27. Diogenes Laertius, *Lives of Eminent Philosophers,* vol. 1, pp. 409–15. Guthrie, *History of Greek Philosophy,* vol. 1, pp. 408–15. I use aphorisms 18 (on learning) and 21 (on Homer).

28. The fragments are numbered as in Kahn, *The Art and Thought of Heraclitus.* Kahn gives the Diels-Kranz numbers as well.

29. See the interpretation given in Kahn, *The Art and Thought of Heraclitus*, pp. 271–74.

30. Aristotle, *Metaphysics* 1010a 14.

31. Plato, *Symposium* 207d.

32. Plato, *Phaedo* 70d–e.

33. A. H. Coxon, *The Fragments of Parmenides*, Assen: Van Gorcum, 1986. D. Gallop. *Parmenides of Elea: Fragments* (I have often depended on his interpretation). W. K. C. Guthrie, *A History of Philosophy*, vol. 2, pp. 1–79. H. Fränkel, *Early Greek Poetry and Philosophy*, pp. 349–70. E. Hussey, *The Presocratics*. G. S. Kirk, J. E. Raven, and M. Schofield, *The Presocratic Philosophers*, 2d ed. G. E. R. Lloyd, *Polarity and Analogy*, pp. 103–107. V. Tejera, "The Metaphysical Poem of Parmenides" (unpublished ms.).

34. Coxon, *The Fragments of Parmenides*, pp. 37–40. Diogenes Laertius, *Lives of Eminent Philosophers*, vol. 2, pp. 429–33. Guthrie, *History of Greek Philosophy*, pp. 1–4.

35. Coxon, *The Fragments of Parmenides*, pp. 44–50 (fragment 1). Except where otherwise noted, I follow Coxon.

36. Coxon, p. 58 (fragment 7).

37. Compare the translation by Kahn (fragment 2, p. 55) and Coxon (p. 54, here in parentheses).

38. Coxon, p. 52 (fragment 3). See Kahn, p. 5 and note 18, p. 31, where Kahn says that the concepts of speech and thought are coupled throughout the Way of Truth (2.7–8 [Coxon's fragment 3], 61.8.8, 8.17, 8.35–56, and 8.50).

39. Coxon, pp. 60–62 (fragment 8, lines 1–6).

40. Coxon, p. 66 (fragment 8, lines 19–21).

41. Coxon, p. 66 (fragment 8, lines 22–25). Where Coxon translates, "All full of being," Gallop (p. 69) translates "full of what-is."

42. Coxon, p. 68 (fragment 8, lines 26–30).

43. Coxon, pp. 68–70 (fragment 8, lines 30–36).

44. Coxon, p. 72 (fragment 8, lines 37–38).

45. Coxon, p. 74 (fragment 8, lines 39–49).

46. Coxon, p. 76 (fragment 8, lines 50–55).

47. The last lines of the proem (Coxon, p. 50 [fragment 1], lines 29–32) speak obscurely of the general acceptance of things as they are believed to be because they pervasively appear to be so. See Kahn, pp. 21–23 and Coxon, pp. 168–71.

48. **For India**: To the sources enumerated in note 1, add: B. Allchin and R. Allchin, *The Rise of Civilization in India and Pakistan*, Cambridge: Cambridge University Press, 1982, esp. chap. 12. Gonda, *Vedic Literature*, pp. 361–67. W. Halbfass, *India and Europe*, Buffalo: State University of New York Press, 1988. F. Hardy, "The Classical Religions of India," in S. Sutherland, L. Houlden, P. Clarke, and F. Hardy, eds., *The World's Religions*, London: Routledge, 1988, pp. 586–87. Keith, "The Period of the Later Saṃhitās, the Brāhmaṇas, the Āraṇyakas, and the Upaniṣads," in Rapson, ed., *Cambridge History of India*, vol. 1. H. Kulke, "The Historical Background of India's Axial Age," in S. N. Eisenstadt, ed., *The Origins and Diversity of Axial Age Civilizations, Part I*, Albany: State University of New York Press, 1986. R. S. Sharma, *Aspects of Political Ideas and Institutions in Ancient India*, especially chap. 22, a summary. B. K. Smith, *Reflections on Resemblance, Ritual, and Religion*, New York: Oxford University Press, 1989. F. Staal, "Is There Philosophy in Asia?" in G. J. Larson and E. Deutsch, eds., *Interpreting across Boundaries*, Princeton: Princeton Univertsity Press, 1988, pp. 215–24 (on the meaninglessness of *tat tvam asi* and Vedic ritual).

For Greece: To the sources enumerated in note 21, add: J. Boardman et al., eds., *Cambridge Ancient History*, 2d ed., vol. 4, *Persia, Greece and the Western Mediterranean c. 525 to 479 B.C.*, Cambridge: Cambridge University Press, 1988, chap. 5. Davies, "Religion and State," in *Cambridge Ancient History*, vol. 4. S. C. Humphreys, "Dynamics of the Greek Breakthrough: The Dialogue between Philosophy and Religion"; and C. Meier, "The Emergence of an Autonomous Intelligence among the Greeks"; both in S. N. Eisenstadt, ed., *The Origins and Diversity of Axial Age Civilizations* (see this note, above). G. E. R. Lloyd, *Magic, Reason and Experience*, Cambridge: Cambridge University Press, pp. 234–67; *Polarity and Analogy*, Cambridge: Cambridge University Press, 1987. C. Meier, "The Emergence of an Autonomous Intelligence among the Greeks," in Eisenstadt, *The Origins and Diversity of Axial Age Civiliations, Part I*.

49. Davies, "Religion and State," p. 384.

50. Gonda, *Vedic Literature*, pp. 362–63.

51. Lloyd, *Polarity and Analogy*, pp. 272–94; *The Revolutions of Wisdom*, pp. 137–38.

52. Heraclitus, fragments 63–65, in Kirk, *The Art and Thought of Heraclitus*, pp. 57–59. Fragment 66 adds, "It is law also to obey the counsel of one." For Parmenides, see Coxon, *The Fragments of Parmenides*, p. 39.

53. "The Concept of Experience in the Encounter between India and Europe," in Halbfass, *India and Europe*.

54. Heraclitus, fragment 90 (in Kahn), and *Bṛhadāraṇyaka* 4.3.6 (trans. Edgerton, p. 140). I agree with the conclusion of Kahn, *Art and Thought of Heraclitus* (pp. 298–99), as against the implication of West, *Early Greek Philosophy and the Orient* (p. 183), that this similarity is not evidence enough to show direct influence.

55. Edgerton, *Beginnings of Indian Philosophy*, p. 171 (*Chandogya Upaniṣad*, chap. 6.2).

56. Coxon, *The Fragments of Parmenides,* p. 64 (fragment 8, lines 7–11).

Chapter 3. The Beginnings of Moral Philosophy

1. **On Confucius himself and on the general development of Confucianism**: H. G. Creel, *Confucius: The Man and the Myth,* New York: John Day, 1949. R. Dawson, *Confucius,* Oxford: Oxford University Press, 1981. D. C. Lau, trans, *Confucius: The Analects,* Hong Kong: Chinese University Press, 1983, "Appendix 1" (I have made much use of both Lau's translation and his long introduction). J. K. Shryock, *The Origin and Development of the State Cult of Confucius,* New York; Century Co., 1932. Watson, *Ssu'ma Ch'ien, Grand Historian of China,* New York: Columbia University Press, 1958, pp. 50–54, 169–74 (includes a review of the evidence for Confucius' life).

On Confucius' Doctrine: First come the more developed histories of Chinese Philosophy: Fung Yu-lan, *A History of Chinese Philosophy,* 2 vols., Princeton: Princeton University Press, 1955² (contains many translated excerpts; written from a kind of Neo-Confucian standpoint, later repudiated by Fung). A. C. Graham, *Disputers of the Tao,* La Salle: Open Court, 1989 (the author is a pioneer in deciphering early Chinese logic; written from a philosophically analytical viewpoint). C. Hansen, *A Daoist Theory of Chinese Thought,* New York: Oxford University Press, 1992 (onesided but penetrating and strikingly consistent); see the discussion in H. Lenk and G. Paul, eds., *Epistemological Issues in Classical Chinese Philosophy,* Albany: State University of New York Press, 1993). B. I. Schwartz, *The World of Thought in Ancient China,* Cambridge: Harvard University Press, 1985 (sets Chinese philosophy in a broad cultural context).

To these histories there should be added Kung-chuan Hsiao's *A History of Chinese Political Thought,* Princeton: Princeton University Press, 1797 (an extended, careful study). See also H. Fingarette, *Confucius—The Secular as Sacred,* New York: Harper & Row, 1972 (an influential essay). D. L. Hall and R. T. Ames, *Thinking Through Confucius,* Albany: State University of New York Press, 1987 (attempts to renew the way in which Confucius is perceived).

Translations of Confucius: *The Analects,* trans. D. C. Lau (see above in this note); also published by Penguin, without the Chinese text and the appendices). *The Analects,* trans. R. Dawson, New York: Oxford University Press, 1993. *The Analects of Confucius,* trans. A Waley, London: Allen & Unwin, 1938. *Confucian Analects, The Great Learning, and the Doctrine of the Mean,* trans. J. Legge, reprinted New York: Dover, 1971 [1893]. *The Wisdom of Confucius,* trans. Lin Yutang (clear and simplified; contains, among other translations from the Confucian Classics, the *Analects* classified by subject). There are two new good translations of the *Analects,* published too late to be consulted for the present chapter. The one is by Chichung Huang (New York: Oxford University Press, 1977) and the other by Simon Leys (a pen name for Pierre Ryckmans) (New York: Norton, 1997). Huang prefaces his translation with a discussion of Confucius' main terms, and follows it with a careful account of Confucius' life and a collection of brief biographies of his students. Leys tries "to reconcile learning with literature." His notes compare the ideas of the *Analects* with those of various European thinkers, ranging from C. S. Lewis, to Carl Jung, Pascal, John Henry Newman, Elias Canetti, C. P. Snow, La Bruyère, Miguel de Unamuno, and Nietzsche.

2. Quoted from Ssu-ma Ch'ien's biography of Confucius in Watson, *Ssu-ma Ch'ien, Grand Historian of China*, p. 169.

3. From Ssu-ma Ch'ien, in Watson, *Ssu-ma Ch'ien, Grand Historian of China*, pp. 173–74.

4. I thank the Sinologist, Yoav Ariel, for the immediately preceding characterization of the aim of the *Analects* as a whole.

5. For what follows on *shang jen*, see Hall and Ames, *Thinking Through Confucius*, pp. 255–68.

6. Confucius, *The Analects*, trans. Lau, p. xl.

7. Hall and Ames, *Thinking Through Confucius*, pp. 268–75.

8. For Mencius, I have used the histories of philosophy by Fung, Graham, Schwartz, and Hsia (see note 1 above). The two translations I have consulted are *Mencius*, translated by D. C. Lau, Harmondsworth: Penguin, 1970; and *The Works of Mencius*, translated by J. Legge, reprint New York: Dover, 1970. "The Background of the Mencian Theory of Human Nature," in A. C. Graham, *Studies in Chinese Philosophy and Philosophical Literature*, Albany: State University of New York Press, 1990, has been very helpful, as has A. H. Yearly, "A Confucian Crisis: Mencius' Two Cosmogonies and Their Ethics," in R. W. Lovin and F. E. Reynolds, *Cosmogony and Ethical Order*, Chicago: University of Chicago Press, 1985. On Mencius' conception of "human nature" (*jen-hsing*) see two articles, both in *Philosophy East and West* 47.1 (January 1997): Kwong-loi Shun, "Mencius on *Jen-hsing*," pp. 1–20; and I. Bloom, "Human Nature and Biological Nature in Mencius," pp. 21–32.

9. Legge, *The Works of Mencius*, pp. 16, 17.

10. Yearly, "A Confucian Crisis: Mencius' Two Cosmogonies and Their Ethics," p. 315.

11. *Mencius*, trans. Lau, p. 82.

12. Kao-tzu's debate with Mencius is found in *Mencius* 6.A.1–6. For an explanation of the argument, see "On Mencius' Use of the Method of Analogy in Argument," in *Mencius*, trans. Lau, pp. 235–63.

13. J. S. Cikoski, "On Standards of Analogic Reasoning in the Late Chou," in the *Journal of Chinese Philosophy* 2.3 (June 1975, p. 354). For further references see D. Daor and B.-A. Scharfstein, "In Answer to Antony Flew: The Whiteness of Feathers and the Whiteness of Snow," *Journal of Chinese Philosophy* 6 (1979), pp. 37–53.

14. Hsün Tzu, *Basic Writings*, trans. B. Watson, New York: Columbia University Press, 1963, p. 158.

15. **Background, biography, and history**: W. Rhys Davids, *Buddhist India*, reprint Delhi: Banarsidass, 1971. R. Gombrich, *Theravāda Buddhism*, London: Routledge & Kegan Paul, 1988. G. P. Malalasekera, "Buddha," in the *Encyclopaedia of Buddhism*, ed. G. P. Malalasekera, vol. 3, Sri Lanka: Government of Sri Lanka, 1973, pp. 357–80. K. R. Norman, *Pāli Literature*, Wiesbaden: Harrassowitz, 1983 (a survey of canonical Hinayana literature). K. H. Potter, ed., *Abhidharma Buddhism to 150 A.D.* (vol. 7 of the *Encyclopedia of Indian Philosophies*), Delhi: Banarsidass (in addition to the paraphrases of early Buddhist literature, which are apt to be curt and dry, there are four helpful introductory chapters: "The Historical Buddha and His Teachings," "The Buddhist Way to Liberation," "The Development of Abhidharma Philosophy," and "A Few Abhidharma Categories." H. W. Schumann, *The Historical Buddha*, London: Arkana, 1989. V. Seth, *Study of Biographies of the Buddha*, New Delhi: Akay Book Corporation, 1992 (Buddha's life, divided into its episodes, with quotations from and references to mostly Pali and Sanskrit sources). E. J. Thomas, *The Life of Buddha as Legend and History*, London: Kegan Paul, Trench, Trubner & Co., 1931.

Histories with emphasis on philosophy: H. Akira, *A History of Indian Buddhism: From Śākyamuni to Early Mahāyāna*, Hawaii: University of Hawaii Press, 1990. E. Conze, *Buddhist Thought in India*, London: Allen & Unwin, 1962. A. K. Warder, *Indian Buddhism*, 2d ed., Delhi: Banarsidass, 1980. Takasaki Jikido, *An Introduction to Buddhism*, Tokyo: Toho Gakkai, 1987.

Traditional Buddhist histories of Buddhism: Bu-ston, *History of Buddhism*, trans. E. Obermiller, Heidelberg: Harrassowitz, 1931, 1932 (two parts bound together). Taranatha, *Tāranātha's History of Buddhism in India*, trans. Lama Chimpa and A. Chattopadhyaya, ed. D. Chattopadhyaya, reprint Delhi: Banarsidass, 1990.

Birth stories: E. W. Burlingame, *Buddhist Parables*, reprint Delhi: Banarsidass, 1991. J. G. Jones, *Tales and Teachings of the Buddha*, London: Allen & Unwin, 1979. K. Khoroche, trans., *Once the Buddha Was a Monkey: Arya Śura's* Jatakamala, Chicago: University of Chicago Press, 1989.

Translated texts: Wm. T. de Bary, ed., *The Buddhist Tradition* in India, China & Japan, New York: Modern Library, 1969. *Dialogues of the Buddha (Digha Nikāya)*, trans. T. W. Rhys Davids. 3 vols., reprint London: Luzac, 1971–1973. A. I. Embree, ed., *Sources of Indian Tradition*, vol. 1 (the texts are mostly those that appear in de Bary's anthology). The Middle Length Saying (Majjhima-Nikāya), trans. I. B. Horner, 3 vols., London: Pali Text Society, 1954–1959. *Thus Have I Heard: The Long Discourses of the Buddha: Dīgha Nikāya*, trans. M. Walshe, London: Wisdom Publications, 1987.

Attempts to clarify, formulate, or systematize the earliest thought: S. Collins, *Selfless Persons*, Cambridge: Cambridge University Press, 1982. T. Egardt, *Faith and Knowledge in Early Buddhism*, Leiden: Brill, 1977. P. Griffiths, *On Being Mindless*, La Salle: Open Court, 1986. K. N. Jayatilleke, *Early Buddhist Theory of Knowledge*, London: Allen & Unwin, 1963. R. E. A. Johannsen, *The Dynamic Psychology of Early Buddhism*, London and Malmo: Curzon Press, 1979; *The Psychology of Nirvāṇa*, Garden City: Doubleday, 1970. D. J. Kalupahana, *Causality: The*

Central Philosophy of Buddhism, Honolulu: The University of Hawaii Press, 1975. D. Keown, *The Nature of Buddhist Ethics*, Basingstoke and London, 1992. P. Masefield, *Divine Revelation in Pāli Buddhism*, Colombo: Sri Lanka Institute of Traditional Studies and London: Allen & Unwin, 1986. K. H. Potter, ed., *Abhidharma Buddhism to 150 A.D.* (see above, under "Background, biography, and history"). R. R. Sarathchandra, *Buddhist Psychology of Perception*, Colombo: Ceylon University Press, 1958. T. Vetter, *The Ideas and Meditative Practices of Early Buddhism*, Leiden: Brill, 1988.

16. See, e.g., Akira, *A History of Indian Buddhism*, p. 20. Malalasekera, *Buddha*, p. 358.

17. I have tried to give something of the flavor of both the more fabulous accounts and the earlier, less fabulous ones, but to avoid unrestrained eclecticism. From Buddha's birth to his renunciation, I follow the fabulous introduction to the *Jātaka*, the *Nidāna-kathā*. For a translated excerpt, see Thomas, *The Life of Buddha*, pp. 41–43.

18. For the Buddha's ascetic period, I have used accounts attributed to the Buddha himself, namely, the "Discourse on the Ariyan Quest" and "Greater Discourse to Saccaka," in Horner, *The Middle Length Sayings*, vol. 1 (*Majjhima-Nikāya* 1). See the corresponding translations in Walshe, *Thus Have I Heard*, and the analysis in Vetter, *The Ideas and Meditative Practices of Early Buddhism*, pp. 3–6, and Erghardt, *Knowledge in Early Buddhism*, pp. 75–83.

19. Horner, trans., *The Middle Length Sayings*, vol. 1, p. 301. I quote the corresponding translation from Vetter, *The Ideas and Meditative Practices of Early Buddhism*, p. 4.

20. I thank Dr. Ornan Rotem for drawing my attention to the Buddha's initial reluctance and later change of mind. For the account as given in the *Majjhima-nikāya*, see Thomas, *The Life of Buddha*, pp. 80–83. For the significance to later Buddhism of the Buddha's reluctance, see "The Silence of the Buddha and its Madhyamic Interpretation," in G. M. Nagao, *Mādhyamika and Yogācāra*, Buffalo: State University of New York Press, 1991.

21. To describe the Buddha's death, I have used "The Book of the Great Decease," in Davids, *Dialogues of the Buddha*, vol. 2.

22. Jātaka Story 261. See Jones, *Tales and Teachings of the Buddha*, p. 89.

23. Jayatilleke, *Early Buddhist Theory of Knowledge*, chaps. 4, 8.

24. Ibid., pp. 203, 378.

25. Jayatilleke, *Early Buddhist Theory of Knowledge*, pp. 172, 175. Schumann, *The Historical Buddha*, pp. 200–201 (*Aṅguttara Nikāya* [*Gradual Sayings*] 3.65).

26. Masefield, *Divine Revelation in Pāli Buddhism*, pp. 45–55.

27. For a detailed effort to identify who is meant, see Jayatilleke, *Early Buddhist Theory of Knowledge*, chap. 5, esp. pp. 243ff.

28. "Lesser Discourse to Māluṅkya (Putta), in *The Middle Length Sayings (Mahajjima-Nikāya)*, trans. Horner, vol. 2, pp. 97–102.

29. See, in particular, S. Collins, *Selfless Persons*, Cambridge: Cambridge University Press, 1982. Y. Hoffmann, *The Idea of Self—East and West*, Calcutta: Firma KLM, 1980. R. E. A. Johansson, *The Dynamic Psychology of Early Buddhism*, London: Malmo: Curzon Press, 1979. Y. Kurunadasa, *Buddhist Analysis of Matter,* Colombo: Department of Cultural Affairs, 1967, chap. 8 (on the irreducible factors of material existence [that is, of *rupa,* "the sphere of visibility"] as envisaged in Theravada Buddhism). T. Stcherbatsky, *The Soul Theory of the Buddhists*, reprint Varanasi: Bharatiya Vidya Praksan, 1970.

30. "Sermon on the Marks of Non-Soul" *(anattalakkhaṇa-sutta),* cited in Thomas, *The Life of Buddha,* pp. 88–89.

31. *Dialogues of the Buddha,* vol. 1, trans. T. W. Rhys Davids (*Potthapada Sutta [The Soul Theory]*). Ibid., pp. 248–51; 251 quoted.

32. Ibid., p. 252.

33. Ibid., pp. 262–63.

34. This section is heavily influenced by Johannson, *The Dynamic Psychology of Early Buddhism.* All the books on Buddhism deal with the Buddhist doctrine of causality. For a monograph on the subject see D. J. Kalupahana, *Causality: The Central Philosophy of Buddhism,* Honolulu: The University of Hawaii Press, 1975.

35. Collins, *Selfless Persons,* pp. 103–10. Kalupahana, *Causality.* Thomas, *The Life of Buddha,* p. 193–99.

36. R. E. A. Johannsen, *The Dynamic Psychology of Early Buddhism.* London and Malmo: Curzon Press, 1979.

37. Ibid.

38. P. J. Griffiths, *On Being Mindless,* La Salle: Open Court, 1986, esp. chap. 1. R. E. A. Johannson, *The Psychology of Nirvana,* Garden City: Doubleday, 1970. J. W. de Jong, *Buddhist Studies,* Berkeley: Asian Humanities Press, 1979, pp. 43–51, 69–75 (review of Welbon, below). L. de la Vallée Poussin, *The Way to Nirvāṇa,* Cambridge: Cambridge University Press, 1917 (a lucid introduction to the early conceptions; see also the same author's "Nirvana" in J. Hastings, ed., *Encyclopaedia of Religion and Ethics*). Th. Stcherbatsky, *The Conception of Buddhist Nirvāṇa,* reprint The Hague: Mouton, 1965. G. R. Welbon, *The Buddhist Nirvāṇa and Its Western Interpreters,* Chicago: University of Chicago Press, 1968.

39. Vetter, *The Ideas and Meditative Practices of Early Buddhism,* p. 57 (*Mahajjima-nikāya* 1, p. 487). This passage can also be found in Horner, *Middle Length Sayings,* vol. 2, pp. 165–66.

40. *Shvetashvatara Upanishad* 1.13. See *The Thirteen Principal Upaniṣads*, trans. R. E. Hume, London: Oxford University Press, 1934, p. 396; and Deussen, *Sixty Upaniṣads of the Veda*, trans. V. M. Bedekar and G. B. Palsule, Delhi: Banarsidass, 1980, vol. 1, p. 308 (the translation is rather different from Hume's, but its substance is the same).

41. *Dialogues of the Buddha*, trans. Davids and Davids, vol. 2, p. 91 (*Dīgha Nikāya* 2.86 (*Mahāparinibānna Suttana [The Book of the Great Decease]*, section 24); or *Thus Have I Heard*, trans. Walshe, pp. 236–37. See D. Keowan, *The Nature of Buddhist Ethics*, for an assessment of Buddhist doctrines, early and late, in terms of Buddhist ethics.

42. **Social, religious, and political background**: K. J. Dover, *Greek Homosexuality*, London: Duckworth, 1978; *Greek Popular Morality in the Time of Plato and Aristotle*, Oxford: Blackwell, 1974. R. Garland, *Introducing New Gods: The Politics of Athenian Religion*, Ithaca: Cornell University Press, 1992. M. H. Hansen, *The Athenian Democracy in the Age of Demosthenes*, Oxford: Blackwell, 1991. A. J. L. van Hoff, *From Autothanasia to Suicide: Self-Killing in Classical Antiquity*, London: Routledge, 1990. R. Parker, *Athenian Religion: A History*, Oxford: Oxford University Press, 1996. D. R. Stuart, *Epochs of Greek and Roman Biography*, Berkeley: University of California Press, 1928.

Accounts of Socrates or Socratic thought: T. C. Brickhouse and N. D. Smith, *Plato's Socrates*, Oxford University Press: New York, 1994; *Socrates on Trial*, Oxford University Press: Oxford, 1989. O. Gigon, *Sokrates*, Berne: Artemis, 1947 (2d ed., not at my disposal, 1979). G. Fine, "Inquiry in the *Meno*," in R. Kraut, ed., *The Cambridge Companion to Plato*, Cambridge: Cambridge University Press, 1992. P. Friedländer, *Plato*, vol. 1, New York; Pantheon, 1958, chaps. 6–9. W. K. C. Guthrie, *A History of Greek Philosophy*, vol. 3, Cambridge: Cambridge University Press, 1969. V. de Magalhaes-Vilhena, *Le problme de Socrate*, Paris: Presses Universitaires, 1952. T. Penner, "Socrates and the Early Dialogues," in R. Kraut, ed., *The Cambridge Companion to Plato*. E. de Strycker and S. Slings, *Plato's Apology of Socrates*, Leiden: Brill, 1994. G. Vlastos, *Socrates*, Cambridge: Cambridge University Press, 1991; *Socratic Studies*, Cambridge: Cambridge University Press, 1994.

Translations: *The Dialogues of Plato*, trans. R. E. Allen, vol. 1, New Haven: Yale University Press, 1984. Plato, *Early Socratic Dialogues*, ed. T. J. Saunders, Harmondsworth: Penguin, 1987. Xenophon, *Conversations of Socrates*, trans. H. Tredennick and R. Waterfield, London: Penguin, 1990.

Reputation and influence: Diogenes Laertius, *Lives of the Eminent Philosophers*, rev., 2 vols., trans. R. D. Hicks, Cambridge: Harvard University Press, 1931, 1938 (for Socrates and his disciples; e.g., Aeschines, Crito, Antisthenes). A. J. Droge and J. D. Tabor, *A Noble Death: Suicide and Martyrdom among Christians and Jews in Antiquity*, San Francisco: HarperSanFrancisco, 1992. J. Ferguson, ed., *Socrates: A Source Book*, London: Macmillan for the Open University, 1970 (begins with Diognes Laertius and continues through the earlier Middle Ages). W. Jaeger, *Paideia*, vol. 2, Oxford: Oxford University Press, 1944, chap 2. H. Spiegelberg, ed., *The Socratic Enigma*, Indianapolis: Bobbs-Merrill, 1964 (until the recent present).

43. Plato, *Gorgias*, 461e.

44. Brickhouse and Smith, *Plato's Socrates*, p. 174.

45. Diogenes Laertius, *Lives of Eminent Philosophers* 2.40; trans. Hicks, vol. 2, p.171.

46. Strycker and Slings, *Plato's Apology of Socrates,* pp. 86–89, 153–55.

47. Garland, *Introducing New Gods*, chap. 7.

48. Allen, *The Dialogues of Plato*, vol. 1, p. 124. For returning injustice for injustice, see the Dover, *Greek Popular Morality*, pp. 180–83 (on friends and enemies), 192–95 (on magnanimity); and Vlastos, *Socrates*, chap. 7.

49. Trans. in Guthrie, *A History of Greek Philosophy*, vol. 3, p. 451.

50. *Meno* 70aff., 79cff; *Protagoras* 319aff.

51. Vlastos, *Socrates*, chap. 8.

52. Penner, "Socrates and the Early Dialogues," pp. 125–31; Vlastos, *Socrates*, chap. 2.

53. R. Robinson, *Plato's Earlier Dialectic*, 2d ed., Oxford: Oxford University Press, 1953. Vlastos, *Socrates*, chaps. 1, 5.

54. As translated in Vlastos, *Socratic Studies*, p. 43.

55. Vlastos, *Socrates*, p. 115; *Socratic Studies*, p. 19.

56. Paraphrase from Allen, *The Dialogues of Plato*, vol. 1, pp. 84–85.

57. Saunders, ed., Early Socratic Dialogues, pp. 95–96.

58. "The Socratic Elenchus: Method Is All," in Vlastos, *Socratic Studies*, p. 4. See also Brickhouse and Smith, *Plato's Socrates*, chap. 1, "Socratic Method."

59. Vlastos, *Socrates*, pp. 117–31. See also Allen, *The Dialogues of Plato*, pp. 133–50, and his translation of the *Meno* in the following pages; and Fine, "*Inquiry in the* Meno," who is skeptical of Vlastos' interpretation, which I have adopted.

60. Aristotle, *Metaphysics*, vol. 2, trans. H. Tredennick, Cambridge: Harvard University Press, 1935, p. 197.

61. This account of what Antisthenes found in Socrates is somewhat incautiously extrapolated from Diogenes Laertius, *Lives of Eminent Philosophers*, trans. Hicks, vol. 2, pp. 5, 7, 11–13, on Antisthenes.

62. See the excerpts from Justin Martyr translated in Ferguson, *Socrates*, p. 305. See also Droge and Tabor, *A Noble Death*, chap. 2.

63. Nietzsche, *The Gay Science*, trans. W. Kaufmann, New York: Vintage Books (Random House), 1974, p. 272 (section 340); *The Will to Power*, trans.

W. Kaufmann, New York: Random House, 1967, pp. 236, 244 (sections 432, 441, both of 1888).

64. S. Kierkegaard, *The Concept of Irony, with Continual Reference to Socrates*, trans. H. V. Hong and E. H. Hong, Princeton: Princeton University Press, 1989, p. 271.

65. Ibid., p. 198.

66. B. Russell, *A History of Western Philosophy*, London: Allen and Unwin, 1945, p. 142.

67. L. Wittgenstein, *Culture and Value*, Oxford: Blackwell, 1977, p. 14e (1931).

68. K. R. Popper, *Conjectures and Refutations*, London: Routledge and Kegan Paul, 3d rev. ed., 1969, p. 183.

69. *Mencius*, trans. Lau, pp. 160–61.

70. *The Dialogues of Plato*, trans. Allen, vol. 1, p. 163.

71. Thomas, *The Life of Buddha*, p. 89; from the *Anattalakkhaṇa-sutta* or *Pañca-sutta* (*Samyutta-nikāya* 3.66).

72. For a recent comparison of Confucius with Socrates, see F. Jullien, *Le détour et l'accès: Stratégies du sens en Chine, en Grèce*, Paris: Grasset, 1995, pp. 253–54, 264.

73. Confucius, *The Analects*, trans. Lau, p. 155.

74. *Mencius*, trans. Lau, p. 82.

75. The Buddha's exhortation to his monks is from *Dialogues of the Buddha*, trans. Davids, vol. 1, p. 79 (*Sāmaññaphala Sutta* 43).

Chapter 4. Early Logical Relativism, Skepticism, and Absolutism

1. For at attempt, using both anthropology and philosophy, to describe and find a way between the extremes, see B.-A. Scharfstein, *The Dilemma of Context*, New York: New York University Press, 1989.

2. **General**: A. L. Basham, *History and Doctrines of the Ājīvikas*, London: Luzac, 1951 (see index under *Jain-a, -ism;* and under *Mahavira*). J. Charpentier, "The History of the Jains," in E. J. Rapson, ed., *The Cambridge History of India*, vol. 1, Cambridge: Cambridge University Press, 1935. H. Jacobi, "Jainism," in J. Hastings, ed., *Encyclopaedia of Religion and Ethics*, New York: Scribners, 1928. P. S. Jaini, *The Jaina Path of Purification*, Berkeley: University of California Press, 1979. B. K. Matilal, *The Central Philosophy of Jainism (Anekānta-Vāda)*, Ahmedabad: L.D. Institute of Indology, 1981. W. Schubring, *Religion of the Jainas*, Calcutta: Sanskrit College,

1966. F. Williams, *Jaina Yoga,* London: Oxford University Press, 1963. M. Winterniz, *History of Indian Literature,* rev. ed., vol. 2, Delhi: Banarsidass, 1983, section 4.

Philosophy: Of the following books, the most useful to me have been Basham, Frauwallner, Tatia, Vidyabhusana, and especially Matilal, because of their attention to the often obscure historical development of Jain philosophy. A. L. Basham, *The Ājīvikas,* London: Luzac, 1951. Frauwallner, *History of Indian Philosophy,* vol. 1, chap 5; vol. 2, chap. 8. S. Mookerji, *The Jaina Philosophy of Non-Absolutism.* Delhi: Banarsidass, 1944. Y. J. Padmarajiah, *Jaina Theories of Reality and Knowledge,* Delhi: Banarsidass, 1963. R. Singh, *The Jaina Concept of Omniscience,* Ahmedabad: L. D. Institute of Indology, 1974. N. Tatia, *Studies in Jaina Philosophy,* Banaras: Jain Cultural Research Society, 1951. S. C. Vidyabhusana, *A History of Indian Logic,* part 2, section 1, reprint, Delhi: Banarsidass, 1971.

Translation: There are translated texts in Embree, *Sources of Indian Tradition,* vol. 1, and Radhakrishnan and Moore, *A Source Book in Indian Philosophy.* However, only the latter book, pp. 260–68, contains a text on relativism (from the thirteenth century). Umasvati/Umasvami, *Tattvārtha Sūtra: That Which Is,* San Francisco: HarperCollins, 1994.

3. Charpentier, "The History of the Jains," pp. 151–63.

4. Winternitz, *History of Indian Literature,* vol. 2, p. 419 (from the *Āyāraṃga-Sutta*).

5. Tatia, *Studies in Jaina Philosophy,* pp. 17–22.

6. This is a problem of which Frauwallner (*History of Indian Philosophy,* vol. 2, chap. 8) is particularly aware. He constructs an early Jain system from the writings of two early systematics, Umasvati (Umasvami), of perhaps the second century A.D., who is schematic, and Kundakunda, of perhaps the fourth century, who is more philosophical. I have found the relation between the names of the various viewpoints and the explanations and examples given to be rather confusing.

7. Matilal, *The Central Philosophy of Jainism,* p. 18 (from the *Bhagavatī Sūtra* 9.386).

8. Matilal, *The Central Philosophy of Buddhism,* pp. 20–21 (from the *Bhagavatī Sūtra* 2.1.90).

9. Tattia, *Studies in Jaina Philosophy,* pp. 23–24 (*Bhagavatī Sūtra* 2.1.90).

10. Umasvati, *Tattvārtha Sūtra* 1.34 Trans. pp. 23. See the exposition, drawn from early commentators, and the translator's note, pp. 24–27. See also Matilal, *The Central Philosophy of Jainism,* pp. 43–46; and Vidyabhusana, *A History of Indian Logic,* pp. 170–71. For a more extensive explanation, incorporating later thought, see Padmarajiah, *Jaina Theories of Reality and Knowledge,* chap. 10.

11. Umasvati, *Tattvārtha Sūtra,* p. 24 (commentary to 1.34).

12. Matilal, *The Central Philosophy of Jainism,* pp. 53–54. For an account including late sources, see Padmarajiah, *The Jaina Theories of Reality and Knowledge,* chap. 11.

13. Matilal, *The Central Philosophy of Jainism*, pp. 37, 38 (Kundakunda, *Pravacanasāra*, chap. 2, verses 7, 8).

14. Matilal, *The Central Philosophy of Jainism*, p. 38 (Amritacandra Suri, comm. on *Pravacanasāra*, chap. 2, verse 8).

15. The formulation of Samantabhadra (600 A.D.), who adds three more exotic possibilities. See Vidyabhusana, *A History of Indian Logic*, pp. 184–85.

16. Matilal, *The Central Philosophy of Jainism*, p. 31 (Siddhasena Divaraka, *Sanmati-tarka*, chap. 1, verse 28). See also Tatia, *Studies in Jaina Philosophy*, p. 22.

17. **Date and composition of the book**: A. C. Graham, "How Much of *Chuang-tzu* did Chuang-tzu Write?" in A. C. Graham, *Studies in Chinese Philosophy and Philosophical Literature*, Albany: State University of New York Press, 1986; "Reflections and Replies," in H. R. Rosemont, ed., *Chinese Texts and Philosophical Context*, La Salle: Open Court, 1991. Liu Xiaogan, *Classifying the Zhuangzi Chapters*, Ann Arbor: University of Michigan, Center for Chinese Studies, 1994 (I know this book only from its review, by L. Kohn, in *Philosophy East and West* 46.3 [July 1996], pp. 420–24). Liu dates the final compilation about 200 B.C.E., considerably earlier than does Graham, and regards the book as a reflection of the views of three schools rather than (Graham's) four. H. Roth, "Who Compiled the *Chuang-tzu*," in Rosemont, ed., *Chinese Texts and Philosophical Contexts*.

Interpretation: Apart from the histories of Chinese philosophy named in note 1 of the previous chapter, and apart from the translations noted just below: A. Allinson, *Chuang-Tzu for Spiritual Transformation: An Analysis of the Inner Chapters*, Albany: State University of New York Press, 1989. C. Hansen, "A Tao of Tao in Chuang-tzu," in V. Mair, ed., *Experimental Essays on Chuang-tzu*, Honolulu: University of Hawaii Press, 1983. C. Harbsmeier, "Conceptions of Knowledge in Ancient China," in H. Lenk and G. Paul, eds., *Epistemological Issues in Classical Chinese Philosophy*, Albany: State University of New York Press, 1993. H. Roetz, "Validity in Chou Thought: On Chad Hansen and the Pragmatic Turn in Sinology," in Lenk and Paul, eds., *Epistemological Issues in Classical Chinese Philosophy*.

Translations: A. C. Graham, trans., Chuang-tzu, *The Seven Inner Chapters and Other Writings from the Book* Chuang-tzu, London: Allen & Unwin, 1981. J. Legge, trans., *The Texts of Taoism*, London: Oxford University Press, 1891. V. H. Mair, *Wandering the Way*, New York: Bantam Books, 1994. M. Palmer, *The Book of Chuang Tzu*, London: Arkana (Penguin Books), 1996. B. Watson, *The Complete Works of Chuang-tzu*, New York: Columbia University Press, 1968. Kuang-ming Wu, *The Butterfly as Companion: Meditations on the First Three Chapters of the Chuang-tzu*, Albany: State University of New York Press, 1990.

18. For a translation of Ssu-ma Ch'ien's life of Chuang-Tzu, see Fung Yu-lan, *A History of Chinese Philosophy*, vol. 1, p. 221 (*Shih Chi*, chap. 63).

19. *Chuang-tzu*, trans. Graham, p. 120; *The Complete Works of Chuang-tzu*, trans. Watson, pp. 216–17 (*Chuang-tzu*, chap 20).

20. Graham, "How Much of *Chuang-tzu* Did Chuang-tzu Write?"; "Reflections and Replies," pp. 279–83. Roth, "Who Compiled the *Chuang-tzu*?" See also Liu Xiaogan, *Classifying the Zhuangzi Chapters*.

21. *Chuang-tzu,* chap. 2, lines 1–59. Trans. Graham, *Chuang-tzu,* pp. 48–51 (with matter inserted from elsewhere); Legge, *The Texts of Taoism,* part 1, pp. 176–78; Watson, *The Complete Works of Chuang-tzu,* pp. 36–38; Wu, *The Butterfly as Companion,* pp. 135–38.

22. *Chuang-tzu,* chap. 2, lines 60–68. Trans. Burton, p. 38; trans. Graham, p. 51; trans. Legge, part 1, p. 180; trans. Wu, p. 138.

23. *Chuang-tzu,* chap. 2, lines 85–94. Trans. Graham, p. 52; trans. Watson, p. 39; trans. Legge, part 1, pp. 181–82; trans. Wu, pp. 139–40.

24. *Chuang-tzu,* chap. 2, lines 85–107. Trans. Graham, pp. 52–53; trans. Watson, pp. 39–40; trans. Legge, part 1, pp. 182–83; trans. Wu, pp. 139–41 (see commentary, pp. 173–75, 193–95).

25. *Chuang-tzu,* chap. 2, lines 154–60. Trans. Graham, p. 55; trans. Watson, p. 43; trans. Legge, part 1, p. 187; trans. Wu, pp. 144–45.

26. *Chuang-tzu,* chap. 2, lines 163–69. Trans. Graham, p. 56; trans. Watson, p. 43; trans. Legge, part 1, p. 188; trans. Wu, p. 145.

27. *Chuang-tzu,* chap. 2, lines 177–81. Trans. Graham, p. 57; trans. Legge, part 1, p. 189; trans. Watson, p. 44; trans. Wu, p. 146 (commentary, pp. 204–205).

28. *Chuang-tzu,* chap. 2, lines 205–19. Trans. Graham, p. 58; trans. Watson, pp. 45–46; trans. Legge, part 1, pp. 191–92; trans. Wu, p. 148.

29. *Chuang-tzu,* chap. 2, lines 273–79. Trans. Graham, p. 60; trans. Legge, pp. 195–96; trans. Watson, p. 48; trans. Wu, pp. 152–53.

30. *Chuang-tzu,* chap. 2, lines 295–305. Trans. Graham, p. 61; trans. Legge, part 1, p. 197; trans. Watson, p. 49; trans. Wu, p. 148 trans. Wu, p. 153.

31. For a discussion of various interpretations of the butterfly dream, see Allinson, *Chuang-Tzu,* chaps. 6, 7. See also Graham, *Chuang-tzu,* pp. 21–22, note p. 61; and Wu, *The Butterfly as Companion,* pp. 175–78, 191–93, 375–77. My first interpretation is close to Graham's, and my preferred one essentially that of Wu.

32. *Chuang-tzu,* chap. 2, lines 255, 261, 263. Trans. Burton, pp. 47–48; trans. Graham, pp. 59–60; trans. Wu, p. 151.

33. *Chuang-tzu,* chaps. 27, 33. Trans. Burton, pp. 303–304, 373; trans. Graham, pp. 106–107, 283 (see also pp. 25–26); trans. Legge, pp. 142–43, p. 228; Wu, *The Butterfly as Companion,* pp. 262–64.

34. *Chuang-tzu,* chap. 33. Trans. Graham, p. 283.

35. **General accounts of the sophists:** Guthrie, *A History of Greek Philosophy,* vol. 3, Cambridge: Cambridge University Press, 1969. G. B. Kerferd, *The Sophistic Movement,* Cambridge: Cambridge University Press, 1981. J. de Romilly, *The Great Sophists in Periclean Athens,* Oxford: Oxford University Press, 1992.

Translated sources: R. K. Sprague, ed., *The Older Sophists*, Columbia: University of South Carolina Press, 1972.

36. Xenophon, *Memorabilia* 1.6.13.

37. Plato, *The Sophist*, in F. M. Cornford, *Plato's Theory of Knowledge*, p. 331.

38. Protagoras, fragment 4, in Sprague, ed., *The Older Sophists*, p. 20.

39. Protagoras, fragment 1 (Plato, *Theaetetus* 151e–152a), as translated in Sprague, ed., *The Older Sophists*, p. 19. On the various interpretations of this sentence, see Guthrie, *History of Greek Philosophy*, vol. 3, pp. 188–92.

40. Plato, *Theaetetus* 158b.

41. Ibid., *Theaetetus* 161c, 166d–167d.

42. Plato, *Philebus* 58a. Fragment 26; Sprague, ed., *The Older Sophists*, p. 39.

43. *Gorgias' Encomium of Helen* 14; trans. Sprague, ed., *The Older Sophists*, p. 53.

44. *Meno* 70b, as translated in R. E. Allen, *The Dialogues of Plato*, vol. 1, New Haven: Yale University Press, 1984, p. 151. See also fragment 1a, from Philostratus, in Sprague, ed., *The Older Sophists*, p. 31.

45. Aristophanes, *The Birds*, line 1694; translated in Sprague, ed., *The Older Sophists*, pp. 33–34.

46. Sextus Empiricus, *Against the Schoolmasters* 7.65, reporting on Gorgias, *On the Nonexistent or On Nature,* in Sprague, *The Older Sophists*, pp. 42–46; Sextus Empiricus, *Outlines of Pyrrhonism*, Cambridge: Harvard University Press, 1933, vol. 1, pp. 41–45. See Kerferd, *The Sophists Movement*, pp. 78–84, 93–100.

47. **Surveys of the dialogues one by one**: P. Friedländer, *Plato*, 3 vols., New York: Pantheon, 1958, 1964, 1969. W. K. C. Guthrie, *History of Greek Philosophy*, vol. 4, 1975; vol. 5, 1978. On Guthrie's two volumes, see the comments in C. J. de Vogel, *Rethinking Plato and Platonism*, Leiden: Brill, 1986, chap. 3. V. Tejera, *Plato's Dialogues One by One*.

Translation: *The Collected Dialogues of Plato*. ed. E. Hamilton and H. Cairns, New York: Pantheon, 1961.

Theory of ideas: H. Cherniss, *The Riddle of the Early Academy*, Berkeley: University of California Press, 1945, lecture 1. Friedländer, "Eidos," in vol. 1 of his *Plato*. G. Fine, *Aristotle's Criticisms of Plato's Theory of Forms*, Oxford: Oxford University Press, 1933 (technical). J. Moravcsik, *Plato and Platonism*, Oxford: London, 1992. D. Ross, *Plato's Theory of Ideas*, Oxford: Oxford University Press, 1951.

Selected commentaries: Apart from the commentaries in Friedländer, Guthrie, and Moravcsik, see: For the Parmenides, R. E. Allen, *Plato's Parmenides*, Oxford: Blackwell, 1983; F. M. Cornford, *Plato and Parmenides*, reprint New York: Liberal Arts Press, 1957; V. Tejera, "The Dialogism of Plato's Parmenides," unpublished ms. For the Sophist, R. S. Bluck, *Plato's Sophist*, Manchester: Manchester

University Press, 1975; F. M. Cornford, *Plato's Theory of Knowledge,* London: Routledge & Kegan Paul, 1935; and F. J. Pelletier, *Parmenides, Plato, and the Semantics of Not-Being,* Chicago: University of Chicago Press, 1990 (a careful comparison and discussion of various interpretations).

Essays: J. C. Klagge and N. D. Smith, eds., *Methods of Interpreting Plato and His Dialogues (Oxford Studies in Ancient Philosophy, Supplementary Volume),* Oxford: Oxford University Press, 1992. R. Kraut, ed. *The Cambridge Companion to Plato,* Cambridge: Cambridge University Press, 1992. V. Tejera, "The Hellenistic Obliteration of Plato's Dialogism," in G. A. Press, ed., *Plato's Dialogues,* Lanham: Rowman & Littlefield, 1993.

Ancient anecdotes: A. S. Reginos, *Platonica: The Anecdotes Concerning the Life and Writings of Plato,* Leiden: Brill, 1976.

48. Reginos, *Platonica,* chap. 1.

49. Diogenes Laertius, *Lives of the Eminent Philosophers,* vol. 1, p. 281 (3.5–6).

50. *Phaedrus* 275–77.

51. Plato, *Apology* 34a, 38b; *Phaedo* 59b.

52. The reference is to Aristotle's *Physics* 209b 11–17. On the subject of the unwritten teachings, see Guthrie, *History of Greek Philosophy,* vol. 5, chap. 8, and Ross, *Plato's Theory of Ideas,* chap. 9. A number of other passages in Aristotle attribute or appear to attribute teachings to Plato or his followers that are unknown in the dialogues. The Seventh Letter ascribed to Plato, which is used as evidence, is a controversial reed to lean upon. It does ascribe certain doctrines to Plato himself; if it is genuine, it represents the older Plato; and it is by and large compatible with his later dialogues.

53. See F. E. Peters, *Greek Philosophical Terms,* New York: New York University Press, 1967.

54. In describing Socrates, I cited Aristotle's *Metaphysics* 1078b9–32. Here *Metaphysics* 987129–b14 is added to the evidence, as cited in Ross, *Plato's Theory of Ideas,* p. 154.

55. For a relatively full, historically oriented account of Pythagorean thought see Guthrie, *History of Greek Philosophy,* vol. 1, chap. 4. Aristotle's statements, all from the *Metaphysics,* are cited on p. 229.

56. Plato, *Cratylus;* trans. Jowett, *The Collected Dialogues of Plato,* ed. Hamilton and Cairns, p. 474.

57. *Plato's Parmenides,* trans. Allen, p. 13. The following paraphrase and discussion of the *Parmenides* are much influenced by Allen.

58. Ibid., pp. 4–6.

59. Matilal, *The Central Philosophy of Jainism,* p. 19 (*Bhavagatī Sūtra* 9.386).

60. Vidyabhusana, *A History of Indian Logic,* p. 185.

61. *Chuang-tzu,* chap. 2, lines 95–99. Trans. Graham, *Chuang-tzu,* p. 52.

62. Sprague, *The Older Sophists,* p. 13.

63. Ibid., p. 43, much compressed.

64. F. M. Cornford, *Plato's Theory of Knowledge,* London: Routledge & Kegan Paul, 1935, pp. 294–95.

65. *Chuang-tzu,* chap. 3, lines 5–29.

66. *Chuang-tzu,* chap. 2, line 223. Trans. Graham, p. 58; trans. Wu, p. 148. *Chuang-tzu* chap. 3. On *shen,* especially in Chuang-tzu, see Wu, *The Butterfly as Companion,* pp. 319–21.

67. On the importance of ignorance to Chuang-tzu and its frequent profession, see Wu, *The Butterfly as Companion,* pp. 190–91, 207, 210–12. See also Harbsmeier, "Conceptions of Knowledge in Ancient China," pp. 23–24.

68. *Chuang-tzu,* chap. 2, lines 203–204; chap. 22, line 61. Trans. Graham, pp. 58, 162; (first quotation) trans. Wu, p. 148.

69. Plato, *The Apology* 41c–42a, in Allen, *The Dialogues of Plato,* vol. 1, pp. 103–104. *Chuang-tzu,* chap. 2, lines 245, 249. Trans. Burton, p. 47 (quoted); trans. Graham, p. 59; Trans. Wu, p. 150.

70. On Plato's interest in the relativist's arguments see L. Raphals, "Skeptical Strategies in the *Zhuangzi* and *Theaetetus,*" *Philosophy East and West,* July 1944. For the rest, see Plato, *Euthydemus* 286b, *Cratylus* 383a–b, 391b–e, 422d. In the *Cratylus,* Plato's Socrates reaches the conclusion that names may be given by conventional agreement, but they can be rightly given only by those who know the unchanging reality. See Kerferd, *The Sophist Movement,* chap. 7.

Chapter 5. Early Rational Synthesis

1. The quotation in the subtitle is from Watson's translation of the latter part of the first sentence of section or book 23 of Hsün-tzu's writings.

Historical, political, and social background to Hsün-tzu: Cho-Yun Hsu, *Ancient China in Transition,* Stanford: Stanford University Press, 1965. Cho-Yun Hsu and K. M. Lindhoff. *Western Chou Civilization,* Yale: Yale University Press, 1988. D. Twitchett and M. Loewe, eds. *The Cambridge History of China,* vol. 1 (Cambridge: Cambridge University Press, 1986, chaps. 12–14. J. Needham, *Science and Civilization in China,* vol. 2, chap. 9 (On Confucians, science, etc.).

Philosophy: The histories of Chinese philosophy by Fung, Graham, Hansen, and Schwartz, and of Chinese political thought by Hsiao (see chap. 3, note 1). R. T. Ames, *The Art of Rulership: A Study in Ancient Chinese Political Thought,* Honolulu:

University of Hawaii Press, 1983. F. W. Mote, *Intellectual Foundations of China*, 2d ed., New York: Knopf, 1989 (succinct). Knoblock, *Xunzi* (see immediately below). D. J. Munro, *The Concept of Man in Early China*, Stanford: Stanford University Press, 1961.

Translations: H. H. Dubs, *The Works of Hsüntze*, London: Probsthain, 1928, Hsün Tzu: *Basic Writings*, trans. B. Watson, New York: Columbia University Press, 1963. J. Knoblock, *Xunzi: A Translation and Study of the Complete Works*, 3 vols. Stanford: Stanford University Press, 1988, 1990, 1994.

Studies: A. S. Cua, *Ethical Argumentation: A Study in Hsün Tzu's Moral Epistemology*, Honolulu: Hawaii University Press, 1985; "The Possibility of Ethical Knowledge: Reflections on a Theme in the *Hsün Tzu*," in H. Lenk and G. Paul, eds., *Epistemological Issues in Classical Chinese Thought*, Buffalo: State University of New York Press, 1993. R. Eno, *The Confucian Creation of Heaven*, Albany: State University of New York Press, 1990. A. Graham, "The Background of the Mencian Theory of Human Nature," in Graham, *Studies in Chinese Philosophy and Philosophical Literature*. D. S. Nivison, "Hsun Tzu and Chuang Tzu," in H. Rosemont, ed., *Chinese Texts and Philosophical Contexts*, La Salle: Open Court, 1991. H. Roetz, "Validity in Chou Thought," in Lenk and Paul, eds., *Epistemological Issues in Classical Chinese Thought*.

2. Knoblock, *Xunzi: A Translation and Study of the Complete Works*, vol. 1, pp. 11–12 (p. 11 quoted).

3. *Hsün-tzu* section or book 15. See Knoblock, trans., *Xunzi*, vol. 2, pp. 211–34 and the equivalent in Dubs, *The Works of Hsüntze*, and Burton, *Hsün Tzu*.

4. Knoblock, trans., *Xunzi*, vol. 2, pp. 20–27.

5. Ibid., pp. 31–35 (p. 35 quoted).

6. This is the careful verdict of Knoblock, *Xunzi*, vol. 1, p. 120. The whole of chapter 7 in on the text's history and authenticity.

7. Ibid., chap. 3.

8. *Xunzi (Hsün Tzu)* 1.13.

9. See Knoblock, vol. 3, book 22; Watson, *Hsün Tzu*, section 22; Dubs, *The Works of Hsüntze*, book 22; and Cua, *Ethical Argumentation*. The translation by Graham, *Disputers of the Tao*, pp. 261–67, is particularly incisive.

10. *Hsün-tzu* 3.22.1a–b. See Graham, *Disputers of the Tao*, pp. 260–61; Knoblock, *Xunzi*, vol. 3, p. 127.

11. *Hsün-tzu* 3.22.1c–2a. Graham, *Disputers of the Tao*, p. 262; Knoblock, *Xunzi*, vol. 3, p. 128.

12. *Hsün-tzu* 3.22.2c. Knoblock, *Xunzi*, vol. 3, p. 128.

13. *Hsün-tzu* 3.22.2d. Knoblock, *Xunzi*, vol. 3, p. 129.

14. *Hsün-tzu* 3.22.2f–h. Graham, *Disputers of the Tao*, p. 265–66; Knoblock, *Xunzi*, vol. 3, pp. 130–31.

15. *Hsün-tzu* 3.22.3f. Graham, *Disputers of the Tao*, p. 267; Knoblock, *Xunzi*, vol. 3, pp. 132–33 (p. 132 quoted). See Roetz, "Validity in Chou Thought," pp. 81–82, for an attempt to specify the meaning of the terms translated as *link* or *join*, *proposition* or *sentence*, and so on.

16. *Hsün-tzu* 22.3f. Knoblock, *Xunzi*, vol. 3, p. 133.

17. *Hsün-tzu* 22.3a–c. Graham, *Disputers of the Tao*, pp. 263–64; Knoblock, *Xunzi*, vol. 3, p. 130.

18. *Hsün-tzu* 22.6a. section 22. Knoblock, *Xunzi*, vol. 3, p. 136; Watson, *Hsün Tzu*, p. 152.

19. See Knoblock, *Xunzi*, vol. 1, chap. 5. For a fuller picture of the cosmology of the time see Graham, *Disputers of the Tao*, pp. 313–70.

20. *Hsün-tzu* 9.65–67. See Watson, *Hsün Tzu*, p. 44. I follow Graham, *Disputers of the Tao*, pp. 242–444.

21. *Hsün-tzu* 17.1. Knoblock, *Xunzi*, vol. 3, pp. 14–15; Watson, *Hsün Tzu*, pp. 79–80.

22. *Hsün-tzu* 17.7–8. Knoblock, *Xunzi*, vol. 3, pp. 18–19; Watson, *Hsün Tzu*, pp. 83–85 (p. 85 quoted).

23. See the sober exposition in J. D. Barrows, *The World within the World*, London: Oxford University Press, 1988, chap. 7.

24. *Hsün-tzu* 17.3a. Knoblock, *Xunzi*, vol. 3, p. 16; Watson, *Hsün Tzu*, pp. 81–82.

25. *Hsün-tzu* 17.2a–b. Knoblock, *Xunzi*, vol. 3, pp. 14–15; Watson, *Hsün Tzu*, pp. 79–80.

26. *Hsün-tzu* 17.10. Bodde, *The Works of Hsüntze*, p. 183; Graham, *Disputers of the Tao*, p. 240 (its bold, incisive translation quoted); Knoblock, *Xunzi*, vol. 3, pp. 20–21; Watson, *Hsün Tzu*, p. 86.

27. *Hsün Tzu* 21.8. Knoblock, *Xunzi*, vol. 3, pp. 108–109; Watson, *Hsün Tzu*, pp. 133–35.

28. *Hsün-tzu* 21.9 and 4.11. Knoblock, *Xunzi*, vol. 3, pp. 110–11; vol. 1, pp. 193–94 (p. 194 quoted).

29. *Hsün-tzu* 21.7b. Knoblock, *Xunzi*, vol. 3, p. 107; Watson, *Hsün Tzu*, p. 131. The quotation is from Cua, "The Possibility of Ethical Language," p. 166.

30. *Hsün-tzu* 23.1a. Knoblock, *Xunzi*, vol. 3, p. 150 (quoted); Watson, *Hsün Tzu*, p. 157.

31. *Hsün-tzu* 23.1c. Knoblock, *Xunzi*, vol. 3, p. 152 (quoted); Watson, *Hsün Tzu*, pp. 158–59.

32. *Hsün-tzu* 23.1b. Knoblock, *Xünzi*, vol. 3, p. 151 (quoted); Watson, *Hsün Tzu*, pp. 157–58.

33. *Hsün-tzu* 9 ("On the Regulations of a King"), esp. 9.16a. Knoblock, *Xunzi*, vol. 2, pp. 94–112 (esp. pp. 103–105; Watson, *Hsün Tzu*, pp. 33–55. See also *Hsün-tzu* 18 ("Rectifying Theses") and 19 ("Discourse on Ritual Principles").

34. *Hsün-tzu* 9.16b, 9.17 (in Dubs, numbered 9.12–13, 9.14). Dubs, *The Works of Hsüntze*, pp. 137–39, 140–41; Knoblock, *Xunzi*, vol. 2, pp. 105, 106.

35. *Hsün-tzu* 21.1–2. Knoblock, *Xunzi*, vol. 3, pp. 100–101; Watson, *Hsün Tzu*, pp. 121–22.

36. *Hsün-tzu* 21.4. Knoblock, *Xunzi*, vol. 3, pp. 102–103 (103 quoted); Watson, *Hsün Tzu*, pp. 125–26.

37. *Hsün-tzu* 2.4; trans. Knoblock, *Xunzi*, vol. 1, p. 153.

38. Knoblock, *Xunzi*, vol. 1, pp. 143–49.

39. *Hsün-tzu* 2.11; trans. Knoblock, *Xunzi*, vol. 1, p. 157.

40. *Hsün-tzu* 1.14; trans. Knoblock, *Xunzi*, vol. 1, p. 142.

41. The quotation accompanying the subtitle is from Aristotle, *Metaphysics* 1072a. Trans. H. Tredennick, Cambridge: Harvard University Press, vol. 2, 1935, p. 147.

Historical, political, and social background: K. C. Dover, *Greek Popular Morality in the Time of Plato and Aristotle*, Oxford: Blackwell, 1974. M. H. Hansen, *The Athenian Democracy in the Age of Demosthenes*, London: Blackwell, 1991. D. M. Lewis, J. Boardman, J. K. Davies, and M. Ostwald, eds., *The Cambridge Ancient History*, 2d ed., vol. 5, *The Fifth Century B.C.*, Cambridge: Cambridge University Press, 1992.

Life: J. Barnes, "Life and Works," in Barnes, ed., *The Cambridge Companion to Aristotle* (see just below). Diogenes Laertius, *Lives of the Eminent Philosophers*, trans. Hicks, pp. 445–83. I. Dühring, *Aristotle in the Ancient Biographical Tradition*, Göteborg: Acta universitatis gothburgensis 58, 1957.

General surveys: J. Barnes, ed., *The Cambridge Companion to Aristotle*, Cambridge: Cambridge University Press, 1995. I. Dühring, *Aristotleles*, Heidelberg: Carl Winter, Universitätsverlag, 1966. W. K. C. Guthrie, *A History of Greek Philosophy* (1981). A. Idel, *Aristotle and His Philosophy*, Chapel Hill: University of North Carolina Press, 1982. T. H. Irwin, *Aristotle's First Principles*, Oxford: Oxford University Press, 1988. W. D. Ross, *Aristotle*, 5th ed., London: Methuen, 1949. F. Solmsen, *Aristotle's System of the Physical World*, Ithaca: Cornell University Press, 1960.

Translations: *Aristotle's Categories and De Interpretatione*, trans. J. L. Ackrill, London: Oxford University Press, 1963. *The Complete Works of Aristotle (The Revised Oxford Translation)*, ed. J. Barnes, 2 vols., Princeton: Princeton University

Press, 1984. *The Works of Aristotle*, vol. 12, *Select Fragments*, trans. D. Ross, London: Oxford University Press, 1952.

Politics: E. Barker, *The Politics of Aristotle,* London: Oxford University Press, 1946 (translation with extensive commentary). *Aristotle's Politics, Books III and IV,* trans. R. Robinson, London: Oxford University Press, 1962 (translation with extensive commentary). J. Day and M. Chambers, *Aristotle's History of Athenian Democracy,* Berkeley: University of California Press, 1962.

Ethics: H. H. Joachim, *The Nichomachean Ethics,* London: Oxford University Press, 1951. M. Nussbaum, *The Fragility of Goodness,* Cambridge: Cambridge University Press, 1986, part 3. R. Kraut, *Aristotle on the Human Good,* Princeton: Princeton University Press, 1989.

Other relevant subjects: G. Fine, *Aristotle's Criticism of Plato's Theory of Forms,* Oxford: Oxford University Press. 1993 (technical). V. Kal, *On Intuition and Discursive Reasoning in Aristotle,* Leiden: Brill, 1988. G. E. R. Lloyd, *Aristotelian Explorations,* Cambridge: Cambridge University Press, 1996 (on the tensions between Aristotle's a priori views and the empirical data he encountered and felt it necessary to take account of). C. Lord, *Education and Culture in the Political Thought of Aristotle,* Ithaca: Cornell University Press, 1982. G. A. Kennedy, *Aristotle on Rhetoric,* New York: Oxford University Press, 1991 (translation with extensive commentary). D. K. W. Modrak, *Aristotle: The Power of Perception,* Chicago: University of Chicago Press, 1987.

The ancient commentators: R. Sorabji, ed., *Aristotle Transformed,* London: Duckworth, 1990.

42. *Nicomachean Ethics* 1096a.

43. *Politics* 1327b. Except when otherwise indicated, the quotations below from Aristotle are all from *The Complete Works of Aristotle*, ed. Barnes.

44. Aristotle, *Select Fragments*, trans. Ross, pp. 65, 67 (Cicero, *Atticus* 12.40.2; Plutarch, *Moralia* 329b and Strabo 1.4.9 [quoting Eratosthenes]). See Dühring, *Aristoteles*, p. 12.

45. *On the Parts of Animals* 645a.

46. The learned, painstaking Ingmar Dühring believes that Aristotle's school, in the sense of an institution, was founded not by Aristotle but by his successor, Theophrastus, but the traditional account seems to me more plausible. See Guthrie, *History of Greek Philosophy*, vol. 6, pp. 38ff.

47. Diogenes Laertius, *Lives of Eminent Philosophers*, trans. Hicks, vol. 1, pp. 455, 457 (5.12–13).

48. Diogenes Laertius, *Lives of Eminent Philosophers* 5.18, 20.

49. *Physics* 994a27–29.

50. *Physics* 192b9–193a. For Aristotle's doctrine of potentiality and actuality see especially book 9 of the *Metaphysics*. For expositions see Guthrie, *A History of*

Greek Philosophy, vol. 6, pp. 119–29; Irwin, *Aristotle's First Principles*, pp. 223–38; Ross, *Aristotle*, pp. 176–78.

51. *Physics* 192b9–193a. On form and matter see Guthrie, *A History of Greek Philosophy*, vol. 6, chap. 6 and pp. 226–32; Irwin, *Aristotle's First Principles*, pp. 238–47; Ross, *Aristotle*, pp. 73–75.

52. The examples are from *Metaphysics* 1025a; and see 1026b. On substance or substance and accident see Guthrie, *A History of Greek Philosophy*, vol. 6, pp. 146–49, 203–22; Irwin, *Aristotle's First Principles*, chap. 12; Ross, *Aristotle*, pp. 165–67.

53. Aristotle, *Prior Analytics*, trans. E. S. Forster, Cambridge: Harvard University Press, 1960, p. 31.

54. As translated in Modrak, *Aristotle: The Power of Perception*, p. 160.

55. For this comparison of induction and deduction, see *Topics* 105a. For Aristotle's explanation of demonstration and science see the *Posterior Analytics* and, on the science of being, the *Metaphysics*, books 3, 4, 6. Guthrie, *A History of Greek Philosophy*, vol. 6, chaps. 10 (on demonstration) and 11 (on the science of being); Irwin, *Aristotle's First Principles*, chaps. 1–3; Ross, *Aristotle*, pp. 41–61.

56. See Guthrie, *A History of Greek Philosophy*, vol. 6, chap. 15; Irwin, *Aristotle's First Principles*, chaps. 15–21; Ross, *Aristotle*, chaps. 7, 8.

57. Solmsen, *Aristotle's System of the Physical World*, esp. pp. 112, 175–81, 248–49, 290–92, 308–13, 379–82.

58. *Nicomachean Ethics* 1096a.

59. *Hsün-tzu* 22.3. Knoblock, *Xunzi*, vol. 3, p. 133; Watson, *Hsün Tzu*, p. 147. Where Watson translates, "analogies should be drawn which are not forced or false," Knoblock translates, "inferences should be made from the characteristic category of a thing, but not to the point of introducing fallacies." The general meaning seems to be about the same.

60. *De interpretatione* 16a.

61. *Topics* book 1.

62. *Hsün-tzu* 5.8; trans. Knoblock, *Xunzi*, vol. 1, p. 209.

63. Trans. Kennedy, *Aristotle On Rhetoric*, p. 121.

64. (Pseudo)-Aristotle, *Physiognomics*, 806b, 810.

65. *Hsün-tzu* 5.1; trans. Knoblock, vol. 1, p. 204.

66. *Hsün-tzu* 17; trans. Watson, p. 80.

67. *Hsün Tzu* 9.16a. My version is a compromise among translations. See also the translation and comments in Needham, *Science and Civilization in China*, vol. 2, pp. 21–24.

68. See, e.g., Aristotle, *On the Soul* 414a29–415a14. Since the original is confusing, see also the account in Guthrie, *History of Greek Philosophy*, vol. 6, chap. 14.

69. *History of Animals* 586b.

70. *Politics* 1256b21–22.

71. *The Complete Works of Aristotle*, ed. Barnes, vol. 2, pp. 1988, 1986.

72. *On Virtues and Vices* 1251b; *Politics* 1352a, 1253a, 1324a.

73. *Politics* 1253a31–37.

74. *Nicomachean Ethics* 1103a19–26.

75. *Nichomachean Ethics* 1179b–1180a.

76. Knoblock, *Xunzi*, vol. 1, p. 47.

77. *Hsün-tzu* 19.2c. Knoblock, *Xunzi*, vol. 3, pp. 60–61.

78. *Nicomachean Ethics* 1109b.

79. *Nicomachean Ethics* 1106b–1107a.

80. *Hsün Tzu* 20.2. Knoblock, *Xunzi*, vol. 3, p. 82; Watson, *Hsün Tzu*, pp. 114–15.

81. Aristotle, *Politics* 1339a–1342b (quoted words from 1340a 20–24, and 1342a 20–25).

82. *Hsün-tzu* 1.8, 1.9, 3.2 (quoted), 3.4. Knoblock, *Xunzi*, vol. 1 (p. 174 quoted).

82. *Nicomachean Ethics* 1122a–1125a.

84. *Nichomachean Ethics* 1094b.

85. *Politics* 1253a27–29. In *The Complete Works of Aristotle*, ed. Barnes, vol. 2, p. 1988.

86. *The Complete Works of Aristotle*, ed. Barnes, vol. 2, p. 1861.

Chapter 6. Early Varieties of Atomism

1. This on atomism and alphabetization is, of course, no more than a conjecture. For a comparison of the various writing systems see F. Coulmas, *The Writing Systems of the World*, London: Blackwell, 1989.

2. **Greek and Roman atomism**: D. Sedley, "Philosophical Allegiance in the Greco-Roman World," in M. Griffin and J. Barnes, eds., *Philosophia Togata*, London: Oxford University Press, 1989. D. Furley, *Cosmic Problems: Essays on Greek*

and Roman Philosophy of Nature, Cambridge: Cambridge University Press, 1989. H. Jones, *The Epicurean Tradition*, London: Routledge, 1989. M. Nussbaum, *The Therapy of Desire*, Princeton: Princeton University Press, 1994, chaps. 4–7.

Atomism: Diogenes Laertius, *Lives of Eminent Philosophers*, books 9, 10, trans. R. D Hicks, vol. 2. D. Furley, *The Greek Cosmologists*, vol. 1, Cambridge: Cambridge University Press, 1987; *Two Studies in the Greek Atomists*, Princeton: Princeton University Press, 1967. A. J. Festugière, *Epicurus and His Gods*, Oxford: Blackwell, 1955. W. K. C. Guthrie, *A History of Greek Philosophy*, vol. 2, chap. 8 (on Leucippus and Democritus). W. R. Knorr, "Infinity and Continuity: The Interaction of Mathematics and Philosophy in Antiquity," in N. Kretzman, ed., *Infinity and Continuity in Ancient and Medieval Thought*, Ithaca: Cornell University Press, 1962. F. D. Miller, "Aristotle against the Atomists," in N. Kretzman, ed., *Infinity and Continuity in Ancient and Medieval Thought*. J. M. Rist, *Epicurus*, Cambridge: Cambridge University Press, 1972. G. Rodis-Lewis, *Épicure et son École*, Paris: Gallimard, 1975. R. Sorabji, "Atoms and Time Atoms," in N. Kretzman, ed., *Infinity and Continuity in Ancient and Medieval Thought*.

Roman atomism: D. R. Dudley, ed., *Lucretius*, London: Routledge & Kegan Paul, 1965. D. P. Fowler, "Lucretius and Politics," in Griffin and Barnes, eds., *Philosophia Togata*. C. Segal, *Lucretius on Death and Anxiety*, Princeton: Princeton University Press, 1990.

Translations with commentary: Epicurus, *The Extant Remains*, trans. C. Bailey, Oxford: Oxford University Press, 1926. G. S. Kirk, J. E. Raven, and M. Schofield, trans., *The Presocratic Philosophers*. A. A. Long and D. N. Sedley, *The Hellenistic Philosophers*, Cambridge: Cambridge University Press, 1987. A. A. Long, *Hellenistic Philosophy*, vol. 1, London: Duckworth, 1974. Lucretius, *De Rerum Natura*, trans. C. Bailey, 3 vols, London: Oxford University Press, 1947; trans. W. H. D. Rouse, rev. M. F. Smith, rev. 2d ed., Cambridge: Harvard University Press, 1982.

3. The quoted words about Leucippus and the statements about Democritus are from Diogenes Laertius, *Lives of Eminent Philosophers*, vol. 2, in his accounts of the two philosophers.

4. Diogenes Laertius, *Lives of Eminent Philosophers*, vol. 2, pp. 537–41.

5. Cicero, *De natura deorum* 1.33, trans. H. Rackham, Cambridge: Harvard University Press, 1933, p. 91.

6. Lucretius, *De rerum natura*, vol. 1, pp. 8–18.

7. Lucretius, *De rerum natura*, 1.62–83, 3.31–64 (vol. 1, pp. 179–81, 305).

8. *On Generation and Corruption* 325a28, as translated in Guthrie, *A History of Greek Philosophy*, vol. 2, p. 390.

9. Aristotle, *On the Soul*, 404a.

10. *Letter to Herodotus*, 42; in *Epicurus, the Extant Remains*, trans. Bailey, p. 25.

11. Guthrie, *A History of Greek Philosophy*, vol. 2, pp. 417–19.

12. Kirk, Raven, and Schofield, pp. 410 (entries 548–50), 42 (entries 552–54). All this testimony is from Sextus Empiricus, *Against the Mathematicians*, 7. See these and further excerpts in Guthrie, *A History of Greek Philosophy*, vol. 2, pp. 458–65.

13. Lucretius, *De rerum natura* 2.133–141.

14. For Epicurus, see his *Letter to Herodotus* 56–59. For Lucretius on the size that would result from an infinite number of particles see *De rerum natura* 1.615. See also Bailey's note on the passage in vol. 2, p. 700.

15. *Epicurus*, trans. Bailey, pp. 33–34. See the rather sharper translation in Long and Sedley, *The Hellenistic Philosophers*, p. 39.

16. Aristotle, *On Generation and Corruption*, 316aff. Aristotle's comment is from *On the Heavens*, 303a; he refers back to *Physics* 6.231ff. See the discussion in Guthrie, *A History of Greek Philosophy*, vol. 2, appendix. See also Furley, *Two Studies in the Greek Atomists*, chap. 6; and *Cosmic Problems*, chap. 9.

17. Furley, *Two Studies in the Greek Atomists*, chaps. 1, 2. Sorabji, *Time, Creation and the Continuum*, pp. 371–75.

18. *Physics* 6.104, 10.

19. R. Sorabji, "Atoms and Time Atoms," in N. Kretzman, ed., *Infinity and Continuity in Ancient and Medieval Thought*; *Time, Creation and the Continuum*, London: Duckworth, 1983, chap. 24.

20. Trans. Bailey, vol. 1, pp. 185–86.

21. Trans. Bailey, vol. 1, p. 253.

22. Epicurus, *Letter to Herodotus*, section 39. *Epicurus*, trans. Bailey, pp. 21–23.

23. Lucretius, *De rerum natura* 2.289–93; in Furley, *Two Studies in the Greek Atomists*, p. 178. For an older, rival interpretation, see Lucretius, *De rerum natura*, trans. Bailey, vol. 2, pp. 837–41.

24. See the passage from Diogenes of Oenoanda in Long and Sedley, *The Hellenistic Philosophers*, vol. 1, p. 106.

25. Lucretius, *De rerum natura* 3.307–322, as interpreted by Furley in *Two Studies in the Greek Atomists*, study 2, chap. 4, pp. 198–200.

26. Cicero's summary in *On Ends* 1; in Long and Sedley, *The Hellenistic Philosophers*, vol. 1, p. 112.

27. Rist, *Epicurus*, pp. 102–103, 109.

28. Epicurus, *Letter to Menoecus*; in Long and Sedley, *The Hellenistic Philosophers*, vol. 1, p. 113.

29. Epicurus, *Vatican Sayings* 27, 41; in Long and Sedley, *Hellenistic Philosophy*, vol. 1, p. 156. The statement that philosophy should expel suffering is Porphyry's quotation from Epicurus, as in Long and Sedley, p. 155.

30. Epicurus, *Principal Doctrines*, 11; in *Epicurus*, trans. Bailey, p. 97.

31. Rist, *Epicurus*, chaps. 6, 8.

32. *Fragments*, frag. 32, in *Epicurus*, trans. Bailey, p. 111.

33. *Letter to Menoeceus*, 124, 125 (quoted); as in *Epicurus*, trans. Bailey, p. 85.

34. See "Mortal Immortals: Lucretius on Death and the Voice of Nature," chap. 6 of Nussbaum, *The Therapy of Desire*.

35. Translated Rouse, p. 195.

36. Lucretius, *De Rerum Natura* 3.919–22; trans. Rouse, p. 261.

37. Ibid., 3.931–77 (967–68 and 977 quoted).

38. Although in the text I deal with the Indian atomism only of the Naiyayikas and the Buddhists, for those interested in reading further, I add references to the Ajivikas, whose atomism is apparent only in late sources, and to the Vaisheshika. A description of relatively early Jain atomism can be found in Umasvati, *Tattvārtha Sūtra* (see bibliography of chapter 4) and in Gangopadhyaya (see immediately below).

Indian atomism in general: M. Gangopadhyaya, *Indian Atomism*, Calcutta: Bagchi & Co., 1980 (mostly an original, annotated translation of sources). H. Jacobi, "Atomic Theory (Indian)," in J. Hastings, *Encyclopaedia of Religion and Ethics*, New York: Scribner's, 1928.

Ajivikas: A. L. Basham, *History and Doctrines of the Ājīvikas*, London: Luzac, 1951.

Vaisheshika and Nyaya: The two schools, which were soon regarded as allied and which coalesced about the eleventh century A.D., are often expounded together. For their separate and joint history see S. C. Vidyabhusana, *A History of Indian Logic*, reprint, Delhi: Banarsidass, 1971. S. Bhaduri, *Studies in Nyāya-Vaiśeṣika Metaphysics*, Poona: Bhandarkar Oriental Research Institute, 1947. C. Bulcke, *The Theism of Nyāya-Vaiśeṣika: Its Origin and Early Development*, Delhi: Banarsidass, 1947. S. Dasgupta, *A History of Indian Philosophy*, vol. 1, chap. 8. E. Frauwallner, *History of Indian Philosophy*, vol. 2 (on the Vaisheshika). W. Halbfass, *On Being and What There Is: Classical Vaiśeṣika and the History of Indian Ontology*, Albany: State University of New York Press, 1992. S. N. Junankar, *Gautama: The Nyāya Philosophy*, Delhi: Banarsidass, 1978. A. B. Keith, *Indian Logic and Atomism*, Oxford: Oxford University Press, 1921. B. K. Matilal, *Nyāya-Vaiśeṣika*, in J. Gonda, ed., *A History of Indian Literature*, Wiesbaden: Harrassowitz (a brief, lucid, and authoritative summary, but not helpful for the subject of atomism). K. H. Potter, ed., *Indian Metaphysics and Epistemology: The Tradition of Nyāya-Vaiśeṣika up to Gaṅgeśa*, vol. 2

of the *Encyclopedia of Indian Philosophies*, Princeton: Princeton University Press, 1977 (contains detailed paraphrases of the works of the period it deals with). S. Radhakrishnan, *Indian Philosophy*, 2d ed., London: Allen & Unwin, vol. 2, 1931. J. Sinha, *A History of Indian Philosophy*, vol. 1, Calcutta: Sinha Publishing House, 1956, chaps. 8, 9.

Translations of Nyaya sources: *Nyāya: Gautama's Nyāya Sūtra with Vātsyāyana's Commentary*, trans. M. Gangopadhyaya, Calcutta; Indian Studies, 1982 (the translation is the same as in Gangopadhyaya, *Indian Atomism* [see above], but *Indian Atomism* has extensive explanations). *The Nyāya-Sūtras of Gautama*, trans. G. Jha, 4 vols., reprint Delhi: Banarsidass, 1984. Prashastapada, *Padārthasaṃgraha of Praśastapāda*, trans. G. Jha, reprint, Varanasi: Chaukhamba Orientala, 1982. Radhakrishnan and Moore, trans., *A Source Book in Indian Philosophy*.

39. Dasgupta, *A History of Indian Philosophy*, vol. 3, pp. 531–33.

40. *Chāndogya Upaniṣad* 8.9. The sources for Indian materialism, along with interpretative articles, are collected in D. Chattopadhyaya, ed., *Cārāvaka/Lokāyata*, New Delhi: Indian Council of Philosophical Research, 1990.

41. *Sāmañña-phala Sutta* 23. See Chattopadhyaya, ed., *Cārāvaka/Lokāyata*, p. 48. The quoted sentences are from the paraphrase in Basham, *History and Doctrines of the Ājīvikas*, p. 15. See also Dasgupta, *History of Indian Philosophy*, vol. 3, pp. 521–22.

42. For the various theories on the origin of Indian atomism see Gangopadhyaya, *Indian Atomism*, pp. 39–54.

43. Ibid., pp. 40–44.

44. Matilal, *Nyāya-Vaiśeṣika*, p. 77, and, in detail, Vidyabhusana, *History of Indian Logic*, pp. 46–50. On the grounds that the Nyaya Sutra 4.2.25 is directed against Nagarjuna, who is presumed to have lived during the second century C.E., it has been usual to assign "Gautama" the same date. However, a recent verdict, in Potter, ed., *The Tradition of Nyāya-Vaiśeṣika up to Gaṅgeśa*, p. 221, is that "we have not the vaguest idea who wrote the Nyaya Sutras or when he lived." This is apart from the compiled nature of the work.

45. There is a brief summary of the contents of the Nyaya Sutras in Matilal, *Nyāya-Vaiśeṣika*, pp. 78–79, a detailed one in Potter, *The Tradition of Nyāya-Vaiśeṣika*, pp. 221–238, and a quite elaborate one in Vidyabhusana, *A History of Indian Logic*, pp. 54–114. There is also a good one in Junankar, *Gautama*.

46. *Nyāya*, trans. Gangopadhyaya, 1.1.1, p. 3.

47. H. Nakamura, *A History of Early Vedānta Philosophy*, part 1, Delhi: Banarsidass, 1983, pp. 331–34.

48. *Bhāṣya* 1.1.1. Trans. in Gangopadhyaya, *Nyāya*, pp. 3–4.

49. *Bhāṣya* 1.1.23, 2.1.7. Ibid., pp. 33, 77.

50. *Bhāṣya* 4.2.16–30. Ibid., pp. 359–62.

51. *Sūtras* with *bhāṣya* 4.2.31–37. Ibid., pp. 362–67.

52. Vātsyāyana's comment on 1.1.3, p. 13; in Jha's translation, vol. 1, p. 102.

53. *Bhāṣya* to *sūtra* 1.1.7. Trans. Gangopadhyaha, *Nyāya*, p. 19.

54. Vātsyāyana's commentary *(bhāṣya)* to 1.1.1. *Nyāya*, trans. Gangopadhyaya, p. 3.

55. *Bhāṣya* 1.1.7. Trans. Gangopadhyaha, *Nyāya*, p. 19.

56. *Bhāṣya* 2.2.65. Trans. Gangopadhyaya, *Nyāya*, p. 125. See also *bhāṣya* to 2.1.61; trans. p. 123.

57. *Sūtra* and *bhāṣya* 2.1.18 with *bhāṣya*. Trans. Gangopadhyaya, *Nyāya*, p. 85.

58. *Bhāṣya* 2.1.18–20. Trans. Gangopadhyaha, *Nyāya*, pp. 85–89. I have found it helpful to read the same passages, much extended by notes and the subcommentary in Jha's translation, vol. 2, pp. 648–60; but except where noted, I have kept the subcommentary out of my selective paraphrase.

59. *Bhāṣya* 3.1.3. Trans. Gangopadhyaha, *Nyāya*, pp. 172–73.

60. *Bhāṣya* 3.1.6. Ibid., pp. 175–76.

61. *Bhāṣya* 3.1.4. Trans. ibid., pp. 173–74. See also 4.1.10–11, trans. pp. 284 ff., on rebirth.

62. *Bhāṣya* 4.1.54–57. Trans. ibid., pp. 316–20.

63. Ibid., *sūtras* and *bhāṣya* 1.1.22–23, pp. 27–32. See also 1.1.9 in Jha's translation, vol. 1, pp. 211–12. Uddyotakara's subcommentary, pp. 215–16, is even more emphatic. On the Nyaya view of *duhkha* see Matilal, *Logical and Ethical Issues of Religious Belief*, Calcutta: University of Calcutta, 1982, *"Duḥkha."*

64. *Bhāṣya* 3.1.3. Trans. Gangopadhyaha, *Nyāya*, *bhāṣya* 4.1.21, pp. 290–91. What I call a somewhat bold paraphrase in based on p. 291, which I think is a somewhat bold translation. See the same passage in Jha's translation, vol. 4, pp. 1460–61. On theism in early Nyaya and Vaisheshika see Bulcke, *The Theism of Nyāya-Vaiśeṣika*. Bulcke (p. 17) believes that the theism was borrowed from Yoga. According to him, the existence of God was not denied but did not serve as an important subject for speculation.

65. Gangopadhyaya, *Indian Atomism*, p. 129.

66. *Bhāṣya* 2.1.34. Trans. Gangopadhyaya, *Indian Atomism*, p. 288.

67. *Bhāṣya* 2.1.35. Trans. Gangopadhyaya, *Indian Atomism*, p. 289.

68. *Nyāya-sūtra* 4.2.4.

69. Ibid. 4.2.6.

70. *Nyāya-sūtra* and *bhāṣya* 4.2.7. Trans. Gangopadhyaya, *Nyāya*, pp. 345–46 and Gangopadhyaya, *Indian Atomism*, pp. 303–304.

71. *Nyāya-sūtra* and *bhāṣhya* 4.2.10. Trans. Gangopadhyaya, *Nyāya*, pp. 346–47 and *Indian Atomism*, pp. 308–309. For "later complications" see *Indian Atomism*, p. 309. The illustration of thread and cloth is from Uddyotakara's *vārtika*, in Jha's translation, vol. 4, pp. 1592–93.

72. *Nyāya-sūtra* and *bhāṣhya* 4.2.11–12. Trans. Gangopadhyaya, *Nyāya*, pp. 346–49 and *Indian Atomism*, pp. 311–15.

73. *Nyāya-sūtra* and *bhāṣhya* 2.1.36. Trans. Gangopadhyaya, *Nyāya*, pp. 100–101 and *Indian Atomism*, pp. 290–92. Jha's translation, vol. 2, pp. 764–66.

74. *Bhāṣhya* 2.1.36. Trans. Gangopadhyaya, *Nyāya*, pp. 104–106 and *Indian Atomism*, pp. 298–300. Jha's translation, vol. 2, pp. 771–73.

75. Trans. Gangopadhyaya, *Nyāya*, pp. 126–27 and *Indian Atomism*, p. 353. Jha's translation, vol. 4, pp. 1605–1606.

76. *Bhāṣhya* 4.2.17.

77. Trans. Gangopadhyaya, *Nyāya*, p. 358 and *Indian Atomism*, p. 141. See Jha's translation, vol. 4, p. 1618.

78. Subcommentary of Uddyotakara to Nyaya Sutra 2.17. See Gangopadhyaya, *Indian Atomism*, p. 128 and Jha's trans., vol. 4, pp. 1606–1608. Jha interprets the word *truti* in the *sutra* as *dyad* rather than *triad*, but the general sense of the argument remains the same.

79. 4.2.23–24. *Nyāya*, trans. Ganghopadhyaya, pp. 356–59; Jha trans., vol. 4, pp. 1616–28.

80. **Buddhist atomism**: N. Dutt, *Buddhist Sects in India*, Calcutta: Firma KLM, 1970. S. Chaudhury, *Analytical Study of the Abhidharmakośa*, Calcutta: Firma KLM, 1983. Hirakawa Akira, *A History of Indian Buddhism from Śākyamuni to Early Mahāyāna*, Honolulu: University of Hawaii Press, 1990. C. A. F. Rhys Davids, "Sarvāstivādins," in Hastings, *Encyclopaedia of Religion and Ethics*. T. Jikido, *An Introduction to Buddhism*, Tokyo: Toho Gakkai, 1987. Y. Kurunadasa, *Buddhist Analysis of Matter,* Colombo: Department of Cultural Affairs, 1967, chap. 8 (on atomism as understood in Theravada and Vaibhashika Buddhism). É. Lamotte, *Histoire de Bouddhisme Indien*, Louvain: Publications Universitaires, Institut Orientaliste, 1958 (there is an English translation, not at my disposal). W. M. McGovern, *A Manual of Buddhist Philosophy*, vol. 1, London: Kegan Paul, Trench, Trubner & Co., 1923, part 2. L. de la Vallée Poussin, "Sautrantika," in Hastings, *Encyclopaedia of Religion and Ethics*. L. Silburn, *Instant et cause: le discontinue dans la pensée philosophique de*

l'Inde, Paris: Vrin, 1955. Th. Stcherbatsky, *Buddhist Logic*, reprint 2 vols, S-'gravenhage [The Hague]: Mouton, 1958 [1932]; *The Central Conception of Buddhism*, London: Royal Asiatic Society, 1923. A. K. Warder, *Indian Buddhism*, 2d ed., Delhi: Banarsidass, 1980. **Translations**: Gangopadhyaya, *Indian Atomism*, pp. 85–119. Stcherbatsky, *The Central Conception of Buddhism*, pp. 76–92 (trans. of Vasubandhu, *Abhidharmakośa* 5. 24–26). Vasubandhu, *L'Abhidharmakośa de Vasubandhu*, trans. L. de la Vallée Poussin, 6 vols., Brussels: Institut Belge des Hautes tudes Chinoises, reprint 1980 [1971]. Vasubandhu, *Abhidharmakośabhāṣyam*, English trans. (with reference to the original) by L. M. Pruden from the French trans. of L. de La Vallée Poussin, 4 vols, Berkeley: Asian Humanities Press, 1988–90. I have found this translation useful even though it has been criticized.

81. See Lamotte, *Histoire du Bouddhisme Indien*, pp. 663–64; and, especially, L. de La Vallée Poussin, introduction to Vasubandhu, *Abhidharmakośabhāṣyam*, trans. Pruden, vol. 1, pp. 1–4. Gangopadhyaya, *Indian Atomism*, pp. 10–17.

82. That the primary particles never exist in an isolated state is declared in more than one passage, e.g., *Abhidharmakośabhāṣyam*, trans. Pruden, vol. 1, p. 70 (1.13); *L'Abhidharmakośa*, trans. Poussin, vol. 1, p. 25. See the *Abhidharmakośabhāṣyam*, trans. Pruden, vol. 1, p. 185 (2.22); McGovern, *A Manual of Buddhist Philosophy*, vol. 1, pp. 118–28; and Stcherbatsky, *Buddhist Logic*, vol. 1, pp. 97–98, 190–92.

83. *Abhidharmakośabhāṣyam*, trans. Pruden, vol. 1, p. 186 (2.22); *L'Abhidharmakośa*, trans. Poussin, vol. 1, pp. 145–46.

84. To the references of the preceding note, add *Abhidharmakośabhāṣyam*, trans. Pruden, vol. 1, pp. 68–70 (1.12–13), 184–90 (2.22); vol. 2, pp. 474–75 (3.85–88). *L'Abhidharmakośa*, trans. Poussin, vol. 1, pp. 21–23, 143–49. Stcherbatsky, *Buddhist Logic*, vol. 1, p. 101.

85. Vasubandhu, *Abhidharmakośabhāṣyam* 1.21–23; trans. Pruden, vol. 1, pp. 184–188 and especially, notes 95, 107, pp. 332–33. The equivalent pages in vol. 1 of Poussin's French translation, *L'Abhidharmakośa of Vasubandhu* are 143–49 (where the notes are at the bottom of the pages). For the arrangement of the atoms of the different sense organs, see the Pruden trans., vol. 1, pp. 122–26 (*Ab*. 1.44–45).

86. *Abhidharmakośabhāṣyam*, trans. Pruden, vol. 2, p. 474.

87. *Abhidharmakośabhāṣyam*, trans. Pruden, vol. 1, chap. 1, pp. 120–21, with notes 188, p. 148, and 190, p. 140. The equivalent pages (including the notes) in Poussin's translation are 89–91. See also Lamotte, *Histoire du Bouddhisme Indien*, p. 664–68.

88. W. H. Newton-Smith, *The Structure of Time*, Routledge and Kegan Paul, 1984, pp. 114–21.

89. Stcherbatsky, *The Central Conception of Buddhism*, p. 38.

90. *Abhidharmakośabhāṣyam*, trans. Pruden, vol. 2, p. 474 (3.85); *L'Abhidharmakośa*, trans. Poussin, vol. 2, p. 177.

91. See the tables in Stcherbatsky, *The Central Conception of Buddhism*, pp. 95–107.

92. *Abhidharmakośabhāṣyam*, trans. Pruden, vol. 1, pp. 59–61 (1, 6); *L'Abhidharmakosa*, trans. Poussin, vol. 1, pp. 8–11. There is perhaps a distinction to be drawn here between space and ether. McGovern, *A Manual of Buddhist Philosophy*, pp. 110–11, thinks that for the Sarvastivadins, merely empty space, the external space element (*akasha-dhatu*, in the Chinese translation, *k'ung*) is regarded as conditioned or caused. Space in this sense—that of gaps or cavities—is light and darkness, a kind of color, and day and night. For the Sarvastivadins, says McGovern, what is unconditioned is ether (in the Chinese translation, *hsüh-k'ung*), in the sense of an omnipresent, invisible, unimpeding, unimpeded substance. See Pruden's translation of the *Abhidharmakośa* 1.27, vol. 1, pp. 49–50, or Poussin's, vol. 1, pp. 49–50.

93. Silburn, *Instant et cause*, p. 256.

94. On the Sarvastivada school see Dutt, *Buddhist Sects in India*, pp. 134–83; and the *Abhidharmakośabhāṣyam*, trans. from Poussin's translation into English by Pruden, vol. 1, pp. xxx–lxii, 1–53. In *The Central Conception of Buddhism*, pp. 76–91, Stcherbatsky translates a complete debate between a Sarvastivadin and a Buddhist opponent.

95. Stcherbatsky, *The Central Conception of Buddhism*, pp. 5, 77–82. The same text is (re)translated by Pruden, in *Abhidharmakośabhāṣyam* 5.24–26, vol. 3, pp. 806–11 (the argument continues through p. 820).

96. Such is my perhaps mistaken interpretation of Schterbatsky, *The Central Conception of Buddhism*, p. 40 and Silburn, *Instant et Cause*, pp. 256–57, 262.

97. *Abhidharmakośabhāṣyam*, trans. Pruden, vol. 3, pp. 808–10 (5.25–26); *L'Abhidharmakośa of Vasubandhu*, trans. Poussin, vol. 4, pp. 51–55. See Stcherbatsky, *The Central Conception of Buddhism*, pp. 79–80.

98. See the exposition in Jikido, *An Introduction to Buddhism*, pp. 120–21; and Silburn, *Instant et cause*, pp. 262–63, 271. There is an exposition and defense in D. Bastow, "The Mahā-Vibhāṣa Arguments for Sarvāstivāda," *Philosophy East and West* 44.3 (July 1994).

99. See Furley, *Cosmic Problems*, p. 225, where he contrasts not only Aristotle but Aristotelians in general with atomists.

100. For the fortunes of Epicureanism up to the seventeenth century, see H. Jones, *The Epicurean Tradition*, London: Routledge, 1989. Gassendi, the philosophical reviver of atomism, saw himself as an Epicurean.

101. H. C. von Baeyer, *Taming the Atom*, New York: Random House, 1992, chap. 9.

Chapter 7. Hierarchical Idealism

1. Plotinus, *Enneads* 4.8.8, 5.1.12.3–14. See Atkinson, *Plotinus: Ennead V.1*, p. lxvi.

2. See the analytically clear expansion of *Enneads* 5.1.5.16–19—an obscure use of Plato's unknown number theory—in Atkinson, *Plotinus: Enneads V.1*, pp. 20–21 and 109–23.

3. The quotation of the subtitle is from Proclus, *Elements of Theology*, trans. Dodds (see following note), p. 17. That on Plotinus is from Porphyry, "On the Life of Plotinus and the Order of His Books" 1; in *Plotinus*, trans. Armstrong (see just below), vol. 1, p. 3.

History and intellectual background of philosophy: A. H. Armstrong, ed., *The Cambridge History of Later Greek and Early Medieval Philosophy*, Cambridge: Cambridge University Press, 1967. A. Dihle, *Greek and Latin Literature of the Roman Empire*, London: Routledge, 1994. E. R. Dodds, *The Greeks and the Irrational*, Berkeley: University of California Press, 1952. R. T. Wallis, *Neo-Platonism*, London: Duckworth, 1972.

Biography: Porphyry, *On the Life of Plotinus and the Order of His Books*, in Plotinus, *Enneads*, trans. A. H. Armstrong, vol. 1; Porphyrius, *Über Plotins Leben*, vol. 5 of *Plotins Schriften*, trans. R. Harder, Hamburg: Meiner, 1958 (annotated).

Monographs: H. J. Blumenthal and A. C. Lloyd, eds., *Soul and the Structure of Being in Late Neoplatonism*, Liverpool: Liverpool University Press, 1982 (contains a chapter on Proclus). A. Charles-Saget. *L'Architecture de divin: Mathmatique et philosophie chez Plotin et Proclus*, Paris: Les Belles Lettres, 1982. L. P. Gerson, *Plotinus*, London: Routledge, 1994. P. Hadot, *Plotinus or the Simplicity of Vision*, Chicago: University of Chicago Press, 1989. A. C. Lloyd, *Anatomy of Neoplatonism*, Oxford: Oxford University Press, 1990. J. M. Rist, *Plotinus*, Cambridge, Cambridge University Press, 1967.

Translations: PLOTINUS: *Enneads*, trans. A. H. Armstrong, 7 vols., Cambridge: Harvard University Press, 1966–1988. *Enneads*, trans. S. MacKenna, abridged J. Dillon, London: Penguin, 1991.

PROCLUS: *A Commentary on the First Book of Euclid's Elements*, trans. G. R. Morrow, Princeton: Princeton University Press, 1970. *Elements of Theology*, trans. E. R. Dodds, 2d ed., London: Oxford University Press, 1963. *Proclus's Commentary on Plato's* Parmenides, trans. G. R. Morrow and J. Dillon, Princeton: Princeton University Press, 1987. *Théologie Platonicienne*, trans. H. D. Saffrey and L. G. Westerinck, 4 vols., Paris: Les Belles Lettres, 1968–1981.

Annotated partial translations: M. Atkinson, *Plotinus: Ennead V. 1*, Oxford: Oxford University Press, 1983. J. Bussanich, *The One and Its Relation to Intellect in*

Plotinus, Leiden: Brill, 1988. P. Hadot, *Traité 38* [*Enneads* 6.7], and *Traité 50* [*Enneads* 3.5], Paris: Cerf, 1988, 1990.

4. Porphyry, ibid., 3; trans. p. 9.

5. *Enneads* 6.7.14. Trans. Armstrong, vol. 7, p. 135.

6. Prophyry, ibid., 8; trans. p. 29.

7. Porphyry, ibid., 23; trans. p. 71.

8. Plotinus, *Enneads*, trans. MacKenna, p. 334.

9. Plotinus, *Enneads* 5.1.8, trans. Atkinson, *Plotinus: Ennead V.1*, p. lxii and notes pp. 186–92. On Plotinus' faithfulness and faithlessness to Plato see also Dodds, "Tradition and Personal Achievement in the Philosophy of Plotinus," *Journal of Roman Studies* vol. l, 1960, pp. 1–7; and Rist, *Plotinus*, pp. 179–87.

10. There are accounts of Proclus's life in the respective introductions to Morrow's translation of Proclus's commentary on Euclid and to Saffrey and Westrink's translation of the *Théologie platonicienne*, which also describes the Platonic, that is, Neoplatonic school of Athens, which Proclus came to head.

11. On the late Classical philosopher-saint, see Dihle, *Greek and Latin Literature of the Roman Empire*, p. 488.

12. Proclus, *Théologie platonicienne*, vol. 2, trans. Saffrey and Westrink, pp. clxxxvii–xix; and the text of the *Théologie* 1.1–5, pp. 5–26, with the corresponding notes, pp. 130–39. The only dialogue explicitly rejected by Proclus is the *Epinomis*— see note 3 (for p. 23), p. 138.

13. Charles-Saget, *L'Architecture divine*, pp. 189–90, 209. Proclus, *A Commentary on the First Book of Euclid's Elements*, trans. Morrow, pp. xxvi–xxvii.

14. Bussanich, *The One and Its Relation to Intellect in Plotinus*, pp. 1, 3–6.

15. Armstrong, *The Cambridge History of Later Greek and Early Medieval Philosophy*, pp. 211–12.

16. Some of the following description of the philosophy of Plotinus and Proclus draws from B.-A. Scharfstein, ed., *Philosophy East/Philosophy West*, New York: Oxford University Press and Oxford: Blackwell, 1978, pp. 212–13.

17. Plotinus, *Enneads* 6.9.8.1–7.

18. Ibid., 5.9.8.

19. Ibid., 3.8.11.

20. Ibid., 3.6.7; trans. Armstrong, vol. 3, p. 241.

21. Ibid., 4.3.18–19, 4.4.1–2.

22. *Enneads* 2.4.7; trans. Armstrong, vol. 2, pp. 121–23.

23. Ibid., 3.6; trans. Armstrong, vol. 3, p. 237. On Plotinus' conception of matter, see Gerson, *Plotinus*, pp. 108–15, 192–94.

24. Ibid.; trans. Armstrong, vol. 3, p. 239.

25. Ibid., 3.6; trans. Armstrong, vol. 3, pp. 241–43.

26. *Enneads* 1.8.3; trans. Armstrong vol. 1, pp. 283–85. Once, Plotinus even calls matter "a sort of ultimate form" (ibid., 5.8.7; vol. 5, p. 259).

27. Ibid.; trans. Armstrong, vol. 7, p. 303.

28. Trans. Bussanich, *The One and Its Relation to Intellect in Plotinus*, p. 202.

29. *Ennead* 4.7.2; trans. Bussanich, *The One and Its Relation to Intellect in Plotinus*, pp. 8–9.

30. Ibid., p. 8. See comm. p. 9.

31. The following account of justification of the priority of oneness in the philosophy of Plotinus and Proclus is mostly drawn from B.-A. Scharfstein, *Ineffability*, Albany: State University of New York Press, 1993, pp. 149–53. For the sources in Proclus, see the first six propositions in *The Elements of Theology*, trans. Dodds, pp. 3–7; and *Théologie platonicienne*, trans. Saffrey and Westerink, vol. 2, book 2, chap. 1, pp. 3–14.

32. Proclus, *Théologie platonicenne*; trans. Saffrey and Westrink, vol. 2, book 2, chap. 1, p. 5; and supplementary note, p. 79.

33. Proclus, *The Elements of Theology*, trans. Dodds, p. 5.

34. *Enneads*, 5.5.11; trans. Armstrong, vol. 5, p. 17.

35. Trans. Armstrong, vol. 5, p. 59.

36. Proclus, *Elements of Theology*, trans. Dodds, p. 17.

37. Bussanich, *The One and Its Relation to Intellect in Plotinus*, pp. 97–98, citing *Enneads* 2.2.17.64–75; 5.1; 6.4.12; 4.3.18.13–20.

38. Wallis, *Neoplatonism*, p. 157.

39. Proclus, *A Commentary on the Book of Euclid's Elements*, trans. Morrow, p. xxxiii.

40. *The Elements of Theology*, trans. Dodds, pp. 3, 185.

41. Charles-Saget, *L'Architecture du divin*, pp. 231–34. The phrase "axiomatics of perfection" is from p. 253.

42. Proclus, *The Elements of Theology*, props. 35–51, with Dodds' notes. See also his notes to prop. 65.

43. *Enneads* 5.6.1.

44. *Enneads* 5.6.5.

45. *Enneads* 6.8.13.

46. Proclus, *A Commentary on Plato's Parmenides*, trans. Morrow and Dillon, p. 427.

47. *Vākyapadīya*, 1.14 (see bibliography note 48).

48. **Indian philosophy of language**: M. Biardeau, *Théorie de la connaissance et philosophie de la parole dans le brahmanisme classique*, Paris: Mouton/Ecole pratique de hautes Etudes, 1964. H. G. Coward, *Sphoṭa Theory of Language*, Deli: Banarsidass, 1980. H. G. Coward and K. K. Raja, eds., *Encyclopedia of Indian Philosophies*, vol. 5, *The Philosophy of the Indian Grammarians*, Princeton: Princeton University Press, 1990 (with an extensive introduction, detailed paraphrases, and many blank pages containing names of members of the school about whom nothing but their names is known). B. K. Matilal, *Epistemology, Logic, and Grammar in Indian Philosophical Analysis*, the Hague: Mouton, 1971; *The Word and the World*, Delhi: Oxford University Press, 1990 (a lucid general introduction). D. S. Ruegg, *Contributions à l'histoire de la philosophie linguistique indienne*, Paris: Boccard, 1959.

Monographs: R. Herzberger, *Bhartṛhari and the Buddhists*, Dordrecht: Reidel, 1986. K. A. S. Iyer, *Bhartṛhari*, Poona: Deccan College, 1969; *The Vākyapadīya: Some Problems*, Poona: Bhandakar Research Institute, 1982. D. Śastri, *The Philosophy of Word and Meaning*, Calcutta: Calcutta Sanskrit College, 1959.

Translations: Bhartrhari, *The Vākyapadīya*, cantos (chaps.) 1, 2, trans. K. R. Pillai, Varanasi: Banarsidass, 1971. (Since Iyer [see just below] omits verses 108 through 115 in Bhartriharis's first chapter, the numbering in Pillais's equivalent translation differs from 108 and on.) Bhartṛhari, *Vākyapadīya Brahmakaṇda*, trans. M. Biardeau, Paris: Boccard, 1964. *The Vākyapadīya of Bhartṛhari*, chap. I, trans. K. A. S. Iyer, Poona; Deccan College, 1965; *The Vākyapadīya of Bhartṛhari*, chap. 3, part 1, trans. Iyer, Delhi: Banarsidass, 1971; *The Vākyapadīya of Bhartṛhari*, chap. 3, part 2, Delhi: Banarsidass, 1973; *The Vākyapadīya of Bhartṛhari*, kanda (chap.) 2, Delhi: Banarsidass, 1977 (this volume has not been available to me).

Passages from Bhartrihari that appear here have sometimes been modified by me from one or more of the above translations. Aklujkar, "An Introduction . . ." (see just below) says that because Iyer's translation, the only complete one—is meant to convey the general sense of the original—it often does not attempt to get at the exact meaning of a knotty Sanskrit passage. Biardeau's French translation of the first book is more helpful in this regard, Aklujkar says (pp. 19–20).

Articles: A. Aklujkar, "An Introduction to the Study of Bhartr-Hari," in S. Bhate and J. Bronkhorst, eds., *Bhartṛhari: Philosopher and Grammarian*, Delhi: Banarsidass, 1994 (first published Bern: Lang, 1993). J. E. M. Houben, "Bhartṛhari's *Samaya*/Helārāja's Saṃekta," *Journal of Indian Philosophy* 20.3 (June 1992); "Bhartṛhari's Solution to The Liar and Some Other Paradoxes," *Journal of Indian Philosophy* 23.4 (December 1995). F. Staal, "Sanskrit Philosophy of Language," in *Current Trends Linguistics* 5, 1969. D. N. Tiwari, "Bhartṛhari's Philosophy of Relation between Word and Meaning," *Journal of the Indian Council of Philosophical Research* 11.2 (January–April 1994). F. Tola and C. Dragonetti, "Some Remarks on Bhartrhari's Concept of Pratibha," *Journal of Indian Philosophy*, June 1990.

49. E.g., in the *Bṛhadāraṇyaka Upaniṣad* 4.1.2.

50. For a historical sketch of the place of language in Indian philosophy, see Coward and Raja, eds., *The Philosophy of the Grammarians*, pp. 3–32. See also Ruegg, *Contributions à l'histoire de la philosophie linguistique indienne* . . .

51. The dating and sequence of philosophers proposed by Frauwallner and accepted by Iyer are as follows: Vasurata, Bhartrihari's guru, 430–490 C.E.; Bhartrihari, 450–510; Dignaga, 480–540.

On the poet Bhartrihari and his possible identity with the grammarian, see: Iyer, *Bhartṛhari*, p. 2. D. H. H. Ingalls, *An Anthology of Sanskrit Court Poetry*, Cambridge: Harvard University Press, 1965, pp. 40–43. B. S. Miller, *The Hermit and the Love-Thief: Sanskrit Poems of Bhartrihari and Bilhaṇa*, New York: Columbia University Press, 1978. A. K. Warder, *Indian Kavya Literature*, vol. 4, Delhi: Banarsidass, 1983, pp. 121–22. M. Winternitz, *A History of Indian Literature*, vol. 3, Delhi: Banarsidass, 1963 [1922], pp. 256–58.

52. *Vākyapadīya* 2.482; trans. Pillai, p. 146.

53. Most manuscripts take the third book to be part of the *Vākyapadīya*. Ashok Aklujkar, who is preparing a critical edition of the text, emphasizes that the three books are largely independent of one another. Their position is consistent enough to be that of a single author, he says, but they do not build up an argument that proceeds consecutively from one book to another. (See Aklujkar, "An Introduction . . . ," pp. 22–28; and *Vakyapadiya*, trans. Pillai, p. xxvii.)

54. Iyer, *The Vākyapadīya of Bhartṛhari*, chap. 1, pp. xii–xv.

55. Ibid., pp. 84, 90.

56. *Vākyapadīya* 1.133. For Bhartrihari's attitude toward revelation and tradition, see Iyer, *Bhartṛhari*, pp. 92–97.

57. Some of the following account of Bhartrihari's philosophy is drawn from B.-A. Scharfstein, *Ineffability*, Albany: State University of New York Press, 1993. The principles of Bhartrihari's philosophy are given a particularly brief, clear, orderly summary, to which there is no equivalent in Bhartrihari himself, by Ashok Aklujkar in Coward and Raja, *The Philosophy of the Grammarians*, pp. 122–26. Aklujkar's summary makes Bhartrihari sound more organized and modern than he in fact is. Aklujkar's following, detailed summary brings out the linguistic side of Bhartrihari's philosophy with particular clarity. The account I give below omits many of the points of even Aklujkar's brief summary, as it does of Bhartrihari's own grammatical observations, but it remains relatively close to the way in which Bhartrihari and his commentators expressed themselves.

58. *Vākyapadīya*, 1.107–15.

59. Iyer, *Bhartṛhari*, pp. 66–67, 153; Iyer, *The Vākyapadīya: Some Problems*, pp. 15–17.

60. Commentary to *Vākyapadīya* 1.44; trans. Iyer, chap. 1 (i.e., vol. 1), p. 53.

61. *Vākyapadīya* 1.44–46.

62. *Vākyapadīya* 1.47–49.

63. *Vākyapadīya* 1.51–53, with comm. Iyer, *Bhartrhari*, pp. 153–54.

64. *Vākyapadīya* 2.208–209 (the opponents in question are the exponents of Mimamsa). Iyer, *Bhartṛhari*, pp. 143–44, 183; and Staal, "Sanskrit Philosophy of Language," pp. 509–14. The Neo-Vedantist philosopher Shankara was also opposed to the *sphota* doctrine. See Chakrabarti, "Sentence-Holism, Context-Principle and Connected-Designation *Anvitabhidhana*," *Journal of Indian Philosophy*, March 1989, where the Mimamsa and Nyaya positions are compared with the sentence holism of Bhartrihari, Quine, and others. For the word-sentence controversy In Indian thought, see the "Introduction to the Philosophy of the Grammarians," Coward and Raja, eds., *The Philosophy of the Grammarians*, pp. 63–97; and Matilal, *The Word and the World*, pp. 106–19.

65. *Vākyapadīya* 2.421, 438–39.

66. *Vākyapadīya* 3.1, comm. and 2.414.

67. Iyer, *Bhartṛhari*, p. 62.

68. *Vākyapadīya* 2.324; trans. Pillai, p. 110.

69. Iyer, *Bhartṛhari*, pp. 192–93; Iyer, *The Vākyapadīya: Some Problems*, pp. 25–26.

70. *Vākyapadīya* 2.327–282, 345.

71. *Vākyapadīya* 1.73.

72. *Vākyapadīya* 2.7, 8 and 3.4.1–2 (including Iyer's explanation, pp. 121–22). Also Iyer, *Bhartṛhari*, p. 86.

73. Iyer's explanation of *Vākyapadīya* 3.3.24. In *The Vākyapadīya of Bhartṛhari*, chap. 3, p. 91.

74. Trans. Iyer, p. 90.

75. *Vākyapadīya* 3, part 1: 3.3.27 comm. and 3.3.28; trans. Iyer, p. 92.

76. *Vākyapadīya* 1.131, 142. The image of the blind man running is from 1.41. The line of grammarians, with its temporary eclipse by "the followers of dry logic," is described at the end of chapter 2 (2.476–81).

77. *Vākyapadīya* 2.138; trans. Pillai, p. 69.

78. For the discussion on the adequacy of words and of the instruments of knowledge, see *Vākyapadīya* 2.134–42. The clever logicians are from elsewhere: *Vākyapadīya* 2.34. See Iyer, *Bhartṛhari*, chap. 4; and Iyer, *The Vākyapadīya: Some Problems*, lecture 3. That grammar can realize true, indescribable knowledge: *Vākyapadīya* 2.234.

79. Tola and Dragonetti, "Some Remarks on Bhartṛhari's Concept of Pratibha," pp. 109–10. The knowledge of children is based on the residual traces of the words they used in previous lives (*Vākyapadīya* 1.121).

80. Trans. Pillai, pp. 71–72.

81. *Vākyapadīya* 2.151; Pillai translation, p. 72.

82. *Vākyapadīya*, 1.35. Iyer, *Bhartṛhari*, pp. 88–92; *The Vākyapadīya: Some Problems*, pp. 56–58.

83. *Vākyapadīya* 2.156–58, 214–15.

84. *Vākyapadīya* 2.46 (on the single letter), 2.247 (on praise and blame).

85. Trans Iyer, pp. 109, 110, 112, 113.

86. *Vākyapadīya* 1.119, with comm.

87. *Vākyapadīya* 1.121 and comm; trans. Iyer, p. 109. In Pillai, verse no. 122.

88. *Vākyapadīya* 1.121, comm.; trans Iyer, p. 109.

89. Matilal, *The Word and the World*, p. 134, interpreting difficult texts from the earliest commentary to the *Vākyapadīya* 1.124 and trying to clarify what is unclear in Iyer's translation, pp. 111–12.

90. *Vākyapadīya* 1.123–25, comm.; trans. Iyer, pp. 110–12.

91. Trans. Iyer, pp. 105–6.

92. My rendition.

93. Trans. Iyer, pp. 1–2. See Iyer, *Bhartṛhari*, p. 101.

94. Śastri, *The Philosophy of Word and Meaning*, pp. 27–28.

95. Iyer, *Bhartṛhari*, p. 100.

96. Ruegg, *Contributions à l'histoire de la philosophie linguistique*, p. 67, drawing on Helaraja, Bhartrihari's commentator.

97. *Vākyapadīya* chap. 3, part 2, trans. Iyer, section 9 (pp. 36–74). See Iyer, *Bhartṛhari*, pp. 111–30; "Introduction to the Philosophy of the Grammarians," in Coward and Raja, *The Philosophy of the Grammarians*, pp. 38–44; Śastri, *The Philosophy of Word and Meaning*, chap. 2.

98. *Vākyapadīya* 1.2 and 1.3, both with comm.

99. *Vākyapadīya* chap. 3, part 2: 9.1.3, 4, 5, 8, 9, 14, 41.

100. Ibid., 9.18, 19 (quoted). See Iyer, *Bhartṛhari*, p. 101 and the exposition in Coward and Raja, eds., *The Philosophy of the Grammarians*, p. 154.

101. *Vākyapadīya* chap. 3, part 2: 9.1.12.

102. Ibid., 3.9.62, with comm.

103. Ibid., 3.6.26, 28; 3.7.40, 42 (quoted); trans Iyer, pp. 146, 172.

104. *Vākyapadīya* 1.130, comm.

105. *Vākyapadīya* 1.15.

106. *Vākyapadīya* 1.137 comm.

107. Ibid. And see *Vākyapadīya* 2.314–15; trans. Pillai, p. 108.

108. Trans. Iyer, p. 1.

109. *Vākyapadīya* 1.4.

110. *Vākyapadīya* 1.142. See "Introduction to the Philosophy of the Grammarians," in Coward and Raja, eds., *The Philosophy of the Grammarians*, pp. 44–50.

111. *Vākyapadīya* 1.142, 1.5.

112. *Vākyapadīya* 1.31, 142, 51, all with comm. Coward and Raja, eds., *The Philosophy of the Grammarians*, pp. 48–50, 138–53 (paraphrase of *Vākyapadīya*, chap. 2). Pillai, *The Vākyapadīya*, pp. 36–146.

113. See B.-A. Scharfstein, *Ineffability*, Albany: State University of New York Press, 1993, chaps. 4, 5.

Chapter 8. Developed Skepticism

1. The quotation just above is from *Sextus Empiricus*, trans, Bury, vol. 1, p. 9 (*Outlines of Pyrrhonism* 1.10). Mates (*The Skeptic Way*, pp. 30–32) insists on the difference between *doubt*, which, he says, implies understanding, and *aporia*, a state of bafflement.

History of Hellenistic philosophy and of skepticism: V. Brochard, *Les sceptics grecs*, 2d ed., reprint, Paris: Vrin, 1959. R. J. Hankinson, *The Sceptics*, London: Routledge, 1995. A. S, Long, *Hellenistic Philosophy*. Diogenes Laertius, *Lives of Eminent Philosophers*, trans. R. D. Hicks, 2 vols., Cambridge: Harvard University Press, 1925. C. L. Stough, *Greek Skepticism*, Berkeley: University of California Press, 1969.

Collections of articles: M. Burnyeat, ed., *The Skeptical Tradition*, Berkeley: University of California Press, 1983. J. C. Klagge and N. D. Smith, eds., *Oxford Studies in Ancient Philosophy, Supplementary Volume 1992: Methods of Interpreting Plato and His Dialogues*, Oxford: Oxford University Press, 1992. M. Schofield, M. Burnyeat, and J. Barnes, eds., *Doubt and Dogmatism*, Oxford: Oxford University Press, 1980.

Monographs: J. Annas and J. Barnes, *The Modes of Scepticism*, Cambridge: Cambridge University Press, 1985. J. Barnes, *The Toils of Scepticism*, Cambridge: Cambridge University Press, 1990. B. Mates, *The Skeptic Way: Sextus Empiricus's Outlines of Pyrrhonism*, New York: Oxford University Press, 1996. H. Tarrant, *Scepticism or Platonism? The Philosophy of the Fourth Academy*, Cambridge: Cambridge University Press, 1985.

Translations: Annas and Barnes, *The Modes of Scepticism* (see *monographs*, just above). B. Mates, *The Skeptic Way* (particularly clear) (see *monographs* just above). A. A. Long and D. N. Sedley, *The Hellenistic Philosophers*, vol. 1. Cambridge: Cambridge University Press, 1987. Sextus Empiricus, *Sextus Empiricus*, 4 vols., trans. R. G. Bury, Cambridge: Harvard University Press, 1933–49 (see the appreciation and criticism of Bury's translation in Mates, *The Skeptic Way*, pp. 220–22).

2. Diogenes Laertius 9. 116.

3. Sextus Empiricus, *Against the Logicians* 2.191, and *Outlines of Pyrrhonism* 1.236–41; and "Scepticism in the Medical Schools," chap. 13 of Hankinson, *The Sceptics*.

4. For attempts to delineate his individual character as a philosopher, see Brochard, *Les sceptiques Grecs*, pp. 326–27.

5. Diogenes Laertius, *Lives and Opinions of Eminent Philosophers* 9.61, 63; trans. Hicks, vol. 2, pp. 475, 477 (quoted). On Pyrrho and India, see the discussion in Hankinson, *The Sceptics*, pp. 58–65 (59 quoted). Hankinson also discusses (pp. 52–53) Pyrrho's reported approval of Democritus, perhaps because Democritus so emphasized the inability of humans to know the full truth about reality—atoms.

6. Ibid. 9.62; vol. 2, p. 475.

7. Long and Sedley, *The Hellenistic Philosophers*, p. 15. The report of Timon's account of Pyrrho's thought is from Eusebius (c. c.e. 260–340), who repeats what he read in Aristocles (second century c.e.), of whose history of philosophy there remain only fragments and testimonies. For an explanation of this position attributed to Pyrrho, see Long and Sedley, pp. 16–17; Hankinson, *The Sceptics* (who provides a careful translation and discussion of this passage), pp. 59–63; and Stough, *Greek Skepticism*, pp. 18–26.

8. Diogenes Laertius, *Lives and Opinions of Eminent Philosophers*, 9.70; trans. Hicks, vol. 2, p, 483.

9. The reason for Pyrrho's apparent inconsistency may be that although he rejected all theory, he preached and reacted as he felt was just. See Brochard, *Les sceptiques Grecs*, pp. 60–64; and Hankinson, *The Sceptics*, pp. 667–68. Sedley ("The Motivation of Greek Skepticism," in Burnyeat, ed., *The Skeptical Tradition*, p. 19) suspects that Aenesidemus (first century c.e.) adopted Pyrrho as the head of the skeptical lineage mainly because his school needed to prove its historical priority over its skeptical rival, the (Platonic) New Academy.

10. Cicero, *Academica* 2.76–77.

11. See Hankinson, *The Sceptics*, pp. 74–91, on Arcesilaus (on "Plato Scepticus," pp. 83–85). On Plato interpreted as a skeptic, see also J. Annas, "Plato the Skeptic."

12. See Diogenes Laertius, *Lives of the Eminent Philosophers*, vol. 2, pp. 155 (7.45–46) and 159–65 (7.49–54). See also the passages and critical discussion in Long and Sedley, *The Hellenistic Philosophers*, pp. 236–43. Hankinson, *The Sceptics*, pp 106–108, on the conditions required by the Stoics for an impression to be "cataleptic"; chap. 11 summarizes what Sextus contains on (and against) "the criterion of the agent," "the instrumental criterion," and "the criterion 'according to which.'" On the problems with the translation of *phantasia* as *impression* see Mates, *The Skeptical Way*, pp. 32–41.

13. Sextus Empiricus, *Against the Professors* 7, as translated in Long and Sedley, *The Hellenistic Philosophers*, p. 461. For the positions of Arcesilaus and Carneades see also P. Coussin, "The Stoicism of the New Academy," in Burnyeat, ed., *The Skeptical Tradition*, and, especially for Carneades, Tarrant, *Scepticism or Platonism?* in the same collection. See also Hankinson, *The Sceptics*, pp. 94–115.

14. Long and Sedley, *The Hellenistic Philosophers*, p. 462.

15. Cicero, *Academica*, 1.43–46, in Sedley and Long, *The Hellenistic Philosophers*, p. 438; or as translated by H. Rackham in Cicero, *De Natura Deorum, Academica* (the two works in one volume), Harvard: Harvard University Press, 1951, pp. 449–55. The passage on refusing to answer questions is from Cicero, *De finibus* 2.2, as quoted in J. Annas, "Plato the Sceptic," in J. C. Klagge and N. D. Smith, eds., *Oxford Studies in Ancient Philosophy*, supplementary volume 1992, *Methods of Interpreting Plato and His Dialogues*, Oxford: Oxford University Press, 1992, p. 45.

16. Sextus Empiricus, *Against the Professors* 7.159–65, in Long and Sedley, *The Epicurean Philosophers*, pp. 460–61. See also Plutarch, *Against Colotes* 1122A–F, in Long and Sedley, p. 450.

17. On Carneades see Diogenes Laertius, *Lives of Eminent Philosophers* 4.62–66; Long and Sedley, *The Hellenistic Philosophers*, pp. 448–67; and Hankinson, *The Sceptics*, pp. 94–115.

18. Hankinson, *The Sceptics*, p. 95, quoting Eusebeus.

19. Cicero, *Academica* 2.104; in Hankinson, *The Skeptics*, p. 112.

20. Sextus Empiricus, *Against the Professors* 7.176–84, in Long and Sedley, *The Hellenistic Philosophers*, pp. 452–53. See also the preceding section from Sextus Empiricus on pp. 451–52.

21. A later part of the same passage, Sextus Empiricus, *Against the Professors* 7.176–84, in Long and Sedley, *The Hellenistic Philosophers*, p. 453. The quoted words are as translated in Hankinson, *The Sceptics*, p. 111.

22. Sextus Empiricus, *Outlines of Pyrrhonism* 1. 226–31. Trans. Bury, vol. 1, pp. 139–43.

23. Ibid. 1.70.8–9. Trans. Bury, vol. 1, p. 7.

24. Ibid. 1.14–15. Trans. Bury, vol. 1, p. 11.

25. Ibid. 1.20. Trans. Bury, vol. 1, p. 15; and Hankinson, *The Sceptics*, p. 274 (more cautious in translating *logos* by *definition* rather than *essence*).

26. Ibid. 2.10. Trans. Bury, vol. 1, p. 157; and Hankinson, *The Sceptics*, p. 281.

27. Ibid., 1.23–24. Trans. Bury, vol. 1, p. 17.

28. Ibid. 1.27–28. Trans. Bury, vol. 1, p. 157; and Hankinson, *The Sceptics*, p. 288.

29. Ibid., 1.28–29; vol. 1, pp. 19–21.

30. See, Hankinson, *The Sceptics*, on Aenesidemus, pp. 120–36, and on the ten modes, chap. 9, The fullest description of the modes is in Sextus Empiricus, *Outlines of Pyrrhonism*, 1.36–163. Most of this is translated in Long and Sedley, *The Hellenistic Philosophers*, vol. 1, pp. 473–83. For a translation and discussion, together with parallel passages from Diogenes Laertius and Philo of Alexandria, see Annas and Barnes, *The Modes of Scepticism*. There are briefer versions of the modes in Diogenes Laertius 9.78–88, and Philo Judaeus (Philo of Alexandria) (c. 13 B.C.– c. 45 C.E.), an earlier source, with only eight modes.

31. Sextus Empiricus, *Outlines of Pyrrhonism* 1.148, 155, 158. Trans. Annas and Barnes, *The Modes of Skepticism*, pp. 152–53. On the ten modes, see the commentary in Mates, *The Skeptic Way*, pp. 234–52.

32. Sextus Empiricus, *Outlines of Pyrrhonism* 3. 280–81.

33. The quotation just above is the opening salutation of Nagarjuna's most famous work, the *Mūlamadhyamikakārikā*, as translated in Lopez, *A Study of Svātantrika*, p. 41.

History of Buddhist philosophy: Tibetan Buddhist: Bu-ston, *History of Buddhism*, trans. E. Obermiller, Heidelberg: Harrassowitz, 1931–32. Taranatha, *Tarānātha's History of Buddhism*, trans. Lama Chima and A. Chattopadhyaya, reprint Delhi: Banarsidass, 1990.

Modern: E. Conze, *Buddhist Thought in India*, London: Allen & Unwin, 1962; *A Short History of Buddhism*, London: Allen & Unwin, 1980. D. J. Kalupahana, *A History of Buddhist Philosophy*, Honolulu: University of Hawaii Press, 1992. C. V. Kher, *Buddhism as Presented by the Brahmanical Systems*, Delhi: Satguru Publications (Indian Books Centre), 1992, pp. 559–60, 618–20. P. Williams, *Māhāyana Buddhism*, London: Routledge, 1989.

Histories or studies of Madhyamika as a whole: T. R. V. Murti, *The Central Philosophy of Buddhism*, London: Allen & Unwin, 1955. G. N. Nagao,

Mādhyamika and Yogācāra, Albany: State University of New York Press, 1991. R. H. Robinson, *Early Mādhyamika in India and China*, Madison: University of Wisconsin Press, 1967. D. S. Ruegg, *The Literature of the Mādhyamika School of Philosophy in India*, Wiesbaden: Harrassowitz, 1981. T. E. Wood, *Nāgārjunian Disputations*, Honolulu: University of Hawaii Press, 1994.

Commentarial traditions: M. D. Eckel, *Jñānagarbha on the Two Truths*, Albany: State University of New York Press, 1987. C. W. Huntington, Jr. (with G. N. Wangchen), *The Emptiness of Emptiness*, Honolulu: University of Hawaii Press, 1989. D. S. Lopez, *A Study of Svātantrika*, Ithaca: Snow Lion Publications, 1987. C. Rizzi, *Candrakīriti*, Delhi: Banarsidass, 1988 (based on trans. of chap. 1 of Chandrakirti's commentary). P. Della Santina, *Madhyamaka Schools in India*, Delhi: Banarsidass, 1986.

Tibetan interpretations: J. I. Cabezon, *A Dose of Emptiness*, Albany: State University of New York Press, 1992. J. Hopkins, *Meditation on Emptiness*, London: Wisdom Publications, 1983. Newland, G., *The Two Truths*, Ithaca: Snow Lion Publications, 1992. Tsong Khapa, *Tsong Khapa's Speech of Gold in the* Essence of True Eloquence, trans. A. A. F. Thurman, Princeton: Princeton University Press, 1984. Tson-kha-pa, *Calming the Mind and Discerning the Real*, trans. A. Wayman, New York: Columbia University Press, 1978.

History of Western interpretations: R. Hayes, "Nāgārjuna's Appeal," *Journal of Indian Philosophy*, December 1994, pp. 331–61. A. P. Tuck, *Comparative Philosophy and the Philosophy of Scholarship*, Oxford: Oxford University Press, 1990.

Monographs and single-author collections of articles: P. Fenner, *The Ontology of the Middle Way*, Dordrecht: Kluwer, 1990. Chr. Lindtner, *Nagarjuniana*, Copenhagen: Akadimsk Forlag, 1982 (contains translations of lesser-known works). G. Nagao, *The Foundational Standpoint of Mādhyamika Philosophy*, Albany: State University of New York Press, 1989; *Mādhyamika and Yogācāra*, Albany: State University of New York Press, 1991. A. M. Padhye, *The Framework of Nāgārjuna's Philosophy*. V. Venkata Ramanan, *Nāgārjuna's Philosophy as Presented in the Mahā-Prajñāparamitā-Śāstra*, Rutland/Tokyo: Tuttle, 1966.

Selected articles: S. Biderman, "Scepticism and Religion: On the Interpretation of Nagarjuna," in R. W. Perett, ed., *Indian Philosophy of Religion*, Dordrecht, 1989. G. Bugault, "Logic and Dialectics in the *Madhyamakakārikās*," *Journal of Indian Philosophy* (hereafter *JIP*) 11.1 (March 1983). S. S. Chakravarti, "The Mādhyamika *Catuṣkoṭi* or Tetralemma," *JIP* 8.3 (September 1980). B. Galloway, "Some Logical Issues in Madhyamaka Thought," *JIP* 17.1 (March 1989). R. N. Ghose, "The Modality of Nāgārjuna's Dialectics," *JIP* 15.3 (September 1987). R. P. Hayes, "Nāgārjuna's Appeal," *JIP* 22.4 (December 1994). Yu-kwan Ng (Ng Yu-kwan), "The Arguments of Nāgārjuna in the Light of Modern Logic," *JIP* 15.4 (December 1987). C. W. Huntington, Jr., "The System of Two Truths in the Prasannapadā and the Madhyamakāvatāra," *JIP* 11.1 (March, 1983). Chr Lindtner, "Atisa's Introduction to the Two Truths, and Its Sources," *JIP* 9.2 (June 1981). B. K. Matilal, "Buddhist Logic and Epistemology," in B. K. Matilal and R. D. Evans, eds., *Buddhist Logic and Epistemology*, Dordrecht: Reidel, 1986. I. Mabbett, "Is there a Devadatta in the House: *Nāgārjuna's Vigrahavyāvrtanī and the Liar Paradox*," *JIP*

24.3 (June 1996). Oetke, "On Some Non-Formal Proofs of the Madhamikākarikās," in D. S. Ruegg and L. Schmithausen, eds., *Earliest Buddhism and Madhyamaka*, Leiden: Brill, 1990; "Remarks on the Interpretation of Nāgārjuna's Philosophy," *JIP* (September 1991). K. C. Patel, "The Paradox of Negation in Nāgārjuna's Philosophy," *Asian Philosophy* 4.1 (1994). D. S. Ruegg, "Does the Madhyamaka Have a Thesis and Philosophical Position?" in Matilal and Evans, eds., *Buddhist Logic and Epistemology*. M. Siderits, "The Madhyamaka Critique of Epistemology" I, II, *JIP* 8.4 (December 1980) and 9.2 (June, 1981); "Nāgārjuna as Anti-Realist," *JIP* 16.4 (December 1988). P. M. Williams, "Some Aspects of Language and Construction in the Madhyamaka," *JIP* 8.1 (March 1980); "On the Interpretation of Madhyamaka Thought," *JIP* 19.2 (June 1991).

Translations with commentary: Nagarjuna: *The Conception of Buddhist Nirvāṇa*, trans. Th. Stcherbatsky, reprint The Hague: Mouton, 1965. *The Dialectical Method of Nāgārjuna (Vigrahavyāvartanī*, abbr. *VV)*, trans. K. Bhattacharya, Delhi: Banarsidass, 1978. Nagarjuna's *Seventy Stanzas*, trans. D. R. Komito, Ithaca: Snow Lion Publications, 1987. *A Translation of his Mūlamādhyamikākarikā* (abbr. *MMK)*, trans. K. K. Inada, Tokyo: The Hokuseido Press, 1970. Chr. Lindtner, "Ātiśa's Introduction to the Two Truths, and Its Sources" (see *Articles* above). F. J. Streng, *Emptiness*, Nashville: Abingdon Press, 1967. Wood, *Nāgārjunian Disputes* (see *Histories or Studies*, just above)—contains four translated karikas from the *MMK* and two from the *VV*.

Bhavaviveka: "Bhāvaviveka's *Prajñāpradīpa*," trans. W. L. Ames, *JIP* 23.3 (September 1995).

Candrakirti: *Cinq chapitres de la Prasannapadā*, trans. J. W. de Jong, Paris: Guethner, 1949. *The Emptiness of Emptiness*, trans. C. W. Huntington, Jr. with Geshi Namgyal Wangchen, Honolulu: University of Hawaii Press, 1989 (trans. of stanzas surviving in Tibetan translation of *The Entry into the Middle Way (Madhyamakāvatāra)*. *Lucid Exposition of the Middle Way*, trans. M. Sprung, Boulder: Prajna Press, 1979. *Prasannapadā Madhyamakavṛtti*, trans. J. May, Paris: Adrien-Maisonneuve, 1959.

Santideva: *The Bodhicaryāvatāra*, trans. K. Crosby and A. Skilton, Oxford: Oxford University Press, 1995 (chap. 9 is an exposition of Madhyamaka philosophy, with refutations of Hinayana, Yogachara (Mind Only), Samkhya, and Nyaya views).

34. I draw what I say of Tibetan tradition from Bu-ston, *History of Buddhism*, part 2, pp. 122–30.

35. Nāgārjuna, *Mūlamadhyamikakārkikā* (hereafter *MMK*) 24.10. Trans. Inada, in Nāgārjuna, *A Translation of His Mūlamadhymaikākarikā*, p. 146.

36. Bugault, "Logic and Dialectics in the *Madhyamikākārikas*," p. 22.

37. *MMK* 2.8. Trans. Bugalt, "Logic and Dialectics," p. 38; Inada, p. 46; and Streng, *Emptiness*, p. 184.

38. *MMK* 13.8. Trans. Bugalt, p. 60.

39. *MMK* 18.8. Trans. Inada, p. 115.

40. See G. Bugault, Logic and Dialectics in the *Madhyamikārikās*; Chakravarti, "The Mādhyamika Catuṣkoṭi or Tetralemma"; R. N. Ghose, "The Modality of Nāgārjuna's Dialectics"; Ng Yu-kwan, "The Arguments of Nāgārjuna in the Light of Modern Logic"; Staal, *Universals*; and Woods, *Nāgārjunian Disputations*.

41. Chandrakirti's commentary on Nagarjuna's first chapter is translated in Stcherbatsky, *The Conception of Buddhist Nirvāṇa* and in Sprung, *Lucid Exposition of the Middle Way*, chap. 1. Rizzi, *Candrakīrti*, a brief book all on the first chapter, is more an extended paraphrase than a translation.

42. Ramanan, *Nāgārjuna's Philosophy*, pp. 26, 28, 57–62, with endnotes; Ruegg, *The Literature of the Madhyamaka School*, p. 7, notes 14, 15. Despite the consensus of both Mahayana tradition and modern scholarship, Hayes objects that, "in the absence of solid evidence, there is no reason for assuming that Nagarjuna's attitude toward Buddhist scholasticism was antagonistic" (Hayes, "Nāgārjuna's Appeal," p. 374, note 15).

43. Williams, "Some Aspects of Language and Construction in the Madhyamaka," pp. 1–2, 33.

44. *MMK* 1.1. Modified from Inada's translation, p. 38.

45. *MMK* 1. 1–3. Translated Stcherbatsky, *The Conception of Buddhist Nirvāṇa*, p. 71, comm. verse 1, pp. 92–165; verses 2–3, pp. 165–67. The corresponding commmentary in Sprung, *Lucid Exposition of the Middle Way*, pp. 36, 42–43, 65–66. The whole of *MMK* 1—without Chandrakirti's commentary—is in Inada's translation, pp. 38–42, and Sprung's translation, pp. 183–84. The quoted passage is Nagarjuna is *MMK* 1.3, as translated by Sprung, *Lucid Exposition of the Middle Way*, p. 66.

46. A paraphrase of *MMK* 1.4, mostly following Sprung pp. 67–68.

47. *MMK* 1.4. Trans. Stcherbatsky, p. 71. Comm., pp. 167–70. Comm. Sprung, pp. 66–68.

48. An explanation of *MMK* 1.5. See Stcherbatsky, *The Conception of Buddhist Nirvana*, pp. 170–71; Sprung, *Lucid Exposition of the Middle Way*, p. 68.

49. On *MMK* 1.7. See Stcherbatsky, pp. 172–73; Sprung, p. 70.

50. *MMK* 1.9. See Stcherbatsky, pp. 174–75; Sprung, pp. 71–72.

51. *MMK* 1.11, 13–14. Stcherbatsky, pp. 177–80; Sprung, pp. 72–74.

52. Matilal points out that *pratijñā* is defined in the Nyaya Sutra "as the statement . . . which states what is to be proven . . . Hence, when Nāgārjuna says 'nasti mama pratijñā' [*Vigrahavyāvartanī*, verse 29] he obviously means that he has no stated thesis of his own and therefore should not be faulted" (Matilal, "Buddhist Logic and Epistemology," p. 26).

53. *MMK* 1.1. Trans. Inada, p. 39.

54. Ruegg, "Does the Mādhyamika Have a Philosophical Thesis?" pp. 232–35. Some Tibetan commentators argue that, properly interpreted, Madhyamaka has no theses at all. This view is refuted by the Tibetan philosopher, Tsong Khapa (1357–1419) and his school. See *Tsong Khapa's Speech of Gold in the* Essence of True Eloquence, trans. Thurman, pp. 331–36. See also Williams, "On the Interpretation of Madhyamaka Thought," pp. 199–204.

55. See the brief analysis of Nagarjuna's replies made in Lindtner, *Nagarjuniana*, pp. 74–75.

56. *VV*, verses 21–29. Trans. Bhattacharya, *The Dialectical Method of Nāgārjuna*, pp. 17–24.

57. *The Dialectical Method of Nāgārjuna (Vigrahavyāvartanī)*, verses 30–33. Trans. Bhattacharya, pp. 24–27.

58. Ibid., verses 35–39. Trans. Bhattacharya, pp. 27–29.

59. Ibid., verses 40–51, pp. 30–35, with ellipses and omissions.

60. Ibid., verses 52–56. Trans. Bhattacharya, pp. 35–39.

61. Ibid., verses 61–64. Trans. Bhattacharya, pp. 40–42.

62. *MMK* 25.19–20. With Chandrakirti's explanation, Stcherbatsky, *The Conception of Buddhist Nirvāṇa*, p. 205; Sprung, *Lucid Exposition of the Middle Way*, pp. 259–60. See also the translation in Wood, *Nāgārjunian Disputations*, pp. 304.

63. *MMK* 25.21–23. Stcherbatsky, pp. 206–7. Sprung, pp. 260–62 (262 quoted).

64. The quotation in the subtitle above is the first sentence of Jayarashi's book. On the probable pun see See Franco, *Perception, Knowledge and Disbelief*, p. 69 and note 1. Franco translates: "This dreadful [book], the lion of annihilation of [all] principles, was indeed [composed] by me."

65. **Sources and discussions of Charvaka**: D. Chattopadhyaya, ed., *Cārvāka/ Lokāyata*, Mew Delhi: Indian Council of Philosophical Research, 1990.
   Summary of Charvaka positions and responses to them: J. Sinha, *A History of Indian Philosophy*, vol. 1, Calcutta: Sinha Publishing House, 1956, chap. 7.
   Paraphrase: E. Solomon, *Indian Dialectics*, vol. 2, pp. 526–47, 572–81.
   Translation with commentary: E. Franco, *Perception, Knowledge and Disbelief: A Study of Jayarāśi's Skepticism*, Stuttgart: Franz Steiner Verlag, 1987. There is a translated excerpt on the refutation of the Nyaya doctrine of inference in Radhakrishnan and Moore, *A Source Book in Indian Philosophy*, pp. 236–46.
   For Jayarashi's date, see Franco, *Perception, Knowledge and Disbelief*, p. 12.

66.. Ibid, p. 71.

67. Nyaya Sutras 1.1.4, in my free version.

68. As summarized in Franco, *Perception, Knowledge and Disbelief*, note 19, p. 311.

69. Franco, *Perception, Knowledge and Disbelief*, pp. 75–77 (*Tatt.* 1.12). The argument that nothing benefits all people is from p. 127 (*Tatt.* 1.1bab). For an outline of the whole argument see the clear exposition in Matilal, *Logical and Ethical Issues of Religious Belief*, pp. 55–59.

70. Ibid., p. 79, *Tatt.* 1.13.

71. Ibid., pp. 77–83.

72. Selected and paraphrased from Franco, *Perception, Knowledge and Disbelief*, pp. 91–91. W. Ruben has a brief summary of these arguments, which he calls "meaningless hair-splittings." See Chattopadhyaya, *Cārvaka/Lokāyata*, pp. 508–10.

73. I paraphrase from Vidyananda, as given in Franco, op. cit. (note 69 above), p. 33.

74. Uddyotakara (sixth century C.E.), in his subcommentary to the Nyaya Sutras 1.2.4, *The Nyāya Sūtras of Gautama*, trans. Jha, vol. 3, p. 523. See Franco, op. cit., p. 35.

75. Franco, *Perception, Knowledge and Disbelief*, p. 69 and note 6, pp. 300–301.

76. Franco, *Perception, Knowledge and Disbelief*, p. 245. For Jayarashi's attack on the Buddhist denial of universals, see pp. 253–57.

77. The quotation accompanying the subtitle above is the introductory verse to the *Khaṇḍanakhaṇḍakhādya*, trans. Jha, vol. 1, p. 3.
Critical expositions or paraphrases: S. Dasgupta, *A History of Indian Philosophy*, vol. 2, Cambridge: Cambridge University Press, 1932, pp. 125–47. B. Matilal, *Logical and Ethical Issues of Religious Belief*, Calcutta: Calcutta University Press, 1982, pp. 59–65 (short, clear, simple); *Perception*, Oxford: Oxford University Press, 1986, pp. 65–68, 135–40; "Skepticism and Mysticism in Indian Philosophy," unpublished lecture delivered at Tel-Aviv University in 1979. C. Ram-Prasad, "Knowledge and the 'Real' World: Śrī Harṣa and the *Pramāṇas*," *Journal of Indian Philosophy* 21.2 (June 1993); "The Provisional World: Existencehood, Causal Efficiency and Śrī Harṣa," *Journal of Indian Philosophy* 23.2 (June 1995). J. Sinha, *A History of Indian Philosophy*, vol. 3, Calcutta: Sinha Publishing Co., 1971. E. Solomon, *Indian Dialectics*, 2 vols., Ahmedabad: B. J. Institute of Learning and Research, 976, 1978, vol. 2, pp. 547–72, 581–610.
Translations with Commentary: P. Granoff, *Philosophy and Argument in Late Vedanta: Śrī Harṣa's* Khaṇḍanakhaṇḍakhādya, Dordrecht: Reidel, 1978 (preface and commented translation). *The* Khaṇḍanakhaṇḍakhādya *of Shri Harsha*, 2 vols., trans. G. Jha, reprinted Delhi: Sri Satguru Publications, 1986 [1911–1918]. Not surprisingly, the translator warns (vol. 1, p. xvi) that "the nature of the text is such that many passages must have been not understood or at best imperfectly understood by me." To avoid compounding confusion, I give chapter and section numbers as in Jha, which, though old, is the only full, published translation. The

numbers in parentheses are his paragraph numbers, which run consecutively through each of the two "chapters"—*books* would be a better designation. Granoff gives references to the editions she uses.

78. Granoff, *Philosophy and Argument in Late Vedānta*, pp. 6–2, notes 5, 6; and M. Krishnamachariar, *History of Classical Sanskrit Literature*, reprint Delhi: Banarsidass, 1989, pp. 177–84. For the symbolism of Shriharsha's epic poem, see Granoff's note, pp. 252–53.

79. *Khaṇḍana* 1.1 (4–9). Trans. Granoff, pp. 72–74; Jha, pp. 4–5.

80. *Khaṇḍana* 1.1 (10). Trans. Granoff, p. 74; Jha, vol. 1, p. 5.

81. *Khaṇḍana* 1.1 (11–13). Trans. Granoff, pp. 75–76; Jha, vol. 1, pp. 5–7.

82. *Khaṇḍana* 1.1 (27). Trans. Granoff, p. 82; Jha, vol. 1, pp. 10–11.

83. *Khaṇḍana* 1.1 (28–31). Trans. Granoff p. 83; Jha, vol. 1, pp. 11–12.

84. *Khaṇḍana* 1.1 (34–36). Trans. Granoff, p. 86; Jha, vol. 1, pp. 12–14.

85. *Khaṇḍana* 1.5 (87–89). Trans. Granoff, pp. 136–37; Jha, vol. 1, p. 40.

86. *Khaṇḍana* 1.5 (90). Trans. Granoff, p. 140; Jha, vol. 1, p. 41.

87. *Khaṇḍana* 1.5 (93, 97). Trans. Granoff pp. 140–41, 44; Jha, pp. 41–42, 43–44.

88. *Khaṇḍana* 1.5 (98), 1.6 (99). Trans. Granoff, pp. 144, 145 (quoted); Jha, vol. 1, p. 44.

89. *Khaṇḍana* 1.6 (100). Trans. Granoff, pp. 145–46 (145 quoted); Jha, vol. 1, pp. 44–45.

90. *Khaṇḍana* 1.6 (100). Trans. Granoff, pp. 146; Jha, vol. 1, pp. 44–45.

91. *Khaṇḍana* 1.6 (101). Trans. Granoff, pp. 146 (146); Jha, vol. 1, p. 46.

92. *Khaṇḍana* 1.6 (102) quoting *Bṛhadāraṇyaka Upaniṣad* 4.4.19. Trans. Granoff, p. 148 (quoted); Jha, vol. 1, p. 46.

93. *Khaṇḍana* 1.7 (107). Trans. Granoff, p. 149–50; Jha, vol. 1, pp. 48–49.

94. *Khaṇḍana* 1.7 (112–13). Trans. Granoff, pp. 153–54; Jha, vol. 1, pp. 52–53.

95. *Khaṇḍana* 1.7 (117–19). The words "all things are different" or, in Granoff's translation, "all is different," occur in paragraph 119. Trans. Granoff, p. 159 (quoted); Jha, vol. 1, pp. 55–56. Granoff notes (p. 234, note 107) that the commentators see "all is different" as a worldly rather than scriptural statement. The quotation fits the rival, dualistic Vedanta of Madhva (1199–1278 C.E.) rather than the monistic school to which Shriharsha belongs.

96. *Khaṇḍana* 1.7 (120). Trans. Granoff, p. 159; Jha, vol. 1, p. 55–57.

97. *Khaṇḍana* 1.10 (152–53). Trans. Granoff, pp. 192–93; Jha, p. 75.

98. *Khaṇḍana* 1.10 (160). Trans. Granoff, p. 198–99; Jha, vol. 1, p. 77 (quoted).

99. See Granoff, *Philosophy and Argument in Late Vedānta*, pp. 5–31.

100. *Khaṇḍana* 1.13 (174). Trans. Granoff, p. 4; Jha, vol. 1, p. 82.

101. Jha, ibid., p. 83.

102. *Khaṇḍana* 2.4 (151–52, 157, 166). Jha, vol. 2, pp. 187, 197, 206 (numbering below page).

103. Granoff, *Philosophy and Argument in Late Vedānta*, pp. 4 (quoted), 53–54.

104. Dasgupta, *A History of Indian Philosophy*, vol. 2, p. 146.

105. Bimal Matilal, in his preface to Granoff, *Philosophy and Argument in Late Vedānta*, p. x.

106. *Khaṇḍana*, 2.4 (205). Trans. Jha, vol. 2, p. 247 (numbering at bottom of page).

107. On Sextus's use of the charges of infinite regress and circularity, see J. Barnes, *The Toils of Scepticism*, Cambridge: Cambridge University Press, 1990, chaps. 2, 3.

108. *Sextus Empiricus*, trans. Bury, vol. 1, pp. 163–64.

109. Bhattacharya, *The Dialectical Method of Nāgārjuna*, p. 25.

110. Franco, *Perception, Knowledge and Disbelief*, pp. 69–70.

111. Long and Sedley, *The Hellenistic Philosophers*, p. 462 (attributed to the Academics generally).

112. Franco, *Perception, Knowledge and Disbelief*, pp. 103, 125, 127.

113. *Khaṇḍana* 1.6 (101). Trans. Granoff p. 146 (quoted); Jha, vol. 1, p. 46.

114. Translated Hankinson, *The Sceptics*, p. 219. See also the translation by Bury, *Sextus Empiricus*, vol. 1, pp. 341–43.

115. Stcherbatsky, *The Conception of Buddhist Nirvāṇa*, pp. 168–69.

116. Radhakrishnan and Moore, *A Source Book in Indian Philosophy*, pp. 242–43 (*Tatt.* 7).

117. Franco, *Perception, Knowledge and Disbelief*, p. 267.

118. *Khaṇḍana* 6.6 (139). Trans. Jha, vol. 2, p. 179 (or, in the numeration at the top of the page, continuous with that of vol. 1, p. 637). The ants are mentioned in paragraph 128, p. 164 (622).

119. Sextus Empiricus, *Outlines of Pyrrhonism*, 2.204; trans. Bury, vol. 1, p. 283. For Sextus on inference, see Hankinson, *The Sceptics*, pp. 201–12.

120. Ibid., 2.205–10; trans. Bury, vol. 1, pp. 285–87.

121. On Nagarjuna's expression of the doctrine and the subsequent Buddhist debate, see Lindtner, "Ātiśa's Introduction to the Two Truths, and Its Sources." For Tibetan responses, see Cabezon, *A Dose of Emptiness* and Newland, *The Two Truths*. Like early modern expositors, Hindu philosophers stigmatized Madyamaka as nihilism—see Kher, *Buddhism as Presented by the Brahmanical Systems*, pp. 559–60, 618–20. In *Nāgārjunian Disputations*, Wood has recently given a detailed defense of the nihilistic interpretation, according to which neither the self nor the dharmas are real (p. 5)—even the mind is unreal. By this interpretation, the phenomenal world is real in only a qualified sense and the absolute is not real at all (pp. 211, 279–80). Wood says that although this view is radical, it may not be possible to refute it as logically inconsistent.

122. The words of Chandrakirti, *Prasannapadā*, ed. L. de la Vallée Poussin, p. 536; as in Huntington, "The System of the Two Truths . . . ," p. 98.

123. From Nagarjuna's *Short Treatise of Pulverization (Vaidalya-prakaraṇa).* Meant to reduce Nyaya concepts as well as philosophers to dust, this "is without compare the most lively and amusing of all texts ascribed to Nagarjuna, full of sophistries as it is" (Lindtner, *Nagarjuniana*, p. 87).

124. Patel, "The Paradox of Negation in Nāgārjuna's Philosophy," pp. 28–29.

125. Siderits, "Nāgārjuna as Anti-Realist," p. 321.

126. M. Siderits, "Thinking on Empty: Madhyamaka Anti-Realism and Canon of Rationality," in S. Biderman and B.-A. Scharfstein, eds., *Rationality in Question*, Leiden: Brill, 1989.

Chapter 9. Religio-Philosophical Synthesis

1. **History of philosophy and philosophical context**: S. Dasgupta, *A History of Indian Philosophy*, vol. 1, Cambridge: Cambridge University Press, 1932; A. B. Keith, *Indian Logic and Atomism* [1921], reprint New York: Greenwood Press, 1968. B. K. Matilal, *Epistemology, Logic, and Grammar in Indian Philosophical Analysis*, The Hague: Mouton, 1971; *Logic, Language and Reality*, Delhi: Banarsidass, 1985; *Perception*, Oxford: Oxford University Press, 1986. S. Radhakrishnan, *Indian Philosophy*, 2d ed., London, Allen and Unwin, 1929, vol. 2, chaps. 2, 3; J. Sinha, *A History of Indian Philosophy*, vol. 1. Calcutta: Sinha Publishing House, 1956.

Monographs on the school: S. Bagchi, *Inductive Reasoning: A Study of Tarka and Its Role in Indian Logic*, Calcutta: Calcutta University Press, 1953. S. Bahaduri, *Studies in Nyāya-Vaiśeṣika Metaphysics*, Poona: Bhandarkar Oriental Research Institute, 1947. S. Chatterjee, *The Nyāya Theory of Knowledge*, Calcutta: University of Calcutta, 1950. W. Halbfass, *On Being and What There Is: Classical Nyāya-Vaiśeṣika and the History of Indian Ontology* (with a brief appendix of translated ontological texts), Albany: State University of New York Press, 1992. B. K. Matilal, *Nyāya-Vaiśeṣika*, Wiesbaden: Harrassowitz, 1977. K. H. Potter, "Introduction to the Philosophy of Nyāya-Vaiśeṣika," in K. H. Potter, ed., *Encyclopedia of Indian Philosophies*, vol. 2, *Nyāya-Vaiśeṣika* (see below).

Controversy with Buddhists: C. V. Kher, *Buddhism as Presented by the Brahmanical Systems*, Delhi: Indian Books Centre, 1992 (contains much on Nyaya responses, but omits Udayana). D. N. Shastri, *Critique of Indian Realism*, Agra: Agra University, 1964.

Detailed commentary: G. Chemparathy, *An Indian Rational Theology: Introduction to Udayana's Nyāyakusumāñjali*, Vienna: De Nobili Research Library, 1972.

Translations, mostly with commentary: *Ātmatattvaviveka of Udayana*, Part I, trans. C. V. Kher and S. Kumar, Delhi: Eastern Book Linkers, 1987. M. Tachikawa, *The Structure of the World in Udayana's Realism: A Study of the Lakṣaṇāvalī and the Kiraṇāvalī*, Dordrecht: Reidel, 1981 (see review by P. K. Sen, *Journal of Indian Philosophy* 11.3 (Sept. 1983), pp. 315–22). Udayana Acharya, *The Kusumāñjali or Hindu Proofs of the Existence of a Supreme Being*, trans. E. B. Cowell [1864], reprinted Varanasi (Banaras): Bharat-Bharati, 1980.

Paraphrases of Udayana's works: K. H. Potter, ed., *Encyclopedia of Indian Philosophies*, vol. 2, *Indian Metaphysics and Epistemology: The Tradition of Nyāya-Vaiśeṣika up to Gaṅgeśa* (hereafter *Nyāya-Vaiśeṣika*), Princeton: Princeton University Press, 1977. J. Vattanky, *Gangesha's Philosophy of God*, Madras: Adyar Library and Research Centre, 1984, pp. 87–119 (careful paraphrases of the sections relating to God in Udayana's *Ātmatattvaviveka, Nyāyakusumāñjali*, and *Kiraṇāvalī*).

2. Tachikawa, *The Structure of the World in Udayana's Realism*, p. 13.

3. On Udayana's life and works, see Chemparathy, *An Indian Rational Theology*, pp. 20–33 (p. 27 quoted); Matilal, *Nyāya-Vaiśeṣika*, pp. 96–97; and Tachikawa, *The Structure of the World in Udayana's Realism*, pp. 14–17.

4. Chemparathy, *An Indian Rational Theology*, p. 28.

5. See the stories (some come in more than one version) in Chemparathy, *An Indian Rational Theology*, p. 28; Potter, ed., *Nyāya-Vaiśeṣika*, p. 522; and Shastri, *Critique of Indian Realism*, p. 120.

6. Chemparathy, op. cit., pp. 34–35.

7. Potter, in Potter, ed., *Nyāya-Vaiśeṣika*, pp. 203–7.

8. The account that follows is based mainly on Chemparathy, *An Indian Rational Theology*, references for which I give. I also use the Introduction (pp. 102–111) and paraphrases in Potter, *Nyāya-Vaiśeṣika*. The summary in Sinha, *History of Indian Philosophy*, vol. 1, pp. 668–73, and (for the nine proofs I refer to) 680–92, are readable, clear, and relatively full. The text of the proofs can be found in Cowell's translation. This translation, made with the help of Indian pandits who

gave their explanations in Sanskrit or Bengali, dates back to 1864 and should therefore be read with caution. Its calculation into verses (karikas) is in part mistaken (Chemparathy, p. 37, note 64).

9. For this proof, I follow Chemparathy, An Indian Rational Theology, pp. 86–90.

10. Chemparathy, op. cit., pp. 87–88 (from Udayana, Kiraṇāvalī 97.10–12).

11. Potter, Nyāya-Vaiśeṣika, pp. 582–83. For the brief text of the argument see Cowell's translation, pp. 67–68.

12. Chemparathy, op. cit., p. 85.

13. Ibid., pp. 140–49, 153, 159.

14. Chemparathy, op. cit., pp. 90–92.

15. Ibid., p. 90.

16. Chemparathy, op. cit., pp. 138–40, 148–49.

17. Ibid., pp. 92–94.

18. Ibid., pp. 94–95.

19. Ibid., pp. 52–53. See also the paraphrase in Potter, Nyāya-Vaiśeṣika, pp. 572–73 and Cowell's translation, pp. 29–31.

20. Ibid., pp. 95–97.

21. Ibid., pp. 97–98.

22. Chemparathy, op. cit., pp. 98–99.

23. Ibid., pp. 99–103.

24. See the references given by Sinha, History of Indian Philosophy, vol. 1., p. 684.

25. Chemparathy, op. cit., pp. 104–8.

26. Atoms of the four material elements and of the manas are eternally small. Only time, space, and soul are supremely great and, therefore, eternal See Chemparathy, An Indian Rational Theology, p. 104; and Udayana's Kiraṇāvalī, as translated in Tachikawa, The Structure of the World in Udayana's Realism, pp. 121–22.

27. Apart from Chemparathy, op. cit., pp. 104–7, see Frauwallner, History of Indian Philosophy, vol. 2, pp. 93–94, 136–38, 157–60 (in this English translation of Frauwallner's German, the term apekṣābuddhi, here called relating cognition, is called observing knowledge and reflective knowledge). In On Being and What There is, Halbfass translates the term as relational cognition.

28. Chemparathy, op. cit., pp. 29–30, 73.

29. The quotation just above is from Chu His, *Learning to be a Sage*, p. 98.

History of Neo-Confucianism: C. Chang, *The Development of Neo-Confucian Thought*. vol. 1, New York: Bookman, 1957. Kai-wing Chow, *The Rise of Confucian Ritualism in Late Imperial China*, Stanford: Stanford University Press, 1994 (on the "gentrification" of Confucianism from the seventeenth century and on by way of the insistence on ritual (instead of the "learning of principle"), the recovery of "pure," untainted Confucianism, and the puritanical restriction of women and of popular art and literature). Wm. T. De Bary, *The Message of the Mind* in Neo-Confucianism, New York: Columbia University Press, 1989; *Neo-Confucian Orthodoxy and the Learning of the Mind-and-Heart*, New York: Columbia University Press, 1981; "The Uses of Neo-Confucianism: A Response to Professor Tillman," *Philosophy East and West* 43.3 (July 1933). Fung Yu-lan (Yu-lan Fung), *A History of Chinese Philosophy*, vol. 2, Princeton: Princeton University Press, 1953. A. S. Graham, *Two Chinese Philosophers: Ch'eng Ming-tao and Ch'eng Yi-ch'uan*, London: Lund Humphries, 1958. Needham, J., *Science and Civilisation in China*, vol. 2, Cambridge: Cambridge University Press, 1956. C. M. Schirokauer, "Chu Hsi's Political Career: A Study in Ambivalence," in A. F. Wright and D. Twichett, eds., *Confucian Personalities*, Stanford: Stanford University Press, 1962.

Anthologies of studies: Wm. Theodore de Bary, ed., *The Unfolding of Neo-Confucianism*, New York: Columbia University Press, 1975. Wing-tsit Chan, ed., *Chu Hsi and Neo-Confucianism*, Honolulu: University of Hawaii Press, 1986.

Monographs on Chu Hsi: D. M. Munro, *Images of Human Nature*, Princeton: Princeton University Press, 1988. H. C. Tillman, *Confucian Discourse and Chu Hsi's Ascendancy*, Honolulu: University of Hawaii Press, 1992.

Translations: Ch'en Ch'un, *Neo-Confucian Terms Explained*, trans. Wing-tsit Chan, New York: Columbia University Press, 1986 (by a close disciple of Chu Hsi). Chu Hsi, *Learning to Be a Sage*, trans. D. K. Gardner, Berkeley: University of California Press, 1990. Chu Hsi and Lü Tsu-Ch'ien, compilers, *Reflections on Things at Hand*, trans. Wing-tsit Chan, New York: Columbia University Press, 1967. Wing-tsit Chan, trans., *A Source Book in Chinese Philosophy*, Princeton: Princeton University Press, 1963.

Relations with European philosophy (especially Malebranche and Leibniz): J. Ching and W. Oxtoby, eds., *Discovering China: European Interpretations in the Enlightenment*, Rochester: University of Rochester Press, 1992, chaps. 1, 2, 4–6, 11. G. W. Leibniz, *Discourse on the Natural Theology of the Chinese*, trans, H. Rosemont and D. J. Cook, Honolulu: University Press of Hawaii, 1977. D. E. Mungello, *Leibniz and Confucianism: The Search for Accord*, Honolulu: University Press of Hawaii, 1977.

30. The claim was made by Chu Chen to the emperor Kao-tsung in 1136. See Tillman, *Confucian Discourse and Chu Hsi's Ascendancy*, pp. 20–21.

31. The relative importance of the movement's immediate, eleventh-century ancestors became a sensitive issue. Apart from the two Ch'eng brothers, Chu Hsi emphasized the contributions (in descending order of attention and, probably, of importance to him) of Chang Tsai (1020–1077), Shao Yung (1012–1077), and

Chou Tun-I (1017–1073). (See Tillman, *Confucian Discourse and Chu Hsi's Ascendancy*, pp. 114–19.)

32. From a letter presented in person by Ch'en Ch'un to Chu Hsi in 1190. See Ch'en Ch'un, *Neo-Confucian Terms Explained*, trans. Chan, p. 198. See also pp. 7–8.

33. Schirokauer, "Chu Hsi's Political Career, pp. 183–85 (184 quoted); Tillman, *Confucian Discourse and Chu Hsi's Ascendancy*, pp. 143–44, 255–56.

34. Tillman, *Confucian Discourse and Chu Hsi's Ascendancy*, pp. 40–41. Chan, *A Source Book in Chinese Philosophy*, pp. 602–4 (for the seedlings and weeds), and 646–53; Ch'en Ch'un, *Neo-Confucian Terms Explained*, pp. 168–73. For criticism of Chu Hsi's knowledge of Buddhism, see C. Wei-hsun Fu, "Chu Hsi on Buddhism," in Chan, ed., *Chu Hsi and Neo-Confucianism* (the fragment of Chu Hsi's poem I quote is from p. 378).

35. Chu Hsi, *Learning to Be a Sage*, pp. 13–20.

36. Chu Hsi, *Learning to Be a Sage*, 4.2, 4.3 (p. 128).

37. Ibid., pp. 21–22.

38. Ibid., p. 139.

39. Ibid., p. 151.

40. See Munro, *Images of Human Nature*. I have drawn especially from the translations from Chu Hsi on pages 57 (clear water), 81 (the bright mirror), 84 (still water), 121 (the seed).

41. On the Taoist origin of the terms see Fung Yu-lan, *History of Chinese Philosophy*, vol. 2, pp. 438–42. The term *Great Ultimate* also occurs in the "Appended Remarks," attributed to Confucius, of the *Book of Changes*. See Tillman, *Confucian Discourse and Chu Hsi's Ascendancy*, pp. 216–22.

42. Yu Yamanoi, "The Great Ultimate and Heaven in Chu Hsi's Philosophy," in Chan, ed., *Chu Hsi and Neo-Confucianism*, pp. 79–87 (p. 86 quoted). Yu also contends (pp. 87–89) that the Principle of Heaven (*T'ien-li*) fits loosely into Chu's philosophy and has a role that can sometimes be reversed with that of Principle. See also Hsü Fu-kuan, "Chu Hsi and the Ch'eng Brothers," also in Chan, ibid., pp. 54–55.

43. The quotation is from Ch'un, *Neo-Confucian Terms Explained*, section 144 (p. 118).

44. For the texts from Chu Hsi on which the common way out is based, see Yu Yamanoi, "The Great Ultimate and Heaven in Chu Hsi's Philosophy," Chan, ed., *Chu Hsi and Neo-Confucianism*, p. 81. The text on principles that I paraphrase is from a brief statement by Chu Hsi on the difference between Buddhism and Confucianism, as translated in Chan, *A Source Book in Chinese Philosophy*, p. 603.

The second solution was suggested to me by Galia Patt-Shamir, whose doctoral dissertation involves Chu Hsi's philosophy.

45. Fung Yu-lan, *History of Chinese Philosophy*, vol. 2, pp. 534–35. The tree metaphor is from Chu's *Conversations of Master Chu, Arranged Topically*, as translated in Munro, *Images of Human Nature*, pp. 118–19.

46. Tillman, *Confucian Discourse and Chu Hsi's Ascendancy*, pp. 216–22.

47. For the meanings of *li*, see Chan in Chu Hsi and Lü Tsu-ch'ien, *Reflections on Things at Hand*, pp. 367–68; Graham, *Two Chinese Philosophers*, pp. 8–21; Needham, *Science and Civilisation in China*, vol 2, pp. 472–89, 490–93; and N. Nicolas-Vandier, in S. Aroux, ed., *Les notions philosophiques*, vol. 2, Paris: Presses Universitaires, 1990, pp. 2960–61.

For *ch'i*, see Graham, *Disputers of the Tao*, pp. 351–54; Needham, op. cit., pp. 475–76; I. Robinet, "Qi," in S. Aroux, op. cit., vol. 2, pp. 2970–71; Schwartz, *The World of Thought in Ancient China*, pp. 179–84.

48. Ch'en Ch'un, *Neo-Confucian Terms Explained*, section 135 (pp. 112–13).

49. Ch'en Ch'un, *Non-Confucian Terms Explained*, section 147 (p. 119).

50. See Chan, *A Source Book in Chinese Philosophy*, pp. 623, 634–38. The two brief quotations are from pp. 634 (section 105), 635 (section 105). The statement on soul and consciousness is from pp. 637–38 (section 113), the quotation from p. 637.

51. Ch'en Ch'un, *Neo-Confucian Terms Explained*, pp. 48–50 (50 quoted). See also Chan, *A Source Book in Chinese Philosophy*, pp. 597–600, 622–26.

52. Chu Hsi, in Chan, *A Sourcebook in Chinese Philosophy*, p. 641.

53. Ibid., pp. 641–42.

54. Ibid., p. 641.

55. Ibid., p. 643.

56. Ch'en Ch'un, *Neo-Confucian Terms Explained*, pp. 69–70.

57. Chu Hsi, "A Treatise on Jen," in Chan, trans., *A Source Book in Chinese Philosophy*, pp. 593–97. S. Hitoshi, "Chu Hsi's 'Treatise on Jen,'" in Chan, ed., *Chu Hsi and Neo-Confucianism*. Tillman, *Confucian Discourse and Chu Hsi's Ascendancy*, pp. 70–82.

58. Chu Hsi, "A Treatise on Jen," p. 594.

59. Ibid., pp. 595–56.

60. Ibid., p. 89. Confucius is quoted from the *Analects* 15.23. "For if what is harbored" is from p. 90.

61. Chu Hsi, *Learning to Be a Sage*, trans. Gardner, 6.12 (p. 164).

62. The quotation following ths subtitle above is from Rahman, *Prophecy in Islam*, p. 35.

Historical background: M. G. S. Hodgson, *The Venture of Islam*, vol. 2, Chicago: University of Chicago Press, 1974.

Histories of culture, thought, or philosophy: H. Corbin, *Histoire de la philosophie islamique*, Paris: Gallimard, 1964 (there is an English translation). M. Fakhry, *A History of Islamic Philosophy*, New York: Columbia University Press, 1970. S. Pines, "Philosophy," in P. M. Holt, A. K. S. Lambton, and B. Lewis, eds., *The Cambridge History of Islam*, vol. 2, Cambridge: Cambridge University Press, 1970. F. E. Peters, *Aristotle and the Arabs,* New York: New York University Press, 1968. E. I. J. Rosenthal, *Political Thought in Medieval Islam*, Cambridge: Cambridge University Press, 1958. F. Rosenthal, *Knowledge Triumphant: The Concept of Knowledge in Medieval Islam*, Leiden: Brill, 1970. J. Schacht, ed., *The Legacy of Islam,* 2d ed., London: Oxford University Press, 1974. M. Montgomery Watt, *Islamic Philosophy and Theology*, Edinburgh: Edinburgh University Press, 1962; *Muslim Intellectual: A Study of al-Ghazali*, Edinburgh: Edinburgh University Press, 1963. M. J. L. Young, J. D. Latham, and R. B. Serjeant, *Religion, Learning and Science in the 'Abbasid Period*, Cambridge: Cambridge University Press, 1990. M. Montgomery Watt, *Islamic Philosophy and Theology*, Edinburgh: Edinburgh University Press, 1962.

Special subjects: I. A. Bello, *The Medieval Islamic Controversy between Philosophy and Orthodoxy*, Leiden: Brill, 1989. H. A. Davidson, *Al-Farabi, Avicenna, and Averroes on Intellect: Their Cosmologies, Theories of the Active Intellect, and Theories of Human Intellect*, New York: Oxford University Press, 1992; *Proofs for Eternity, Creation and the Existence of God in Medieval Islamic and Jewish Philosophy*, New York: Oxford University Press, 1987. M. Fakhry, *Ethical Theories in Islam*, Leiden: Brill, 1991. G. F. Hourani, *Reason and Tradition in Islamic Ethics*, Cambridge: Cambridge University Press, 1985. G. E. von Gruenebaum, ed., *Logic in Classical Islamic Culture*, Wiesbaden: Harrassowitz, 1970. P. Morwedge, ed., *Neoplatonism in Islamic Thought*, Albany: State University of New York Press, 1992. S. H. Nasr, *An Introduction to Islamic Cosmological Doctrines*, Harvard: Harvard University Press, 1965. F. Rahman, *Prophecy in Islam: Philosophy and Orthodoxy*, London: Allen & Unwin, 1858. F. Rosenthal, *The Classical Heritage in Islam*, London: Routledge & Kegan Paul, 1965 (wide-ranging anthology of Islamic sources). H. A. Wolfson, *The Philosophy of Kalam*, Cambridge: Harvard University Press, 1976.

Monographs on Avicenna (and Al-Farabi): S. M. Afnan, *Avicenna*, London: Allen & Unwin, 1958. H. Corbin, *Avicenna and the Visionary Recital*, Princeton: Princeton University Press, 1960. A.-M. Goichon, *La philosophie d'Avicenne et son influence en Europe médiévale*, Paris: Adrien-Maisonneuve, 1944. L. E. Goodman, *Avicenna*, London: Routledge, 1992. D. Gutas, *Avicenna and the Aristotelian Tradition*, Leiden: Brill, 1988 (contains many translated excerpts). P. Heath, *Allegory and Philosophy in Avicenna (Ibn Sina)*, Philadelphia: University of Pennsylvania Press, 1992 (with a translation of a work attributed to Avicenna—the book's second part contains a particularly lucid summary of the main lines of Avicenna's philosophy). A. R. Netton, *Al-Farabi and His School*, London: Routledge, 1992.

Translations: Avicenne, *La Métaphysique du Shifā*, trans. G. C. Anawati, 2 vols., Paris: Vrin, 1978, 1985. A. J. Arberry, *Avicenna on Theology*, London: John

Murray, 1951. Averroes, *On the Harmony of Religion and Philosophy*, trans. G. F. Hourani, London: Luzac, 1961. W. E. Gohlman, *The Life of Ibn Sina*, Albany: State University of New York Press, 1974. A. Hyman and J. J. Walsh, eds., *Philosophy in the Middle Ages*, pp. 233–62. M. Mahdi, ed., *Medieval Political Philosophy: A Sourcebook*, Boston: Free Press, 1963 (chaps. 5–7). Ibn Khaldun, *An Introduction to History: The Muqaddimah*, trans. F. Rosenthal, abridged by. N. J. Dawood, London: Routledge and Kegan Paul and Secker and Warburg, 1967. F. Rahman, *Avicenna's Psychology*, London: Oxford University Press, 1952.

63. For relatively full accounts of his life see Afnan, *Avicenna*, and Goodman, *Avicenna*.

64. For Avicenna's intention, see the Prologue to *The Cure* as translated in Gutas, *Avicenna and the Aristotelian Tradition*, pp. 50–51.

65. Morwedege, ed., *Neoplatonism and Islamic Thought*.

66. On the Intelligences as angels and on the number and nature of the celestial spheres, see H. Corbin, *Avicenna and the Visionary Recital*, chap. 2; and P. Heath, *Allegory and Philosophy in Avicenna (Ibn Sina)*, pp. 35–52.

67. This is according to Avicenna's *Cure (Shifaʾ)*; but this two-phase emanation of human thought " is not integrated with what Avicenna writes elsewhere on the subject of human thought" (Davidson, *Al-Farabi, Avicenna, and Averroes on Intellect*, pp. 91 [esp. note 74] and 92, drawing on *Shifa: De Anima* 242–47).

68. Gutas, op. cit., pp. 261–65. See also Davidson, *Proofs for Eternity, Creation, and Existence . . .* , pp. 282–310, which is a summary and commentary on Avicenna's proof of existence as in appears in the *Najat (The Salvation)*, the *Ishārāt (Pointers and Reminders)*, as well as the *Shīfaʾ (The Cure)*, on the last of which almost alone my summary depends. There is an English translation in Hyman and Walsh, *Philosophy in the Middle Ages*, pp. 240–46 (*al-Shifaʾ, al-Ilāhīyyāt* 1.6–7). For a French translation, see Avicenne, *La Métaphysique de Shifa*, vol. 1, pp. 113–22.

69. Goodman, *Avicenna*, p. 64, puts the foregoing argument in a neat skeletal form. Davidson, op. cit., is quite detailed. My account of the proof in *The Cure (Shifa)* remains fairly close to the limited part of the text I summarize.

70. On the nondemonstrativeness of the proof, see Davidson, *Proofs for Eternity, Creation and the Existence of God . . .* , op. cit., pp. 298–99. On the "superaddition" of existence to essence, see Goodman, *Avicenna*, pp. 72–73.

71. Gutas, *Avicenna and the Aristotelian Tradition*, p. 74; from *On the Rational Soul*, probably Avicenna's last work.

72. Goodman, *Avicenna*, p. 155, from *Shifa (The Cure), De anima* 1.1. Avicenna repeats the "experiment" and explains at some length in *Isharat (Pointers and Reminders)*. The passage is translated by Goodman on pp. 157–58 (in contrast with Gutas, he translates the name of the source as the *Book of Hints and Pointers*).

73. Gutas, *Avicenna and the Aristotelian Tradition*, p. 74; from Avicenna, *On the Rational Soul*.

74. Ibid., pp. 73 (quoted), 159–65 (165 quoted).

75. Ibid., op. cit., p. 170, 172.

76. Gohlman, *The Life of Ibn Sina*, pp. 28–31; Gutas, ibid., pp. 27–28.

77. Gutas, ibid., pp. 181–82.

78. Ibid., p. 184.

79. Ibid., pp. 184–87.

80. Ibid., pp. 31, 35.

81. Rahman, *Prophecy in Islam*, p. 38.

82. Rahman, *Prophecy in Islam*, pp. 37–38. Heath, *Allegory and Philosophy in Avicenna*, p. 90.

83. Rahman, *Prophecy in Islam*, p. 39.

84. Ibid., pp. 40–42.

85. Ibid., p. 42; from the *Risāla al-Aḍḥawīya* (*Immolation Treatise on the Destination*).

86. Ibid., pp. 44–45; from the same work by Avicenna.

87. Ibid., pp. 45–52.

88. Gutas, *Avicenna and the Aristotelian Tradition*, pp. 225–34.

89. Hourani, *Reason and Tradition in Islamic Ethics*, chap. 14. See the comments of Gutas, *Avicenna and the Aristotelian Tradition*, and the freer translation in Arberry, *Avicenna on Theology*.

90. Heath, *Allegory and Philosophy in Avicenna*, pp. 89–100. Corbin, *Avicenna and the Visionary Recital*, is a detailed, academically eloquent exposition of these themes in Avicenna.

91. Gutas, *Avicenna and the Aristotelian Tradition*, pp. 304–307.

92. Heath, *Allegory and Philosophy in Avicenna*, pp. 98–100.

93. From *Avicenna on Prayer* (*Risāla fī Māhiyyati 'l-Ṣalat*), as translated in Goodman, *Avicenna*, pp. 167–68. See the translation in Arberry, *Avicenna on Theology*, pp. 50–63; pp. 64–76; "The After-life" (from *Najat*) is also relevant.

94. The *Book of the Prophet Muhammad's Ascent to Heaven* (*Miʿrāj Nāma*), Heath, *Allegory and Philosophy in Avicenna*, p. 150. This work is not universally accepted as Avicenna's, but it surely expresses his point of view.

95. The quotation following the subtitle above is from Isaiah 35:5. It is quoted by Maimonides at the end of the *Guide*. Trans. Pines, p. 638.
   Historical and cultural background: S. W. Baron, *A Social and Religious History of the Jews*, 2d ed., vol. 8, *The High Middle Ages: Philosophy and Science*, New York; Columbia University Press, 1958.

History of philosophy: I. Husik, *A History of Mediaeval Jewish Philosophy*, New York: Macmillan, 1930. C. Sirat, *A History of Jewish Philosophy in the Middle Ages*, Cambridge/Paris: Cambridge University Press/Editions de la Maison des Sciences de l'Homme, 1985.

Special subjects: H. A. Davidson, *Proofs for Eternity, Creation and the Existence of God in Medieval Islamic and Jewish Philosophy*, New York: Oxford University Press, 1987. A. Dhanana, *The Physical Theory of Kalam: Atoms, Space, and Void in Basrian Mu'tazili Cosmology*, Brill: Leiden, 1994. I. Efros, *The Problem of Space in Jewish Medieval Philosophy*, Columbia: Columbia University Press, 1917. J. van Ess, "The Logical Structure of Islamic Theology," in G. E. von Grunebaum, ed., *Logic in Classical Islamic Culture*, Wiesbaden: Otto Harrasowitz, 1970. L. E. Goodman, ed., *Neoplatonism and Jewish Thought*, Albany: State University of New York Press, 1992, M. Kellner, *Dogma in Medieval Jewish Thought*, Oxford: Oxford University Press, 1986; *Maimonides on Human Perfection*, Atlanta: Scholars Press (Brown University), 1990. S. Pines, *Studies in Islamic Atomism*, Jerusalem: Magnes Press, 1997 (trans. of a thesis first published in Berlin, in 1936, as *Beiträge zur islamischen Atomenlehre*). H. A. Wolfson, *The Philosophy of the Kalam*, Cambridge: Harvard University Press, 1976; *Repercussions of the Kalam in Jewish Philosophy*, Cambridge: Harvard University Press, 1979.

Monographs and articles on Maimonides: A. Altmann, *Essays in Jewish Intellectual History*, Hanover: University Press of New England (for Brandeis University Press), 1981. A. Hyman, ed., *Maimonidean Studies*, vol. 1, New York: Yeshiva University Press, 1990. M. Idel, *Maimonide et la mystique juive*, Paris: Éditions du Cerf, 1991. M. Kellner, *Maimonides on Judaism and the Jewish People*, Albany: State University of New York Press, 1991. O. Leaman, *Moses Maimonides*, London: Routledge, 1990. S. Pines, "Maimonides," in P. Edwards, ed., *The Encyclopedia of Philosophy*; and "The Philosophic Sources of *The Guide of the Perplexed*," in Maimonides, *Guide of the Perplexed*. A. Ravitsky, "The Secrets of the Guide to the Perplexed: Between the Thirteenth and Twentieth Centuries," in Twersky, ed., *Studies in Maimonides* (see just below). L. Strauss, "How to Begin to Study *The Guide of the Perplexed*," in Maimonides, ibid. I. Twersky, ed., *Studies in Maimonides*, Cambridge: Harvard University Press.

Translations: There is a notable, three-volume edition of *The Guide of the Perplexed* (*Le Guide des égarés traité de Théologie et de Philosophie par Moise ben Maimon dit Maimonide*) containing a critical version of the Arabic text, a translation into French, and notes by S. Munk, Paris, 1856–1866; reprint Paris: Maisonneuve, 1970. There is also an older translation into English, in three volumes, by M. Friedländer, London 1881–1885; reprinted, without notes, New York: Dover, 1956. A newer, sometimes more accurate translation is that by S. Pines, Maimonides, *The Guide of the Perplexed*, Chicago: Chicago University Press, 1963. L. E. Goodman, trans., *Rambam: Readings in the Philosophy of Moses Maimonides*, New York: Viking Press, 1976, contains extensive, especially readable translations from the *Guide*; each translated section has an introduction and is followed by an analysis.

96. P. M. Holt, A. K. S. Lambton, and B. Lewis, eds., *The Cambridge History of Islam*, vol. 2, Cambridge: Cambridge University Press, pp. 224–29, 424–29.

97. J. Levinger, "Was Maimonides 'Rais al-Yahud' in Egypt?" in I. Twersky, *Studies in Maimonides*, Harvard: Harvard University Press (Harvard University Center for Jewish Studies), 1990.

98. G. L. Blidstein, "Where Do We Stand in the Study of Maimonidean Halakhah?" in I. Twersky, *Studies in Maimonides*. Kellner, *Dogma in Medieval Jewish Thought*, chap. 1.

99. Pines, "Philosophic Sources of *The Guide of the Perplexed*," pp. lix–xl. I have taken the last sentence from Pines, p. lx, note 4, in Pines, because it seems grammatically clearer than the version Pines uses in his main text.

100. Maimonides, *Guide of the Perplexed* 1 (6a). Trans. Pines, p. 10.

101. Ibid., p. 28 (chap. 1.5).

102. Ibid., pp. 30, 69 (chaps. 1.5, 1.32). See S. Klein-Braslavy, "King Solomon and Metaphysical Esotericism According to Maimonides," in Hyman, ed., *Maimonidean Studies*, vol. 1. On the history of the interpretation of Maimonides' esotericism see E. Schweid, "Religion and Philosophy: The Scholarly Debate between Julius Guttmann and Leo Strauss," in Hyman, ed., *Maimonidean Studies*, vol. 1; and A. Ravitsky, "The Secrets of the Guide to the Perplexed: Between the Thirteenth and the Twentieth Centuries," in Twersky, ed., *Studies in Maimonides*.

103. Maimonides, *The Guide of the Perplexed*, trans. Pines, p. 7 (1.4b).

104. Ibid.

105. Al-Farabi makes the preceding points in the *Harmonization of the Opinions of Plato and Aristotle* and the introduction to his *Paraphrase of Plato's Laws*. See Muhsin Mahdi, "Philosophical Literature," In Young, Latham, and Serjeant, eds., *Religion, Learning and Science in the Abbasid Period*, pp. 80–87. The quotation (from elsewhere in Al-Farabi) is from p. 87.

106. Maimonides, *Guide of the Perplexed* 1 (9a), trans. Pines, pp. 15–20. The quoted passages are from p. 15.

107. Ibid. 1.73 (111a). Trans. Pines, p. 203.

108. Ibid., 1.71 (95a, 96a, 98b). Trans. Pines, pp. 178, 179, 183 (1.71).

109. Ibid., 1.71 (98b). Trans. Pines, p. 182.

110. Maimonides, *Guide of the Perplexed* 1.73 (113a–114b). Trans. Pines, pp. 206–209.

111. Trans. Pines, pp. 181.

112. Ibid., introduction to Part 2. Trans. Pines, pp. 235–41.

113. Ibid., 2.15 (33a–33b). Trans. Pines, pp. 291–92.

114. Ibid., 2.22 (49a). Trans. Pines, p. 319.

115. Ibid., 2.18, as cited in Davidson, *Proofs for Eternity*, pp. 73–74, 76ff.

116. Ibid., 2.22 (48b–49a). Trans. Pines, pp. 317–18; p. 318 quoted. See Davidson, *Al-Farabi, Avicenna, and Averroes, on Intellect*, pp. 199–200.

117. As he points out, Maimonides taught Ptolemy's *Almagest* to the student to whom he addressed the whole *Guide of the Perplexed* (see chap. 24 of the *Guide*).

118. Ibid., 2.22 (49a). Trans. Pines p. 318.

119. Ibid., 2.19 (42a–43a). Trans. Pines, pp. 306–308 (2.19). See the summary in Davidson, *Proofs for Eternity, Creation, and the Existence of God*, p. 198; and see the whole of chap. 6, on arguments from the concept of particularization.

120. Trans. Pines, p. 310.

121. Davidson, *Al-Farabi, Avicenna, and Averroes on Intellect*, pp. 197–207. See also A. L. Ivry, "Maimonides and Neoplatonism" and L. E. Goodman, "Maimonidean Naturalism," in Goodman, ed., *Neoplatonism and Jewish Thought*.

122. Maimonides, *Guide of the Perplexed* 2.23 (55b). Trans. Pines, pp. 329–30.

123. Ibid., 2.27 (57a). Trans. Pines, p. 332.

124. Ibid., 71.1 (97b). Trans. Pines, p. 182.

125. Ibid., 2.32 (73b). Trans. Pines, p. 361.

126. Ibid.

127. Ibid., 2.32 (74a) 2.33 (74b), 2.35 (77a). Trans. Pines, pp. 362, 363, 367. The quoted words are as translated in Goodman, *Rambam*, pp. 381, 382.

128. *The Guide of the Perplexed* 3.27 (60b). Trans. Pines, p. 511.

129. Ibid., 3.54 (134a). Trans. Pines, p. 635.

130. See the account of the differences between Al-Farabi and Avicenna, on the one hand, and Maimonides, on the other, in Davidson, *Al-Farabi, Avicenna, and Averroes on Intellect*, pp. 197–206.

131. Maimonides, *Guide of the Perplexed* 2.35, 36, 2.45 (97b) (quoted). Trans. Pines, p. 403.

132. Shem Tov ben Joseph Falaquera, *Moreh ha-Moreh (Guide to the Guide)*, p. 43; as cited and translated in Sirat, *A History of Jewish Philosophy in the Middle Ages*, p. 189.

133. For Ibn Tibbon's interpretation, see Ravitsky, "The Secrets of the Guide to the Perplexed," pp. 185–86.

134. Ravitsky, "The Secrets of the Guide to the Perplexed," pp. 165–68.

135. Goodman, *Rambam*, p. 431. See also Kellner, *Maimonides on Human Perfection*. According to this moderate reading, Maimonides' aim is to teach that "the highest perfection available to Jews is the imitation of God through the observance of the commandments of the Torah" (p. 61).

136. For the Greek literary forms in relation to Arabic ones, see L. Goodman, "The Translation of Greek Materials into Arabic," in Young, Latham, and Serjeant, eds., *Religion, Learning and Science in the Abbasid Period*.

137. Leaman, *Moses Maimonides*, p. ix.

138. Maimonides, *Guide of the Perplexed* 3.18.

139. Ibid., 3.54 (134a, 135b). Trans. Pines, pp. 635, 638.

140. Ibid., 3.54 (135a). Trans. Pines, p. 637.

141. Ibid., 3.27 (61a). Trans. Pines, p. 511.

142. Mahdi, "Philosophical Literature," p. 86.

143. Maimonides, *Guide of the Perplexed* 1.35 (42a). Trans. Pines, p. 80.

144. Pines, "Limitations," as quoted in Sirat, *A History of Jewish Philosophy in the Middle Ages*, p. 202.

145. According to two summaries: Ravitsky, "The Secrets of the Guide to the Perplexed," pp. 186–87; and Sirat, *A History of Jewish Philosophy in the Middle Ages*, pp. 201–203; both citing S. Pines, "The Limits of Human Knowledge according to al-Farabi, Ibn Bajja and Maimonides," in I. Twersky, ed., *Studies in Medieval Jewish History and Literature*, vol. 1, Cambridge: Harvard University Press, pp. 82–109.

146. Translator's introduction to Maimonides, *Guide of the Perplexed*, pp. lxxviii–xcii.

147. L. Strauss, "How to Begin to Study *The Guide of the Perplexed*," in Pines, trans., *The Guide of the Perplexed*, pp. xix (where references to *The Guide* are given), xvii. See also Ravitsky, "The Secrets of the Guide to the Perplexed," p. 178.

148. Strauss, "How to Begin to Study the *Guide of the Perplexed*," p. li.

149. Ibid., p. lvi.

150. K. H. Green, *Jew and Philosopher: The Return to Maimonides in the Jewish Thought of Leo Strauss*, Albany: State University of New York Press, 1993, pp. 135–36. See also pp. 114–15.

151. The quotation that accompanies the subtitle above is from Thomas Aquinas, *Summa Theologiae* 1a.1.1. Trans. Gilby (Blackfriars' ed.), vol. 1, p. 9.
   Intellectual and specifically philosophical background: C. E. Butterworth and B. A. Kessel, eds., *The Introduction of Arabic Philosophy into Europe*, Leiden, Brill, 1994. R. C. Dales, *The Intellectual Life of Western Europe in the Middle Ages*,

rev. ed., Leiden: Brill, 1992. E. Gilson, *Reason and Revelation in the Middle Ages*, New York: Scribner's, 1952. G. Leff, *Paris and Oxford Universities in the Thirteenth and Fourteenth Centuries*, New York: Wiley, 1968. F. van Steenberghen, *Aristotle in the West*, Louvain: Nuwelaerts, 1955; *Thomas Aquinas and Radical Aristotelianism*, Washington, D.C.: Catholic University of America Press, 1980.

Histories of philosophy: E. Gilson, *History of Christian Philosophy in the Middle Ages*, New York: Random House, 1955. M. Haren, *Medieval Thought: The Western Intellectual Tradition from Antiquity to the Thirteenth Century*, London: Macmillan, 1985 (brief and lucid). N. Kretzmann, A. Kenny, and J. Pinborg, eds., *The Cambridge History of Later Medieval Philosophy*, Cambridge: Cambridge University Press, 1982 (topical, with more emphasis than usual on logic). G. Verbeke, *The Presence of Stoicism in Medieval Thought*, 1983.

Particular philosophical issues: E. Booth, *Aristotelian Aporetic Ontology in Islamic and Christian Thinkers*, Cambridge: Cambridge University Press, 1983. R. C. Dales, *Medieval Discussions of the Eternity of the World*, Leiden: Brill, 1990. H. A. Davidson, *Al-Farabi, Avicenna, and Averroes on Intellect*, New York: Oxford University Press, 1992; *Proofs for Eternity, Creation and the Existence of God in Medieval Islamic and Jewish Philosophy*, Oxford: Oxford University Press, 1987. M. G. Henninger, *Relations: Medieval Theories 1250–1325*, Oxford: Oxford University Press, 1989. A. Kenny, *The Five Ways*, London: Routledge & Kegan Paul, 1969; *The God of the Philosophers*, Oxford: Oxford University Press, 1979.

Summaries of Aquinas' philosophy: B. Davies, *The Thought of Thomas Aquinas*, Oxford: Oxford University Press, 1992. B. E. Gilson, *The Christian Philosophy of St. Thomas Aquinas*, New York: Random House, 1956. E. Weber, "Thomas d'Aquin," in J.-F. Mattéi, ed., *Les oeuvres philosophiques*, Paris: Presses Universitaires de France, vol. 1, 1992, pp. 865–69 (summaries of Aquinas' major works).

Articles: J. A. Aertsen, "Aquinas' Philosophy in Its Historical Setting," in Kretzmann and Stump, *The Cambridge Companion to Aquinas* (see just below). D. B. Burrell, "Aquinas and Islamic and Jewish Thinkers," in Kretzmann and Stump (see below). C. E. Butterworth and B. A. Kessel, eds., *The Introduction of Arabic Philosophy into Europe*, Leiden: Brill, 1994. B. G. Dodd, "Aristoteles Latinus," in Kretzmann, Kenny, and Pinborg, eds., *The Cambridge History of Later Medieval Philosophy* (see above). E. Grant, "The Effect of the Condemnation of 1277," in Kretzmann, Kenny, and Pinborg. N. Kretzmann and E. Stump, eds., *The Cambridge Companion to Aquinas*, Cambridge: Cambridge University Press, 1993. N. Kretzmann, "Philosophy of Mind," In Kretzmann and Stump. C. H. Lohr, "The Medieval Interpretation of Aristotle," In Kretzmann, Kenny, and Pinborg. J. Owens, "Aristotle and Aquinas," in Kretzmann and Stump. E. P. Mahoney, "Sense, Intellect, and Imagination in Albert, Thomas, and Siger," in Kretzmann, Kenny, and Pinborg.

Anthologies of translations: Thomas Aquinas, *Basic Writings*, 2 vols., ed. A. Pegis, New York: Random House, 1945 (long excerpts from the *Summa Theologica* (as translated by Father Lawrence Shapcote and corrected) supplemented with one long excerpt from the *Summa Contra Gentiles*. *Philosophical Texts*, ed. T. Gilby, London: Oxford University Press, 1951. *Selected Political Writings, ed. A. P. D'Entrèves, Oxford: Blackwell, 1970. Theological Texts*, ed. T. Gilby, London: Oxford University Press, 1955.

Full translations: The *Summa Theologiae* has two full translations, one of which, known as the English Dominican translation and named *The Summa Theologica* (22 vols., London, 1912–1936), is actually by L. Shapcote. This is the translation used in the anthology edited by Pegis (see above). The other, the Blackfriars edition, is in sixty-one volumes, London: Blackfriars in conjunction with Eyre & Spottiswoode, 1964–80. Each volume, with Latin text facing the English translation, has a different translator, who supplies extensive notes and explanatory appendices. I have used the translation of *On the Truth of the Catholic Faith: Summa Contra Gentiles*, the philosophically more important work, by A. C. Pegis, J. F. Anderson, V. J. Bourke, and C. J. O'Neill, 6 vols., Garden City: Doubleday, 1955–57. For other translated works see the bibliography in Haren, *Medieval Thought* (above).

152. Quoted in Davies, *The Thought of Thomas Aquinas*, p. 9. Davies cites A. Ferrua, ed., *Thomas Aquinatis vitae fontes praecipuae*, Alba, 1968, pp. 318ff.

153. Lohr, "The Medieval Interpretation of Aristotle," pp. 87–88.

154. Davies, *The Thought of Thomas Aquinas*, p. 7.

155. For an explanatory catalogue of Aquinas' works see Gilson, *The Christian Philosophy of St. Thomas Aquinas*, pp. 381–439.

156. Aquinas, *On the Truth of the Catholic Faith: Summa Contra Gentiles* 1.2.3. Trans. Pegis, vol. 1, p. 61.

157. *Summa Theologiae* 1a.1.8.2. Trans. Gilby, Blackfriars ed., vol. 1, p. 31.

158. E. Panofsky, *Gothic Architecture and Scholasticism*, New York: Meridian Books, 1957, pp. 44, 46–47.

159. *Summa Theologiae* 1a.1.1. Trans. Gilby, Blackfriars ed., vol. 1, pp. 5–9.

160. *Summa Theologiae* 1a.2.1. Trans. T. McDermott, Blackfriars ed., vol. 2, pp. 5–9.

161. For a philosopher's careful, clear exposition, see Kenny, *The Five Ways*. Not surprisingly, Kenny thinks that the five ways fail because they depend too heavily on medieval cosmology. The text I follow for the *Summa Theologiae* is that of vol. 2 of the Blackfriars edition, translated by T. McDermott, pp. 13–18. The corresponding text in *The Basic Writings of Saint Thomas Aquinas*, ed. by Pegis, is in vol. 1, pp. 21–24.

162. Albertus Magnus refers to Maimonides in *Summae Theologiae* 2, tr. 1, q. 4, a.5, partic. 3. I copy this reference from R. Sorabji, *Time, Creation and the Continuum*, London: Duckworth, 1983, p. 197, note 32.

163. The relation between Muslim, Jewish, and Christian proofs and discussed with full documentation in Davidson, *Proofs for Eternity, Creation and the Existence of God in Medieval Islamic and Jewish Philosophy*, New York: Oxford University Press, 1987. The text in Aquinas' *Summa Theologiae* (1a.46) relevant to

creation and eternity is translated by T. Gilby in vol. 8 of the Blackfriars translation. Appendix 2, pp. 152–57, contains a translation of Aquinas' opuscule, "On the Eternity of the World." Dales, *Medieval Discussions of the Eternity of the World* is a monograph on the subject with long translated excerpts from the opuscule.

164. From Siger of Brabant, *Quaestiones in Metaphysicam* 3.15, as quoted in Lohr, "The Medieval Interpretation of Aristotle," p. 90.

165. On Averroes' doctrine of the intellect, see Davidson, *Al-Farabi, Avicenna, and Averroes on Intellect*, chaps. 6–8.

166. On Siger see E. P. Mahoney, "Sense, Intellect, and Imagination in Albert, Thomas, and Siger," in Kretzman, Kenny, and Pinborg, eds, *The Cambridge History of Medieval Philosophy*, chap. 30. See also Steenberghen, *Thomas Aquinas and Radical Aristotelianism*, pp. 29–74.

167. Mahoney, "Sense, Intellect, and Imagination in Albert, Thomas, and Siger" (see previous note), pp. 614–15.

168. *Summa Theologiae* 1a.75–89. Apart from the general books on Aquinas, see Kretzmann, "Philosophy of Mind," and Mahoney, "Sense, Intellect, and Imagination in Albert, Thomas, and Siger."

169. *Summa Theologiae* 1a.85.1, ad 1. Trans. Pegis, *Basic Writings of Saint Thomas Aquinas*, vol. 1, p. 814.

170. *Summa Theologiae* 1a.85.1. Kretzmann, "Philosophy of Mind," pp. 138–45.

171. *Summa Theologiae* 1a.75.2–4. Trans. Suttor, Blackfriars ed., vol. 11, pp. 11–21.

172. Ibid., 1a.75.6. Trans. Suttor, Blackfriars ed., vol. 11, pp. 27–29.

173. Ibid., 1a.118.2–3.

174. Ibid., 1a.76.6, 7. Trans. Suttor, Blackfriars ed., vol. 11, pp. 77, 81. The reference to Aristotle is to *De Anima* 412b6–9.

175. Ibid., 1a.76.8. Trans. Suttor, Blackfriars ed., vol. 11, pp. 115, 117. On the exception of the passive intellect, see E. P. Mahoney, "Sense, Intellect, and Imagination" (note 149 above), p. 607.

176. *Summa Theologiae* 1a.89.1. As trans. in Pegis, ed., *Basic Writings of Saint Thomas Aquinas*, vol. 1, pp. 851–54 (854 quoted).

177. Dales, *Medieval Discussions of the Eternity of the World*, pp. 38–49, 75–77.

178. On the philosophical problem of the eternity of the world as a whole see Dales, *Medieval Discussions of the Eternity of the World*; and Davidson, *Proofs for Eternity, Creation and the Existence of God in Medieval Islamic and Jewish Philosophy*.

For various arguments used at different times by Aquinas, see Dales (just above), pp. 97–108, 116–17, 132–40; and Van Steenberghen, *Thomas Aquinas and Radical Aristotelianism*, pp. 1–27.

179. Aquinas, *On the Eternity of the World* 1. Trans. by Gilby in the *Summa Theologiae*, Blackfriars ed., vol. 8, p. 153. See also Burrell, "Aquinas and Islamic and Jewish Thinkers," pp. 72–73.

180. Aquinas, *On the Eternity of the World* 4. Trans. by Gilby in the *Summa Theologiae*, Blackfriars ed., vol. 8, p. 153.

181. Ibid., 6, 8, 11. Trans. pp. 154, 155.

182. Dales, *Medieval Discussions of the Eternity of the World*, p. 136. The same text, *On the Eternity of the World* 14, is translated by Gilby in the *Summa Theologiae*, Blackfriars ed., vol. 8, p. 156.

183. Aquinas, *On the Eternity of the World* 19, 20. Trans. Gilby, in the *Summa Theologiae*, Blackfriars ed., vol. 8, p. 157.

184. Lohr, "The Medieval Interpretation of Aristotle" (see preceding note), p. 88. The proposition is the 154th. The 40th, that the intellectual virtues are the highest, make the same social point. On the condemnation of 1277 and its aftermath, see Dale, *Medieval Discussions of the Eternity of the World*, chaps. 9, 10; and Van Steenberghen, *Aristotle in the West*, chap. 9.

185. On Aquinas' many references to the Stoics see Verbeke, *The Presence of Stoicism in Medieval Thought*, pp. 15–16, 39–40, 42, 63–64, 69–70, 91–94). On his unity in variety see Booth, *Aristotelian Aporetic Ontology in Islamic and Christian Thinkers*, pp. 205–206.

186. Van Steenberghen, *Aristotle in the West*, pp. 183–84.

187. The words of the eighth-century physician and translator Hunayn ibn-Ishaq, in Gutas, *Avicenna and the Aristotelian Tradition*, p. 206. For the influence of Neoplatonism and Aristotelianism on Jewish philosophy, see Sirat, *A History of Jewish Philosophy in the Middle Ages*, chaps. 3, 5; and for their influence on Christian philosophy, see Haren, *Medieval Thought*, chap. 1.

188. For Avicenna, see the summary in Gutas, op. cit., pp. 260–61.

189. On the philosopher's reaction see, e.g., Davidson, *Proofs for Eternity, Creation and the Existence of God in Medieval Islamic and Jewish Philosophy*, pp. 203–209 and elsewhere.

190. Bello, *The Medieval Islamic Controversy between Philosophy and Orthodoxy*, p. 10.

191. Ibid., and Averroes, *On the Harmony of Religion and Philosophy*. trans. Hourani, p. 5.

192. Averroes, *On the Harmony of Religion and Philosophy*, p. 53 (of trans.). See also note 86.

193. Ibid., p. 47 (of trans.).

194. Ibid., p. 48.

195. Ibid., p. 50.

196. Ibid., p. 51.

197. Ibid., p. 61.

198. Ibid., p. 70.

199. Munro, *Images of Human Nature*, pp. 12–16, 113, 129–31.

200. Averroes, *Risāla al-Aḍḥīwa*; translate Rahman, *Prophecy in Islam*, p. 42. For the qualifications, see p. 77, note 39.

201. Al-Farabi, *Siyāsāt*. Trans. Rahman, *Prophecy in Islam*, p. 40.

202. Kellner, *Maimonides on Judaism and the Jewish People*, pp. 26–27.

203. Ibid., p. 30.

204. Ibid., pp. 34–40.

205. J. Sinha, Indian Psychology, vol. 1, Calcutta: Sinha Publishing House, 1958, pp. 336–37.

206. Ibid., p. 342.

207. Ch'in Ch'un, *Neo-Confucian Terms Explained*, p. 40.

208. For preceding, Greek and Roman theories of veridical dreams, see Altmann, "Maimonides and Aquinas: Natural or Divine Prophecy," pp. 77–79.

209. Al-Farabi distinguishes two levels of prophecy, only the lower being possible to men whose intellect is not yet perfected. Avicenna's theory allows for the possibility—as earlier described—of instantaneous intuitive scientific knowledge. (See Davidson, *Al-Farabi, Avicenna, and Averroes on Intellect*, pp. 59–61 [61 quoted], 116–23 [on Avicenna]. For the varied reactions of more conservative or literalist thinkers see Rahman, *Prophecy in Islam*, chap. 3.)

210. Altmann, "Maimonides and Aquinas: Natural or Divine Prophecy," pp. 80–82; Leaman, *Moses Maimonides*, chap. 3. See Maimonides, *The Guide of the Perplexed* 2.32, 35, 36.

211. Altmann, "Maimonides and Aquinas: Natural or Divine Prophecy," pp. 82–87.

Chapter 10. Logic-Sensitized, Methodological Metaphysics

1. See *Descartes' Conversation with Burman*, trans. Cottingham, sections 77–79, pp. 46–49.

2. W. Kneale and M. Kneale, *The Development of Logic*, London: Oxford University Press, 1962, pp. 320–45.

3. **History of philosophy or logic**: B. K. Matilal *Nyāya-Vaiśeṣika*, vol. 6.2 of *A History of Indian Literature*, ed. J. Gonda, Wiesbaden: Harrassowitz, 1977. K. Potter, ed., *Indian Metaphysics and Epistemology: The Tradition of Nyāya-Vaiśeṣika up to Gaṅgeśa*, vol. 2 of *Encyclopedia of Indian Philosophies*, Delhi: Banarsidass, 1977. K. Potter and S. Bhattacharyya, eds., *Indian Philosophical Analysis: Nyāya-Vaiśeṣika from Gaṅgeśa to Raghunātha Śiromaṇi*, vol. 6 of *Encyclopedia of Indian Philosophies*, Delhi: Banarsidass, 1993. J. Sinha, *A History of Indian Philosophy*, vol. 1, Calcutta: Sinha Publishing House, 1956. D. N. Shastri, *Critique of Indian Realism: A Study of the Conflict between the Nyāya-Vaiśeṣika School & the Buddhist Dignaga School*, Agra: Agra University, 1964. S. C. Vidyabhusana, *A History of Indian Logic*, reprint, Delhi: Banarsidass, 1971 [1921] (still helpful but, because old, to be used with caution).

Studies: S. Bagchi, *Inductive Reasoning: A Study of Tarka and Its Role in Indian Logic*, Calcutta: Sinha, 1953; S. Chatterjee, *The Nyāya Theory of Knowledge*, Calcutta: The University of Calcutta, 1950. C. Goekoop, *The Logic of Invariable Concomitance in the Tattvacintāmaṇi*, Dordrecht: Reidel, 1967 (consistently translates Navya-Nyāya logic into symbolic logic). D. H. Ingalls, *Materials for the Study of Navya-nyāya Logic*, Cambridge: Harvard University Press, 1951 (contains extensive translated excerpts). P. K. Mandal, "Some Problems of Perception in Navya-Nyāya," *Journal of Indian Philosophy* 15.2 (June 1987). B. K. Matilal, *Epistemology, Logic, and Grammar in Indian Philosophical Analysis*, The Hague: Mouton, 1971; *Logic, Language and Reality*, Delhi: Banarsidass, 1985; *The Navya-nyāya Doctrine of Negation*, Harvard: Harvard University Press, 1968; *Perception: An Essay on Classical Indian Theories of Knowledge*, Oxford: Oxford University Press, 1986. F. Staal, *Universals*, Chicago: University of Chicago Press, 1988. S. C. Vidyabhusana, *A History of Indian Logic*, reprinted Delhi: Banarsidass, 1971 [1921].

Extended summaries: See Potter and Bhattacharyya (above) for a long paraphrase (227 pages), and Vidyabhusana (above) for a briefer paraphrase, of forty-six pages. It is notable that despite the some seventy years separating the book of Potter and Bhattacharyya from that of Vidyabhusana, the former feel it often necessary to complete their summaries by use of the latter's.

Translations with commentary: V. N. Jha, *The Logic of the Intermediate Causal Link*, Delhi: Sri Satguru Publications, 1986. J. Mohanty, *Gaṅgeśa's Theory of Truth*, rev. ed., Delhi: Banarsidass, 1989. S. H. Phillips, "Gaṅgeśa on Characterizing Veridical Awareness," *Journal of Indian Philosophy*, June 1993. T. Wada, *Invariable Concomitance in Navya-Nyāya*, Delhi: Sri Satguru Publications (Indian Books Centre), 1990. J. Vattanky, *Gaṅgeśa's Philosophy of God*, Adyar, Madras: The Adyar Library and Research Centre, 1984.

Translations of later Navya-Nyāya works: Besides Ingalls, *Materials for the Study of Navya-Nyāya Logic,* and Matilal, *The Navya-Nyāya Doctrine of Negation,* both noted above, see: S. Bhattacharyya, *Gadādhara's Theory of Objectivity*, 2 vols., New Delhi/Delhi: Indian Council of Philosophical Research/Banarsidass, 1990. K. H. Potter, *The Padārthatattvanirūpaṇam*, Cambridge: Harvard-Yenching Institute,

1957. T. Wada, "Gaṅgeśa and Mathurānātha on Siṃhavyāgralakṣaṇa of Vyāpti," *Journal of Indian Philosophy* 23.3 (September 1995).

4. D. Bhattacharya, *History of Navya-Nyāya in Mithila*, Darbhanga: Mithila Institute, 1958, p. 99. I owe this reference to my friend, Karin Preisendanz.

5. *Manikara*. See Matilal, *Nyāya-Vaiśeṣika*, p. 105.

6. The estimate of Vidyabhusana, *History of Indian Logic*, p. 454. Vidyabhusana is a careful scholar but understandably does not say exactly how he arrived at this estimate. Probably it was by adding up the pages of the works, whether printed or in manuscript, that he lists as commentaries.

7. See the partial annotated translation in Phillips, "Gaṅgeśa on Characterizing Veridical Awareness." The corresponding paraphrase in Potter and Bhattacharyya, eds., *Nyāya-Vaiśeṣika from Gaṅgeśa to Raghunātha Śiromaṇi*, pp. 98–100, is far less detailed and far simpler.

8. Matilal, *Nyāya-Vaiśeṣika*, p. 104, quoting D. C. Bhattacharya.

9. For Gangesha's defense of the atomicity of the self, see Potter and Bhattacharyya, eds., *Nyāya-Vaiśeṣika from Gaṅgeśa...*, pp. 148–50.

10. *Nyāya-sūtra with Vātsyāyana's Commentary*, trans. M. Gangopadhyaya, Calcutta: Indian Studies, 1982, pp. 176, 178 (Vātsyāyana, *Nyāyabhāṣya* 3.1.7, 12).

11. Sinha, *History of Indian Philosophy*, vol. 1, pp. 628–41. Udayana's arguments, interspersed with those of others, are found on pp. 631–41. The view that the self acquires consciousness by means of its conjunction with the body and the internal organ or cause is an old one, already found in Vatsyayana. Sinha, p. 641, gives a reference to Varadaraja (1150 C.E.), whose *Tārkikarakṣā* is a manual of philosophy that elaborates on Udayana's views.

12. Mandal, "Some Problems of Perception in Navya-Nyāya," p. 129; from Gangesha, *Tattvacintāmaṇi* (Delhi: Banarsidass, 1974), p. 809.

13. For a relatively detailed description of the views of the various Indian philosophical schools on indeterminate and determinate awareness, see J. Sinha, *Indian Psychology*, vol. 1, Calcutta: Sinha Publishing House, 1958; and Chatterjee, *The Nyāya Theory of Knowledge*, chap. 9. For the Nyaya view, see also Matilal, *Perception*, pp. 342–53. Matilal's discussion of *jñāna* in *The Navya-nyāya Doctrine of Negation*, chap. 2, is philosophically the most careful of which I know. For Gangesha's particular view, see Potter and Bhattacharyya, eds., *Nyāya-Vaiśeṣika from Gaṅgeśa...*, pp. 151–64; and Vidyabhusana, *History of Indian Logic*, pp. 418–20 (brief and clear).

14. Potter and Bhattacharyya, eds., pp. 150–55 (the quoted passage is from p. 152). See Matilal, *Perception*, pp. 160–67.

15. Potter and Bhattacharyya, eds., *Nyāya-Vaiśeṣika from Gaṅgeśa...*, pp. 170–71.

16. See Potter, ed., *The Tradition of Nyāya-Vaiśeṣika up to Gaṅgeśa*, pp. 171–85; Potter and Bhattacharyya, eds., *Nyāya-Vaiśeṣika from Gaṅgeśa . . .*, 69–81; Vidyabhusana, *History of Indian Logic*, pp. 420–25; Sinha, *History of Indian Philosophy*, vol. 1, pp. 700–10; and Wada, *Invariable Concomitance in Navya-Nyāya*.

17. Goekoop, *The Logic of Invariable Concomitance in the Tattvacintāmaṇi.* p. 111. Goekoop translates this verbal form into symbolic logic (p. 116). Matilal's translation of Gangesha's "conclusive definition" can be found on p. 176 of Potter and Bhattacharyya, eds., *Nyāya-Vaiśeṣika from Gaṅgeśa . . .*

18. Potter and Bhattacharyya, eds, *Nyāya-Vaiśeṣika from Gaṅgeśa . . .*, pp. 182–83, 191–92. Sinha, *History of Indian Philosophy*, vol. 1, p. 711.

19. See the account, with supporting quotations from Gangesha's *Tattvacintāmaṇī*, in Bagchi, *Inductive Reasoning*, pp. 32–37. See also Matilal, *Perception*, pp. 164–67, 178.

20. Bagchi, *Inductive Reasoning*, pp. 38–44. See also Matilal, *Perception*, pp. 167–70.

21. Potter, and Bhattacharyya, eds., *Nyāya-Vaiśeṣika from Gaṅgeśa . . .*, pp. 117–18. Sinha, *History of Indian Philosophy*, pp. 724–25. Sinha gives as reference Gangesha, *Tattvacintāmaṇī* (Bibliotheca Indica, Calcutta), pp. 253–55, 256, 271, 279–80.

22. Bagchi, *Inductive Reasoning*, pp. 48–49.

23. Potter and Bhattacharyya, eds, *Nyāya-Vaiśeṣika from Gaṅgeśa . . .*, p. 183. See also, Bagchi, *Inductive Reasoning*, pp. 46–51; Matilal, *Perception*, pp. 172–79; Sinha, *History of Indian Philosophy*, vol. 1, pp. 710–13, 724–25.

24. For his proofs for God's existence, see Potter and Bhattacharyya, *Nyāya-Vaiśeṣika from Gaṅgeśa . . .*, pp. 211–26; Sinha, *History of Indian Philosophy*, vol. 1, pp. 735–62; and Vattanky, *Gaṅgeśa's Philosophy of God*. Vattanky contains an analysis, translation, and commentary.

25. Vattanky, *Gaṅgeśa's Philosophy of God*, p. 169.

26. Vattanky, *Gaṅgeśa's Philosophy of God*, pp. 33–38. My text refers, among the rest, to Dharmakirti's verses numbered 13–15, 17–18, 25, and 27, on pages 34–35.

27. For the (here incomplete) sequence of arguments on God's bodilessness and singleness, see the summary in Potter and Bhattacharyya, eds, *Nyāya-Vaiśeṣika from Gaṅgeśa . . .*, pp. 221–24 (brief but helpful); Sinha, *History of Indian Philosophy*, vol. 1, pp. 756–62 (a longer, usually lucid summary); and Vattanky, *Gaṅgeśa's Philosophy of God* (translation (pp. 200–238) and commentary (pp. 327–404). The language of the translation itself is compressed and sometimes forbiddingly technical. The relevant part of the summary in Potter and Bhattacharyya is only a few pages long, so I have not given detailed references to it.

28. Vattanky, *Gaṅgeśa's Philosophy of God*, pp. 201–202, 324–26.

29. Ibid., pp. 234, 394–95. With the help of Vattanky's commentary and Potter and Bhattacharyya's summary, I have expanded the language of the original, which has a formulaic brevity. The give and take between objector and counterobjector and the original sequence of arguments have been retained.

30. Ibid., pp. 234–35, 395.

31. Ibid., pp. 235, 395.

32. Ibid., pp. 235, 396.

33. Ibid., pp. 235, 396.

34. Ibid.

35. Ibid., pp. 235, 397.

36. Ibid., pp. 236, 397–99.

37. Ibid. pp. 237, 399.

38. Ibid., pp. 237, 399–400.

39. **Biography**: S. Gaukroger, *Descartes: An Intellectual Biography*, Oxford: Oxford University Press, 1995 (clear, careful, thoughtful). B.-A. Scharfstein, *The Philosophers*, pp. 125–42. J. R. Vrooman, *René Descartes*, New York: Putnams, 1970.

History of philosophy: G. H. R. Parkinson, ed., *The Renaissance and Seventeenth-century Rationalism*, London: Routledge, 1993. R. A. Watson, *The Downfall of Cartesianism, 1673–1712*, The Hague: Nijhoff, 1966. On the history of the term *idea* see K. Neumann, *idee*, in J. Ritter and K. Gründer, eds, *Historisches Wörterbuch der Philosophie*, Schwabe: Basel/Stuttgart, vol. 4, 1976, esp. pp. 103–105.

Studies: L. J. Beck, *The Metaphysics of Descartes: A Study of the Meditations*, London: Oxford, 1965. J. Cottingham, "Descartes: Metaphysics and the Philosophy of Mind," in Parkinson, ed., *The Renaissance and Seventeenth-Century Rationalism*. S. Gaukroger, Descartes: Metaphysics and the Philosophy of Mind," in Parkinson, ed., *The Renaissance and Seventeenth Century Rationalism*. H. Gouhier, *La pensée métaphysique de Descartes* Paris: Vrin, 1971; *La pensée religieuse de Descartes*, Paris: Vrin, 1924; *Les premiéres pensées de Descartes*, Paris: Vrin,, 1958. R. Lefèvre, *La bataille du "cogito,"* Paris: Presses Universitaires de France, 1960; *Le criticisme de Descartes*, Paris: Presses Universitaires de France, 2958. G. Rodis-Lewis, *L'anthropologie cartésienne*, Paris: Presses Universitaires de Paris, 1990; *L'oeuvre de Descartes*, 2 vols., Paris: Vrin, 1971. N. K. Smith, *New Studies in the Philosophy of Descartes*, New York: St. Martin's Press, 1952.

Translations: *Descartes' Conversation with Burman*, trans. J. Cottingham, Oxford: Oxford University Press, 1976. *The Philosophical Works of Descartes*, 3 vols. Cambridge: Cambridge University Press, 1984, 1985, 1991, trans. J. Cottingham, R. Stoothoss, D. Murdoch; vol. 4, with A. Kenny as well. *Treatise of Man*, trans.

T. S. Hall, Cambridge: Harvard University Press, 1972. *The World*, trans. M. S. Mahoney: Abaris Books, 1979.

40. *Treatise on Man* 131, in Cottingham, Stoothoff, and Murdoch, *Philosophical Writings of Descartes*, vol. 1, p. 100.

41. Ibid., p. 101.

42. *Principles of Philosophy* 4.199–202, ibid., pp. 285–88.

43. *Discourse on Method*, part 2, in Cottingham, Stoothoff, and Murdoch, trans., *Philosophical Writings of Descartes*, vol. 1, p. 119.

44. Ibid., p. 120.

45. Letter of February 22, 1638, to Antoine Vattier. See also Gaukroger, "Descartes: Methodology," p. 187.

46. Cottingham, Stoothoff, and Murdoch, *Philosophical Writings of Descartes*, vol. 2, p. 56.

47. From the second set of replies, Cottingham, Stoothoff, and Murdoch, *Philosophical Writings of Descartes*, vol. 2, p. 100.

48. "Conversation with Burman," section 44. Trans. Cottingham, p. 28.

49. Ibid., section 48. Trans. Cottingham, pp. 30–31.

50. Letter to Mersenne, May 27, 1630. *The Philosophical Writings of Descartes*, ed. Cottingham et al., vol. 3, p. 25. For Descartes's approval of the idea of a rational, universal language see p. 13 (letter to Mersenne, Dec. 18, 1629).

51. *Principles of Philosophy*, part 1, principle 21. *The Philosophical Writings of Descartes*, vol. 1, p. 200. See Cottingham, "Descartes: Metaphysics and the Philosophy of Mind," pp. 212–14.

52. On Descartes's religion, see Gouhier, *La pensée religieuse de Descartes*.

53. Pascal, *Pensées, pensée* 84 (in L. Lafuma's numbering; in J. Brunschvicg's, 79). Trans. A. J. Kreilsheimer, *Pascal, Pensées*, Harmondsworth: Penguin Books, 1966, p. 52. For the influence of Descartes on Newton, see J. Herivel, *The Background to Newton's* Principia, Cambridge: Cambridge University Press, pp. 35, 42–43ff., 50–53, 231.

54. Hegel, *Introduction to the Lectures on the History of Philosophy*, sect. F; trans. T. M. Knox and A. V. Miller, Oxford: Oxford University Press, 1985, p. 183.

55. *Thus Spoke Zarathustra*, Part I, sect. 4, "On the Despisers of the Body." *The Portable Nietzsche*, trans. W. Kaufmann, New York: Viking Press, 1954, p. 146.

56. Nietzsche, *The Will to Power*, sect. 436. Trans. W. Kaufmann, New York: Random House, 1968, p. 240.

57. Edmund Husserl, *Cartesian Meditations*, trans. D. Cairns, the Hague: Nijhoff, 1960, p. 6.

58. K. Jaspers, *Descartes und die Philosophie*, Berlin: de Gruyter, 2d ed., 1947.

59. Lefèvre, *La bataille du cogito*, pp. 229–30, and *Le criticisme de Descartes*, pp. 229–30.

60. A. R. Damasio, *Descartes' Error: Emotion, Reason and the Human Brain*, New York: Grosset/Putnam, 1994, p. 250.

61. Ibid., p. 251.

62. **Biography**: R. Ariew, "G. E. Leibniz, Life and Works," in Jolley, ed., *The Cambridge Companion to Leibniz* (see just below). Cambridge: Cambridge University Press, 1995. G. E. Guhrauer, *Gottfried Wilhelm Freiherr von Leibniz*, 2 vols., reprint Hildesheim: Olms, 1966. B.-A. Scharfstein, *The Philosophers*, pp. 165–74.

History of philosophy: N. Jolley, ed., *The Cambridge Companion to Leibniz*, Cambridge: Cambridge University Press, 1995, chaps. 3 (S. Brown, "The Seventeenth-Century Intellectual Background), 13 (C. Wilson, "The Reception of Leibniz in the Eighteenth Century").

Studies: Y. Belaval, *Leibniz: Initiation à sa philosophie*, Paris: Vrin, 1956. D. Blumenfeld, "Leibniz's Ontological and Cosmological Arguments, in Jolly, ed., *Leibniz*. N. D. Garber, "Leibniz: Physics and Philosophy," in Jolley, ed., *Leibniz*. Jolley, "Leibniz: Truth, Knowledge and Metaphysics," in G. H. R. Parkinson, ed., *The Renaissance and Seventeenth-Century Rationalism*, London: Routledge, 1993. G. Martin, *Leibniz: Logic as Metaphysics*, Manchester: Manchester University Press, 1964. C. Mercer and R. C. Sleigh, Jr., "Metaphysics: The Early Period to the *Discourse on Metaphysics*," in Jolley, ed., *Leibniz*. G. H. R. Parkinson, *Leibniz on Human Freedom*, Wiesbaden: Franz Steiner Verlag, 1970; *Logic and Reality in Leibniz's Metaphysics*, Oxford: Oxford University Press, 1966. G. H. R. Parkinson, "Philosophy and Logic," in Jolley, ed., *Leibniz*. D. Rutherford, "Metaphysics: The Late Period"; "Philosophy and Language in Leibniz"; in Jolley, ed., *Leibniz*. R. C. Sleigh, *Leibniz and Arnauld: A Commentary on Their Correspondence*, New Haven: Yale University Press, 1990. C. Wilson, *Leibniz's Metaphysics*, Manchester; Manchester University Press, 1989.

Relations with Descartes and Spinoza: Y. Belaval, *Leibniz critique de Descartes*, Paris: Gallimard, 1960. G. Friedmann, *Leibniz et Spinoza*, 3d ed., Paris: Gallimard, 1974.

Interest in Chinese thought: J. Ching and W. Oxtoby, *Discovering China: European Interpretations in the Enlightenment*, Rochester: University of Rochester Press, 1992. D. E. Mungello, *Curious Land: Jesuit Accommodation and the Origins of Sinology*, Honolulu: University of Hawaii Press, 1989; *Leibniz and Confucianism: The Search for Accord*, Honolulu: University of Hawaii Press, 1977. J. Needham, *Science and Civilisation in China*, vol. 2, Cambridge: Cambridge University Press, 1956.

Translations: *Descartes' Conversation with Burman*, trans. J. Cottingham, Oxford: Oxford University Press, 1976. *The Discourse on Metaphysics*, trans. P. G. Lucas and L. Grint, corrected ed., Manchester: Manchester University Press, 1961. *Discourse on the Natural Theology of the Chinese*, trans. H. Rosemont, Jr., and D. J. Cook, Honolulu: University of Hawaii Press, 1977. *The Leibniz-Arnauld Correspondence*, trans. H. T. Mason, Manchester: Manchester University Press, 1967. The

Leibniz-Clarke Correspondence, trans. H. T. Mason, Manchester: Manchester University Press, 1956. *Logical Papers*, trans. G. H. R. Parkinson, Oxford: Oxford University Press, 1966. *New Essays on Human Understanding*, trans. P. Remnant and J. Bennett, Cambridge: Cambridge University Press, 1981. *Philosophical Papers and Letters*, trans. L. E. Loemker, 2d ed., Dordrecht: Reidel, 1969. *Philosophical Writings*, trans. M. Morris and G. H. R. Parkinson, rev. ed. London: Dent, 1973. *Theodicy* (Abridged), trans. D. Allen, Indianapolis: Bobbs-Merrill, 1966.

63. Leibniz, *Philosophical Papers and Letters*, pp. 463–64.

64. *New Essays on Human Understanding*, chap. 6, section 2. Trans. Remnant and Bennett, p. 398.

65. Mungello, *Curious Land*, pp. 192–97 (192 quoted). Rutherford, "Philosophy and Language in Leibniz."

66. Leibniz, *Discourse on the Natural Theology of the Chinese*, trans. Rosemont and Cook, pp. 157–58. See also Lach, "Leibniz and China," pp. 104–108; Mungello, *Curious Land*, pp. 312–28; and Needham, *Science and Civilisation in China*, vol. 2, pp. 340–45.

67. Friedmann, *Leibniz et Spinoza*, pp. 123–24, 25–52, 285–86, 309–14.

68. Friedmann, *Leibniz et Spinoza*, pp. 123–24, 25–52, 285–86, 309–14.

69. Belavel, *Leibniz critique de Descartes*, pp. 60, 67 (quoted), 69.

70. Letter of February 1/11, 1686, in Leibniz, *Philosophical Papers and Letters*, p. 319.

71. Letter of June 22/July 2, 1679, Leibniz, *Philosophical Papers and Letters*, p. 211.

72. Ibid.

73. Essay of 1695 ("A New System of the Nature and the Communication of Substances, as Well as the Union between the Soul and the Body"), Leibniz, *Philosophical Papers and Letters*, p. 456.

74. Ibid., p. 457.

75. *The Leibniz-Clarke Correspondence*, p. 15 (Leibniz's "Second Paper").

76. Ibid., p. 16.

77. *The Leibniz-Clarke Correspondence*, p. 36 (Leibniz's "Fourth Paper").

78. "First Truths," c. 1680–84, Leibniz, *Philosophical Papers and Letters*, p. 268.

79. Ibid.

80. *The Leibniz-Arnauld Correspondence*, pp. 14–16 (to Arnauld, April 12, 1686).

81. Leibniz, *Philosophical Papers and Letters*, p. 519 (letter of June 23, 1699).

82. *The Leibniz-Clarke Correspondence*, trans. Alexander, Leibniz's Third Paper, pp. 25–27; Fourth Paper, pp. 36–45; Fifth Paper, pp. 66–75. See also Garber, "Leibniz: Physics and Philosophy," pp. 301–321.

83. Leibniz, *Philosophical Papers and Letters*, p. 456 ("A New System on the Nature and the Communication of Substances, as well as the Union between the Soul and the Body," 1695.

84 Leibniz, *Philosophical Papers and Letters*, p. 646 (*Monadology, 47*).

85. Ibid., p. 67 (*Monadology, 7*).

86. Leibniz, *Philosophical Papers and Letters*, pp. 515–16 (Letter to de Volder, April 3, 1699).

87. Leibniz, *New Essays on Human Understanding*, pp. 472–73.

88. Leibniz, *New Essays on Human Understanding*, p. 55.

89. Ibid.

90. Ibid., p. 56.

91. Ibid., pp. 188–89.

92. Ibid., p. 192.

93. See the thoroughgoing chap. 4, "Freedom and Contingency," in Sleigh, *Leibniz and Arnauld*; and see Parkinson, *Leibniz on Human Freedom*, pp. 7–12.

94. Sleigh, *Leibniz and Arnauld*, pp. 87–89.

95. Sleigh, *Leibniz and Arnauld*, p. 61, depending on Leibniz's letters to Arnauld of April 12 and July 14, 1686.

96. From Leibniz, *De libertate*, as quoted in Sleigh, *Leibniz and Arnauld*, p. 82.

97. I. O. Wade, *The Intellectual Development of Voltaire*, Princeton: Princeton University Press, 1969, pp. 691–93. For more detail, see the same author's *Voltaire and Candide*, Princeton: Princeton University Press, 1959.

98. See, e.g., L. W. Beck, "From Leibniz to Kant," in R. C. Solomon and K. M. Higgins, eds., *The Age of German Idealism,* London: Routledge, 1993, pp. 5–14.

99. Jolley, "Leibniz: Truth, Knowledge, and Metaphysics," p. 414. See also the eventually appreciative evaluation by Wilson in *Leibniz's Metaphysics*, pp. 304–31.

100. Needham, *Science and Civilisation in China*, vol. 2, p. 499.

101. Cook and Rosemont, "Leibniz and Chinese Thought" (p. 96 quoted).

102. Letter of June 28, 1643, to Elisabeth. See *The Philosophical Writings of Descartes*, trans. Cottingham et al., vol. 2, pp. 227–28.

103. *The Vedānta Sūtras of Bādarāyaṇa with the Commentary by Śaṅkara*, trans. G. Thibault, 2 vols., reprint Dover: New York, 1962, vol. 1, p. 14 (1.1.1); vol. 2, p. 14 (2.3.17).

104. Leibniz, *New Essays on Human Understanding*, trans. Remnant and Bennett, p. 212 (book 2, chap. 21).

105. Wilson, *Leibniz's Metaphysics*, pp. 234–49, especially. pp. 246–47.

106. Vattanky, *Gaṅgeśa's Philosophy of God*, p. 246.

107. J. E. LeDoux, "Emotion, Memory and the Brain, *Scientific American* June 1994, p. 38. See the same author's *The Emotional Brain*, New York: Simon and Schuster, 1996, pp. 163–74, 283–89.

108. Adams, *William Ockham*, vol. 1, p. 156.

109. G. W. Leibniz, *Philosophical Papers and Letters*, ed. L. E. Loemker, 2d ed., Dordrecht: Reidel, 1969, pp. 127–28, 306 (quoted) ("Preface to an Edition of Nizolius," 1670). See also Blumenfeld, "Perfection and Happiness in the Best Possible World," pp. 385–90.

Chapter 11. Immanent-Transcendent Holism

1. The quotation following the subtitle is from Shankara, as quoted in Siegel, *Fires of Love, Waters of Peace*, p. 9. Siegel gives as reference the *Saundaryalaharī*, ed. W. Norman Brown, Cambridge, 1958, 35.

Background, history of philosophy: S. Dasgupta, *A History of Indian Philosophy*, vols. 1, 2, Cambridge: Cambridge University Press, 1932 (on Shankara and Shankara's school); *Indian Idealism*, Cambridge: Cambridge University Press, 1933. J. N. Farquhar, *The Religious Quest of India*, London: Oxford University Press, 1920. C. V. Kher, *Buddhism as Presented by the Brahmanical Systems*, Delhi: Sri Satguru Publication (India Books Centre), 1992. H. Nakamura, *A History of Early Vedānta Philosophy*, Delhi: Banarsidass, 1983. B. N. K. Sharma, *The Brahmasūtras and Their Principal Commentaries: A Critical Exposition*, 3 vols., Bombay: Baharatya Vidya Bhavan, 1971–1978. J. Sinha, *A History of Indian Philosophy*, vol. 3, Calcutta: Sinha Publishing House, 1971 (on post-Shankara Vedantists from c.e. 900–1700). S. Radhakrishnan, *Indian Philosophy*, vol. 2, London: Allen & Unwin, 2d rev. ed., 1931.

History or nature of particular philosophical concepts: N. B. Chakraborty, *The Advaita Concept of Falsity*, Calcutta; Sanskrit College, 1967. W. Halbfass, *Tradition and Reflection*, Albany: State University of New York Press, 1991. R. R. Dravid, *The Problem of Universals in Indian Philosophy*, Delhi: Banarsidass, 1972.

M. Hulin, *Le principe de l'ego dans la pensée indienne classique, la notion d'Ahamkara*, Paris: Collège de France, Institut de civilisation indienne, 1978. B. Kar, *The Theories of Error in Indian Philosophy*, Delhi: Ajanta Publications, 1979. E. Lott, *Vedantic Approaches to God*, New York: Harper & Row, 1980. E. A. Solomon, *Avidyā—A Problem of Truth and Reality*, Ahmedabad: Gujarat University, 1969.

 General books on Shankara or Advaita Vedanta: P. Deussen, *The System of the Vedānta*, reprint New York: Dover, 1973 [1912]. E. Deutsch, *Advaita Vedānta*, Honolulu: East-West Center Press, 1969. A. Kuppuswami, *Śrī Bhāgavatpadā Śankarācārya*, Varanasi: Chowkamba Sanskrit Series Office, 1972. G. C. Pande, *Life and Thought of Śankarācārya*, Delhi: Banarsidass, 1994. N. Isayeva, *Shankara and Indian Philosophy*, Delhi: Sri Satguru Publications (India Books Centre) and Albany: State University of New York Press, 1993. K. H. Potter, ed., *Advaita Vedānta up to Śaṁkara and His Pupils* (vol. 3 of *Encyclopedia of Indian Philosophies*, ed. K. Potter), Delhi: Banarsidass, 1981.

 Monographs: S. Biderman, *Reality and Illusion in the Philosophy of Śaṅkara*, unpublished doctoral thesis, Tel-Aviv University, 1974. F. X. Clooney, *Theology after Vedanta: An Experiment in Comparative Theology*, Albany: State University of New York Press, 1993 (a respectful comparison of the theology and interpretive methods of Shankara's school with that of Aquinas' *Summa Theologiae*). N. K. Devaraja, *An Introduction to Śaṅkara's Theory of Knowledge*, Delhi: Banarsidass, 1962. P. Hacker, *Vivarta*, Mainz: Akademie der Wissenschaften und der Literatur in Mainz. K. S. Murty, *Revelation and Reason in Advaita Vedānta*, Waltair: Andhra University and New York: Columbia University Press, 1959. T. Vetter, *Studien zur Lehre und Entwicklung Śaṅkaras*, Vienna: De Nobili Research Library, 1979.

 Articles: V. S. Ghate, "Śaṅkaracharya," in J. Hastings, ed., *Encyclopaedia of Religion and Ethics*, New York: Scribners, 1928. P. Hacker, "Śaṅkara der Yogin und Śaṅkara der Advaitin," in *Festschrift für Erich Frawallner*, ed. G. Oberhammer, Vienna: Indologische Institut der Universität Wien, 1968. J. G. S. Hirst, "The Place of Teaching in Śaṁkara's Theology," *Journal of Indian Philosophy* (hereafter *JIP*) 18.2 (June 1990). S. Kaplan, "The Yogācāra Roots of Advaita Idealism?" *JIP* 20.2 (June 1992). R. King, "Śunyatā and Ajāti: Absolutism and the Philosophies of Nāgārjuna and Gauḍapāda," *JIP* 17.4 (December, 1989). B. K. Matilal, "A Note on Śaṁkara's Theodicy," *JIP* 20.4 (December 1992). S. Mayeda, "The Advaita Theory of Perception," in *Festschrift für Erich Frawallner*, ed. Oberhammer. C. R. Prasad, "Dreams and Reality: The Śankarite Critique of Vijnañāvāda," *Philosophy East and West* 43.3 (July 1993). S. Rao, "Two 'Myths' in Advaita," *JIP* 24.3 (June 1996). A. Sharma, "Is Anubhava a Pramāṇa According to Śaṅkara?" *Philosophy East and West* 42.3 (July 1992); "Karma and Reincarnation in Advaita Vedānta," *JIP* 18.3 (September 1990); "Śaṅkara's Attitude to Scriptural Authority as Revealed by His Gloss on Brahmasūtra 1.1.3," *JIP* 10.2 (June 1982). J. Taber, "Reason, Revelation and Idealism in Śaṅkara's Vedānta" *JIP* 9.3, (September 1981). K. N. Upadhyaya, "Śaṅkara on Reason, Scriptural Authority and Self-Knowledge,"*JIP* 19.2 (June 1991).

 Translations: Of the School of Vedanta: E. Deutsch and J. A. B. van Buitenen, eds., *A Source Book of Advaita Vedānta*, Honolulu: University of Honolulu Press, 1971.

OF GAUDAPADA: *The Āgamaśāstra of Gauḍapāda*, trans. V. Bhattacharya, Delhi: Banarsidass, 1943. *Dispelling Illusion: Gaudapada's "Alātaśānti,"* trans. D. A. Fox: Albany: State University of New York Press, 1993.

OF SHANKARA: *The Bṛhadāraṇyaka Upaniṣad with the Commentary of Shankārā-charya*, trans. Swami Madhavananda, Mayavat, Almora: Swami Virewarananda Advaita Ashram, 1934 (date of preface). *A Thousand Teachings: The* Upadeśasāhasrī *of Śaṅkara*, trans. S. Mayeda, Albany: State University of New York Press, 1992. *The Vedānta Sūtras of Bādarāyaṇa with the Commentary by Śaṅkara*, trans. G. Thibaut, 2 vols., reprint New York: Dover, 1962 [1890, 1896]. A. Sharma, *The Hindu Gita*, La Salle: Open Court, 1986 (chap. 4 has translated fragments and commentary on them). L. Siegel, *Fires of Love, Waters of Peace*, Honolulu: University of Hawaii Press, 1983 (a contrast of the poems attributed to Shankara with those of the erotic poet, Amaru).

Competing interpretations of Vedanta: Sinha (see above), *A History of Indian Philosophy*, vol. 3, chap. 1 (on Bhaskara); vol. 4 (on Ramanuja and Nimbarka). Further: Lott (see above), *Vedantic Conceptions of God*; J. B. Carmen, *The Theology of Rāmānuja*, New Haven: Yale University Press, 1974; and B. N. K. Sharma, *Philosophy of Śrī Madhvācārya*, rev. ed., Delhi: Banarsidass, 1986.

2. See the relatively full account of the sources for Shankara's life in Pande, *Life and Thought of Śaṅkarāchārya*, chap. 1.

3. Ibid., pp. 31–32, 80–81.

4. Ibid., p. 88.

5. Ibid., pp. 83–85. As Pande points out, Shankara's presumed references to Gauḍapāda are at the end of his commentary to the *Mandukya Upanishad* (the authenticity of which has been suspected) and in his commentary to the *Brahma Sutras* 1.4.14 and 2.1.9.

6. Ibid., pp. 85–87.

7. Pande, *Life and Thought of Śaṅkarācārya*, pp. 278–99. See also Isayeva, *Shankara and Indian Philosophy*, pp. 62–68, 79–80.

8. Dasgupta, *A History of Indian Philosophy*, vol. 5, p.3. There are also stories that he persecuted Buddhists and Jains. See Farquhar, *An Outline of the Religious Literature of India*, p. 175.

9. Ibid., p. 63.

10. Ibid., pp. 361–65. See also Farquhar, *An Outline of the Religious Literature of India*, pp. 174–76.

11. Pande, *Life and Thought of Śaṅkarācārya*, pp. 32, 337–65.

12. Mayeda, *A Thousand Teachings*, p. 9, note. 26, who speaks only of Sringeri. Isayeva, *Shankara and Indian Philosophy*, p. 93, says that the title was also conferred on the heads of the Kanchi monastery.

13. Pande, *Life and Thought of Śankarācārya*, p. 103.

14. Mayeda, trans, *A Thousand Teachings: The* Upadeśasāhasrī of *Śankara* 1.17.9. Trans. p. 161.

15. *The Brihadaranyaka Upanishad with the Commentary of Shankaracharya*, trans. Madhavananda, p. 448.

16. Ibid., 2.1.11. Trans. Thibaut, vol. 1, pp. 315–17. See Halbfass, "Human Reason and Vedic Revelation in Advaita Vedānta," chap. 5 of his *Tradition and Reflection*, especially pp. 153–56, 160, 180. Halbfass draws on Vetter, *Studien zur Lehre und Entwicklung Śankaras*. See also Deutsch, *Advaita Vedānta*, pp. 86–97; Upadhyaya, "Śankara on Reason, Scriptural Authority and Self-Knowledge"; and Clooney, *Theology after Vedānta*, pp. 103–6.

17. I say that the name Vedanta Sutra is late on the authority of Nakamura, *A History of Early Vedānta Philosophy*, pp. 425–26.

18. Potter, ed., *Advaita Vedānta up to Śamkara and His Pupils*, p. 119.

19. Shankara, *Commentary on the Vedānta Sūtras (Brahmasūtrabhāṣyam)* 1.1. Trans. in *The Vedānta Sūtras of Bādarāyaṇa with the Commentary by Śankara*, trans. Thibault, vol. 1, p. 3. Thibault's introduction, pp. xxxii–lxxxv, is a paraphrase of the whole commentary; and there is a detailed paraphrase in Potter, ed., *Advaita Vedānta up to Śamkara and His Pupils*, pp. 120–180.

20. Shankara, *Commentary on the Vedānta Sūtras* 1.1, trans Thibault, vol. 1, pp. 4–6. See also ibid. 1.1.5 and 1.2.6, trans. Thibaut, vol. 1, pp. 51, 113.

21. *Commentary on the Vedānta Sūtras* 1.1. References to Shankara's commentary will hereafter be to *Commentary*. The passage quoted is as translated in Thibault, vol. 1, p. 9. On the internal organ (*manas*) see *Commentary* 2.3.34, trans. Thibaut, vol. 2, p. 48.

22. *Commentary* 1.1. Trans. Thibault, vol. 1, p. 9.

23. *Commentary* 1.1.1. Trans. Thibault, vol. 1, p. 14.

24. Trans. Thibault, vol. 2, p. 14.

25. Shankara, *Commentary* 2.3.7. Trans. Thibault, vol. 2, p. 15.

26. Ibid., 1.2. Trans. Thibault, vol. 1, pp. 14–15.

27. Ibid., 1.4.15. Trans. Thibault, vol. 1, p. 266.

28. Ibid., 2.3.9. Trans. Thibaut, vol. 2, pp. 19–20.

29. Ibid., 4.3.14. Trans. Thibaut, vol. 2, pp. 394–95 (p. 395 quoted).

30. *Commentary* 2.1.31. Trans. Thibaut, vol. 1, p. 355.

31. Ibid., 1.1.3. Trans. Thibaut, vol. 1, p. 20.

32. *Commentary* 1.1.11. Trans. Thibaut, vol. 1, p. 63.

33. *Commentary* 2.1.33. Trans. Thibaut, vol. 1, p. 357. For the Lord as all-pervading, see 1.23; trans. Thibaut, vol. 1, p. 111.

34. Trans. Thibaut, vol. 1, p. 328–29.

35. Solomon, *Avidyā*, pp. 117–19, 120–21 (on *viparaya*). The references to the Vedanta Sutra are to 3.3 (*vidyā* as *subject of learning*) and 3.2.3 (*māyā*). For *māyā*, see J. Gonda, *Change and Continuity in Indian Religion*, the Hague: Mouton, 1965, chap. 6.

36. Solomon, *Avidyā*, chap. 10.

37. Ibid., chap. 12. The analogy of space in a jar is from *Gauḍapādakārikā* 3.3, 4, 7, 8, 10. For the power of maya, see the *Gauḍapādakārikā* 3.19, 1.17, 2.31 (ibid., Solomon, pp. 203, 207–209).

38. *Bṛhadāraṇyaka Upaniṣad* 4.3.22. Trans. (with Shankara's commentary) by Madhavananda, p. 665.

39. *Commentary* 4.1.3. Trans. Thibaut, vol. 2, p. 340. See Solomon, *Avidyā*, pp. 230–31.

40. Ibid., 4.1.4. Translated Thibaut, vol. 2, pp. 340–41.

41. Solomon, *Avidyā*, pp. 230–31, citing Shankara's commentary on the *Bṛhadāraṇyaka Upaniṣad* 4.3.20.

42. See Sinha, *A History of Indian Philosophy*, vol. 3, chap. 8.

43. *Commentary* 2.1.14. Trans. Thibaut, vol. 1, pp. 323–26 (p. 326 quoted). See Murty, *Reason and Revelation in Advaita Vedānta*, chap. 7.

44. Ibid., 4.1.15. Trans. Thibaut, vol. 2, p. 358. See Murty, *Reason and Revelation in Advaita Vedānta*, chap. 8.

45. See Kher, *Buddhism as Presented by the Brahmanical Systems*, chap. 11 (confined to his commentary to the Vedanta Sutras). Deutsch and van Buitenen, eds., *A Source Book of Advaita Vedānta*, pp. 92–103, 207–13, contains extended excerpts from Shankara's criticisms of Buddhism. See also Pande, *Life and Thought of Śaṅkarācārya*, chap. 9, and Isayeva, *Shankara and Indian Philosophy*, chap. 5.

46. Shankara, *Commentary* 2.2.18. Trans. Thibaut, vol. 1, pp. 400–404; my paraphrase is from p. 403.

47. Ibid., 2.2.19. Trans Thibaut, pp. 404–407; my paraphrase from pp. 406–407.

48. Ibid., 2.2.22–23. Trans Thibaut, pp. 410–11.

49. *Commentary* 2.2.25. Trans. Thibaut, vol. 1, pp. 413–15 (413, 414 quoted).

50. Trans. Thibaut, vol. 2, p. 415.

51. *Commentary* 2.2.28. Trans. Thibaut, vol. 1, p. 418.

52. Ibid. Trans. Thibaut, vol. 2, pp. 420–21.

53. Ibid.

54. For the estimates of the relationship between Gaudapada, Nagarjuna, and Shankara see the books of Isayeva and Pande on Shankara. See also D. A. Fox, *Dispelling Illusion*, pp. 29–32; and Kaplan, "The Yogācāra Roots of Advaita Idealism?" The *Sarva-darśana-siddhanta-saṅgraha* 4.1.7, 4.1.10, doubtfully attributed to Shankara, has a brief but, so far as I can see, correct characterization of Madhyamaka (Isayeva, *Shankara and Indian Philosophy*, pp. 186–87, 189).

55. *Commentary* 2.2.32. Trans. Thibaut, vol. 1, p. 427.

56. Trans. Thibaut, vol. 1, pp. 427–28.

57. *The Vedānta Sutras with the Commentary by Rāmānuja* 2.2.7. Trans. Thibaut, p. 513.

58. Ibid. 1.1.1. Trans. Thibaut, p. 39.

59. For a full description of Shankara's views, see Deussen, *The System of the Vedānta*.

60. The theological modes of interpretation of Shankara and his followers are spelled out in Murty, *Revelation and Reason in Advaita Vedanta*, and in Clooney, *Theology after Vedānta*. Clooney compares the interpretive structures of the *Summa Theologiae* with those of the commentaries to the Brahma Sutra.

61. See Isayeva, *Shankara and Indian Philosophy*, pp. 239–40.

62. The quotation just above is from Spinoza, *Ethics* 5.42, schol; trans. Curley, p. 617.

Background and biography: J. Freudenthal, *Die Lebensgeschichte Spinozas*, Leipzig: Von Veit, 1899 (basic documents). D. Levin, *Spinoza*, New York: Weybright & Talley, 1970. Y. Kaplan, *From Christianity to Judaism: The Story of Isaac Orobio de Castro*, Oxford: Oxford University Press, 1989. H. Méchoulan, *être Juif à Amsterdam au temps de Spinoza*, Paris: Albin Michel, 1991. R. H. Popkin, *The Third Force in Seventeenth-Century Thought*, Leiden: Brill, 1992. I. S. Révah, "Aux origines de la rupture Spinozienne," *Revue des éltudes Juives,* 4th series, vol. 3, fascicules 3–4 (July–Dec., 1964); *Spinoza et le Dr. Juan de Prado*, The Hague: Mouton, 1959. S. von Dunin Borkowski, *Spinoza*, 4 vols., 1910–1936, Münster. Y. H. Yerushalmi, *From Spanish Court to Italian Ghetto*, New York: Columbia University Press, 1971. B.-A. Scharfstein, *The Philosophers*, New York: Oxford University Press, 1980, pp. 149–56 (psychological interpretation). A. M. Vaz Dias and W. G. van der Tak, *Spinoza Mercator et Autodidactus*, The Hague: Nijhoff, 1932. A. Wolf, *The Oldest Biography of Spinoza*, London: Allen & Unwin, 1927. Y. Yovel, *Spinoza and Other Heretics*, 2 vols., Princeton: Princeton University Press, 1989.

History of philosophy: H. W. Blom, "The Moral and Political Philosophy of Spinoza," in G. H. R. Parkinson, ed., *The Renaissance and Seventeenth-century Rationalism*, London: Routledge, 1993. G. H. R. Parkinson, "Spinoza," in Parkinson, ed., op. cit. R. Popkin, *The History of Scepticism from Erasmus to Spinoza*, rev. ed., Berkeley: University of California Press, 1979.

Monographs and articles: METHOD: H. de Dijn, "Conception of Philosophical Method in Spinoza," *Review of Metaphysics* 40 (September 1986). J. I. Friedman, "Spinoza's Denial of Free Will in Man and God," in J. Wetlesen, ed., *Spinoza's Philosophy of Man*, Oslo: Universitetsforlaget, 1978. H. G. Hubbling, *Spinoza's Methodology*, Assen: Van Gorcum, 1964; "A Short Survey of Recent Spinoza Research," in Wetlesen, ed., *Spinoza's Philosophy of Man*. D. J. O'Meara, *Pythagoras Revived: Mathematics and Philosophy in Late Antiquity*, Oxford: Oxford University Press, 1989. A. Charles-Saget, *L'Architectur du divin*, Paris: "Les Belles Lettres," 1982. H. Schüling, *Die Geschichte der axiomatischen Methode im 16. and beginnenden 17. Jahrhundert*, Hildesheim: Olms, 1969.

METAPHYSICS AND THEORY OF KNOWLEDGE: E. M. Curley, *Spinoza's Metaphysics*, Harvard: Harvard University Press, 1969. L. Lermond, *The Form of Man: Human Essence in Spinoza's* Ethic, Leiden: Brill, 1988. G. H. R. Parkinson, *Spinoza's Theory of Knowledge*, Oxford: London, 1964. L. C. Rice, "Mind Eternity in Spinoza," *Iyyun, The Jerusalem Philosophical Quarterly* 41 (July 1922).

PSYCHOLOGY: B. Alexander, "Spinoza und die Psychoanalyse," *Chronicon Spinozanum*, vol. 5 (1927). D. Bidney, *The Psychology and Ethics of Spinoza*, New Haven: Yale University Press, 1940. J. Neufeld, *Emotion, Thought and Therapy*, London: Routledge & Kegan Paul, 1977.

RELIGION AND POLITICS: R. J. McShea, *The Political Philosophy of Spinoza*, New York: Columbia University Press, 1968. L. Strauss, "How to Study Spinoza's Theologico-Political Treatise," *Proceedings of the American Academy from Jewish Research* 17 (1947–48), New York: Bloch, 1948; *Spinoza's Critique of Religion*, New York: Schocken, 1965.

Commentaries: H. Joachim, *Spinoza's* Tractatus de Intellectus Emendatione, London: Oxford University Press, 1940. J. Bennett, *A Study of Spinoza's* Ethics, Cambridge: Cambridge University Press, 1984 (regards the concluding pages of the *Ethics* as "an unmitigated and seemingly unmotivated disaster" [p. 57]). M. Gueroult, *Spinoza*, 2. vols, Hildesheim: Olms, 1968, 1974 (through only *Ethics* book 2. H. S. Wolfson, *The Philosophy of Spinoza*, 2 vols., Cambridge: Harvard University Press, 1934—a mostly syllogistic reconstruction based on medieval philosophy.

Translations: *The Collected Works of Spinoza*, vol. 1, trans. E. Curley, Princeton: Princeton University Press, 1985. *The Correspondence of Spinoza*, trans. A. Wolf, London: Allen & Unwin, 1928. *Ethic*, trans. W. H. White, rev. A. H. Stirling, 4th ed., London: Oxford University Press, 1923. *Ethics*, trans. A Boyle, rev. G. H. R. Parkinson, London: Dent, 1989. *The Political Works*, trans. A. G. Wernham, London: Oxford, 1958. *Tractatus Theologico-Politicus*, trans. S. Shirley, Leiden: Brill, 1989.

Influence and assessments (no more than a suggestive selection): F. M. Barnard, "Spinozism," in P. Edwards, ed., *The Encyclopedia of Philosophy*. O. Bloch, ed., *Spinoza au XXe siècle,* Paris: Presses Universitaires de France, 1993. Bayle,

Historical and Critical Dictionary, Selections, trans. R. H. Popkin, Indianapolis: Bobbs-Merrill, 1965. L. W. Beck, *Early German Philosophy*, Cambridge: Harvard University Press, 1969, pp. 352–68, 385–87. O. Bloch, ed., *Spinoza au XXe Siècle*, Paris: Presses Universitaires de France, 1993. R. L. Colie, *Light and Enlightenment*, Cambridge: Cambridge University Press, 1957. G. Friedmann, *Leibniz et Spinoza*, rev. ed., Paris: Gallimard, 1962. Gilson, *God and Philosophy*, New Haven: Yale University Press, 1941. L. Kolakowski, "Pierre Bayle, critique de la métaphysique Spinoziste de la substance," in L. Dibon, ed., *Pierre Bayle*, Paris: Vrin, 1959. G. Santayana, *Persons and Places*, New York: Scribners, 1944. J. S. Spink, *French Free-Thought from Gassendi to Voltaire*, London: Athlone Press, 1960. P. Vernière, *Spinoza et la pensée française*, 2 vols., Paris: Presses Universitaires de France, 1954. J. H. Zammito, *The Genesis of Kant's* Critique of Judgment, Chicago: University of Chicago Press, 1992, chaps. 11, 12.

Comparison with Vedanta: R. K. Tripathi, *Spinoza in the Light of the Vedanta*, Banaras: Banaras Hindu University, 1957.

63. Vaz Dias and van der Tak, *Spinoza Mercator et Autodidactus*.

64. Méchoulan, *Etre Juif à Amsterdam . . .*, pp. 22–30. See Spinoza's tribute to Amsterdam's freedom toward the end of the *Tractatus Theologico-Politicus* (chap. 20).

65. Méchoulan, *Etre Juif à Amsterdam au temps de Spinoza*, pp. 32–34.

66. Ibid., pp. 37–41. See also Yerushalmi, *From Spanish Court to Italian Ghetto*, pp. 44–46, and Révah, *Spinoza et le Dr. Juan de Prado*, pp. 276ff.

67. Méchoulan, *Etre Juif à Amsterdam . . .*, pp. 48–58.

68. "The Marranos of Amsterdam," in Popkin, *The Third Force in Seventeenth-Century Thought*, pp. 162–64.

69. As translated in Popkin, *The Third Force . . .*, p. 160. See Révah, *Spinoza et Prado*, pp. 57–58.

70. "Spinoza's Relations with the Quakers in Amsterdam," in Popkin, *The Third Force in Seventeenth-Century Thought*, p. 121.

71. Ibid., p. 61; as translated in Kaplan, *From Christianity to Judaism*, pp. 133–34. For the other report see Révah, *Spinoza et le Dr. Juan de Prado*, pp. 66–68; translated in Kaplan, op. cit., p. 134.

72. *Tractatus Theologico-Politicus* chap. 20. Trans. Shirley, p. 297. Also trans. Wernham in Spinoza, *The Political Works*, p. 239.

73. Wolf, *The Correspondence of Spinoza*, pp. 49–57, where Spinoza's more intimate correspondents are named and described.

74. "The Religious Background of Seventeenth-Century Philosophy," in Popkin, *The Third Force in Seventeenth-Century Philosophy*, p. 275.

75. Wolf, *Correspondence of Spinoza*, letter 30, p. 206.

76. Quotation from *Tractatus Theologico-Politicus*, chap. 12; trans. Shirley, p. 211.

77. A. Wolf, trans., *The Oldest Biography of Spinoza*, pp. 155–56.

78. In *An Investigation of the Laws of Thought*, London, 1854, the English logician George Boole (1815–1864) finds logical flaws in the first book of the *Ethics*, including vagueness of definitions and axioms, which he tries to remedy.

79. See Lodewijk Meyer's introductory comment to *Descartes' "Principles of Philosophy,"* in *The Collected Works of Spinoza*, trans. Curley, vol. 1, p. 229.

80. Letter 83, to Tschirnhaus. Wolf, *The Correspondence of Spinoza*, p. 365.

81. De Dijn, "Conceptions of Philosophical Method in Spinoza," p. 68.

82. Letter 10. Trans. Wolf, *The Correspondence of Spinoza*, p. 109.

83. Letter 37, to Bouwmeester. Wolf, *The Correspondence of Spinoza*, pp. 227–28.

84. Quotation from the end of the preface to *Ethics*, book 3. Trans. Curley, p. 492.

85. *The Collected Works of Spinoza*, trans. Curley, p. 402.

86. "Untraditionally"—see Wolfson, *The Philosophy of Spinoza*, vol. 1, pp. 64–65.

87. *Metaphysics* 1070b.36–1971a.1.

88. *Ethics*, trans. Boyle, pp. 33, 34.

89. Ibid., p. 40.

90. Ibid., p. 84 (preface to part 3).

91. *The Collected Works of Spinoza*, trans. Curley, pp. 518–520.

92. *The Collected Works of Spinoza*, trans. Curley, vol. 1, p. 584.

93. Ibid., p. 607.

94. Ibid., p. 607.

95. Ibid., p. 612.

96. Ibid., p. 612.

97. Ibid., p. 615.

98. Bennett, *A Study of Spinoza's* Ethics, chaps. 3–5. Curley, *Spinoza's Metaphysics*, chap. 1. Gueroult, *Spinoza*, vol. 1, chap. 1; appendixes 3, 10. Wolfson, *The Philosophy of Spinoza*, vol. 1, chaps. 2, 7, 11.

99. Wolfson, ibid., pp. 75–75. "Prior in nature," *Ethics* 1, prop. 1.

100. *Short Treatise* 1.2.2. See Wolfson, *The Philosophy of Spinoza*, pp. 71–72, 97–98.

101. Ibid., p. 66. Spinoza explicitly rejects the term *accident* in the *Cogitata Metaphysica* 1.1.

102. *The Correspondence of Spinoza*, letter 64 (to Schuller). Trans. Wolf, p. 307.

103. Letter 63. See Wolfson, *The Philosophy of Spinoza*, vol. 1, pp. 238–41.

104. *The Correspondence of Spinoza*, trans. Wolf, letter 64 (to Schuller), p. 308. See Wolfson, vol. 1, pp. 244–49.

105. Wolfson, *The Philosophy of Spinoza*, vol. 1, pp. 372–75.

106. Gueroult, *Spinoza*, vol. 1, chap. 13 ; vol. 2, chap. 18. Wolfson, *The Philosophy of Spinoza*, vol. 1, chap. 12; vol. 2, chap. 17.

107. For Aristotle, see *De Anima* 431–32. The comparison is made in Wolfson, *The Philosophy of Spinoza*, vol. 2, pp. 164–67. In the light of Gueroult, *Spinoza*, vol. 2, pp. 493–95, I have also drawn on Spinoza's *Short Treatise* for the understanding of his distinction difference between will and desire.

108. *The Complete Works of Spinoza*, vol. 1; trans. Curley, p. 442.

109. Gueroult, *Spinoza*, vol. 2, chaps. 11–17. Parkinson, *Spinoza's Theory of Knowledge*, chaps. 7–9. Wolfson, *The Philosophy of Spinoza*, vol. 2, chap. 16.

110. Parkinson, *Spinoza's Theory of Knowledge*, pp. 163–64, 170–73.

111. *The Collected Works of Spinoza*, vol. 1, trans. Curley, pp. 612–13.

112. Rice, "Mind Eternity in Spinoza." Wolfson, *The Philosophy of Spinoza*, vol. 2, chap. 20. See also L. Lermond, *The Form of Man*, pp. 72–75.

113. See the bibliography of assessments and reactions. Vernire, vol. 1, gives a broad picture, but mainly confined to France.

114. "Spinoza," in Bayle's *Historical and Critical Dictionary*, trans. Popkin; pp. 301, 303 quoted. See Vernire, *Spinoza . . . ,* vol. 1, pp. 288–306.

115. Vernière, *Spinoza . . . ,* vol. 2, pp. 495–527. I. O. Wade, *The Intellectual Life of Voltaire*, Princeton: Princeton University Press, 1969, pp. 693–711 (for Voltaire's emanative God, proposed in the essay, *Tout en Dieu*, see p. 741).

116. Kant, *Critique of Judgment*, sec. 73; in Zamitto, *The Genesis of Kant's Third Critique*, pp. 252–60.

117. See M. A. Nowak, R. M. May, and K. Sigmund, "The Arithmethics of Mutual Help," and D. W. Pfennig and P. W. Sherman, *Kin Recognition*, both in the *Scientific American* of June 1995; and R. Wright, *The Moral Animal*, New York: Pantheon, 1994.

118. *Tractatus Theologico-Politicus*, chaps. 1, 2. E.g., in Shirley's translation, p. 71.

119. Wolfson, ibid., pp. 81–86. See the account of Avicenna in the present book. For Spinoza, see the *Ethics* 1.4–6.

120. See H. A. Davidson, *Alfarabi, Avicenna, and Averroes on Intellect*, New York: Oxford University Press, 1992, pp. 34–43, 56–57, 109–10, 201–202; and L. Goodman, *Avicenna*, London: Routledge, 1992, p. 163–72.

Chapter 12. *Perceptual Analysis, Realistic and Idealistic*

1. See, e.g., Leibniz's reply in 1702 to Bayle's criticism, in G. W. Leibniz, *Philosophical Papers and Works*, trans. L. E. Loemker, 2d ed., Dordrecht: Reidel, 1969, p. 578.

2. The definitions of *idea* are from the *New Shorter Oxford English Dictionary*, ed. L. Brown, Oxford: Oxford University Press, 1993. For an elaborate, historically documented account of the philosophical use of *idea*, see the entry *idee* in J. Ritter and K. Gründer, eds, *Historisches Wörterbuch der Philosophie*, Schwabe: Basel/Stuttgart, vol. 4, 1976, pp. 51–134. For *idealism*, see pp. 30–45.

3. Quoted from the novelist William Gibson, the inventor of the term (*Time*, special issue on cyberspace, spring 1995, p. 2).

4. *Laṅkāvatāra Sūtra,* 184. Trans. in Conze, ed., *Buddhist Texts*, p. 207.

5. The quotation subtitle following is from the *Laṅkāvatāra Sūtra*, 184; trans. in Conze, ed., *Buddhist Texts*, p. 207.

General reference books: *Les Notions philosophiques*, ed. by S. Auroux, Paris: Presses Universitaires de France, 1990. *Les Oeuvres philosophiques*, ed. by J.-F. Mattéi, Paris: Presses Universitaires de France, 1991.

History of Buddhist religion and philosophy: Tibetan Buddhist: Bu-ston, *History of Buddhism*, trans. E. Obermiller, Heidelberg: Harrassowitz, 1931–32 (two parts in one volume). Taranatha, *Tāranātha's History of Buddhism*, trans. Lama Chima and A. Chattopadhyaya, reprint Delhi: Banarsidass, 1990.

Modern: Buddhist Thought Alone: A. Bareau. W. Schubring, and C. von Führer-Haimendorf, *Die Religionen Indiens*, vol. 3, Stuttgart: Kohlhammer, 1964. E. Conze, *Buddhist Thought in India*, London: Allen & Unwin, 1962; *A Short History of Buddhism*, London: Allen & Unwin, 1980. D. J. Kalupahana, *A History of Buddhist Philosophy*, Honolulu: University of Hawaii Press, 1992. A. B. Keith, *Buddhist Philosophy*, Oxford: Oxford University Press, 1923. T. R. V. Murti, *The Central Philosophy of Buddhism*, London: Allen and Unwin, 1955. P. Williams, *Mahāyāna Buddhism*, London: Routledge, 1989. A. K. Warder, *Indian Buddhism*, 2d ed., Delhi: Banarsidass, 1980.

In the Context of Indian Thought: S. Dasgupta, *A History of Indian Philosophy*, vol. 1, Cambridge: Cambridge University Press, 1932; *Indian Idealism*, Cambridge: Cambridge University Press, 1933. C. V. Kher, *Buddhism as Presented by the*

Brahmanical Systems, Delhi: Satguru Publications (Indian Books Centre), 1992. D. N. Shastri, *Critique of Indian Realism*, Agra: Agra University, 1964. Th. Stcherbatsky, *Buddhist Logic*, 2 vols., S'-Gravenhage [The Hague]: Mouton, 1958 [1932]. M. Winternitz, *History of Indian Literature*, vol. 2, rev. ed., Delhi: Banarsidass, 1983.

IN THE CONTEXT OF CHINESE AND JAPANESE THOUGHT: K. S. Chen, *Buddhism in China*, Princeton: Princeton University Press, 1964. Fung Yu-lan, *A History of Chinese Philosophy*, vol. 2, Princeton: Princeton University Press, 1953. G. N. Nagao, *Mādhyamika and Yogācāra*, Albany: State University of New York Press, 1991. D. Matsunaga and A. Matsunaga, *Foundation of Japanese Buddhism*, vol. 1, Tokyo: Buddhist Books International, 1974. D. Y. Paul, *Philosophy of Mind in Sixth-Century China*, Stanford: Stanford University Press, 1984. J. Takakusu, *The Essentials of Buddhist Philosophy*, Bombay: Asia Publishing House, 1956 (original ed., Honolulu: University of Hawaii Press, 1947).

IN THE CONTEXT OF TIBETAN THOUGHT: Tsong Khapa, *Ocean of Eloquence: Tsong Kha Pa's Commentary on the Yogācāra Doctrine of Mind*, trans. G. Sparham, Albany: State University of New York Press, 1993 (on the *alaya* consciousness and the ego consciousness); *Tsong Khapa's Speech of Gold in the* Essence of True Eloquence, trans. A. A. F. Thurman, Princeton: Princeton University Press, 1984.

Monographs and one-author collections of articles: A. K. Chatterjee, *The Yogācāra Idealism*, Delhi: Banarsidass, 2d ed., 1975. M. D. Eckel, *Jñānagarbha on the Two Truths*, Delhi: Banarsidass, 1992 [1987]. E. Frauwallner, *On the Date of the Buddhist Master of the Law Vasubandhu*, Rome: Instituto Italiano per il Medio ed Estremo Oriente, 1951. P. J. Griffiths, *On Being Mindless*, La Salle: Open Court, 1986. G. M. Nagao, *Mādhyamika and Yogācāra*, Albany: State University of New York Press, 1991. O. Rotem, *A Study of Idealism: With Constant Reference to Berkeley and Vasubandhu*, unpublished M.A. thesis, Tel-Aviv University, 1991. D. T. Suzuki, *Studies in the Laṅkāvatāra Sūtra*, Boulder: Prajna Press, 1981 [1930]. G. Tucci, *On Some Aspects of the Doctrines of Maitreya[nātha] and Asaṅga*, Calcutta: University of Calcutta, 1930. T. W. Wood, *Mind Only: A Philosophical and Doctrinal Analysis of the Vijnanavada*, Hawaii: University of Hawaii Press, 1991.

Articles: E. Hamlin, "Discourse in the Laṅkāvatāra Sūtra," *Journal of Indian Philosophy* (hereafter *JIB*) 11.3 (September 1983). J. Hopkins, "A Tibetan Contribution on the Question of Mind-Only in the Early Yogic Practice School," *JIP* 20.3 (September 1992). S. Kaplan, "The Yogācāra Roots of Advaita Idealism?" *JIB* 20.2 (June 1992). M. Kapstein, "Mereological Considerations in Vasubandhu's 'Proof of Idealism'" (*Vijñaptimātrasiddhiḥ*), *Idealistic Studies*, 1987. R. King, "Yogācāra and Its Relationship with the Madhyamaka School," *Philosophy East and West* 44.4 (October 1994). B. K. Matilal, "A Critique of Buddhist Idealism," in L. Cousins et al., eds., *Buddhist Studies in Honour of I. B. Horner*, Dordrecht: Reidel, 1974. A. C. C. McDermott, "Asaṅga's Defense of *Ālayavijñāna*," *JIB* 2 (1973). O. Rotem, "Vasubandhu's Idealism: An Encounter between Philosophy and Religion," *Asian Philosophy* 3.1 (1993). W. Waldron, "How Innovative Is the *Ālayavijñāna*," Part 1, *JIB* 22.3 (September 1994); Part 2, *JIB* 13.1 (March 1995). Walpola Rahula, "Asaṅga," in *Encyclopaedia of Buddhism*, ed. G. P. Malalasekera, vol. 2, fascicle 1, Colombo: Government of Ceylon, 1966. L. Schmithausen, "A Note on Vasubandhu and the Laṅkāvatārasūtra," *Asiatic Studies* 46.1 (1992).

Translations: ANTHOLOGIES: E. Conze, ed., *Buddhist Texts Through the Ages*, Oxford: Cassirer, 1954. E. Frauwallner, trans., *Die Philosophie des Buddhismus*, Berlin: Akademie-Verlag, 1958.

SUTRAS: *The Large Sutra on Perfect Wisdom*, trans. E. Conze, Berkeley: University of California Press, 1975. *The Teaching of Vimalakīrti (Vimalakīrtinirdeśa)*, trans. E. Lamotte; English trans. S. Boin, London: Pali Text Society, 1976. *A Treasury of Mahāyāna Sūtras* (from the Mahāratnakūta Sūtra), trans. ed. G. C. C. Chang, Delhi: Banarsidass, 1991 (original ed. Pennsylvania State University Press, 1983).

MAITREYA/ASANGA: *Madhyānta-Vibhanga: Discourse on Discrimination between Middle and Extremes*, trans. Th. Stcherbatsky, New Delhi: Oriental Books Reprint Corp. [1936]. Wood, *Mind-Only* (see *Monographs*), chap. 1.

ASANGA: *Mahāyāna-sūtrālaṃkāra*, ed. and trans. (French) S. Lévi, 2 vols., Paris: Librairie Ancienne Honoré Champion, 1907, 1911 (the attribution to Asanga is doubtful). *Mahāyānasūtralaṃkāra*, trans. S. V. Limaye, Delhi: Sri Satguru Publication (Indian Books Centre), 1992. *The Realm of Awakening: Chapter 10 of Asaṅga's* Mahāyānasaṅgraha, trans. P. J. Griffiths, N. Hakamaya, J. P. Keenan, and P. L. Swanson, New York: Oxford University Press, 1989. *La Somme du Grand Véhicule d'Asanga*, trans. E. Lamotte, 2 vols. Louvain: L'Institut Orientaliste de l'Université Catholique de Louvain, 1973 [1938]. Wood, *Mind Only*.

VASUBANDHU: *A Buddhist Doctrine of Experience*, trans. T. A. Kochumuttom, Delhi: Banarsidass, 1982. *Seven Works of Vasubandhu*, trans. S. Anacker, Delhi: Banarsidass, 1984. *Treatise in Thirty Verses on Mere-Consciousness*, trans. S. Ganguly, Delhi: Banarsidass, 1992. "The Trisvabhāvakārikā of Vasubandhu," trans. F. Tola and C. Dragonetti, *JIB* 11.3 (September 1983). "Vasubandhu's 'Refutation of the Theory of Selfhood' *(Ātmavādapratisedha)*," trans. J. Duerlinger, *JIB* 17.2 (June 1989). *Wei Shih Er Shih Lun or The Treatise in Twenty Stanzas on Representation-Only*, trans. C. H. Hamilton, New Haven: American Oriental Society, 1938. *Vijñaptimātrata Siddhi (with Sthiramati's Commentary)*, trans. K. N. Chatterjee, Varanasi: Kishor Vidya Niketan, 1980 (translations of the *Viṃśatikā* and *Triṃśikā*). Wood, *Mind Only*.

PARAMARTHA (OR VASUBANDHU): S. B. King, *Buddha Nature*, Albany: State University of New York Press, 1991 (translation of the *Buddha Nature Treatise*).

HSÜAN-TSANG: Wing-tsit, Chan, trans., *A Source Book in Chinese Philosophy*, Princeton: Princeton University Press, 1963, pp. 370–95. *Ch'eng Wei-shih Lun: The Doctrine of Mere-Consciousness*, trans. Wei Tat, printed in Hong Kong, copyright Wei Tat. *Vijñāptimātratasiddhi: Le Siddhi de Hiuan-tsang, trans. L. de La Vallée Poussin*, 2 vols, Paris: Librairie Orientaliste Paul Geuthner, 1929; index vol., 1948.

BHAVAVIVEKA: "Bhāvaviveka's Critique of Yogācāra Philosophy in Chapter XXV of the *Prajñāpradīpa*," in Chr. Lindtner, *Miscellanea Buddhica*, Copenhagen: Akademsk Forlag, 1985.

DHARMAKIRTI: *Santānāntara-siddhi (Establishment of the Existence of Other Minds)*, trans. Th. Stcherbatsky, in *Papers of Th. Stcherbatsky*, trans. from the Russian by H. C. Gupta, Soviet Indology Studies No. 2, *Indian Studies Past and Present*, 1969 [1922]. Wood, *Mind Only*, app 2. Trans. Hidenori Kitagawa, "*A Refutation of Solipsism*" (annotated translation of the *Santānāntarasiddhi), Journal of the Greater India*

Society, vol. 14, nos. 1, 2, Calcutta 1955; reprinted in *A Study of Indian Classical Logic—Dignāga's System*, Tokyo, 1965, pp. 405–39 (under the general Japanese name of *Indo Koten Ronrigaku no kenkyu, Jinna (Dignaga) no taikei*. The dialogue survives only in Tibetan.

RATNAKĪRTI: *An Eleventh-Century Buddhist Logic of 'exists': Ratnakīrti's Kṣaṇabhaṅgasiddiḥ Vyatirekātmikā*, trans. A. C. S. McDermott, Dordrecht: Reidel, 1969. Wood, *Mind Only*, app. 4. K. Mimaki, *La réfutation bouddhique de la permanence des choses . . . et La preuve de la momentanité des choses . . .* Paris: Institut de civilisation indienne, 1976.

TSONG KHA PA (see above, IN THE CONTEXT OF TIBETAN THOUGHT).

6. The story is as told in the oldest extant biography, by Paramartha, who lived during the first half of the sixteenth century. See Walpola Rahula, "Asanga," pp. 133–34.

7. This conversation, the words of which I have modified, are excerpted from an unknown biography by Chi-tsang, who lived at the end of the sixth and beginning of the seventh century. See Frauwallner, *On the Date of the Buddhist Master of the Law Vasubandhu*, pp. 49–50.

8. Bu-ston, *History of Buddhism*, trans. Obermiller, part 2, pp. 143–44.

9. P. May, in Matti, ed., *Les oeuvres philosophiques*, vol. 2, p. 3984.

10. Chang, ed., *A Treasury of Mahāyāna Sūtras*, chap. 12 (sutra 46, "Mañjuśri's Discourse on the Paramita of Wisdom," p. 107. On the absolute in Buddhism, especially Mahayana, see *The Teaching of Vimalakīrti*, trans. Lamotte, pp. lx–lxxi.

11. *The Large Sutra on Perfect Wisdom*, trans. Conze, p. 56.

12. Ibid., p. 145.

13. Suzuki, *Studies in the Laṅkāvatāra Sūtra*, pp. 241–83 (p. 242 quoted, from Laṅkāvatāra Sūtra 30–31).

14. Anguttara-nikaya 1.6; in Conze, ed., *Buddhist Texts*, p. 33.

15. Chang, ed., *A Treasury of Mahāyāna Sūtras*, chap. 12 (sutra 39), "The Elucidation of Consciousness," p. 229. The preceding paraphrased passages are from the same sutra, pp. 225–27.

16. For the following exposition of the *Vimshatika* and *Trimshika*, I have had at hand the translations of Anacker (*Seven Works of Vasubandhu*), Chatterjee (*Vijñapti-Mātrata-Siddhi*), Frauwallner (in *Die Philosophie des Buddhismus*), Kochumuttom (*A Buddhist Doctrine of Experience*), Wood (*Mind Only*), and Hamilton's translation from Hsüan Tsang's Chinese (*Wei-shih-er-shih-lun*). Wood translates only a little of Vasubandhu's commentary, for which Kochumuttom substitutes his own. Chatterjee translates the subcommentary as well as the commentary of the *Vimshatika* and Sthiramati's commentary to the *Trimshika*. I have followed Frauwallner more often than anyone else.

17. See the translation of this part of verse 17 and its commentary in Griffiths, *On Being Mindless*, pp. 83–84.

18. A Chinese commentator seems to have discussed why there were versions varying from twenty to twenty-three verses (Wood, *Mind Only*, p. 247, note 4).

19. Hsüan-tsang, *Vijñaptimātratasiddhi*, trans. La Vallée Poussin, vol. 1, p. 431 (commentary to Vasubandhu, *Triṃśikā*, verse 17). Also in Chan, *A Source Book of Chinese Philosophy*, pp. 391–92; Fung, *A History of Chinese Philosophy*, pp. 326–27; and Wood, *Mind Only*, p. 95.

20. Dharmakīrtī, *Establishment of the Existence of Other Minds*, trans. Stcherbatsky. See Wood, *Mind Only*, pp. 107–31 (a critical discussion) and 207–18 (a comprehensive synopsis). Wood's synopsis preserves more of the byplay of the reasoning than does my rapid paraphrase, which does not distinguish between Dharmakirti's text and Vinitadeva's commentary. I have checked my synopsis against Kitagawa's free, annotated translation into English (my references are to the 1965 reprint). There is a short summary of the dialogue in Stcherbatsky, *Buddhist Logic*, vol. 1, pp. 521–24.

21. Kitagawa, "A Refutation of Idealism," p. 409.

22. Sutras 1–4. Trans. Stcherbatsky, *Establishment*, pp. 85–87; Kitagawa, "A Refutation," pp. 409–10.

23. Sutras 5–26. Trans. Stcherbatsky, *Establishment*, pp. 87–93; Kitagawa, "A Refutation," pp. 410–14.

24. Sutras 27–33. Trans. Stcherbatsky, *Establishment*, pp. 94–95; Kitagawa, "A Refutation," p. 414.

25. Sutras 50–52. Trans. Stcherbatsky, *Establishment*, pp. 100–102; Kitagawa, "A Refutation," p. 418.

26. Sutras 53–59. Trans. Stcherbatsky, *Establishment*, pp. 103–105; Kitagawa, "A Refutation," pp. 418–20.

27. Sutras 60–65. Trans. Stcherbatsky, *Establishment*, pp. 105–109; Kitagawa, "A Refutation," pp. 420–23.

28. Sutras 66–82. Trans. Stcherbatsky, *Establishment*, pp. 109–13; Kitagawa, "A Refutation," pp. 423–26.

29. Sutras 88–93. Trans. Stcherbatsky, *Establishment*, pp. 117–19; Kitagawa, "A Refutation," pp. 428–29.

30. Chatterjee's translation (*Vijñāpti-mātrata-siddhi*), is helpful because it contains Sthiramati's commentary. Ganguly, *Treatise in Thirty Verses on Mere-consciousness*, translates from the Hsüan-tsang's Chinese and the Chinese translation of Dharmapala's Chinese, which it compares with Sthiramati's Sanskrit commentary.

31. Fung, *A History of Chinese Philosophy*, vol. 2, p. 311. See Hsüan-tsang, *Vijñaptimātratasiddhi*, trans. La Vallée Poussin, vol. 1, pp. 156–57 (commentary to *Trimśika*, verse 4.

32. For a description of the roles that the store-consciousness fills, see Waldron, "How Innovative Is the *Ālayavijñana*," Part II, pp. 28–29.

33. Waldron, "How Innovative Is the *Ālayavijñāna*," Part II, p. 31.

34. Ibid., p. 32.

35. *Madhyānta-vibhāṅga* 1.13, 14. Trans. Wood, *Mind Only*, p. 12. See the *Madhyānta-vibhāṅga Discourse*, trans. Stcherbatsky, pp. 76, 81—a different, much less cautious translation, with Vasubandhu's commentary and Sthiramati's comment on it. On the Yogachara interpretation of emptiness, see Nagao, *Mādhyamika and Yogācāra*, chaps. 5, 13.

36. *Madhyānta-vibhāṅga Discourse*, trans. Stcherbatsky, pp. 19–20, 23–26.

37. Wood, *Mind Only*, pp. 55, 56.

38. That Asanga's use of *thoughtless thought* is, in its context, relatively new, is asserted by Lamotte in his translation of the *Mahāyānasaṃgraha*. See *La somme du grande véhicule*, vol. 2, p. ix.

39. See Wood, *Mind Only*, who takes such contradictions with logical seriousness, pp. 56–60. I take it that the doctrine makes such contradictions necessary—they give emptiness what anthropologist call a "thick" description—thick, at least, for the metaphysical imagination.

40. Walpola Rahula, "Asanga," pp. 142–43. See the *Mahāyāna-Sūtralamkāra (Ornament of the Mahāyāna Sūtras)* 9.15, 21, 24, 26, 31, 37. Although this work may not be by Asanga, its commentary is probably by Vasubandhu. Whoever its author, the work is central to Yogachara, and its concepts and temper of thought resemble those of Asanga in the *Mahāyānasaṅgraha*—see especially chap. 10 in Lamotte's translation and the *Realm of Awakening* (an English translation of chap. 10, with translators' variants and excerpts from different commentaries). E.g., Asanga asserts that Buddha is neither many nor one in *Mahāyānasaṅgraha* 10.3b. King, *Buddha Nature*, based on a work attributed to Vasubandhu, gives a comprehensive view of the metaphysical Buddha doctrine.

41. Eckel, "Bhāvaviveka's Critique of Yogācāra Philosophy in Chapter XXV of the Prajnapradipa," pp. 25–44.

42. Ibid., p. 75.

43. The quotation just above is from John Locke, *Essay Concerning Human Understanding* 2.1.19.
Philosophical background and history: P. Bayle, *Historical and Critical Dictionary, Selections*, trans. R. H. Popkin, Indianapolis: Bobbs-Merrill, 1965. Y. Hoffmann, *The Idea of Self—East and West: A Comparison between Buddhist Philosophy and the*

Philosophy of David Hume, Calcutta: KLM Private, 1980. N. Malebranche, *La Recherche de la vérité*, in Malebranche, *Oeuvres*, vol. 1, ed. G. Rodis-Lewis, Paris: Gallimard, 1979. G. H. R. Parkinson, ed., *The Renaissance and Seventeenth-Century Rationalism*, London: Routledge, 1993. R. H. Popkin, *The High Road to Pyrrhonism*, San Diego: Austin Hill Press, 1980; *The Third Force in Seventeenth-Century Thought*, Leiden: Brill, 1992. N. Rodis-Lewis, *Nicolas Malebranche*, Paris: Presses Universitaires de France, 1963. Scharfstein, *The Philosophers*, New York: Oxford University Press, 1980 (psychological biographies). J. W. Yolton, *Perceptual Acquaintance*, Oxford: Blackwell, 1984. R. A. Watson, "Foucher, Simon," in *The Encyclopedia of Philosophy*, ed. Edwards. J. R. Weinberg, *Ockham, Descartes, and Hume*, Madison: University of Wisconsin Press, 1977.

Biography: M. Cranston, *John Locke*, London: Longmans, 1957. K. Dewhurst, *John Locke, Physician and Philosopher*, London: The Wellcome Historical Medical Library, 1963. W. N. Hargreaves-Mawdsley, *Oxford in the Age of John Locke*, Norman: University of Oklahoma Press, 1973.

Monographs and articles: R. I. Aaron, *John Locke*, 3d ed., London: Oxford University Press, 1971. P. Alexander, *Ideas, Qualities and Corpuscles: Locke and Boyle on the External World*, Cambridge: Cambridge University Press, 1985. M. Ayers, *Locke*, 2 vols., London: Routledge, 1991. J. G. Clapp, "Locke, John," in Edwards, ed., *The Encyclopedia of Philosophy*. J. W. Yolton, *Locke and the Compass of Human Understanding*, Cambridge: Cambridge University Press, 1970. J. W. Yolton, ed., *John Locke: Problems and Perspectives*, Cambridge: Cambridge University Press, 1969.

Texts: *An Essay Concerning Human Understanding*, ed. P. H. Nidditch, London: Oxford University Press, 1975. *Epistola de Toleranta: Letter on Toleration*, ed. R. Klibansky, trans. J. W. Gough, London: Oxford University Press, 1968. *John Locke on Education*, ed. P. Gay, New York: Teachers College, Columbia University Press, 1964. *Two Tracts on Government*, ed. P. Abrams, Cambridge: Cambridge University Press, 1967. *Two Treatises of Government*, ed. P. Laslett, Cambridge: Cambridge University Press, 1964.

44. Locke, *Essay on Human Understanding* 4.3.16. See Alexander, *Ideas, Qualities and Corpuscles*, p. 8.

45. Yolton, *Locke and the Compass of Human Understanding*, p. 59, note 1.

46. Cranston, *John Locke*, p. 100.

47. See Locke's account of intuition and demonstration in the fourth book of the *Essay Concerning Human Understanding* (*Essay* 4.2.8–14), and his use of Descartes' *cogito ergo sum* argument (ibid., 4.9.3; ed. Nidditch, p. 618).

48. Ibid., pp. 11–13, 82.

49. Ibid., p. 159.

50. *Some Thoughts Concerning Education*, section 174.

51. This characterization is more developed in Scharfstein, *The Philosophers*, pp. 159–61.

52. For a favorable assessment, worked out in nuanced detail, see the concluding pages of each of the two volumes of Ayer's *Locke*.

53. *Essay on Human Understanding*, ed. Nidditch, p. 47.

54. From the *Oxford English Dictionary*, as in the glossary of Nidditch's edition of the *Essay*. See also Alexander, *Ideas, Qualities and Corpuscles*, pp. 92–93, 97–100.

55. Ayers, *Locke*, vol. 1, pp. 16–17, and chap. 5 (ideas as images).

56. *Essay*, ed. Nidditch, p. 104.

57. Ibid., pp. 105–6.

58. Ibid., p. 106.

59. Ibid., p. 88.

60. Ibid., p. 119.

61. Ibid., p. 120.

62. Ayer, *Locke*, vol. 1, chap. 29.

63. See Ayer, *Locke*, vol. 2, chap. 14. Locke arrived at his views carefully, but because of his informal, often diffuse way of writing, he needs a defender such as Ayer.

64. **Biography**: A. Luce, *The Life of George Berkeley, Bishop of Cloyne*, rev. facsimile ed., New York: Greenwood Press, 1968. J. O. Wisdom, *The Unconscious Sources of Berkeley's Philosophy*, London: Hogarth Press and Institute of Psycho-Analysis.

Monographs and articles: H. B. Acton, "Berkeley, George," in Edwards, ed., *The Encyclopedia of Philosophy*. A. A. Luce, *The Dialectic of Immaterialism*, London: Hodder and Stoughton, 1963. R. H. Popkin, "Berkeley and Pyrrhonism," "Berkeley's Influence on American Philosophy," "David-Renaud Boullier and Bishop Berkeley," and "The New Realism of Bishop Berkeley," all in Popkin, *The High Road to Pyrrhonism* (see above). I. C. Tipton, *Berkeley: The Dialectic of Immaterialism*, London: Methuen, 1974.

Texts: *Philosophical Works*, rev. ed., ed. M. R. Ayers, Dent: London, 1975. In the case of *Three Dialogues between Hylas and Philonous*, which is not divided into numbered sections, I have given page references to the standard edition, *The Works of George Berkeley*, ed. A. A. Luce and T. E. Jessop, 9 vols., London: Nelson & Sons, 1948–1957, as well as to the edition edited by Ayers.

Comparison: O. Rotem, *A Study of Idealism: With Constant Reference to Berkeley and Vasubandhu*, unpublished M.A. thesis, Tel-Aviv University, 1991.

65. Ibid., pp. 41–42.

66. *De Motu* section 11.

67. Ibid., section 17.

68. Ibid., sections 71, 72.

69. This struggle is the main theme of Luce, *The Dialectic of Immaterialism*.

70. As is more fully said in *Principles*, section 89.

71. For the mutual necessity of inactive perception and active perceiver, see *Philosophical Notebooks*, no. 673. This passage of my exposition depends on Luce, *The Dialectic of Immaterialism*, chaps. 8, 11.

72. For Berkeley's early dependence on Malebranche's rules of method, and the dependence of his *Theory of Vision* on Malebranche's *Investigation of Truth (La Recherche de la vérité)*, see Luce, *The Dialectics of Immaterialism*, pp. 62–64.

73. Malebranche, *La Recherche de la vérité*, book 1, chapter 10; ed. Rodis-Lewis, p. 89.

74. *De la recherche de la vérité*, book 3, part 2, chap. 6; ed. Rodis-Lewis, p. 346.

75. Ibid, "Sixth Clarification" *(VIe Éclaircissement)*; ed. Rodis-Lewis, pp. 831–32.

76. Ibid., pp. 832–34.

77. Ibid., pp. 834–36.

78. Ibid., pp. 838–39.

79. "Pyrrho," in Bayle, *Historical and Critical Dictionary*, trans. Popkin, p. 198.

80. Ibid., pp. 199–200. On Bayle's "super-Pyrrhonism," See Popkin, "Pierre Bayle's Place in Seventeenth-Century Scepticism."

81. See Berkeley's *Principles*, sections 89, 96.

82. Berkeley, *Principles*, introduction, secs. 21, 22.

83. H. S. Thayer, *Meaning and Action: A Critical History of Pragmatism*, Indianapolis: Bobbs-Merrill, 1968, appendix 5, "Berkeley and Some Anticipations of Pragmatism."

84. See *Principles*, sec. 59.

85. Berkeley, *Philosophical Works*, ed. Ayers, p. 188. In the standard Luce and Jessop ed., vol. 2, p. 237.

86. Ayers ed., p. 238. Luce and Jessop ed., vol. 2, p. 238.

87. Ayres ed., pp. 188–89; Luce and Jessop, vol. 2, p. 238.

88. Ayres ed., p. 194. Luce and Jessop ed., vol. 2, pp. 245–46.

89. Ayres ed., pp. 195–96. Luce and Jessop ed., vol. 2, pp. 247–48.

90. Second dialogue. Ayers ed., pp. 169–70 (170 quoted). Luce and Jessop ed., vol. 2, pp. 214–15. See the similar passage in the third dialogue, Ayers ed., pp. 182–83, and Luce and Jessop ed., vol. 2, pp. 230–31.

91. Hume, *Enquries concerning Human Understanding* 12.1, note; ed. Selby-Bigge, p. 155.

92. I. Kant, *Prolegomena to Any Future Metaphysics*, appendix; trans. P. Lucas, Manchester: Manchester University Press, 1953, pp. 145–46. See also Kant, the *Critique of Pure Reason* B71, B274, A368-70, A377-78. And see N. K. Smith, A Commentary to Kant's "Critique of Pure Reason," 2d ed., London: Macmillan, 1923, pp. 153–61, 306–309.

93. Popkin, "Berkeley's Influence on American Philosophy."

94. E. Husserl, *The Crisis of European Sciences and Transcendental Phenomenology,* section 23; trans. D. Carr, Evanston, Ill.: Northwestern University Press, 1970, pp. 88–90; *Logical Investigations*, 2 vols, London: Routledge and Kegan Paul, 1970 [Halle, 1900), trans. J. N. Findlay, vol. 1, Investigation 2, sections 28–31, pp. 394–401. W. James, *Essays in Radical Empiricism*, New York: Longmans Green, 1938 (1912), pp. 10–11. See Popkin, "Berkeley's Influence on American Philosophy," pp. 344–45. And see H. S. Thayer, *Meaning and Action: A Critical History of Pragmatism*, Indianapolis: Bobbs-Merrill, 1968, appendix 5, "Berkeley and Some Anticipations of Pragmatism." There is an interesting, somewhat enigmatic tribute to Berkeley in G. Santayana, "Apologia Pro Mente Sua," in P. A. Schilpp, *The Philosophy of George Santayana*, Evanston, Ill.: Northwestern University, 1940, p. 574 (accompanied by criticism, p. 534).

95. **Biography and letters**: "Hume's Autobiographies," appendix to Norton, ed., *The Cambridge Companion to Hume* (see below). *The Letters of David Hume*, ed. J. Y. T. Grieg, 2 vols., London: Oxford University Press, 1932. E. C. Mossner, *The Life of David Hume*, Austin: University of Texas Press, 1954. N. K. Smith, *The Philosophy of David Hume* (see below), chap. 24.

Monographs and articles: D. G. C. MacNabb, "Hume, David," in Edwards, ed., *The Encyclopedia of Philosophy*. D. F. Norton, *David Hume*, Princeton: Princeton University Press, 1982. D. F. Norton, ed., *The Cambridge Companion to Hume*, Cambridge: Cambridge University Press, 1993. Noxon, *Hume's Philosophical Development*, London: Oxford University Press, 1973. N. K. Smith, *The Philosophy of David Hume*, London: Macmillan, 1941. J. P. Wright, *The Sceptical Realism of David Hume*, Manchester: Manchester University Press, 1983.

Texts: *An Abstract of "A Treatise of Human Nature,"* 1740, ed. J. M. Keynes and P. Sraffa, Cambridge: Cambridge University Press, 1938. *Essays: Moral, Political and Literary*, Oxford: Oxford University Press, 1963. *Hume's Dialogues Concerning Natural Religion*, ed. N. K. Smith, 2d ed., New York: Social Science Publishers, 1948. *A Treatise of Human Nature*, ed. L. A. Selby-Bigge, London: Oxford University Press, 1896.

Reactions: H. H. Bracken, *The Early Reception of Berkeley's Immaterialism 1710–52*, The Hague: Nijhoff, 1966. K. Lehrer, *Thomas Reid*, London: Routledge, 1989. Popkin, *The High Road to Pyrrhonism* (see above).

96. Hume, *Letters*, ed. Grieg, vol. 1, p. 1. For the same text, with modernized spelling, see *The Cambridge Companion to Hume*, ed. Norton, p. 351. The whole letter is also reprinted in Mossner, *The Life of David Hume*, pp. 611–15.

97. Mossner, *The Life of David Hume*, p. 73.

98. From a letter to Gilbert Eliot of Mindi, 18 Feb., 1751. In *Letters*, vol. 1, p. 154.

99. *Letters*, vol. 1, p. 13. In Norton, ed., *The Cambridge Companion to Hume*, p. 346.

100. *Letters*, vol. 1, pp. 16–17. In Norton, ed., *The Cambridge Companion to Hume*, pp. 348–49.

101. *Treatise* 1.4.7. Ed. Selby-Bigge, p. 264.

102. From Hume's essay, "Of National Characteristics," as quoted in "Hume's Racism Reconsidered," in Popkin *The Third Force in Seventeenth-Century Thought*; p. 65.

103. Hume, *An Abstract of A Treatise of Human Nature.*

104. J. C. A. Gaskin, "Hume on Religion," in Norton, ed., *The Cambridge Companion to Hume.*

105. Hume, *Treatise*, introduction. Ed. Selby-Bigge, p. xx.

106. On Hume's conception of ideas, see Yolton, *Perceptual Acquaintance*, chap. 10.

107. *Treatise*, ed. Selby-Bigge, p. 2.

108. Ed. Nidditch, pp. 1–3 (p. 1 quoted).

109. For the growing attention paid to what Hume called "the anatomy of the mind," with its detailed descriptions and therapeutic goal, see Yolton, *Perceptual Acquaintance from Descartes to Reid*, pp. 181–82.

110. Ibid., p. 8.

111. Ibid., p. 24 (quoted).

112. Ibid., esp. pp. 34–35.

113. Ibid., pp. 39–40.

114. Ibid., p. 80.

115. Ibid., p. 134.

116. Ibid., p. 158; and Malebranche, *Recherche de la vérité* 6.2.3, ed. Rodis-Lewis, pp. 646–47.

117. *Treatise*, ed. Nidditch, pp. 158–59.

118. Ibid., p. 170.

119. Ibid., p. 189.

120. Ibid., pp. 252, 253.

121. Ibid., pp. 254–55.

122. Ibid., p. 261.

123. *Treatise*, introduction. Ed. Nidditch, p. xviii.

124. Yolton, *Perceptual Acquaintance*, pp. 165–67.

125. Ed. Nidditch, p. 199.

126. Appendix, *Treatise*, ed. Selby-Bigge, p. 629. For *irresistible* and *permanent*, see 1.4.4; p. 225.

127. Ed. Nidditch, pp. 267–69, 273.

128. In the *Enquiry concerning Human Understanding*, Hume praises as best "the Academic or Sceptical Philosophy" (sec. 5, part 1; ed. Nidditch, p. 41). See "Hume's Pyrrhonism and Critique of Pyrrhonism," in Popkin, *The High Road to Pyrrhonism*.

129. See Rotem, *A Study of Idealism*.

130. *Twenty Verses*, verse 3.

131. Ibid., verse 4.

132. See Hoffmann, *The Idea of Self—East and West*.

133. Locke's theory of abstract ideas as particular appearances to represent patterns by which to classify real things is somewhat of a departure from ordinary nominalism. See Ayer, *Locke*, vol. 1, chap. 27, and for a clear declaration of minimalism by Locke, *Essay on Human Understanding* 4.17.8; ed. Nidditch, pp. 680–81.

134. I. Stewart, *Nature's Numbers*, New York: Basic Books, 1995, pp. 145–46.

135. T. Reid, *An Inquiry into the Human Mind on the Principles of Common Sense*. In *The Works of Thomas Reid*, reprinted, Hildesheim: Olms, 1983 [1895]. As quoted in K. Lehrer, *Thomas Reid*, Routledge: London, 1989, pp. 77–78.

Chapter 13. Fideistic Neo-Skepticism

1. I. Kant, *Critique of Pure Reason,* p. B74. Trans. N. K. Smith, London: Macmillan, 1933, p. 93.

2. J. D. Foley, "Interfaces for Advanced Computing," *Scientific American,* October 1987. B. Sherman and P. Judkins, *Glimpses of Heaven, Visions of Hell: Virtual Reality and Its Implications,* London: Hodder & Stoughton, 1992. K. Pimental and K. Teixeira, *Virtual Reality,* New York: McGraw-Hill, 1993, give a clear and fairly detailed explanation of the techniques used.

3. R. P. Hayes, *Dignaga on the Interpretation of Signs,* Dordrecht: Kluwer, 1988, p. 230.

4. The quotation accompanying the heading is from the opening of Dignaga's Pramāṇasamuccaya (hereafter *PS*), trans. Hattori in *Dignaga, On Perception,* p. 23. Hattori's translation of *pramāṇa-bhūta* as "Personification of the Means of Cognition" seems mistaken. *Bhūta* probably means no more than *is* in the predicative sense of a copula, but Dharmakirti understands it as *has become* (possibly, as Ruegg has argued, it should be understood as *like,* meaning that the Buddha is similar to means of knowledge). I owe this note to my two expert friends, Eli Franco and Ornan Rotem.

5. Bu-ston, *History of Buddhism,* vol. 2, p. 149. Tāranātha, *History of Buddhism in India,* pp. 181–85, puts the life somewhat differently and adds details. See also Hattori, *Dignāga, On Perception,* pp. 1–11; Stcherbatsky, *Buddhist Logic,* vol. 1, pp. 31–34.

6. Bu-ston, *History of Buddhism,* p. 150.

7. My words on the difficulties of understanding and the poor translation follow Hayes, *Dignaga on the Interpretation of Signs,* pp. 224, 227-28.

8. **General background to the Buddhism of the period**: L. Joshi, *Studies in the Buddhistic Culture of India (During the Seventh and Eighth Centuries c.e.),* Delhi: Banarsidass, 1967.
History of the relevant Buddhism: Tibetan: Bu-ston, *History of Buddhism,* trans. E. Obermiller, two parts in one volume, Heidelberg: Harrassowitz, 1931, 1932. *Tāranātha's History of Buddhism in India,* trans. Lamba Chimpa and A. Chattopadhyaya, reprint Delhi: Banarsidass, 1990 (1970).
Modern: E. Frauwallner, "Dignāga, sein Werk und Entwicklung," *Wiener Zeitschrift für die Kunde Süd- und Ostasiens* 3, 1959. D. J. Kalupahana, *A History of Buddhist Philosophy* (Nagarjuna's faithfulness to the original precepts of Buddhism is stressed, but Dharmakirti is regarded as not a true exponent of Buddhism and is therefore omitted). S. Vidyabhusana, *A History of Indian Logic* (antiquated but still sometimes useful). Th. Stcherbatsky, *Buddhist Logic,* 2 vols., reprint S'-Gravenhage [The Hague]: Mouton, 1958. A. K. Warder, *Indian Buddhism,* 2d ed., Delhi: Banarsidass, 1980. P. Williams, *Mahāyāna Buddhism: The Doctrinal Founda-*

tions, London: Routledge, 1989 (only mentions Dignaga and does not take up Dharmakirti, but gives an excellent background).

Expositions emphasizing debate of Buddhists with other schools: R. R. Dravid, *The Problem of Universals in Indian Philosophy,* Delhi: Banarsidass, 1972. C. V. Kher, *Buddhism as Presented by the Brahmanical Systems,* Delhi: Sri Satguru Publications, 1992. S. Mookerji, *The Buddhist Philosophy of Universal Flux,* Calcutta: University of Calcutta, 1935. N. J. Shah, *Akalanka's Criticism of Dharmakīrti's Philosophy,* Ahmedabad: L. D. Institute of Indology (based on criticism by a Jain philosopher). D. N. Shastri, *Critique of Indian Realism,* Agra: Agra University, 1964.

Some relevant Tibetan interpretations: A. C. Klein, trans., *Knowing, Naming and Negation,* Ithaca: Snow Lion Publications, 1991 (annotated translations of three Tibetan [Gelukba] texts interpeting Dignaga and Dharmakirti); *Knowledge and Liberation,* Ithaca: Snow Lion Publications, 1986.

Relevant monographs: E. Franco, *Dharmakīrti on Compassion and Rebirth,* Vienna: Arbeitskreis für Tibetische Studien Universität Wien, 1997. B. K. Matilal, *Perception,* Oxford: Oxford University Press, 1988. L. Silburn, *Instant et cause,* chap. 8. Th. Stcherbatsky, *The Central Conception of Buddhism and the Meaning of the Word "Dharma,"* London: Royal Asiatic Society, 1923; *La théorie de la connaissance et la logique chez les bouddhistes tardifs,* Paris; Paul Geuthner, 1926 (even though superseded by the author's later work, of interest because of its organization). T. Vetter, *Erkenntnisprobleme bei Dharmakīrti,* Vienna: Österreichische Akademie der Wissenschaften.

Articles: R. S. Y. Chi, "Diṅnāga and Post-Russell Logic," in Matilal and Evans, eds., *Buddhist Logic and Epistemology* (see just below). E. Franco, "Did Dignāga Accept Four Types of Perception?" *Journal of Indian Philosophy* (hereafter *JIP*) 21.3 (September 1993); "The Disjunction in *Pramāṇavārttika, Pramāṇasiddhi* Chapter Verse 5c," in E. Steinkellner, ed., *Studies in the Buddhist Epistemological Tradition,* Osterreichische Akademie der Wissenschaften, Vienna, 1991. "Once Again on Dharmakīrti's Deviation from Dignāga on *Pratyakṣabhāṣa,*" *JIP* 14.1 (March 1986); "On the Interpretation of Pramāṇasamuccaya(vṛtti) I,3d," *JIP* 12.4 (December 1984); "Valid Reason, True Sign," *Wiener Zeitschrift für die Kunde Südasiens* 34 (1990); "Was the Buddha a Buddha?" *JIP* 17.1 (March 1989); "Yet Another Look at the Framework of the *Pramāṇasiddhi* Chapter of *Pramāṇavārttika, Indo-Iranian Journal* 37 (1994); "Zum religiösen Hintergrund der buddhistischen Logik, *Berliner Wissenschaftliche Gesellschaft e.V., Jahrbuch, 1990,* Berlin: Berliner Wissenschaftliche Gesellschaft, 1990, pp. 177–93. J. Ganeri, Dharmakīrti on Inference and Properties," *JIP* 18.3 (September 1990). R. Gupta, "Dharmakīrti's Theory of Language," in Doboom Tulku, ed., New Delhi: Tibet House and Aditya Prakashan, 1990. R. Hayes, "Diṅnāga's Views on Reasoning *(Svārthānumāṇa), JIP* 8.3 (September 1980); "On the Reinterpretation of Dharmakīrti's *Svābhavahetu," JIP* 15.4 (December 1987). S. Katsura, "Dharmakīrti's Theory of Truth," *JIP* 12.3 (September 1984). J. May, "Candrakīrti," "Dharmakīrti," and "Dignaga," in J.-F. Mattei, ed., *Les oeuvres philosophiques,* 2 vols., Paris: Presses universitaires de France, 1992, vol. 2. B. K. Matilal and R. E. Evans, eds., *Buddhist Logic and Epistemology,* Dordrecht: Reidel, 1986. S. H. Phillips, "Dharmakīrti on Sensation and Causal Efficiency," *JIP* 15.3

(September, 1987). R. K. Sharma, "Dharmakīrti on the Existence of Other Minds," *JIP* 13.1 (March 1985). E. Steinkellner, "Die Entwicklung des Kṣanikātvānumānam bei Dharmakīrti," in G. Oberhammer, ed., *Festschrift für Erich Frauwallner*, Leiden: Brill (*Wiener Zeitschrift für die Kunde Süd- und Ostasiens* 12–13 [1968/1969]).

Translations or monographs with extensive translated excerpts: DIGNAGA: *Dignāga's Ālambanaparīkṣavṛtti*, trans. F. Tola and C. Dragonetti, *JIP 10.2* (June 1982). *Dignāga, On Perception*, trans. M. Hattori, Cambridge: Harvard University Press, 1968. R. P. Hayes, *Dignaga and the Interpretation of Signs*, Dordrecht: Kluwer, 1988. R. P. Hayes and B. S. Gillon, "Introduction to Dharmakīrti's Theory of Inference as Presented in *Pramāṇavārtikka Svopajñavṛtti* 1–10," *JIP* 19.1 (March 1991). R. Herzberger, *Bhartṛhari and the Buddhists*, Dordrecht: Reidel, 1986.

DHARMAKIRTI: *Dharmakīrti's Hetubindiḥ*, part 1, trans. E. Steinkellner, Vienna: Österreichische Akademie der Wissenschaften, 1967. *Nyāya-bindu*, trans. Th. Stcherbatsky, in *Buddhist Logic* (see above), vol. 2. *Pramāṇavārtikka II*, with Prajnagupta's commentary, in Franco, *Dharmakīrti on Compassion and Rebirth* (see above, under monographs). *The Pramāṇavārttikam of Dharmakīrti [Kārkikās I–LI]*, trans. S. Mookerjee and H. Nagasaki, Nalanda: Navya Nalanda Mahavihara, 1964. *Dharmakīrti's Pramāṇaviniścayaḥ*, chap. 1, trans. T. Vetter, Vienna: Österreichische Akademie der Wissenschaften, 1966; chap. 2, trans. E. Steinkellner, Vienna; Österreichische Akademie der Wissenschaften, 1979. *Santānāntara-siddhi*, in H. D. Gupta, trans., *Papers of Th. Stcherbatsky*, Delhi: Indian Studies Past and Present, Soviet Indology Series. No. 2, 1969. R. Herzberger, *Bhartṛhari and the Buddhists* (see above).

9. Bu-ston, *History of Buddhism*, p. 154.

10. To see how his system can be pieced together, follow the notes, for example, in Katsura, "Dharmakīrti's Theory of Truth."

11. For Dharmakirti on Buddha as a *pramāṇa* see Franco, "The Disjunction in *Pramāṇavārttika, Pramāṇasiddhi* Chapter Verse 5C." For Franco's later view, see "Yet Another Look at the Framework of the *Pramāṇasiddhi* Chapter of *Pramāṇavārttika.*"

12. *Dharmakīrti's Pramāṇaviniścaya*, trans. Vetter, chap. 1, p. 31.

13. Stcherbatsky, *Buddhist Logic*, vol. 1, p. 36.

14. Franco, "Yet Another Look at the Framework of the *Pramāṇasiddhi* Chapter of *Pramāṇavārttika*," pp. 244–47.

15. See the note in Hattori, *Dignāga, On Perception*, p. 77.

16. E. Franco, "On the Interpretation of Pramāṇasamuccaya(vṛtti) I, 3d," *JIP* 12.4 (1984), p. 397. See also Franco's *Dharmakīrti on Compassion and Truth*, pp. 38–39 and chap. 4. To make the reading of the passage easier, I have removed the translator's brackets around the explanatory words he has added—the brackets are mine. Compare Hattori, *Dignāga, On Perception*, p. 25, and Hayes, *Dignaga on the Interpretation of Signs*, p. 134. See also Herzberger, *Bhartṛhari and the Buddhists*, pp. 115, 120.

17. Hattori *Dignāga, On Perception*, p. 27 (*PS* 1.6ab).

18. Hattori *Dignāga, On Perception*, p. 28 (*PS* 1.7cd–8ab). See also Hayes, *Dignaga on the Interpretation of Signs*, p. 139.

19. *Nyāya-Bindhu* 1.6, in Stcherbatsky, *Buddhist Logic*, vol. 2, pp. 24–25.

20. *Ālambanaparīkṣā*. Trans. Hayes, *Dignaga on the Interpretation of Signs*, p. 175.

21. Ibid., p. 177.

22. Ibid. I have run together Dignaga's prose commentary and his verse (translated as ordinary prose) without marking the difference.

23. Hayes, "Diṅnāga's Views on Reasoning" (pp. 233, 242 for the decisiveness of the negative criterion), and Hayes, *Dignaga on the Interpretation of Signs*, pp. 181–83. See also Franco, "Valid Reason, True Sign."

24. Hayes, *Dignaga on the Interpretation of Signs*, pp. 165–68.

25. Franco, "Valid Reason, True Sign," pp. 206–207.

26. Hayes, pp. 183–96 (p. 185 quoted).

27. Hayes, *Dignaga on the Interpretation of Signs*, pp. 212–16, 238, 297, depending on *PS* 2.4 and 5.15.

28. Herzberger, *Bhartṛhari and the Buddhists*, pp. 129–30.

29. Ibid., pp. 134–37. Franco (personal communication) thinks this view of Dignaga's views is mistaken.

30. Franco, "Valid Reason, True Sign," p. 208, translating from *The Pramāṇavārttikam of Dharmakīrti*, ed. R. Gnoli, Rome, 1960, p. 20, verse 31. See also *The Pramāṇavārttikam of Dharmakīrti*, trans. Mookerji and Nagasaki, p. 77.

31. Stcherbatsky, *Buddhist Logic*, vol. 1, pp. 181–83, has a list of fourteen applicable Sanskrit terms, mostly superlatives.

32. *Pramāṇavārttika* (hereafter *PV*) 3.123–25, as translated somewhat freely from Vetter's translation in *Erkenntnisprobleme bei Dharmakīrti*, p. 38. See Stcherbatsky's translation of an analogous passage from the *Nyāya-bindhu* 2.2 in *Buddhist Logic*, vol. 2, pp. 50–51.

33. *PV* 2, 130–32, as interpreted by Shah, *Akalanka's Criticism of Dharmakīrti's Philosophy*, pp. 202–203. On the vividness of a pure perceptual awareness, see Stcherbatsky, *Buddhist Logic*, vol. 1, pp. 186–89.

34. *PV* 1.32, 33, and comm. Trans. Mookerjee and Nagasaki, pp. 79–82.

35. Hayes, "Diṅnāga's Views on Reasoning," pp. 230–34. See also Hayes and Gillon, "Dharmakīrti's Theory of Inference," pp. 30–34.

36. *PV* 1.34 and comm. Trans. Mookerjee and Nagasaki, pp. 83–85 (p. 85 quoted).

37. Trans. Mookerjee and Nagasaki, pp. 85–86 (p. 86 quoted).

38. *PV* 1.37. Trans. Mookerji, pp. 83–85 (p. 85 quoted).

39. Ibid., comm. 1.37. Mookerjee and Nagasaki, pp. 87–88.

40. Trans. Mookerjee and Nagasaki, p. 89. The just-preceding quotation is from verse 1.38, p. 88.

41. For Dignaga, see Hattori, *Dignāga on Perception,* note pp. 93–94. I follow Dharmottara, a Kashmirian follower of Dharmakirti, of about 800 c.e., as his views as reported in later commentaries. See Stcherbatsky, *Buddhist Logic,* vol. 2, pp. 313–18, 330–33 for the sources, and vol. 1, pp. 204–209.

42. The preceding paragraph and the remainder of this section on perception is indebted to Katsura, "Dharmakirti's Theory of Truth," whose references include Dharmakirti's *PV* and *Hetubindu.* In this section, when I give a reference to *PV* without a page reference, it is borrowed from Katsura.

43. Stcherbatsky, *Buddhist Logic,* vol. 1, p. 81, drawing on Kamalashila.

44. *PV* 3.247–48.

45. *PV* 1.42 and comm. Trans. Mookerjee and Nagasaki, pp. 91–93.

46. Trans. Mookerjee and Nagasaki, p. 94.

47. Ibid., 1.51. Trans. Mookerjee and Nagasaki, p. 112.

48. Stcherbatsky, *Buddhist Logic,* vol. 1, pp. 211–13.

49. Katsura, "Dharmakīrti's Theory of Truth," pp. 218–19, where the references to Dharmakirti's works are given.

50. *PV* 2.1a–c, 2.1.5c. Katsura, "Dharmakīrti's Theory of Truth," pp. 219, 220.

51. Katsura, "Dharmakīrti's Theory of Truth," pp. 224–26. See also the beginning of Dharmakirti's *Nyāya-bindhu,* with Dharmottara's copious commentary, in Stcherbatsky, *Buddhist Logic,* vol. 2, pp. 1–11.

52. Katsura, "Dharmakīrti's Theory of Truth," pp. 224–26.

53. I base this statement on the argument of Hayes, *Dignaga on the Interpretation of Signs,* pp. 179–81.

54. This is the conclusion of Hayes's *Dignaga on the Interpretation of Signs,* pp. 311–12.

55. *PV* 2.31c–d, as cited by Vetter, *Erkenntnisprobleme bei Dharmakīrti,* p. 33.

56. Franco, "Yet Another Look at the Framework of *Pramāṇasiddhi* Chapter of *Pramāṇavārtikka*"; "Zum religiösen Hintergrund der buddhistischen Logik," *Berliner Wissenschaftliche Gesellschaft e.V., Jahrbuch, 1990,* Berlin: Berliner Wissenschaftliche Gesellschaft, 1990, pp. 177–93; and "Was the Buddha a Buddha?"—a review of T. Vetter's. *Der Buddha und seine Lehre in Dharmakīrtis Parmāṇavārttika,* Vienna: Arbeitskreis für Tibetische und Buddhistische Studien, 1984. Vetter, *Enkenntnisprobleme bei Dharmakīrti,* pp. 31–34.

57. The quotation in the subtitle is from the *Critique of Pure Reason* A536/B564, trans. Smith, p. 466.

The bibliography that follows is limited to particularly relevant or recent books.

Social and historical background: E. Reicke, *Der Gelehrte in der deutschen Vergangenheit,* Leipzig: Steinhausen, 1900. J. G. Sheehan, *German History 1770–1866,* Oxford: Oxford University Press, 1989.

Life and connection of life with philosophy: B.-A. Scharfstein, *The Philosophers.* H.-J. de Vleeschauwer, *The Development of Kantian Thought,* London: Nelson and Sons, 1962. K. Vorländer, *Immanuel Kant: Der Man und das Werk,* 2 vols. Leipzig: Meiner, 1924.

History of philosophy: L. W. Beck, *Early German Philosophy: Kant and His Predecessors,* Cambridge: Harvard University Press, 1969.

Dictionaries: H. Caygil, *A Kant Dictionary,* Oxford: Blacwell, 1995. R. Eisler, *Kant-Lexikon,* Hildesheim: Olms, 1930.

Monographs: S. J. Al-Azm, *The Origins of Kant's Arguments in the Antinomies,* London: Oxford University Press, 1972. H. E. Allison, *Kant's Theory of Freedom,* Cambridge: Cambridge University Press, 1990; *Kant's Transcendental Idealism,* New Haven: Yale University Press, 1983. M. Friedman, *Kant and the Exact Sciences,* Cambridge: Harvard University Press, 1992. A. Brook, *Kant and the Mind,* Cambridge: Cambridge University Press, 1994. P. Guyer, *Kant and the Claims of Knowledge,* Cambridge: Cambridge University Press, 1987. K. Reich, *The Completeness of Kant's Table of Judgments,* Stanford: Stanford University Press, 1992. A. W. Wood, *Kant's Rational Theology,* Ithaca: Cornell University Press, 1978. J. H. Zammato, *The Genesis of Kant's Critique of Judgment,* Chicago: University of Chicago Press, 1992.

Articles: M. S. Gram, ed., *Interpreting Kant,* Iowa City: University of Iowa Press, 1982. P. Guyer, ed., *The Cambridge Companion to Kant,* Cambridge: Cambridge University Press, 1992. D. Henrich, *The Unity of Knowledge,* Cambridge: Cambridge University Press, 1994.

Translations: I. Kant, *Anthropology,* trans. M. J. Gregor, the Hague: Nijhoff, 1974; *Critique of Judgement,* trans. J. C. Meredith, London: Oxford, 1952; *Critique of Pure Reason,* trans. N. K. Smith, London: Macmillan, 1933; *The Kant-Eberhard Controversy,* trans. H. E. Allison, Baltimore: Johns Hopkins University Press, 1973; *Logic,* trans. R. S. Hartman and W. Schwarz, reprint, New York: Dover, 1988; *Opus postumum,* trans. E. Förster and M. Rosen, Cambridge: Cambridge University Press, 1993. *Prolegomena to Any Future Metaphysics.* trans. P. G. Lucas, Manchester: Manchester University Press, 1953; *Selections,* ed. L. W. Beck, New York: Macmillan, 1988.

Critics, apostates, heirs: H. E. Allison, *The Kant-Eberhard Controversy,* Baltimore: Johns Hopkins University Press, 1973. L. W. Beck, "From Leibniz to Kant," in R. C. Solomon and K. M. Higgins, eds., *The Age of German Idealism,* London: Routledge, 1993. J. Bransen, *The Antinomy of Thought: Maimonian Skepticism and the Relation between Thoughts and Objects,* Dordrecht: Kluwer, 1991. S. H. Bergman, *The Philosophy of Solomon Maimon,* Jerusalem: Magnes Press, 1967. G. Di Giovanni, "The First Twenty Years of Critique: The Spinoza Connection," in Guyer, ed., *The Cambridge Companion to Kant* (see above). G. Di Giovanni and H. S. Harris, trans., *Between Kant and Hegel: Texts in the Development of Post-Kantian Idealism,* Albany: State University of New York Press, 1985.

58. For biographical details, see Scharfstein, *The Philosophers,* pp. 210–30.

59. Letter to Christian Garve, August 7, 1783, in Kant, *Philosophical Correspondence 1759–99,* trans. A. Zweig, Chicago: University of Chicago Press, 1967.

60. "Preface to Second Edition," p. Bxvi. Translated Smith, *Immanuel Kant's Critique of Pure Reason,* pp. 21–22.

61. Ibid., pp. Bxvii–xviii. Trans. Smith, pp. 22–23.

62. Friedman, *Kant and the Exact Sciences,* p. 21.

63. Ibid., pp. Bxviii–xix. Trans. Smith, p. 23.

64. Ibid., p. Bxix, note a. Trans. Smith, p. 23.

65. Ibid.Trans. Smith, p. 24.

66. Ibid., p. Bxxv. Trans. Smith, pp. 26–27.

67. Ibid., p. Bxxviii. Trans. Smith, p. 28.

68. Ibid., p. Bxxx. Trans. Smith, p. 29.

69. Ibid., pp. A687/B715. Trans. Smith, p. 560.

70. Ibid., pp. A701/B729. Trans. Smith, p. 569.

71. Ibid., pp. A4–5, 7–9/B11–14. Trans. Smith, pp. 44–51, 48–51.

72. Ibid., p. B19. Trans. Smith, p. 55.

73. Ibid., p. B56. Trans. Smith, p. 22.

74. Ibid., pp. A11/B24. Trans. Smith, p. 58.

75. For this and the next paragraph, on time, the references are, respectively, to the rather short sections on space and time in the first part of the *Critique of Pure Reason.*

76. Kant, *The Critique of Pure Reason,* pp. Axiv/Bix.

77. Ibid., pp. A80–81/B106–107. That no others are possible Kant says in the *Prolegomena,* para. 23.

78. Kant, *Critique of Pure Reason,* pp. A67/B92. Trans. Smith, p. 104. The subject is taken up in Reich, *The Completeness of Kant's Table of Judgments,* on which I have drawn here.

79. It is possible, though artificial, to compile an analogous table of the judgments and categories of Buddhist logic. Such a table would presumably be acceptable to Dignaga and Dharmakirti. For an attempt, see Stcherbatsky, *Buddhist Logic,* vol. 1, pp. 252–56.

80. Translated Smith, p. 112.

81. Trans. Smith, pp. 146, 148.

82. Trans. Smith, p. 148.

83. Al-Azm, *The Origins if Kant's Arguments in the Antinomies,* p. 1.

84. Ibid., pp. A422/B449–50. Trans. Smith, p. 394.

85. *Prolegomena,* section 52b; trans. Lucas, pp. 105–106). In Roman rhetoric, an antimony (from the Greek *anti-nomos, a contradiction in a law or between two laws*) is a form by which opposed arguments are presented side by side. The form was used in seventeenth-century jurisprudence to bring out differences between laws. (See Caygill, *A Kant Dictionary,* p. 75).

86. *Critiques of Pure Reason* B452. See Al-Azm, *The Origins of Kant's Arguments in the Antinomies,* p. 141.

87. Trans. Smith, pp. 269–70.

88. Kant, *Critique of Pure Reason,* pp. Bxviii (note), A49/B62. Trans. Smith, pp. 23, 87.

89. Trans. Smith, p. 466.

90. Kant, *Reflexionen,* reflection 6317 (*Kant's Handschriftliche Nachlass* in the Akademie edition, vol. 18, p. 626). As translated in Guyer, *Kant and the Claims of Knowledge,* p. 353. See also *The Critique of Pure Reason* (B71–72), where Kant says that in natural theology we do away with the conditions of time and space from God's intuition because if we did not and considered them conditions of things in themselves, as the conditions of all existence they would have to be conditions of God's existence as well.

91. Kant, *Critique of Pure Reason,* p. A251. Trans. Smith, pp. 268–69.

92. See the perplexity concerning the thing in itself expressed in Allison, *Kant's Transcendental Idealism,* pp. 241–42 and the discussion of the thing in itself as "cause" (e.g., A190/B235, A358, A380, A494/B522), pp. 247–54. The solution is as expressed on p. 254. Guyer, *Kant and the Claims of Knowledge,* insists (p. 79) that "Kant's definition of experience itself is indeed ambiguous" and that Allison is quite wrong to contend that Kant asserts only innocuous analytic propositions (pp. 336–43). According to Guyer (p. 334), Kant "says that there are *things* which are actually not in space and time or possessed of spatial and temporal form."

93. Kant, *Critique of Pure Reason*, p. A100. Trans. Smith, p. 132.

94. Ibid., p. A114. Trans. Smith, p. 140.

95. I. Kant, *Anthropology from a Pragmatic Point of View*, trans. M. J. Gregor, pp. 52–53.

96. Henrich, *The Unity of Reason*, p. 80; quoting Kant, Vorlesungen hber Metaphysik, ed. K. H. L. Politz, reprinted, Darmstadt: Wissenschaftliche Buchgesellschaft, 1975 (1821), pp. 205–207.

97. Giovanni and Harris, *Between Kant and Hegel*, pp. 20–25, and 107–13 (from the *Aenesidemus*).

98. In Kant's "Open letter on Fichte's *Wissenschaftslehre*," dated August 7, 1799. See also Kant, *Philosophical Correspondence 1759–99*, trans. Zweig, pp. 253–54, in which Kant speaks of treacherous, deceitful friends.

99. Vleeschauwer, *Development of Kantian Thought*, pp. 166–98.

100. Trans. Hattori, pp. 24–25.

101. Stcherbatsky, *Buddhist Logic*, vol. 2, pp. 12–19 (without commentary).

102. *Critique of Pure Reason*, trans. Smith, pp. 92, 93. The two German terms have been inserted by me.

103. Ibid., p. Bxxxvi. Trans. Smith, p. 33.

104. *Prolegomena to any Future Metaphysics That Will Be Able to Present Itself as a Science*, trans. Lucas, p. 9 ("Preface").

105. Dharmakirti, quoted in Herzberger, *Bhartṛhari and the Buddhists*, p. 221. On *svabhāva* in this sense, see Hayes, "On the Reinterpretation of Dharmakīrti's *Svabhāvahetu*" and Hayes and Gillon, "Introduction to Dharmakirti's Theory of Inference as Presented in *Pramāṇavārttika Svopajñavṛtti* 1–10."

106. Herzberger, *Bhartṛhari and the Buddhists*, pp. 226, 237 (note 51).

107. The example of the baby, given by Dharmottara, is as given in Herzberger, *Bhartṛhari and the Buddhists*, p. 223.

108. Ibid., pp. 227–30 (p. 227 quoted). The preceding description of Dharmakirti's ideal objects depends on Herzberger's controversial interpretation in chapter 5 of *Bhartṛhari and the Buddhists*. Herzberger defends Stcherbatsky's Kantian conception of Dharmakirti's philosophy. I own that the details of this doctrine of ideal linguistic objects are obscure to me. In "Dharmakīrti's Theory of Language," Rita Gupta contends that Herzberger exaggerates by making what Dharmakirti sees as exceptional cases into the norm.

109. See Allison, *Kant's Transcendental Idealism*, chap. 13.

110. For a characterization of Stcherbatsky and his work, see V. Lysenko, "On Certain Intellectual Stereotypes in Buddhist Studies as Exemplified in Th.

Stcherbatsky's works," *Journal of Indian Council of Philosophical Research*, 9.2 (January–April, 1992)—the article is much less negative than its title would lead one to expect (my remark on Stcherbatsky's belief stems from p. 89). R. Hayes, "Nāgārjuna's Appeal," *Journal of Indian Philosophy*, December 1994, pp. 331–38. A. P. Tuck, *Comparative Philosophy and the Philosophy of Scholarship*, Oxford: Oxford University Press, 1990, is primarily a description of the varying interpretations of Nagarjuna and their dependence on the philosophies that happen to be current.

111. See in particular Stcherbatsky's *Buddhist Logic*, 2 vols, reprinted the Hague: Mouton, 1959 [1930], vol. 1, pp. 177–78, 200–203, 228, 271–74, 436–43, 482–84, 531–36; vol. 2, index, "Kant." T. R. V. Murti, *The Central Philosophy of Buddhism*, London: Allen and Unwin, 1955, pp. 123–24.

112. Hayes, *Dignaga on the Interpretation of Signs*, pp. 15–16.

113. This formulation comes from the *Upādāyaprajñaptiprakaraṇa*, attributed to Dignaga and preserved in a Chinese translation. See Herzberger, *Bhartṛhari and the Buddhists*, pp. 113–14, and the reference in Hattori, *Dignāga, on Perception*, p. 8.

114. E. Conze, *Thirty Years of Buddhist Studies*, Oxford: Cassirer, 1967, pp. 231–32. Conze is speaking of the parallel between Nagarjuna and Kant, but his words apply equally well to the parallel between Dignaga/Dharmakirti and Kant. For an account of Stcherbatsky's interpretation of Buddhism, especially Nagarjuna, in the context of European Buddhism, see A. P. Tuck, *Comparative Philosophy and the Philosophy of Scholarship: On the Western Interpretation of Nāgārjuna*, New York: Oxford University Press, 1990, pp. 36–47.

115. K. H. Potter, *Presuppositions of India's Philosophies*, New Delhi: Prentice-Hall of India, 1965, p. 191.

116. Jacques May, quoted in E. Conze, *Thirty Years of Buddhist Studies*, p. 234, note 1.

117. C. W. Huntington, Jr. with Geshé Namgyal Wangshen, *The Emptiness of Emptiness*, Honolulu: University of Hawaii Press, 1989, p. 28. Huntington is writing primarily about Nagarjuna, but I assume that he would say much the same about Dignaga and Dharmakirti.

118. R. P. Hayes, *Dignaga on the Interpretations of Signs*, Dordrecht: Kluwer, 1988, chap. 2.

119. Ibid., chap. 4.

120. Chandrakīrti, *Prasannapadā*, pp. 58.14ff. See *Lucid Exposition of the Middle Way*, trans. Sprung, pp. 53–97; and Th. Stcherbatsky, *The Conception of Buddhist Nirvāṇa*, reprint, the Hague: Mouton, 1965 [1927], pp. 140–64. Candrakīrti, *Prasannapadā Madhyamakavṛtti*, trans. May, Paris: Adrien-Maisonneuve, 1959, pp. 253–59, is a disorganized, perhaps interpolated attack on the point-instant theory.

May, "Dharmakīrti," gives a brief and lucid summary of Chandrakirti's writings. Ruegg, *The Literature of the Madhyamaka*, pp. 71–81, is more dense and detailed.

121. Stcherbatsky, *The Conception of Buddhist Nirvāṇa,* pp. 141–42; and Sprung, *The Lucid Exposition of the Middle Way,* pp. 53–54.

122. Chandrakīrti, *Prasannapadā* 1.74. Trans. Stcherbatsky, *The Conception of Buddhist Nirvāṇa,* pp. 161–62.

123. Friedman, *Kant and the Exact Sciences,* pp. 136 (quoted), 1.

124. Allison, *Kant's Transcendental Idealism,* p. 319. At this point, my whole account is derived from Allison, chap. 15.

125. Trans. Smith, p. 472.

126. Trans. Smith, pp. 168–69.

127. For a discussion of Kant's view of self-awareness in relation to the noumenon, see Brook, *Kant and the Mind,* pp. 246–59.

128. Kant, *Critique of Judgement,* pp. 208–209.

129. Translated Smith, p. 478. At this point I am following Allinson, *Kant's Theory of Freedom,* chap. 2. The quotation occurs on p. 48.

130. *Opus Postumum,* trans. Förster and Rosen, p. 239; from the Akademie edition 21.36.

131. On Dharmakirti's Idealism, see Vetter, "Erkenntnisprobleme bei Dharmakīrti," pp. 77–83.

132. Trans. Phillips, "Dharmakīrti on Sensation and Causal Efficiency," p. 243–44. Phillips points out that this theme runs through all of *PV* 2.342–43.

133. Trans. Smith, p. 90.

134. Huntington and Wangchen, *The Emptiness of Emptiness,* pp. 7–8, 134. In an extended review of the book, which he recommends, Paul Williams finds that its translation of Chandrakīrti assumes the authors' interpretation and therefore cannot be used to support it (Williams, "On the Interpretation of Madhyamaka Thought," pp. 210–14).

Afterword

1. *The Essays of Michel de Montaigne,* trans. M. A. Screech, London: Allen Lane, 1991, p. 576 (from "An Apology for Raymond Sebond").

2. Halbfass, *India and Europe,* p. 356.

3. D. Twitchett, *The Writing of Official History under the T'ang,* Cambridge: Cambridge University Press, 1992, pp. 84–91.

4. B. Watson, *Ssu'ma Ch'ien,* New York: Columbia University Press, 1958, p. 190.

5. For books on the historiography of European philosophy, see the heading *European philosophy* in note 7 of chapter 1. On Aristotle as historian of philosophy, see Braun, *Histoire de l'histoire de la philosophie,* pp. 16–20.

6. Ibid., pp. 33–36.

7. Ibid., pp. 119–37. For the history's eminent readers, see p. 121.

8. Ibid., pp. 126, 135.

9. Ibid., pp. 184–203.

10. Ibid., pp. 193–94.

11. G. W. F. Hegel, *Introduction to the Lectures on the History of Philosophy,* trans. T. M. Knox and A. V. Miller, Oxford: Oxford University Press, 1985, p. 5.

12. See Halbfass, *India and Europe,* chap. 6, and Glasenapp and Sommerfeld (note 7, chap. 1). The quotation on Chinese religion is from Hegel's *Lectures on the Philosophy of Religion* (of 1827), one-volume ed., ed. P. C. Hodgson, Berkeley: University of California Press, 1988, p. 249.

13. *The Essays of Michel de Montaigne,* trans. Screech, London, pp. 1209–10. As Screech notes, Montaigne quotes Quintilian 10.3.6, "explaining why peasant and uneducated folk speak more directly and less hesitantly."

14. L. Wittgenstein, *Culture and Value,* Oxford: Blackwell, 1978, p. 44e. *The Essays of Michel de Montaigne,* trans. Screech, p. 1258 *(Of Experience).*

15. See the translations of Chuang-tzu by Graham, Mair, and Watson. The translation used here is from A. Birrell, *Chinese Mythology,* Baltimore: Johns Hopkins University Press, 1993, p. 100. Birrell translates Hun Tun's name as Confusion, which seems to me confusing, so I have substituted Formless, another translation she suggests.

16. This ambiguous passage is from the famous hymn, *Rigveda* 10.129.

17. *The Essays of Michel de Montaigne,* trans. Screech, p. 707 ("On Glory"). After consulting the original text I have changed the translation somewhat.

18. See, e.g., N. Cartwright, *How the Laws of Physics Lie,* Oxford: Oxford University Press, 1983.

Bibliography

The bibliography required for this book varies greatly from chapter to chapter. I have therefore thought it helpful to the reader to make each chapter bibliographically independent, except for occasional cross references. In the endnotes, every philosopher discussed separately has a separate bibliography, which is divided into sections within which the entries are alphabetized. Although relatively large, these bibliographies are intended not to be exhaustive but to reflect the books and articles the author had at hand when composing this history. The presence of a book or article in these lists does not necessarily mean that I think it is a good one, nor does its absence, even assuming that I know of it, mean that I think it is a poor one. The bibliographies simply tell the reader of what raw materials the history is constructed. Unlike the text of this book, all titles in the bibliographies are given with diacritics.

The brief general bibliography that follows is made up of more or less current books that deal with comparative thought or philosophy as a whole or with India or China as a whole. Relevant books not mentioned here can be found in the bibliographies of the first chapter.

For comparative philosophy as a whole, the most useful reference work is the *Encyclopédie philosophique universelle*, published in Paris by the Presses Universitaires de France, under the direction of André Jacob. Its four volumes—the second and third each divided into two separate books— are, *L'univers philosophique*, ed. by A. Jacob, 1989; *Les Notions philosophique*, ed. by S. Auroux, 1990; *Les Oeuvres philosophiques*, ed. by J.-F. Mattéi, 1991; and *Les Textes philosophiques*, ed. by R. Arnaldez and A. Doremus, 1992. In volumes 2 and 3, extensive separate sections are devoted to Occidental philosophy, Asiatic philosophy, and the "conceptualization of traditional [so-called 'primitive'] societies." Another general reference book, published too late to be made use of here, is *The Companion Encyclopedia of Asian Philosophy*, edited by B. Carr and I. Mahalingam, London: Routledge, 1997. Its six main sections, divided into relatively brief chapters by different authors, are devoted respectively to Persian, Indian, Buddhist, Chinese, Japanese, and Islamic philosophy.

Of general histories of philosophy, the most useful for comparative philosophy is the three-volume *Histoire de la philosophie*, written by a large number of specialists under the direction of Brice Parain and Yvon Belavel, Paris; Gallimard, 1969-1973. The work of a single author, David Dilworth's *Philosophy in World Perspective: A Comparative Hermeneutic of the Major Theories* (New Haven: Yale University Press, 1989) attempts to show that all philosophical theories "fall under four generic types, themselves systematically related—Sophistic, Democritean, Platonic, and Aristotelian" (p. 7). Hajime Nakamaura discusses the basic intellectual traits of the different philosphical traditions in the *Ways of Thinking of Eastern Peoples: India-China-Tibet-Japan*, Hawaii: East-West Center Press, 1964; and in *A Comparative History of Ideas*, 2d ed., London: KPI, 1986 (distributed by Routledge and Kegan Paul).

In *Contemporary Philosophy*, edited by Guttorm Fløistad, vol. 7, *Asian Philosophy*, Dordrecht: Kluwer, 1993, a variety of authors characterizes the philosophies of India, China, Korea, and Japan. Two recent books of essays take comparative philosophy as their direct subject: *Interpreting across Boundaries*, edited by G. J. Larson and E. Deutsch, Princeton: Princeton University Press, 1988; and *Culture and Modernity: East-West Philosophic Perspectives*, Honolulu: University of Hawaii Press, 1991. Another book of essays relevant to comparative philosophy as a whole is *Rationality in Question: On Eastern and Western Views of Rationality*, edited by S. Biderman and B.-A. Scharfstein, Leiden: Brill, 1989.

For the justification of the comparison of the intellectual attitudes of widely different peoples, see G. E. R. Lloyd, *Demystifying Mentalities*, Cambridge: Cambridge University Press, 1990; D. Shaner, Shigenori Nagatomo, and Yuasa Yasuo, *Science and Comparative Philosophy*; and B.-A. Scharfstein, *The Dilemma of Context*, New York: New York University Press, 1989.

Extensive bibliographical material on Indian philosophy can be found in the *Bibliography of Indian Philosophies*, 2d ed., Delhi: Banarsidass, 1984, the first volume of the *Encyclopedia of Indian Philosophy*, edited as a whole by Karl Potter; there is a recent revised edition. For Buddhism in particular, see also H. Nakamura, *Indian Buddhism*, Osaka: KUFS Publication, 1980. Bibliographical material on China and Chinese thought can be found in Joseph Needham's *Science and Civilisation in China*, Cambridge: Cambridge University Press. The generally relevant volumes are the first two: *Introductory Orientations* (1954), and *History of Scientific Thought* (1956). Volume 7, part 1, *Language and Logic in Traditional China*, by C. Harbsmeier, to be published in late 1997, when the present book will have been completed, promises to be the most detailed discussion of its subject matter and will doubtlessly have the most elaborate bibliography. There is also a good general bibliography in Derk Bodde, *Chinese Thought, Society, and Science*, Honolulu: University of Hawaii Press, 1991, which is careful and, within its limits, thoroughgoing.

Note on Author

✵

Born April 12, 1919, in New York City. Taught at Brooklyn College and briefly at Columbia University, the Teachers' Institute of the Jewish Theological Seminary, and the University of Utah. Married to Ghela Efros. One child (who is, not by accident, a book designer). In 1955, moved to Israel, where he founded the department of philosophy of Tel-Aviv University, then just in its inception.

social bias: (U.S.) American, democratic
religious bias: secular Jewish
philosophical bias: empirical, loosely Pragmatic
most impressive teacher of philosophy: Harry Wolfson
relevant weaknesses: inadequate command of languages and mathematical logic, tendency to disregard cultural and disciplinary boundaries (attempts at rash comparisons and syntheses), relative lack of fear of error, incomplete freedom from biases
relevant strengths: broad interests (art, music, literature, psychology, and the exact and social sciences), tendency to disregard cultural and disciplinary boundaries (attempts at far-reaching comparisons and syntheses), relative lack of fear of error, relative freedom from cultural and disciplinary biases

Index

✳

To simplify the reading of this book, I have omitted the diacritics that are used in scholarly transliteration from Sanskrit. The convention is to represent ś and ṣ by *sh,* and *c* by *ch.* However, I have used diacritics in bibliographies and bibliographical citations. This is because it may be essential to know the exact title of a book or article in order to find it. In the index that follows, Sanskrit names and terms appear with their diacritics. When the form with diacritics has fewer letters than the form that appears in the text, it is added in parentheses.

Transliterations from Arabic, like those from Sanskrit, omit almost all diacritics except in bibliographies. With respect to Chinese, the Wade-Giles transliteration (named after the sinologists Thomas Wade [1818–95] and Herbert Giles [1845–1935]) is followed here because it is used in almost all of the books I cite. However, the *Pinyin (phonetic spelling)* transliteration, officially adopted by the People's Republic of China in 1979, has become dominant, so I have added in parentheses the *Pinyin* equivalent of all the Chinese names and terms. The *Pinyin* symbols that deviate radically from the pronunciation of their English equivalents are: initial *c* (pronounced *ts*), *q* (pronounced *ch* as in *chart*), *x* (pronounced *sh*), *z* (pronounced *ts*), and *zh* (pronounced *j* as in *just*).

I thank Dr. Ornan Rotem for adding most of the Sanskrit diacritics and thank Dr. Galia Patt-Shamir for going over the *Pinyin* transliterations.